The Global Art
of Soccer

Soccer [International Football] in 56 Languages

1	ayaktopu	Turkish [Türkçe]
2	balompié	Spanish dialect
3	bóng đá	Vietnamese [Tiếng Việt]
4	calcio	Italian [Italiano]
5	fitbaw	Scottish [Scots] sometimes written fitbaa
6	fodbold	Danish [Dansk]
7	football	English (international), French [Français]
8	fotbal	Romanian [Română], Czech [Čeština]
9	fotbale	Walon
10	fotball	Norwegian [Norsk]
11	fotboll	Swedish [Svenska]
12	foutbol	Haitian Creole [Kreyòl Ayisyen]
13	fudbal	Serbian [Srpski] Српски
14	fusbol	Yiddish ייִדיש
15	fußball	German [Deutsch]
16	futbal	Slovak [Slovenčina]
17	futbalo	Esperanto
18	fútbol	Spanish [Español or Castellano], Galego
19	futbol	Catalan [Català], Turkish [Türkçe]
20	futbola	Basque [Euskera]
21	futboll	Albanian [Shqip]
22	futbols	Latvian [Latviešu Valoda]
23	futebol	European Portuguese and Brazilian [Português]
24	fuzbal	Slovenian slang [Slovenščina]
25	jalgpall	Estonian [Eesti Keel]
26	jalkapallo	Finnish [Suomi]
27	kandanda	Swahili [Kiswahili]
28	knattspyrna	Icelandic [Íslenska]
29	kopaná	Czech [Čeština]
30	labdarúgás	Hungarian [Magyar],
31	nogomet	Bosnian [Bosanski], Croatian [Hrvatski], Slovenian [Slovenščina]
32	palluni	Sicilian [Sicilianu]
33	piłka nożna	Polish [Język Polski]
34	putbol	Tagalog [Filipino]
35	sacar	Irish [Gaeilge]
36	schutte	Swiss German [Schwyzerdütsch]
37	sepakbola	Indonesian [Bahasa Indonesia]
38	soccer	English (Australia, Canada, USA)
39	soka	Swahili [Kiswahili]
40	sokker	Afrikaans
41	vakapi	Guaraní [Avañe'ẽ]
42	voetbal	Dutch [Nederlands]
43	⠋⠕⠕⠞⠃⠁⠇⠇	Braille
44	ποδόσφαιρο	Greek Ελληνικά
45	ფეხბურთი	Georgian ქართული
46	Футбол	Russian Русский, Bulgarian Български, Ukrainian Українська
47	כדורגל	Hebrew עִבְרִית
48	فوتبال	Persian [Fârsi] فارسی
49	كرة القدم	Arabic العربية
50	足球	Chinese 中文
51	サッカー	Japanese 日本語
52	축구	Korean 한국어
53	ฟุตบอล	Thai ภาษาไทย
54	फ़ुटबॉल	Hindi हिन्दी
55	ফুটবল	Bengali [Bānglā] বাংলা
56	👐👌👍👎✌️✋	Langage des Signes [Sign language]

The Global Art of Soccer

Richard Witzig

CusiBoy Publishing
New Orleans

© 2006 by Richard Witzig
All rights reserved. No part of this publication may be reproduced in any form or by any means without the written permission of CusiBoy Publishing. Published 2006
CusiBoy Publishing
76 OK Avenue
New Orleans, LA 70123

10 09 08 07 06   1 2 3 4 5

Witzig, Richard
    The global art of soccer / Richard Witzig.
      p. cm.
    Includes bibliographical references and index.
    ISBN 0-977-66880-0 (pbk.)
    1. Soccer.   2. Art and Soccer   3. Football – international.

Cover design: Fred and Richard Witzig.

Printed in the USA by Garrity Printing, New Orleans.
The paper used in this publication meets the minimum requirements of the American National Standard for Informational Sciences – Permanence of Paper for printed Library Materials, ANSI Z39.48-1992.

www.theglobalartofsoccer.com

CONTENTS

	Foreword	vii
	Preface	ix
	Acknowledgements	xi
	About the Cover	xii

Part 1: Soccer Essence & Evolution — 1
1. Joy of Soccer — 3
2. Art of Soccer — 15
3. Soccer and Identity — 31
4. Soccer: Social and Political — 59
5. Soccer Business and Marketing — 77
6. Soccer Injury and Illness — 99

Part 2: Soccer Excellence — 129
7. Best Players of the Modern Era 1958 – 2006 — 131
8. Best Teams of the Modern Era 1958 – 2006 — 195
9. World Cup 2002 — 221
10. World Cup 2006 — 297

Part 3: Soccer Chronicles — 321
11. Soccer at the Top of the World — 323
12. Soccer at the End of the World — 339
13. Soccer Dishonor — 347

Part 4: Soccer Future — 361
14. Soccer: The USA Way — 363
15. The Penalty Paradox — 379
16. Soccer Future — 389
17. Soccer Resources and References — 407

Part 5: Epilogue — 421
18. Modern Soccer Odyssey — 423

Appendix 1	455
Postscript	457
Index	459
About the Author	464
Photos	465

FOREWORD

Soccer has been a big part of my life, and I even wrote two books about my experiences. But when I read this book by Richard Witzig, it further established in my mind just how important soccer is in our world.

Primarily an inspiring book on soccer art, *The Global Art of Soccer* delves deeper into what soccer means for the human experience. At the same time, Richard has researched new and important history of the game that should not be ignored, lest we repeat our mistakes.

Each chapter of the book takes the reader beyond the game itself, where issues that in the past were considered taboo are depicted in great extent, for example: intolerance, politics, international conflicts, xenophobia, and exclusiveness. Dr. Witzig's chapter on soccer injury and illness crystallizes exactly how critical soccer is for human development, as soccer is the only world sport that can make a significant positive impact on the HIV/AIDS epidemic. People are dying, and soccer power can deliver the necessary education for relief of suffering for individuals and communities.

Richard also nicely lays out the developments of recent FIFA World Cups, and makes a succinct case for the best players and teams in the Modern Era (1958-2006). He then tackles the hidden history of the 1936 "Nazi" Olympic soccer tournament, another example of how soccer could have helped humanity in a time of need. His chapters on soccer in unusual environments and his own soccer odyssey are also fascinating. Finally, he takes on the future of the game, and the nearly limitless possibilities of how soccer can help improve the world.

This book is aimed at the soccer fan intent on exploring the important dynamics of soccer in the world. If you are such a person, you are in for a singular and spellbinding ride. And yes, even though I was a serious player, I am still a very serious fan, and very anxious to maximize the potential of the sport I love. For that I am grateful for the contributions Richard has made in the writing of *The Global Art of Soccer*.

EMMANUEL "MANNO" SANON

Emmanuel "Manno" Sanon played for the Haitian national team from 1969-1977. During a four-year period, Sanon scored 47 goals for Haiti, and he was the leading scorer in the 1973 CONCACAF tournament that qualified Haiti for the 1974 West Germany World Cup [Figure 1].

In West Germany, Haiti was drawn in the "Group of Death" comprising Italy, Argentina, and Poland. The semi-professional Haitians were sometimes outmatched against the professional Europeans, but still Sanon managed to break Dino Zoff's record streak of twelve consecutive games without a goal conceded, after he rounded the stellar goalkeeper in scoring one of the goals of the tournament (he also scored against Argentina). Sanon then turned professional and played for Beerschot in Belgium and the San Diego Sockers in the USA. In 1994, Sanon was voted to *France Football's* Top 100 World Cup Players from 1930-1990 ("Les 100 Héros de la Coupe du Monde"). He managed the Haitian national team in 1999-2000, and was voted the Haitian Athlete of the Century.

Manno Sanon's two books are "Toup Pou Yo" ["Take That," the rallying song of the Haitian team during the 1974 World Cup] Part One & Part Two, and he maintains a superb Haitian football website at www.haitifoot.com.

For Massiel
and the boys
Stephan and Derek
for all
the emotions
they bring.

PREFACE

My formative years were spent in the United States of America (USA), not yet a breeding ground for international soccer[1] stars. Growing up in the USA in the 1960s and 1970s meant being exposed to large doses of the "Big Four" sports; baseball, basketball, ice hockey, and USA-football.[2] Minor market sports such as track and field, tennis and lacrosse also influenced my adolescent life. With so many other competing professional sports (the New York-New Jersey area has nine Big Four professional teams)[3], soccer was an afterthought in the galaxy of USA sport right through to the 1990's.

Fortunately I was raised in northern New Jersey, a region containing many first and second-generation immigrants who had introduced and nurtured local soccer development. During the latter part of the 20th century, Argentines, Armenians, Brazilians, Central Americans, Colombians, Dutch, Eastern Europeans, English, French, Germans, Ghanaians, Greeks, Irish, Koreans, Polish, Peruvians, Nigerians, Scots, Swiss, and West Indians (among others), all contributed to the development of soccer in the Greater New York-New Jersey area. In my school team, we had players from Armenian, Brazilian, Colombian, English, French, Greek, Irish, Swiss, and other backgrounds playing on a unified team. Therefore, from an early age I associated soccer with the celebration of human diversity.

Playing in amateur, university, and semi-professional teams exposed me to players from virtually every country in the Americas (North, Central, and South America), Europe, parts of Africa (Cameroon, Nigeria, Ghana, South Africa, Morocco, Kenya, Sierra Leone, Gambia) and Asia (Iran, Malaysia, South Korea, Thailand). I could visit with representatives of many of the world's populations simply by interacting with soccer players in the New Jersey-New York area. These interactions necessarily influenced my budding worldview, routing me to a philosophy of tolerance and sparking an insatiable curiosity of the human condition. As the reader peruses this book, one cannot help but appreciate the profound variety of given and family names in the world of soccer, which fully represent the diversity of mankind.

Having learned about the world's peoples by playing soccer inside and outside the USA, I admit taking full advantage of soccer being the world's game. During my career in medicine and working in soccer-playing countries, I would often be invited to participate in soccer games and tournaments. These games ranged from the amateur level – with fellow doctors on their hospital courts or with worker and university student teams -= to scrimmaging with professional soccer teams in their stadiums. These overseas soccer encounters resulted in the formation of instant critical relationships with individuals I would never have had the chance to be acquainted with otherwise. Soccer became a vital social connection to share with new peoples and cultures, complementing a significant professional medicine and public health relationship.

---

[1] In this book, "soccer" and "football" are occasionally and unavoidably used interchangeably, as they refer to the same game as sponsored worldwide by the *Fédération Internationale de Football Association*, most popularly known by its acronym, FIFA.

[2] The USA version of "football," more similar to rugby and currently represented professionally by the National Football League (NFL), is referred to as *USA-football* in this book. "American football" is not used because Central and South American peoples and nations all consider themselves "Americans." To illustrate this point, three prestigious soccer clubs named "América" from the Western Hemisphere have their insignias illustrated below. There are dozens of smaller "América" teams existing in Central and South America.

América – Mexico City   América – Rio Preto, Brazil   América – Cali, Colombia

[3] Giants & Jets (USA-football), Yankees & Mets (baseball), Knicks & Nets (basketball), and the Rangers, Islanders & Devils (ice hockey).

The inspiration for writing *The Global Art of Soccer* arose from the global passion for the sport that is the world's game, and of respect for soccer's innate people connection that assisted me in promoting critical health issues in communities. The book title pays tribute to soccer's unparalleled aesthetic and social qualities that give rise to universal enjoyment of the game.

The contents of *The Global Art of Soccer* are drawn from a multitude of observations and experiences spanning a forty-year period of playing and watching soccer with thousands of individuals in many corners of the world. The thought behind this book was not to repeat old histories already documented by capable witnesses, but to further develop a new synthesis of soccer ideas often oversimplified in a purely sports framework (Chapter 13 is the only exception to the "old history" rule in the book, as the critical events described therein have never been adequately explored or explained). This approach intends to make the reader think about where soccer has been, where it presently stands, and what the future might be for "the beautiful game." The material within will hopefully enable the reader to appreciate the impact of society on soccer, and equally, the underestimated importance of soccer in the world. While proposed to be a thinking person's book on soccer, *The Global Art of Soccer* is intended more for soccer aficionados than academicians.

The book also seeks to present familiar and favorite soccer themes in new ways. Playing styles, the essence of the game, and soccer's place in sport and world history are explored. Players and teams are looked at in a fresh light; placing players by position, ranking teams by best offenses, midfields, and defenses, and an overall ranking of teams by nation or club. Players and teams from the pre-1958 era (referred to as the Legends Era) are not included in the listings, simply because the scarcity of game film makes direct and thorough investigation and comparison impossible. Many classic soccer volumes by previous soccer poets have already characterized the top players and teams of that era, and shall not be repeated here.

Despite protestations that sport is independent of politics, soccer is an integral part of the socio-political fabric of nations. As such, soccer is truly the *world sport*, and often the initial contact and most common interest between nations with little commonality. I have endeavored to explain and explore the human rights aspects of soccer in society (health, civil, and economic rights), and how those rights play an increasingly prominent part in soccer culture and its role in the future of humanity. Now is the time to envision the 'beautiful game" – soccer – as more than just a sport, but as taking its rightful place in the artistic and intellectual splendor of humanity.

Please enjoy this book as I have enjoyed writing it; and share the wonderful world of local and international soccer with family and friends the world over.

Richard Witzig
April 26, 2006
New Orleans

Acknowledgements

This kind of book takes extensive research and fact checking as well as being in many places at once, and the work would not be nearly as complete without the selfless collaboration of many friends and colleagues listed below. However, the final responsibility and accuracy of all data presented rests solely with the author.

I would like to express my sincere appreciation to:

- Anand Roy, Allison Tauman, Stephanie Maxwell, Jason Forsythe, and Ursula Hopkins for reviewing the manuscript and performing superb copy-editing and content critique work; Pierre Dejace for content review and translations, and Mae Lupatkin for her review and encouragement.
- Emmanuel "Manno" Sanon for his interview and foreword contribution.
- Herb Austin, Keith West, Chris Haraszti, Vladimir Chachanidze, Obiefuna Okoye, Eric Bennett, Dan Yafet, Peter Alegi, Ricky Shanks, Aldo Panfichi, Asieb Sekandarzad, Michael Blake, Edgar Martín del Campo, Nadim Salomon, and Aron Tendler for fact-checking; Bella Tendler, Salima and Aliyya Haque, Gagik Karapetyan, Adi Nadimpalli, Ali Banaie, Uros Stanic, Edith Haari, Alexandra Ihringova, Ragnheiður Elíasdóttir, Peter Palencik, and Liana Stoicescu for linguistics assistance; Pastor Shapiama, Beto, Jesus, Nacho Guardia, Angela Cimadevilla, Chantal Cruyff, Johan Cruyff, Marta Ríos i Bonet, and Michael Ströck for photographic and graphic assistance; Steve Styron for computer support; Christoph Winter for communications assistance; and David and Alex Maxwell for expert computer and graphics assistance.
- The coaching and administrative staff of Club Cienciano of Cusco, Peru; especially Coaches Ramón Quiroga (1997) & Freddy Ternero (2001), administrator Juvenal Silva, club doctor Américo Alviz, and the entire Cienciano team; who arranged an invitation to their centenary kickoff and welcomed me to their training sessions at Huaro, Sacsayhuamán and Estadio Inca Garcilaso de la Vega in Cusco, and later invited me to team celebrations at the Recopa championship in Fort Lauderdale in 2004.
- Juan Valdivieso, the legendary "El Mago," in Lima, Carlos Tovar in Chancay, and Teófilo "Nene" Cubillas in Lima – three Peruvian soccer legends who all graciously consented to interviews at short notice in Peru.

Special thanks are extended to:

- My parents Fred and Jane Witzig, for all the guidance and love they have given me (and thanks Dad for help with the cover design), and my sister Margrit, whose persistent encouragement in youth helped my confidence.
- My wife Massiel, who not only contributed to book content and logistics, but kept our family life sailing as smoothly as possible during the execution of this work.

In memoriam (for they so loved the game and humanity):

- David Shelton, global human rights activist – like Camus, a rare goalkeeping gem.
- Bruce Heckinger, global environmentalist – Tasmanian ecology and soccer ambassador.
- Fritz Leandre, global footballer – we all miss your soccer art and camaraderie.
- McColvin Scott, global physician – played soccer karate-style "for kicks."

About the Cover

The cover is designed as a poster model presenting a 90 degree perspective difference between soccer thought (the title and languages of soccer) and the soccer dynamic (represented by the photo of the child with ball).

The cover photo is of an 18-month old toddler already interested in and playing soccer well. Note the perfect running form as he addresses the ball, about to kick with his left foot. Aha! Perhaps a new Tostão or Liam Brady in the making. Not even having outgrown his baby fat, he was showing such promise.

Shortly after this photo was taken, this boy entered the world of a child with autistic spectrum disorder (also called ASD or autism). He stopped playing soccer, because he developed difficulty expressing himself in all his actions. Today, with intensive therapy and infinite love from people around him, he is making strong progress back towards the original potential demonstrated in the earlier picture.

ASD is a poorly understood neurological condition – autistic symptoms often surface in a child that has seemingly developed normally up to two years old. What is known is that autism will likely rob a child of developing his full potential if not diagnosed early on, and treated promptly and intensively. Autism is increasing in incidence worldwide – diagnosed in up to 1 in 166 children – and research as to its etiology and optimal treatment has so far been delayed and limited.

A portion of the author sales of this book goes to autism, AIDS, malaria, and tuberculosis research and treatment.

Soccer Essence & Evolution

Chapter One

The Joy of Soccer
From The Simplest Game to the Beautiful Game

"Football is a part of I. When I play the world wakes up around me." *Bob Marley*

"The greatest joy I get is watching fans rise to their feet when I do something unexpected." *Ronaldinho*

"Happy now, they went to play ball at the court…with this, the masters of Xibalba were defeated by Hunahpu and Xbalanque."
From the *Popol Vuh*, the Mayan Book of the Dawn of Life.

Baby Joy

A baby's first toy is likely to be a rattle, introducing Baby to the sights and sounds of the world. Once Baby learns to roll over and sit up, his next toy is likely to be a colored plastic ball ¼ to ½ his size. Baby holds it, pulls it, pushes it, and watches it roll away. With the ball, Baby is introduced to the possibilities of movement controlled by his own desire and invention. As Baby discovers the possibilities of time and space from ball play, he laughs so hard he nearly falls over.

The ball Baby receives is closest to a soccer ball, a large colored ball that can be manipulated in any fashion.[1] Baby learns much about the world from such a ball and human interaction with it, and discovers the joy of soccer as an introduction to the joy of life.

Baby then learns to walk and is soon running – he is a toddler now. At 15 months, he can manipulate the ball with his feet, keeping it in front of him as he shuffles ahead.[2] At 18 months he kicks the ball repeatedly – dribbling really – and his kicking technique is surprisingly good (see cover photo). He walks the ball into the goal to examine the net. At two years old, he kicks the ball to Mom or Dad, happily waiting for the return pass. As soccer is an intuitive game, his training has begun simply because he is playing. He does not need a coach, only a parent or sibling to participate with him. Soccer coaching comes much later and may not always be beneficial, as poor coaching can destroy the intuitive parts of the game that are its essence.

---

[1] Baby is unlikely to receive a basketball, baseball, hockey puck, or a USA-football because they are impractical and simply not as fun. A baseball, basketball or hockey puck is too dense and heavy, and a USA-football is too erratic in its wobble to entertain an infant for very long.

[2] According to the German version of the Denver Developmental Scale for Infants and Toddlers (*Denver Entwicklungsskalen*), toddlers are able to play soccer (*spielt Fussball*) from the age of 15 months. German pediatricians can be trusted to have rigorously tested this developmental milestone.

Eventually the toddler becomes an adult, and if he pays attention, the soccer world will have much to teach him. Albert Camus, the 1957 Nobel Prize winning writer, said, *"All that I know most surely about morality and obligations, I owe to football."*[3] Even after Camus was diagnosed with tuberculosis at the tender age of seventeen, he never lost his soccer passion and included soccer references in his work. For example, in his novel *The Fall* (*La Chute*, 1956), Camus declared the only places he felt happy and relaxed were in a theatre or a soccer stadium. Camus' soccer observances testify that by experiencing the emotions, successes and failures, and social relations integral to the game – soccer can be one of life's grand instructors.

Historical Joy

To fully appreciate the joy of soccer it is useful to know the history of the sport, including the evolution of soccer's ancestral ballgames, and how they have influenced the world at large.

Ancestral Ball Games

Soccer's origins are ancient – far older than any modern team sport. Soccer's precursors developed independently as simple ball games in various world sites in millennia past. For example, four ball games are known to have developed in different parts of the world more than 2000 years ago:

(1) A round ball game called ***Tsu-Chu*** (蹴鞠 or 蹴踘) was played in China more than 2,500 years ago, and involved kicking a leather ball through a hole in a silk cloth.

(2) ***Episkyros*** (επισκυρος) was played in Greece more than two millennia ago.

(3) ***Harpastum*** was popular in Rome more than 2000 years ago. It is thought (but not proven) that the Roman game was influenced by episkyros. Harpastum was likely exported in some form to many foreign lands the Roman Empire conquered around 2000 years ago – including much of Europe and England.

The exact rules for these three ball games have been lost, except they involved a round ball made of a stuffed animal bladder or stitched leather skins, and were fiercely competed.

(4) New research reveals that the first ancestral soccer game likely originated in the New World, as ancient ***American ball games*** were contested as long ago as 1,500 B.C. One of the oldest American ball-fields is located in the archeological digs at Paso de la Amada in Mexico, and is estimated to be 3,500 years old. The object of these games was to advance a heavy solid rubber ball into goals without the use of the hands. Native Americans played similar ball games for millennia over a wide geographical range, from the Hohokam people in the north (straddling modern-day USA and Mexico), the Aztecs in central Mexico, to the Mayas in the highlands of southern Guatemala. A recent museum exhibit and book, *The Sport of Life and Death: The Mesoamerican Ballgame*, extensively documents the evolution of the American games.[4]

The *Quiché Maya* people inhabiting the highlands of southern Guatemala have a special relationship with their version of the ancestral ballgame, as it was incorporated into their *creation myth* – the story of origin in which a culture explains the how and why its people came into existence. In the Quiché Maya creation story of *Popol Vuh*, two sets of Hero Twins confront the Lords of Death in a football match. The second Hero Twins (Hunahpu and Xbalanque) eventually defeat the evil Lords of Xibalba, and metamorphose to become the immortal sun and moon, signifying the continuation of the Quiché Maya people. It is an

---

[3] This quote is sometimes translated as "Everything I learned about life I learned on the football pitch," quite a comprehensive statement from a university team goalkeeper. Camus played in his native Algeria for the Racing Universitaire de'Alger team from 1928-30.

[4] *The Sport of Life and Death: The Mesoamerican Ballgame*. 2001. M. Whittington, ed. Thames & Hudson, NY., and Hill, WD, Blake, M, Clark, JE. *Ball Court Design Dates Back 3,400 Years.* Nature, 392, 30/04/1998, pp.878-9.

extraordinary occurrence that an ancestral ball game contributes to the foremost anthropological event of an ancient people – their creation myth.[5]

The *Aztec* version of the ancestral soccer game was called **Tlachtli** (*tlachco* was the actual ball court), which used a solid rubber ball weighing at least 4.4 pounds (ouch!), four times heavier than a modern soccer ball. The hands were prohibited from manipulating the ball in any manner (the favored passing and shooting methods were with the hips, thighs, shoulders, and upper arms), and the object of the game was to put the ball through one of two stone hoop goals [Figure 1A]. A variant style allowed hip-girder type leather belts to protect the body from the dense rubber. Some matches were so important that it is postulated that the losers were sacrificed to their people's gods.

These ancient American ballgames used the first rubber balls, providing for a ball bounce similar to modern soccer. Because the rubber plant is an indigenous species, rubber was unknown outside the Americas until 500 years ago. Indeed, when Hernán Cortés and his men arrived in the New World from Spain and witnessed bouncing rubber balls, they were convinced an independent spirit possessed the balls. The modern soccer fan might argue that perhaps they were right![6]

More recent ancestral games similar to soccer include:

(1) **Kemari**: This ancient Japanese ballgame developed in the Yamato Imperial Court about 1,400 years ago, and was likely influenced by the Chinese tsu-chu. The object of the game was to keep the ball (a ten-inch diameter deerskin-covered ball stuffed with sawdust) up in the air using only the feet, and then kick it to the next player. Therefore, kemari is likely the world's first form of football "juggling" or "keepie-up." The field size for kemari was variable, although traditionally cornered by four trees.

There is no victory or defeat in kemari – very Zen, no? After the Imperial Court started kemari, first the samurai class and eventually the common folk adopted it. Marco Polo was supposedly exposed to kemari in China and brought the game back to Europe, but this claim has never been verified. When British sailors first played football in Japan in 1873, the amused locals assumed the Brits were playing a version of kemari. Kemari is still played at Shinto shrines for seasonal festivals.

(2) **La Soule**: This ballgame favoring kicking became the rage in the Normandy area in France 1000 years ago, and involved getting a large wood or leather ball into the "goal" of an opposing village, which was often a pond.

(3) **Street football games** (from 1827 called **Shrovetide football**) resembling soccer have been contested for at least eight centuries in Britain. The noble class repeatedly banned these games, as they were thought to waste time and idle the mind. Many British monarchs in the past millennium, including Edward II[7], Edward III (1349), Richard II (1389), Henry IV (1401), and Henry VIII (1540)[8] issued proclamations banning football, calling it the "vulgar recreation." Far be it for the serfs to have a little fun when they could be conserving their energy and laboring longer for their feudal masters! Needless to say, the football bans were unsuccessful, and the people continued their footballing ways.

---

[5] The *Popol Vuh* is also called "The Mayan Book of the Dawn of Life." Interpretation from Dennis Tedlock's book *Popol Vuh*. 1996. Touchstone. Also, at www.uwec.edu/greider/Indigenous/Popol_Vuh/Popol%20Vuh.htm.
[6] A ball court was also found in the Casma Valley in Peru in an archeological site of an extinct culture. This site at Pampa de las Llamas-Moxeke has now been dated as the oldest ball court, about 3600 years old. It is a mystery why cultures 2,500 kilometers apart would have similar ball court designs. See Pozorski T, and Pozorski, S. *An I-Shaped Ball-Court Form at Pampa de las Llamas-Moxeke, Peru*. Latin American Antiquity, 6(3), 1995, pp. 274-280.
[7] On 13 April 1314, Edward II issued this edict banning football: "Forasmuch as there is great noise in the city caused by hustling over large balls from which many evils may arise which God forbid; we command and forbid, on behalf of the King, on pain of imprisonment, such game to be used in the city in the future." This ban was enforced by the mayor of London, and is said to be the first written documentation of football.
[8] Henry VIII banned football in 1540, although there is evidence he had probably played it himself, as he ordered what is thought to be the first pair of football boots in 1526.

Even *The Bard* William Shakespeare commented on this ruling class view of the ancestral soccer game in two plays, *Comedy of Errors* and *King Lear*. In *Comedy of Errors*, Shakespeare alludes to Dromio of Ephesus being kicked about like a football by an insane master, and Dromio requests to be "encased in leather" (like a football) in order to be protected from the blows. In *King Lear*, the King and Kent gang up on Oswald, cursing him with a variety of phrases, including the final insult "you base foot-ball player." Kent trips up Oswald in the service of the King, thus recording the first "intentional" or "professional" football foul in literature.[9,10]

After the English Civil Wars from 1642 to 1651, Oliver Cromwell was more successful at suppressing football games. But after the Restoration in 1660, street football became more popular than ever, and was eventually legalized by Charles II of England in 1681.

(4) **Calcio**: This Italian ball game has been played in the streets of Florence since at least the year 1410, and possibly started centuries earlier. Indeed, soccer in Italy is still affectionately and officially referred to as "calcio" (even the Italian Professional Football League is called the *"Lega Calcio,"* website www.lega-calcio.it/). The original form of calcio had twenty-seven men on each team, allowed the use of the hands, and basically resembled a tactical street fight with a ball.

Calcio may have brought forth the *first organized ballgame strategy*. Since scoring was rare in calcio, might one of the first tactics have been similar to the *catenaccio* (derived from the Latin *catena* or "chain") defense so favored by Italian soccer in recent decades? The original calcio is still played in Italy at exhibitions and festivals, especially in Florence

(5) **Native North American football**: The Pilgrim settlers arrived in Massachusetts in 1620, around the same time Shakespeare was writing of football. There they found Native Americans already playing an indigenous ball game called *pasuckquakkohwog*, meaning, "they gather to play ball with the foot." Many North American indigenous groups had their own variation of this ancestral soccer game.

Modern Soccer Development

Out of this diverse evolution of ballgames emerged a more disciplined game of football among the English upper class secondary schools in the early 1800's. At Cambridge in 1848, ballgames were finally divided into two sports either allowing the use of the hands (rugby) or forbidding the use of the hands (football) – these were called the *Cambridge Rules*. The early rugby-type rules later influenced distinct sports allowing the use of hands such as *USA-football, Canadian football*, and *Australian Rules football*; these "football" games are popular only in their respective countries.

English club Sheffield FC (founded in 1857) – acknowledged to be the world's oldest football club – used a modified form of the Cambridge rules known as the *Sheffield rules* until 1878 (when they finally adopted the BFA Laws).[11] The newly-formed British Football Association (BFA) met in the Freemason Tavern in London on 25 October 1863, and shortly thereafter, on 8 December 1863, codified the first *Laws of Football*. The BFA document was often called the *London Rules* of what was formally called *Association Football*. These first soccer rules were thirteen simple "Laws" expressed in a scant 528 words on one page (Appendix I), but one hundred and forty-two years later, the 2005 FIFA version of the Laws

---

[9] *Comedy of Errors*, Act ii, sc. I,1.83. Last words of *Dromio of Ephesus* to Adriana: "Am I so round with you as you with me, that like a football you do spurn me thus? You spurn me hence, and he will spurn me hither; If I last in this service, you must case me in leather" (in this old English dialect "round" means "plain-spoken" and "spurn" means to "kick away"). Shakespeare likely wrote this in 1589-1593, but it was not published until 1623.

[10] *King Lear*, Act i, 4.95. *King Lear* (to Oswald): O, you sir, you, come you hither, sir. Who am I, sir? *Oswald*: My lady's father. *Lear*: My lady's father! My lord's knave. You whoreson dog! You slave! You cur! *Oswald*: I am none of these, my lord; I beseech your pardon. *Lear*: Do you bandy looks with me, you rascal? [Striking him]. *Oswald*: I'll not be striken, my lord. *Kent*: Nor tripped neither, you base foot-ball player. [Tripping up his heels]. *Lear* (to Kent): I thank thee, fellow; thous servest me, and I'll love thee.

[11] The Sheffield FC – Hallam FC derby, dating from 1861, is the oldest football derby in the world (Chapter 3).

of Football has seventeen Laws comprised of thousands of words detailed on 83 pages.[12] Only four more Laws, but many more words and specifics are apparently required to regulate modern professional soccer.

In summary, while the Laws of Football were codified in the Old World, it appears some of the deepest roots of the game are in the New World, where the availability of rubber provided a bouncing ball for the contestants to shoot into goals without the use of hands.

The fact that many of these early ballgames developed independently throughout the world speaks to the human essence of these proto-football arts, and the separate evolution of soccer-like ballgames is almost as if the human collective consciousness willed the game of soccer into being.

Name Games

What is known as *soccer*[13] in the United States of America (USA) is known as *football*[14] in most of the world. The latter term is most logical, since soccer is the only international team sport primarily executed with the feet.

Oxford University student Charles Wreford-Brown is acknowledged to have created the word concept of *soccer* in 1886 from a slang combination of *Association Football*.[15] The abbreviation *Assoc.* was itself abbreviated into "socca" in 1889, "socker" in 1891, and eventually "soccer" in 1895.[16] The term *soccer* instead of *football* was subsequently adopted in only a few countries such as the USA, Canada and Australia,[17] where other "football" games derived from rugby had developed. Although the word "soccer" was conceived in England, it is seldom used there due to non-competition for the word and concept of "football."

The sport called "football" in the USA is called either *USA-football* or *NFL* (National Football League) *Football* in the rest of the world (the latter name popularized by the global spread of computer games). The objective of USA-football is to advance an *elliptical ball carried in the hands* by running or passing in set plays over lines to score. Only rarely is the egg-shaped ball kicked with the feet, and then, ironically only by renegade soccer specialists. A more accurate name for USA-football would be *handball*, but this name is already used by the Olympic sport of *team handball* that is dominated by European nations.

The name "*LineCrushBall*" has been proposed for USA-football, as the game is fixated on crossing the ball over lines while the defense tries to (literally) crush the ball carrier and/or passer. While rugby and Australian Rules football have continued the time-honored tradition of not wearing any protective equipment, USA-football and Canadian football have evolved into a techno-robotic game in which nearly every part of the body is protected against contact injury by plastic, metal or even bulletproof Kevlar Not a game for the light-hearted, but a modern day big-business form of gladiator-ball.

The football versus rugby distinction was not fully understood by USA universities when the game first appeared in the 1860s. The first professed competitive USA-football game between two teams took place in New Brunswick, New Jersey on 6 November 1869, between the Rutgers and Princeton universities (Rutgers won, 6-4). *But that game was actually the first official soccer* (or "international football") *game in the USA, as in that game, the "London Rules" were used.* Those rules forbade the use of hands, mandated the use of a round ball, and points were made by kicking the ball into goals. Contrary to some

---

[12] Listed at the FIFA website at: www.fifa.com/en/regulations/regulation/0,1584,3,00.html#.
[13] When discussing soccer in the USA, the terminology *international football* may be used to distinguish it from *USA-football*, which places soccer in proper historical and geographic context.
[14] *Football* (English), *fútbol* (Spanish), *futebol* (Portuguese), *fussball* (German), *voetbal* (Dutch), etc. See cover.
[15] Wreford–Brown went on to captain the England national team twice between 1894 and 1898.
[16] Online Etymology Dictionary at: www.etymonline.com/index.php?search=soccer&searchmode=or.
[17] The Australian Soccer Association changed its name to Football Federation Australia in December 2004, thereby downgrading by one the few countries in the world that actively use "soccer." The Australian national team nickname of the "Socceroos" will likely be less used after the change.

USA sport historians, this match was without a doubt far closer to modern soccer than USA-football.[18]

The hands-allowed rugby style and egg-shaped ball only entered the USA university landscape in the mid-1870s. The *first game of definite USA-football origins was played between the Harvard and Yale universities in New Haven, Connecticut on 13 November 1875 (Harvard won 4-0). This first USA-football game still used a round ball and allowed soccer style kicked goals*, but also permitted hand-carried touchdowns.[19] The Intercollegiate Football Association (composed of Harvard, Yale, Columbia and Princeton universities) only mandated a replacement from the round ball to the egg-shaped ball in 1876. Despite the dominant use of the hands in USA-football, a creative novel name for this new rugby cousin never emerged. As a result, "football" was continually used for USA-football, and so it erroneously remains more than a century later.

New World, Old World, All World

The USA was the first country outside of England to organize a soccer club in 1862 – the Oneida Football Club in Boston, Massachusetts. For unclear reasons, the Oneida club only had a lifespan of four years (Chapter 14).

At the same time soccer was making inroads in the USA and mainland Europe, Englishman Charles Miller introduced soccer to Brazil in 1894.[20] Soccer spread rapidly throughout South America, ensuring that the first clubs were formed by the beginning of the 20th century in mainland Europe and South America.

Despite the profound impact of soccer in British history, a soccer museum appeared in the USA nineteen years before one opened in England. The USA *National Soccer Hall of Fame and Museum* opened in 1982, and is located in Oneonta, New York State, about a three-hour drive northwest of New York City.[21] The British *National Football Museum* officially opened in 2001 in Preston, the home of the Preston North End club team that won the first English Football League title in 1888.[22] The Preston museum is actually located on two sides of the club's Deepdale Stadium, with space reserved for future expansion around the entire stadium.[23] Both museums are well worth a visit for fans from any country.

Today, soccer is the most popular global game played by virtually every nation, and the theme of the most popular sporting event in the world – the FIFA World Cup. FIFA, the international federation of soccer associations, has more member nations and territories than even the United Nations (FIFA had 207 members at the end of 2005, while the United Nations had 191).[24] Fledgling political entities such as Palestine competed in the elimination rounds for the 2002 and 2006 World Cup tournaments.

---

[18] Rutgers University, the state university of New Jersey, still claims this was the first university USA-football match (www.scarletknights.com/football/history/first_game.htm). This is all the more unfortunate, as New Jersey has historically been responsible for much of the USA's soccer development (and is one of the author's alma maters - Chapter 18). The NFL website slightly more accurately states that the game was a "college soccer football game" using the London Rules (http://www.nfl.com/history/chronology/1869-1910).

[19] The first Harvard-Yale game was actually predated by two developmental games between the Harvard (USA) and McGill (Canada) universities on 14-15 May 1874 in Massachusetts. Additionally, a Canada-football style game was first played between the Montreal Foot Ball Club and Quebec City on 12 October 1972 in Quebec.

[20] Miller was actually born in Brazil to expatriate parents but schooled in England. For a complete investigation of Miller's impact on soccer in Brazil see Josh Lacey's book, *Charles Miller: The Man Who Brought Football to Brazil*, published in 2005 by Tempus.

[21] USA National Soccer Hall of Fame and Museum site: www.soccerhall.org/home.htm.

[22] The (British) National Football Museum website at www.nationalfootballmuseum.com. The Preston squad was undefeated in a 22-game season in 1888-89, a feat not duplicated by a top division team until 2004, when Arsenal of London completed the 38-game season undefeated. Arsenal then broke Nottingham Forest's 42-game undefeated streak in 2004, improving the record to 49 games. Preston just missed promotion to the Premiership in 2005.

[23] Four of the 2005 Women's European Soccer Championship matches were held at Preston's Deepdale Stadium.

[24] FIFA is the *Fédération Internationale de Football Association*.

Why the World Plays Soccer

This section could also be titled, *"What is so different about soccer from other team sports that make it the overwhelmingly preferred team game worldwide?"*

Soccer is by far the dominant team sport in the world. In some Latin American areas soccer is simply called *pelota* ("ball") – as if the only ball game existing or imaginable is soccer. This illustrates the central cultural position soccer occupies in Latin American countries, and indeed in many other countries around the globe.

Basketball is now the second most popular team sport worldwide, but has emerged as the most popular national sport only in a few countries such as the Philippines. *Baseball* is played as the national sport in a few Central and South American countries (Cuba, Dominican Republic, Nicaragua and Venezuela) that were historically dominated by the USA's colonial and trade influence. However, soccer is currently gaining on baseball in both Venezuela and Cuba.[25] Japan has a national baseball league, but the country is rapidly becoming soccer-mad with the establishment of the professional J-League.

Outside of North America and Europe, USA-football and ice hockey are unpopular. There are several reasons for the lack of global participation in these other sports:

(1) *They require specialized equipment*, making them implausible for poorer nations to equip teams.
(2) *The general philosophy of soccer differs from these other Western sports.*
   a. Baseball is a slow non-continuous game akin to cricket, with a statistical component best absorbed by fans with numerical infatuations.
   b. Ice hockey is designed for northern countries that have natural ice, and requires a stick to handle a puck.
   c. USA-football is burdened with arcane and frequently changing rules, not to mention the overt violence of the game.
(3) USA-football and baseball are *static games*. The only constant in these games are the frequent interruptions, making them the antithesis of free-form play that people love to see in soccer.

Scoring of the various games is interesting to compare. Total basketball scores are in the three digits, USA-football scores are in the double digits, baseball scores are usually in the high single or double digits, while soccer games are almost always in the single digits. High scoring sports seem important only in the USA, where the viewing public seemingly needs scoring gratification every few minutes to sustain its interest.

The less frequent but more significant scoring aspect of soccer is more apropos of life itself. One does not normally have a significant success every few seconds, like basketball, or every few minutes, like USA-football or baseball. A good moment or success naturally arrives more selectively, and there is usually "good" tension and anticipation involved. An accomplishment, a union, or a birth is a rare and usually anticipated life event. Soccer is more like life; the apprehension and anticipation are high, and when a goal is attained, there is a great emotional release. It appears that being gratified all the time – as one potentially is in the rampant materialism of the consumer culture – is a surefire recipe for glorified boredom. An antidote for apathy in the world outside the USA has certainly been soccer.

Another important difference between the Big Four USA sports and soccer is that soccer players have much more autonomy, and therefore responsibility, of the action of their sport. The Big Four sports games are typically interrupted every few seconds or minutes, each stoppage providing an opportunity for yet more player encouragement and strategizing by the coaching staffs. USA-football is the most extreme, having each play of the game scripted by the coaches. Soccer play is the exact opposite of this over-strategized sport model, with

---

[25] Venezuela has so far never appeared in the soccer World Cup, but had excellent results at the end of the 2002 World Cup qualifying tournament. Cuba participated in the third World Cup in Italy in 1938, and recently qualified for the Gold Cup (CONCACAF Championship) in 2003.

players only allowed to be coached before the game and during the half-time period. Soccer player autonomy is further established by the rule that allows only three players of the starting eleven to be substituted during a match. In contrast, the Big Four sports allow for *complete substitution* of all starting players in a game.

All of the above factors were nevertheless ignored in a mathematical modeling study from the Los Alamos National Laboratory (New Mexico, USA) released in January 2006 *that concluded* – after analyzing results of 300,000 matches of the Big Four sports and soccer – *soccer is the most exciting of the sports*. The study mainly measured the *unpredictability of games* with soccer having the highest "upset frequency," thereby providing hard scientific evidence that soccer is the most exhilarating and competitive of the major sports.[26]

Some team sports such as *team handball, ice hockey, field hockey, water polo* and *lacrosse* do have similar game objectives and dynamic playing strategies as soccer. The common strategy of these sports is to bring the ball (or puck) up the field by a series of inventive coordinated passes and/or dribbles culminating in a shot on a goal. Where all of these sports (and baseball, basketball, and USA-football) differ with soccer, is that *only one small part of the body – the hands – is involved in the ball (or puck) playing aspect*.

Hand Play versus Unlimited Play

As toddlers mature into childhood they learn how to control their world by using their hands, and hand play (or usage) is the dominant physical behavior in adult society. We humans have a prehensile thumb and have taken full advantage of it, especially in the sports necessitating an instrument to manipulate a ball or a puck (such as hockey and lacrosse).

However, most body motions in soccer involving non-hand parts of the body to control the ball are *unique to soccer and foreign to other sports*.

Herein lays the beauty of the game: *soccer has the common team strategies and objective, BUT the whole body is used to manipulate the game object* (the soccer ball). As the soccer ball can be controlled by any part of the body except for the arms, the dictum of soccer seems to be, "we have removed the easier aspects of hand play, now start practicing with the whole body."

This unrestrained whole body play is a sizeable component of what makes soccer limitless and fascinating, and continually sparks the imagination of people worldwide. Soccer is like a dance form – be it salsa, free-form jazz or ballet – and a perfect soccer form is a poetic dance with a ball using the entire body.

Team and Individual Play

Soccer is the simplest team game, played on a large field with eleven players on each team, with only the goalkeepers using their arms and hands to protect their goals. The game is essentially a continuous flow of improvised play interrupted only momentarily by substitutions, penalties or injuries. There are no "timeouts" as mandated either by the rules or by modern "television breaks."

Players on the team maintaining possession of the ball attempt to advance the ball toward and into the opposing goal, but must instantly metamorphose into defensive players the moment their team loses possession.

A large part of the enjoyment derived from playing soccer is watching other players on the field as they explore the nuances of the game – how to beat another player, creating space, running into space, maintaining awareness and anticipating where other players are as they move, threading a pass, intercepting, tackling, touch trapping, passing, and shooting. An intuition develops of what your teammates will do because of your long practice and game experience with them, and there is constant satisfaction when one anticipates what your teammates will do in advance of the opposition.

---

[26] Los Alamos study available at: http://cnls.lanl.gov/~ebn/pubs/sports/sports.pdf.

During the game, players make mental notes of what the opposition is doing, and cannot ignore the fine plays that the opposing players create. The initial appreciation is curiosity, as a player does not yet have a definite sense for what constitutes the opposition's individual talents or team cohesiveness. That awareness is continually accumulated during the game.

If a soccer player finds himself beaten by a fine move by an opposition player, he might be thinking, "That was slick, just how did he do that?" even as he tries to track the player down. This kind of mental note taking perfectly combines the aesthetic and tactical appreciation that embodies the thinking soccer player. Dutch soccer legend Johan Cruyff famously said, "Football is a game you play with your brain," and he was entirely correct. No other sport yet offers the *right brain – left brain*, or *aesthetic and spontaneous* yet *technical and tactical* challenge of free-form international football.

The Ageless Joy of Soccer

Soccer joy does not necessarily diminish with age, as it can be created and appreciated long into the golden years. A splendid example was the 2001 "Goal of the Year" contest in Germany, with the "Wonder Goals" supplied by the usual stars of the German First Division: German stars Michael Ballack and Gerald Asamoah, Brazilian striker Marcio Amoroso, and Peruvian whiz kid Claudio Pizzaro. But the winner (with 21% of the vote) was Kurt Meyer, an *octogenarian* playing with amateur club Post Recklinghausen Seniors. Meyer had scored a wonder goal from a near-impossible angle that was best appreciated and nominated by the voters. Only an insurmountable joy for the game can keep somebody performing into his eighties.[27]

As soccer is enjoyed near the end of life, a reminder to celebrate the arrival of new life came in the 1994 World Cup, when Brazil striker Bebeto honored both his goal and the recent birth of his child. Thus was born the cradle-rocking celebration, as Bebeto was joined by his teammates Mazinho and Romário [Figure 1B].

Seamless Joy of Soccer

The joy and beauty of soccer is spreading out into other models, specifically "small-ball" games played with fewer players on more compact fields. These forms have the advantage of giving players more time "on the ball" per minute. These newer soccer forms include: (1) *Futsal (futebol de salão* – Portuguese, *futbol de salón* – Spanish), (2) *indoor soccer*, and (3) *beach soccer*.

Futsal

The name Futsal is derived from the Spanish/Portuguese root words for *fut* (for football) and *sal* (for room, or indoors). Despite the name, Futsal matches are not restricted to indoor venues and are often performed outdoors. Futsal has so far generated several international synonyms: *futbol sala*, FDS (*futebol de salão*), *futbolito, futbito* or *five-a-side*.[28]

Futsal is a five versus five-player soccer format (one goalkeeper and four other players) designed to develop skills of youth players. In contrast to indoor soccer in the USA, Futsal does not allow any ball-play off sidewalls – thereby necessitating a higher skill level to keep the ball within the boundary lines. Futsal rules also do not allow excessive bodily contact as occurs in regulation soccer, therefore resulting in fewer player injuries [Figure 1C] (the complete rules of Futsal are listed at the FIFA website www.fifa.com).

There have been five FIFA Futsal World Championships, with Brazil (surprise!) winning the first three in 1989, 1992, and 1996. The 2000 Futsal World Championship was

---

[27] Lucien Laurent, the French international who scored the first ever goal in a World Cup match (opening game of the 1930 World Cup), was another individual who played amateur soccer into his eighties. He died in 2005 aged 97.
[28] Futsal was developed in 1930 in Uruguay by Juan Carlos Ceriani, and was likely independently developed in São Paulo, Brazil around the same time. The first rules were published in Brazil in 1936. The International Federation for Futebol de Sala (FIFUSA) was formed in Brazil in 1971, and FIFA adopted the game in 1989. Many Brazilian players credit playing Futsal in their youth with giving them superior technical skills as professionals.

held in Guatemala, and the Spaniards finally beat the Brazilians 4-3 in the Final. Still, Brazilian Futsal star Manoel Tobias had 19 goals in that tournament (outscoring all but five of the sixteen teams in the competition), and six of the top nine scorers were Brazilian. In the 2004 tournament in Chinese Taipei, Spain again beat Brazil, this time on penalty kicks in the semi-final, and went on to beat Italy in the Final to claim their second Futsal World Championship in a row.

The USA did fairly well in the early Futsal World Cups, finishing third in 1989 and second in 1992. However, they were eliminated early in 1996 and did not even qualify for the 2000 competition, an alarming trend that suggested USA soccer technique was less competitive. However, the USA did qualify for the 2004 Futsal World Championship and progressed to the second round again, only to lose all three games. Official Futsal rules will have to be widely established in the USA for it to be consistently competitive in the Futsal World Cup.

The rapidly evolving popularity of Futsal is staggering: seventy countries were involved in qualifying for the 2004 FIFA Futsal World Championship held in Chinese Taipei, and professional Futsal leagues are currently flourishing in Spain, Portugal, Russia and Brazil. Many experts have suggested that similar to the summer Olympics hosting regulation soccer competitions, a Futsal competition should be included in each future Winter Olympic Games.

Indoor Soccer USA-Style

Indoor soccer has been played in the USA for decades. The Major Indoor Soccer League (MISL) even outlasted the outdoor North American Soccer League (the NASL folded in 1984), and in 2006 still has a seven-team league (website at www.misl.net).

USA indoor soccer modifies the regulation soccer rules to make the game seem "more attractive" to the USA sports fan, which of course includes higher scoring games. Indoor soccer is played on a variety of hard indoor and artificial fields with special rules regarding offside and substitutions. The most important difference from regular soccer or Futsal is that indoor soccer allows play off perimeter walls surrounding the field of play. This rule makes for a technically less-demanding game (because mistakes are "forgiven" by the wall), and is therefore inferior to Futsal for optimal youth development.

Beach Soccer

Beach soccer is the newest form of organized soccer, and is five-a-side soccer played barefoot on a field of sand without shoes (socks are permitted). One major difference with Beach Soccer versus Futsal is that there is a "penalty box" similar to ice hockey, where penalized players must sit idle for two minutes.

Beach soccer started in Brazil decades ago, and was promoted by Beach Soccer World Wide (BSWW - www.beachsoccer.com) in the 1990s. BSWW is independent of FIFA, so the World Champion Beach Soccer competitions were not FIFA-sanctioned until the first FIFA Beach Soccer World Cup in 2005 in Brazil, which FIFA coordinated with the already experienced BSWW.[29] The 2005 Cup took place on a specially constructed field in the most densely populated place on the planet – the famous Copacabana Beach in Rio de Janeiro, Brazil.

BSWW had earlier managed to enlist such star players as Eric Cantona (France), Alain Sutter (Switzerland), Daniele Massaro and Pietro Vierchowod (Italy), Thomas Ravelli (Sweden) and Julio Salinas (Spain) in their ten world tournaments prior to 2005. Brazil (surprise!) won nine out of the ten annual BSWW World Championships of Beach Soccer, including the last in 2004 against Spain by a score of 3-2.

With the talismanic Cantona coaching, France won the inaugural 2005 FIFA Beach Soccer World Cup, on a penalty kick competition after a 3-3 tie match with Portugal. Host

---

[29] The FIFA Beach Soccer World Cup is the only FIFA-sponsored tournament that uses "soccer" in all languages instead of "football" (see www.fifa.com/en/index.html under Men's and Youth Tournaments in four languages), which is rather odd since it is yet another form of soccer invented in Brazil.

Brazil had been eliminated by Portugal after a penalty kick competition in the semi-finals, and eventually took third place.

Soccer Sportsmanship

Soccer has long adopted one of the highest forms of sportsmanship to celebrate the conclusion of matches – the *soccer jersey exchange* between individuals of the opposing teams. The shirt jersey exchange is most common in international matches between two national or club teams. Although this does not always occur, no other team sport can routinely claim this tradition that documents the joy of sports competition between peoples.

The most heartwarming exchange in the 2002 FIFA World Cup took place at the conclusion of the 3rd place game between the host South Korean team and the dynamic Turkish squad, as the teams circled the stadium arm in arm. That celebration was a picture perfect positive image of the unity of soccer.

Soccer Fan's Joy

The rest of this book details much about the fan's enjoyment of the game, the sense of community a club team can provide, and the appreciation of player and group skills. Soccer brings the world together, and it is the fans that truly support and appreciate all aspects of the sport.

The Official Emblem of the 2006 FIFA World Cup Germany supports this idea, as it is composed of three fans (perhaps a family of father, mother, and child) of neutral colors enjoying the spectacle of the World Cup, which is represented by a stylized World Cup trophy. It is the first Official Emblem of all the FIFA World Cups that represents the fans themselves.[30]

Soccer's Eternal and Universal Appeal

Soccer's absolute uniqueness in human history and modern sport cannot be summed up better than this anonymous quote:

Football's eternal and universal appeal can be largely attributed to the unique balance that it strikes between simplicity and sophistication. It is simple enough that it can be played anywhere with only one necessary object, a ball, and yet so sophisticated in that each country retains its own footballing culture, each match its own flavor, each team its own tactics. This diversity gives football a richness that few sports can match.

Summary of Soccer Joy Essentials

- Soccer is humanity's most popular sport, enjoyed by more than 250 million active players worldwide in the year 2006.
- Soccer is omnipresent because it is the simplest and most intuitive game people can enjoy.
- Soccer is simple because the game object is a ball, the rules are few and concise, and the game itself is a continuous flow of athletic and strategic possibilities.
- Soccer joy commences early on, beginning when a toddler walks.

---

[30] For the duration of this book, whenever "World Cup," "FIFA World Cup," "Futsal World Cup," "FIFA U-17 World Cup," "FIFA U-20 World Cup," et cetera, are mentioned, they refer to the trademarked events sponsored by FIFA (*Fédération Internationale de Football Association*) – such as the FIFA World Cup^{TM}.

Chapter Two

The Art of Soccer

Soccer is a game you play with your brain. *Johan Cruyff*

A game without goals is like a day without sunshine. *Alfredo Di Stéfano*

Art and the Art of Soccer

Art has many definitions, ranging from one-word synonyms to encyclopedic efforts attempting to thrash out a concept of Art. One-word synonyms of art include skillfulness, ingenuity, aptitude, craftsmanship, knowledge, expertise, adroitness, dexterity, mastery, knack, faculty, trickery, cunning, guile and cleverness. However, despite the best attempts by thesaurus writers, no single word can do justice to define soccer artistry. Perhaps all the synonyms added together would describe the sublime skills of the soccer artist.

A simple definition of art that efficiently applies to the art of soccer is
"The use of skill and imagination in the production of beauty."

In Britain soccer has been called the "working class ballet," and the sport's aficionados appreciate that beautiful soccer is truly an art form. For many individuals soccer is more than just a game – for some it is their dominant art form and practically a way of life.

The *Laws of Football* frame the canvas for the world art form, but the soccer artists create the dynamic image that is the Art of Soccer. Players must endure at least a decade-long apprenticeship attaining knowledge and practicing soccer skills just in order to develop into competent soccer craftsmen. The best craftsmen, accentuated by intense desire for the sport, have the ability to harness their imagination and improvise in any situation. But in order to innovate spontaneously they must first be technical experts of soccer, possessing the highest level of physical skill that will allow that improvisational expression. Without superb technique their ideas will dissolve into chaos, as they cannot be properly executed. Only a select group of players combine these attributes of imagination, improvisation and superb technique, which is what separates a master soccer artist from an ordinary soccer craftsman.

Soccer Art may be separated into three areas: the Physical Art, the Mental Art and the Cultural Art. This chapter reviews the first two Arts, while Chapter 3 examines the Cultural Art of soccer under the title *Soccer and Identity*.

PHYSICAL ART of SOCCER
Ball and Body Movements

Difference Between Soccer and Other Sports

The physical moves of soccer distinguish it from all other sports. Exciting soccer is all about feint and sleight of hand and foot – tricking your opponent as to where the ball is going. Other sports simply do not have the high intensity of feints and trick technique as when a player is controlling a soccer ball (often called "dominating" the ball).

Also unique to soccer is the manipulation of the game object – the soccer ball – on the body. No other sport allows for the interplay and expression of the body with the object of the game. Because of this characteristic the soccer ball is often spoken of as a feminine entity, and in some parts of the world such as Brazil players idly converse about caressing and sleeping with the soccer ball. The USA Big Four sports (baseball, basketball, USA-football, ice hockey) require the game object (a different type of ball or puck) to get from point A to point B – *but prudishly only with the hands thank you very much.*

Indeed, no other sport allows for *juggling* moves of the game object (and it would be illegal in most other sports). Juggling a soccer ball consists of keeping a ball off the ground using any part of the body except the arms below the shoulders. Foot to thigh to shoulder to head to chest to heel to sole of the foot, nearly the whole body is available for play in soccer. The juggling world record was broken often until current record holder Nicolai Kutsenko of the Ukraine juggled a full day (actually 24:30 hours) in 1995 with more than 100,000 ball touches. Other athletes have juggled a ball while running a full marathon, walking up and down stairs, or even climbing a ladder![1] These are amazing accomplishments, but that kind of skill alone may not translate into the array of skills needed to perform at a professional level. Still, juggling is a classic warm-up skill, and anybody who has seen Maradona, Pelé, or Ronaldinho juggle will have marveled at their skill.

Receiving the Ball

Receiving the ball is called "trapping," the goal of which is to bring the ball under close control quickly. The term *"trapping"* originated from the classic technique of stopping the ball between the foot and the ground, which ensnared, or "trapped" the ball. This technique is less preferred today because of the rapid movement of the game and more precise ways of controlling the ball without mandating use of the ground, but the terminology persists. Two salient points regarding the art of trapping are:

1. *Trapping is a fluid skill as passes arrive in a variety of angles and velocities.* [No two traps are alike.]

2. *The ability to make the optimal trap is often dependent on the quality of the pass.* [A poor pass may lead to an off balance trap or a dangerous "50-50" (or contested) ball].

There are many body areas and dozens of techniques to trap the ball:
- Standard trapping surfaces include the inside, outside, sole, or the top of the foot.
- Inside, outside and top of thigh are also common trapping areas.
- The whole chest area can be used to trap the ball down to the feet or to a teammate, or to pop the ball up for a bicycle kick.
- The top of the shoulder is a legal area to trap balls in the air, but referees may incorrectly call a handball.
- The forehead may be used to receive the ball if the player is skilled enough.[2]

---

[1] All sorts of football juggling records are listed at www.recordholders.org/en/list/ball.html.
[2] Brazil youth player Kerlon invented a move in 2004 called the "seal dribble," whereupon he evades defenses by running with the ball on his forehead.

Areas of the body not normally used to trap are located on the dorsal aspect (back) of the body because of the lack of control, as well as sensitive areas on the ventral (abdominal) side:
- The back of the leg (the calf muscles: gastrocnemius and soleus) and the back of the thigh (hamstring area) are not recommended for trapping because of difficult control as well as the "shock" potential to these tightly wound muscles. A defender may stop a shot accidentally with those areas if no other method is available.
- The shin area due to lack of control (with or without shin pads).
- The groin area is not intentionally used to trap due to the risk of genital injury.
- The back area is not used due to lack of control.
- The neck and facial area are not used to trap due to risk of injury.
- The butt or "ass" trap is a practical joke trap done from a high ball and is not useful in game situations except for entertainment value (Rodney Marsh, the "Clown Prince of Soccer," occasionally used this method).

The above are guidelines for the average player. No doubt Maradona, George Best, Pelé or soccer jester Marsh could have trapped the ball with their noses if they had to.

The physics of trapping the ball are straightforward, as Newton's Third Law of Motion predicts that "for every action, there is an equal and opposite reaction." This law explains that if a ball traveling at *x* speed hits a wall (or a foot) it will travel back at *x* speed minus any frictional forces encountered. Therefore, to execute a proper trap, the foot (or other body part) must cushion the ball by quickly withdrawing, thereby allowing the ball to immediately decelerate to a near stop. A proper trap requires this critical adjustment that allows for immediate control of the ball.

Another trapping imperative is the *direction in which the ball is immediately controlled has to be calculated in advance*. Therefore, *tactical trapping is also the first act of dribbling*.

Sending the Ball

Sending the ball is either "passing" or "shooting."

There is more passing than trapping action in soccer because many of the touches of the ball are "first-time" touches, meaning the ball was redirected without the necessity of bringing the ball under personal control. In essence, "one-touch" passing is the *simultaneous receiving and sending of the ball*. These first-time exchange passes between two players are often called a "give and go" or a "wall" pass.

Ideally, *the path the ball takes on a pass should be unimpeded*. Once the defense gets a touch on the ball, all imaginings of team coordination are temporarily thrown into chaos until possession is regained.

Passing

Passing is another skill in which the most creative players excel. Passing involves at least five separate skills – (1) *vision*, (2) *positioning*, (3) *timing*, (4) *pass angle*, and (5) *weight*.

(1) *Vision*: Players must first use their imagination to predict where to pass. As the game unfolds before him, the player must anticipate where his teammates and opponents will be in the next few seconds and transport the ball to the optimal place.

(2) *Positioning*: A player may need to get himself into the proper position to pass. That is, when the desired pass angle is already guarded he must maneuver himself and the ball to create the most favorable pass angle to the desired space. The best passers can create the space for themselves by dribbling or feinting for a clear pass.

(3) *Timing*: A player must select the optimal timing of the pass – exactly when to release the ball to allow another player to run through and gather it without violating the offside rule.

(4) *Pass angle*: The proper pass angle requires intuitive geometrical knowledge that accounts for each pass opportunity. Allowing for balls taking to the air, the pass angle is

actually a dynamic vector in 3-dimensional space (the reader may now refer back to notes from geometry class).

(5) *Weight*: This is perhaps the most difficult passing skill to execute consistently. The proper weight of a pass is defined as *how hard (or "heavy") the ball must be hit to arrive at the selected area at the proper time*. Taking into account the weather and field conditions, an innate differential calculus is required by the expert passer.

Passing can be initiated with many parts of the body, but passing with the feet is by far the most common. The inside, outside, heel and instep are all used in various ways. The inside is mostly used for accurate passes across the body, while the outside of the foot is used for passes on the same side of the body. The instep pass is used for distance, flight and accuracy. Combining the instep with the inside or outside of the foot will create an in-swinging or out-swinging pass, respectively. The heel can be used for a back-heel or step-over heel flip pass.

After the feet, the head provides the impetus behind the next most common passes (the forehead is used as it is the hardest part of the cranium and the use of other parts of the face or head may result in injury). The whole body is involved in every heading action, best demonstrated by the *diving header* technique below. The chest, thigh, and knee are also used for passing (chest passes in particular have become more sophisticated as one-touch passes to a teammate).

Diving header phases: commitment and extension, execution, and full follow-through.

When a teammate is unmarked (free or unguarded) behind a closely guarded player receiving a pass, the best option may be to simply run over the ball (by letting it pass through or by the legs). This fake-play of the ball is called *dummying* the ball. Pelé was the master at "selling" a dummy – faking out the defender without ever touching the ball. Pelé would put his whole body into the feint, and his marker would be sprawled over where he thought the ball would be if Pelé had controlled it. More recently, his compatriot Rivaldo sold a beautiful dummy to set up Ronaldo's second goal of the 2002 World Cup Final against Germany. Of course, if the teammate is not aware that a dummy is a possibility, he will also be faked out. That is why familiarity of teammates' style of play is so important.

In some situations the best option is to pass the ball through an opponent's legs, either to the same player (in a dribbling action) or to another player. This same-player move is inexplicably called a "nutmeg" in England (also, to "nut" or "meg" a player), but in the West Indies it is just as curiously called a "salad." In Latin America there are various terms used to describe this action: "tunél" (tunnel), "sala" (exit), "ventana" (window), or even "camote" (sweet potato). Some nicknames are intuitive while others are merely cute.

Special passing skills include passing with the heel of the foot, either softly for accuracy or across the body for power. Heel play in tight quarters is the fastest growing aspect of the soccer passing game. The heel can occasionally be used in aerial play, as the foot is usually lifted up across the body and the ball is flicked on to a teammate with the heel. Alfredo Di Stéfano used to score goals with a behind-the-back heel shot called a *talón* shot. Another spectacular move with the heel is to launch the body forward into the air, arch the back, and shoot the ball with a back-heel action. This very difficult move is a kind of reverse bicycle kick (see below) and was one of the Brazilian Zico's specialties. Finally, while dribbling, one can simply run over the ball pretending to play it, and back pass it to a teammate as the natural stride lifts up the heel to meet the oncoming ball (the step-over heel flip pass).

Another type of pass involving the heel – in this case the inside of the heel combined with the sole of the opposing foot – was perfected by Vladislav Bogićević of Yugoslavia (member of the 1974 World Cup team) and the New York Cosmos. This pass involves both feet when the player is advancing forward and is met by a defender; the ball is pulled back by the sole of the foot very quickly towards the back of the opposite foot, while the opposite heel simultaneously pirouettes towards the oncoming ball to send it out at a 45 degree angle on the opposite side of the kicking foot. The move is virtually impossible to defend against because it confuses defenders into thinking, "Wait a minute, he's pulling the ball back where? Oh, there it goes…" This pass is named the *"pullback-heel pass"* or the *Bogićević special* until somebody has a better idea. It is fitting that a Yugoslavian popularized this move that included a sole of the foot technique, as the Yugoslavians were often called "the Brazilians of Europe." It was the Brazilian soccer artists that popularized the sole of the foot soccer moves that are less popular in Europe (possibly due to cold and wet conditions that make sole of the foot moves more difficult).

The pullback-heel pass is a good move while advancing towards the goal with a teammate, either to safely pass to him or to score past the goalkeeper at a 45-degree angle. When advancing from the left, you must shoot with the right heel, when advancing from the right, pullback with the right foot and shoot with the left heel. The goalkeeper will be as mystified as a defender, but this is not a recommended shooting technique because of the high skill level and there are easier ways of scoring. Additionally, all moves involving the sole of the foot are best done on a dry field. This lesson was demonstrated in the 1997 MLS Cup final between DC United and the LA Galaxy, when DC United was leading 2-1 and threatening to score again in the final minutes in the rain. The brilliant Marco Etcheverry tried a *Bogićević special* just a few yards from the right side of the goal (he is left-footed) and whiffed on it, missing a sure goal to make it 3-1. DC United still won, but Marco likely felt a bit sheepish afterwards. If Bolivian international Etcheverry had trouble doing this move on goal, it is probably best to use it just in midfield play and fool your goalkeeper only in practice.

Another move perhaps best left on the practice field is the *behind the back pass*. The kicking foot swings behind the planted non-kicking foot and strikes the ball with the instep. This "hot dog move" can be done stationary or running, but doing it while running is extremely difficult to execute well. Diego Maradona once centered the ball perfectly with his left foot from the right side while running with this move, and another Argentine player converted for goal. Outrageous! It is only a matter of time before somebody uses this move on a penalty kick attempt (but not recommended here because of high skill level required).

Shooting

Shooting is a specialized form of passing, and more goals are scored by accuracy than from pure power. The object of shooting is the same as passing (to propel the ball to a designated place at the proper time) except that place is an area of the goal unguarded by the goalkeeper. The most successful goal scorers understood that many shots require less than full power to attain optimum placement in the goal. Pelé, Johan Cruyff, Diego Maradona, Jimmy Greaves and Romario were all experts in pinpoint passing the ball into the net.

The pass angle combined with the weight of the pass determines the *pass placement* (called the *shot placement* if meant to shoot on goal), which is the when and where the soccer ball is delivered. The effectiveness of the shot placement (whether or not a goal is scored) is also dependent on the velocity and trajectory of the shot. Straight shots or curving shots that are below the goal crossbar are more effective with higher velocity. Shots hit below the center of the ball to create a "knuckle" effect also can be hit with high velocity. Shots meant to bounce before goal can also generally be hit hard. If a shot depends at all on gravity, such as on "dry leaf" or "banana" shots, there will be an optimum velocity that will place the ball in the net without traveling harmlessly above the crossbar.

The intuitive calculus of angles, ball speed, drag of wind and field surface, and gravity can be computed electronically, but the resulting shot on the field is derived from countless years of experience and practice. Those eager to further explore the mathematics and physics of soccer should consult John Wesson's book, *The Science of Soccer*.

Also crucial to striking an optimal shot is the position of the body, especially the body feint as a player shoots the ball. If a player can convince the goalkeeper by his body position (especially the knee position of his shooting leg) that he will shoot the ball into the right corner but still place it in the left corner, he has an advantage over the athletic abilities of the keeper. This mastery of body feinting is especially important in taking penalty kicks.

Finally, the speed of the collection of the pass and shot is very important, as speed of technique may often surprise the defense and goalkeeper, leaving them split seconds of reaction time behind.

Some players are better at calculating angles quicker and have more composure in front of the goal than others. These are the goal scorers of the team, the center forward or "number 9" (in the current popular formation of 4-4-2, with four defenders, four midfielders, and two strikers, the two strikers are likely number 9 and 11). Those who can create in addition to scoring goals are the magical "number 10s" (often called *fantasistas* in South America), as were many of the great attacking midfielders and creative strikers. The "number 10" usually plays "in the hole," slightly behind the two strikers.

Striking the Ball

A soccer ball may be struck in many different ways to obtain distinctive ball effects. The most basic way of striking the ball is under the center, which will elevate the ball depending on the foot angle and contact speed. Passes on the ground have to be struck near the center to avoid popping the ball into the air.

One difficult method is to strike the ball at high velocity exactly at the center of the ball (or fractionally above) to produce an unpredictable "knuckle" effect. The ball is struck at full force and results in minimal or no rotation of the ball. With no top- or backspin to smoothly guide its path, the football is maneuvered by wind currents and gravitational effects determined by the imperfections of the ball itself. The result is a powerfully struck ball that may first move left and back right again, or move up and down rapidly and unpredictably. Toto Schillaci's famous shot in 1990 World Cup had this unpredictable up and down motion as it dropped behind the Uruguayan keeper Alvez. The Brazilian Eder was another such free-kick specialist with the ability to fool a goalkeeper with this demanding shot (see Chapter 18).

Dribbling

Dribbling can be thought of as a special form of passing – that of passing to oneself. The intention is similar, to control the ball on an offensive move. The move can be forward, sideways or even backwards, as the ball will eventually advance forward if kept under control by one person or team.

There are numerous dribbling moves, a few of which are listed below.

A famous maneuver involving feint and trickery is the *Cruyff turn,* named for Johan Cruyff of Holland. The player feints going forward or to kick, but instead pulls the ball back with the middle inside of the foot behind the planted leg, thus quickly reversing direction. The player can then set off dribbling, pass or shoot rapidly with the other foot. The Cruyff turn is nearly impossible to defend because the ball is protected behind the planted leg, making a direct challenge a likely foul play.

A more demanding South American version of the Cruyff turn is the *"side push-pullback."* This technique has a feint built into the first movement. Starting in one place, the player pushes the ball at a 90-degree angle with the outside of his foot, and when the ball reaches the end of the foot reach, pulls the ball back fluidly with the toe of the foot behind the planted leg.

The Brazilian ball magician Roberto Rivelino's version of a reverse-direction move would be to show the ball to the opponent like a matador shows his red cape to a bull, then swerve to the left while trodding on the ball thereby jerking it to the left (Rivelino was a lefty). As the ball reached the end of his leg reach, he would whip it back in front of him to go off in the opposite direction. That move truly played havoc with defenders' minds.

A distant variation of the Cruyff special is the *"dominant leg whip-around,"* using a player's dominant leg because of the level of difficulty. Instead of pulling the ball back with the inside of the foot, the player steps on the ball with the sole of his foot then curls it around the back of the non-dominant foot to exit in front of that foot. Like the *"side push-pullback,"* the first part of the move has the body (and defense) leading right, while the second part has the ball exiting left. The Brazilian Ronaldo is an expert in this movement.

A *"pullback"* move is when the sole of the foot pulls the ball back in the 180 degree opposite direction. It is an essential move for any middle level player, but a radical *double pullback* was part of Grenada national team striker Barry James' repertoire (see Chapter 18). BJ would execute two pullbacks in a row, faking the defense that he was retreating one way but quickly reversing to attack again. BJ would lean so far back doing the double he looked like he was defying gravity. The most remarkable part of the BJ double pullback was the speed of which he could execute it – whoosh, whoosh, and the defense was left hanging. BJ would then use the resultant defensive confusion to shoot or pass off to an open teammate.

The fake pullback move keeps the defense honest when they anticipate a pullback or Cruyff turn. Simply step on the top of the ball, pull it back slightly, then lean forward and roll it ahead.

The *stepover* is a feint move made famous by many members of the Brazil team, especially Rivelino, Tostão and Pelé. This involves faking dribbling with one leg, but instead stepping over the ball from the inside or outside of the body. The defender leans in the direction of the feint, while the offensive player is free to change direction with the added space resulting from the move. A superb example of the power of the stepover was Ronaldinho's massive stepover at full speed against England in the 2002 World Cup that completely unbalanced Ashley Cole and the English defense. The move allowed him to slip the ball to an unmarked Rivaldo, who slotted it home from 16 yards for the equalizing goal (Brazil won the game 2-1 after Ronaldinho's winning free-kick goal from distance – see Chapter 9). Robinho of Brazil and Cristiano Ronaldo of Portugal are two other modern stepover experts. The stepover is sometimes labeled a "lollipop" move (a "show-off" or "hot-dog" technique) in which the ball direction does not actually change despite the consumption of a lot of energy. So the stepover is really a feint or setup move for a ball-moving technique, and an expert technician can ensure his energy expenditure is rewarded when he rounds his defender.

There are many dribbling moves involving both feet with the ball going in a back and forth motion mystifying the defender. One unusual move involves the dominant foot heeling the ball back onto the inside of the other foot, whereupon the ball pops out ahead of the player on the dominant foot side and the player can dribble away – a wall pass to oneself. It is another "stun" move whereby the time the defender figures out where the ball is, the offensive player is already away. This is even of a higher skill level than the *pullback-heel pass* (*Bogićević special*), and both moves are usually executed on the player's dominant side. This can be called the *"heel-opposite foot self wall pass,"* a move Pelé mastered.

Another dribbling wall-pass is where the player uses the defender as the wall (*defender-wall-pass*). This was another of Pelé's specialties, as he would poke the ball off the opposition's shin back to himself, and, by the time the defender had realized what had happened, Pelé was long gone. Pelé also used to deliberately kick the ball off the inside of a defender's leg to have it pop out on the side he was already running to recover it – a modified *nutmeg self-pass* off the defender.

Many of these complex movements are interesting in that no body feint is necessary to fool the defense, as the move itself incorporates adequate feinting maneuvers.

Special, Skill, or "Trick" Moves

The *bicycle kick* is the most spectacular – yet the most opportunistic and desperate – move that exists in soccer. Ideally, it should occur only on air balls in the goal areas, either to shoot on goal offensively or to clear a goal shot defensively. The "bicycle" is performed as such: the player jumps up into the air, leans back, pumps his non-kicking foot forward and then backwards to get momentum, then meets the ball with the instep of the kicking foot. The legs move in different directions in a scissor movement. Offensively the bicycle is partly a blind shot done by "feel," as the player is kicking backwards and must concentrate on the ball hitting his foot exactly. He must therefore take cues of where the goal is located, even before the shot is attempted. A defensive bicycle kick is a desperation move to clear the ball from the goalmouth, and need not be aimed like an offensive bicycle kick.

A bicycle kick performed between the goal areas is usually a wasted move that could be substituted by a safer simple overhead kick. The midfield area contains more space to create, and passes in that area should demand more accuracy than a bicycle kick can safely deliver. Furthermore, there is no need to do an airborne maneuver unnecessarily, as there is always a small risk of injury. The player must land on his upper back area supported by his arm(s), preferably rolling over onto his side at the same time to cushion the fall. Done correctly, there is no pain and little risk of injury.

A perfectly taken bicycle kick is a thing of beauty, even if it just misses the goal like Marcelo Balboa did with his "bicycle" in the USA vs. Colombia 1994 World Cup game.[3] Bicycle kicks were another of Pelé's specialties, and his compatriot Rivaldo is also an expert. Rivaldo's chest trap setting up his dramatic 18-yard bicycle kick goal against Valencia in the last game of the 2001 Spanish League dramatically completed his hat-trick, and sent Barcelona through to the Champion's League competition.

In Latin America, the bicycle kick is called a *chilena*, *chalaca,* or *bicicleta*, depending on which country you are visiting. The bicycle kick was likely invented in Chile (hence *chilena*), although Brazilian legend Leonidas da Silva made the kick famous at the 1938 World Cup in France.

A player must be courageous and in the right frame of mind to successfully execute a bicycle kick. For example, a bicycle kick opportunity may result from a poor centering pass that the player cannot otherwise propel towards goal by foot or head. The player must have the thought in his mind already, "If the pass comes behind me, I'll try a bicycle kick." Without that thought possibility, he probably will not be prepared when the rare opportunity arises. In this sense, the bicycle kick is both a spontaneous and planned maneuver.

A move related to the bicycle is the *scissors* (*tijera* in Spanish) kick. It is basically a bicycle kick done on an angle rather than upside down [next page]. The player still needs to stabilize his body with the non-kicking leg, and scissor the legs to get momentum for the actual shot, which is often taken at a 90-degree angle to the ground (instead of 180 degrees like the bicycle kick).

A move called a *clam digger* occurs when a player grasps the ball firmly between the heels, then jumps up and whips the ball forward around the body on either side. Done with enough force it will go over the opponent's head facing the player. This is seen more on the practice field, but the Brazilian Denilson has done it in competitive games.

---

[3] Balboa's bicycle kick has its own exhibit at the *USA Soccer Hall of Fame* in Oneonta, New York.

Proper volleying technique is a necessary skill for both bicycle and scissor kicks: Getting set in the right position, exact eye contact with ball, and full follow-through.

Mexican national striker Cuauhtémoc Blanco invented a piece of trickery known as the "*Cuauhtémoc hop*," which involves leaping through a gap between opposing defenders clutching the ball between his ankles (almost a forward *clam digger*). Another difficult move is the *rainbow*, (*arco iris* in Spanish, *roulette* in French). This move is done stationary, or on the run in a game by a ball wizard such as Pelé or Djalminha, both of Brazil.[4] Both feet grab the ball at the same time while the feet are both pointed forward, the dominant foot in front with the non-dominant trailing. The non-dominant foot pulls the ball up the back leg of the dominant foot, and by the running motion, the ball kicks off the dominant heel and is elevated over the player's head. If a rainbow is executed perfectly, the player can continue running and collect the ball over his and the defenseman's head, without missing a stride. The best recent example of a *rainbow* was in the first Brazil-Turkey game in the 2002 World Cup, when İlhan Mansiz of Turkey outrageously flipped the ball over Roberto Carlos' head (Chapter 9). Roberto Carlos had to foul Mansiz from behind to stop the spectacular play from continuing, and was lucky not to receive a yellow card for his transgression.

Defending

A soccer team must defend *en masse* (all together), because if they do not have ball possession everybody is a defender. Strikers who show the initiative to defend are invaluable, and there are few players who defend poorly who are not a liability to their teams (The Brazilian Romario is one of these rare players who comes to mind).

Soccer defending means to engage in maneuvers intended to recover the ball from the opposing team. Good defending requires anticipation of the moves of the offensive team, resulting in interrupting play and intercepting the ball. This is more difficult than it appears, and as a result the defending team often relies on the second recovery option – unforced

---

[4] The "rainbow" is popularly known as a "Jay Jay Okocha" in Germany, because of this Nigerian national team player's skill in executing the move.

errors of the offensive team. Unforced errors usually occur from an overly ambitious or poorly placed pass.

How does one defend against sophisticated soccer trickery? What are the secrets of anticipating an opponent's actions and/or thoughts? Consulting a 2000-year-old martial art regarding self-defense, one learns that *kung-fu* masters were trained to concentrate on their opponent's body at mid-chest level. This allows their peripheral vision to alert them to movements of the four limbs, and to track the direction of their opponent. However, in soccer this method may result in the defender losing track of the direction of the ball. Mystical martial art methods do not necessarily work in soccer, because the ball may not be going where the center of the body is initially headed.

On the other hand, watching only the ball and not the man will leave a player open to sleight-of-foot magic tricks – here is the ball, there it is gone. The ball may not follow a logical path when under a skilled ball handler's control.

Therefore, the best defenders study an individual's moves by closely observing *both the ball and the player's body*, and watching for breaks in technique. Anticipation or "mind reading" is a key skill; the player who can put himself in the ball handler's shoes understands better the dynamic possibilities of ball and man. With experience, a defender can anticipate what might be happening in the offensive schemes, and close down the passing angles to intercept the ball. Defenders should also work in synchrony (double-teaming) by turning an opponent into another defender. Turning an opponent into the sideline also gives the offensive player less room and potential to create danger.

Good defense is underappreciated because as soon as the ball is recovered, the team immediately switches to an offensive mode. Therefore, a defensive success of an interception lasts just a moment, while offensive moves may be made of a dozen or more touches involving many team players. Therefore, in terms of ball movement during games, offensive time of possession far exceeds defensive time of possession.

Finally, the best defenders are also good offensive players, both in their ability to distribute and attack on the ground or in the air. Despite an increasing trend to create more specialized roles for players, a top defender should have excellent two-way skills.

Summary of Soccer Ball and Body Movements

The above descriptions of the dynamic body and ball actions of soccer will inevitably fall short of satisfying the reader. Mere two-dimensional ink on paper – although amplified by the infinite dimensions of the human imagination – is not adequate to teach the soccer apprentice proper techniques. The masterwork on teaching soccer movements was published in 1965 by legendary Hungarian coach Árpád Csanádi, but it is slightly dated and would benefit from including all the new techniques of the past forty years. Two good more recent books on the subject by David Spurdens (*World Soccer Skills,* published in 1984) and Simon Clifford (*Play the Brazilian Way,* published in 1999) attempt to show the most challenging and beautiful soccer movements, but both fall short despite good photography sequences.[5] The best solution for teaching special skills is by live demonstration or the simulated three dimensions of video. As videotaping did not exist in the 1960s and 1970s one could only learn "live" from the best players available. If a video series were made with star players incorporating all the moves of these two books, it would be a stunner. A video of the 2002 World Cup highlights film is a good beginning for learning moves, and Clifford has made an interesting video (*Learn to Play the Brazilian Way*) to accompany his book.

After making a spectacular move or shot in a game, players are sometimes asked to repeat it in practice but find they cannot duplicate the move. This is because although expert technique is learned, each shot presents a new and different challenge. Tennis master Bjorn

---

[5] Csanádi's book was the 684 page *Soccer: Technique-Tactics-Coaching*, published in Hungary by Corvina Press and Athenaeum. It was simply titled "Labdarúgás" in the original Hungarian (see cover), and was a comprehensive work that also introduced important new concepts such as nutrition that are now integral to modern soccer training.

Borg said he never hit a tennis ball the same twice, and so it is the same in soccer. This is important to remember when watching professionals that perform actions differently from standard soccer instruction, as they have already graduated from the mechanized practice of school soccer. Although soccer fundamentals must be learned well in order to elevate above the rest, dogmatic soccer technique is frequently spontaneously amended to reach the highest levels.

One sunny day in 1987 at Fordham University in New York City a skinny Italian kid executed a perfect "rainbow" over his defender in a pickup game. He was a new immigrant, fresh off the boat and full of talent, and one had to admire the thought, technique and sheer sauce of the attempt and success of the move. This is why true aficionados never get bored with "street soccer." If you have just paid good money and watched a pitifully cynical and violent professional game, venture out another day and play or watch some soccer in your neighborhood. You are just as liable to see quality play that is full of surprises.

Body Types in Soccer

Body Sizes

Soccer is the Everyman sport. There is no perfect soccer body, although it is said that *"legs of a sprinter, lungs of a marathoner"* is a good template for a soccer player. One of the equities of soccer is that unique individuals, short or tall, stout or slim, have excelled at the highest level. Players need only have well-developed lower extremities (from hip to foot), coordination and endurance.

Shorter players between 158-168 centimeters (5'2" to 5'6") tall, such as António Simões of Portugal, Alain Giresse of France, Anthony "Pitufo" de Avila of Columbia and Diego Maradona of Argentina all excelled in club and international play. Tall field players (greater than 190 centimeters, or 6'3") such as Alejandro Villanueva from Peru, Ralf Edström from Sweden, and John Carew from Norway did not allow their higher center of gravity be a hindrance to excellent play.[6]

Before the English played Hungary's "Magical Magyars" at Wembley Stadium on 25 November 1953 in one such "Game of the Century," a local player overconfidently commented, "Look at that little fat chap. We'll murder this lot." The "little fat chap" was the solidly-muscled Ferenc Puskas, who then proceeded to dismantle the English defense as Hungary easily won 6-3 (see Chapter 7). Looks can be deceiving in soccer.

There may be a theoretical optimal balance between body height, speed and center of gravity in soccer, but in reality this is not obvious. Most of the great players presented in Chapter 7 are from 5'6" (168 cms) to 6'2' (188 cms), a span of only eight inches (20 cms) – very much the size of the "average man." Interestingly, extra-tall individuals such as African basketball players Hakeem Olajuwon (208 cms, 6'10") and Dikembe Mutumbo (213 cms, 7 feet) developed their athletic abilities playing soccer before discovering basketball.

Soccer players rarely weigh over 200 lbs (90 kilos), as the physical demands of the sport dictate that players cannot carry that weight and compete for 90 or 120 minutes. So no matter the given body type, a player can excel in soccer as long as he is in tremendous physical shape and has the drive to fulfill his optimal ability.

An estimated 95 percent of the world's adult male population can play soccer with the average body size delineated above. USA-football and basketball cannot make this claim, as both sports rely on the philosophy "bigger and taller is better." Although height ranges from 5'8" to 6'10" (173-208 cms), more than eighty percent of all USA-football professional players weigh over 100 kilos, with some weighing more than 140 kilos! Professional basketball players are getting bigger all the time – up to 7'5" (223 cm) and 140 kilos. At a

---

[6] Taller players are increasingly entering the professional soccer ranks, such as strikers Peter Crouch of England and Jan Koller of the Czech Republic – both about 6'7" (201 centimeters).

professional level, these two sports have become limited to less than 10% of the world's adult male population.

Ice hockey players are also getting larger, in part due to the inherent violence of the North American approach to the game (in contrast to the more artful European passing style). Baseball players come in a variety of larger sizes due to the inherent static nature of the game, and the increasing desire for more home runs. Gone forever it seems are the smaller skilled players such as Maurice Richard and Yvan Cournoyer in hockey, and Phil Rizzuto and Billy Martin in baseball. These two sports are limited by body size to approximately 50 percent of the world's adult male population.

In summary, with regard to body size, soccer is an inclusive sport while the Big Four USA sports are already exclusive sports that are becoming increasingly restricted. Soccer is truly the world sport in that almost anybody has the raw potential to play at the highest level.

Soccer Physique and Physical Attributes

At first glance many top soccer players do not look like top-flight athletes. Their finely tuned lower extremities combined with a marathoner's lung capacity are easily concealed, making players such as Roberto Baggio or Zinedine Zidane look more like accountants than top skill athletes.

Raw speed by itself is overrated in soccer. Rather than speed, *quickness*, especially the ability to explode from a standstill in the first few steps (1 to 3 meters), is a more useful attribute in soccer. Most top players were not speedsters in the sense of a sprinter, but they developed the ability to move quickly with the ball and out-feint the opposition in those most important first two to five steps. Players such as Roberto Baggio, George Best, Johan Cruyff, Kenny Dalglish, Diego Maradona, Pelé and Zico all had that initial explosive ability.

Quickness alone is not enough, either. The ability to move the ball with the body at optimal speed, to change speed and direction at will, and to develop and change a dribbling rhythm – all these skills are necessary to continually beat players. This ability *to control the ball at optimal speed* is in theory within the reach of any player of any size. The Argentine Juan Román Riquelme is a modern master of soccer quickness and ball control, and more rarely, is able to consciously change the cadence of the play.

Speed and coordination can be further developed through physiologic training, which together with excellent technique and understanding of the game results in an improved player.

USA "Best Athletes" Myth

It is often incorrectly claimed the USA has not become a soccer power because all the "best athletes" play the Big Four sports.[7] As shown above, this is a fallacious argument, as many of those athletes are oversized and over-muscled, and in fact, would have difficulty playing a sport that demands maximum flexibility. There are plenty of USA citizens with the Paolo Maldini, Gerd Müller or Pelé body types. What truly matters in the evolution of a master player are the spirit and the desire to train, learn and innovate. Simply stated, soccer ability results from developed talent and passion.

Where is soccer headed with regard to body type? Hopefully, the soccer body type will stay within reach of most of the world's population. However, if the level of violent "professional" fouls continues or increases in the future, soccer may see the disappearance of players the size of Maradona or Baggio, only to be replaced by huskier types deemed more immune to injury. This would be a massive blow to the world game of soccer.

---

[7] Even if one assumes the preposterous idea of USA "best athletes" all playing the USA Big Four professional sports, they were doing poorly by 2006. The USA Olympic basketball team made up of professional players barely won a bronze medal in 2004, and the USA professional baseball team were eliminated in the second round of the inaugural World Baseball Classic in March 2006 (Japan beat amateurs Cuba in the Final). Both of the all-professional USA teams competed against teams that often incorporated semi-professional or even amateur players.

MENTAL ART of SOCCER

The Thought of Art

Art has a creative and emotional base. Art represents a way of thinking – a voyage from a feeling within resulting in a physical manifestation of that emotion.

Spatial imagery and spontaneous creativity are prized abilities generally acknowledged to develop in the right side of the brain (intuitive), while strategy and analysis are abilities honed and maintained mostly through the left side of the brain (logical). Nobody understood this better than Johan Cruyff, whose mantra was "football is a game you play with your brain."

By intuition, experience, and analysis, a player can anticipate what the next ball and player moves should be on offense or defense. A soccer master maps out the most fortuitous evolving options in the physical chess match of soccer. The major difference is that unlike the static stature of the chess pieces, options change moment-to-moment in soccer. That is the mind-body dynamic that creates the beautiful game of international football. Regardless of a player's impressive physical talents, his usefulness will also be gauged on his ability to continually analyze – even prophesize – the action in the game.

Mind-Body Improvisation: The Zen of Soccer

Another attribute a top player must develop is *vision*. Vision requires the ability to predict the game as it unfolds, and to constantly know where the other players are on the field.

When a player knows where his opponents and teammates are at all times, he is truly a master of position play. He is like a Zen master, "feeling" where his opponents and teammates are by utilizing his developed peripheral vision. This ability is obviously enhanced when a player is intimately familiar with his teammates' playing habits. The best creative passers have this "field sense" ability, and often appear to have "eyes in the back of their head."

The companion skill of this soccer Zen awareness is the technique to dribble without looking at the ball, to bring the ball along by feel rather than sight. Players who combine these difficult skills, like Roberto Baggio, Johan Cruyff, Diego Maradona, Pelé, Ronaldinho, Juan Román Riquelme, and Zinedine Zidane, are rare and spectacular.

Practiced invention involves learning the movements of teammates in practice so a player can coordinate his game with them. *Discovered invention* refers to the observation of opposition movements during the game, so any discovered weaknesses can be exploited. Added to this dynamic supply of knowledge is the *spontaneous invention* that occurs in tight quarters during the game, when an individual must rely on instinctual or spontaneous movements to extract himself and the ball from a dangerous situation. These invention skills are similar to those of a jazz musician – jazz provides a framework melody (practiced) with instrumental refrains (discovered) and improvisational free play (spontaneous). Since there may be 1,000 touches on the ball in a single soccer game, there are plenty of opportunities for players to "play the notes right."

As a result of these multiple mental skills that are developed over time, soccer is both a right brain (spontaneous and creative) and a left brain (calculating and analyzing) game, and therefore the quintessential *complete brain game.*

Psychology and Mental Fortitude

Peruvian international Teófilo "Nene" Cubillas (Chapter 7) agrees with Cruyff's view when he stated, "soccer is mostly mental." But Cubillas also made clear that his view includes the critical psychological preparation necessary in the sport.

According to Cubillas, individual and team attitude is the great mental equalizer in soccer matches. A player's attitude matures as a result of the training and mentorship received in development, and proper attitude development should result in a permanent "can-do" and "striving-to-be-the-best" mind-set. Further experience brings the proper mature attitude in important matches, even under extremely adverse circumstances such as unfamiliar stadiums in foreign lands.

Specific environments may improve attitude; that is why most teams have a better record playing at home (the "home team advantage"), and some "inferior" teams beat "superior" teams in important games. Overconfidence is a foolish attitude because less-experienced and/or talented teams can still out-hustle and out-create the favorite. Any team, no matter how highly rated, still must perform in every match. With the proper mind-set, one can play at a higher level or "above one's level" because of cohesive team and positive individual attitudes.

A good example of "playing above one's level" was the Greek national team, which was given virtually no chance of winning the 2004 European Championships. But the Greeks emerged as champions by defeating France, the Czech Republic and hosts Portugal (twice), thereby demonstrating the strength of their team unity.

Adapting to and Accepting the Playing Environment

A team often seems to play above their normal level in front of their home fans. Large countries with good quality teams such as Mexico and the United States have long found it difficult to prevail at smaller Central American and Caribbean venues with squadrons of rabid fans. For example, Jamaica was unbeaten in more than fifty consecutive home games at their National Stadium in Kingston that is nicknamed "The Office."

But besides playing in front of a hostile crowd, there are other physical aspects that coaches need to take into account. Temperature and humidity can vary widely from the location a team normally trains to where a game takes place, and players should have time to accustom themselves to these new conditions. But all these factors are complicated when the issue of altitude is brought into the equation.

Altitude is the great physiologic equalizer, and needs to be prepared for mentally as well as physically. As the altitude increases, there is less oxygen available for consumption, and fitness becomes more important than usual. A team trained at altitude for a home game not only knows the temperature and humidity levels and how the ball plays in that climate, but also has adapted their play to altitude and is likely fitter as a result.

Denver, called the Mile High City because of its altitude of 1650 meters (5280 feet), is the hometown of the Colorado Rapids, the highest Major League Soccer (MLS) team. However, well-conditioned athletes do not have much difficulty adapting to mile-high altitude on short notice. Mexico City is located at 2300 meters above sea level (7500 feet), and has an added complication of a malignant smog condition. The air pollution gives an additional level of uncertainty to visiting players, and players complain as much of the smog conditions as of the elevated altitude. Because of the smog, it is probably not advisable to bring players to Mexico City to train before the game, but to train at high altitude in a pollution-free zone, as there is no acclimation regimen for smog. Whether it was the altitude, smog and/or fine play of the Mexican national team, they maintained a streak of 52 unbeaten matches in the massive Azteca stadium in Mexico City, until they lost to Costa Rica's team in the 2001 World Cup qualifiers.

Art versus Non-Art in Soccer

A detailed discussion of soccer tactics and playing styles is beyond the scope of this book, but they do require an understanding of soccer art. Rivaldo's thoughtful statement at the 2002 World Cup, "*Destroying the opponent is easy, but creating the game is difficult,*" refers to much of football today, in which teams prefer to punish or "destroy" the opposition, as opposed to creating an authentic aesthetic that is practical and pleasing to the eye.

Art, when it is good, is enthralling; when bad, it can be appalling. Just as soccer artists create beauty, the destroyers produce hideous acts of ugliness. Bad soccer art is essentially "non-art," as there is nothing artful about it.

The Argentine team Estudiantes de La Plata promoted a bad soccer art form in the late 1960s, which was unfortunately successful in competitions. Playing ugly, violent, cynical, unimaginative and uninspiring soccer (a style called *el antifútbol* ["anti-football"] in Argentina), they wore down teams playing imaginative and fair play soccer. Many teams have since discovered this tactical option, and emphasize high work-rate, dubious tackling, goal packing, non-creative "negative" soccer.

Some teams do this through tactics; they start with the *catenaccio* (chain) goal-packing defense, and then produce even more negative tactics. If the offense nears the 18-yard box, they will bring a player down hard before the foul can result in a penalty kick (the oxymoronic "professional foul" – there is nothing professional about it). While the catenaccio itself can be a serious and creative tactical style provided it is coupled with an incisive counterattack arising from the defense, some modern teams unfortunately adapt it as a singular and negative defensive strategy.

Below is a summary table of the dominant attributes of the *Art of Soccer* versus the *Non-Art of Soccer*. The first eleven characteristics apply to the players and teams, while the last two can also be applied to the fans.

	Art	Non-Art
1	Technique	Physique
2	Stylistic Play	Hack Play
3	Possession	Lockdown
4	Diagonal Ball	Square Ball
5	Daring	Safe
6	Creative	Destructive
7	Imaginative	Violent
8	Clean Play	Dirty Play
9	Play the Ball	Play the Man
10	Fair Play	Cheating
11	Sportsmanship	Win at any Cost
12	Aficionados	Hooligans
13	Diversity	Xenophobia

Human Art evolved as a form of magical illustration, and the simple rationale of that art was to captivate the human spirit.[8] Is not soccer art an ongoing illustration of magic in time and space, and captivation of the spirit?

---

[8] The magical illustrations of the 30,000 year old Chauvet cave paintings in France are thought to be the oldest documented human Art.

Chapter Three

Soccer and Identity
The Cultural Arts of Soccer

My way of life was chosen 26 years ago. It is football. Football makes me human.
Gheorghe Hagi

A football team represents a way of being, a culture.
Michel Platini

The Existential Art of Soccer

Why do people all over the world watch soccer in their neighborhood spaces, parks and stadiums? Soccer is of course Pelé's "beautiful game," but people also attend for the feeling of community as they watch "their boys" play (or "throw some art") on the opposing team. In this way, soccer is integral to the formation of community identity throughout the world.

Culture is the social dynamic of identity, and for that reason this chapter is subtitled *The Cultural Arts of Soccer*. Human diversity is the biological mirror of culture, which evolved from an awareness of both individual and community identity. Therefore, this chapter examines the development and interaction of soccer culture with individual and community identity.

In writing this book, *world soccer* was chosen as a vital example of both the diversity and basic similarities between peoples. Not the artificial similarities imposed by brazen cultural impositions of "globalization,"[1] but an existential link between peoples that permeates beyond the conventional boundaries of societies. I was searching for an essential reality by which people globally could identify with on a local level, an entity that empowers them to articulate their own community dynamics. Soccer is very often that cultural force.

I could just as well be writing about medicine and public health in the world, but a surprising truth is that *world soccer may be as or more important to the human spirit than the current availability of Western medicine*. After all, much of the world lacks "modern" medicine, but few parts of the world lack the deceptively simple and elegant art of soccer.

---

[1] An example of this type of soccer "globalization" is the increasing practice of hyper-rich clubs (such as Manchester United and Real Madrid) marketing their super-expensive wares (such as team shirts) to poorer populations in other continents. This mega-marketing of the rich comes at the expense of locals supporting their own teams, players and ultimately, their own football culture. For example, at the 2004 Copa America in Peru, an official replica jersey of 2003 Copa Sudamericana and Recopa (SuperCup) champion Cienciano cost 70 soles ($20), while the comparable Manchester United or Real Madrid jersey was 230 soles ($65). The price difference represents a minimum of $45 profit leaving the country for each shirt.

Despite the massive and urgent need for health care in Africa[2], a majority of Africans lack that human right yet still play football as children and remain supporters of the sport. Nelson Mandela, the national hero and ex-President of South Africa, recognized the tremendous effect of soccer when he told Mark Fish[3] *"We can reach far more people through sport than we can through political or educational programs. In that way, sport is more powerful than politics."*

First Century, Second Century

Soccer is presently in its second full century of development. The first rules were drawn up in a London pub on 26 October 1863, and English clubs that were founded in the 19th century celebrated their centennials years ago (Manchester United 1878-1978, Tottenham Hotspur 1882-1982, Arsenal 1886-1986, Liverpool 1892-1992). Notts County was the first formed soccer league club, dating from 1862. By 1888, the first Football League started with twelve League founding members concentrated well north of London in the Midlands of England. The dozen founding clubs were Accrington, Aston Villa, Blackburn Rovers, Bolton Wanderers, Burnley, Derby County, Everton, Notts County, Preston North End, Stoke, West Bromwich Albion and Wolverhampton Wanderers. A Second Division was started in 1892 with an additional twelve teams.

There was a twenty to thirty year delay in soccer club formation in many parts of the world, as British and other European engineers, entrepreneurs, and adventurers exported their new national sport in the late 19th and early 20th centuries. These "expats" helped found or inspired the formation of sport and soccer clubs in their adopted lands. Many of the expats were professionals, such as engineers, and therefore soccer was often established first in the local upper and ruling classes, but then quickly filtered down to the lower classes. Often the ruling class at that time discarded soccer in favor of cricket or tennis, as the masses made soccer their game.

As a result, many professional clubs outside of England are just now celebrating a century of soccer competition. In Europe, recent celebrants were Barcelona (1899-1999), Ajax of Amsterdam (1900-2000), and Real Madrid (1902-2002). These three clubs are of such reputation that weighty books have already been written to celebrate their centennial histories. Real Madrid celebrated in style as they won the European Championship (against Bayer Leverkusen of Germany) and World Club Championship (against Olimpia of Paraguay) in their centenary year; Olimpia was also celebrating their centenary year. Flamengo was the first club founded in Brazil in 1895 and Fluminense followed in 1902, making the "Fla-Flu" Rio de Janeiro soccer derby the oldest and most significant in South America. The Brazilians also celebrated the centennial of the Sao Paulo league in 2002 (1902-2002).

Because of the popularity of soccer, the sport rapidly spread to nearly all the countries of the world, even those outside the vast empire that England controlled at the beginning of the 20th century. For example, British rail workers helped launch soccer in many countries in South America, a location where Britain had scant political power. They also brought in other British customs such as the bowler hat; even today in the Andean highlands of Ecuador, Peru and Bolivia, the indigenous market and *campesina* women proudly wear their locally made felt bowler hats.

The British simultaneously introduced two other team sports besides soccer into their colonial empire and beyond. Cricket and rugby both accompanied and competed against

---

[2] Africa leads the world in AIDS, malaria and infant mortality deaths. Changing these grim statistics is beyond the capability of the Sub-Saharan African economies, but a mere $10 billion per year from the world economy could avert 5 million preventable human deaths per year – most of them innocent children.
[3] Mark Fish is a skillful and charismatic "white" South African player who performed for "black" professional teams Jomo Cosmos and Orlando Pirates. He later signed for Lazio (Italy) and Bolton (England), and subsequently played a part in the renaissance of Charlton in the English Premiership before retiring in 2005.

early soccer development, and many soccer clubs started out as cricket clubs. For example, the Flamengo club of Brazil was originally a cricket club, and the first champion of the Italian Serie A was the Genoa Cricket & Athletic Club in 1898.

Cricket is still far more popular than soccer in some Commonwealth countries such as India and Pakistan. Both of these large nations (the second and sixth largest populations in the world, respectively) have not yet appeared in the FIFA Football World Cup Finals, although India was to have competed in 1950 tournament, but withdrew after they were not permitted to compete barefoot (as they were used to playing at the time).[4] In the West Indies soccer has caught up with cricket in popularity, but not yet in success. The West Indies cricket team was dominant through the 1980's and became world champion in 1989, but only Jamaica (1998), Haiti (1974) and Cuba (1938) have so far advanced to the World Cup Finals.

Some clubs that have professional soccer teams have names that reflect other sports such as bicycling (Ciclista Lima of Peru), or tennis (Tennis Borussia "TeBe" of Berlin, Germany & Lawn Tennis of Lima, Peru). These teams are becoming insignificant, as both Ciclista and Lawn Tennis were knocked out of the Peruvian first division in the 1990's, while "TeBe" was relegated from the German Second Division in 2000 – not a great record for teams that ignore soccer in their official names.

Clubs that did not have a primary British link to their development often had a secondary link, meaning that a native person had seen or played with British expatriates, and then formed their own club. Still other clubs formed *de novo* after getting a rulebook and seeing another local club play. But whichever way clubs were formed, by the 1920's most clubs worldwide had severed their links with this British heritage. The reasons for this were several: (1) the First World War took attention away from sport, (2) professionalism was introduced in many countries with many British authorities remaining opposed, (3) the refusal of Britain to join FIFA, and finally (4) the refusal of the English team to engage in play against other nations' teams, often in a manner that implied their obvious superiority.

But this "superiority" had rapidly become a myth, for by insulating themselves from foreign competition, Britain overlooked the rapid worldwide development of the game. They missed the marvelous ball control game from South American teams such as Peru in 1936 and Brazil in 1938, and the dynamic Argentine soccer that was supplying national team players to Italy and Spain. Even the Swiss, who invented the *catenaccio*, or link-defense (chain) and counterattack game, had little influence on the British in that era.[5]

One of the great ironies in soccer history is that the country that codified the rules and first developed organized soccer ("Association Football") then isolated themselves from many international soccer developments before 1950. After all, soccer had "originated" in England, and the English were quite certain they possessed the best team in the world, and until 1950, England had not even bothered to enter the first three soccer World Cup tournaments (1930, 1934, and 1938). But in their first World Cup in 1950, the "colonies across the pond" gave them a big surprise, as the USA beat England 1-0.[6] There in Brazil, England was effectively eliminated by their former colonies in what is still the greatest upset in the soccer history.[7] And in 1953, the hammer blow came, when the superb "Magical

---

[4] Soccer is still most prominent in the Kerala and West Bengal states in India.

[5] The Italians are often said to have invented catenaccio, but they will confirm they only refined it to an art in the 1960s and 1970s.

[6] USA's goal was scored by Haitian-born Joe Gaetjens; he eventually returned to Haiti and was "disappeared" (and assumed murdered) on 8 July 1963 by dictator "Papa Doc" Duvalier's Tonton Macoute secret police.

[7] Greece winning the 2004 European Championship is a close second for greatest upset in a large soccer competition.

Magyars" Hungary team soundly defeated England 6-3 in London, and again 7-1 in the return match in Budapest.[8]

These results confirmed that English overconfidence in their soccer history had failed to surpass the innovations that had occurred in the rest of the world during their soccer hibernation. However, Britain's absence from the international soccer scene may have made the global game stronger, as national soccer federations were able to find their own identities without undue interference from the British Isles.

It was not until the mid-1960s that England could claim to be the best, when host England captured the 1966 World Cup and Manchester United won the 1967 European Championship.

English Language Invades the World of Soccer

By virtue of some British helping or inspiring to organize new clubs, some clubs bypassed their native language and created an English language name or partial name.

Country	Club	City
Argentina	Boca Juniors	Buenos Aires
	River Plate	Buenos Aires
	Nueva Chicago	Buenos Aires
	Racing	Avellaneda
	Newell's Old Boys	Rosario
	Arsenal	Sarandí
Austria	Rapid	Vienna
Bolivia	The Strongest	La Paz
	Blooming	Santa Cruz
Brazil	Corinthians	São Paulo
Chile	Wanderers	Santiago
	Rangers	Talca
Czech Republic	Bohemians	Prague
France	Racing	Strasbourg
	Red Star 93	Paris
Italy	Genoa*	Genoa
	A.C. Milan*	Milan
Japan	Kashima Antlers	Kashima
	Grampus Eight	Nagoya
	JEF United	Ichihara
	Red Diamonds	Urawa
Peru	Sport Boys	Callao
	Sporting Cristal	Lima
Portugal	Sporting	Lisbon
Romania	Rapid	Bucharest
Spain	Athletic Bilbao	San Sebastian
	Racing	Santander
Switzerland	Young Boys	Bern
	Grasshoppers	Zurich
Uruguay	Wanderers	Montevideo
Yugoslavia	Red Star	Belgrade

*These clubs use the English spelling of their Italian cities, instead of Genova and Milano.

---

[8] This game harkened the arrival of the softer and lighter form-fitting boot, as the English marveled that the Hungarians appeared to be wearing "slippers" when they entered the field. English overconfidence was destroyed by the superior technique and control demonstrated by the Hungarians, resulting in the lopsided score.

The above table shows interesting examples of clubs from sixteen countries that made the choice of an English language team name in a non-English speaking country. The tendency to name and retain soccer clubs in English rather than the national language pays homage to the British influence in the world development of the game, and the role of British expatriates in bringing the game to their new nations. English club names that appear in more than one non-English speaking country include Racing, Rapid, Wanderers, Sporting and Red Star.

Some anglicized names' origins remain mysteries. For example, Frenchman Jules Rimet (FIFA President from 1921 to 1954) formed the *Red Star 93* club in Paris in 1897 but never disclosed exactly what the club name meant, and he brought its significance to his grave. Some clubs with full or partial English language team names are listed on the previous page.

One of the few soccer teams using a team name in a language other than their own or English is the Yokohama F Marinos. Marinos is Spanish for "mariners" or "sailors," which reflects the port status of Yokohama.

Club Identity

Clubs were initially formed with the intent of members playing football amongst their friends. Therefore many clubs initially targeted a subclass of society for their membership.

Clubs were founded by a wide variety of groups. Some clubs originally identified with the rich, landed or bourgeois society, while others were formed by a union between the lower middle and poor classes. When two teams were formed in one town, often one team was favored by the ruling class and the other by "the masses." Some *derbies* (or rivalry games) still reflect this historical trend within the same city. So it was that the famous *"Fla-Flu"* rivalry in Rio de Janeiro began; Fluminense was founded by the wealthy and Flamengo became "the people's club." Other examples of "rich vs. poor" city derbies are River Plate vs. Boca Juniors (Buenos Aires), and Universitario vs. Alianza (Lima). Sometimes a club nickname gives the origin away, for example, River Plate is known as "los Millionarios" ("the Millionaires").

Regionalism and class have shaped some club rivalries; this is especially true in Italy, as there is a general rivalry between the richer northern clubs (in Milan and Turin) versus the poorer southern clubs (in Rome and Napoli).

Some clubs are distinguished by cultural and political differences. This is perhaps best demonstrated in Spain, in which the autonomous regions of the Basque Country (País Vasco), Catalonia and Galicia have produced the powerhouse clubs of Athletic Bilbao (Spain's oldest major club, founded 1898), Barcelona (founded 1899), and Deportivo de La Coruña (founded 1906), respectively.

Derbies with religious overtones are less common, but the Glasgow, Scotland derby of Rangers (Protestant) - Celtic (Catholic) is still the biggest intra-city clash in Europe. This derby is called "The Old Firm" because the clubs are the two oldest major teams in the country (Rangers founded in 1873, Celtic in 1888), and are considered the "football establishment" in Scotland. Despite the recent increasing diversity of the teams, this derby still has a religious overtone, which has seeded a history of gratuitous hooligan violence.

Certain teams, such as Palestino of Chile, were formed by distinct ethnic groups in their Diaspora. Palestinians formed the club in Santiago in 1920, and incredibly, the third and fourth generation players of Palestinian ancestry have since been recruited to play for recent Palestine World Cup team qualifying efforts.

With the increase of international communication, the Internet, the Bosman ruling (see Chapters 4 & 5), and clubs signing more foreign players, club fan bases are much more diverse than their narrow origins. Rich people may now support the "poor teams," and vice versa, and club supporters often encompass all classes. There is now no excuse to be a blinkered religious fanatic about The Old Firm when both teams are signing internationals of all ethnicities and religions.

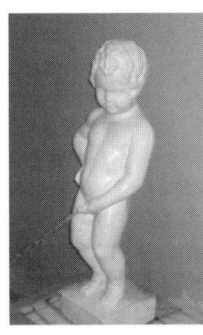
Another way clubs form an identity is by utilizing a mascot or nickname. Many of these are animal names that are cute (Periquitos of Palmeiras, Newcastle Magpies) or ferocious (Monterrey Tigers). Other names are semi-macho types (the Gunners of Arsenal, The Musketeers of Gremio). Still other teams have borrowed their nicknames; the South African Mamelodi Sundowns are also known as "the Brazilians." Some names are decent and innocuous (Southampton Saints, Fulham Cottagers and the Osaka Sakura - a cherry tree in blossom), while some are bizarre such as The Colchoneros (mattress makers) of Atlético Madrid, and the Botafogo Manequinho (the peeing boy) of Rio de Janeiro.[9]

The Argentine league, however, wins the prize for the most dubious and notorious nicknames. The Argentine Primera División has Los Bichos (The Bedbugs) of Argentino Juniors, Los Bosteros (The Stinkards) of Boca Juniors, Los Canallas (The Scoundrels) of Rosario Central, and even Los Quemeros (The Arsonists) of Huracán. However, the contest for the award of the most dubious and/or notorious nickname is between Los Pincharrates (The Rat Jabbers) of Estudiantes de la Plata and Los Leprosos (The Lepers) of Newell's Old Boys. While Pincharrates receives the *Bizarro award* (what is a Rat Jabber?), Los Leprosos wins the *Most Notorious Nickname* award. The Newell's story is "Los Leprosos" was chosen because there was a leprosarium near the stadium, and it possibly was a sympathetic naming for those afflicted with the disease.

In the future, Newell's Old Boys will benefit from a new nickname, because the disease of leprosy will be eradicated from humanity. The World Health Organization has developed an effective triple-drug leprosy cure, and the eradication of leprosy is scientifically possible with the proper international cooperation.[10] Perhaps Newell's new nickname could be Los Viejos (The Old Men) or Los Abuelos (The Grandpas) – either would be tame in comparison with the other Argentine league team names.[11]

Individual Player Identity

Early on, individual player identity was shaped by whether a player could support himself financially from the game. In the late 19th and early 20th century, soccer clubs were all-amateur outfits, and players either needed to be independently wealthy or have an individual sponsor. But professionalism crept into the game in the 1920's and became the norm in the 1930's, except in holdout Britain. Even though soccer clubs employed so-called professionals, the reality was they were not highly paid and usually held regular jobs. Only the real superstars could make a comfortable living off football in the early days.

The British Football Association (FA) wanted to keep football an amateur sport, and made such an issue out of professionalism that they withdrew from FIFA in 1928, and did not participate in a World Cup until 1950.

Up to the 1960s player identity was characterized by an effective bondage to one club, as the clubs set the salary structure and completely controlled transfer activities. There were two main options for star players to obtain a more lucrative contract: either play in a renegade league outside FIFA control (such as Alfredo Di Stéfano did in the rebel Colombian league in the 1950s), or transfer to an Italian or Spanish team that was paying the highest salaries (such as Welshman John Charles, who played for Juventus).

---

[9] Botafogo's Manequinho probably takes its primary inspiration from the Manneken Pis statue in Brussels that was erected in 1619, and is often interpreted as an expression of freedom. The above photo of a Manequinho is from a Manneken Pis copy at the patisserie francaise Croissant D'Or in New Orleans, USA.
[10] The situation of human leprosy is exactly the same as the eradication of polio and the control of AIDS in the world. Both are scientifically possible with the proper international organization and cooperation.
[11] Italian soccer fans in general are nicknamed *tifosi*, because they supposedly act as if they have *typhus fever*.

In November 1960, the Player's Football Association (PFA) led by Jimmy Hill finally succeeded in abolishing the *maximum wage rule* in England (salaries had been capped at about £20 per week before). British players were thereafter theoretically free to negotiate their salaries.

By the time England won the 1966 World Cup, soccer was changing financially, with salaries creeping up because of labor organization and greater awareness of player rights. British soccer players began to assert themselves in contract talks, and some left their national leagues to enter the new North American Soccer League in the USA in the 1960s and 1970s. There was an increased flow of players across national boundaries, even from the socialist East. For example, Polish midfield wizard Kazimierz Deyna was finally allowed to work in Western Europe and the USA near the end of his career.

With the advent of more advertising revenue in the 1980s, especially from placing advertisements on shirts, salaries began to progressively increase. But salaries began to skyrocket after the 1995 Bosman ruling, which allowed players to be free agents once they were out of contract. Salaries increased so fast that many clubs began to spend more money on players than they received in revenues, and some clubs went into financial crisis or even bankruptcy.

Today, top soccer players make millions of dollars a year, although not quite approaching the stratospheric levels of USA basketball or baseball salaries. In the second and lower soccer divisions, salaries drop off dramatically, but often allow players to still make a living at soccer. The lower division players live among "the masses," as even the superstars of the game once did.

Certain leagues pay much higher salaries than others; for example, the Mexican league pays higher than the Brazilian or Argentine leagues. Players are aware of this reality, and are often looking for a bigger payoff in another country. In 2004, there were more than one thousand Brazilian and Argentine players making a living playing soccer out of their countries, and all were earning more money than they could have made in their own country. As player prices have risen and South American economies have stagnated, the exportation of talented soccer players represents a larger percentage of country GNP each successive year.

Many soccer leagues have relaxed their foreign player requirements, with the Italian Serie A finally easing restrictions in 2001. As a result, good players from around the world have a chance to enter one of the European leagues (Spanish, Italian, German or English leagues), which are considered the best along with the Brazilian and Argentine leagues. Top players can nearly dictate when they want to leave their clubs, and sometimes seek out lucrative transfers.

Three players from Real Madrid who were World Players of the Year are good examples of top players on the move, searching until they have found their ideal job. Ronaldo moved from Barcelona to Inter Milan to Real Madrid, Zinedine Zidane from Juventus to Real Madrid, and Luis Figo from Barcelona to Real Madrid. Players and agents may reap a fat percentage of the transfer fee from their moves, possibly making player movement more attractive from a financial standpoint.

The idea of loyalty to one club, originally cultivated by a bondage relationship between player and club, has now become quaint, and the days of players staying with one club for their career are likely over. Ex-England captain Tony Adams finished a 19-year career with Arsenal in 2002, and Ex-Italy captain Paolo Maldini completed 20 years at AC Milan in 2005, but their experiences likely represent the last of an era.

World Cup Soccer Identity

The world's biggest sporting spectacle is the FIFA World Cup, which is contested every four years. The qualifying rounds for the World Cup Finals include more countries and political entities (207 Football Associations in 2005) than are members of the United Nations (191 Member States in 2004). It has been said that FIFA could eliminate all war in the world simply by refusing to allow offending countries to qualify for the World Cup. Because much of the world is soccer-mad, there might be some truth to this speculative sentiment.

Even countries that by their colonial history had USA sports imposed as their national game (Cuba and Nicaragua for baseball, the Philippines for basketball) still manage to field national soccer teams for the World Cup qualifiers. Countries such as Pakistan and India that were influenced by British colonialism and adopted cricket as their national sport also field national soccer teams. New countries (ex-Soviet Union republics), broken-away countries (Croatia, Slovenia), and even a political entity (Palestine) all field national teams. Nobody wants to be left out of the world phenomenon and human drama of football.

But how is it that FIFA started qualifying nations as competition entrants, and what does it mean in a changing world that is finally becoming comfortable with its own human diversity?

FIFA requires that the national entrants for the World Cup or Olympic soccer competition must have an active unified Football Association that is the undisputed organizer of the nation's soccer activities, and an established league.

The World Cup competition is arranged around these Football Associations, which represent nations or semi-autonomous regions. This is why not only England, but Northern Ireland, Wales and Scotland all have their own national teams. Although they are all part of Great Britain, each has their own distinct Football Association and soccer league.

FIFA stipulates that there must not be competing national soccer federations, such as existed in the USA in the early part of the 20th century. Two soccer federations – the American Football Association (AFA) and the American Amateur Football Association (AAFA) – merged to form the United States Football Association (USFA), which was finally accepted into FIFA in 1913. The old USFA organization is now known as the *United States Soccer Federation* (USSF) or *US Soccer* (www.ussoccer.com).

Newly independent countries must first form a Football Association; only then may they apply for FIFA membership. In this way Croatia went from independence to qualifying for the World Cup Finals in only seven years (1991-1998), and finished an impressive third in the 1998 World Cup. Croatia and Slovenia qualified for the 2002 World Cup, both once having been part of greater Yugoslavia.

There have been some complaints about the relatively open-door entrance policy of FIFA membership. FIFA admits virtually any political entity, no matter how small or if not represented in the United Nations. Hence there are states such as Puerto Rico or American Samoa represented by "national teams." These are entities that are parts of the United States, but have a different legal status and cultural history from the mainland. The Faroe Islands (Denmark), Bermuda (England), Netherlands Antilles (Holland), and Martinique and Guadeloupe (France), are others that have parent countries yet compete independently.

Even tiny states such as San Marino (pop. 28,000) and Montserrat (pop. only 4,400 after the 1995 Soufriere Hills volcanic eruption) field national soccer teams. Admitting tiny states can dilute the overall quality of soccer tournaments, and San Marino routinely lost games by double-digit goals and had never won an international game in more than 70 tries until beating fellow minnow Liechtenstein 1-0 in 2004. With Archie Thompson scoring 13 goals, Australia beat American Samoa in a record 31-0 2002 World Cup qualifying loss, and that was only two days after the Aussies had broken the previous record by beating Tonga 22-0!

What does this massive soccer inequality prove? Only that those tiny states do not have the ability to play with larger, more organized and better-funded states. But there are occasional upsets, such as in 2004 when the Melanesian island nation of Vanuatu (population 200,000) beat New Zealand (population 4 million) 4-2, and Italy lost 2-0 to Iceland (Italy has 58 million people while the population of Iceland is only 294,000). And during one traumatic week in 2004 European group qualifying for the 2006 World Cup, minnow Albania beat reigning European Champions Greece 2-1, Liechtenstein (population 33,000) tied European Finalist Portugal 2-2, and Andorra (population 70,000) beat Macedonia 1-0. Perhaps those results are what make playing these usually mismatched games worthwhile.

Nations and Peoples in Soccer Organizations

The Changing Concept of Nations

The World Cup is a soccer contest of nation versus nation, but what exactly is the current status of nationhood? After all, the second half of the 20th century has witnessed the greatest migrations humanity has ever experienced. In this modern post-colonial era, nations have of necessity embraced population diversity and become functional inclusive states, if only to maintain the public order. A nation such as Germany, once nearly all German, now finds Eastern Europeans, Turks, Slavs, Africans, and members of other ethnicities among its populace. Their national football team mirrors this diversity, as players with Polish (Jürgen Grabowski, Miroslav Klose), Turkish (Mehmet Scholl), Panamanian (Kevin Kuranyi) and African ancestry (Gerald Asamoah, born in Ghana) have prominently appeared with the national team.

The people of Spain speak four different languages in four distinct regions, each of which could conceivably be a separate nation. The four regions are *Castilla-La Mancha* where they speak Castilian Spanish in the capital of Madrid, *Catalonia* where they speak Catalan in the capital of Barcelona, *País Vasco* where Basque (Euskara) is spoken in the capital of Vitoria, and *Galicia* where they speak Galician (Galego) in the capital of La Coruña. But after the Spanish Civil War (1936-1939), the fascist dictator Francisco Franco declared the usage of regional languages illegal as part of his strategy to crushing peripheral resistance. But during those dark years of repression the soccer stadiums, such as Barcelona's Camp Nou stadium, remained safe refuges where people could preserve their linguistic culture.

Although today the diverse regions of Spain possess more autonomy from Madrid, it remains a special match when one of the regional club teams plays Real Madrid. However, the current Spanish national team has players from all areas of Spain, and the regional languages are now spoken freely.

Italians separate themselves into northern and southern, and by cities and regions: Milanese, Romans, Neapolitans, Sardinians and Sicilians. Diego Maradona understood the underdog status of the southern Italians, and became a local hero after he helped to twice bring the *scudetto* (Italian championship) to Napoli (1986-87 and 1989-90).

France has incorporated all ethnicities (North and West Africans, Arabs and Polynesians), which were once part of their colonial empire and beyond. Their 1998 World Champion squad was a compact version of world diversity.

Central and South American nations are composed of diverse populations, and their ancestry is a mix of indigenous, European, Asian and African contributions. In this vein, Brazil has always been a multiethnic nation.

Asian and African nations had colonial borders imposed on them, often fusing multiple ethnic groups together in artificial political unions. Perhaps not surprisingly, many civil wars ensued that caused untold human suffering for decades. Half a century later, these now independent countries are still becoming familiar with positive aspects of their diverse populations, and are finally emerging in the soccer and political worlds (often in that order).

Although the overwhelming global movement has been towards population diversity, a setback for such diversity has been the recent disintegration of the original multiethnic

The Changing Concept of Individuals within Nations

If nation-states are the World Cup qualifying entrants, what does this mean for the individual teams and competitors?

In the past, national teams were often of one "race," pure and homogenous; certainly Adolf Hitler wanted the German and Austrian teams to be of the purest Aryan breeding (see Chapter 13). At the same time, most of the rest of the world was adapting and becoming more tolerant of other ethnicities, and soccer often played a significant part in that transformation. That tolerance still has not been perfected with respect to all ethnic groups and in all areas, but it is progressively improving. Soccer certainly has the potential to play a major role in increasing tolerance of world diversity in the 21st century.

The world is continually changing, with socio-political conflicts resulting in refugees crossing borders and the borders themselves being altered. Despite the seemingly continual strife in the world, the World Cup has seen only seven players who have appeared for two separate nations.

Luis Monti and Attilio DeMaria played for the Argentine World Cup team in 1930, then were recruited as *oriundi* (foreigners with Italian heritage) to play for the World Cup winning Italian side in 1934. That Italian side recruited two other Argentinean oriundi who had not played for Argentina in 1930, Raimundo Orsi and Enrique Guaita Monti was the midfield general, while Orsi and Guaita were the wingers in a 2-3-5 system. A substitute winger on the 1934 team was Brazilian oriundi Anfilogino Guarisi, so in total, five oriundi were recruited for the 1934 Italian team.

The 1962 Spain World Cup team had three players of foreign origin. José Santamaria had already played for Uruguay and Ferenc Puskas for Hungary in the 1954 World Cup. Puskas was an essential cog of the great Real Madrid teams of the late 1950s and early 1960s, and his Argentine teammate Alfredo Di Stéfano was also on the 1962 Spanish World Cup team, but could not perform because of injury.

José Altafini (known also as "Mazzola" in Brazil) played in Brazil's first games in the 1958 World Cup Finals as a nineteen-year-old, but was replaced by the even younger prodigy seventeen-year old Pelé for the final games. Altafini then moved to Italy and played for his new country in the 1962 World Cup, and subsequently had a long and superb club career in Italy. Altafini scored the two goals that won the European Cup for AC Milan in 1963, and ten years later played for Juventus in their 1973 European Cup Final loss to Ajax.

Robert Prosinecki and Robert Jarni both performed for Yugoslavia in the 1990 World Cup, and then helped the newly independent Croatia to an impressive 3rd place finish in the 1998 World Cup. Prosinecki and Jarni were also on the 2002 Croatia World Cup team.

Not counted in the above statistics is 1934 Austrian World Cup team member Franz Wagner, who because of the Nazi annexation of Austria in March 1938 was forced to be on the 1938 Germany World Cup team. The star of that 1934 Austrian team, the elegant creative midfielder Matias Sindelar (known as the "Man of Paper" for his feinting ability and slim build), could not tolerate the Nazi aggression of Austria, and apparently committed suicide shortly after the 1938 World Cup.

FIFA recently declared that players may no longer perform for more than one national team in their career, even if they possess multiple citizenships. Thus, young players must choose one nation to represent for the duration of their international careers. For example, Owen Hargreaves of Bayern Munich had to choose between Canada, England, Germany and Wales (he chose England). Kevin Kuranyi is of Panamanian, Hungarian, and German ancestry and grew up in Brazil, but chose to play for Germany.

Even if a player has already appeared for a national team, there may be other reasons to obtain a European Union nationality. Young Santos star Diego, having already played for the Brazil national team, investigated acquiring an Italian passport (he is of part-Italian heritage) in order to ease his transfer to a European team (he eventually moved to Porto in Portugal).

Perhaps because there are so many top-quality Brazilian players, some of them have searched outside their home country for a national team with an eye toward appearing in a World Cup. In 2004, FIFA ruled that players must have a "clear connection to that country," which they defined as living in a country for at least two years, or having a parent or grandparent who was born there. This ruling was brought on by a situation whereby the Qatar national team wanted to draft three Brazilian players (including Bundesliga leading scorer Ailton), none of whom had lived or worked in Qatar before. Also disturbing were the rumors of large payouts to players who would add a nationality and play for Qatar.

The best example of the trend of Brazilians playing for other national teams surfaced in the 2004 African Nation's Cup championships held in Tunisia. The host country had persuaded Francileudo Santos and José Clayton, two Brazilians who had played for Tunisian soccer clubs, to don their country's uniform. Both Santos and Clayton were part of the Tunisia team that secured their first ever African championship, beating Morocco 2-1. Santos scored the first goal in the Final, and along with Mali's Frederic Kanouté, was voted the best striker of the tournament.

Diversity in National Teams

The modern reality is that almost every country or nation-state is multiethnic, whether it occurred by fiat in the ex-colonial countries, by natural evolution as in some European nations, or by a combination of both mechanisms as in the USA. The dynamics of multiethnic societal construction have been variable, and in the modern era each viable nation must eagerly embrace its diversity for its own social harmony.

This applies to national soccer teams as well. This requires that the coaching staff be sensitive to individual needs and player requirements to promote good team camaraderie. *Above all, this means respect from everybody on the team for his teammates,* regardless of ethnicity and/or religion.

One need look no further to evaluate the impact of diversity than examine the makeup of 1998 World Cup winner France. The French team had players of Sub-Saharan African heritage (Marcel Desailly, Ghana, and Patrick Veira, Senegal), West Indian heritage (Lilian Thuram and Thierry Henry, Guadeloupe), Asian heritage (Christian Karembeu, the Pacific Islands of New Caledonia), North African heritage (Zinedine Zidane, Algerian Kabyles), Middle Eastern heritage (Youri Djorkaeff, Armenian), Basque heritage (Bixente Lizarazu), and South American heritage (David Trezeguet, Argentine). Many of these French players are of multiethnic heritage, and they were in every sense a "world" team and champion.

However, the 1998 France squad was only the fifth "world team" to win the World Cup – the first four teams were Brazilian (1958, 1962, 1970, 1994). All Brazil teams feature multiethnic individuals characteristic of that country after immigration waves of Portuguese, African, German, Japanese and other groups, which over centuries blended in with the indigenous Amerindian population.

The French however, can righteously claim to have embraced diversity in their national football program more fervently than other European nations, as they were the first European country to integrate non-European players into their national team (the Italian *oriundi* were foreign ethnic Italians). As early as the 1938 World Cup, the French had African and Arab players on their national team. A search of the French national team players since 1938 reveals many players of Armenian, Dutch, Spanish, Italian, German, Basque, Polish, Western Pacific and Asian Indian ancestries, and various other African and Arab ancestries.

Other European countries have slowly embraced the emerging societal diversity in their soccer squads. Holland, Sweden, England, Norway, and lastly Italy and Germany are currently reaping the benefits of a diverse national team, positively reflecting the new social dynamics of their populations.

Players with some African ancestry performed for the first time in the Italian and unified German national teams in 2001 (Fabio Liverani for Italy and Gerald Asamoah for Germany[12]). This is obviously a positive symbol of societal diversity, although both countries are still gripped by prominent racist activity at many soccer grounds (especially Liverani's Lazio club). FIFA, UEFA, and the national Football Associations are belatedly addressing the horrors of xenophobia, ethnophobia, and racism in football.

Diversity in Club Teams

In the late 1940s and early 1950s, renegade Colombian league teams not under FIFA control such as Millionarios brought together players from various South American nations (such as Alfredo Di Stefano of Argentina – see Chapter 7). Real Madrid copied this trend, as their all-World squads of the late 1950s prominently featured South Americans and other non-Spanish individuals. But these clubs were the exceptions, as most club teams were mono-ethnic within relatively homogenous nations.

Club team makeup has changed radically in the last 30 years. When Ajax won their European Cup treble in 1971-72-73, and Bayern Munich their European Cup treble in 1974-75-76, they were basically all-Dutch and all-German teams. Contrast those teams with the starting lineup of the 2001 European Champions League winners Bayern Munich team, which featured a Ghanaian (Sammy Kuffour), a Swede (Patrik Andersson), a Frenchman (Willy Sagnol), a French Basque (Bixente Lizarazu), a Canadian-English-Welsh (Owen Hargreaves), a Brazilian (Giovane Elber), a Bosnian (Hasan Salihamidzic), and a German of Turkish heritage (Mehmet Scholl). On the Bayern substitute bench was a Paraguayan (Roque Santa Cruz), an Italian-Swiss (Cirico Sforza), and another Brazilian (Paulo Sergio). The Valencia team was as diverse, with a Norwegian (John Carew), an Italian (Amedeo Carboni), two Argentines (Mauricio Pellegrino and Pablo Aimar) a Guadeloupe-French (Jocelyn Angloma), a Yugoslavian (Miroslav Djukic) and a Slovenian (Zlatko Zahovic) performing amongst Spaniards of various ethnicities.

Club teams sought to maximize their flexibility after the European league rules changed to allow a quota of foreign players on the field. Some teams went to great lengths to arrange multiple passports for players in order to field their best eleven. European Union (EU) country passports were increasingly issued to foreign players (especially South Americans) on flimsy ancestral evidence. These passports were obtained so players could evade restrictive foreign player rules, and perform as modern "club oriundi" in various countries.

A citizenship scandal erupted in 2001 as many players' passports from European Union countries were suspected to have been obtained on false pretenses. Many of these fraudulent passports were obtained from Portugal, Greece or Italy, and resulted in investigations, fines or suspensions of involved players and administrators.[13]

New rules further opening up European leagues to players of any nationality seemed likely to nullify this illegal passport trend. Italy later opened up their league to more foreigners in 2001, making the Veron-Cragnotti scandal moot. And Ajax of Amsterdam, which already has an impressive local youth development program, had nearly 20 foreign players on its books in 2003.

Some decry the increasing importation of players as coming at the expense of local talent. This may be somewhat true, but it is also likely that local talent will improve as a

---

[12] William Hartwig, the son of a USA soldier father and a West German mother, played for the West German national team in 1979, making him the first of African ancestry to perform on a "German" national team.

[13] In one prominent case, Lazio owner Sergio Cragnotti was accused of using false documents to obtain an Italian passport for Argentine national midfielder Juan Sebastian Veron, as Veron's new dual citizenship meant that Lazio could field an extra non-EU player in the 2000 league competition. However, both Veron and Cragnotti were eventually exonerated on technicalities.

result of new competition. The two most critical conditions to the increasing influx of players from poor countries to rich countries are; (1) newly imported soccer youth must not be abused in any way by European clubs (teams must provide education, reasonable and flexible contracts, and adhere to European Union labor laws), and (2) the players' countries and clubs of origin must be justly compensated in order to improve soccer development back home. Otherwise, a completely "free trade globalization" system of player movement will always favor the rich and European clubs, and remain one of exploitation on both an individual and country basis.

Through recent actions some English Premiership teams are in the forefront of the foreign/domestic player debate. Chelsea fielded an all-foreign team for the first time in any England league game in 1999, and Arsenal went one better in 2005 when it fielded the first all-foreign 16-man squad (meaning all the substitutes were non-English as well). These and other similar incidents appear to be leading to an UEFA/FIFA reaction, which will likely result in progressive new "home player" requirements in the coming years, in order to ensure that each team is fielding at least *some* national talent.

Intolerance of Diversity in Soccer: Racism, Ethnophobia and Xenophobia
Definitions of Intolerance

Intolerance of others has been the bane of humanity since time immemorial, causing virtually all wars between peoples.

Racism has been the term used to denote prejudice against a group deemed to be another "race." Since "race" is an indefinite term that analytical scientists have abandoned, "racism" is understood to be a general prejudice against a group that somehow appears different.

Ethnophobia denotes prejudice against a specific ethnic group. The Greek root words translate to "fear of [an] ethnic[ity]". Interestingly, most overtly violent xenophobic actions in the last century have been directed against ethnicities rather than "races."

Xenophobia translates as "fear of the foreign," meaning prejudice against any non-dominant group that differs by ethnicity, religion or other perceived characteristic. Xenophobia is probably the best term to designate all intolerance issues, but until now, this term has carried the least emotional and historical gravitas.

It is significant to note that both ethnophobia and xenophobia carry the root word "phobia," meaning, "fear." For *what is intolerance except fear and ignorance of the unknown (and that "unknown" is other living and breathing human beings)?* Only progressive political will and quality education can bring an end to the ignorance that fuels the irrational fear of other peoples.

Soccer is uniquely qualified to bridge the perceived "otherness" between peoples, and to guide communities toward fraternity and away from conflict. As the world sport, one could argue that it is the *responsibility* of soccer and its true supporters to put forth the maximum effort to do just that.[14]

---

[14] In both the Introduction and in Chapter 18, the author refers to his youthful soccer experiences in the USA as an introduction to and appreciation of human diversity. However, some individuals have not had a totally positive experience – even in a traditional soccer country like Germany. The author interviewed one player born of a German mother and an Asian father who had been in the Hamburg SV system. His experience within the Hamburg youth team was good, as there were other players from Turkey, Ghana, Spain, and the former Yugoslavia forming a "multiethnic constellation" (as he termed it). However, after his youth career, he was exposed to the often xenophobic atmosphere of the German minor leagues (what he described as "narrow-minded attitude towards other cultures"). Those negative experiences drove him to compete in less popular sports like basketball, surfing and tennis, as he felt more comfortable in those more open-minded environments.

Examples of Intolerance

Among the most prominent examples of ethnic, "racial" and religious intolerance in soccer history are Nazi Germany's intolerance of non-Aryans and Jews in the 1930s, the Franco regime's intolerance of regional ethnicities, the blame placed on Brazil's "black" players for World Cup losses in 1938 and 1950, the rich Northern clubs versus the poor Southern clubs in Italy, and the "Catholic" Celtic club versus the "Protestant" Rangers club in Glasgow, Scotland. As always happens with intolerance, there are people and entities that benefit from this classic "divide and rule" strategy of humanity – be it governments, politicians, the ruling class, or major armament manufacturers.

Players of African ancestry emerged in British football in the 1970s, but the racist abuse they suffered *actually increased in the 1980s* as hooliganism began to rise during the conservative Thatcher/Tory era. Poor and ignorant British hooligans were too socially and politically unsophisticated to realize that their xenophobic actions undermined their own social position, by reinforcing the ruling conservative Tory political views favoring the landed and upper classes.

Intolerance is still a problem in soccer, as the following recent examples illustrate:

- England's 30,000-member official national football team fan club *England Members Club* had to be disbanded in 2001 because of uncontrolled hooliganism and racist behavior. The club was reorganized with a new code of conduct, including the prohibition of bigoted chants. The new club is called *englandfans.*
- Oxford, England, home of famous Oxford University, is supposed to be a bastion of intellectual enlightenment. However, it is also the home of Oxford United, whose coach and ex-England player Mark Wright made racist remarks to a referee in 2001. Wright was fined, suspended, and ultimately resigned from his position.
- After the Rome (Roma—Lazio) derby in January 2005, Lazio player Paolo Di Canio gave a straight-arm fascist salute to Lazio supporters. As Lazio was former fascist dictator Benito Mussolini's favorite team, his right-wing granddaughter expressed her appreciation of Di Canio's idiotic gesture.
- German football officials launched a "Red Card" program of rejection of violence and racism against foreigners, but racism in the lower divisions in Germany is still unchecked. After suffering horribly from xenophobic jeers in Halle on 25 March 2006, FC Sachsen Leipzig's Nigerian player Adebowale Ogungbure sarcastically gave a "Nazi salute" to the crowd to counter their fascist actions. Incredibly, Ogungbure was then charged (later rescinded) with "unconstitutional behavior" for making the salute (which is illegal in Germany). If the German and FIFA authorities are not more vigilant, right-wing hooligans that are well-practiced in the lower German divisions pose a real threat of disrupting the 2006 Germany World Cup by targeting the national teams involved.
- During one of Spain's training sessions in 2004, national team coach Luis Aragonés made a racist remark regarding France and Arsenal player Thierry Henry that was recorded on tape. Aragonés claimed that he was only trying to motivate one of his players by using "colloquial language," and was fined only 3000 euros (£2,060) by the Spanish Football Association.
- A friendly match between England and Spain in 2004 (won by Spain 1-0) was marred by racist chanting in Madrid's Bernabeu stadium against some of England's players with some African heritage FIFA fined the Spanish FA only $87,000.
- FC Barcelona's Cameroon striker Samuel Eto'o suffered xenophobic abuse while visiting Spanish teams Zaragoza and Santander in the 2005-2006 season, but the clubs were fined less than € 10,000 for each offense. Eto'o understandably wanted to walk off the field at Zaragoza, but his team asked him to persevere.

Switzerland is an idyllic country set in the Alps that has a long history of tolerance with its near neighbors, as the Swiss confederation (the *Confoederatio Helvetica*) is actually made up of German, French, Italian and Romansch speaking peoples. But Kubilay Türkyilmaz, a Swiss player of Turkish heritage, decided to retire from his own national team in early 2001 *because of xenophobic abuse from his fellow citizens.*[15] At the time of his retirement, Türkyilmaz had 32 Swiss goals in 60 Swiss appearances. The record holder was Swiss legend Max Abegglen with 34 goals (including three of Switzerland's five goals against Nazi Germany in the 1938 World Cup) in 68 games, in an age when goals were easier to come by. Türkyilmaz played his last game before retirement for Switzerland on 10 November 2000 against Slovenia, scoring two goals at the age of thirty-three.

Fortunately, Türkyilmaz decided to return to play for the national team through the 2002 World Cup qualifiers, although Switzerland ultimately did not qualify. He continued scoring goals, and is now the Swiss co-scoring leader with Abegglen, with 34 goals in 62 games.

Hooliganism and Soccer Violence

There is no question that hooliganism is a major cause of the intolerance documented above. Hooligans are fanatics to a cause, willing to bridge any opening to promote their view to the world. Their causes vary from vehement support of their club to abusing foreign players and planning violence from a religious or ethnic base. When hooligans turn to physical and verbal violence, they are transformed into urban terrorists causing fear among the general populace.

Gerald Asamoah was the first German of African ancestry to play for the unified German national team, and he scored in his debut win over Slovakia. Asamoah, who had declined invitations to play for his native Ghana, said, "I just want to show a few idiots that a black man can do some good for Germany." The idiots he was referring to were xenophobic hooligans.

Hooliganism has been the bane of international football, especially in England and Italy, and increasingly in Eastern Europe. Hooliganism has expanded to other countries, and has occasionally led to deaths, as when a crowd of Turkish hooligans killed two Leeds fans attending the Leeds – Galatasaray game in April 2001. Hooligans have also fueled stadium crowd disasters, especially the Heysel Stadium disaster at the 1985 European Cup Final in Brussels, when hooligans pushed forward and thirty-nine fans were crushed to death in the ensuing panic. It is clear that hooliganism must be contained if future stadium disasters causing loss of life are to be avoided.

The activist Emma Goldman said, "The most violent element in society is ignorance." This phrase applies perfectly to zealously xenophobic and violent hooligans, as they know nothing about world culture and history, and promote terror from an intellectual and emotional void.

---

[15] Türkyilmaz was an elegant striker with a nose for the goal, and tops a list of modern outstanding Swiss players, including striker Stephan Chapuisat and midfielders Heinz Hermann and Cirico Sforza. Significantly, his national team performances seemed to get better with age, as in his last six games (including four World Cup qualifiers and two European Championship qualifiers), he scored 12 goals.

Solutions to the Human Rights Issue of Intolerance

FIFA has finally recognized the stains of xenophobia, ethnophobia and racism on their sport, and has started investigating the causes and potential solutions. In a meeting during the 2001 World Youth Championships in Argentina, FIFA examined the issue and passed a resolution intending to confront the specter of racism in soccer.[16] The United Nations High Court of Refugees sponsored a worldwide conference on intolerance and racism in South Africa in 2001, and FIFA sent a small delegation.

In some instances, the FAs first need to clean their own houses. Referee Gurnam Singh finally won a tribunal decision and financial award against the English Football League after it was found that other English referees were promoted over him despite their lower performance marks. The instigators of the discrimination within the English league were not significantly punished, and therefore there is little deterrence to prevent this happening again in English football in the future.

A "neutral" view expressed by the ex-Italy coach Giovanne Trapattoni is that soccer has little responsibility to fight racism. Trapattoni said racism "must be fought first in the family and then in the schools. The stadium is not the place." He is correct in the first statement, but not in the second. Unfortunately, if nothing is done in the stadiums, the hooligans will understand this as permissiveness, which would translate to them as tacit approval. The Italian FA is finally beginning to understand this reality, and is finally taking steps to punish teams whose fans exhibit racist behavior.

However, in 2006 the most egregious violations of xenophobic behavior have occurred in Europe, especially Spain, Italy, Germany, and some Eastern European nations. Many European nations already have laws against xenophobic behavior, and still the local FAs fail to address the issue seriously. The Spanish FA should be ashamed at fining teams less than €1,000 for allowing their home hooligans to abuse international players. Since the FAs have not taken effective measures, UEFA and FIFA must immediately enact serious deterrents such as team suspensions and bans from UEFA/FIFA competitions to stop the madness.

FIFA and the Football Associations can neither afford to be neutral or lax in the human-rights violations of xenophobia, which are specifically outlined in the United Nations Declaration of Human Rights (http://www.un.org/Overview/rights.html). A positive sign occurred in the England-Holland and Ireland-Portugal international friendly matches played 9 February 2005, when both Holland and Portugal relinquished their national colors to play in half-white/half-black uniforms symbolizing their anti-racist stance. The England shirts carried a "No To Racism" message on the front.

International football has the potential to demonstrate the most comprehensive example of successful diversity in the world if, and only if, FIFA and the Football Confederations (especially UEFA since most violations occur in this Confederation) and Associations are serious about combating xenophobia in their sport.[17] FIFA is belatedly making noises about punishment for racist behavior of fans at the 2006 Germany World Cup, but it is a stop-gap measure rather than a well-thought out and executed policy.

---

[16] Players have been rightly puzzled over what to do when confronted with xenophobic actions by hooligans. They want to continue playing the beautiful game, but they are smart enough to realize that there are more important things than football – such as making a stand against xenophobia in the stadium and society. Additionally, it is almost impossible for human emotions not to be affected by blind ignorance and hatred, and one naturally wants to avoid this negative energy at any cost. Even Albert Einstein experienced blind hatred, and he explained his intellectual/emotional method of controlling negative energy thrown his direction: "Arrows of hate have been aimed at me too. But they have never hit me, because somehow they belonged to another world with which I have no connection whatsoever."

[17] What is likely necessary for FIFA to make a worldwide impact against xenophobia is the incorporation of a positive message on soccer uniforms for the decade 2006-2015, so that soccer becomes synonymous and inseparable with human diversity. Rather than a negative "No To Racism" phrase, a positive phrase such as "Humanity Matters," "Diversity Rules," or "Stand Up, Speak Up," might be more effective at fully engaging all soccer supporters for the decade, which will hopefully result in eliminating blatant xenophobia from the game.

Team Identity and Rivalry

Fans identify with teams for several reasons: (1) proximity to their neighborhood, town or city, (2) team success, (3) favorite players or style, or (4) other specific characteristics of a team.

Teams historically drew fans from their own geographic base, and to a great degree this is still true today. An intra-city *derby* is a rivalry between two teams of the same city or region.[18] These rivalries tend to be intense but are often good-natured because of the need to co-exist in the same living space.

Intra-City Derbies

Brazil has a wealth of clubs to choose from in certain cities:

Rio de Janeiro:	Flamengo	Fluminense	Vasco da Gamma	Botafogo
São Paulo:	São Paulo	Santos	Corinthians	Palmeiras
Belo Horizonte:	Cruzeiro	Atletico Mineiro		
Porto Allegre:	Gremio	Internacional		
Salvador:	Bahia	Vitoria		

Argentina club team derbies are located mainly in Buenos Aires:

Buenos Aires:	River Plate	Boca Juniors	Velez Sarsfield
	Huracán	San Lorenzo	Banfield
Avellaneda:	Independiente	Racing	
Rosario:	Rosario Central	Newell's Old Boys	
La Plata:	Estudiantes	Gimnasia y Esgrima	

Peru rivalries are concentrated in the capital Lima and in the mountains:

Lima:	Alianza Lima	Sporting Cristal	Universitario
	Sport Boys		
Mountain derby:	Cienciano - *Cusco*	Melgar - *Arequipa*	

England city and region derbies: Londoners traditionally supported the clubs nearest their neighborhoods, which are spread out all over the Greater London area. Arsenal – Tottenham has traditionally been the biggest derby in London, but may soon be equaled by Arsenal – Chelsea and Tottenham – Chelsea if all remain top teams.

Northeast:	Arsenal	Tottenham
Northwest:	Queen's Park Rangers*	
East:	West Ham	
Central:	Chelsea	Fulham
North:	Watford*	
South:	Charlton	Wimbledon*^

The three largest English same-city derbies outside of London are:

Liverpool:	Liverpool	Everton
Manchester:	Manchester United	Manchester City
Birmingham:	Aston Villa	Birmingham City

A historical derby between English teams in the Midlands:

Midlands:	West Bromwich	Wolverhampton*

*[Not in Premiership (Top Division) in 2005-2006 season]
^[moved to Milton Keynes in 2003; see Chapter 5]

---

[18] The term "derby" was likely borrowed from a traditional Shrovetide football match (see Chapter 1) between the two halves of Derby, a city in central England.

Italy city derbies:
Milan:	AC Milan	Internazionale
Rome:	Roma	Lazio
Turin:	Juventus	Torino
Genoa:	Genoa	Sampdoria

Germany city derbies:
Munich:	Bayern Munich	Munich 1860*
Hamburg:	Hamburg	St. Pauli*
Ruhr derby:	Dortmund	Schalke 04

*[Not in First Division in 2005-2006 season]

Spain city derbies:
Madrid:	Real Madrid	Atlético Madrid	Rayo Vallecano
Barcelona:	Barcelona	Espanyol	
Seville:	Sevilla	Real Betis	
Basque derby:	Real Sociedad	Athletic Bilbao[19]	
Galician derby:	Celta Vigo	Deportivo de la Coruña	

Portugal city derbies:
Lisbon:	Benfica	Sporting
Oporto:	Porto	Boavista

Turkey derbies:
Istanbul:	Galatasaray	Fenerbahçe	Beşiktaş

Scotland city derbies:
Glasgow:	Celtic	Rangers
Edinburgh:	Hibernian	Heart of Midlothian

Egypt derby:[20]
Cairo:	Al-Ahly	Zamalek

The Celtic – Rangers derby (also known as the "Old Firm clash") is probably the *most significant intra-city derby* in Europe, enhanced because of the historical religious tensions surrounding the two Glasgow clubs. Rangers has been the club of the city's Protestant community, while Celtic has been supported by Catholics, many who had Irish ancestors immigrate to Glasgow at the end of the 19th century. Thus the notorious Protestant – Catholic political and cultural conflict that has consumed Northern Ireland for the past 350 years eventually became the unfortunate focus of a football derby in Scotland.

Rangers refused to play any Catholic player until 1989, when forward Mo Johnston was signed by then coach Graeme Souness (not entirely accurate – see below).[21] Celtic had

---

[19] Athletic Bilbao has continued to employ only Basque players, while Real Sociedad employs players of many ethnicities and foreigners. Athletic Bilbao's last title came in 1984 when many teams were still comprised of one ethnicity, a very rare situation today.

[20] Al-Ahly versus Zamalek is Africa's most important derby, and is contested so fiercely that it is usually officiated by a foreign referee. The author utilized the Egyptian fanaticism for soccer in 2004 when confronted with a critically wounded Egyptian patient who spoke little English. After greeting him with *As-salaam Alaikum* (Arabic, "Peace be upon you"), the author inquired *Zamalek or Al-Ahly?* The patient immediately said "Zamalek!" – thrusting his fist in the air. He then made a good recovery.

[21] This is the popular history, but Rangers had previously signed Catholic players before, such as John Spencer in 1985 and Hugh O'Neill in 1976. O'Neill was a USA university graduate, and was a leading goal scorer for the Rangers reserve team that won the treble. Perhaps most significant was South African Don Kitchenbrand, who concealed his Catholic faith in the 1950s in order to play for Rangers (after all, Laurie Blyth had preceded him at Rangers in 1951-52 but had to leave after his Catholic faith was discovered). Kitchenbrand played very well for Rangers – even scoring five goals in a game in 1956.

employed Protestants, but persisted in flying the Irish tricolor at the stadium. Today, both teams have gone international and hired good players from around the globe regardless of ethnicity or religion. A recent Celtic hero was the multi-ethnic 2001 Golden Boot winner (most goals in Europe) and Sweden player Henrik Larsson, who scored more than 50 goals in their 2000-2001 championship campaign.

This does not mean that Scottish football is free of religious tension, as a Hibernian player received a yellow card against Rangers because he crossed himself as he walked off the field at halftime. The referee interpreted what would be a routine motion in South America as a provocation to a partisan Scotland crowd.

The biggest Italian intra-city derbies are the Milan derby between AC Milan and Internazionale, and the Rome derby between Lazio and Roma. The Roma – Lazio derby is probably the fiercest in Italy, as the Milan derby is cushioned by the fact that the San Siro stadium is the home stadium for both teams. Still, Inter fans rioted in 2005 while being eliminated from the Champions League by AC Milan in the San Siro, and the match was defaulted to AC Milan.

The Flamengo-Fluminense, or "Fla Flu" derby, is the oldest and most significant intra-city derby in Rio de Janeiro and Brazil, which is closely rivaled by the Boca Juniors – River Plate "Superclásico" Buenos Aires derby in Argentina. Both derbies have legitimate claims of being the biggest rivalry in South America.

Inter-City Derbies

Each of Spain's four major cultural and linguistic regions has representative teams in the *Primera Liga*. The *Castilla* region has Real Madrid, Atlético Madrid and Rayo Vallecano, *Catalonia* has Barcelona and Espanyol, the *Basque region* has Real Sociedad, Athletic Bilbao, and Alavés, and *Galicia* has Deportivo La Coruña and Celta Vigo. The league has even branched out to island teams such as Mallorca in the Mediterranean (in the top division in 2005-2006), and the Canary Island teams of Tenerife and Las Palmas in the Atlantic Ocean.

The biggest inter-city derby in the world is in Spain, the Barcelona – Real Madrid rivalry. Tensions run high, partly because Real Madrid has been viewed as the team of the ruling establishment, while Barcelona was a steadfast symbol of resistance to oppression. During the fascist period, Franco banned regional languages except the Castilian Spanish spoken in Madrid, and until Franco's death in 1975, the Barcelona football stadium (the Camp Nou since 1956) was one of few safe havens where Catalan could be spoken freely. Although Real Madrid was the dictator's preferred football club, some Real Madrid players such as Alfredo Di Stéfano interacted with Juan Carlos de Borbón (Spain's future king who favored a democratic system), and was even an invited guest player for the Barcelona team.

Few players have transferred between Barcelona and Real Madrid, as they could be seen as betraying the team. Even in recent times, when the clubs employed players from France (Zidane), Portugal (Figo), Brazil (Rivaldo, Ronaldo, Ronaldinho, Roberto Carlos), England (McManaman, Beckham, Owen), Argentina (Saviola), Mexico (Marquez), Sweden (Larsson), Cameroon (Eto'o) and Holland (Kluivert, Van Bronckhorst), there is still an awareness of the old Spanish Civil War battles. Luis Figo still meets up with a rude crowd reception at the Camp Nou in Barcelona, as he is one of few to have transferred directly from Barcelona to Real Madrid. Figo was even accosted in the 2004 European Championship Final while playing for Portugal, when a hooligan ran onto the field and threw a Barcelona scarf at him.

The biggest out-of-city derby after Barcelona – Real Madrid is probably Liverpool – Manchester United, since these have been the most successful British clubs of the past 40 years (Manchester United last won the Champion's League in 1999, and Liverpool in 2005). However, the ascendance of London clubs Arsenal and more recently Chelsea will possibly create new passionate derbies with the northern teams that may rival the traditional Liverpool – Manchester United spectacle.

The big Dutch derbies are all inter-city affairs since the big three teams are located in different cities. The Ajax – Feyenoord match is called "*De Klassieker*" – the National Derby. Almost every Dutch title is predictably won by Ajax (Amsterdam), Feyenoord (Rotterdam) or PSV (Eindhoven).

Inter-Nation Club Rivalries

Authentic club rivalries between different nations' clubs do not really exist because of the infrequency and unpredictability of when they will next play each other. Generally though, special interest is piqued when Spanish and Italian league teams clash in competitions, because those two leagues are generally acknowledged to be the most competitive in the world.

The "Old Firm" Scottish teams of Celtic and Rangers have investigated entering the English Premier division, and if successful, they will likely strike up notable rivalries with top English teams.

National Team Rivalries

It is difficult to maintain a national team rivalry because of the infrequency of the games. But there are three examples of "national team derbies" that are worth mentioning, one in Europe, one in South America, and one cross-continental.

Holland vs. Germany: With a population of 16 million, Holland is the most successful modern era small football nation (Uruguay is the most successful small nation ever with two World Cup wins). But despite excellent player technique and style, the Dutch often appear over-anxious when playing Germany, and German discipline has frequently won out over the Dutch flair. For example, after the 1974 World Cup Final in which Germany beat Holland 2-1, Johan Cruyff tried to explain away the result by saying, "Germany didn't win the Cup – we lost it."

The Dutch are still testy about being occupied by Nazi Germany during World War II, and they place great faith in their football team to defeat Germany. David Winner's book *Brilliant Orange* best details the modern Holland fixation with Germany and this national team football rivalry. France, Denmark, Belgium, Poland and Switzerland also remember the conflict when playing Germany, but perhaps not to the extent of Holland's football spectators.

Argentina vs. Brazil: Nearly always the top two nations in South America, Brazil is usually seen as the poorer and Argentina the richer neighbor (although the income gap is closing as hard times have hit Argentina). Argentina is always convinced that they can win against anybody, and while Brazil has always had mercurial talent, they have at times lacked team cohesiveness. These two teams meet frequently because of the mandatory nature of the South American World Cup qualifiers.

England vs. Argentina: This derby began with the hotly contested match in the 1966 World Cup, in which Argentine captain Antonio Rattin was expelled and England coach Alf Ramsey called the Argentine team "animals." The derby gained political implications after the 1982 war over the tiny Falklands/Malvinas island chain. After losing the war, Argentina gained "revenge" in a 1986 World Cup win with Maradona getting both goals; one a cheat goal known as the "Mano de Dios" (Hand of God) goal, and the other a solo slalom goal voted "FIFA Goal of the Century." The 1998 World Cup brought another confrontation, with Argentina prevailing on penalty kicks after David Beckham was sent off for petulantly kicking Diego Simeone. England won the 2002 World Cup match with Argentina, as Beckham's penalty kick provided the only goal of the match.

Football Styles

The progressive change in football equipment design and materials in the last fifty years has contributed greatly to the dynamic style identity of the sport itself. Soccer teams originally adopted a traditional and conservative uniform dress bereft of even a club's crest; this has now exploded into hundreds of choices of jerseys, shoes and even multiple advertisements on the uniforms. Soccer style has progressed from a minimalist style (1880s to the 1950s), to a classic style (1958-1984), to a transition style (1984-1994), to the present overdone multi-marketing style (1994 onwards).

In exchange for invaluable uniform advertising space, multinational sports clothing and equipment companies (Adidas, Nike, Puma, Reebok, Umbro, Lotto, etc.) are actively engaged in a capital battle to outfit top club and national teams. Needless to say, the advertisements themselves bring no tradition or contribution to the game, just a cash infusion for the owners and players. Soccer fans have not benefited because the ticket prices have continued to climb, and fans are forced to view their favorite club uniforms as continuous billboard propaganda. A review of progressive soccer design and style over time is useful in order to bring the modern big-business soccer style into context.

Uniforms

The soccer uniform is made up of the five "S's": shirt, shorts, socks, shoes and shin guards (FIFA declared protective shin guards as a mandatory part of the uniform in 1990). Soccer uniforms have changed radically in material and style over the past century, reflecting both design changes and technological advances in fabrics.

Shirts

The first soccer shirts (also called a jersey) were of cotton fabric and represented the color scheme of teams; Manchester United wore red, Tottenham Hotspurs wore white, and so on. Some teams had simple color patterns of stripes or a diagonal red slash.

Teams concocted their color schemes in intriguing ways. The St. Etienne club of France wears green and white because of the greengrocer's shop colors that founded the club. Boca Juniors of Argentina wears blue and yellow taken from the national colors of a Swedish ship that was coincidentally moored on the Plate River in Buenos Aires. Cerro Porteño of Paraguay wears a red and blue stripe design as a compromise for the colors of two political parties. Some teams simply borrowed their colors from their founders' favorite teams (often English teams); for example, Juventus of Italy borrowed the black and white stripe shirt design from Notts County, Dinamo Moscow the blue and white kit from Blackburn, Athletic Bilbao the red and white stripes of Sunderland, and poetically, Atlético Madrid adopted the same kit from Athletic Bilbao. However, it was Leeds who borrowed the all-white kit of Real Madrid.

Shirts were initially devoid of club crest or markings, but eventually teams affixed their club crest to the center or upper left hand side of the jersey front. Numbers had already been introduced on the backs of the shirts in the 1930s - original numbers were from 1 to 11. In an early 2-3-5 tactical scheme, the goalkeeper wore number 1, defenders wore 2 and 3, midfielders 4 through 6, and forwards wore 7, 8, 9, 10, and 11. As tactical schemes evolved to 3-3-4, 4-3-3, 4-4-2, and so on, the classic 1-11 shirt numbers still had the keeper first at #1 and ended on the forward line. Since substitutions were first allowed in 1970, it is a rare occurrence that a team only fields players with the classic 1-11. Higher numbers have been accepted for starting players for decades; Eusebio (#13) and Johan Cruyff (#14) popularized this trend as superstars with a number other than 1 to 11.[22] Still, the mystique endures of a "number 10" player who can both create and score, no matter what number he actually wears.

---

[22] Shirt numbers have gone higher and higher for no apparent reason, except perhaps player preference. In 2005, French international Bixente Lizarazu wore number "69" at Bayern Munich.

In the 1970s, the kit manufacturers placed their insignias on the shirts. However, a special situation arose when Puma sponsored Johan Cruyff, and he insisted his Adidas-designed Holland shirt have only two stripes instead of their branded three!

The 1980s introduced blatant shirt advertising unrelated to football, which unfortunately persists to this day. Virtually all clubs have a sponsor(s) advertisement that dominates the club crest on the front of the shirt. Barcelona and Athletic Bilbao of Spain remain the only top-level clubs that purposely have no uniform sponsor, thereby retaining the fullest integrity of their club identity.

Jersey materials have evolved from cotton to polyester and other synthetics, and shirt designs have gotten fancier. Jersey design reached an all-time low in 1996 in the USA when the newborn Major Soccer League (MLS) had several unfortunate garish shirt designs. The MLS jersey designs with jagged patterns and contrasting colors were difficult to look at even when players were standing still. Some English team jerseys in the 1990s were also hideous, with one yellow-green abomination described as "canary cack" by Norwich fans. Fortunately, classic shirt designs are starting to come back into favor again.

Traditionally, national team shirts are designed with the colors of the nation's flag. However, Holland (orange) and Italy (blue) do not use the colors of their flags for their national team shirts. These two countries have retained the colors of their active (Holland's "House of Orange") or retired (Italy's "House of Savoy") monarchy houses. It is ironic that full-fledged democracies take their colors from the anti-democratic institution of monarchy.

Goalkeeper shirts have evolved from monotone to multicolor patterns. Goalkeeper Jorge Campos of Mexico was a major contributor to the spicing up of goalkeeper jerseys in the 1990s, although Peru's Juan Valdivieso wore fancy sweaters in the 1930s. The technical result of an extravagantly colored goalkeeper jersey is unknown – do players aim at the attraction or away from it? It is possible that the more garish and fluorescent shirts might enable smart players to aim away from the colors and into the goal corners.

Juan Valdivieso (center) models his colorful goalkeeper sweater in the 1936 Olympics (Chapter 13).

Mass consumerism has initiated yet another change in soccer shirts: clubs now redesign their soccer jerseys yearly so as to entice fans into buying the annual "new" style. National team jerseys change at a minimum every four years for the World Cup qualifying. The main incentive for shirt variation is financial, as advertisers and clubs can sell more shirts and bring in revenue. But the yearly shirt change leaves the fans short-changed; the club history is trivialized and the fans are blatantly solicited to buy the current incarnation of the *advert-shirt*.

Shorts

The first uniforms in the late 1800s and early 1900s included long cotton pants descending so far down that they practically met the high socks. Only the knees were showing in these first uniforms, illustrating the Victorian clothing norms of the day. Those pants eventually became true shorts, finally culminating in the "mini-shorts" worn in the 1978 and 1982 World Cups. By then, shorts were made of polyester. Thereafter, shorts became longer and baggier again, until they are once again trending lower towards the knees, and may be accompanied by short support tights underneath.

While shorts were initially one color, today they are multicolor as they typically carry insignias of the team and the manufacturer, a number and trim. Some shorts even carry advertising on the front and/or back (see Chapter 5).

Sleeveless Shirts and Shirt-Short Combination

The Cameroon national team experimented with a basketball-style sleeveless shirt at the 2002 African Nations Cup, which they won after beating Senegal in a penalty-kick contest in the Final. FIFA subsequently banned Cameroon from using the sleeveless design at the 2002 World Cup.

For the 2004 African Nations Cup, the *Indomitable Lions*[23] then introduced a one-piece combined shirt and short "bodysuit". This time, FIFA banned the new uniform style before the competition, but Cameroon used it anyway (and lost in the quarterfinals). FIFA then fined Cameroon US $ 155,000, and initially docked them 6 points from the 2006 World Cup qualifying competition, which would have doomed their chances of appearing in that competition. FIFA later rescinded the point penalty, but the issue has not yet died. The Puma company was the provider of both new-style kits, and is intent on deciding the issue in the legal system.

The uniform message is clear: neither nations or multinationals have the power to flaunt the Laws of the Game, at least how they are currently interpreted by FIFA as a separate shirt and short.

Socks

Socks were originally wool or cotton and worn up to the knee. Polyester and polyester blends were introduced in the 1960s, and the thinner socks may have allowed the players a better feel of the ball.

At the same time, some skill players had abandoned the use of the optional shin guards because they felt the guards inhibited their play, and they adopted the habit of wearing their socks around their ankles. Today most players wear their socks up, often tied up with sock ties and taped low down to keep the now mandatory shin guards in place. Advertising has not escaped the socks, which often have the manufacturer's name on them.

Shoes

Soccer shoes (also called soccer "boots") were originally made of heavy bovine leather with leather studs on the soles. Lighter kangaroo leather was later incorporated into the shoe, with metal and plastic studs screwed into the sole. Eventually the complete sole of the boot was manufactured from molded plastic.

The studs themselves had a circular footprint. The shoes were always all black, until 1949, when Adidas placed three stripes on their shoes (which symbolized co-founder Adi Dassler's three sons).[24] When West Germany won the World Cup in 1954, they wore the three-stripe Adidas.

The 1950s Hungarian team revolutionized the use of the lighter boot. Before the England-Hungary match at Wembley in 1953, the English players thought the "Magical

---

[23] The *Indomitable Lions* is the nickname for the Cameroon national soccer team.
[24] Ironically, Adi had just split with his Adidas co-founder brother Rudolph, who founded rival Puma in 1948.

Magyars" team would be a pushover because they appeared to be "wearing bedroom slippers." However, Hungary dominated the game and won 6-3.

The last twenty years have brought about a revolution in soccer boot design, much of it superfluous and geared towards marketing. Today, soccer boots are commonly made of man-made materials rather than leather. The laces may be off-center and/or hidden - a custom made lace-less boot may not be far off. New soccer studs copy the baseball "slash" cleat sole design; however, the new footprint design has not yet been shown to be safer or superior to conventional circular studs. The increasing use of new-generation synthetic turf will doubtlessly lead to the evolution of a custom-made shorter stud design.

Whereas shoes were once all black, there are literally hundreds of color combinations currently available, potentially making shoes the most garish part of a players ensemble. Shoes may be tinted any color from silver to gold to red to white, even a ridiculous "champagne." They may carry special designs painted on or ingrained in the shoe along with the manufacturer's insignia. The modern shoe design is less important for matching the team uniform than to enhance the player's endorsement package (especially since a team's players all wear their own shoes).

Despite tremendous shoe development and propaganda in the past twenty years, there has in essence been no major improvements in soccer boot function. Players using the classic style black kangaroo-leather boot with a circular stud footprint still perform at the same level as those using newer champagne-synthetic-off-center-laces-slash-footprint boots. As "black is basic" in international fashion, a player can never look bad in a black boot.

Shin Guards

Shin guards were originally worn under wooly socks in the late 1800s. In the 1950s and 1960s many players preferred to play without shin pads, as skill football had demonstrated its superiority to the brute force soccer styles.

Many of the best players at that time played with their socks down to their ankles, an act that since 1990 would be illegal by FIFA rules. The socks-down style was the street fashion of the skill players - the hack men were still wearing shin pads. Pelé often went without shin pads until professional hacks tried to incapacitate him. Despite being the constant target of hack men, George Best disdained shin pads, as did Teófilo Cubillas, Mario Kempes and Michel Platini in their early years until the 1980s. Cubillas always wore his socks down and never wore shin pads in his 20-year career, saying, "I never felt comfortable with shin pads because I would not feel the same control of the ball."

Many players started using shin pads again in the 1980s, as hard play again became the fashion. Shin pads became larger and bulkier, and were available with unwieldy ankle discs and Achilles tendon protectors. Unfortunately, all of this extra padding necessarily takes away from the skill of the game, as the players just do not have the same feel for the ball on their feet.

The best example of this shin pad phenomenon was Diego Maradona, who was the constant target of slower (both physically and mentally) defenders. Maradona went from playing without shin guards for Boca Juniors in Argentina in the late 1970s, to wearing shin guards, ankle and Achilles protectors while playing for Napoli in the Italian league in the late 1980s.

The exact reasons why FIFA mandated shin guards to be worn in all professional matches just before the 1990 World Cup in Italy are unknown, but a circulating rumor was that FIFA was motivated by an irrational fear of HIV transmission from leg injuries. With all players thus shin guard armored, perhaps it was no surprise that Germany won the 1990 World Cup with their *power soccer* style, and that Brazil won in 1994, albeit atypically (for Brazilians) playing very physical soccer and scoring no goals in the Final. Both the 1990 and 1994 Final matches were the most uninteresting in the history of the World Cup.

Fortunately, France made stylish soccer successful again in 1998, which Brazil continued with their 2002 World Cup win. Lighter shin guards have appeared, some as small as 6 inches long, which serve to limit the bulk of conventional shin pads. Perhaps not accidentally, many in the skillful Brazil national team have adopted these shin guards, so as not to be encumbered in their creativity and goal of total ball mastery.

Advertisements

Advertisements were increasingly placed on soccer shirts since the 1970s, until they were nearly ubiquitous in the 1990s (with Spanish clubs FC Barcelona and Athletic Bilbao notable exceptions to the trend). These advertisements nearly always distort the shirt design. Many adverts are already known to the public as brands, and are neither customized nor intended to blend with the shirt design. Indeed, sponsors prefer their advert to clash with the club shirt, so as to make a deeper impression on the psyche of the fan (now called the "consumer"). As an unhappy consequence for the fans, adverts dominate and belittle their favorite club shirts, which carried their classic club design for decades or even a century.

The worst part of the modern marketing blitz is that fans cannot buy a pure advert-free club shirt. However, in the USA MLS jerseys were sold under a reverse concept - to receive the advertising on the shirt, one had to pay $10 extra! Is anybody really daft enough to pay an extra $10 to put an advert on his or her club team shirt?

Shirts may carry multiple advertisements on the front, back and sleeves. Adverts are placed on shorts, socks and shoes, and even undershirts and shin pads have become potential advertising space. If shirt-adverts are ugly and historically incorrect, pants-adverts are beyond *gauche*.

Unfortunately, it will be very difficult to dislodge propaganda from soccer uniforms, as the advertising monies are too large for most clubs to ignore.

Soccer Hairstyles

Hairstyles are perhaps the most outwardly individual characteristic, and soccer hair fashion has mirrored societal changes. Before the 1960s, all players had conservative short hair because that was the norm. Then the Beatles grew their hair long and the players followed suit - George Best was even dubbed "the fifth Beatle" for his lengthening locks. Later on, Rodney Marsh and the "Mavericks" (see References) in England, Günther Netzer and Wolfgang Overath in Germany, the whole Dutch team, and many of the Argentine team led by Mario Kempes all had shoulder length tresses that rock stars would have been proud to flaunt. That was also the era of the *mullet*, a hairstyle with a short front and long back (known as *vokuhila* in Germany, slang for ***vo**rne **ku**rz **hi**nten **la**ng, or "short front long back"*). Jairzinho of Brazil, Paul Breitner of Germany, and Kevin Keegan of England innovated with giant Afros or permanents. Among goalkeepers, the Argentine Hugo Gatti led the way with heavy-metal style locks.

The 1980s brought a backlash of hirsute moderation, but the 1990s brought big hair back with a vengeance. Headbands controlled the long locks of Claudio Caniggia and Alexi Lalas, Roberto Baggio had his "divine ponytail," and the USA defensive duo of Marcelo Balboa and Jeff Agoos were also pony-tailed. Carlos Valderrama of Columbia maintained his leonine blonde Afro, while his compatriot Rene Higuita preserved his black Medusa locks. Ruud Gullit, Frank Rijkaard, and Edgar Davids of Holland, Cobi Jones of the USA, Christian Karembeu of France, and Henrik Larsson of Sweden, all maintained a dreadlocks style (a historically authentic African style) brought to international prominence by Jamaican reggae star Bob Marley.

The Samson super-long midback blonde hair of skill midfielders Alain Sutter of Switzerland (1994 World Cup) and Emmanuel Petit of France (1998 World Cup) reached the extreme of positive football hirsutism, and these two share the record of longest hair from quality footballers.

In the mid-90s there was a movement towards shaving all hair; Gianluca Vialli from Italy, Ronaldo and Roberto Carlos from Brazil, and Frank LeBoeuf and Fabien Barthez from France led that charge. This style appeared to follow the baldheaded styles of professional basketball players from the USA, and represented the extreme of negative football hirsutism, reaching the finite limit of baldness.

The short hair phenomenon reached absurd proportions when then coach of Argentina Daniel Passarella stated that no "long-haired" player would be placed on the 1998 Argentine World Cup squad. Passarella himself had sported Beatle locks in the 1978 World Cup, and had played alongside Mario Kempes, the king of the longhairs and the MVP of that World Cup. Their coach had been Cesar Menotti, who still sported long hair into his fifties. Why Passarella would come up with such a foolish rule was incomprehensible, particularly since it placed at risk the play of Argentina's heir to Kempes' goal and hair throne, Gabriel Batistuta. Batistuta was known for his rock-star hair for years, but more importantly he was known as "Batigol" for his prodigious goal output for club and country. Cutting his hair under such duress could hardly have bolstered his confidence or relations with Passarella. In the end, Batistuta did a modified cut and played, but not up to his usual brilliant standard.

Passarella and his rule also cost Argentina the services of Real Madrid midfielder Fernando Redondo, who had been integral to the 1994 Argentina World Cup team. Redondo, who had declined to play for Argentina in the 1990 World Cup because of philosophical differences with the coaching staff, would sit out the 1998 Cup because of the hair hassle. The owner of shoulder length straight black hair, he was not about to alter his appearance to suit Passarella's fantasies. Redondo always did follow his own drum – he once declined to play in an Argentine friendly because he had a university exam that could not be postponed. Diego Maradona was aghast at Redondo's educational priorities.

There are still more hair trends evolving. USA player DaMarcus Beasley sports the smart and practical cornrow style that was another recent NBA fashion and also a classic African style.

The latest and perhaps most unfortunate trend is coloring the hair, usually from dark to blond. As if these overly self-absorbed and pampered men needed any more self-attention, many are furiously dyeing their hair. Maradona himself may have kicked this trend off when he bleached his forelock yellow-white in the early 1990s. This trend came to full fruition during the 2002 World Cup with Japanese, Korean and African players leading the way with their bleached white, blonde, brown or red hair.

The Native American Mohawk and Mohican hairstyle (with hair shaved from the sides leaving a central line of hair) was prominent in the 2002 World Cup, and was likely started months before the Cup by English player David Beckham in one of his ever-changing hairdos. A few other players joined him in Mohawk-land, most notably Clint Mathis' hack-job "styled" by his amateur hair-groomer roommate Pablo Mastroeni. Turkish midfielder Umit Davala cut his long hair and showed up with a wide stripe Mohawk, and Japanese defender Kazuyuki Toda changed from bleach-blond to a red-rooster dyed Mohawk. Roberto Carlos and Fabien Barthez were the best baldies of the 2002 tournament, and Cobi Jones, Emile Mpenza and Ferdinand Coly had the best dreadlocks.

There were two new interesting hairstyles at the 2002 Cup. İlhan Mansız wore his long hair up in a samurai-style, making him look like a Japanese Dragonball character as he ran around defenders (Beckham later copied this look at Real Madrid). Ronaldo felt he needed a change before the semi-finals, so he shaved off all his hair except a blunt forelock, apparently in imitation of a Brazilian cartoon-character. Maybe he thought it brought him luck, but he quickly and appropriately went back to his former classic look.

Taribo West of Nigeria receives the "outer-space" hairstyle award with a two pigtail-bead style, which he has maintained for some years. How does West dare head the ball with those beads? Ouch.

Soccer as Surrogate Religion, or Religions Accommodating Soccer?

The exploration of human identity cannot ignore the historical importance of religion, which ranges from decentralized spiritual groups to bureaucratic organized religions.

Soccer is presently more important than organized religion for millions of aficionados - even acting as a surrogate religion for some fanatics. Certainly this is nothing new to the legions of women who never see their men in a church, mosque or temple, but whose partners never miss a home game of their favorite club or country.

Religions have shown signs of willingness to accommodate the spectacle of soccer and the World Cup. The movie "The Cup" documents young refugee Tibetan Buddhist monks' fascination with soccer, culminating with their success in arranging to watch the France 1998 World Cup by satellite television. Talk about inspiring the spirit!

The popular movie *Bend it Like Beckham* illustrates the effects that a love of soccer may have on an immigrant Asian Indian family in Britain, and the resulting clash between the new (women's soccer) and older values (religion and patriarchy).

There are excesses, however, such as the unveiling of a small gold-leafed relief statue of David Beckham in a Buddhist site in Thailand. And even the ancient Taoism-influenced martial art of Shaolin Kung-Fu has embraced soccer, if you believe the improbable story line of the Hong Kong movie *Shaolin Soccer* (re-released in English in 2004).

Regardless of soccer's impact on religion, the spiritual importance of soccer for young people is very real. Soccer's potential for positive values ascends from the commitment that youth place in the simplest of games. By virtue of being the world's game, soccer has the opportunity, and many say the responsibility, to increase young people's self-confidence, sense of community and personal integrity. This will happen when human rights are at the forefront of organized football policy, racism and xenophobia are driven from the game, and local soccer is respected globally (Chapter 16). When these responsibilities are fulfilled, soccer may be properly valued as an empowering cultural Art of Humanity.

Chapter Four

Soccer: Social and Political

Winning isn't everything. There should be no conceit in victory and no despair in defeat.
Matt Busby[1]

Soccer and Social Relations

Food, water, and shelter are basic material human necessities, but sparks of hope and happiness are also essential for human survival. To address these critical emotional needs, aid workers at massive wretched refugee camps in Africa discovered that camp dwellers' spirits rose immediately once plastic balls were introduced, as the children momentarily forgot their abject misery to play the beautiful game. Play is integral to a child's happiness everywhere, and soccer fulfills this role brilliantly. Indeed, soccer and a child's joy are often manifestly entwined, and a happy child is a healthier child.[2]

Nonetheless, many people view soccer as incidental in life – a mere sporting fancy of youth.[3] This chapter aims to illustrate that despite past denials, it is impossible to separate the social, historical, and political facets of life from events in the soccer world.

Soccer *is* an integral part of the world, and as such has unfortunately contributed to the unseemly aspects as well as the best moments of life. FIFA's recent efforts against racism and violence in soccer demonstrate that they have somewhat modified their passive attitude from just a decade ago.[4] But until the soccer authorities present a more proactive stance, it is unlikely that soccer will affect its relevant and potentially massive influence over the problem triad of ethnophobia, violence, and political intrigue – all of which involve football as part of the world.[5]

---

[1] Matt Busby was *Manchester United* coach from 1945-1971, including the 1968 European Championship team.
[2] To its credit, FIFA has started the "Sport-in-a-Box" program, with each box providing equipment for forty children in poor schools and communities.
[3] Even some top officials of FIFA have at times underestimated soccer's relationship to the world-at-large. When he was the FIFA General Secretary during the run up to the 1994 World Cup, Josep Blatter said, "Violence, political and racial issues have bothered or damaged other sports. Since 1972, there have been problems in the Olympic Games. We have not had such problems in FIFA." Some nifty propaganda, but times have changed; Blatter is now President of FIFA, and he has necessarily become more of a realist.
[4] After non-governmental organizations such as Kick It Out (www.kickitout.org) and Football Unites, Racism Divides (FURD at: www.furd.org) had battled racism and hooligan violence in soccer for more than a decade, FIFA presented an Extraordinary Congress Resolution on 7 July 2001 following their first FIFA Conference against Racism in Football (http://www.fifa.com/u20/2001/media/resolution-E.pdf). This was the effective start of FIFA confronting this significant human rights problem, but so far FIFA's efforts have been less than convincing.
[5] Political intrigue includes any human rights violation against players or fans, including protection from those who express fascist sentiments in word and deed at soccer venues.

Soccer and Human Diversity
Great Britain

Scottish players provided the initial diversity in English football clubs in the latter part of the 19th century, followed by Irish and Welsh players.[6] Four distinct Football Associations evolved in Britain, meaning that there would be the four "national teams" of England, Northern Ireland, Scotland, and Wales.[7] This division of Britain into four separate "football states" based on geography and ethnicity has resulted in smaller talent pools for the individual teams, and probably a reduced success rate than a united British team would have brought.[8] How England would have loved to have access to Northern Ireland's ball wizard George Best, Scotland's quicksilver "number 10" Kenny Dalglish, or Wales' electrifying forward Ian Rush over the years.

As England's foreign empire collapsed after World War II it received a consequential influx of immigrants (especially West Indians and Asians), but the English FA was initially reluctant to include any of their "new-look" citizens in the national team. In truth, Great Britain was still catching up with the rest of the world in 1978, when there was hardly any diversity in British football. Glasgow Rangers was still all Protestant, Glasgow Celtic was nearly all Catholic, and the first South Americans had just arrived in England in the form of World Cup winners Ossie Ardiles and Ricardo Villa. These two Argentine adventurers were successful in improving the Tottenham Hotspur club, although Ardiles was forced into temporary soccer exile in France by the time the Malvinas/Falklands War arrived (Villa had already left Tottenham). After that absurd little war, Ardiles returned to lead Tottenham to the 1984 UEFA Cup championship.

In 1978, the outstanding English player of West Indian descent was Laurie Cunningham, an explosive forward with Orient and West Bromwich Albion who could absolutely disorient the opposition. Cunningham finally broke England's "color" barrier when he played (and scored) against Scotland in an under-21 match on 27 April 1977. Cunningham was so skilled that in those years in which few British players were going abroad, venerable Real Madrid of Spain signed him immediately. Sadly, Cunningham only had six appearances for England before a serious knee injury affected his career. Cunningham's West Brom teammate Cyrille Regis – a versatile and powerhouse center forward – did not get much of a chance with the national team either.

Viv Anderson was the first of African heritage to appear for the full England team on 29 November 1978, but he was a defensive back who by himself could not threaten the uninspiring English national team style at that time (significantly, Anderson reportedly received death threats for breaking the full national team barrier).

The attitude of the English FA and people only began to change when John Barnes – who had impressed during his years at Elton John's Watford club – was selected for England. After Barnes' remarkable dribbling goal against Brazil in a friendly match at the Maracana in

---

[6] In the late 1800s Scottish players were seen as the "ringers" of an English team, as they brought more sophisticated dribbling skills to the English game. The initial England-Scotland match took place on 30 November 1872, and is acknowledged as the first international soccer game ever played (it ended 0-0). Guyana-born Andrew Watson was the first *amateur* British player of African origin when he played for Scotland against England in 1881 – one of his three international appearances for Scotland. The first *professional* British player of part African heritage was Arthur Wharton (part Scottish, Grenadian, and Ghanaian); his story is best documented in Phil Vasili's *The First Black Footballer: Arthur Wharton 1865-1930: An Absence of Memory*.

[7] The four Football Associations of England, Scotland, Wales and Northern Ireland still make up a large part (four of eight members) of the International Football Association Board (IFAB), the entity that oversees the Laws of Football. FIFA controls the other four voting positions.

[8] Despite a tremendous reputation, England has won only one World Cup (at home in 1966) and no European Championships in the modern age of soccer from 1958-2006. There was discussion of a unified Great Britain team participating at the 2008 Beijing Olympics and the 2012 London Olympics, but this proposal now appears doomed.

Brazil in 1984 (which was rated the *Best Goal of the Year in Brazil*), more people began to see the value of some diversity and technical flair in the English national team.[9]

After Anderson, Cunningham, Regis, and Barnes were capped as the first English nationals with some African ancestry; Paul Parker, Des Walker, Ian Wright and Paul Ince (who became England captain) all had success in the national team in the 1990s.[10] The 2002 World Cup team had Rio Ferdinand, Sol Campbell, and Ashley Cole starting in defense, with Emile Heskey as a "holding forward" up front, and with the emergence of winger Shaun Wright-Phillips the 2006 team continues to represent England's evolving diversity.

Europe

Even as they were also losing their own foreign empires, other colonial nations incorporated their new citizens into soccer earlier and more successfully than England. Spain and France had immigrant players on their national teams from the 1910s and 1930s, respectively, and Portugal integrated the fantastic Mozambique duo of Eusébio and Mario Coluna in the 1960s.[11] And after Holland's colony of Dutch Guiana became independent Surinam in 1975, first and second generation Surinamese helped win the 1988 European Championship for Holland. Dutch soccer players with some Surinamese heritage include best players Ruud Gullit and Frank Rijkaard (see Chapter 7), as well as Edgar Davids, Patrick Kluivert and Clarence Seedorf. These individuals played an integral part of the Dutch national team and big Dutch club (Ajax, Feyenoord and PSV Eindhoven) successes in the last 25 years.[12]

Soccer Introduction and Integration in the Americas

Soccer Arrival

Soccer arrived in South America in the late 1800s with British expatriates working in a variety of administrative and technical jobs. Charles Miller is singled out for introducing soccer to Brazil in 1894, when he returned from attending high school in England with a soccer ball and a rule book.[13]

The "expats" were primarily exposed to the upper socioeconomic classes because of their education and skills, and they soon introduced all the British games to their adopted lands, including cricket, rugby, and polo. However, these sports only retained the interest of the elite classes, and as a result they barely exist in the Americas today. So although soccer was first introduced to the upper classes, the working classes quickly adopted the sport and formed their own clubs.

Soccer, Slavery, and Its After Effects

Slavery was abolished in Latin America earlier than the USA; and African-Latinos and indigenous Americans became legally integrated into those American societies faster than in the USA. But despite the abolition of slavery after the USA Civil War in 1865, African-

---

[9] Barnes' career is well documented in his book *Barnes: The Autobiography* (2000 – written with Henry Winter). Barnes was England's first player of African heritage (he was born in Jamaica) to play in a World Cup, coming on in the 76th minute when England was losing 0-2 against Argentina in 1986. In those short 14 minutes he made a goal for Gary Lineker and several other chances, and almost upstaged Diego Maradona.

[10] Although when Ian Wright was the English First Division top scorer in 1991, he was unbelievably not chosen for England's 1992 European Championship squad. Andy Cole was another quality forward of African heritage who did not get enough time in the English national team.

[11] The Filipino Paulino Alcántara played on the Spanish national team, scoring six goals in five games. He is still FC Barcelona's top scorer with 374 goals in 375 games from 1912-1927 (see Chapter 7).

[12] However, the so-called self-destructive tendencies of the Netherlands national team seem to have continued from when it was an all-Dutch ethnic affair. The disconnect from their sumptuous soccer talent is said to come from the liberal Dutch mentality that enables them to speak their mind, thereby theoretically reducing team discipline. Or, perhaps the Netherlands has also been unlucky, especially on penalty kick competitions that they have mostly lost (see David Winner's book *Brilliant Orange: The Neurotic Genius of Dutch Soccer*).

[13] *God is Brazilian* by Josh Lacey (2005) provides a good summary of the Miller era.

Americans were excluded from most USA team sports until after World War II ended in 1945, and many were systematically excluded from civil and other human rights until 1964.[14]

In Peru – like many places where the African Diaspora exists – "black" players were not immediately accepted into the original sport clubs. This rapidly changed, as the inaugural photo of club team Alianza Lima taken around 1901 shows players of mixed Spanish-Inca ethnicity with dark complexions, and the 1912 team photo clearly shows an African-Peruvian present along with others of mixed ethnicity. Already in this era, Peru had begun to develop soccer while utilizing all of its rich ethnic patterns. By the 1920s, African-Peruvians were fully included into many clubs, especially Alianza Lima, which was variously called the club of the *barrio* (neighborhood), the *obreros* (workers), and the *pueblo* (people). After Alianza integrated early on, the club subsequently introduced many important players such as Peruvian legend Alejandro Villanueva, who first performed for Alianza in 1927 (see Chapter 13).

Today, Alianza Lima is still seen as a club of the *pueblo*, partly because their Matute Stadium resides in La Victoria, a lower-class section of Lima. But in reality the Alianza Lima club is supported throughout the country by a wide range of diverse Peruvians. From an informal survey of taxi drivers over the past ten years, the author could detect no ethnic pattern in their support for Alianza, Universitario or Sporting Cristal (the "Big Three" clubs of Lima). Currently, some African-Peruvians support Universitario, some *mestizo* (mixed ethnicity) Peruvians support Sporting Cristal, and some ethnic Spanish Peruvians support Alianza – or any other combination thereof. This is perhaps because Peru is one of the most diverse countries on the planet, and their people have intermixed freely for centuries in a much more accepted lifestyle than the segregated practices of English colonial or USA societies.[15] Although the Spanish conquerors vehemently imposed their culture on the indigenous Incas, they did intermarry into the partially vanquished communities. An early example of this cultural trend was the half-Inca half-Spanish *Inca Garcilaso de la Vega*, the foremost Peruvian historian of the 16th century (see Chapter 11).[16]

African-Brazilians were also kept from playing in Brazil's original clubs, but by the 1920s and 1930s they had infiltrated most of the teams, demonstrating their ambition and soccer skills. The first Brazilian star was the multiethnic *Arthur Friedenreich,* son of a German father and a Brazilian mother, who effectively broke the Brazilian color barrier in 1909 at age seventeen. He finished his soccer career in 1935 at the age of forty-three, and still holds the all-time Brazil and world scoring record with 1329 goals.[17] Another Brazilian star was *Leonidas da Silva* (known as Leonidas in the unique one-name system in Brazil), who was a sensation at the 1938 World Cup Finals when he finished top scorer with eight goals. Unfortunately, Leonidas and Tim (another multiethnic Brazilian) were "rested" during the semi-final against Italy, and Brazil lost the match 1-2. It is still unresolved whether they were rested because of overconfidence and/or racism on the part of the Brazilian soccer administration. Leonidas is generally credited for introducing the spectacular overhead *bicycle kick* into popular play.

---

[14] The year 1964 is NOT a typographical error – the "Jim Crow" laws of the southern USA states prohibited African-Americans from exercising their federal right to vote until the 1964 Civil Rights Act was passed, a delay of 99 years (1865 to 1964) following the Civil War (1861-1865). Many experts assert that African-Americans have still not received full human rights in the USA, as they have never been compensated in any meaningful way for four hundred years of chattel and economic slavery.

[15] For documentation of Peru's human diversity see: *No Hay País Más Diverso* [No Country More Diverse]. C. Iván Degregori, Ed. 2000. Lima, Pontificia Universidad Católica del Perú/Instituto de Estudios Peruanos.

[16] *Inca Garcilaso de la Vega*'s name still graces the public football stadium in the historic Inca capital city of Cusco. Thankfully, Peru still retains much of its historical integrity, and names stadiums after important national figures instead of multinational corporations with no historical connections.

[17] Although Friedenreich's goal total is larger than Pelé's career total of 1281 goals, it was accomplished in an amateur and semi-professional era when it was easier to score goals. Some claim Friedenreich's total is 1239 goals.

Still, all was not equitable in Brazilian football after Friedenreich and Leonidas broke the barriers. Although clubs such as *Vasco da Gama* (effectively a "Portuguese" club) and *Flamengo* integrated very early on, others such as Flamengo's archrival *Fluminense* (of the massive "Fla-Flu" derby) waited until the 1950s to diversify.

However, soccer was integrated in the USA much earlier than the indigenous sports of basketball, baseball, and USA-football. Even though most USA sports were subservient to segregation in the first half of the 20th century, soccer was able to evade much of that systemic xenophobia because of its inherent internationalism and vibrant connections to ethnic and immigrant communities. Still, when Pelé was considering signing for the New York Cosmos in 1974, his advisors counseled him that a significant social disadvantage could be that he would *"be black in the USA"* – in order to differentiate from his life in Brazil where he rarely experienced overt racism.

Soccer and Pan-Americanism

At about the same time in the 1950s, Argentine physician Ernesto "Che" Guevara was exploring the power of soccer in South America. Guevara was obviously a soccer fanatic, and must have lamented his lack of access to soccer after he moved from Argentina and Mexico to the baseball nation of Cuba. In his book *Mi Primer Gran Viaje* ("My First Big Trip" in Spanish, called "The Motorcycle Diaries" in English), which chronicles his motorcycle trip around South America, his entry from Bogotá, Columbia on 6 July 1952 reads, "Tomorrow I'm off to see *Millionarios* play *Real Madrid* in the cheapest stand."[18] Guevara was referring to the "Blue Ballet" of Alfredo Di Stéfano's *Millionarios* club from Bogotá, Colombia, who played against Spain's club team *Real Madrid* (which became Di Stéfano's eventual destination in Europe). Guevara had recognized that soccer was an integral part of Latin American culture and a potential link to revolutionary change – an idea incorporating the Pan-American theme he had developed on his trip.[19]

Modern Soccer and Diversity

In summary, ethnic prejudice by both individuals and soccer institutions was evident throughout the 20th century, but despite occasional traumatic setbacks (some prominent in recent years), has diminished over time. It is essential to understand the history behind these events so mankind does not repeat these horrific errors in the 21st century and beyond.

---

[18] At the time Guevara witnessed the Millionarios – Real Madrid game, Millionarios was a member of the renegade Colombian league that was beyond FIFA control.

[19] Guevara played soccer in his youth, usually limited to goalkeeping duties because of his frequent asthma attacks. Guevara became Fidel Castro's right-hand man in the Cuban revolution, and was later a proponent of the socialist "permanent revolution." Guevara was eventually assassinated in 1966 in Bolivia with crucial assistance from the USA's CIA (Central Intelligence Agency).

Argentina's 1986 World Cup winning captain Diego Maradona has an obvious devotion to his compatriot Guevara, as he displays a prominent tattoo of his face (as shown in his official autobiography), as does Argentine national team player Juan Sebastian Veron (boxer Mike Tyson also displays a tattoo of Guevara). Maradona is friendly with Castro, and he underwent an apparently successful cocaine detoxification program in Cuba. Che could never have imagined that multi-millionaire athletes would tattoo his facial likeness on their bodies.

Women's Soccer

Because of women's unequal social and legal status worldwide (compared to men), women's soccer development faces all of men's soccer problems and more.[20]

The biggest success in women's soccer so far has been the USA national team, which in a span of thirteen years twice won the FIFA Women's World Cup (1991 and 1999) and the Olympic Gold Medal (1996 and 2004). USA women's soccer development was originally boosted by the landmark 1972 Title IX federal statute, which mandated equitable university sports programs regardless of gender.[21] After an initial sluggish period to enforce the statute, sport funding increased proportionately and women were able to increase their athletic competitiveness in the university setting.

Because of the dearth of professional soccer opportunities available for women, the USA university system actually accelerated women's soccer development, as opposed to stunting men's soccer in the USA (see Chapter 14). Presently there are many top-rated women's university teams spread throughout the United States, which essentially functioned as minor league teams for the USA national team and Women's Major League Soccer (WMLS - the now defunct women's professional league). With this splendid organizational capacity in place, the USA will likely continue being a world power in women's soccer.

Women's soccer has also been a notable success in Europe (particularly in Germany, Norway, Sweden, Italy and England). Perhaps not surprisingly, North America and Europe are the two areas in the world where women have the most developed societal and legal rights (although in many instances women still do not have the same legal rights as men). Close behind in success are teams in Asia and South America, specifically China and Brazil.

"Women are the Future of Soccer"

When asked about the future of soccer, Michel Platini stated that "women are the future of soccer." Platini's stance is an activist one, because the oppressive conditions that women faced in Europe and the USA in the 20th century (no voting rights, inferior employment opportunities and wages, oppressive legal structure, etcetera) still exist in much of the world in the 21st century. Thus Platini is effectively calling for a worldwide revolution in women's cultural and political rights, from which women's soccer will benefit. And vice versa, the growth of women's soccer in the world is potentially an important catalyst for expansion of women's human rights [Figure 4A].

A prime example could be South Africa. If the women's game succeeds there – in the process empowering women to stand up for themselves and families – the South African family and society would be strengthened.[22] However, the stark reality is that in those areas of the world without comprehensive women's rights, there will not be much women's soccer – even in countries such as Iran that have already constructed soccer-obsessed societies. World soccer (through FIFA and its Confederations and FAs) will need to redress this blatant gender discrimination in the same way it is finally confronting xenophobia affecting soccer.[23]

---

[20] Because of the availability of women's specialty soccer materials this book offers only a cursory introduction of this important soccer subject, and will defer detailed discussion of the women's game to more expansive sources.

[21] The statute is officially known as TITLE IX OF THE EDUCATION AMENDMENTS OF 1972, 20 U.S.C. §§ 1681 – 1688. Passed in 1972, it was not widely implemented until the early 1980s.

[22] South African women are fighting against local and legal customs that award all property to a deceased husband's family – thereby leaving the wife and children destitute. This harmful tradition has led to widespread suffering of women and children in South Africa, especially as the AIDS epidemic has dramatically influenced family dynamics.

[23] Women were legally prohibited from attending soccer matches in Iran for 26 years (from the 1979 revolution until 25 April 2006), until President Mahmoud Ahmadinejad declared the ban null and void shortly before the 2006 World Cup. Previously, women (sometimes disguised as men) had entered the stadiums and "illegally" watched Iran's national team matches. The 1 March 2006 Iran – Costa Rica match at Azadi Stadium in Tehran was the last time the police enforced the previous ban on ticket-bearing women who went to cheer their national team (Azadi is Persian for "Freedom").

The lesson learned from the USA experience is that even in a democracy, changes in statutory law will likely be necessary to advance both women's rights and women's soccer.[24]

Women's Soccer in England

Shortly after England's men's soccer league started in 1888, women began playing scheduled soccer matches. As early as 1895, a women's game attracted 8,000 spectators to Crouch End in London. However, the all-male English FA felt threatened and banned women's soccer in 1902 – meaning that they would punish clubs that allowed women use of their facilities. This changed slightly during World War I, when for the first time many English women left home to work in wartime factories. The engineering firm of Dick, Kerr began sponsoring a women's team in Preston in 1917, and in due course the *Dick, Kerr's Ladies team* attracted a massive crowd of 53,000 spectators to a game in Everton in 1920. Shortly thereafter, they went on a tour of the United States where they even played against men's teams, often winning. When the war was over, the English FA conveniently reconfirmed its ban in 1921 and women were forced back into the home – bureaucratically vetoed from the physical, social and spiritual exercise of soccer.

Women's soccer in England slowed down considerably thereafter. And yet, after another world war (World War II) in which women were a significant economic force had ended, the *FA again banned women's soccer and absurdly called it "evil"* in 1946. Today, England has an improving women's national team, but the fact remains that the English FA suppressed their women for much of the 20th century.

Women's Soccer in France

Women's soccer in France enjoyed a sixteen-year period of success and popularity between 1910-1926. A French women's team toured England in 1920 and 1921, with only the *Dick, Kerr's Ladies* able to beat them. However, by 1926 women's soccer was again dormant in France, doomed by local patriarchal social forces.

So when Michel Platini says that "women are the future of soccer," one can rest assured he is aware of the long history of women's soccer, as well as the attempts to suppress it by male dominated FAs on the European continent and elsewhere.

Women's Quality Soccer in the World

As any fan of the FIFA Women's World Cup can testify, women play a fluid game with plenty of skill for fans to admire. In addition to the USA's success, Germany (2003) and Norway (1995) have also won the Women's World Cup, and China lost the 1999 World Cup Final only by penalty kicks to the USA. Brazil also has an excellent women's national team, but women's soccer there came up against a sexist backlash in the late 1990s. Let us hope this can be reversed quickly – Brazilians should aspire for soccer style and success for their women just as they do for their men.

Women's Soccer Injuries

While girls and women are increasingly playing competitive soccer worldwide, they are apparently sustaining severe joint injuries at a significantly higher rate than men. This alarming development needs to be closely monitored during the future development of the women's game (see Chapter 6).

---

[24] *Democracy* is defined by "the rule of the majority" or "one person, one vote" criteria – a standard *not* fulfilled during the 2000 USA presidential election (the USA uses the electoral college system that was imposed when half the country kept slaves). In 2000, Bush actually had 539,947 votes less than opponent Al Gore – who would have been President in a truly democratic election. Applying the correct definition of democracy, it is accurate to state that USA democracy was suspended and replaced by a *representative republic* (or "unrepresentative republic" as many USA citizens more accurately characterize it) after 2001.

Women's Soccer Resources

Because of the success of the USA women's national team, more books about women's soccer are found on the shelves of USA bookstores than there are of men's soccer. These books include many biographies of the World Cup winning USA players, stories of their successful World Cup experiences, and skills books by the players themselves. Some players such as star striker Mia Hamm have a handful of admiring books on the shelves.

Despite their highest ever ranking of 4th in the world in 2006, there has not yet been the massive excitement generated for the USA men's national soccer team as there has been for the women champions. While the USA men have to compete with baseball, basketball, USA-football and other men's professional sports, USA women's soccer has only had to compete with a new professional women's basketball league for fans of women's team sports.

Soccer and Monarchy
Italian Blue

It seems somewhat peculiar that the Italian tricolor red, white and green flag is not primarily represented in their national soccer team uniform. Italy purloined their blue national team color from the abolished House of Savoy monarchy, which existed in Italy for over 900 years, but was finally forced into exile in 1946 after its association with Mussolini and fascism was exposed. Still, the blue shirts of the national team remain as indelible as the Italian culture and soccer style.

Dutch Orange

The Netherlands tricolor red, white, and blue flag is also not primarily represented in their national soccer uniform, as their orange shirts represent the House of Orange monarchy that still "rules" the Dutch people. The impressive irony of this situation is that a liberal people in a progressive democratic country have their national soccer team representing a monarchy's colors on the field. The best solution would be to retire the monarchy and keep the classic shirts as a token to soccer history (like Italy). After all, whoever witnessed the "total soccer" of the "Clockwork Orange" (also known as the Orange Machine - *Naranja Mechanica* Sp.) in the 1974 and 1978 World Cups could not imagine the Dutch in anything other than their wonderful orange shirts.

Soccer and Politics

Soccer and politics are often inseparable because soccer is part of most *community life* (which in turn is run by local and regional politics). *Soccer politics* are political dynamics that shape the sport of soccer, and can be roughly divided into those aspects internal to soccer authority (FIFA and the FAs) and those external (outside FIFA/FA control).

Some soccer administrators claim they should be apolitical, although this is a position distant from reality. As the end of 2005 FIFA contained 207 members – more countries and states than the 191 of the United Nations (UN). Some FIFA members such as Palestine did not even have a defined homeland.

As an example of institutional and international soccer politics, FIFA sometimes elects to artificially separate conflicting states using strategies similar to the UN. For example, the UN places India in their South-East Asia Region (SEAR) while neighbor Pakistan is assigned to the Eastern Mediterranean Region (EMRO) – even though the Mediterranean Sea is 2,000 miles (3,000 kilometers) from Pakistan. Conversely, FIFA places both India and Pakistan in the Asian Football Confederation (AFC) without apparent difficulty. However, FIFA places Israel in the European group (UEFA) while Palestine is placed in Asia (AFC) – even though some land governed by the Palestinian Authority (the Gaza Strip) is west of any Israeli territory.

FIFA Organizational Politics

The internal politics and finances of FIFA became notorious in 2001-2002, causing serious harm to the reputation of the soccer organizing authority.

First, FIFA's marketing partner ISL/ISMM went bankrupt in 2001, costing FIFA a loss of between $32 and $116 million. As a result, the second through fifth FIFA Club World Championships were cancelled from 2001 to 2004, with the competition resuming only in December 2005.[25] Second, shortly before the 2002 World Cup, an attempt was made by FIFA general secretary Michel Zen-Ruffinen to topple President Sepp Blatter on a charge of widespread corruption. However, Blatter gained re-election and was able to out-maneuver Zen-Ruffinen, who was subsequently fired. Unfortunately, the corruption charges were never seriously examined by an objective external agency, an action that could have strengthened FIFA's short and long-term organizational integrity.

FIFA President Josep Blatter's predecessor was Joao Havelange, a top-down autocrat who ran FIFA like a personal fiefdom. Judging from his first eight years in the top job, Blatter has borrowed some of Havelange's managerial style. Suffice it to say, the internal world of regional and international soccer administration has not always been pretty.[26]

FIFA and the Football Associations (FAs)
The World Cup

The World Cup has so far been held in every FIFA Confederation in the world except Africa (CAF) and Oceania (OFC). CAF has a large presence in FIFA with 53 countries, but OFC has only 11 members (twelve before Australia joined Asia in 2006). The European and American regions have the most significant past in hosting the World Cup, with Europe (UEFA with 52 members) hosting ten times and North, Central, and South America (CONMEBOL combined with CONCACAF has 45 members) hosting seven times. Asia (AFC with 46 members) hosted the World Cup once, in 2002.

Future World Cup hosting will most likely revolve on a geographic basis. Italy hosted the World Cup in 1990, the USA hosted in 1994, France hosted in 1998, and Japan and South Korea hosted in 2002. Germany then won the 2006 hosting in a FIFA vote that – were it not

---

[25] Sao Paulo beat Liverpool 1-0 in the Final held in Tokyo.
[26] Readers wishing to delve into the subject of the internal politics of FIFA would benefit from pursuing David Yallop's book, *How They Stole the Game: The Book the FIFA President Tried to Ban.*

for an abstention instead of a promised vote from New Zealand – should have confirmed South Africa's winning bid. The 2006 Cup vote was a poor example of a world body conducting its business.

South Africa was named to host the 2010 World Cup in a later meeting. The geographic rotation that has already fortuitously taken place would mean the Americas would host in 2014 (probably Brazil), Asia in 2018 (possibly China), Europe in 2022 (possibly Great Britain, Holland/Belgium, or Turkey/Greece), and Africa would host again in 2026 (possibly a group of North African and/or West African nations).

Oceania will no longer be able to host a World Cup by itself, as the one confederation country combination possibility (Australia – New Zealand) is no more with Australia withdrawing from the OFC.[27] Although the New Zealand national team participated in the 1982 World Cup, their team quality is often suspect and they will have difficulty qualifying against the 5th placed South American teams.

FIFA head Sepp Blatter has suggested having a World Cup every two years instead of four years, but Europe (European Cup) and South America (Copa America) already host powerful regional tournaments in the years between World Cups. World Cup qualifying requires more than a full year to complete, so it is doubtful that the Cup can be scheduled more frequently than every four years. The four year schedule also lends a sense of suspense that would be impossible to create every two or even three years between World Cups.

Many people are in agreement with Blatter, however, in that they would like to see more meaningful international tournaments between the World Cups. The Confederations Cup – with only six country winners of their respective Confederations participating – is unlikely to fill this role even if the national teams can be persuaded to field their strongest teams. This appears to be a losing cause, as even Michel Platini sees the Confederations Cup as a doomed competition by 2010 – even though his home country France was champion in 2001 and 2003.

Independence of the FAs
FIFA appropriately insists on the independence of all national FAs. This means that if a government interferes with their country's FA functions, FIFA will punish that action by suspending the country from actively competing in FIFA sanctioned play. This action effectively temporarily ceases national team activity, which happened to Guinea and Greece in 2001 and threatened Nigeria in 2005.

Sometimes, governments attempt to keep a "check and balance" on national FA activities. Perhaps the most interesting example of this was when Pelé was Brazil Minister of Sport from 1994-1997, and the Brazilian FA (the CBF – *Confederaçao Brasileira de Futebol*) was run by Ricardo Teixeira, FIFA President Joao Havelange's son-in-law. Teixeira ran the Brazilian FA in an autocratic style and substance that did not suit the unique needs of Brazilian football. Indeed, Brazilian football was in such shambles by the late 1990s (from rampant corruption, exploitation of players, and players abandoning the country) that USA's *Newsweek* magazine put a report of Brazil's soccer administration chaos on their international issue cover. Pelé did try to clean up Brazilian soccer by promoting a reform law – popularly called the "Pelé Law" – but by the time the law was passed after years of debate by the Brazilian Congress, it was so diluted it was nearly useless, a situation which Pelé sadly recognized.

A Brazil Congressional inquiry in 2000-2001 followed the passage of the ineffectual reform law, and it reached a devastating conclusion of the Brazilian soccer administration. According to Senator Alvaro Dias, the CBF was "truly a den of crime, disorganization,

---

[27] In 2005, Australia applied to enter the Asian Football Confederation (AFC) under the theory that it would be easier for Australia to qualify for the World Cup by beating Asian teams rather than the 5th place South American team. Ironically, Australia eliminated Uruguay on penalties to qualify for the 2006 World Cup (their last as Oceania representatives), and started playing Asian Nations Cup games even before the 2006 World Cup had begun.

anarchy, incompetence and dishonesty." The report recommended that seventeen people – including CBF President Teixeira – face criminal charges of tax evasion, fraudulent foreign exchange operations, and illegal embezzlement of funds from the federation or clubs. However, charges were never filed, and Teixeira was reelected to the CBF Presidency for a fifth time in 2003.

Club & National Team Politics

Clubs are becoming more protective of their players as "investments," which comes at the expense of player involvement in national team play. This is likely a conscious effort of the large clubs to make the club team championships appear equal in stature to the World Cup. But while *club teams* are for the most part tightly controlled, secretive, and hire whomever they wish; *national teams* are beholden to a nation with their players restricted to citizens of that nation. Indeed, that is one of the main attractions of international play, as nations must perform with the individuals they develop. Since they cannot buy new players, the question of money in international national play has so far been much less important than international club play.

Fundamental Structural and Ideology Differences Between Clubs and Countries

Clubs are increasingly volatile organizations, and even excellent players are shifted from club to club every few years. Not so with national teams, thanks to sensible FIFA rules that ensure players perform for one country for life. Because the national teams have player continuity, the fans can appreciate their compatriots' skills that much longer within a team (players enjoy the continuity also). Conversely, the club fan never really knows when his favorite player is going to leave in today's soccer business atmosphere, as club team continuity has become a quaint idea of the past. In this day of disposable goods, fans witness the disposable player – once his supposed usefulness is gone, so is the player.

Club teams are increasingly complaining that their contracted players are performing for their national teams and putting them at risk for injury without any compensation arrangement. While the club teams do pay the players, they also realize their players are adding value to the club because of the honor of representing their respective national teams. After all, all teams want the prestige of having as many "national team players" as they can.

Charleroi versus FIFA case

However, the 2006 *Charleroi case* may force a change in the present *laissez-faire* arrangement when the legal challenge is finished The case revolves around a Moroccan midfielder named Abdelmajid Oulmers that played for Belgian team *Sporting Charleroi*. While playing for his nation of Morocco, he was injured in a game against Burkina Faso, and Charleroi is seeking financial compensation for his subsequent 8-month injury absence. Charleroi is a small club that is now being backed by the so-called G14 clubs – a group of 18 large European clubs that wield the most financial power in club soccer worldwide (G14 website at. www.g14.com). The G14-backed *Charleroi versus FIFA* will first be heard in a Belgian civil court, and will almost certainly be appealed to the European Court of Justice for final judgment.

Surely, there will be movement towards allowing national FAs to help buy injury insurance for their players whilst they are on national team duty. However, most FAs would not be able to pay the exorbitant salaries for their players who perform for the G14 teams. This scenario would effectively remove the best players in the world from playing with poorer national teams, while the richer national teams would have no obstructions to fielding their best players. It also would take money out of FIFA's and the Confederations' hands that is supposed to be democratically developing soccer in poorer countries – those same countries that the G14 teams continually raid raw and developed talent from with nary a cent for recompense.[28]

National Excitement Still Beats Club Fervor

Even with many nations moving from near mono-ethnicity to multicultural societies, there remains an enhanced mystique of representing a country – a geographical and political entity – rather than a business product such as a modern soccer club. Tim Vickery, in a 2006 column for BBC Sport, pointed out that soccer globalization created the now common multi-national club squads that resulted in increasing the quality gap between the giant clubs (the G14) and the smaller clubs. However, soccer globalization at the international level has *done the reverse* by helping raise quality outside of the big European countries, thereby allowing foreign players to gain more experience in Europe and making their national teams more competitive. Additionally, since national teams representing geographical and political entities have more natural gravitas in the world (i.e., more importance to positively affect social interactions), Vickery is convinced that "international football is the most fascinating and most powerful force in the game." These are some of the reasons why the World Cup will remain the top soccer competition – more important than any imaginable club competition.

Players engaging in the beautiful game for both club and country create an extraordinary spectacle for legions of diverse fans. While it is true that clubs pay most of the wages of the national team players, it is also true that when players excel in national team play more fans will want to watch them at their club venues – thereby bringing in more club revenues. That is the exchange that club soccer and national team soccer have orchestrated, which has so far boosted the romance of world soccer to its zenith. Any future radical tinkering of this tender bargain between club and country may deflate soccer's mystique in the world.[29]

---

[28] FC Barcelona is belying its democratic club structure by belonging to the G14, and thereby participating in the Charleroi charade. Barcelona is a unique club, with a structure that other clubs should emulate, and should not seek to support a movement protecting the capital of the powerful at the expense of the weak in world soccer.

[29] Few players have dared to defy their clubs to play for their homelands. In 1975, Portuguese club Porto discouraged their creative midfielder Teófilo "Nene" Cubillas from playing in the 1975 Copa America for Peru – presumably because it would interfere with his club duties. However, Cubillas was determined to help his country win the Copa, and he paid his own way to the Final and helped Peru win the replay in Caracas.

Soccer and Conflict

Over millennia, sport has been proposed to help train the human body for war. But conversely, sport in the modern age can allow humans to "blow off steam" – thus helping avoid warfare.

In the author's experience, it is the profound desire of the masses of people to avoid violent conflict, as it is often a minority of humans (individuals and their organized groups) that instigate wars. This elite minority usually has a distinct interest in controlling situations through power, politics, and propaganda, as wars are fought over land, resources, religion and ideology, and/or ethnic identity.

Wars are most often unequal, with one side having inherent material and/or strategic advantages over the other. However, an underdog side may still rise up and win, particularly if the war has taken place on their soil (e.g. Vietnam) – a true "home-field" advantage.

Because soccer is the world sport of humanity, it has unfortunately been affected by its share of military conflicts.

Soccer and Extreme Nationalism After World War Two

Nationalism may generally be defined as pride in one's nation, yet in its extreme form develops into an unappealing attitude exalting one nation, religion and/or ethnicity above all others. While nationalism in moderation may allow for mutual cultural respect, unchecked extreme nationalism has been one of the most divisive and destructive forces in human history.

The 1950s Hungary teams starring Czibor, Kocsis, Hidegkuti, and Puskas were a formidable force, unexpectedly losing 2-3 to West Germany in the 1954 World Cup Final. Many of their players elected to go into exile after the Soviet invasion of Hungary in 1956. Hungary subsequently did not pass the first round of the World Cup in 1958, and was eliminated by finalist Czechoslovakia in the 1962 Cup.

Thereafter, it was up to the Soviet Union and East Germany to demonstrate soccer excellence in the socialist nations. The Soviet Union duly won the initial European Championship in 1960, and also did well in the 1962 and 1966 World Cups. East Germany's seminal soccer feat was beating eventual winners West Germany in the first round of the 1974 World Cup Finals.

But in the World Cup qualifying competition in November 1973, the Soviet Union declined to play Chile in Santiago's Estadio Nacional (National Stadium), in the intercontinental playoff that directly determined which country would qualify for the 1974 World Cup Finals. Chile was newly controlled by a fascist military junta headed by Augusto Pinochet, and the Estadio Nacional (which had been the site of the 1962 World Cup Final) had perversely been converted into a concentration camp, and torture and execution zone after the *coup d'otat* (on 11 September 1973). Many of Chile's working intelligentsia and cultural figures had just been assassinated by Pinochet's henchmen in that stadium and the Estadio Chile in September and October 1973. Chile's greatest singer-poet, Victor Jara, had been murdered at the Estadio Chile (on 15 September 1973), and under those horrific circumstances, the Soviet Union honored the innocent Chilean dead by refusing to play. Unfortunately, FIFA did not move that important match's venue to a neutral country, which would have been the only appropriate protocol.

Prior to the 1978 World Cup held in Argentina, some claim that the Argentine players were oblivious to the military junta's serious human rights abuses. However, some of the players and coach César Menotti were very conscious of such abuses and held anti-dictatorship convictions, but they also had a vision of bringing happiness to the Argentine people – if only for a short time – by winning the World Cup.

Soccer and War

War has of course affected soccer as much as any other part of impacted societies. The most infamous dictators of the 20th century (Hitler, Franco, Mussolini – see Chapter 13) took great interest in soccer as societal controlling tool.

Ukraine Soccer in World War II

Germany controlled the Ukraine during much of the Second World War, and the local soccer league was closed during that time.[30] During the 1941-1943 occupation of Kiev, some members of the disbanded Dynamo Kiev team began a new team with a new name – FC Start. The Nazis invited them to play various German teams during June and July 1942. FC Start defeated all six Nazi teams (including a select German XI) despite being warned that they could be shot if they won. One version of the story is that most of the players were arrested after the last game and killed in a notorious Kiev ravine killing zone called Babyn Yar on 9 August 1942.[31] Although this version cannot be verified (there is still Ukrainian denial and guilt as many were complicit with the Nazis, and many would like to believe that story), there is a monument in Kiev commemorating the FC Start team. In addition, this story is said to have inspired *Escape to Victory*, a World War concentration escape movie starring Pelé, Bobby Moore, Ossie Ardiles, Michael Caine, Max Von Sydow and Sylvester Stallone, and directed by John Huston. Still, the movie does not credit the plot to any historical event.

The El Salvador – Honduras Border "Football War"

Tensions were high in the El Salvador-Honduras border zone in 1969, just before a crucial World Cup qualifying match between the two countries. Each country won their home game, which unfortunately featured abusing the away fans. The playoff game in Mexico City on 26 June 1969 was won by El Salvador 3-2, and Honduras broke diplomatic relations the next day. On 14 July 1969, El Salvador invaded Honduras, ostensibly in retaliation for the abuse of Salvadorans in Honduras. The war lasted six days but killed 2,000 people (mainly civilians) – all for the macho idiocy of military and political "leaders" in both countries. It took a more than a decade for a final peace settlement to be brokered.

El Salvador went on to beat Haiti and travel to the 1970 Mexico World Cup as the CONCACAF representative. They lost all three of their games there, allowing nine goals and scoring none. Twelve years later (after the peace settlement), both countries qualified for the 1982 Spain World Cup, tying 0-0 in a preliminary match. El Salvador scored one goal in this Cup, but allowed thirteen (including 10 from Hungary). Honduras fared better, tying host Spain and Northern Ireland and only losing to Yugoslavia 0-1. That is the extent of World Cup Finals experience from these two neighboring countries in Central America whose leaders exploited the senseless xenophobia and extreme nationalism between them to start a "soccer war."

Yugoslavia and Soccer

Yugoslavia was called "The Brazil of Europe" for their high-technique soccer, as their team appeared in nine World Cup Finals. The Yugoslavia team was made up of a mixture of ethnicities in some cases historically antagonistic by culture, religion, language, and/or historical events – yet was successful while they played the beautiful game.

But after the dictator Josip Tito died in 1980, ethnic tensions increased in the country. By 1992, Yugoslavia had fractured into the five countries of Croatia, Slovenia, Bosnia and Herzegovinia, Macedonia, and Serbia and Montenegro. Since that time, however, these new nations have together already qualified five teams into World Cup Finals (Croatia 3, Slovenia

---

[30] Many of the Soviet Union's best players originated from the Ukraine.
[31] Babyn Yar is the site of the infamous massacre of at least 33,771 individuals – mostly Jews – that were shot to death by the Nazis during the 48 hours of 29-30 September 1941. A estimated total of 100,000 people were murdered by the Nazis in Babyn Yar before they were driven out of Kiev in 1943.

1, Serbia and Montenegro 1), thereby continuing their soccer excellence despite earth-shattering changes in their social lives.

Soccer Affecting War
Pelé and the Biafra Conflict

Soccer has not stopped any full wars to date, with exception of a 48-hour ceasefire during the Biafra War. Below is a short rendition of that area and conflict.

Despite winning their independence in the late 1950s and 1960s, most African countries were left with arbitrary borderlines imposed by the colonial powers, which utterly failed to respect either ethnic or geographic boundaries. For that reason, it was perhaps inevitable that some ethnic groups would take up arms for self-determination, and by 1967, western Nigeria was locked in a civil war with the southeastern part of the country called Biafra. The Biafrans were seeking independence but were outnumbered and outgunned, and were soon being slaughtered and starved to death by the Nigerian army.

A two-day cease-fire was arranged when Pelé arrived in Nigeria to play a game with his Brazilian Santos team in 1969, in order that the country could respect and enjoy the presence of "the King" of the Beautiful Game. But after Pelé left, the killing continued, and Biafra ultimately surrendered at great human cost (one million war-related deaths). But soccer had won the peace for some days, and perhaps with some deft negotiations could have won more.[32]

After the Biafra war ended, southeastern Nigeria began to rebuild. The *Enugu Rangers* team (of the former Biafra capital of Enugu) came into immediate prominence and won five national championships between the years of 1975 and 1983. Since then, Nigeria's multiple ethnic groups have all produced star players, and as a team they have performed admirably, winning the 1996 Olympic tournament with their under-23 team. But there is still much room for improvement for the Nigerian team in the World Cup, where team unity and preparation has not yet reached its full potential. Nigeria just missed qualifying for the 2006 World Cup Finals, despite equal points and a better goal difference (+14 to +6) than Angola (Angola qualified with a better head-to-head record).

More recently, Nigeria's Enyimba team from Aba (also in the former Biafra) won the 2003 and 2004 African Club Championship – the first repeat champions since TP Englebert of Zaire in 1967-1968.[33]

Israel's Palestinian Players

The violent conflict between Palestinians and Israelis over justice and the right to live in certain areas of the Mideast has dragged on for more than 50 years, and unfortunately shows no sign of abating.

However, Israel has many Palestinians living within its borders, and some are good enough to star on the Israeli national soccer team. Two Israeli Palestinians – Abbas Suan and Walid Badir – were the heroes against Ireland and France, respectively, as their goals secured 1-1 draws for Israel in an impressive 2006 World Cup qualifying effort. Israel finished level on points with eventual qualifiers Switzerland, but had a worse goals against record.

Some of Israel's club teams are well integrated. Hapoel Bnei Sakhnin represents a Palestinian town in Israel, is financially backed by a rich Russian Jew, and has Muslims, Christians, and Jews playing in unison.

---

[32] That is the potential power of soccer and its top players, should they choose to exercise it in areas of conflict. Some players such as retired France national team member David Ginola have been active in the movement to eliminate land mines from the world – an admirable use of his soccer-derived popularity.
[33] It should be noted that TP Englebert won over Asante Kotoko of Ghana in 1967 because Kotoko were not informed of a replay after the two initial drawn games

If Palestinian players can help Israel almost qualify for the World Cup, and participate successfully in Israeli league teams, serious politicians should ask themselves why cooperation in other societal avenues seems virtually impossible.[34]

Other Palestine Issues and Soccer

Palestine is a political entity (the "Palestinian territories") made up of Palestinians that live in the Gaza Strip, East Jerusalem, and what is left of the West Bank. Despite the Gaza Strip being west of all Israeli territory, Palestine competes in the AFC (Asian Football Confederation) while Israel competes in the European UEFA (presumably so they will not compete directly). The Palestinian and Israeli Football Federations have long histories – both being founded in 1928.

Although the Palestine team is improving (it beat Guam 11-0 on 1 April 2006), it failed to qualify for the 2002 or 2006 World Cups. One fascinating aspect of Palestine's team is that several members come from the Palestinian Diaspora in Chile, which even has a top division team named *Palestino* (www.palestino.cl).

Because Palestine is under constant violent threat, the national team routinely trains in Ismailia, Egypt, and plays their "home" games in Doha, Qatar rather than the Palestine Stadium in Gaza. The Palestine Stadium was bombed by the Israeli Air Force in April 2006, causing the suspension of local games.[35]

George Weah and Liberia

George Weah was a skillful forward who had a starring role in many club team successes, most notably as the central striking figure for AC Milan's great teams (see Chapters 7 & 8). Weah was consensus World Player of the Year in 1995 – the first African player to win this award. Both Weah and Abedi Ayew Pelé from Ghana never had the chance to shine in the World Cup for their nation, unlike top Cameroon players such as Roger Milla and Thomas N'kono.

Weah financed the Liberian national soccer team through years of civil war conflict and reconciliation, and almost achieved his goal of bringing Liberia to the World Cup Finals for the first time in 2002. Liberia led Africa's toughest qualifying group – containing powerhouses Nigeria and Ghana – until the final game when Nigeria beat Ghana 3-0 to win the group by one point. In a very real way, the national soccer team was the only unifying force during those violent years in Liberia. Weah tried marshalling that unifying force by running for President of Liberia in 2005, and came in a respectable second.

---

[34] Israelis and Palestinians are remarkably alike in that they strongly value family life and education, and are even closely linked genetically in the human family. Perhaps an apt comparison would be the Northern Ireland conflict, which also involved people of remarkable similarity in a long religious and political war. Religion and historical events have conspired to destroy any semblance of peace in the Mideast, and any human breakthrough distracting from the chaotic violence is surely welcome.

[35] After the bombing event FIFA spokesman Jerome Champagne said, "Hitting a football stadium is absolutely counterproductive for peace, because today football is the only universal tool that can bridge gaps." FIFA has subsequently vowed to repair the damaged stadium, as they have helped rebuild soccer infrastructure in Israel.

Soccer and the Iraq War

Iraq dictator Saddam Hussein – like Hitler, Mussolini and Franco (Chapter 13) – had a keen interest in national soccer performance, to the point of placing his sadistic son Uday in charge of Iraq's Olympic and Football organizations. Reports that Uday ordered the physical abuse and even torture of Olympic and national soccer team players began to leak out long before Hussein was deposed. FIFA examined these charges in 1997, but gave a clean report after a superficial investigation (likely players who felt their life was threatened would not admit to their abuse).[36] As a result, Iraq was allowed to continue playing in FIFA-sponsored tournaments (the 1998 and 2002 World Cup qualifying tournaments), and participated in the 2000 and 2004 Olympics – even qualifying the soccer team for the 2004 Athens Olympic Games after Saddam Hussein had been deposed in 2003.

Iraqi Soccer Players and Bush

After the non-UN sponsored USA-led invasion of Iraq in 2003, George W. Bush used the example of the 2004 Iraqi Olympic soccer team success in speeches and even a 2004 election campaign advertisement. The Iraqi players quickly contested Bush's claims to be helping Iraq – accusing Bush of war crimes and exhorting the remaining USA military to respect their sovereignty and immediately exit their country.[37] The Iraq team subsequently came in an amazing fourth in the Olympic tournament.

Despite the ongoing strife in Iraq that is approaching civil war status, the national team is still playing well, beating China 2-1 in March 2006.

International Soccer Fans Recognize Bush Iraq Lies

In his recent book *Y El Fútbol, Dónde Está?* [Where is Soccer?], Argentine coach Ángel Cappa writes of what he experienced as the world's impression of the Iraq war:

> When Bush launched all the Imperial weight for a war of annexation against Iraq, most of the world recognized it as illegitimate and illegal, despite the lying arguments they tried to hide the truth that was so evident that nobody could not notice it. Soccer people also uncovered the real reason of the aggression, after which they put decision into action........exhibiting a poster "BUSH, THERE IS OIL IN THE SOCCER FIELD OF UNIÓN."[38]

Cappa only gives this example, but other posters against the war have appeared in stadiums in South America and Europe.

Iraqi Kidnappers Were Fans of Italian Soccer

Iraqi kidnappers let a hostage, Italian reporter Giuliana Sgrena, go free after a direct appeal from Roma (and Italy) star Francesco Totti (he wore a shirt during a game that read "Free Giuliana" that one of the kidnappers saw on television). Although direct cause and effect of her release cannot be proven, the Iraqi obsession with soccer (and with the kidnappers obsession with Roma and Totti in particular) apparently allows for an international soccer appeal for human rights to be respected by persons with even the most dishonorable intentions.[39]

---

[36] The IOC suspended the Iraqi Olympic panel for a year pending investigation of the allegations.

[37] In an August 2004 speech, Bush said, "The image of the Iraqi soccer team playing in this Olympics, it's fantastic, isn't it? It wouldn't have been free if the United States had not acted." Grant Wahl's *Sports Illustrated* interviews in August 2004 (http://www.commondreams.org/headlines04/0819-05.htm) document the Iraqi coach and players' poignant and emphatic disagreement with Bush's comments.

[38] UNIÓN is a first division team in Argentina. Cappa's direct quote, "Cuando Bush lanzó contra Irak todo el peso el Imperio en un guerra de anexión que buena parte del mundo rechazó por ilegitimia e ilegal, apeló a unos argumentos mentirosos que trataban de ocultar una verdad tan evidente que a nadie pasó inadvertida. La gente de fútbol tampoco desconocía el motivo real de esa agresión, a pesar de la campaña mediática que se puso en practica........exhibieron una pancarta durante un partido que revelaba, con sencillez e ironía, lo que EE.UU. trataba de esconder. Decía la pancarta: BUSH, EN LA CANCHA DE UNIÓN HAY PETRÓLEO."

[39] However, after Sgrena was released, accompanying Italian intelligence officer Nicola Calipari was killed by USA forces after they mistakenly fired on the car in which Sgrena was being driven to safety, and Sgrena was wounded as well.

Internal Conflict, Human Rights and Soccer

The most contentious World Cup hosting site since Mussolini's Italy in 1934 was Argentina in 1978. Argentina was a democracy when it was selected to be the World Cup host in 1974, but by World Cup time in 1978 Argentina was run by a ruthless military junta. It was the time of brutal military repression and of *desparecidos* (the disappeared), as young progressive individuals deemed a nuisance to the junta were systematically kidnapped and killed, their families never knowing their fate.

When Colombia hosted the 2001 Copa America, the Argentine national team declined to send a team, claiming security issues in Colombia.[40] However, all other CONMEBOL nations competed as Colombia won a spirited competition. If Argentina had entered the competition, it would have been excellent training for their younger players, which would likely have improved their nation's poor 2002 World Cup performance.

China has already been awarded the 2007 FIFA Women's World Cup and 2008 Olympics, and many think it will be the site of the next Men's World Cup in Asia. Multinational companies are salivating at getting an opportunity to promote their goods to the largest market in the world. However, China is routinely cited for human rights abuses, and FIFA must monitor improvements in human rights before considering China as a viable candidate for a future Men's World Cup Finals site.

---

[40] Colombia has been engaged in a low-level drug and guerilla war for the past four decades.

Chapter Five

Soccer Business and Marketing

Deporte Rey – "*The King of Sports*" *Soccer's moniker in Spain*

Football without fans is nothing. *Jock Stein[1]*

Soccer BIG Business

Beyond pure soccer is the world of soccer business and marketing, which has dramatically changed the sport in the last twenty years. Soccer success always primarily depended on the quality of the soccer art, but more recently business forces have placed equal faith in the quantity and quality of marketing their "soccer product." The current soccer business model is in many ways analogous to the movie industry – as regardless of the quality of the art produced, both soccer clubs and movie studios will hype their product for maximum profits. Nowadays, it is *not just the sport that professes to entertain*, because multi-million dollar soccer marketing campaigns also aim to add entertainment value to their obvious propaganda mission.

However, *over-marketing* may backfire, as decreasing live audiences in some world soccer markets (such as Italy) suggest. Although soccer is *El Deporte Rey*, the King can always be brought down through greed and corruption. One need only consult with football critic Shakespeare (Chapter 1), or his friend Hamlet.

Tottenham Hotspur: Stock Exchange Listing & the Advert-Shirt

Watching the 1983 Tottenham Hotspurs in London was a joy, not only because of their considerable talent directed by Argentine creative midfielder Ossie Ardiles, but also because their uniforms were aesthetically pleasing. Dressed in a superb white and off-white shimmy stripe with blue trim, their team crest *Audere est Facere* ("To Dare is To Do," *Latin*) took pride in the front of the shirt.

---

[1] Jock Stein (1922-1985) was a legendary coach of Glasgow Celtic and the Scottish national team. He was the first non-Catholic coach hired by Celtic, and was the first coach of the first British team to win the European Championship. He led Scotland to the 1982 World Cup where they went out on goal difference to the Soviet Union. He died during Scotland's match against Wales in 1985 that helped them qualify for the 1986 World Cup (after they beat Oceania champion Australia).

But in October 1983 the Tottenham club was the first English top division football club to be listed on the London Stock Exchange (initial share price was only 20 pence). At nearly the same time Tottenham rolled out a comprehensive advertising campaign directed by the Saatchi and Saatchi consulting firm. It was a good year for Spurs as they finished in fourth place in the league, thereby qualifying for the 1984 UEFA Cup competition.

But on 16 December 1983, Tottenham joined the burgeoning soccer propaganda faction[2] with a jersey emblazoned with HOLSTEN across the center, with the Spurs crest relegated to the upper left – almost as an afterthought.[3] Spurs were now selling something on their shirt – was it cows or milk…or beer? It was certainly not purely soccer anymore.

As it happened, Tottenham won the 1984 UEFA Cup with the HOLSTON advert-shirt, beating defending champions Anderlecht on penalties in the return match in London.[4] Maybe the advert-shirt would be a lucky charm for Spurs? Hardly so, as aside from winning the 1991 FA Cup in extra-time, Tottenham has won nothing of note in the succeeding two decades.

Nonetheless, from then on in Britain *soccer was selling*, and selling more than just soccer. Players were converted into moveable advertising billboards to make more money for their clubs, which in turn propped up the price of the newly floated clubs on the stock exchanges. The 1980s British soccer advertising fashion then became the template for soccer business in much of the world, with soccer uniforms used as propaganda venues for beer, telephones, electronics, insurance, airlines, soap – virtually everything.

The Demise of the Community Club Atmosphere

Up until the 1970s, fans supported their local team, and "their boys" used to be men living in the same neighborhood who made a slightly higher paycheck than the average club supporter. Now players are international athletes traded like market commodities, receiving more in a week than their supporters earn in a year, and *definitely not* living in the same neighborhood. Indeed, many English fans have lost the desire to support their local teams, as they have been seduced by propaganda produced by the "BIG" teams from London, Manchester, or Liverpool. Such is the price of an overwhelming "marketing success" for English football.

As a result, the professional game has in many ways become more attuned to the demands of advertising than the wishes of supporters. Fans drawn by the Art of professional soccer are fading fast because of propaganda overload, over-pricing, and cultural neglect. Televised soccer matches are now routinely edited so empty stands are not visible to the viewers. But the owners are not so bothered, as sky-high revenues from previously negotiated television contracts are guaranteed anyway.[5]

---

[2] On 24 January 1976, Southern League team Kettering Town was the first English team to have shirt advertising, which was immediately banned by the English FA until 1977. In 1983, Notts County, the oldest football league club in the world (founded in 1864) and Queens Park Rangers (QPR) placed advertising on their English First Division football jerseys (Notts County had MONARCH and QPR had GUINNESS). Other countries in Europe had predated English First Division soccer advertising. In Germany, Borussia Dortmund had Dutch tobacco sponsor SAMSON as early as 1976.
[3] Tottenham lost their initial match with the advert-shirt 2-4 to Manchester United.
[4] Author was present in Tottenham's White Hart Lane stadium for the 1984 UEFA Cup Final won on penalties (more on penalties in Chapter 15).
[5] European league television contracts are extremely lucrative. In 2005, the French league received £428 million, the English league £341 million, the Italian league £255 million (with Juventus alone receiving £64 million), and the German league £128 million. The Spanish league total figure was unavailable, but Real Madrid alone received £56 million.

Community Link to Clubs

Most soccer teams worldwide list their towns or cities in their names – some examples are Ajax Amsterdam, Alianza Lima, FC Barcelona, São Paulo, Liverpool FC (Football Club), Manchester United FC, PSV Eindhoven, FC Zurich, Bayern Munich, AC Milan, Real Madrid, Sporting Lisbon, Marseilles, and so on. Nicknames are secondary to the club name and are not usually positioned front and center. Over time, soccer clubs establish a relationship and draw their supporters from their own communities. When a team is doing poorly, it does not abandon the local fan base and seek to go afar, but draws from that durable community support. A feeling of stability and continuity of both team and community exists that is beneficial to both.

However, many USA-based teams in many sports have tenuous links to their communities, as clubs are often businessmen's playthings rather than community enterprises. USA sport clubs did not usually arise from community efforts, or if they did, they were eventually bought out by profit-seeking businessmen. Partly because of this trend, USA club nicknames take priority over their locations. This makes it easier for owners to move teams to potentially more lucrative locations – albeit with little consultation with the community or fans. This socially detached USA sports model is commonly called the "franchise model."

The Destruction of Wimbledon FC

Nowhere is the new crass materialism more evident than in London, England, the very birthplace of modern international football. In 2002, the English FA granted the owners of Wimbledon FC – a distinguished South London football club and a founding member of the Premiership League in 1992 – permission to relocate to Milton Keynes, a city 60 miles northwest of London. The English FA thereby allowed the new owners to destroy a club with 113 years of history in one London community (1889-2002). The simple reason was greed, as the new owners wanted more – a new stadium, more fans, *mo' moneeeeey*. Despite their purloined nickname of the MK Dons, they are in no sense a "WimbleDON team" anymore.[6]

As old traditions are forced by the wayside, new traditions are born. And so it was in Wimbledon in 2002-2003 as the local soccer community was rightfully incensed and immediately formed a new club – AFC Wimbledon – whose team was not even entered in the bottom of the professional ranks. The true Wimbledon soccer fans knew their soccer priority was good, clean, attractive football in a community environment. So the Wimbledon Dons were hijacked to Milton Keynes by a greedy owner and misguided English FA? Well, snuff them, the fans said. We will start our own club, our own tradition, and it will be stronger than ever.

Incredibly, *the new amateur AFC Wimbledon team began drawing more fans than the soon-to-be-relegated professional Wimbledon FC* in the English Second Division (now ridiculously called the "Coca-Cola Football League Championship").[7] To ascend to previous and higher soccer highs, the overwhelming majority of Wimbledon soccer fans are willing to wait the five to ten years until their new community club has qualified for the professional Football League.

The new Milton Keynes club makes no pretense for the move, as their website states the MK Dons were formed in 2004, and the year "MMIV" is featured prominently on their new insignia. Still, the Milton Keynes club claims the deep-rooted Wimbledon FC history is rightfully theirs – a position serious English football fans view as outrageous.[8] Perhaps not

---

[6] When USA sports franchises move locales, they are often too lazy and/or unimaginative to choose an appropriate new name. Thus when the New Orleans Jazz basketball club relocated to Utah in 1979, they became the oxymoronic Utah Jazz – a preposterous name theft from the birthplace of Jazz music. The Los Angeles Lakers are located on an ocean, not a lake; all the lakes are in their former habitat of Minnesota. It is a matter of time before the Milton Keynes team will be forced to repatriate the stolen WimbledDON nickname of "the Dons."

[7] The old English First Division is now known as the Barclays Premiership.

[8] Milton Keynes' supercilious attitude has only encouraged English soccer fans to label the club "Franchise FC."

surprisingly, since the club moved to Milton Keynes they were relegated from the English Second Division, and are now positioned at the bottom of the Third Division (now called the "Coca-Cola Football League One"), ready to drop into the old Fourth Division (now called the "Coca-Cola Football League Two"). Perhaps one day in the near future the "reborn" AFC Wimbledon team will vault past the MK team, as they appear to be entities fated for contrary outcomes.[9]

Rather than preserve the one central feature that has made British football great – the community club model – the English FA made a foolhardy decision in sanctioning a USA-style franchise club model for Wimbledon FC. As a result, the English FA has lost trust from *all* football fans, not just the Wimbledon fans.

Which British club will next displace its history? Glasgow titans Celtic or Rangers are itching to join the green money pastures of the English Premiership – would the quickest way be to just up and move to England? Imagine the panic if either Scottish club relocated south to England. Fortunately, the Wimbledon fans are peaceful and determined to go forth with the successful development of their new community club.[10]

International Developments in Club Franchising

Some other interesting developments in the soccer franchise club model occurred outside England in 2003. The Peru First Division team Estudiantes de Medicina - Ica (Medical Students of Ica) packed up and moved to Piura, a city 690 miles (1110 kilometers) to the north, and was subsequently renamed Grau-Estudiantes. The owners were apparently unaffected that the Daniel Alcides Carrión Medical School would of course remain in Ica. In echoes of the Wimbledon-Milton Keynes fiasco, the "new" Grau-Estudiantes club promptly dropped out of the Peru First Division at the end of 2004 and has not yet returned.

A new twist on the franchise club model was made by Mexico's Club Deportivo Guadalajara Chivas, which in 2005 sponsored a new team in the USA MLS (Major League Soccer) called Club Deportivo Chivas USA. Chivas President Jorge Vergara also investigated buying top division clubs in Spain (Atlético de Madrid) and Peru (Universitario) in 2004, which presumably would have been named Club Deportivo Chivas España and Club Deportivo Chivas Peru. That is a lot of goat teams (chivas means "goats" in Spanish). Fortunately, Vergara's plans came to naught.

Also, the MLS San Jose team relocated to Houston for the 2006 season. However, one of the club's first actions was to alienate their prospective Mexican fans (see Chapter 14).

The USA franchise club model is all about money first and the fans second, as they usually have tentative leases and superficial relationships to communities. The USA model also specializes in extracting money from communities, often in the form of special taxes to build new stadiums. This type of corporate welfare amounts to effective blackmail of the general population, as the rich owners petulantly claim they will leave a city if they do not get their new stadium, corporate tax breaks, high profits, etcetera. Public money that should go for health and education instead ends up in already privileged pockets.

However, most of the sporting world is beyond the USA, and based on the experiences of Wimbledon and Estudiantes de Medicina - Ica the franchise club model ends in failure. Outside the USA, it is proven to be a model that only serves to alienate the supporter base and devalue club quality and integrity.

---

[9] There was no stopping the new AFC Wimbledon club in 2004, as they set a new English football record of 78 straight league games without a loss. Milton Keynes barely staved off relegation to the Fourth Division (now called the "Coca-Cola Football League Two") in 2005, but is likely to drop divisions again in 2006.
[10] A similar event occurred in the amateur leagues in north London in 2001. After Enfield FC abandoned its home base, their former supporters formed Enfield Town FC to keep a team in their hometown. As of the 2005-2006 season, Enfield Town FC has ascended to the Southern League Division One where they now *compete directly* with Enfield FC. One of Enfield Town FC's strikers is Rudi Hall, the Golden Boot winner (top scorer with 11 goals) at the 2002 INAS-FID (International Sports Federation for People with Intellectual Disabilities) World Cup in Japan, which England won.

Supporters Most Loyal to Soccer Clubs

Players need not be loyal to their clubs anymore for either business reasons (they will leave for more money and/or their endorsement contracts may be larger than their paycheck), or by necessity (the clubs will sell them at their convenience). The owners have sold out to the advertisers as they jam non-football products down supporters throats with the "all-advertising everywhere" model.[11] Of players, owners and supporters – the most club loyalty now is by far shown by the supporters. Since the fans ultimately control the revenue stream the time is ripe for a backlash, similar to what the financial markets recently experienced (and which was passed down to the average consumer fan). As the USA financial bubble burst in 1999-2001 after massive over-hyping of stocks (the NASDAQ exchange fell over 80%), the soccer bubble could burst as the marketing and cultural abuse of the fans takes its toll.

The fans are finally beginning to exercise their collective power in the new soccer age. Greedy club owners should take note, as they may soon find that their supporters have left to create their own clubs, with new traditions deemed more important than the old establishment. With persistence, intelligence and some luck, communities will continue to be successful stewards of their own clubs. True soccer fans, everywhere, unite!

Soccer as MASSIVE Business – The Globalization Effect

Professional soccer is BIG Business nationally, and can be MASSIVE Business when promoted outside national borders. The soccer business is increasingly reaching outside community and even national borders, as community clubs are increasingly becoming the acquisition properties of rich foreigners and multinational corporations.

English football provides the model of how top dollar – no matter from where it emanates – craves a stake in international soccer. During 2004, there were numerous new globalization money moves attempting to control English football clubs, including: (1) Thailand Prime Minister Thaksin Shinawatra attempted to buy control of Liverpool FC, (2) an Arab group tried to buy financially unstable Leeds United, and (3) USA-football sports mogul Malcolm Glazer attempted and eventually bought control of Manchester United after assuming hundreds of millions of pounds of debt. Previously, newly minted Russian oil billionaire Roman Abramovich had bought Chelsea in 2003, Serb Milan Mandaric bought Portsmouth in 1999, and Egyptian Mohammed al-Fayed had bought Fulham in 1997.[12]

A dubious globalization frontier was reached in 2004, when the new Arsenal stadium at Ashburton Grove (to be opened in 2006) was christened *Emirates Stadium*, after their new sponsor Emirates Airlines. The Ashburton Grove stadium would be the first Premiership stadium named after a corporation not originating in England, and the new sponsor contract "earned" Arsenal £100 million (about $135 million) – apparently enough cash for Arsenal to ditch English tradition.[13]

---

[11] Also called the "living through total marketing" model – see *Individual Propaganda and Societal Impact* later in this chapter.
[12] According to the Russian newspaper *Pravda*, Abramovich was the richest man in Russia in 2005. He gained economic and political power (he is also governor of the Artic Chukotka region of Russia that is home to 80,000 Eskimos) in the 1990s after the breakup of the Soviet Union, becoming a billionaire by a series of inside deals in what has been called "crony capitalism" of the new Russian "oligarchy."
[13] Other Premiership stadiums named after corporations are Reebok Stadium (Bolton), Cellnet Riverside Stadium (Middlesbrough), and the Friend's Provident St. Mary's Stadium (Southampton) – all are originally British companies. Emirates had previously been the shirt sponsor of Arsenal's rival Chelsea.

The Twenty Wealthiest Club Teams in the World

The richest club teams in the world comprise a familiar list that has few year-to-year changes. The 2005 top twenty richest club teams, their sponsor and sponsor business categories are:[14]

1	Real Madrid	Spain	Siemens	Electronics (Germany)
2	Manchester United	England	Vodafone/AIG	Phone/Finance (England/USA)
3	AC Milan	Italy	Opel	Auto (Germany)
4	Juventus	Italy	Tamoil	Petroleum (Libya)
5	Chelsea	England	Samsung	Electronics (Korea)
6	Barcelona	Spain	*Refuses to deface shirt with advertisement*	
7	Bayern Munich	Germany	Deutsche Telecom	Phone (Germany)
8	Liverpool	England	Carlsberg	Beer (Denmark)
9	Internazionale Milan	Italy	Pirelli	Tires (Italy)
10	Arsenal	England	O_2	Phone (Spain)
11	AS Roma	Italy	*Without sponsor*	
12	Newcastle United	England	Northern Rock	Bank (England)
13	Tottenham	England	Thomson	Travel (England)
14	Schalke 04	Germany	Victoria	Insurance (Germany)
15	Lyon	France	Renault Trucks/LG	Auto/Electronics (USA/Korea)
16	Celtic	Scotland	Carling	Beer (Canada)
17	Manchester City	England	Thomas Cook	Travel (Germany)
18	Everton	England	Chang	Beer (Thailand)
19	Valencia	Spain	Toyota	Auto (Japan)
20	Lazio	Italy	INA Assitalia	Insurance (Italy)

England leads the top twenty richest clubs list with eight Premiership representatives, while Italy has five Serie A clubs, Spain's La Liga three clubs, Germany's Bundesliga two clubs, and France's Ligue 1 and Scotland's Premier League are represented by one club. Beer, phone, auto, and electronics interests all sponsored three teams each. The other categories are travel (2), insurance (2), banking, tires, and petroleum. All of these are multinational businesses whose owner nationality may be confusing and changing.[15] The national sponsorship of the richest teams is such: Germany (5), England (3), Italy (2), Korea (2), and Canada, Denmark, Japan, Libya, Spain, Thailand, USA (1 each). Libya and Thailand are nonentities in world soccer, neither having qualified for a World Cup Finals before. Currently, two-thirds (12 of 18) of the sponsored clubs have sponsors outside of their national borders, which reflects the global impact of massive multinational corporations.[16]

With many clubs listed on various stock exchanges, rumors of player transfers may move stock prices. For example, when shareholders speculated that Manchester United would buy Leeds defender Rio Ferdinand in 2001, their stock immediately fell 6% as investors feared a negative impact on the club's bottom line. However, Manchester United's stock price eventually rebounded and it remained the richest soccer club for eight straight years until 2005 (also the richest club team of any world sport, finishing ahead of the USA baseball club New York Yankees). However, Glazer's first move after buying Manchester United was to delist the club from the stock exchange in order to have more direct financial control. Delisting from stock markets will likely be the new strategy of big clubs controlled by one owner as they assume the habits of the franchise model in search of bigger profits.

---

[14] According to accounting firm Deloitte & Touche's 2005 Deloitte Football Money League report, Real Madrid displaced Manchester United from the top spot after eight years. As of March 2006, Serie A team AS Roma was curiously still without sponsor.

[15] Lyon's French sponsor Renault Trucks is owned by Swedish company Volvo, which in turn is owned by the USA automobile company Ford. Thus, the ultimate ownership is from the USA.

[16] Manchester United changed from Vodafone (England) to AIG (American International Group – USA) in 2006.

Club Strategies for Maximizing Globalization Effects ($ Branding $)

European clubs such as Manchester United and Real Madrid are now just as concerned with their "brand image" and "brand marketing" as they are with winning trophies. However, this strategy backfired in 2004 and 2005, as the only trophy won by these two most marketed clubs in the world was the English FA Cup. Despite the 2004 and 2005 season disappointments, their "Big Club" modern business strategies are formed from an apparent three-pronged approach.

First, the colossal clubs – which are ostensibly national symbols – *are seeking to become multinationals in their own right through global marketing of their "brand."* These "Big Clubs" have a new millennium marketing strategy that is not shy about seeking to steal consumer dollars in Asia or elsewhere. Of course, every soccer dollar removed from Asia means less money spent in Asia, so the new soccer imperialism comes at the expense of the more natural event of Asians supporting their own teams. These "globalization" transactions will likely have the same effect as they have had on much of the world economy – the rich get richer and the poor....well, everybody knows the end of this sentence.

Second, these larger teams have found it *profitable to own their own domestic media*, able to control their own television and print exposure that can whip their fans into a virtual frenzy.[17] At the pinnacle of media control is AC Milan, whose owner, none other than Italian Prime Minister Silvio Berlusconi (voted out April 2006), controls several media outlets in Italy. Other prominent examples are Real Madrid and Boca Juniors, which have their own television channels. Real Madrid, not content to be just worldly, has hyped their players as *galacticos* (literally "galactic stars"). What could possibly be next, *universos* ("universe stars")? But the *aficionados* are not so easily fooled by hyperbole; they know soccer art and sportsmanship when they see it, and the *galacticos* do not have a monopoly on either.

Third, large teams seek to *control human resources* (i.e. young players) *not only domestically, but also internationally*. A recent development is the enticement of youth footballers from underdeveloped nations (especially African nations) to sign for European clubs with little or no transfer money. This dubious ethical practice ensures continued pitiful financial conditions for the development of the game in the players' home countries.

Appropriated players are getting younger and younger. In the USA in 2004, DC United acquired fourteen-year old Ghana native Freddy Adu, who was already sought after by Manchester United and other European clubs.[18] But in October 2004, Barcelona went two years younger when they bought 12-year old Argentine Erik Lamela from River Plate.[19] Big European teams are now scouting a 9-year old Brazilian boy (who is not named because he has not yet signed an agreement)!

FIFA has ostensibly ended this potential youth exploitation with a new rule that prevents a player from leaving his club's country before the age of eighteen. By these rules, Freddy Adu will not be able to leave the USA before 2007. But there are ways around this rule, such as bringing players into European countries before they have a domestic soccer agreement. Eighteen-year old Argentine national team player Lionel Messi had been with FC Barcelona since he was thirteen.

The latest method for Big Teams to obtain young talent is through "strategic alliances" between clubs, whereby star players "transfer" from the smaller club to the bigger club. Abramovich's Chelsea club has relationships with PSV Eindhoven and Porto in Europe (with multiple players already sent to Chelsea from each club), and is rumored to have financed

---

[17] The enthusiastic Italian fans are already called the *tifosi* – those who are whipped into a "typhus fever" frenzy.
[18] Adu came to the USA from Ghana when he was eight years old, after his mother won a USA "green card" visa lottery. He was already playing for the USA U-20 team in 2004 at age fifteen, and made his full national debut aged sixteen in 2006. He turns seventeen years old one week before the 2006 Germany World Cup begins.
[19] Barcelona should have kept a tighter hold on their home-developed 15-year old Spaniard Cesc Fabregas, who was swept away by Arsenal for free in 2003 and has subsequently often appeared in their first team. Fabregas made his full Spanish debut in 2006 at age eighteen.

South American Player of the Year Carlos Tévez's move from Argentine club Boca Juniors to Brazilian club Corinthians. If Chelsea has invested in Corinthians, the Brazilian club could act as the South American development club supplying talent for "mother club" Chelsea.

MONEY $$$ Does Not Always Equal Soccer Quality

Fair competition can demonstrate that soccer quality can still supersede mass quantities of money. Some prominent examples of this phenomena occurred in international football in 2003-2004:[20]

(1) Greece – which had never won a game in the finals of a major championship – beat host Portugal twice, holders France, and favorites Czech Republic to win the 2004 European Championship.

(2) Cienciano and *Once Caldas* – two small Andean clubs came out of nowhere to win two South American continental championships. *Cienciano* of Cusco, Peru (their hometown stadium at altitude 3,360 meters) won the 2003 Copa Sudamericana, beating Santos and River Plate, and later beat Boca Juniors in the 2003 Recopa. *Once Caldas* of Manizales, Colombia (at altitude 2,150 meters) beat Boca Juniors in the 2004 Copa Libertadores Final.[21]

(3) Monaco beat the "galacticos" of Real Madrid on away goals after a courageous display, being down by three goals (2-5) after nearly a half in the return game. Discarded Real striker Fernando Morrientes scored two goals in that series, helping to bury his old team that had loaned him to Monaco. Monaco later reached the Champion's League Final, but succumbed to Porto in an entertaining match.

(4) Porto (Portugal) beat Manchester United fairly in their home and away series in the 2004 European Champion's League competition, with subsequent whining from the Manchester delegation that the Porto players were diving and dirty. Porto later won the Final 3-0 against Monaco of France, and the 2004 (and ultimate) Intercontinental Cup against Once Caldas.

(5) English Premiership team *Chelsea* spent over $200 million dollars to acquire several players in the 2003-2004 season – more money than the rest of the other nineteen Premiership clubs combined – and failed to win any titles in 2004.[22]

Even before the Porto-Monaco European Champion's League Final was played, speculation had begun about which of the two "smaller club" coaches and players would leave. While Monaco's coach Didier Deschamps was speculated to join Juventus, Porto coach Jose Mourinho was hired by newly bankrolled (or "oilrolled") Chelsea. Several players from both teams were transferred to "Bigger" teams, some of which had never even won a European championship (Chelsea). These individual transactions would have been inconceivable had a "Big" team won in 2004, and thus began the dismantling of the Porto and Monaco teams after a tremendously successful season by both – actions totally dependent on which way the money flows. But the fans know which teams were superior in the 2003-2004 competitions.

---

[20] In January 2005, the world's most valuable soccer and sport team Manchester United (MUFC) was held to a 0-0 tie by *non-league* Exeter City in the English FA Cup competition. What made the match result more incredible was that it was played at Manchester United's home ground of Old Trafford. Manchester United won the replay at Exeter's stadium 2-0. MUFC tied another non-league team – Burton Albion – away in 2005, but won 5-0 at home.

[21] After the two Finals, Cienciano beat Once Caldas 2-0 in the October 2004 Copa Interandina in Cusco.

[22] By 2006, Chelsea had spent nearly £500 million of Abramovich's controlled Russian oil money (again more than the other 19 teams combined), and succeeded in buying the 2005 and 2006 Premier League Championships. However, they still did not make even the semi-finals of the European Champions League.

USA Interests and International Soccer

Unhappily for the sporting business forces in the USA, the "Big Four" sports have much less influence on world consciousness than international soccer.[23] The USA sport moguls have now realized this and are attempting to make business arrangements with soccer teams to tap into this world market.

An arrangement between the New York Yankees and Manchester United was an example of this unconvincing globalization propaganda phenomenon. The question is this – what do baseball and international soccer have in common? Not much, as soccer continues to gain popularity even in the few countries that support national baseball leagues, such as Japan and Cuba.

USA-football owner (NFL Tampa Bay Buccaneers) Malcolm Glazer figured that instead of making an agreement he might as well buy control of Manchester United. After a protracted financial battle that most fans disdained, Glazer paid 300 pence for each club share, which placed the value of the club at 1.47 billion dollars (most analysts concluded it was an overpayment). The club also assumed significant new debt with the sale. As a result of Glazer's power-grab of the storied Manchester United club there has been strong grassroots resistance on the part of Manchester fan groups – to the point of organizing boycotts of the club's sponsors and starting up a new club in Manchester (similar to AFC Wimbledon).[24] The supporters were alarmed that a USA-football magnate with no English soccer background would treat Manchester United as just a business venture – an entity to be milked for profits. And the amount of debt assumed will ensure ticket prices and other amenities will rise, forcing the fans to subsidize Glazer's takeover.

Other USA-football teams have gone to ridiculous lengths to tap into the international soccer market. For example, the NFL New Orleans Saints have made overtures to their local Latino community to attend their games. Why a Honduran immigrant in New Orleans would give up soccer – the sport of his birthplace and youth – to be seduced by USA-football is beyond logic.

USA multinational corporations such as Coca-Cola and Pepsi have long realized the potential of soccer-associated advertising (sponsorship of leagues, national football associations, club teams, and individuals) to their global bottom line. However, the soccer-based commercials are rarely seen in their home base, as soccer coverage is insignificant on USA television. In a most ironic twist, USA business interests are reluctant to sponsor USA soccer teams, preferring to sponsor "BIG" clubs abroad. They simply forecast a bigger return from overseas soccer advertising than domestic support of the game.

Finally, in this time when the Bush administration has instigated a war in Iraq and the USA military is consistently missing its recruiting quotas, the US ARMY advertises heavily on two channels that broadcast soccer in the USA (*FOX Sports en Español* and *FOX Soccer Channel*). The USA military apparently hopes that recruiting from Spanish-speaking soccer-watching immigrants and lower-class soccer fans will help reverse their increasing manpower deficit generated by the globally unpopular war.[25]

---

[23] The Big Four sports are USA-football, basketball, baseball, and ice hockey, although the latter is waning in popularity after the second lockout in eleven years and a cancelled 2004-2005 season.
[24] Manchester's newest club is the Football Club United of Manchester (also referred to as FCUM, FC United, or FC United of Manchester).
[25] The audience for Fox Sports en Español not only includes USA citizens, but residents who are eligible to join the Army without possessing USA citizenship. Since the US Army does not guarantee foreigners citizenship during or even after a tour of military duty, their military status fits a strict definition of foreign mercenary ("a hired gun"). Some of the foreigners are finally "given" USA citizenship after being killed in action while working for the USA military – at which time that right is obviously useless.

Soccer Labor Rights and Player Finances
Soccer Labor Rights
Soccer clubs were virtually a chattel service for many decades, as players had little control over their finances (which were poor) or even their work-status (players were effectively "owned" by the clubs). The players' financial situation slowly got better after Jimmy Hill, then-Chairman of the Professional Footballers Association, helped force the abandonment of the England maximum wage rule in 1961 (the maximum was £20 a week).

Soccer shirt advertisements brought in new club monies in the early 1980s, and the resulting influx of sponsor money amplified player's salaries to new heights. English footballers who were paid the maximum £20 a week in the early 1960s could receive £20,000 a week or more in 2000 – a 1000-fold increase.[26] Top salaried players are now paid a fortune of *more than £100,000 a week* (not counting endorsements). Even the chasm between the salaries of top stars (making seven figure salaries annually, $1,000,000 – $9,999,999) and regular players (earning in the five figures annually, $10,000 – $99,999) has widened. And to frame the financial contrast between the players and supporters, it is sobering to realize the per capita income of English workers in the last forty years has only doubled from £ 8,000 to £ 16,000 per year. Compared to the average club fan, top players are really paid like stateside (USA) CEOs in the new soccer world (300 times the average worker).

The Bosman Decision
The Bosman case was a turning point in player labor rights. Jean-Marc Bosman was a Belgian player whose career was stifled from the transfer system prevalent in 1990. He belonged to the RFC Liege club until his contract ran out, but his club would not transfer him to the French Dunkerque club without a transfer fee – so he filed suit. He won a decision in the European Court of Justice in 1995 that introduced free agency and blew open the transfer tradition in Europe, and the makeup of clubs has been radically changed ever since (RFC Liege, The Belgian FA, and UEFA lost the case).

The legal decision had two components:

The first concerned the rules of European leagues restricting the number of "foreign" players a domestic league team could sign and actually play on the field simultaneously. These restrictions were deemed to be in conflict with already established rules regarding the free circulation of workers in the European Union (EU – Article 48 of the Treaty of Rome), and the exclusion of foreign players was only justified when it involved the makeup of national teams (in accordance with the 1976 Dona ruling).

The second component affected Bosman himself, for it ruled a transfer fee (called a transfer indemnity) was no longer required for a player to move clubs once he was out of contract. The ruling initially covered players specifically from the European Union (15 countries in 1995 has grown to 25 member countries in 2005), and apparently left non-EU countries' players in somewhat of a "no-man's land." However, more recent cases seem to be protecting non-EU players' rights as well.

A major impact of the Bosman decision was that soccer economic activity could no longer take place in a vacuum outside of standard European community law (including EU law) – soccer-specific labor practices were no longer allowed.[27]

The Bosman decision particularly affected Dutch team Ajax Amsterdam, which appeared in two consecutive European Champions' Cup Finals (winning outright in 1995 and losing on penalties in 1996). Nearly their whole team – which was composed of relatively young players – was pilfered because other "BIG" teams were able to sign them for small or

---

[26] Until the 1970s, "professional" soccer players in Britain often held a second job that supplemented their salaries.
[27] The *Bosman* decision was the European version of USA baseball's *Curt Flood* case that introduced free agency.

no fees. Ajax learned the hard way, and thereafter began to sign their young players to long-term contracts.

Ironically, Bosman himself did not benefit from the ruling, as by the time it went to court his playing career was effectively over. The players making six, seven and eight-figure salaries today owe him a tremendous debt of gratitude.

Soccer Salaries

The European leagues pay the highest salaries; particularly the English, Italian, and Spanish leagues, followed by the Dutch, French, German, and Turkish leagues. As a result of injected oil monies, the Russian league has recently become financially competitive. In Asia, the Middle Eastern states (particularly Qatar and Saudi Arabia) heavily support their national team and leagues through oil monies. The Japan J-League also has relatively high salaries, given that the cost of living is so high.

In the Western hemisphere, one might think that Argentina or Brazil would have the highest salaries simply because of the quality of their leagues and stellar national soccer histories. However, the Mexican league pays the highest salaries and this is a major reason Mexican players do not play abroad very often.

In the USA, Major League Soccer (MLS) was started in 1996 with a unique financial structure concept – *the league would own player rights instead of individual teams* (which would have been the normal arrangement). Teams had their total salaries capped, with the exception that certain "star" players would be sponsored by advertisers. This structure got the league off the ground, but ultimately proved very unpopular with the players, who justifiably felt they were being financially manipulated. The MLS Player's Association took the extraordinary step of filing a class-action lawsuit against the league in 1997, claiming the unique MLS arrangement constituted to an illegal monopoly structure. The lawsuit – which was poorly planned but had some labor law merit – was denied in 2000, and the MLS structure remained basically unchanged.

It is ironic that MLS – in the biggest sports market in the world – pays so poorly when the USA leagues of basketball, baseball, and USA-football outspend even the top European soccer teams on player salaries.[28] Several professional players have earned a pittance while performing in the MLS. An extreme example was Jeff Moore of the NJ/NY MetroStars, who earned only $850 per month while starting thirteen games – a salary amounting to only $200 per game! In comparison, select players in the semi-professional GAFA[29] made as much money in 1976 than did Moore in the professional MLS in 2002 (in *real dollars* not adjusted for inflation, which would make the 1976 dollars much more valuable).

Still, some soccer players in the USA have made big money, but it is mostly in endorsements. Top female player Mia Hamm allowed her professional wages to be cut because of financial problems in the WMLS (Women's Major League Soccer), but her real earnings were mostly endorsements anyway. Despite her sacrifice, the world's "premier women's soccer league" collapsed after the 2003 Women's World Cup. And age is now no barrier to endorsements provided the public relations machine is in place. As a 13-year old in the under-17 USA national team pool, Freddy Adu signed a $1 million endorsement contract with Nike in 2003 – even before signing for a professional team! And once Adu signed a professional contract with D.C. United as a 15-year-old, he was allocated the highest salary in the league ($500,000 per year) – even before playing a game!

Soccer salaries have skyrocketed since the Bosman ruling in 1995, as top salaries have surpassed £100,000 per week (about $135,000) for upper echelon players who perform in the

---

[28] The international soccer salary zenith is about $8-10 million dollars per year, while some USA-based basketball and baseball players receive $15-30 million per year. It is important to note that the international soccer season is at least 10 months, while the basketball and baseball seasons are a maximum of only eight months.

[29] German-American Football Association (see Chapter 18).

English, Italian, and Spanish leagues. There is no sign of this changing even though many clubs have become bankruptcy risks.

Sometimes a team suffers from a poor investment, for example, when players are injured or do not perform well. Examples are:

- Brazilian Ronaldo was paid an enormous salary by Internazionale Milan for three years, during much of which he recovered from a serious knee injury. After the 2002 World Cup where he was top scorer with eight goals, Ronaldo decided he would rather play for Real Madrid. Inter's fans thought they were due some payback for their loyalty, and did not take Ronaldo's departure well (Inter was fortunate to hire quality Argentine striker Hernan Crespo as an interim replacement for Ronaldo). In contrast, Argentine midfielder Fernando Redondo refused his salary from AC Milan when he was recovering from a similar knee injury – reasoning that if he could not play, he should not be drawing a full salary.

- Some players continued to receive huge salaries despite not getting any first team action. A notable duo that played reserve team football at Chelsea in London – but made upwards of £40,000 per week in 2002 – were Australian goalkeeper Mark Bosnich and Dutch defender Winston Bogarde. No wonder many fans are irritated at high salaries and vote with their feet, staying away from live soccer matches. These two players made more in one week warming the bench than most fans do all year! Bosnich was later released by Chelsea after he tested positive for cocaine, so apparently his money was put to poor use.

New Salary Structures

As sport salaries in general have now risen so high as to be obscene, retired star soccer players are in shock at the millions being thrown at even mediocre players. The high salaries added to the poor finances of many clubs has resulted in an effort to create linkage between salaries and performance, which is called *performance-related pay* (PRP). For example, PRP could reward players when clubs are promoted and qualify for international tournaments, or for individual performance targets. The PRP effort is building in Britain, where several clubs are at risk of imploding financially from foolish salary exuberance and shoddy administration practices.

Ironically, it may be that financially stable clubs such as Manchester United are leading the way for PRP rather than clubs facing serious financial woes that would conceivably benefit the most. After teenage sensation Wayne Rooney signed for Manchester United from Everton in 2004 on a transfer fee of £27 million, his salary rocketed to £50,000 a week with PRP bonuses built into the contract.

Salary Summary

After all the discussion above, it is sobering to realize that some mediocre players today make much more money than Pelé – then the world's greatest player – did in real terms (accounting for inflation and GDP per capita). And that is a major concern – that the gargantuan monies paid today to some players do not even guarantee real quality. That is the point when one knows that the soccer business is strangling itself in a furious race for "success" – whatever that means to the various soccer institutions (is it spectator satisfaction, soccer aesthetics, financial rewards, trophies, media coverage, and/or good societal deeds?).

Soccer's Financial Difficulties

Despite being the world's most popular sport, soccer can only get so massive. Considering the salary inflation over the last decade when many clubs paid exorbitant prices for players, it is no surprise that several clubs have entered "into administration" to avoid outright bankruptcy, and even more are on the brink of financial instability. Some examples of this foolish financial fallout are:

- *Leeds United* (England –2004 # 16 richest club) fell from being a Champion's League semi-finalist in 2001 to dropping out of the Premiership in 2004, and remained in danger of bankruptcy until it received a takeover bid from ex-Chelsea chairman Ken Bates in January 2005 (Bates had sold out his Chelsea share for a handsome profit to Roman Abramovich in 2003)
- Beloved Lega Calcio team *Fiorentina* (Italy) filed for bankruptcy in 2002, only to be resurrected in 2003.
- *Borussia Dortmund* (Germany – 2004 # 10 richest club) had a debt of £100 million in 2004, and was in danger of being suspended from the Bundesliga despite recent league championships (1995, 1996, 2002) and top attendance figures.
- Christian Vieri and Ronaldo, (both on £4.1 million a year) and Álvaro Recoba (£5.5 million a year), voluntarily pledged a 10% pay cut to help their cash-strapped *Internazionale* club (Italy –2005 # 9 richest club).
- *Real Madrid* (Spain – 2005 #1 richest team) would have a debt of $245 million had they not sold their training facility in a plush deal to the Madrid government.

Community groups are emerging in Britain that are intent on preserving the roots and spirit of the game. One group, Clubs in Crisis (www.clubsincrisis.com), has its stated purpose to save clubs from financial collapse, explaining, "If the football club you love and support is in financial trouble, has directors with dubious intentions, or if your home ground is being sold from under your feet, let us and everybody else know so we can raise the profile of your plight and generate support. Where possible and where needed we will try to give advice or help on some of the ways to unseat your particular tyrant. This applies both to league clubs and non-league clubs, in any country." Supporters Direct (www.supporters-direct.org) is another English group concerned about the fundamentally undemocratic structure of many football clubs and the rampant and accelerating commercialization of the game.

Marketing and Advertising

Club Team Advertising

By the time Tottenham won the 1984 UEFA Cup at home, the club's shirt was emblazoned with a large and ugly advertisement. The era of shirt propaganda had arrived in English football, and what a shame. Only a die-hard or aesthetically deficient fan would buy one of the new hideously defaced jerseys, and many fans subsequently refused to become walking billboards for products not related to the sport. The overbearing shirt propaganda just does not make sense to many fans, and affects their sense of proper integrity of the game.

The clubs could *sell some shirts without the advertisements*, but instead the advertisements have taken over the shirt. The players are not just playing for their club, but for HOLSTEN, JVC, CARLSBERG, XEROX, SONY, PARMALAT or BUD. Fans would likely be willing to pay more to wear a pure team shirt devoid of advertising, but it is difficult to find a jersey without propaganda, as it is not in the economic interests of the sponsor or even the players who are now receiving much heftier salaries.

In this respect one must admire FC Barcelona, as "Barça" is the last big club to preserve their shirt adorned with only team crest and colors.[30,31] Presumably, FC Barcelona could command nearly $20 million per year for shirt rights, but their more than 100,000 member club allows "people power" to flourish over the false identity of overt shirt advertising. But it may be only a question of time of how long Barça can hold out against the seemingly unlimited (and sometimes ill-begotten) cash supplies of their competitors. The financial pressure of Spain's La Liga is tremendous, and the small but powerful Nike swoosh has already found its way onto the front of the Barça shirts. Hopefully, FC Barcelona will not change their relatively pure status as soccer's only superclub propaganda holdout.

Some soccer clubs have nearly always been sponsored by a company. Two examples are Dutch club PSV Eindhoven (sponsored by electronic giant Phillips) and German club Bayer Leverkusen (sponsored by pharmaceutical firm Bayer – Leverkusen's shirt insignia even looks like Bayer's best known product Bayer Aspirin). But even these teams did not dare place a non-soccer advertisement on their shirts until the 1970s. The MLS club located in New Jersey now (as of March 2006) calls itself the *New York Red Bulls*– a form of extreme marketing that brands a team name with a product (this subject is further addressed in Chapter 14).

Advertising on WHAT?

Soccer advertising has gone completely out of control, often to the point of absurdity. Some clubs have had advertisements not only on the front and back of their shirts, but also on the front (groin) and back (butt) of the shorts (pants)! What businesses would conceivably want to advertise in those locations [see photo next page]?[32]

It is routine to have advertising on the shoes (the shoemaker's propaganda), and now all parts of the uniform account for some advertising revenue. One can even see the shin guard manufacturer's logo through a white pair of socks.

---

[30] Club Athletic Bilbao has also so far resisted the placement of non-soccer related propaganda on their soccer jerseys.

[31] In 2005, there was a rumor that Barça would carry the word "Shanghai" on the front of their shirts, in order to advertise the upcoming 2008 Olympics in China. Fortunately, any rumored deal collapsed, and Barcelona still retained their classic shirt and integrity intact (China's serious human rights issues could compromise FC Barcelona's historical image). However, 2006 has brought new shirt-advert rumors of Austrian bookmaker Betandwin – also not a good bet for Barcelona prestige.

[32] Perhaps a hemorrhoid cream on the back, and a condom manufacturer on the front? Why not a public health service ad to prevent sexually-transmitted diseases? After all, soccer players belong to the population cohort most at risk (18-34 year old men – see Chapter 6).

Long after the propaganda aesthetic line has been crossed, FIFA may have belatedly realized that there should be a limit to advertising of their sport. In 2002, FIFA informed the Mexican FA that it should ban advertising on players' socks and shorts, but the Mexicans refused, reporting that they could lose $40 million if the sponsors' names were erased.

In addition, several leagues have made a bizarre decision to allow advertisements on referee uniforms. Advertisements on the team shirts is bad enough, but the referee's job is hard enough without them having to worry who they are sponsoring or if they are getting a bad deal from being a walking billboard. And is nobody worried about refereeing neutrality and integrity?

Cienciano's (Peru) goalkeeper Oscar Ibáñez shows off an advertisement on his shorts as he enters the field for the second half of the 2003 Recopa against Boca Juniors (Chapter 11).

The Airlines Advert-Shirt Curse

Strangely enough, soccer shirt sponsorship may not necessarily help a company's bottom line. A good example is the Peruvian First Division, where there has been an uncanny association between the sponsoring airline and subsequent bankruptcy.

The only shirt propaganda in the Peruvian First Division in 1992 was for the sponsoring *Faucett* airline, the largest Peruvian airline at the time. However, within five years *Faucett* went out of business after a horrific plane crash.[33] *AeroPeru* then took over the First Division sponsorship, but within two years they went bankrupt as well, so *AeroContinente* took over the advertising. *AeroContinente* has now lost much of its momentum, so in 2001 the *TANS* military airline made a contract with the league. After nine years and four different airlines, the shirt advertising contract for the Peruvian league appears to be less of a boon than a curse, and its recent history does not inspire confidence.

---

[33] Elmer Faucett was the first person to fly across the Andes mountains in 1922, and he became a founder of the first commercial airline in Peru in 1928. After a Faucett Airlines 737 crashed outside of Arequipa in 1996, killing all 110 persons aboard in Peru's worst aviation disaster, the airline ceased operations in 1997.

Soccer Cup Advertising

Advertising has now found its way into the most sacred of soccer institutions, the actual championships and/or Cups themselves. Placing a name on a cup was formerly reserved for a leader who dedicated his life to the service of soccer. For example, Jules Rimet, President of FIFA for 33 years (1921-1954), had his name placed on the first World Cup trophy. The Jules Rimet Trophy was acquired permanently by Brazil in 1970, as they were the first nation to win the Cup three times.[34] FIFA's replacement Cup is simply called the *FIFA World Cup Trophy*.

The South American Cup competitions are named after competing Japanese automobile companies, the Toyota Copa Libertadores and the Nissan Copa Sudamericana. The Toyota Intercontinental Club Cup was one game played between the European and South American champions from 1980-2004 (it was a two-leg non-sponsored competition between 1960-1979).

Because the World Wars interrupted the continuity of the European Cups, the longest continually running soccer cup competition in the world is ironically in the "soccer-deprived" USA. The United States Open Challenge Cup (also called the US Open Cup) – a single-elimination tournament established in 1914 – is open to all amateur and professional soccer teams affiliated with the USSF (*United States Soccer Federation*, also called *US Soccer*, with website at www.ussoccer.com). But in 1999, the U.S. Open Cup's name was amended to the "Lamar Hunt US Open Cup." This is unfortunate, as while Hunt may have financed some of the USA professional soccer teams in the modern era (in his own self – interest of course), he was hardly a societal role model. After all, Hunt had previously tried to *illegally corner the global silver market in 1979-80* with his infamous two older brothers Bunker and Herbert. The price of silver was inflated more than ten-fold during their scheme, and they were eventually found liable for manipulating the silver market.[35] Fortunately the Hunt brothers failed in their scheme, but the immense greed they demonstrated should give pause for desecrating the US Open Cup name. US Soccer is doing a poor job of selling soccer to the public if a greedy disgraced financier is the best role model they can find to grace such an important competition. The fans are not as ignorant of history as the USA soccer authorities seem to think they are, and to them it appears easy money is more important than the integrity of USA soccer (see Chapter 14).

Finally, the fans most often refer to the Cup names without the sponsor antecedents anyway, so it is really a superfluous exercise in branding (the advertisers do not have enough marketing power to actually "brand" the Cups).

FIFA advertising – *Selling FIFA*

Even FIFA is selling itself to the highest bidder. Upon arrival at the FIFA website for the 2002 World Cup (www.fifaworldcup.com), one was greeted by a tasteless movable Budweiser beer advertisement. When one realizes that FIFA is an international organization and people by the millions log on to the site from all over the world every day, these are truly worldwide propaganda. Coca-Cola has been a FIFA sponsor for years, to the point of being strangely represented on the website by the "FIFA Coca-Cola Rankings." These rankings are often bizarrely calculated (see Chapter 9 under France) – one wonders if the judges have drunk too much sugar water before voting.

After the new 2000 World Club Championship competition, FIFA endured the ISL/ISMM insolvency that led to institutional financial weakness – a development that

---

[34] The Jules Rimet was stolen in London prior to the 1966 World Cup in England, only to be found a week later by a dog named Pickles. After Brazil acquired it permanently, it was stolen again, this time in 1983 in Rio de Janeiro Brazil, and was never recovered (it was likely melted down for the gold).
[35] The three Hunt brothers were found guilty in 1988 in the *Minpeco vs. Hunt* jury verdict – but were only fined a pittance of $192 million.

necessitated the procurement of more advertising dollars. The new world club tournament was subsequently cancelled in 2001, and was not restarted until 2005.[36]

FIFA made agreements with fifteen multinational companies as 2002 and 2006 World Cup Official Partners in the following categories:

Multinational	**Business**	**Country**	**Year(s)**
Adidas	Sporting goods	Germany	2002-2006
Anheuser-Busch	Beer	USA	2002-2006
Avaya	Telecommunications	USA	2002-2006
Coca-Cola	Beverages	USA	2002-2006
Continental	Tires	Germany	2006
Deutsche Telekom	Telecommunications	Germany	2006
Fly Emirates	Airline	UAE	2006
FujiFilm	Photography	Japan	2002-2006
Fuji Xerox	Copiers	Japan	2002
Gillette	Shavers	USA	2002-2006
Hyundai	Cars	Korea	2002-2006
JVC	Electronics	Japan	2002
Korea Telecom/NTT	Telecommunications	Korea	2002
MasterCard	Credit cards	USA	2002-2006
McDonald's	Fast food	USA	2002-2006
Philips	Electronics	Holland	2002-2006
Toshiba	Electronics	Japan	2002-2006
Yahoo!	Internet	USA	2002-2006

Interestingly, seven of the official fifteen partners in both 2002 and 2006 are USA-based corporations, originating from a country that until recently had previously ignored international soccer. In 2002, six companies were from the hosting but traditionally soccer-weak nations of Japan (four) and South Korea (two). Three of these six dropped out after the 2002 Japan – Korea World Cup, and for the 2006 Germany World Cup they were replaced by two German companies and the UAE airline. Only two official partners were from the soccer power area of Europe in 2002, specifically Germany and Holland, which increased to four in 2006 (no African, Oceanic, or Central and South American companies were represented either year). These corporations – along with the official suppliers, licensees and broadcasters – were the only commercial entities allowed to claim any direct association with the 2002 and 2006 FIFA World Cup™.

The 2006 FIFA World Cup had much the same advertising lineup as 2002, with one major concession: USA sponsor Anheuser-Busch finally allowed German breweries to serve German beer at the World Cup in Germany. One could not imagine such an historic event in the premier beer brewing country in the world without allowing its superb product to be consumed!

In truth, FIFA has the most attractive sports product in the world, and they should easily be able to make a significant profit. Soccer development worldwide depends on some FIFA monies, but not at the cost of all-consuming propaganda ruining the soccer experience.

---

[36] The World Club Championship (with all continental champions represented) replaced the Intercontinental Cup (played from 1960 to 2004 between the European and South American champions) in 2005.

Total Advertising **Including National Team Advertising**

The new "over-advertising" or "total advertising" in soccer is actually counterproductive to the fan's appreciation of the soccer experience. From a fan's point of view, all the extraneous propaganda is a major turnoff.

Pasting multiple sponsors on uniforms has previously only been part *of individual sports* such as tennis, auto-racing, or golf. In fact, *professional soccer is relatively isolated in this type of total advertising in comparison to other team sports* – even in the advertising-inebriated USA. Perhaps naturally, there has been a backlash to the propaganda overflow, as in many countries "black-market" versions of the official team shirt without adverts are available in street markets. This is evidently the soccer fan/entrepreneur's idea of soccer purity.

National team shirts have historically been free from adverts, except for the kit maker logo. The kit makers (often multinationals in their own right) have now taken over the design and production of team shirts, routinely outsourcing the national team jerseys. That is why different national teams – Brazil and USA, for example – have the *same exact team shirt design* (only in different colors). Large money payments to the national FAs from these multinationals have made this previously unthinkable design arrangement acceptable and routine.

Of course, the soccer marketing "experts" claim, "It is impossible to over-advertise," as they have to justify their outrageous fees and occupational existence. But the propaganda people have proven to be relentless to the point of obscenity in their pursuit of profit. There is talk now of allowing even national soccer teams to contract with companies to have their logos stamped on the national team shirts. Also previously unimaginable is the arrival of advertising on national team practice gear, as certain national teams (such as the USA, Argentina and England) have allowed multinationals (Phillips, Coca-Cola and Vodafone respectively) to advertise on their official country practice gear.

These recent developments have their roots in the equipment manufacturers placing their relatively small logo on soccer uniforms. The shoes were first affected when Adidas presented their three stripe brand in the 1949 (the West German national team won the 1954 World Cup with Adidas shoes with three stripes). The shirts displayed the manufacturer's logo next, then all equipment sported the maker's logo. Over time, the kit makers became huge sponsors for the national teams – the most famous example being Nike's controversial sponsoring contract of the Brazil national team. The Brazil contract contained a highly irregular clause arranging the playing of several "friendly games" – a marketing tactic that should be determined to be an unethical arrangement between a national team and sponsor. What would happen if a player was injured during one of these "sponsor" games – would Nike have to reimburse the player's club team for time and quality missed?

The direct linkage of multinational corporations to national soccer teams must be immediately contained by FIFA in order to avoid (or continue) compromising the integrity of its international soccer competitions. But it has unfortunately already started; the Irish FA is already allowing replica Ireland national team jerseys to be defaced with a sponsor (Eircom) prominently on the front, and on 17 May 2003 a match between Arsenal and an England XI was played with both teams wearing the same telecommunications O_2 sponsor logo.

If this trend is allowed to continue unchecked, FIFA and the FAs will find out that what they have won in money they have lost in irreplaceable integrity of their sport. A Football Association is supposed to represent a nation's soccer development – not shill for a multinational company's expansion. The official visual and financial linkage of a national team's representative gear to multinational companies will inevitably compromise a nation's soccer integrity, and conceivably could affect sovereignty issues through economic pressures (especially in poorer nations that have much less money than multinationals).

An example of this possibility occurred at the 1998 World Cup Final, in which Ronaldo performed despite suffering a first-time seizure immediately before the game. It was widely rumored that Nike's influence with the Brazilian FA created pressure for Ronaldo to play despite his immediate physical debility (Ronaldo had a seizure before the game – he played but was ineffective). No player should be expected to perform in a competitive match after a seizure (i.e., he would not be cleared by the medical staff to play) – even if he had a known seizure disorder. However, after a long and drawn out investigation before the Brazilian Congress, no definite evidence surfaced to confirm the allegations.

The 2006 World Cup again raised the specter of a multinational company influencing a national team selection. On 3 March 2006 – fully 10 weeks before the 23-man World Cup squad list was due by FIFA – host Germany agreed to allow sixteen players' faces to grace cans of Coca-Cola. The multinational flavored sugar-water producer understood this deal to mean sixteen members of the World Cup team, but the German FA (DFB) was forced to deny it was an official list, as the team roster was not due until over two months later. What is going on besides rampant commercialization and potential interference with team selection? Is this deal good for the game, or for the German team or people?

The lines of both good taste and sovereignty are too easily crossed when a multinational corporation is allowed to advertise on a national soccer team uniform. Sovereignty issues may especially be raised if a multinational advertises on a country's jersey that is not its home country. While England and Ireland have contracted with nationally-based sponsors, Argentina and the USA have gone with overseas sponsors (Reebok and Coca-Cola, and Phillips, respectively). This leaves an indelible negative image of a nation – represented by its national team – pandering to an overseas multinational company. Regardless of national or extra-national sponsors, if FIFA allows companies to place advertisements on national team shirts it could very well spell the end of progressive interest in the World Cup worldwide, as corporations will be seen to be more important than nations. Smaller and poorer nations will view these developments as cultural imperialism at best (as they cannot compete financially in the international propaganda game), and at worst, a threat to their sovereignty.

Only one further action remains to complete "total advertising" – to replace the national team logos altogether with the multinational company logos. Thus, a USA – England match might one day soon be "*Bud versus Guinness*" or "*ATT versus Vodafone.*" Even in this age of rampant globalization, this is (almost) unthinkable. But in order to retain the integrity of the game, FIFA needs to rework their policy of allowing advertising on national team training gear, as they have already been too permissive. This is one area that FIFA should seriously study the Big Four USA sports, to see how they run multi-million dollar operations without resorting to defacing their club uniforms with advertisements.

USA Sports Advertising Compared with International Soccer

In the USA – the marketing capital of the world – other professional sports leagues (baseball, basketball, ice hockey, USA-football) have realized that *uniform advertising is bad for their sports* as it pulls attention away from the players, team, and even the sport itself. The Big Four authorities realize that their fans are coming to see the *team and their players* – not walking billboards.

In the USA major team sport clubs have only the uniform manufacturer and shoe logos on the uniform (both naturally have large contracts with individual players and teams), and the fans have learned to live with these comparatively small decorations. Of course, the fans are also subjected to a plethora of other advertisements on the walls of stadiums and arenas during the course of games, but the accepted wisdom is *just keep the damn soda or beer advertisements off our team.* Amazingly, the USA sports barons have realized this arrangement as important to the integrity of their games, and have not dared to cross this sacred boundary.

But the USA soccer have not followed this sensible domestic trend, as MLS followed the errant international trend of "billboard" uniform advertising. While the MLS resisted shirt advertising for the first five years of its existence (1996-2000), it arrived in a big way in 2001. There are soda sponsors (Pepsi), internet (Yahoo Sports!), cereal (Kellogg's Frosted Flakes), insurance (New York Life), auto (Honda), and beer (Budweiser) advertisements on the back and sleeves of shirts. As of early 2004, the Columbus Crew and DC United clubs were the only clubs not yet displaying sponsors. Whatever happened to the novel idea in the USA that you pay your ticket to go watch soccer rather than moving commercials?

Nevertheless, a huge irony occurred with MLS replica shirt sales. In other countries an *official replica shirt is sold with its sponsor advert* – if you are a team supporter you are forced to wear the advertising as well. But the MLS was initially licensing their shirts *without the advertising for ten dollars less*! The question is who would pay ten dollars extra to prance about like a walking billboard and thereby detract attention from their club? As of 2006, MLS clubs are sensibly back to selling their replica shirts without any adverts (see at Eurosport – www.soccer.com).

Individual Propaganda and Societal Impact

With the advent of the "*living through total marketing*" strategy that is the imposed model for the Western world at this time,[37] top echelon soccer players often make more money through endorsements than salary. As a consequence, player adverts have the potential to influence consumer's minds and wallets more than ever, because the public is assumed to care which products the players endorse (even if not sports related).

No doubt receiving a huge salary takes some talent, but creating and hyper-marketing a player's image can really increase the money. Like never before, certain individuals are now valued more as sign-carriers than their soccer performance. The model for image boosting is English midfielder David Beckham, who has had marginal impact in major tournaments (1998 & 2002 World Cup and 2000 & 2004 European Championship tournaments), but still receives the highest compensation in the world. His marketing image was created in significant part by management agency SFX Sports Group (www.sfxsports.com), a wholly-owned subsidiary of Clear Channel Communications, Inc. (CCCI) [see Figure 5A & B].[38]

Perhaps players do not realize what kind of marketing powers they are buying into, as their agents make the arrangements and the easy cash is too tempting. CCCI is a massive media company that only evolved rapidly after the unfortunate 1996 Telecommunications Act that substantially deregulated the USA radio industry.[39] CCCI now owns more than 1200 radio and 30 TV channels in the USA, and has expanded into worldwide media in 63 countries (www.clearchannel.com). CCCI's mission appears to be the seamless blending of opinionated media and advertising, which by sheer quantity results in the homogenization of USA airwaves. This unprecedented loss of *local control of the airwaves* (once a democratic tenet of the Federal Communications Commission [FCC]) – results in decreased availability of diverse information sources and the suffocation of local programming in the USA – apparently with the world to follow.[40] CCCI has already belied any claim of media neutrality

---

[37] Mankind is currently bombarded 24/7 with advertisements in the home (television, newspapers, internet, email, snail mail) and street (billboards on anything stationary or moving, sound adverts, video). This cacophony of noise and visual pollution is what passes for "civilization" at the beginning of the 21st century. The movie *Koyaanisqatsi* – a Hopi word meaning "crazy life" or "life out of balance" – beautifully sums up the aesthetic chaos of the modern world (www.koyaanisqatsi.org).
[38] Ellis Cashmore's book *Beckham* (Chapter 17) has a full discussion of the Beckham marketing phenomenon.
[39] Before the deregulation of radio occurring with the Telecommunications Act of 1996, no single broadcaster in the USA could own more than four radio stations in one city or more than forty in the country. The USA public can thank ex-FCC chairman and Republican Michael Powell (ex-Secretary of State's Colin Powell's son) for the unwise and ultimately undemocratic deregulation of USA radio channels.
[40] After the 9/11 attack on the Twin Towers in New York City, a "gray list" memo was circulated among CCCI radio personnel that listed 150 songs that were somehow deemed inappropriate to play on their 1000-plus radio

by funding the pro-Iraq war "Rally for America" demonstrations in the USA, and as CCCI acquires more international assets, their right-wing control of information access will spread worldwide. This real-life scenario is reminiscent of George Orwell's mind-controlling "Big Brother" and "Thought Police" concepts in his dystopian book "1984."[41]

Soccer Selling versus Sportsmanship

Soccer has been the world sport for over a century. Soccer popularity and business are booming, and there has been a lot of money made – albeit almost exclusively by already rich people. But there has been a heavy price to pay, as the age of innocence is over for international soccer. The concept of the local club is being seriously threatened as the clubs and athletes alike sell themselves to multinational sponsors' highest bids. The size of the financial spoils can be traced to a winning record and media exposure – but apparently not necessarily in that order anymore. Nowadays, a crack public relations team is a critical club necessity for "success." The greed factor involved has become so immense it is manifestly palpable for the fans, and it does not reflect well on soccer.

Some clubs can over-bid any other club to get the player they want – Chelsea with its Russian oil field money is the best example.[42] But there is a point of no-return, and many other clubs have out-bid and out-paid each other into debt and bankruptcy.

Soccer corruption is on the rise, as referees and players in a number of countries have been accused of fixing games so illegal gamblers can make millions of dollars.[43]

Finally, everybody seems to be marketing something – the players, coaches, clubs, and now, even some referees are making significant amounts of money off the field.[44] Naturally, nearly all teams own their Internet site and store.

Of course, the club directors explain all the new developments by saying," it is for the good of the bottom line," and "we are trying to maximize profits." Few people in management first state, "above all else, we would like to play attractive football." And that is where the fans are left behind.

In short, professional soccer has become massive Big Business, as money first and winning second are more important than sportsmanship – *and there are few awards for sportsmanship in the business world*. Perhaps as a result of declining soccer sportsmanship, the unique tradition (in sport competition) of shirt exchanges at the end of important matches has become less frequent, and the respect shown opponents appears to be on the wane. Much still needs to be done to promote fair play and positive sportsmanship in football, which is likely going to require spreading around the Dollar, Pound, Euro, and Yen more equitably in the soccer world.

---

stations. John Lennon's *Imagine* – a song of peace and human rights that was voted #1 on the 2005 All-Time list by Virgin Radio – was on the list (see all 150 gray list songs and discussion at www.wikipedia.org, and Virgin list at www.virginradio.co.uk/music/top500/vote.html).

[41] Players would perhaps benefit from reading Naomi Klein's books before committing to promotional deals, such as *No Logo: Taking Aim at the Brand Bullies*, and *Fences and Windows: Dispatches from the Front Lines of the Globalization Debate*.

[42] Chelsea signs any player they want – the money coming from Russian oil stocks that would more ethically be owned by the Russian people themselves. As a result, the Premiership has turned into "Chelsea versus The Rest of The League," because the £500 million they have spent in the last three years on signing players is more than the rest of the league put together – not an auspicious development for the league.

[43] Match-fixing has been proven in Germany, Italy, and Slovakia, and is being investigated in France, Greece, and Portugal.

[44] Pierluigi Collina of Italy, generally acknowledged to be the world's best referee from 1998-2002, has performed in several commercials for multinational companies.

Chapter Six

Soccer Injury and Illness

Destroying the opponent is easy, but creating the game is difficult. *Rivaldo*[1]

Train the right way. Help each other out. It's a form of socialism without the politics.
Bill Shankly[2]

Soccer and the Physical Risk of Injury

Soccer players are multi-dimensional athletes possessing a unique skill set (Chapter 1), and at the highest level, soccer is the most physical *team sport* in the world as measured by endurance and agility skills.[3] The physicality of soccer may come as a surprise to USA-football fans, devotees of a sport where although players are required to hit each other on every play, their bodies are cushioned by protective body armor such as helmets, eye shields, shoulder pads, neck protectors, groin cups, butt pads, thigh pads, knee pads and flak jackets (some of which contain bulletproof Kevlar). Ice hockey players have similar equipment as they frequently hit each other; in addition they also have to fear the object (a hard puck reaching 80 mph) and instruments (hockey sticks and sharp ice skates) of the game.

However, soccer has some of the most bone-crushing collisions in any sport. Some collisions are legal and others illegal by the Laws of the Game, but all occur with minimal protective equipment. Since 1990, FIFA has required all players to wear thin plastic shin guards, but that is the extent of soccer's protective equipment.

For proof of soccer's physical intensity one can revisit the 1998 World Cup Final, which featured a high-impact collision between Brazilian ace striker Ronaldo and French goalkeeper Fabian Barthez. Two dynamic colliding masses traveling at top acceleration in opposite directions was living proof of Newton's second Law of Motion.

---

[1] Quote from midfielder-striker Rivaldo after Brazil's 2002 World Cup semi-final win against Turkey.
[2] Legendary coach of Liverpool Football Club.
[3] Soccer requires the optimal combination of agility and endurance, as judged most recently in the ESPN forty-sport survey. Soccer also tied with ice hockey and auto racing for the best analytic aptitude required. Incredibly, soccer ranked below softball in "hand-eye coordination." The panelists probably did not understand that "foot-eye coordination" is the relevant measure for soccer, which would have boosted soccer's score even higher. [www.sports.espn.go.com/espn/page2/sportSkills].

> **Total Force = (Mass x Acceleration)**_{RONALDO} **+ (Mass x Acceleration)**_{F. BARTHEZ}
> or, expressed in mathematical symbols:
> $F_{R+FB} = M_R A_R + M_{FB} A_{FB}$

No pads, no flak jackets, no Kevlar. Although Ronaldo did not have a great chance at a goal, the chance was close enough that his challenge was legal by the Laws of Soccer. Barthez was knocked off his feet, but successfully guarded his goal. Similar physical challenges crop up frequently during games; such as head against head, hand in eye, boot in the groin, ball in the groin, foot against foot, ankle, shin, calf, knee or head. Combine the physical contact with 90 to 120 minutes of constant running, and you do not have a game for the faint-hearted.

The point is that even keeping within the rules, soccer is a very tough game. Members of USA-football teams sometimes try to slur soccer by saying it is a "sissy" game. Soccer players can defuse their misguided gridiron classmates by reminding them of "who is so frail that they need pads to protect them," which shuts them up pretty quick. As far as the "delicate" comments are concerned, nothing could be further from the truth. *Soccer is a game of constant physical challenges that require great courage.*

There are other poignant reminders of the physicality of soccer. Despite an orthopedic revolution in the past twenty-five years, several top soccer players have had their careers shortened or compromised by the continual, and often improper, physical challenges of the game. The abuse that Dutch forward and three-time European Player of the Year Marco Van Basten sustained for years from professional hacks unable to keep up with his pace and skills eventually ended his career. He sustained a serious ankle injury that never properly healed, and he retired at only twenty-nine years of age.[4] Van Basten left soccer fans with many indelible images; none better than one of the greatest goals ever scored in a European Cup Final, when he volleyed the ball from a near-impossible right-sided angle over excellent Soviet goalkeeper Rinat Dasaev into the left corner of the net (1988 European Cup Final: Holland 2-0 over Soviet Union).

Human Body Design and Soccer

The human body evolved over millennia into a sophisticated model designed for the pedestrian stalking and hunting of game, with the occasional leap and sprint away from an agitated carnivore. The *corpus humani* was not designed for playing soccer with its high-speed twists and turns stressing the essentially two-dimensional knee joint[5], and tremendous torque forces placed on the ankle joints. Therefore it is imperative to optimally train and to maintain in prime condition the muscles surrounding the joints, in order to support and relieve pressure of the joint apparatus itself.

It is no surprise that knee and ankle/foot injuries are soccer's most commonly occurring *serious injuries*, defined as missing three or more weeks of play. In addition, all of the muscles of the thigh and leg are vulnerable to kicks or overstraining. In the back of the thigh are the flexor hamstrings, and in the front are positioned the extensor quadriceps and sartorius muscle (the longest muscle in the body). Joining the thigh and lower leg are the quadriceps tendon and patella tendon that cradles the patella, a floating pancake-shaped bone vulnerable to all types of abuse. In the leg, located posterior are both heads of the gastrocnemius and the deeper soleus muscle that unites them and extends to the Achilles tendon; interiorly, the tibialis anterior is responsible for the flexion of the foot, and therefore the directional nuances of a shot. Finally, the legs are anchored by the wondrous and delicate

---

[4] Van Basten also credited some of his failure to recover from his injury to surgical malpractice.
[5] The knee joint, which is the largest joint in the body, appears only to be able to move the lower leg up and down, but it actually has a full 6 degrees of rotational freedom. Although this is not nearly as much as the shoulder, hips, fingers, wrist, or neck, the knee is not strictly two-dimensional.

ankle and foot structure, which man relies on to ambulate 10,000 steps and carry tons of human weight per day.

In short, playing soccer is an abnormal event for the human organism, but one in which the spirit commands us to participate. If the participant is trained properly and is in excellent condition, the risks for injury are lessened and recuperation will be quicker.

Soccer Injuries

In the FIFA medical report from the 1998 World Cup, injuries occurred in the following areas (in order of frequency): 25% knee, 18% thigh, 15% head, 13% ankle, 8% upper extremity, 7% thorax or spine, 6% miscellaneous leg, 6% foot injuries, 5% lower leg, and 3% in other areas of the body.

FIFA's figures showed 143 injuries in 64 matches, an average of 2.23 injuries per game. Team injury totals varied from one to twelve injuries during the competition, and the average injury total was 4.47 per team.

Injuries that drew blood were mostly head lacerations that were stitched and bandaged before the player could continue on the field.

The 2002 FIFA World Cup figures revealed 171 injuries in 64 matches, an average of 2.7 per game; 73% were contact injuries and 27% non-contact injuries. Fully half of the contact injuries (37%) were rated to be caused by foul play.[6] The most significant changes in comparison to the 1998 World Cup figures were a 20% increase in total injuries, with knee injuries decreasing to 13% of total injuries.

Causes of Injuries

Injuries can be placed into two general categories by their causal role in soccer; (1) *intentional injuries* and (2) *unintentional injuries*. It is useful to examine these two categories, as the Laws of the Game can be strengthened to eliminate injuries from the first category and decrease injuries from the second category.

Intentional Injuries

Intentional injuries are of evident cause, which is *intent to injure*. This type of injury is inexcusable and should be punished severely by long suspensions and heavy fines. It is assumed that players at the professional level are skilled enough to PLAY THE BALL AND NOT THE MAN, as dictated by the Laws of the Game. Unfortunately, this most basic of soccer tenets has come under severe attack in the last few decades, as teams will do almost anything to win, even at the cost of destroying the spirit of the game.

A blatant example of an intentional foul occurred in the crucial 1982 World Cup semi-final game between Germany and France, when Frenchman Patrick Battiston advanced on goal and took a shot from outside the penalty area. At the time he shot, Battiston was 3 to 4 meters from the onrushing West German goalkeeper Harald Schumacher. Schumacher did not even try for the ball, but instead, took advantage of Battiston's fair play and vulnerable body position to inflict a deliberate hip and elbow smash to his head, resulting in immediate unconsciousness A demoralized French team saw their compatriot stretchered off, only knowing he was seriously wounded, but not knowing his prognosis or even if he would survive.

Incredibly, Schumacher did not even receive a cautionary yellow card from the impotent referee. The West Germans went on to eliminate the stunned French on penalty kicks after the 3-3 overtime tie, in the World Cup's first ever penalty shootout.

Schumacher's offense should have resulted in an *immediate red card, a year ban from soccer, and probably an assault and battery charge from the local prosecutor*. Asking the

---

[6] Junge, A, Dvorak, J, Graf-Baumann, T. Football injuries during the World Cup 2002. *American Journal of Sports Medicine*. 2004;32:23S-27S.

public prosecutor to step in and file an assault-and-battery charge is an extreme step, but there is precedent in other sports and should be an option for the willful endangering of an opponent's life and livelihood. Recently in the NHL (National [Ice] Hockey League), a player received a probation sentence for assault and battery after slashing another player's face with a hockey stick. A criminal record is an extreme punishment, but Schumacher's attack on Battiston was an extreme case, as Schumacher showed no remorse and Battiston never again played to his optimal ability.

Another serious injury occurred in the 1994 World Cup game between Brazil and the United States. In a challenge near the sideline, Brazilian midfielder Leonardo swung an elbow at the elegant ball-possessing USA midfielder Tab Ramos. Leonardo was proficient enough that the foul did not appear to be a "hack play" caused by a lack of skill. Although his back was partially turned, Leonardo *thought he would be beat and had to take down Ramos by any method available*. His action was an example of NEGATIVE SOCCER at its extreme. Ramos sustained a broken skull, and it was not known if he would ever return to professional soccer. Leonardo's foul was intentional but of slightly lesser degree than Schumacher's. Nonetheless, both were caused by the greed to win, with a willful ignoring of the Laws of Soccer.

Leonardo's foul was emblematic of the modern strategies of "playing not to lose" or "negative football," rather than playing to win by fair play. Many players, including Teófilo Cubillas, have noticed this negative modern football trend. It was sad that the *jogo bonito* (beautiful game) Brazilians were involved in this most cynical type of foul. Leonardo's foul should have resulted in a red card, a suspension of further 1994 World Cup play, and a 10 game suspension for qualifying play for the 1998 World Cup. Leonardo was at least contrite and apologized. Fortunately, Ramos recovered completely and went on to play for the USA again, and played at a high level until his retirement in 2002.

Intent to injure another player is not only unsporting but can backfire on the fouling player. Not infrequently, *players who play the man rather than the ball are themselves injured*. Manchester United midfielder Roy Keane injured himself mis-timing a trip on Alf-Inge Haaland in 1997 (Keane admitted he was "trying to trip him rather than kick him").[7] Keane foolishly (as his injury was self-inflicted) harbored a grudge against Haaland, and he later succeeded in seriously injuring Haaland on a terrible foul that got him red-carded in April 2001. Haaland has since suffered multiple knee operations and was effectively out of the game until he was forced to retire in July 2003. Keane got off with a minimal penalty of a five-week ban and a fine of £150,000, hardly justice for a premeditated foul with disastrous results. Soccer should impose more severe penalties for those players who place machismo and intentional violence above the game.

Soccer refereeing needs to be vastly improved to avert these preventable soccer injuries. Intent to injure has unfortunately developed into an advanced skill for defending players, as they illegally physically challenge the other team's dominant striker, going for the man rather than the ball. Rather than receiving a yellow or red card, these defenders are often ignored or only warned by the referees. *Strict control by the referee is required to punish ANY activity in which a player is going for the man rather than the ball*. Perhaps FIFA should also consider sentencing players to "remedial soccer school" for "failing to show the appropriate degree of skill to play the sport properly" when players engage in non-sporting and dangerous actions on the field. This would add an element of shame to what are often insignificant fines, and may encourage compliance to the Laws of Football.

The spirit of soccer commands players *to play the ball and not the man*. When adhered to, this code results in fair and creative play, and minimal injuries on the field, whether amateur or professional.

---

[7] Keane interview by Sean O'Hagan, *The Observer*, Sunday September 1, 2002. Keane changed the description of this incident in the second edition of his autobiography.

Unintentional Injuries

Unintentional injuries are of three types:
(1) Injuries *caused by lack of skill*.
(2) Injuries that are *accidental and resulting from a fair challenge*.
(3) *Non-contact injuries*.

Lack of skill injuries occur when the opposing player does not have enough skill and/or courage to withdraw his illegal challenge. These injuries occur as a result of a lack of technique and/or negative play (playing not to lose). This is why it can be dangerous to play with "hacks", unskilled booters of balls and body parts. Some *hacks* are simply beginners who get too frustrated at more skilled players going past them, and decide to take a short cut rather than improving their skill level. Others are *professional hacks* employed by teams to hassle skilled ball-handlers. These hit men need to be controlled by the referee and dismissed before they are allowed to injure another player. Professional hacks cannot be permitted to take over professional soccer, as they once did in ice hockey.

A *lack of skill* injury can also be self-inflicted. Paul Gascoigne and Roy Keane both severely injured their knees attempting to make ill-advised and quasi-legal tackles on opposition players. A lack of skill and judgment in performing a proper tackle did them in, and they were each forced to take nearly a year off for rehabilitation.

Fair challenge and accidental injuries are a part of the game, and perhaps can be reduced less by rule changes than by improved physical conditioning and equipment refinement. But some serious accidental injuries may be nearly unavoidable. Peruvian star forward Claudio Pizarro suffered a broken skull in the 2004 Copa America game against Venezuela, after the Venezuelan defender accidentally raised his elbow too high for self-protection while heading the ball. Fortunately, Pizarro healed well and was back playing in 3 months.

Non-contact injuries occur by definition when running or turning without contact. When a player is not warmed up properly, a strained or torn muscle may result. Sometimes a freak turn off the ball will result in as serious an injury as the dreaded torn anterior cruciate ligament (ACL). Some of these injuries are "pitch-induced" by a poorly conditioned field, or by playing on the old-style artificial turf. It is still too early to determine what effect the new generation artificial turf will have on joint injuries in soccer, and this issue should be prospectively studied.

Potential Injuries Caused by Lax Officiating

Injuries can be caused by a referee's lax enforcement of the Laws of the Game. Certain players (often the dominant striker) are constantly subjected to illegal physical abuse. The following is an example of this unfortunate phenomenon.

In a 2001 Spanish League game between Valencia and Athletic Bilbao, the Basque team was intent on defending and occasionally counterattacking. The Valencia center forward, Norwegian national player John Carew, was under constant personal attack from a Bilbao hitman, even when he did not have possession of the ball. He punched, kicked, pushed, pulled, and grabbed Carew, placing him in a position to be injured, and all perfectly visible to the referee and the television viewers. When Carew took a pass, made a splendid quick turn at the 18-yard line, and pounded a magnificent strike past the keeper, it was true vindication for the unfair suffering he had endured. Carew ran down the field celebrating, then placed his index finger over his mouth quieting the Bilbao crowd for the abuse he had taken all afternoon. Then he placed his hand to his ear as if straining to hear their comments after such a tremendous goal. For that quiet celebration, taking no more than 10 seconds, he was red-carded and thrown out of the game by the very referee that ignored all the illegal play by the Bilbao hitman. These inactions and ultimate reaction by the incompetent referee were damaging to soccer fair play and the integrity of the sport.

The referee at a 22 February 2006 European Champions league match between host Chelsea and Barcelona was slightly better. Barcelona starlet Lionel Messi was terrorizing defender Asier del Horno, so del Horno made a studs-up challenge on Messi's left knee – an illegal action that could have ended Messi's career. Perhaps the referee did not clearly see that detail, but a few minutes later del Horno again raised his foot high in a body-check challenge on Messi – this one off the ball as he was already beaten – and the referee appropriately gave him a straight red card. Even though the referee missed the more serious challenge, both merited a red card and del Horno was eventually sent off. Once the skill players are allowed to be kicked off the field by hack plays like del Horno made, that will signal the transition of the "beautiful game" into the "ugly game."[8]

Potential Injuries Caused by Field Conditions or Artificial Turf

Poor field conditions increase the risk for musculoskeletal injury, as the simple act of running may result in a sprained ankle, or worse. Richer countries and those that have a football tradition have better field conditions than poorer nations or those with little tradition. Still, USA clubs with largely an ethnic club tradition had little access to development monies, and consistently played on poor fields until the last decade. USA semi-professional clubs played on threadbare fields such as the Metropolitan Oval (Queens, New York City) or Farcher's Grove (Union, New Jersey), which were far worse than comparable amateur fields in Europe such as the Hackney Marshes in London, England, the largest set of football fields in the world.

The USA-football owners first introduced artificial turf fields in the 1970s in an effort to reduce grass field costs. USA-football professionals were later found to sustain a higher rate of serious knee injuries playing on the artificial turf in comparison to natural grass, and there is little reason to suspect that soccer players would not have suffered the same fate. Other studies showed that bleeding injuries were more common in games played on artificial turf, and this information eventually led to the banishment of artificial turf from many USA-football stadiums.

The New York Cosmos played on the same artificial turf pitch in Meadowlands Stadium that the USA-football New York Giants did in the 1970s and 1980s. Knowledgeable fans were always concerned about injuries that could have occurred to Pelé, Franz Beckenbauer, Johan Neeskens, or others that may have resulted from playing on that first generation artificial turf field, which provided dangerous field conditions for soccer.[9]

Soccer competition on first-generation artificial turf was fortunately an aberration, occurring in some North American Soccer League (NASL) stadiums and a few stadiums in England. The most important English club that installed artificial turf was Queens Park Rangers (QPR) in London. Other English clubs that experimented temporarily with artificial turf were Luton Town, Preston North End, Oldham Athletic, and Stirling Albion. As experience of artificial turf was limited in soccer, there were no comprehensive studies documenting excess injuries compared to natural turf.

FIFA developed standards for the new generation of artificial turf that went into effect July 1, 2004 (International Artificial Turf Standard), in the process adding the words "artificial turf" to the Laws of Football for the first time. While the first generation artificial turf was quite short and hard, the new generation turf has longer plastic blades of "grass" placed on a bed of sand and rubber granules. This new turf is already being used in many soccer stadiums worldwide, such as Scotland's First Division club Dunfermline's stadium.

---

[8] To be fair, del Horno is a skilled player who rarely fouls that blatantly. But Chelsea is a superrich team that is not allowed to fail under coach Jose Mourinho, who complained bitterly about Messi's "acting" skills. In truth, both Mourinho and del Horno are lucky that Messi's career did not end that day at Stamford Bridge.

[9] 1974 World Cup star Emmanuel "Manno" Sanon finished his career in 1983 while playing for the San Diego Sockers on an artificial turf field, tearing his right (supporting leg) ACL in a non-contact injury. Despite five operations, Sanon was not able to continue his professional career.

FIFA is promoting this latest generation of turf for areas where weather conditions or financial considerations affect field conditions. As more new generation turf is used, it is imperative that its use be studied prospectively, in order to document any discrepancies between pitch-induced injuries of the new artificial turf versus natural grass. Preliminary results from UEFA suggest that the new artificial pitches may even be safer than grass, with 3.2 muscular or ligament injuries per 1000 playing hours versus 7.6 on grass.

Women's Soccer Injuries

Soccer is the most physically intense team game, and women perform the same actions on the field as men. Although women possess a lower center of gravity on average, men have heavier muscles, tendons, and ligaments than women.[10] Several orthopedic studies have reported that women suffer serious soccer knee injuries such as a torn ACL two to three times as frequently as men.[11] This increased incidence of injuries in women's soccer merits expeditious investigation by both FIFA and US-Soccer, for the purposes of verification and evaluation of possible solutions for this phenomenon.[12]

If the knee injury disparity between the sexes is confirmed, it may be necessary to modify the women's game to alleviate these excess injuries. It has been shown that better physical preparation with proprioceptive training can help avoid serious injuries such as a torn ACL.[13,14] In addition, optimization of field conditions, new equipment and/or meticulous enforcement or amendment of the Laws of the Soccer might help in the prevention of these injuries.

New equipment might include a shoe with a rotating stud technology to protect the knee from torque injuries experienced under high twisting forces. Diverse field conditions should be studied to determine the environments least conducive to injury. Referees of women's matches must be trained to ensure the level of off-the-ball violence and illegal tackles are kept to a bare minimum, in order to reduce serious injury.

Injury Evaluation and Treatment

Evaluation of Soccer Injuries

A trainer or doctor at field level best evaluates soccer injuries initially. A quick examination can normally determine whether the player is fit to continue playing, or has suffered a potentially serious injury.

After sustaining a serious injury a player goes into *psychological shock*. The shock is initially disbelief that an injury has even occurred. After all, a few seconds ago he was a complete and uninjured person. Therefore, psychological support needs to be provided at the same time by the medical team performing the on-field physical evaluation and treatment. *Physical shock* is fortunately rare on the football field, and occurs with life-threatening injuries (ruptured spleen or heart attacks), heat stroke, or severe allergic reactions.

Until thirty years ago, doctors had to rely on plain X-rays to help diagnose knee injuries, but those were rarely definitive. For a knee injury in 1975, the orthopedic surgeon could only say, "Well, we can open it up and take a look inside." Since that time, there have been three technological revolutions in sports medicine diagnosis and treatment.

---

[10] In addition to hormonal differences to men, women on average have a smaller ACL, smaller femoral notch, and more joint laxity than men; all of which may contribute to a higher injury incidence in women's soccer.
[11] Bjordal, JM, Arnly, F, Hannestad, B, Strand, T. Epidemiology of anterior cruciate ligament injuries in soccer. *American Journal of Sports Medicine.* 1997;25(3):341-5.
[12] FIFA is advocating a series of exercises called "The 11," a good sports injury prevention program – information at: http://www.fifa.com/en/development/medicalsection/0,1236,4,00.html.
[13] Caraffa, A, Cerulli, G, Projetti, et al. Prevention of anterior cruciate ligament injuries in soccer. A prospective controlled study of proprioceptive training. *Knee Surgery, Sports Traumatology, Arthroscopy.* 1996;4(1):19-21.
[14] Heidt, RS, Sweeterman, LM, Carlonas, RL, et al. Avoidance of soccer injuries with preseason training. *American Journal of Sports Medicine.* 2000;28(5):659-62.

- A specialized X-ray invented in 1973 called the CT scan (for *computerized tomography*) gave the specialist an improved chance of making a complicated bone fracture diagnosis without exploratory surgery.
- The introduction of *arthroscopic surgery utilizing fiberoptic technology* in the early 1980s revolutionized potential recovery from joint injuries. In arthroscopic surgery, the surgeon inserts a camera and operates through small incisions, manipulating joint structures with special narrow instruments. The advent of arthroscopy has supplanted the need for long incisions and scars over the knee, resulting in shorter rehabilitation periods.
- MRI (for *magnetic resonance imaging*) scanning was introduced in 1984, and gave a boost to non-invasively diagnosing certain structural injuries such as tendon, ligament, and meniscus ruptures and tears.

As a result of these new imaging and surgical technologies, physicians can perform more accurate pre-operative diagnoses, less invasive surgeries, and follow the post-operative joint recovery non-invasively and with better accuracy.

Bodily Injuries

Because of the total body involvement and high contact level of soccer, virtually any part of the body can be injured. Starting at the top of the body:

Head Injuries

The head and facial areas are critical zones to be protected when in tight quarters, as the most devastating and life threatening soccer injuries occur from facial bone fractures or skull fractures usually inflicted by an elbow, knee, or foot. The penalty for the defender (if he does not get carded) is a mere "dangerous play" call and an indirect free kick, so a player must always be prepared for overly aggressive players and protect his head (cover with arms, and/or withdraw head away from danger).

Simple lacerations are important head injuries. These must be closed at field-side so that there is no blood showing. Only then will a player be allowed back on the field.

If a player shows any signs of change of consciousness or personality after a head injury, this is a medical emergency and he must be brought to a hospital immediately. He may have developed an epidural hematoma in his head (blood leakage between the dural covering of the brain and the non-expansible cranium), which is completely curable if caught in time and drained properly.

There has been some recent discussion that repeatedly heading a soccer ball may inflict chronic brain injury or a Parkinsonian neurological syndrome similar to what some boxers have suffered. There is no direct comparison between the two sports, as boxers sustain multiple direct blows of significant power over all parts of the head, while soccer players propel a lightweight ball solely with the forehead (the strongest part of the skull). Before the advent of waterproof soccer balls in the 1970s, soccer players would routinely head waterlogged heavier balls in rainy conditions, and there are no reports of brain damage in those retired players. As of 2006 there is no scientific evidence that heading a football causes any chronic brain damage in adult players.

It is worth noting however, that soccer is the only team sport rated by the American Academy of Pediatrics (AAP) as a contact/collision sport that does not mandate head protection. Although there has never been any credible evidence of chronic brain injury in children from soccer, it just *makes common sense for children to use a smaller* (size 3 or 4) *and lighter ball than adults*, as they would potentially be most at risk for heading a standard size and weight soccer ball.

As a precaution to such worries, in 2003 FIFA authorized the use of soft padded headbands for head-protection (although such gear has never been proven to be significantly protective). Some women players used this device in the defunct WUSA (Women's United Soccer Association), as well as the 2003 Women's World Cup.[15]

Thorax Injuries

Injuries to the chest are typically rib contusions, strains of the muscle layers between the ribs, or on occasion, fractured ribs. These injuries are most often caused by elbows to the thorax area, and less commonly from a kick (unless the player is a goalkeeper). Thorax injuries are usually nuisance injuries that require a week to a month to recover.

Abdominal and Groin Injuries

The most dangerous injury to the abdomen is a laceration of one of the organs, typically the spleen or rarely the liver. These occur as a result of a direct kick to the area, or by blunt trauma such as a player running into an opposing knee. If a player becomes light-headed and his blood pressure is dropping, he is likely losing blood into his abdomen, which constitutes a medical emergency. Spleen injuries may result in rapid exsanguination, while liver lacerations may not be as acute.

The proverbial "boot in the groin" results in compression of the testicles and a most unpleasant severe nauseous sensation. There are many folk remedies to alleviate such pains: (lie on back, knees up, breathe deeply and/or hold and massage affected area), but these are likely only psychological aids, and the sensation usually passes after a few minutes. These injuries are usually self-limited and heal spontaneously, but occasionally some damage occurs with local swelling or blood emanating from the urethra. These symptoms or any persistent pain should be checked by a physician.

Leg Fractures

Fractures of the leg are less common than joint injuries, but are no less serious. Studies have found that most fractures have resulted from aggressive tacking and foul play (75%), and the majority of fractures (90%) surprisingly occurred while wearing shin guards.[16,17]

It is therefore evident that most severe leg injuries in amateurs are caused by uncontrolled aggression and poor football skills. Professional players injuring one of their colleagues in this manner should be suspended for "defects in soccer competence and professionalism," as their foul play and poor sportsmanship must be adjusted before being allowed on the professional field again.

Joint and Ligament injuries
The KNEE

The knee joint is made up of bones, cartilage, tendons, ligaments, and other connective tissue, with delicate vascular and nerve structures running throughout on the way to the lower leg and foot. The most common serious injuries result in damage to the meniscus located between the surfaces of the two long bones that meet in the knee (the femur in the thigh and the tibia in the lower leg), or any of the four major ligaments of the knee.

Meniscus injuries may occur from pivoting movements, with the ensuing shearing forces on the meniscus surface resulting in a laceration or rupture. With a small laceration, the player may be able to return to play without undue discomfort after the initial swelling resolves. If the laceration is large and results in "locking" of the knee, or there is persistent pain after injury, a surgeon would likely elect to order an MRI and perform an arthroscopy of the knee, in order to remove the offending meniscus fragments.

---

[15] Using an adult size number 5 ball has been shown to cause more distal radius (arm) fractures in goalkeepers less than 15 years of age, as opposed to using a youth sized number 3 or 4 ball. See: Boyd, KT, Brownson, P, Hunter, JB. Distal radius fractures in young goalkeepers: a case for an appropriately sized soccer ball. *British Journal of Sports Medicine*. 2001;35(6):409-11.

[16] Goga, IE, Gongal, P. Severe soccer injuries in amateurs. *British Journal of Sports Medicine*. 2003;37:498-501.

[17] Boden, BP, Lohnes, JH, Nunley, JA, Garrett, WE. Tibia and fibula fractures in soccer players. *Knee Surgery, Sports Traumatology, Arthroscopy*. 1999;7(4):262-6.

The most common serious injury is damage to the anterior cruciate ligament (ACL), which connects the anterior part of the femur with the posterior aspect of the tibia. The ACL is usually ruptured either by rapid deceleration or by twisting the knee, either by the leg being held down by another player when trying to turn, or off-the-ball by a foot stuck in the turf. A completely torn ACL results in profound knee instability, making it possible to walk but impossible to perform the rigorous pivoting moves in soccer. A new ACL is usually fashioned by removing the center of the patellar tendon and placing it in the usual ACL position; a full recovery normally requires up to six-month rehabilitation.

The posterior collateral ligament (PCL) runs from the posterior aspect of the femur to the anterior part of the tibia. The PCL is often injured when other structures are affected, sometimes in conjunction with an ACL tear, or in isolation when the knee joint is hyper-extended.

The medial collateral ligament (MCL) is located on the inner aspect of the knee joint, and the lateral collateral ligament (LCL) on the outer aspect. These are most often stretched or partially torn on extreme isolated movements of the lower leg in relation to the thigh. This can result from a poor tackle, an unfortunate turn, or a foot being hung up on the ball. If the movement is excessive, the ligament may be severed, requiring surgical connection.

The quadriceps and patellar tendons connect the fascia sheath of the quadriceps muscles to the top of the tibia. Inside the patellar tendon is the patella, a floating sesamoid bone shaped like a pancake. Rare soccer injuries include fracture of the patella, or a torn patella and/or quadriceps tendon. All require surgical intervention in order to play soccer again. A knee dislocation will require surgery if the vascular supply running through the knee is compromised, and if not attended to early on the leg rarely has to be amputated below the knee.

Because of the unusual stresses placed on the knees in soccer, serious knee injuries are the most common physical injury to force retirement. Indeed, more than 30% of former professionals will experience chronic pain from osteoarthritis on retirement.[18]

The FOOT

The foot is a complex structure composed of 26 bones, 33 joints, 19 muscles, and 107 ligaments, supporting more than 100,000 pounds of pressure for every mile walked. If any of these structures are injured, the whole foot is affected and the player will be forced to rest and recuperate. Most soccer ankle and foot injuries have been linked to contact-type injuries.[19]

Perhaps the most serious foot-ankle injury is the Achilles tendon rupture, which requires surgery to repair. Full stretching and proprioceptive training before playing should help prevent undue stress on this critical tendon.

Running and repetitive kicking using the instep of the foot can lead to "footballer's ankle", which occurs when excess bone growth (called osteophytes) are produced. These osteophytes can occasionally break off and form free-floating foreign bodies in the joints, resulting in pain and limitation of the range of motion of joints. The treatment is rest, or if the condition is serious, surgical removal of the bone particles.

The foot/ankle complex is the most commonly injured area for soccer players (according to the 2002 World Cup injury statistics), but fortunately most players recover in short order – they may not even report a mild injury or strain to the trainer. Unlike serious knee injuries, ankle injuries are remarkably a rare cause of forced retirement in soccer. An exception was Marco van Basten, who retired at age 29 with a chronic ankle injury, and who notably blamed his retirement as much on medical malpractice as his original ankle injury.

---

[18] Drawer, S, Fuller, CW. Propensity for osteoarthritis and lower limb joint pain in retired professional soccer players. *British Journal of Sports Medicine*. 2001;35;402-408.
[19] Giza, E, Fuller, C, Junge, A, Dvorak, J. Mechanisms of foot and ankle injuries in soccer. *American Journal of Sports Medicine*. 2003;31(4):550-4.

Injury Consequences and Treatment Outcomes

Almost any injury sustained to bone, tendon, or ligament can be treated, but this does not mean that the player will ever return to full fitness or confidence. Judgment should be reserved for the success of all serious injuries requiring reconstructive surgery until a full rehabilitation period has been completed. The surgeon may claim "the operation was a success," but it is the proof on the field that establishes true success.

Muscle strains and tears are commonplace and must be handled carefully. The player must not be rushed back into training, lest he be further injured by the two following mechanisms:

(1) The injury itself could get worse and result in permanent damage, and/or

(2) Unbeknownst to the player himself, he often favors his injured leg by engaging in compensatory body movements, which can result in abnormal stresses and injury of the healthy leg.

The concept of *overtraining* means excess physical activity leading to the break down of more muscle and fibrous tissue than can be immediately replaced or repaired, and should absolutely be avoided when attempting a surgical recovery.

Non-Soccer Inflicted Injuries and Conditions Still Allowing for Soccer Play

As soccer is the all-inclusive game, people with congenital birth conditions or severe injuries sustained outside of soccer can often still play the beautiful game. Four so-called handicapped conditions that would preclude participation in most other team or individual sports are considered below [see Figure 6A and end of chapter]:

Severe trauma

Persons with trauma and/or burns sustained to the chest, head and arms may continue to play competitive soccer. A player with severe burns to the face, chest and arm participated on a Texas all-star team as an integral member of his team. Similarly, the author has observed a boy severely scarred from kerosene burns on his face, chest, arms and legs, playing soccer in a Peruvian Amazon village.

Phocomelia

Phocomelia is a congenital condition most often caused by ingestion of the drug *thalidomide* during pregnancy. In Greek, *phōkē* means "seal", and *melos* is "extremity." Persons with this condition have shortened extremities (arms and/or legs) that resemble the flippers of a seal. The arms are more commonly affected, so if the legs have developed normally, the affected person can play soccer. The author's high school soccer team had a scholar-athlete with upper extremity phocomelia who played high quality soccer, and who later graduated from law school.

Amputee football

When players are missing or lose one extremity, there is no reason to discard soccer as amputee soccer is developing rapidly. In this football style, the rules mandate that outfield players are leg amputees on crutches, and the goalkeepers are single-arm amputees. There is even a soccer World Cup for amputees, and England Amputees captain Steve Johnson won this World Cup three times.

Special Olympics

Since soccer is an easy game to understand, it is an extremely successful Special Olympics team game. Starting in 1979, Special Olympic athletes have entertained crowds with 5 v. 5 and 11 v. 11 competitions, and even an Individual Skills competition. The Special Olympics motto is the ultimate emblem of sportsmanship, "Let me win, but if I cannot win, let me be brave in the attempt."

In addition to the above conditions, England also sponsors football teams for the blind, the deaf, and for athletes with cerebral palsy. Once a player has seen the people affected with the above conditions perform, it is amazing how inspired he will be as he strives to master the universal skills of soccer.

Soccer and Illness

Many illnesses can affect the soccer player, yet a fit player will likely recover enough to resume his previous level of play, or if not, achieve a soccer level he can still enjoy. In fact, soccer can be enjoyed by nearly all people in the world, no matter if they have been ill or rendered handicapped. Soccer can also be used as a sport for rehabilitation purposes.

Much of this section concerns how illnesses affect the individual player, but there have been some illnesses, especially infectious diseases, which have seriously affected soccer as a sport. The most important four of these illnesses are caused by viruses. These infectious viruses were the 1919 influenza pandemic which killed soccer players worldwide, the polio pandemic of the 20th century that crippled many future soccer players, the HIV epidemic that started around 1980 and has seriously affected soccer players in many countries, and the 2003 SARS (Severe Acute Respiratory Syndrome) outbreak, which resulted in the cancellation of the 2003 Women's World Cup in China and subsequent hosting by the USA later that same year.

Illnesses can be broken down into 2 types of conditions: (1) *organic conditions* that can be congenital or induced by microbes, nutritional deficiency, or an autoimmune state; and (2) *toxicity conditions* that are provoked by the ingestion of chemical substances. All may have immediate importance to soccer players.

Organic Disease Conditions
HIV and AIDS

HIV and AIDS are of supreme importance to soccer players, because the HIV virus is spread through sexual contact, and *sexually active young people (who play the most soccer) are most at risk in the community*. It is precisely this age and sex risk present in young athletes that has alarmed sports medicine specialists, as evidenced by a conspicuous picture of an acute HIV conversion skin reaction on the *very first page* of the Oxford Textbook of Sports Medicine.[20]

Although HIV can also spread through unscreened blood transfusions and same-needle usage, the primary mode of transmission worldwide is unprotected sexual intercourse with an infected individual.

Many soccer players grow up in poverty in developing countries. Like nearly all infectious diseases, HIV infection is more common among the poor who lack access to basic information and preventive efforts to avoid the HIV virus. Therefore, it is imperative that all soccer players arm themselves with the information to protect themselves from the virus, or, if they are HIV-infected already, to access the proper health care to protect themselves and their loved ones.

What is AIDS and what is HIV?

The Acquired Immunodeficiency Syndrome (AIDS in English, SIDA in French and Spanish) is a recently discovered infectious disease caused by the Human Immunodeficiency Virus (called HIV, or *VIH* in French and Spanish). Known only since 1981, AIDS is a modern day plague that has so far resulted in the infection of 65 million people and the death of more than 28 million individuals worldwide. The AIDS epidemic has no end in sight, as every prediction made by world experts has been overrun by millions of new cases. Although effective medication to contain (but not cure) AIDS is available, the current international political structure guarantees that the treatment is financially and logistically inaccessible for >90% of those who are infected by HIV.

HIV is a virus that attacks a specific cell in the human body – the CD4 cell – that controls many immune responses to bacteria, fungus, and viruses. HIV often causes an initial

---

[20] Harries, M, Williams, C, Stanish, WD, Micheli, LJ, eds. Oxford Textbook of Sports Medicine, 2nd ed. 1998. Oxford University Press, Oxford, England.

flu-like illness within three months after entering the body, but then lies dormant for five to ten years thereafter. During the dormant period, the person appears well and their status is *HIV-infected*, BUT they may still be unwitting and efficient transmitters of the virus. At the end of the dormant period, the person is left with little resistance to microorganisms, and is then defined as having developed AIDS, as the *Acquired* HIV virus has made their *Immune* system become *Deficient* (hence the name Acquired Immunodeficiency Syndrome).

There is overwhelming scientific evidence that the presence of HIV is necessary for an individual to develop AIDS. Theories to the contrary are not based in science and are counterproductive to public health and control efforts.

How does one acquire the HIV virus?

HIV is both a *sexually transmitted disease* and a *blood-borne transmission disease*.

Any sexual activity involving genitalia contact without barrier protection (e.g., a condom) can result in transmission. HIV can also be transmitted by blood exchange, most commonly through contaminated needles for drug injecting, but may also occur with unsanitary medicine injections, tattooing, or acupuncture. When blood sources are not tested for HIV, contaminated blood transfusions are a source of transmission.

Since there is some blood exchange during the birthing process, a newborn baby has a chance to be HIV-infected if the mother has the HIV virus. Breast-feeding a baby may also transmit the HIV virus from mother to child. Fortunately, mothers who are HIV-infected can take an anti-HIV drug combination prior to birth that will drastically reduce the possibility of HIV transmission to their child (from about 25% HIV infection rate to less than 1% in an optimal treatment scheme).

How can a person avoid the HIV virus?

The best ways to avoid the HIV virus through sexual activity are to:
(1) Completely abstain from sexual activity, or
(2) Use a barrier contraceptive method (condom).

The ideal situation when two people are considering having sexual relations is to test both partners for HIV:

(1) If both are found not to be HIV-infected, they must maintain a monogamous relationship or use barrier contraception.

(2) If one or both partners are found to be HIV-infected, they must practice *safe sex* (using condoms as a barrier method) to prevent the other partner from exposure or re-exposure to HIV.

It should be noted that condoms have been proven to drastically reduce the chances of becoming HIV-infected, but are not absolutely foolproof. In addition, birth control measures such as hormone-based contraceptive pills or injections alone *will not protect either women or men from receiving the HIV virus* – a condom must be used in conjunction with hormonal contraception for adequate prevention.

Avoiding the HIV virus through blood-borne transmission is straightforward – do not receive any injection from anybody unless you are positive the needle is new and sterile. Do not share needles, *ever*, not even once. Insist that any necessary blood transfusion is at a minimum tested for HIV, Hepatitis B, and Hepatitis C.

What would a professional sports club or national team do if a player was found to be HIV infected?

They would likely try and convince him that playing would not be in the best interests of himself, his teammates, the league, or even the sport. There is ample precedence for these opinions and actions.

In 1991, basketball great Ervin "Magic" Johnson of the Los Angeles Lakers faced this problem at the height of his career, forcing his immediate retirement from professional basketball. However, Johnson did return to star on the 1992 Gold medal winning USA

Olympic Basketball "Dream Team" in Barcelona, Spain, *after he had made an announcement that he was HIV-infected*. After his positive experience in the Olympics Johnson wanted to play for the Lakers again, but some of his basketball player peers said they were afraid of possible infection if they played opposite him, and some NBA coaches, administrators, and owners joined in to voice these unsubstantiated fears. A sad and nonsensical element of the episode was that some of the critical players had performed alongside Johnson on the 1992 Olympic "Dream Team." Johnson eventually made abbreviated comebacks in the NBA in 1992 and 1996. In sum, Johnson was embraced by the international basketball and sports community at the Olympic Games, but was pressured to retire after encountering resistance to continue playing professionally in the USA.

Magic Johnson is so far the only NBA basketball player to declare that he has the HIV virus, but there are likely others that are HIV-infected who are either ignorant of the fact or have not gone public. After all, if a superstar like Magic Johnson was forced to retire with HIV, another HIV-infected player would surely reason that he also would also have to retire immediately. While Johnson had several other sources of revenue besides basketball, most players rely solely on basketball as their livelihood. Therefore players facing Johnson's reality may see an HIV-infected status as an impedance to receiving any basketball-related salary – regardless of their ability – and it is likely that players are not even tested because of this fear. Johnson retired immediately with financial security, while many other players would not have that opportunity.[21]

Four-time Olympic gold medalist Greg Louganis (Diving 1976, 1984, 1988) won his last two medals in 1988 knowing he was HIV-infected, and this world-class athlete details his complete story in his autobiography *Breaking the Surface* (he remains healthy in 2006).

Soccer and HIV/AIDS - The Remarkable Story of Eduardo Esidio

The HIV virus entered the professional soccer environment in the early days of the epidemic (early 1980s), but all players except one have avoided divulging their health condition because of the widespread and unwarranted social stigma.

In 1998, an HIV-infected soccer player in Peru was forced to go public under unusual circumstances. Brazilian center forward *Eduardo Esidio* had signed a contract with top Peruvian club Universitario, but during his physical exam, *they tested him for HIV-infection without his knowledge*. The test revealed he was HIV-infected, and the Universitario administration was hesitant about honoring his contract. Esidio needed the Universitario job, as soccer was still his premium occupational skill and best chance to better his family's condition. If he was forced out of this opportunity, other teams could justify taking the same position to avoid signing him, and he would not be able to provide for his family. However, Esidio's case never went to court, as in 1993 Peru had already signed into law a statute banning job discrimination based on HIV status.

Once Esidio performed with the Universitario team, he was an immediate sensation, scoring goals left, right and center. With Esidio providing the goal thrills, Universitario won three straight Peruvian professional soccer championships from 1998-2000. In 2000, he smashed the single season Peruvian goal record when he scored 37 league goals.[22] This accomplishment garnered him the *Top Scorer in South America* and the *World's Second Best Top Division Goal Scorer* of the "Top 50" national leagues from all six continents[23] (as calculated by the International Federation of Football History & Statistics - IFFHS).

---

[21] HIV has also affected amateur basketball in the USA, as Juan Dixon endured the death of his parents from AIDS-related illnesses while he was playing high school basketball. Dixon's superb play resulted in his being named the most valuable player of the 2002 NCAA (National Collegiate Athletic Association) basketball tournament, when he performed for the national champions University of Maryland.

[22] Record had been 32 goals, by Pablo Muchotrigo of Cienciano in 1974 and Ysrael Zúñiga of Melgar in 1999.

[23] Links: www.rsssf.com/miscellaneous/samgboot.html and www.iffhs.de/main/frame/?maintarget=englisch.

In 2001 Esidio transferred to Alianza Lima to help mark Alianza's centenary celebration (1901-2001). Esidio continued his winning ways, marking the 100th year of this famous club by helping Alianza to the Apertura (Opening) championship, thereby ensuring their participation in the 2002 Libertadores Cup.

What was also astounding was how the Peruvian media treated Esidio. Since his HIV-infected status was revealed, he was covered strictly by his performance with virtually no mention of HIV (it is doubtful that the USA media would have responded as maturely in a similar situation). In 2001, Esidio was interviewed on the Peruvian television show *Nadie Se Duerme* ("Nobody Sleeps!"), to explain how well he felt physically and had enjoyed his time in Peru. Interviewing locals on the street in Lima or elsewhere in Peru reveals a consistent opinion of viewing Esidio simply by his excellent deeds as a player and his modest demeanor.

Unfortunately, despite his impressive accomplishments of four titles in a row, Esidio's soccer experience in Peru was not completely smooth. Opposition coach Juan Carlos Oblitas of Sporting Cristal (Lima) commented at the time of Esidio's HIV announcement that he would advise avoiding any action of heading the ball if Esidio was in the vicinity (Oblitas later became the national team coach for Peru's unsuccessful qualifying bid for the 2002 World Cup). And on Christmas Eve, 2000, just after Esidio was signed by Alianza Lima, Universitario club President Flores bizarrely stated that Esidio was going to have serious health problems while playing for Alianza. The Peruvian media took these statements as an injustice to Esidio, which appeared to have been made only because he had changed teams.

Esidio's subsequent performances proved his detractors wrong. In the first 20 games of the 2001 season Alianza lost only once, a memorable 1-0 defeat to Cienciano in terrible conditions in the 11,000 feet altitude of Cusco. It had rained heavily the previous days in Cusco, and the field was saturated with puddles and small lakes. The weather was cool and windy, and rain fell for much of the second half. Paulo Autori, the Brazilian coach of Alianza (later coach of Peru and São Paulo, where he won the 2005 Copa Libertadores and World Club Championship), elected to keep two of his stars on the sidelines for this game –Palinha (Jorge Ferreira da Silva), the Brazilian creative midfielder who previously starred for the 1992-1993 Copa Libertadores and World Club Champions São Paulo and the Brazil national team, and Waldir Saenz, the Peruvian international midfielder-striker. Palinha probably was not bothered as the conditions were distinctly un-Brazilian, but Saenz was not happy – he had performed well in altitude before and would have preferred to play. One player whom Autori did not deny was Eduardo Esidio. Playing as the lone striker, Esidio was the only credible Alianza goal threat in the game, going it alone among multiple lakes and defenders. Once he was knocked down and lay in a puddle of water in the wind-accentuated cold, but just got up and continued playing his game until it was finished.

Esidio had given his best in the most difficult conditions any soccer player could possibly face – extreme altitude, cold, rain, terrible field conditions – and done well [Figure 6B & C]. That is why Esidio's HIV status was never an issue, as he transcended it by his dignity and performance. One trusts that he is receiving the excellent HIV care that is available in Peru and Brazil, and that his health does not become an issue in the future.

Brazil could likely have used Esidio in their disastrous World Cup qualifying in 2001, as he was a tall striker useful with his head and either foot. In addition to being a goal machine, he could dribble and pass with the best. In the Alianza Lima "100th anniversary celebration game" on 14 February 2001 against Colo Colo of Chile, Esidio chased down a ball on the right side, beat two defenders on the dribble, and slotted an improbable but perfectly weighted pass to Palinha, who pushed it precisely in the corner. With hundreds of Brazilian players in demand and performing overseas, the competition was perhaps too fierce for a Brazil spot. But Esidio would have been an inspired choice and would likely have done well, as Brazil had trouble finding a central striker who could work with Rivaldo while Ronaldo was injured.

Soccer and HIV/AIDS — Other Players

Unfortunately, Esidio's success as an HIV-infected player is an exception, as there have been dozens of less fortunate soccer players who have suffered and ultimately died from AIDS.[24] These players are as of yet hidden from history's view, effectively erased by the vicious stigma that permeates nearly all societies in the world, the presence of which signifies a massive global HIV public health failure.[25]

Several of these individuals have been very high profile, including two players who performed in the 1974 World Cup in West Germany and later died of AIDS. Another player performed in his country's World Cup qualifying matches but was unable to claim a place in the team due to chronic illness. *Sizwe Motaung* was a wing defender who played for years for the South African national team (known as the "Bafana Bafana"), eventually becoming a vice captain of the team. He came into prominence in club soccer first with Jomo Cosmos, and then went overseas to play with Tenerife in Spain and St. Gallen in Switzerland. Motaung was a cornerstone of the South African national team, having played in South Africa's first international game after apartheid ended in 1992, the historic African Nations Cup win in 1996, and then helping South Africa enter their first World Cup in 1998 (although he did not appear in the Cup itself). Motaung was forced to retreat into isolation and died penniless in August 2001 of an "undiagnosed illness," widely rumored to be AIDS.

The human cost of HIV/AIDS in southern Africa is unbelievable – nearly one South African in nine suffers from HIV or AIDS. But because of the persistent shame and stigma of HIV/AIDS in South Africa, families are still reluctant to make a diagnosis public. To counter such destructive HIV stigma, former South African President Nelson Mandela disclosed in 2002 that three of his relatives had died from AIDS, and on January 6, 2005 revealed that his only living son had just died of AIDS. Mandela made a plea that should be the human rights mantra of societies worldwide: "We call upon everybody not to treat people who are HIV-positive with stigma. We must embrace and love them."[26]

Another South African, Nkosi Johnson, necessarily became an HIV/AIDS spokesperson at the age of eight – when he was refused entry to school on the basis of his HIV-infection he had received at birth. He was later keynote speaker at the 13th International AIDS Conference in Durban in 2000, pleading with AIDS victims and others to accept HIV as a natural course of events so that they can live life as normally as possible.[27] For his efforts to destigmatize the HIV epidemic, Johnson was named in the Top Ten of the SABC3's poll of South Africa's 100 Great South Africans (far above the three footballers listed in the Top 100). Nkosi died in 2001 aged twelve.

In most countries, HIV-infected players eventually become ill and are forced to retire to a clandestine life of sickness – dying in silence because of the manufactured social stigma of AIDS. Most often they are discovered when they are not just HIV-infected, but have

---

[24] Although aware of other HIV-infected soccer players in the Americas, Europe, and Africa, the author has chosen to discuss only those whose status is already known or have died.

[25] The families of stricken athletes often shun publicity because of stigmatizing reactions from an ignorant public. The tragedy is compounded because if families told their stories more often, the enhanced HIV prevention and education result would save more lives in those players' countries. By allowing their stories to be heard, the deceased players' families could actually save future lives, thus bringing honor to the family. Indeed, there are institutions eager to sponsor just such individuals for motivational and inspirational speaking tours.

[26] Another African leader, President Kenneth Kaunda of Zambia, announced in 1987 that his own son had died of AIDS in 1986.

[27] Nkosi Johnson said, "Care for us and accept us – we are all human beings. We are normal. We have hands. We have feet. We can walk, we can talk, we have needs just like everyone else. Don't be afraid of us – we are all the same," and "Do all you can with what you have in the time you have in the place you are." For more details on Nkosi Johnson, see http://nkosi.iafrica.com/speech/.

developed full-blown AIDS. In that condition medical help is very challenging, and without expert care patients may deteriorate rapidly and die. This is absolutely an avoidable outcome. *Since HIV is a major epidemic problem affecting all populations, HIV is a serious health concern for soccer leagues all over the world.*

Even though players are routinely given physical examinations (especially prior to changing teams), HIV testing is not routinely performed. So if a player is HIV-infected, he may not know until he has full-blown AIDS. This a health catastrophe because if HIV-infection is known earlier and the proper medication started, the player can take care of himself, live a long life, *and most importantly, be counseled on how to securely avoid infecting anyone else that he cares about.*[28]

Infectious Diseases and HIV Risk and Exposure in Soccer

What are the risks of infectious disease and HIV transmission in sports in general, and soccer in particular? HIV transmission risk in general depends on the particular sport, and specifically as to the amount of physical contact that can draw blood.

Boxing is undoubtedly the sport with the highest risk of HIV transmission, as it is an activity whose objective is to physically punish the opponent and actually draw blood. Boxer Tommy Morrison was once WBO and IBC heavyweight champion, but retired shortly after his HIV-infected status became known.[29] However, some countries still do not require HIV testing for boxers.

The American Academy of Pediatrics (AAP) lists boxing and wrestling as the two sports with the highest potential for contamination of injured skin by blood, and by extension, transmission of infectious agents, including Hepatitis B, Hepatitis C, and HIV. Other contact sports, such as rugby and ice hockey, draw blood at a predictable frequency. Sports in which an instrument is essential to the play, such as lacrosse and field hockey, have the potential of instrument-induced injuries drawing blood. USA-football players wear a lot of protective equipment, but blood is routinely drawn by helmet injuries on soft tissues or even the facial area (especially when one helmet comes off). Even so, one study estimated that USA-football players have a potential to transmit the HIV virus in only 1 in 85 million game contacts (or 1 in 170,000 games assuming 500 contacts per game).[30]

Soccer presents a lower risk of transmitting infectious agents than any of the aforementioned sports because of a lesser frequency of drawing blood. The most frequent injury drawing significant blood is the "head-butt" injury, which occurs when two players attempt to head the ball simultaneously. However, it is rare for both players to draw blood on the same collision.

There has only been one report (a letter in the British medical journal *Lancet* in 1990) of a soccer player found to be HIV-infected two months after a head collision with an HIV-infected player; both drew blood on their head wounds.[31] This report *was suggestive but in no way conclusive* of HIV transmission, as no evidence existed that the two players had identical strains of HIV – a necessary test required for transmission verification. Nevertheless, it serves as a warning that any player with an infectious disease needs to have their condition controlled as much as possible to prevent any transmission. In March 2002, FIFA reported a study that estimated no increased risk of contracting the HIV virus during a soccer match.

---

[28] HIV-infected soccer players actually have a wealth of possibilities in today's world, as various organizations, governments, and pharmaceutical agencies would be eager to hire them as credible spokespersons for HIV education and public health.

[29] Tommy Morrison (born Marion Michael Morrison), the great grandnephew of actor John Wayne, appeared with Sylvester Stallone in the motion picture "Rocky V."

[30] Brown, LS, Drotman, DP, Chu, A, Brown, CL, Knowlan, D. Bleeding injuries in professional football: Estimating the risk for HIV transmission. *Annals of Internal Medicine.* 1995;122(4):271-274.

[31] Torre D, Sampietro C, Ferraro G, Zeroli C, Speranza F. Transmission of HIV-1 infection via sports injury (letter). *Lancet.* 1990;335:1105.

In terms of infectious diseases transmission risk in sport, the Hepatitis B virus is much easier to transmit by wound-to-wound contact than HIV, i.e., a smaller inoculum may lead to actual virus infection. Therefore, it is the AAP's recommendation that all athletes participating in any sport with physical contact receive the Hepatitis B vaccine. After receiving the vaccine course, the risk of transmission of Hepatitis B is nearly zero.

HIV Policy in Soccer

Most professional soccer leagues have no policy requiring HIV testing as part of a mandatory physical exam. But should there be a policy? After all, HIV testing is routine in many parts of the world as an important part of a physical examination, if there are even remotely any risk factors for obtaining HIV.

When a soccer HIV policy is developed, it must not be predicated on a player's HIV status automatically determining his fitness status. Many players who are HIV-infected can continue playing for years at a high level under physician supervision; Eduardo Esidio has proven this supposition correct beyond all doubt. If a player has his HIV condition controlled resulting in an extremely low or undetectable HIV virus load in his body, the risk of HIV transmission even with a rare "double head-butt" wound is extremely unlikely. So the medical condition and care of the HIV-infected player is also vital to the safety of the other players.

HIV-infection transmission is only potentially serious when a player is ignorant of or in denial of his infection. This will result in eventual development of full-blown AIDS with much higher levels of HIV in the blood, vastly increasing the minute chance of HIV transmission. So if a player is ignorant or in denial of his HIV infection, it is dangerous not only to himself, but may also be to his fellow players. The social and scientific lesson is crystal clear: *in the sports arena, uncontrolled HIV infection is both an individual and group concern, wherein controlled HIV infection is usually not a concern.*

If an HIV-infected player's physiological condition is deteriorating or he develops full-blown AIDS, it would not be in that player's best health interest to continue playing at a professional level, as the stress from playing top-level soccer may result in an acceleration of his physical deterioration. HIV-infected players must realize that there may be instances when their physician advises them to go on the injury list in order to recover from physical stress or to take a course of therapy, or even to retire from competitive soccer for their own health.

HIV testing in the setting of a routine sport physical exam is vitally important because young people (the age of professional soccer players) are at the most susceptible age for transmission. If done properly, HIV testing would be a valuable public health tool to both prevent new infections and contain HIV transmission by virtue of health education and proper HIV care. Players would know if they were HIV-infected, receive proper treatment, and continue playing. This can happen now even in Africa, as HIV drugs are cheaper because of lower drug prices negotiated by the World Health Organization (WHO) and other institutions.

Two requirements regarding HIV examination for athletes should be that testing must be (1) voluntary and (2) strictly confidential. Although voluntary, players should be counseled that it is definitely in their best interests to know if they are HIV-infected or not, and how to avoid future infections. Those refusing should be re-counseled by the medical staff on each physical examination that testing is in their best health interests. There will likely be a few players refusing out of fear or other reasons, and there should be no discrimination because of their beliefs.

A professional soccer physical evaluation including HIV testing would require cooperation and coordination between the national Football Associations and national health systems. However, support from the international soccer and health agencies, FIFA and WHO, would be essential if this policy is to be promoted.

Unfortunately, it is a reality that persons in the public spotlight may have private information illegally released. In the event of a news leak, these players should be sustained by the team and the media in the way that Eduardo Esidio has been supported. There should also be a legal contingency plan that will protect the privacy and rights of the individual, and ensuring that any parties divulging private medical information be subject to prosecution for violating the law.

All countries should have a law that specifically forbids discrimination of any type against persons who are HIV-infected. People with HIV infection are often tragically stigmatized by individuals and communities; this human rights issue must be addressed worldwide as it is crucial to the control of the HIV epidemic.

Soccer players could be spokesmen for HIV programs in their countries, much like basketball legend Magic Johnson. Remarkably, Johnson also wrote a book specifically addressed to empower adolescents for their protection from HIV, an excellent public health product that should have been more widely and continuously distributed.[32]

There is nothing improper with HIV-negative players doing HIV awareness propaganda. A great commercial and public health video would be two players talking, one HIV-infected and one not HIV-infected, enacting an HIV awareness commercial and video. Can you imagine a video of Esidio alongside some prominent players and human rights advocate Nelson Mandela, talking about their successes and the importance of protecting themselves and others from HIV infection? It would be a great boon to the HIV public health planners in Brazil, South Africa, and the Portuguese-speaking African countries, and would save many lives in these soccer-mad countries. Such is the global power of soccer.[33]

Through a song, HIV/AIDS has played a hidden but prominent part of global soccer celebrations for decades. For example, immediately after Bayern Munich won the 2001 European championship at the San Siro Stadium in Milan, the speakers belted out the song "We Are The Champions" by the British rock group Queen. This Queen song is popular worldwide in many soccer and sporting events, and is one of the many songs written and sung by Queen's brilliant lead singer Freddie Mercury. Mercury died from AIDS in 1991.[34]

HIV/AIDS is a reality in every country that plays soccer, but widespread ignorance and prejudice still shadow infected persons. It is incumbent upon the world community to protect the basic human rights of persons who are HIV-infected, and through education and counseling to help protect those young people in our communities who are most at risk for contracting HIV. The soccer-playing community of young men are at the most particular risk of contracting HIV: indeed, in many countries HIV/AIDS is the major cause of death of men aged 24-40. As the world's sport, soccer (and FIFA and it's Confederations) has a responsibility to fully engage its tremendous popularity to combat the world's largest health threat of the HIV/AIDS epidemic. The world is still waiting for this to happen, and if it does, soccer will be elevated to a higher humanistic phase of development.

---

[32] Earvin "Magic" Johnson. *What You Can Do To Avoid AIDS*. 1992. Time Books, New York. Johnson was a prominent member of President George Bush, Sr.'s advisory National Commission on AIDS (NCA), but he eventually resigned because Bush shamefully did not take action on the specific recommendations of the NCA.

[33] Manno Sanon (see Foreword) is one influential person in soccer that is deeply concerned about the lack of education in soccer and society about the dangers of promiscuity, sexually-transmitted diseases & consequent HIV risk.

[34] Freddie Mercury was born Farrokh Bulsara on November 5, 1946 in Zanzibar, Africa.

Soccer and HIV Prevention

Soccer activities have been used in Honduras, Haiti, Vietnam, and many African countries in pilot programs in order to increase HIV/AIDS awareness and education. "Street theater" techniques have been employed, such as playing a mock soccer game pitting the "HIV/AIDS team" vs. the "HIV prevention team" (the "HIV prevention team" always wins in the end). It is time to escalate these activities to a higher level and enable them to become more integrated and disseminated with prevention programs.

FIFA was involved in some HIV awareness campaigns through their 2002 World Cup activities with UNICEF. On November 20, 2001, UNICEF and FIFA announced a global alliance for children, and FIFA dedicated the 2002 World Cup to children under the banner of "Say Yes for Children". This was the first time a World Cup was officially dedicated to a humanitarian cause. It is worth printing the UNICEF campaign's "Ten Imperatives for Children" here, as all soccer joy starts with children.

1. **Leave No Child Out**
   All forms of discrimination and exclusion against children must end.
2. **Put Children First**
   It is the responsibility of everyone – governments, NGOs, individuals, religious groups, the private sector and children and adolescents themselves – to ensure that children's rights are respected.
3. **Care for Every Child**
   Ensure all children the best possible start in life.
4. **Fight HIV/AIDS**
   Protect children and adolescents and their families.
5. **Stop Harming and Exploiting Children**
   Violence and abuse must be stopped now; sexual and economic exploitation of children must end.
6. **Listen to Children**
   Respect the rights of children and young people to express themselves and to participate in making the decisions that affect them.
7. **Educate Every Child**
   Every child – all girls and boys – must be allowed to learn.
8. **Protect Children from War**
   No child should experience the horrors of armed conflict.
9. **Protect the Earth for Children**
   Safeguard the environment at global, national and local levels.
10. **Fight Poverty**
    Invest in Children. Invest in services that benefit the poorest children and their families, such as basic health care and primary education. Make the well being of children a priority objective of debt relief programs, development assistance and government spending.

It should be noted that every imperative listed will help against the worldwide HIV/AIDS epidemic, which is specifically mentioned as Imperative number Four.

Diabetes

Diabetes is a condition caused by a lack of the hormone insulin, and is called *Type I* or *juvenile diabetes* when it affects young people. The cause is mostly idiopathic (unknown), or assumed to be a viral infection that has affected the ability of the pancreas to produce insulin.

Danny McGrain, a former captain of Scotland and Celtic, is probably the best-known player that successfully managed a football career and diabetes. McGrain was a defensive stalwart who was excellent at breaking forward under control and forming a dynamic duo with Kenny Dalglish. Arsenal's star Charlie Nicholas even rated McGrain his greatest player of all time.

Another more recent success story was Brazilian striker Washington, who almost led Atletico Paranaense to the 2004 Brazilian title with his league-leading 34 goals, despite having diabetes and recovering from surgery for a vascular blockage.

A young person with diabetes can play soccer at a high level with proper treatment including insulin introduced into the body several times a day. He needs to keep a source of sugar at the field at all times, in case he feels light-headed in the event of hypoglycemia.[35] New treatments such as the latest generation of insulin pumps show tremendous promise for diabetes control.

Type II diabetes usually occurs in adults who can still produce insulin, but have an inability to process it properly at the insulin receptors. Obesity is a main cause of Type II diabetes, so staying in shape and playing soccer for a lifetime will drastically decrease one's chances of developing Type II diabetes.

Heart Conditions

Heart conditions occur worldwide, and are either congenital (present at birth) or acquired later in life. Both types need to be recognized by a routine physical examination in order for a young person to play demanding sports safely.

Congenital conditions are multiple and range from mild (mitral valve prolapse) to serious (ventricular and/or electrical heart problems). Some congenital heart conditions require surgery in order to live a normal life.

Acquired heart conditions are of many causes under the age of 40. The most common infectious heart problems in soccer players worldwide may be rheumatic fever complications and South American trypanosomiasis (also called "Chagas disease"). Rheumatic fever is more common in developing countries, while Chagas disease is common in poor areas in South America. There can be an acute involvement of the heart in rheumatic fever, or a chronic lesion that only surfaces at age 40 or later. Chagas disease results in a myocarditis that can enlarge the heart and lead to arrhythmias, and is a leading cause of sudden death on the soccer field in South America (usually caused by a fatal arrhythmia). Coronary heart disease due to poor dietary habits and/or smoking is attacking players more frequently under the age of 40, but is fortunately still rare.

Diagnosis of cardiac conditions requires a health worker well trained in the auscultation of heart sounds. Confirmation of specific heart lesions requires a special ultrasound examination of the heart called an echocardiography. These follow-up tests and corrective surgery may be beyond the capacity of many youngsters in developing countries.

Two Brazilian players died suddenly on the field in 2004 from heart disorders. Sao Caetano defender Serginho was known to have a heart condition, but his club allowed him to play anyway, and they were fined 24 league points for doing so after he died. Additionally, Cameroon international Marc-Vivien Foe died during the semi-final of the 2003 Confederation's Cup.

Nwankwo Kanu is one of the most successful African players ever. After winning the 1993 FIFA U-17 World Championship with Nigeria, the European Cup, Super Cup and Intercontinental Club Championship with Ajax Amsterdam in 1995, and the Olympic soccer gold medal in 1996, Kanu was found to have a heart condition. He had played in hundreds of amateur and professional games to that point, but had never discovered his serious cardiac

---

[35] Brian Scheuer was an inspiration to the author when both were youths, as he played soccer at a high skill level while managing his diabetes.

problem. He underwent successful heart surgery, recovered fully, was named African Footballer of the Year in 1996 and 1999, and participated in the 1998 and 2002 World Cups for Nigeria. As of 2006 he is still playing club soccer for West Bromwich Albion.

Khalilou Fadiga, a 30-year old midfielder who gave an excellent World Cup performance for the 2002 Senegal team, was found to have a heart arrhythmia that required a surgically implanted defibrillator in 2004. Although some Italian physicians opined that Fadiga could be endangering his life if he continued playing, he received a clearance from British physicians and started playing again for his Bolton Wanderers club at the end of 2004.

Developing Country Problems

There are four special medical conditions in the developing world that result in the poor development of children and their lower extremities, thus risking their ability to play soccer at a high level. They are (1) polio, (2) rickets, (3) club foot, and (4) injuries from land mines. These are addressed here as *bona fide preventable medical problems*; everybody can contribute to prevent these conditions from affecting the world's children and their ability to play the beautiful game.

Polio

Polio is a timeless scourge that causes body paralysis (usually of the legs), meningitis, or death. Polio is caused by the poliovirus, and can be prevented by multiple vaccinations with the oral poliovirus vaccine (OPV). There is currently a massive campaign led by the World Health Organization to eradicate polio from the few developing countries that still harbor the disease (campaign website at www.polioeradication.org). Polio would only be the second disease to be eradicated from humanity, as smallpox was eradicated in 1977 after a similar massive international effort. As of 2006, the poliovirus is still active in selected areas in Asia and Africa, especially India and Nigeria. Children with polio are usually prevented from playing soccer, as the affected limb loses coordination and power and withers away from disuse. However, a child occasionally recovers from polio and can perform at a high level in soccer. Comprehensive rehabilitation services are critical to optimal recovery from polio.

Rickets

Rickets is a nutritional-deficiency syndrome resulting from a lack of Vitamin D in the body. Typically occurring in poverty stricken areas from a Vitamin D deficiency in a growing child's diet, rickets may strike in tandem with malnutrition. Endogenous Vitamin D production in the skin is stimulated by sunlight, so a child in the tropics is normally less susceptible to rickets. The typical lesion produced by rickets is severe curvature of the legs, causing an irregular bow-legged gait.

Clubfoot

Clubfoot is a congenital condition known medically as *talipes*. At birth or shortly thereafter in an affected baby, talipes can be noticed when a foot is not growing in the correct direction. With the recognition and prompt low-technology treatment of talipes, the baby will walk and lead a normal life. The treatment required involves placing the affected foot in a cast or brace in the direction that it needs to grow properly [Figure 18A].

A major problem develops if the condition is not recognized promptly or if no treatment is available, and surgery may be necessary if there has been no non-invasive treatment before the baby is 6 months old. In many poor countries children receive no treatment, and their foot grows abnormally into a club shape making it impossible to walk. Another congenital condition manifesting in infancy is *congenital hip dislocation* (CHD), which some poor children do not receive the basic treatment necessary to correct. These children with talipes or CHD are most often consigned to the lowest rung of society's ladder, dragging themselves along by their hands in the dirt (or in a little cart if they are lucky), or on crutches if only one leg was affected. For lack of recognition and a low-tech cure, these children's lives are effectively erased.

Land Mine Injury

Injuries from land mines and cluster bombs are an epidemic in the recent wars of Afghanistan, Angola, Vietnam, Cambodia, Iraq, and other lands. Land mines can be made cheaply (under US $1.00) and are often designed to maim rather than kill an adult, evolving them into tactical weapons used to terrorize civilian communities. When a child steps on an "anti-personnel mine" or "cluster bomblet" the injuries can be quite horrific, and tissue damage requiring amputation of limbs is common. These injuries result in a lifetime loss of production for the individual and his community. The environment is also affected because farmland is made useless by the presence of landmines, as they may detonate 20 years or more from the time they were placed.

Use of land mines and cluster bombs runs counter to the Geneva Convention, and should be opposed by the international soccer community. David Ginola – a quality former French national team striker – has been active in the anti-landmine effort in recent years. The International Campaign to Ban Landmines (ICBL) led by Jody Williams justifiably won the Nobel Peace Prize in 1997 – incredibly just six years after ICBL's inception.

All of the above conditions lead to poor development or destruction of the legs, which are necessary not only to play soccer but to contribute fully to agrarian societies. Soccer players worldwide should be cognizant of these facts, and endeavor to eliminate these conditions in the worldwide soccer community.

The great modern player Garrincha of Brazil was affected by one or more of these conditions. Although Garrincha's left leg was curved outward while the right curved inward, he ingeniously developed a wicked body swerve that could fool even the most astute defender. Depending on which source you read, Garrincha suffered from a birth defect, polio, or malnutrition-induced rickets.[36] Since his condition is sometimes reported as originating from birth, he might have had a congenital leg condition. But polio can strike very young, and one leg shorter than the other is typical for polio but rare for rickets. So it is quite possible Garrincha was a childhood polio survivor with a deformity who later played top-flight soccer. He likely also suffered from malnutrition as he grew up in poverty.

Many countries have more than one of these conditions present -- Afghanistan has all four. A 1999 cartoon from the Peshawar *Frontier Post* (Pakistan) newspaper revealed the Afghan population's predicament in four panels:

1. The first panel shows a boy receiving the OPV polio vaccine drops in his mouth.
2. The second panel shows the boy and his mother walking away happily.
3. The third panel shows an explosion.
4. The final panel reveals the unhappy boy with only one leg, the unhappy result that the OPV vaccine was meant to prevent.

While the boy avoided polio's potential paralysis, he still lost use of his leg because of the ever-present landmines in his country.

---

[36] Ruy Castro's book *Garrincha: The Triumph and Tragedy of Brazil's Forgotten Footballing Hero* claims Garrincha's leg condition was present from birth, which would make it a congenital condition (like clubfoot). It still would not rule out him having had malnutrition (likely) or polio (possible) as well.

TOXICITIES

Toxicity conditions include societal approved substances, as well as doping and addiction conditions. Toxicities are divided into two types, *Legal* and *Illegal*, but all toxicities can be extremely harmful and lead to destruction of the body and even death.

Legal Toxins

There are two very important toxicities that annually lead to millions of deaths worldwide: alcohol and tobacco.

Alcohol

Many soccer players have been caught up in the macho drinking world of the male athlete, especially in the 1960s to 1980s. It is important to realize that different individuals do not have equivalent abilities to detoxify alcohol (ethanol); an equal amount of alcohol will result in a hangover for one individual while resulting in liver damage in another. It is still very difficult (if not impossible) to predict which individuals will be the more susceptible to liver damage. Therefore, it is imperative that if one is going to drink alcoholic spirits, to always imbibe in moderation. Moderation translates to a maximum of one to two beers or glasses of wine per day.

In many poor countries ethanol is cheap, of poor quality, and sometimes contaminated, as peddlers exploit the unhealthy option that temporarily blocks out the horrors of grinding poverty. Sometimes cheap ethanol is mixed with other chemicals, such as methanol, which when ingested leads to toxic blindness or death. Other ethanol impurities such as lead contribute to kidney failure and death.

There have been many players who have suffered from alcohol toxicity, and there have been some great ones. There are five players of the highest caliber that have fought a battle with alcohol: Garrincha, Jimmy Greaves, George Best, Gerd Müller, and Johan Neeskens. They were caught up in the world of alcohol while they were playing, as their superb physical conditioning allowed them to drink and perform while they were young. But they later endured addiction to alcohol and often suffered resultant liver damage. There is usually no cure for liver damage – only the complete cessation of alcohol intake can prevent further damage. In grave cases a liver transplant is necessary for survival, which George Best underwent in 2002. Against doctors' orders, Best drank alcohol again after his transplant, and he subsequently died of liver failure in November 2005 – demonstrating the perilous nature of alcohol addiction. It is only hoped that each of the three living men can completely avoid alcohol for the rest of their lives.

A liver transplant was not an option for Brazilian football wizard Garrincha, who also died from alcoholic liver disease. Despite being one of the world's greatest ever talents, Garrincha fell into the grasp of alcoholism reinforced by the poverty he endured. He played at a time when salaries were low and football clubs virtually owned the players (at that time players had no bargaining power to elevate their salaries or force a move to another team). Although Brazilians had a huge outpouring of sadness for Garrincha when he died in 1983, it came too late to help the "Little Bird."

Smoking

Native Americans used tobacco in sacred rituals for millennia, but did not suffer ill health due to their infrequent religious use. However, after Europeans arrived in the American continent and encountered tobacco it was swiftly marketed worldwide. Today, multinational tobacco companies specifically target young people and market their products worldwide. Unfortunately, tobacco companies have learned that sponsoring sports events will attract teenagers and convert them to smokers for life. The number of young people, especially women, which start smoking today is increasing and is alarming to international public health workers.

Soccer players have not been immune to the allure of smoking, especially since tobacco companies advertised actively in the sport. For example, FIFA allowed tobacco companies to advertise their toxic products at the World Cup Finals as late as the 1986 World Cup. It seems incongruous to mix smoking with soccer, as soccer is the most physically demanding of the team sports. But some players can smoke and succeed for some years, as their youth is enough to camouflage the obvious drop-off in stamina. Ex-players in their 40s, 50s, and 60s begin to suffer the ravages of smoking damage, which are primarily lung, heart, and vascular diseases.

Perhaps the most striking example of a star soccer player smoking was Johan Cruyff. After he retired at thirty-seven years old he became a full-time coach (which is likely more stressful than playing), and his smoking habit probably increased from his playing days. Toxic tobacco smoke – much the same as alcohol – has unpredictable dosage effects on an individual. Some individuals have a very low tolerance for the toxin before they begin to suffer side effects while others have a high tolerance at the same dosage level. Cruyff's individual tolerance was lower and he suffered a heart attack in his early forties. He was forced to immediately give up smoking, and he made a wonderful anti-smoking advertisement for the Catalan Public Health Department that should be broadcast every day all over the world. In the television spot, Cruyff is dressed like a coach in a long trench coat. But he produces a *package of cigarettes and proceeds to juggle it like a soccer ball.* Foot, thigh, chest, head (twice), shoulder – sixteen times in all – and BAM! He kicks the cigarettes away forever [Figure 6D]. Throughout the commercial he speaks in Catalan about the dangers of smoking. It is a very powerful message by one of the greatest players ever.[37]

Fortunately, Cruyff kicked his tobacco habit and remains healthy. Many players have not been able to kick the habit and have succumbed to the ravages of lung cancer, emphysema, heart attack, and stroke brought on by tobacco use. For example, Sócrates of Brazil should take Cruyff's advice and quit smoking before he sustains significant permanent lung damage (Sócrates is also a pediatrician).

The message for soccer players regarding legal substances is: imbibe alcohol only in moderation and *never drink before driving*, and *NO tobacco*. Following this advice can help a player attain his optimal physical state.

Illegal Toxins

FIFA has outlawed dozens of illegal substances to date. These range from illegal drugs like cocaine and heroin, prescription drugs like narcotic painkillers, to over-the-counter drugs containing ephedrine.

FIFA has divided illegal drugs into six categories: (1) stimulants, (2) narcotic analgesics, (3) anabolic steroids, (4) diuretics, (5) peptide and glycoprotein hormones and related substances, and (6) other drugs. Some of the most important drugs and their potential effects on a soccer athlete are described below.

NON-FORMULARY DRUGS
Cocaine
Cocaine – pure pharmaceutical grade

Diego Maradona used cocaine for years until he was caught in 1991 and he subsequently served out a long suspension. Although cocaine is a powerful stimulant, it is unlikely Maradona's performance was enhanced because of the psychological depressant effect between highs. It is certain that Maradona damaged his own playing career by using cocaine, and he is lucky to still be alive in 2006. Imagine the player Maradona could have been if he had dedicated the time to training that he used taking cocaine and recovering from its effects.

---

[37] The Cruyff video was sponsored by the Generalitat de Catalunya (GENCAT) Departament de Salut (Catalan Department of Health) and produced by Barcelona advertising firm Ogilvy. In order to further the anti-smoking public health message it was created to address – Johan Cruyff, Ogilvy, and GENCAT graciously allowed a photo reproduction from the video for this book project (see photos in back of book). The video is still viewable on the GENCAT website at: www.gencat.net/salut/depsan/units/sanitat/html/ca/tabac/doc6816.html.

Like all drug substances, people react differently to different doses. Maradona could easily have overdosed from super-pure cocaine that was undoubtedly provided for him. Or he could have ingested toxic substances that are used to dilute or "cut" the cocaine, such as PCP (phencyclidine, commonly known as "angel-dust"). Cocaine addiction is more of a mental addiction than physical, and may take up to 18 months for a real cure that requires continual reinforcement. Maradona attempted to kick his cocaine habit in Cuba in 2001-2002, but fell critically ill with a severe heart attack in 2004 and entered yet another rehabilitation program (which was ultimately successful).

Argentine national striker Claudio Caniggia was also a user of cocaine and served a suspension. Caniggia quit cocaine and enjoyed a late revival with Rangers of Scotland, and a call-up to the national team for the 2002 World Cup. Hopefully, they have both left their cocaine nightmares behind forever.

Cocaine – unrefined

Refined cocaine is beyond the means of the poor of the world, but the cocaine barons have developed two other cocaine types in order to quickly addict them. In South America, it is the unrefined *pasta basica de cocaina* (PBC) that comes straight out of the jungle labs to be smoked in the slums of the cities. In the developed world, it is *crack cocaine* that is smoked in the ghettoes of North America. Both have the capability to cause death due to the direct toxicity of the cocaine or thru contaminants, and their use precludes any serious soccer activity.

Cocaine - natural

Testing positive for cocaine may not necessarily mean an individual has ingested pharmaceutical grade cocaine. Cocaine comes from refining the coca bush, which is a staple tea source in all Andean countries, as coca tea has been used to combat altitude sickness for centuries in Bolivia, Peru, and Ecuador. When Bolivia beat Brazil 2-0 in La Paz in 1993, two players were found to have trace amounts of cocaine metabolites in their urine after the game. These were deduced to be residues from the local coca tea they drank to help adjust to the altitude, and the players were not fined or suspended. However, since that time, players do not drink coca tea when arriving at altitude, lest they set off the drug testing monitors.

Amphetamines

Amphetamines were used more frequently in the 1960s and 1970s before chemical testing was available. They are generally perceived as performance enhancing, but when they wear off, the depressive effects can severely deplete a professional player's stamina. Players who abused amphetamines were also frequently abusers of alcohol and/or "downers" in an attempt to control their chemical conditioning and mood. Most often that personal control turned out to be an illusion.

Additionally, amphetamine overdose or use in competitive sports may cause sudden death. The latest designer amphetamine (methamphetamine) renders an individual much too unstable to play soccer. Amphetamine doping still continues today, but on a much smaller scale due to effective drug testing and awareness of the medical risks.

Marijuana

Marijuana is less a performance-enhancing drug than a hallucinogen that can adversely affect coordination. Players who have smoked the leaves will urine-test positive for tetrahydrocannibanol (THC), the active ingredient in marijuana. THC can show up in a urine test months after the last use of marijuana, so even if a player occasionally smokes marijuana, he will easily be caught. The toxic danger to marijuana itself is low, but if the marijuana plants have been sprayed with the pesticide paraquat, then there is potential for serious illness or death after smoking.

Heroin, Opium, LSD, Ecstasy

Heroin and opium are hard-core narcotics, and LSD (lysergic acid diethylamide) and Ecstasy (MDMA – methylenedioxymethamphetamine) are synthetic hallucinogens. It is impossible to perform at a professional level with even casual use of these substances. Heroin and opium are frequently causes of overdose deaths, while Ecstasy has caused a number of deaths due to physiologic dehydration. Drug testing for these substances is straightforward, and abuse of these substances is rare in international football.

PRESCRIPTION and PERFORMANCE DRUGS
Steroids

The steroid group encompasses many substances that mimic natural body hormones that control stress and growth characteristics. Anabolic steroids that are structurally similar to the male hormone *testosterone* are the most used steroid class in sport. However, chronic use of these steroids can develop into several classic toxic medical problems: liver damage, sperm malfunction, psychosis, hyperglycemia, diabetes, hypertension, and even death. Why some athletes persist in using such dangerous drugs to artificially "bulk up their body" in an unsportsmanlike fashion is for one reason only – greed.

Steroids have been used extensively in other sports to increase muscle mass and power. Sports such as swimming, track and field, and weightlifting, which have the goal of getting somewhere fastest or lifting the most weight, have most often been the target of steroid users.

Soccer is a much more complicated sport that does not involve repetitive motion challenging the exact same muscle groups. Therefore, it is very doubtful that a player using steroids could get much of a soccer advantage. Additionally, steroid use is fairly easy to detect as they remain in the body a long time, and the prospects of being caught and receiving a long suspension are high. Therefore, the risk-reward ratio for steroid use in soccer is heavily on the risk side.

Several soccer players have been recently cited for steroid abuse in an alarming trend of use of the illegal steroid *nandrolone*, and a recent doping case may even have affected the 2002 World Cup. Key Dutch team members Edgar Davids and Frank de Boer both tested positive for the steroid nandrolone; both denied use of the substance and suspicion centered on the possibility that the steroid was mixed into team nutritional supplements without their knowledge. Nevertheless, they were both suspended through the crucial World Cup qualifying game against Ireland on September 1, 2001. Holland lost 1-0 and was out of the 2002 World Cup. If Holland had won, they would have qualified had they subsequently beat Iran. Instead, Ireland won the playoff with Iran, and went on to an impressive performance in the 2002 World Cup.

The most recent anabolic steroids detected are the "purely synthetic designer steroids." The first, THG (*tetrahydrogestrinone*) was initially detected in prominent USA track and field athletes in the *Balco scandal* in 2003, which resulted in the suspensions of several potential Olympic athletes. So far no soccer players have been suspected of THG usage, and THG has been banned by all international sports agencies. The World Anti-Doping Agency (WABA) reported in 2005 that a second designer steroid, DMT (*desoxy-methyl-testosterone*), had been detected. Unfortunately, the sports world will likely see the continual manufacture of new "designer" steroids.

Narcotics

Legal narcotics (codeine, morphine, and oxycodone) are rarely used by players unless recovering from an operation or illness. However, *Oxycontin* (controlled-release oxycodone) use has become an addiction epidemic in the USA, and resulted in dozens of deaths from overdose. Narcotic use is determined without difficulty in routine drug testing.

EPO

Erythropoietin (EPO) is a natural hormone made in the kidneys, which stimulates the bone marrow to make more red blood cells. The increased red blood cell mass means more oxygen carrying capability that can translate into improved stamina – but at the risk of suffering a stroke as a side effect. EPO use has replaced "blood doping," the practice of withdrawing a unit of blood three weeks prior, and then replacing it just before competition. Since both EPO and blood doping involve manipulation of natural substances (EPO and blood cells, respectively), the monitoring of these doping activities is more difficult.

EPO abuse has been a problem in bicycling contests and some Olympic endurance sports. EPO abuse made news in the soccer world in November 2004, when a Juventus doctor was convicted of providing EPO to club players in the 1990s, a conviction that placed an ethical cloud over the impressive performances of the Juventus team in that era. However, the conviction was overturned on appeal in December 2005.

The international sports groups are currently standardizing the monitoring protocols for EPO use or blood doping. These will likely be a combination of the level of red blood cells in the serum, and/or a measure of the EPO level in the blood.

A natural way to increase EPO and red cell output is to train at altitude for one month or more. Therefore, teams that train at altitude may have a psychological and physiological advantage over teams arriving from sea level.

Over-the-counter DRUGS (OTC)

OTC drugs can be bought without a doctor's prescription and vary by country, as in some countries even narcotics are dispensed without a prescription. For purposes of this section, any drug class not covered in the above section is described as an OTC.

Stimulants

In the 1994 World Cup, Argentine superstar Diego Maradona was found to have ingested illegal ephedrine combined with a few other substances on the FIFA banned drugs list. Maradona claimed that he had innocently taken a cold medicine that contained the drugs. Ephedrine is an OTC drug commonly used in cold medications, but at higher and continuous dosages it is a stimulant that can help with weight loss. It is probable that ephedrine was used intentionally to help Maradona lose weight and get in shape before the 1994 World Cup, but according to FIFA that is an illegal drug action. Maradona suffered a second ban from soccer as a result of his positive test, Argentina did not recover from the psychological blow from the loss of their team leader, and they lost in the second round of the Cup.

Herbal supplements

Ephedra (also known as *ma huang*) is an OTC herbal preparation that contains ephedrine. This herbal preparation is suspected to have caused dozens of deaths in the last decade in the USA, and is especially dangerous in the dehydrated athlete. In 2001 it was banned by the USA-football NFL league, and it was ruled a causative factor in the death of a professional baseball player Steve Bechler in 2003. Routine drug testing records the drug metabolites of this herb combination.

Results of Doping Tests: 2002 World Cup and Other Testing

For the first time in a World Cup Finals, the 2002 edition utilized blood drug testing in conjunction with the standard urine testing. Two hundred and fifty-six players were tested without a single positive doping result, thereby giving the tournament a clean bill of health.

FIFA Chief Medical Officer Jiri Dvorak succinctly summed up the argument why soccer players should not use illegal substances: "It's obvious that football is a simple game, but one which involves a combination of things to make a fantastic player. It requires not only endurance but motor skills, coordination, flexibility, mental fitness - many attributes. It's difficult to believe that there would be a substance that could cover so many physical and mental variables that together makes a good footballer, and this is what we try to explain."

Nutritional Supplements

A good, balanced diet will contain all of the vitamins and minerals that an athlete needs. Athletes are now being pressured to accept nutritional supplements as part of team regimens, which likely have more psychological than physical benefit. While extra water-soluble vitamins (B vitamins) will be excreted in the urine, extra calcium and minerals may occasionally lead to kidney stone formation. Additionally, fat-soluble vitamins (Vitamin A, D & E) may be toxic to the body if taken in amounts greater than advised.

Soccer players and their clubs must be super-vigilant, as some products marketed simply as nutritional supplements may contain performance enhancers, or worse (see the Dutch steroid experience above). There can be no more excuses for positive drug testing results.

Prevention of Disease and Optimization of Performance

Physical Prevention

Physical examination

Children should receive a complete physical examination before they start competitive soccer play. Rarely, sudden death in any sport may be due to a congenital heart condition that may be detected before play.

Routine soccer physical exams for children should include examining the cardiac system (heart) for congenital defects, the musculoskeletal system for assessing old injuries, and to check for hernias.

By the time a child becomes a potentially sexually active adolescent, the physical exam should become more comprehensive, to include checking the blood pressure, rechecking the heart, lungs, abdomen, skin, muscles and joints, and the genitals for lesions or testicular masses (testicular cancer is most common in young men).

Counseling and Instruction

Adolescents need extensive counseling and guidance, including instruction on risk factors for sexually transmitted infectious diseases and safe sex practices, and alcohol, tobacco, and drug avoidance counseling. *The counseling and instructional actions at this age will save many more lives than the actual physical examinations.*

Diet

A balanced diet must be emphasized in adolescence when food is more fashion than sustenance. Excessive "junk food" diets may lead to vitamin deficiencies, kidney stones, obesity, hypertension, and diabetes. A one-a-day complete vitamin tablet can help adolescents receive all the necessary vitamins, but cannot prevent them from becoming obese due to poor dietary habits.

Blood Testing

Consideration should be given to blood testing when an adolescent or young athlete is becoming sexually active. *Knowledge is power*, and if a young person tests negative, then he will know there is a possibility he may test positive in the future if he does not protect himself. He should also insist on his partner being tested, and on entering into a monogamous relationship with the knowledge of their health status.

Blood testing should not just be done for HIV, but also for sexually transmitted viruses Hepatitis B and Hepatitis C. The three-stage Hepatitis B vaccine should be given to all sexually active persons, but there is no Hepatitis C vaccine yet available.

Mental Development

Mental development is enhanced by both *behavioral* and *spiritual* development. Positive behavioral development comes from:
1. Family and community support
2. Mentor availability
3. Reinforcement of good behaviors
    a. Honesty
    b. Humility
    c. Respect for others
    d. Striving for excellence
4. Avoidance of harmful behaviors:
    a. Sexual activity when the individual is mentally unprepared
    b. Unsafe sex
    c. Smoking/Alcohol/Drugs (SAD)

Mental development is also a lifelong spiritual process, with the optimal end result being a person who displays confidence, humility, and a spirit of brotherhood. When one person becomes successful it is most often the result of a whole community – however economically poor – that has nourished the individual's progress. The whole world is a community, and players who lose sight of this reality often fall into bad behaviors, and end up feeling alone and fearful of what their future will be after their soccer career is over.

This chapter is in acknowledgement to three of the best players of the modern era who are also medical specialists: Tostão (ophthalmologist), Sócrates (pediatrician), and Hugo Sanchez (dentist). It is heartening to see colleagues who had the ability to pursue a course in medicine while playing top-flight football.

The universal game – a Peruvian boy excels at fútbol despite a maimed left hand.

Soccer Excellence

Chapter Seven

Best Players of the Modern Era 1958-2006

Get out of the street, Roberto!   Title of *Roberto Rivelino's* autobiography
[as he must have been told countless times in his childhood by his mother]

Soccer Legends (pre-1958)

This chapter and the next present the best soccer players and teams in the *Modern Era of Soccer*, defined as the years 1958-2006.[1] These *Modern Era* players were the inspiration of their club, country, and often the world, as their exploits at international tournaments were increasingly televised in the modern era.

The era prior to 1958 is designated the *Legend Era of Soccer*, whose star players are well documented by other authors with direct experience of that epoch. The pre-1958 *Legend Era of Soccer* included some fantastic players, such as Matthias Sindelar of Austria, Luis Monti of Argentina/Spain, Leônidas da Silva of Brazil, Alejandro Villanueva of Peru, Nándor Hidegkuti of Hungary, Obdulio Varela of Uruguay, Fritz Walter of Germany, Stanley Matthews of England, and Max Abegglen of Switzerland. But because of the dearth of game film available those players are truly legends now, existing most vibrantly in the prose of past soccer poets.

The Modern Era of Soccer 1958-2006

The period from 1958-2006 is deemed the *Modern Era of Soccer* because (1) television was beginning to show soccer to a worldwide audience, (2) tactics began to change from overly offensive schemes to more balanced schemes, (3) players emerged from the dark ages of complete club control and began to fight for decent labor rights, and (4) soccer slowly became globalized, with more players performing in countries other than their native lands.

The years 1958 to 2006 cover a period of forty-eight years and the most recent thirteen World Cup Finals. The Modern *Era of Soccer* starts with the inspirational 1958 Brazil World Cup victory in Sweden, until 2002 the only World Cup win by a country out of their home hemisphere. Brazil won their fifth World Cup Finals in Korea/Japan in 2002, to nearly bookend the Modern Era with the only two World Cup Final winners out of their own hemisphere.

---

[1] Selecting players starting from 1958 relates to author preference of listing players seen personally or on video.

Number and Positions of the Best Players

This chapter features a subjective list of the top one hundred and twenty-five soccer players in the Modern Era, presented in the position they performed the most impressively.

Player roles have evolved in the Modern Era, with a special emphasis on intensified defensive play. The number of defenders on the field was increased from 2 to 3 to 4 or even 5 (such as 3 central defenders and 2 wingbacks), midfielders stayed the same at 3 or increased to 4 or even 5, and strikers were reduced from 5 to 4, to 3 or 2, and in extreme cases, even 1 (the dreaded 4-5-1 formation is unfortunately gaining influence amongst modern teams afraid to commit to creative attack).[2]

Because of position changes over the years, the quantity of outfield players have been averaged and compromised. Therefore, *ten goalkeepers, thirty defenders, forty midfielders,* and *forty-five strikers* have been selected. Obviously these numbers do not fit any tactical formation; they are just a historical approximation of the importance of each position over time.

Some players who performed well at more than one position were placed in the group in which they were most dominant and ranked highest. Only seven players – Welshman John Charles, Argentine Alfredo Di Stéfano, Brazilian Pelé, Germans Franz Beckenbauer and Lothar Matthäus, and Dutchmen Johan Cruyff and Frank Rijkaard – performed brilliantly enough in two distinct positions to be mentioned for both. Charles is the lone mention at defense and striker, Cruyff, Di Stéfano, and Pelé are mentioned at midfield and striker, and Beckenbauer, Matthäus, and Rijkaard at defense and midfield.

Qualifications of the Best Players

Selected players must have performed for their national team by 1994 (the year of the 15th World Cup held in the USA). Therefore, some current featured star players are not included because their careers are too young to evaluate for an "all-time" list (for example, 2004-2005 World Player of the Year Ronaldinho started Brazil national team play in 1999).

Each player must have been a stellar club player and had a significant impact on international football. Most players excelled with both club and country; those that were denied an opportunity to play in the greatest soccer theater, the World Cup, must have overcome their absence with impressive international club play.[3]

"Natural Talent" versus Dedication and Training

The concept of "natural talent" in sport is highly overstated. Star players are not "born" as the sport media constantly declares, but developed and shaped during adolescence and early adulthood. There may be some degree of raw athleticism and coordination that may be translatable to sport in general, but sport-specific athleticism develops according to sport-specific development in adolescence. Despite his refined athleticism, Michael Jordan, one of the best modern era basketball players, did not succeed at professional baseball. Jordan's skills would not be translatable to soccer at a professional level without extensive training for at least a decade, beginning in adolescence.

Raw athletic talent needs to be guided, developed, and most importantly, worked on. Pelé started practicing his *futebol* craft under excellent guidance from his father, Dondinho, whose professional football career was cut short by a severe knee injury. Dondinho was then

---

[2] There have been some outlandish formations recently. The USA played a 3-6-1 formation in the 1998 World Cup (3 defense, 6 midfielders, and 1 striker); thankfully, for the future of soccer, it was a miserable failure.
That USA soccer misadventure and other idiosyncrasies are memorialized in the internet soccer satire magazine *ThreeSixOne* at www.kenn.com/361/threesixone_jul1998.jpg and www.kenn.com/361/index.html.
[3] Note: the *Copa Libertadores* is the South American Club Championship, and the *European Champions Cup* has been renamed the *European Champions League*. The *Intercontinental Cup* is the World Club Championship played between the European Champions League and the South American Copa Libertadores winners from 1960-2004.

available to coach his son from an early age, and Pelé had both the optimal drive and guidance for him to succeed at the sport. There are pictures of Diego Maradona kicking a football when he was two years old; Maradona started early, had the motivation to improve and invent, and received proper coaching along the way.

When people say these individuals had "natural talent," they are implying (perhaps unintentionally) that "they were lucky" and/or "did not have to work so hard." But if the best players did not work hard at their development they would have only been average professionals, and certainly never reached the superlative skill levels they attained.

In addition, natural body size is much less important in soccer than in many other sports (see Chapter 2). Most of the best players presented are from 5'6" (168 centimeters) to 6'2" (188 centimeters), a span of only 8 inches (20 centimeters); and most weighed between 150 and 184 pounds (68 – 83 kilograms).

Players versus Tactics

When given a choice, most astute coaches in the Modern Era would choose *players* over *tactics*, i.e., talented players are considered to be more valuable assets than a "genius coach" with his new system. The important dynamics for a coach to explore and exploit are which players can improve a field position, and which system can be adapted to the individual player strengths.

A successful coach in the Modern Era is most often a shrewd player tactician who knows and cares about his players as individuals. When players are confident their needs are being attended to, they are more likely to forgo individual goals for better team play, which is essential for winning soccer.

In short, a group of talented and motivated soccer players will always be more important than mere tactics. Listed below are the players that any international coach would have loved to have had as the backbone of their teams.

Origins of the Best Players

The *best players in the modern era* list is overly top-heavy with Europeans and South Americans. Only three African nationals, and no Asian nationals are presented in the main list. This is simply because Modern Era soccer has been most dominant in Europe and South America, but in the future best players will be generated from all parts of the world. A list in twenty years will likely include more Africans and Asians as soccer development in those areas of the world is elevated.[4]

However, *most areas of the world have been represented on the list*, as many South Americans are multiethnic, (with ancestry from Asian, African, European, and/or indigenous peoples), and many "European" nationals are multiethnic as well. This means that many ethnic groups in the world are represented on the list, only *not* by traditional nationality.

By perusing this exceptional list, one is exposed to the incredible diversity of the human organism. Football players from all over the globe have come together to form a virtual team – one of unique spatial and temporal creativity. These are a selection of the best soccer artists that epitomize creative soccer, and collectively they form the promise of a positive soccer future.

---

[4] The lack of African and Asians on the list is not due to lack of talent but to lack of opportunity on the world stage until recently. But as an example, one of the greatest strikers of the 20th century was *Paulino Alcántara* from Iloilo in the Visayas area of the Philippines. Alcántara was born in 1896 to a Spanish father and Filipina mother when Spain still controlled the Philippines. He moved to Barcelona in 1910 and made his debut in Barcelona's first team at age 15 in 1912, scoring three goals in an 8-2 win. Alcántara played for Barça until 1927, and remains their all-time goal leader with 374 goals in 375 games. Alcántara also played for both the Filipino and Spanish national teams, and in his initial Spanish appearance he scored both goals in a win against Belgium. Playing for Spain, he scored six goals in five appearances. He is especially remembered for the match against France in Bordeaux in 1922, when his powerful scoring shot perforated the net. Despite his international team success, Alcántara's appearances were rationed by diligent attention to his medical studies.

Player Profile Template
[Data for active players is accurate only to March 30, 2006]

[Player Rank] Name   Country Represented   Birth date [Day/Month/Year]

[Summary of National and Club Career]

Awards: Awards received.
International: Appearances and goals scored.
World Cup: Years played. Appearances and goals scored.
Club: Clubs listed in chronological order [with one exception – if a player returned to a team later in his career, the team name is not duplicated).

Best Goalkeepers

1 Lev Yashin   **(Soviet Union)**   22.10.29

Lev Yashin was known as the "Black Spider" or "Black Octopus" because of his size, agility, and all-black uniform. Yashin had the knack for making impossible saves look routine, and brought good Soviet Union teams farther in international competitions than they otherwise would have progressed.

Yashin's goalkeeping talents helped the Soviet Union win the soccer Olympic Gold in 1956, and the first European Championship in 1960 (the Soviet Union finished second to Spain in 1964). He also led the Soviet Union in three World Cups, where they twice finished first in their group, and progressed to the second round each time (quarterfinals in 1958 & 1962, and semi-finals in 1966). His performances for Dynamo Moscow kept them on top of the Soviet league for more than a decade, winning five Soviet championships.

Yashin was so dominant a force in the nets that in 1963 he became the *only goalkeeper ever* to win the European Footballer of the Year. He also won six European Goalkeeper of the year awards (awarded to the highest rated goalkeeper for European Footballer of the Year), and is credited with 150 penalty kick saves. Not surprisingly, the *FIFA Best Goalkeeper of the World Cup Award* is now called the Yashin Award.

Awards: 1963 European Footballer of the Year.
European Goalkeeper of the Year six times.
2002 FIFA World Cup Dream Team.
Planète Foot (France) best 50 players of all time.
World Soccer's 100 Greatest Footballers of all time.
France Football's Footballer of the Century (# 10).
International: 79 games.
World Cup: 1958, 1962, 1966, & 1970 (did not play); 14 games with 5 shutouts.
Club: Dynamo Moscow.

2 Dino Zoff   **(Italy)**   28.02.42

Dino Zoff was medium in stature but quick on his feet and had excellent positioning and shot-stopping skills. Zoff was Italy's goalkeeper when they won the 1968 European Championship, but he deferred to Enrico Albertosi as Italy lost the 1970 World Cup Final against Pelé's Brazil. Zoff then became Italy's indisputable keeper after the 1972 European Championships, and eventually captained and kept goal impressively for the Italian side that won the 1982 World Cup in Spain. At 40 years old, he was the oldest player at that Cup.

Zoff did not concede a goal for twelve consecutive national team matches (from 7 October 1972 until 15 June 1974) for a total of 1,142 consecutive minutes, an international record. At club level, Zoff won six Italian league championships and the 1977 UEFA Cup with Juventus. The only title that escaped him was the European Cup, which Juventus lost in 1973 and 1983 (when Zoff was 41 years old). After retirement, he coached Lazio (winning the 1990 UEFA Cup) and the Italian national team from 1998-2000.

Awards: 1973 European Footballer of the Year voting, 2nd after Johan Cruyff.
Planète Foot (France) best 50 players of all time.
World Soccer's 100 Greatest Footballers of all time.
France Football's Footballer of the Century (# 18).
France Football's World Cup Top-100 1930-1990.
2004 Pelé/FIFA Best 125 Living Players.
International: 112 games, 0.81 goals against per match.
World Cup: 1970 (did not play) 1974, 1978, & 1982; 17 games with 5 shutouts.
Clubs: Udinese, Mantova, Napoli, Juventus.

3 Gordon Banks (England) 20.12.37

Gordon Banks was average-sized but quick and agile, and his strongest asset was his football knowledge and positional play. An unshakable goalkeeper to build a team around, Banks was instrumental in helping England win their only World Cup in 1966. His overall World Cup record was stellar, with 0.60 goals per game allowed for his career.

Banks is particularly known for *"The Save,"* a reflex save from a brilliant Pelé header in the 1970 World Cup; an action that still appears impossible when viewed on video. Pelé made a picture-perfect downward header aimed inside the post, but Banks somehow dove down and *flicked it over the crossbar*. Banks played with modest clubs in his career, but he won the League Cup with both Leicester City and Stoke City. Banks lost an eye in an accident in 1973, but he came back to play successfully in the NASL (North American Soccer League) in 1977.

Awards: 1972 English Footballer of the Year Award.
France Football's World Cup Top-100 1930-1990.
Planète Foot (France) best 50 players of all time.
World Soccer's 100 Greatest Footballers of all time.
2004 Pelé/FIFA Best 125 Living Players.
International: 72 games.
World Cup: 1962 (did not play), 1966, & 1970; 9 games with 6 shutouts.
Clubs: Chesterfield, Leicester City, Stoke City, Fort Lauderdale.

4 Ubaldo Fillol (Argentina) 21.07.50

Ubaldo Fillol was a goalkeeper with some of the fastest reflexes to ever play the game. Fillol started out as a midfielder, and ended up as a brilliant athletic keeper who kept goal for Argentina in three World Cups. His shot-blocking and positional play was a major reason (along with Mario Kempes and Daniel Passarella) why Argentina was able to win the 1978 World Cup at home.

On the club side, Fillol won three Argentine championships with River Plate, and the South American Super Cup with Racing Club. As a goalkeeper, it was quite a tribute to his abilities that he was in the running for the South American Footballer of the Year many times. Fillol stayed in the game after retirement, coaching Racing in 2004.

Awards: All-Century South America XI Team.
1977 Argentine Player of the Year.
South American Footballer of the Year voting, placed 2nd three times (1978, 1983, 1984), and in the top five three additional years.
International: 58 games.
World Cup: 1974, 1978, & 1982; 13 games with 4 shutouts.
Clubs: Quilmes, Racing Club, River Plate, Argentinos Juniors, Flamengo, Atlético Madrid, Vélez Sarsfield.

5 Sepp Maier   (West Germany)   24.02.44

Sepp Maier was an outstanding athletic and cerebral keeper for the great West Germany and Bayern Munich teams in the 1970s. He was one of the "magic trio" featuring Franz Beckenbauer and Gerd Müller, and all starred for both Bayern Munich and West Germany.

With Bayern Munich, Maier won four West Germany league championships, four West Germany Cups, the 1972 UEFA Cup, three consecutive European Cups (1974, 1975, 1976), and the 1976 Intercontinental Cup.

As the undisputed West Germany goalkeeper, he won the 1972 European championship and the 1974 World Cup with an active style that left no doubt who was running the defense.

Awards: 1975, 1977, & 1978 West Germany Footballer of the Year.
France Football's World Cup Top-100 1930-1990.
2004 Pelé/FIFA Best 125 Living Players.
International: 95 games.
World Cup: 1970, 1974, & 1978; 18 games with 8 shutouts.
Clubs: Bayern Munich.

6 Peter Schmeichel   (Denmark)   18.11.63

Peter Schmeichel was a first-rate shot-stopper; large but agile, and quick off his line. Schmeichel anchored Denmark's surprising conquest of the 1992 European Championship, shutting out the powerful 1990 World Cup-winning German team in the Final.

Schmeichel also kept goal for Manchester United's great teams in the 1990s, keeping a "clean sheet" (shutout) in nearly half of the matches he played. He won five league championships with Manchester United; his last match was the Red Devils' 1999 European Champions' Cup winning match against Bayern Munich. He finished out his career with Manchester City in 2003.

Stylistically, he was one of the few European keepers to advance into scoring positions; he had one international goal and several club goals (including a headed goal against Rotor Volgograd in the 1995 UEFA Cup competition).

Awards: 1995 European Goalkeeper of the year.
1992 & 1993 World Goalkeeper of the year [rated by the IFFHS[5]].
2003 Second non-British inductee into the National Football Museum Hall of Fame (first was Eric Cantona in 2002).
2004 Pelé/FIFA Best 125 Living Players.
International: 129 games with 1 goal.
World Cup: 1998; 5 games with 1 shutout.
Clubs: Hvidøvre, Brondby, Manchester United, Sporting Lisbon, Aston Villa, Manchester City.

7 José Luis Chilavert   (Paraguay)   27.07.65

José Luis Chilavert was a rare combination of a stellar goalkeeper as well as successful free kick and penalty specialist for both club and country. He continued the diversification of the goalkeeper position with outfield play, as had other Latin American goalkeepers Hugo Gatti, Rene Higuita, and Jorge Campos. Chilavert holds the unofficial goalkeeping record of sixty-two goals in official club and country matches.[6]

His most valuable goal for Paraguay was a penalty against Argentina in Buenos Aires, earning Paraguay a World Cup qualifying 1 - 1 draw, and he scored three penalty goals against Argentina in his career. He once had a penalty kick hat trick for his Vélez Sarsfield club against Ferro Carril Oeste, and twice scored from free-play in a game. It must have been intimidating for the opposing keeper to see his large contemporary advancing on set plays attempting to score.

Chilavert led his club Velez Sarsfield to the ultimate prizes in 1994, the Copa Libertadores and the Intercontinental Club Cup. Rock-solid in goal, Chilavert mobilized a good Paraguayan side into extra-time against a great French team in the 1998 World Cup Finals, by which Paraguay lost 1-0 by a golden goal (in sudden-death overtime). He led Paraguay again in the 2002 World Cup, in which he played three games. His positional play was superb against eventual runner-up Germany, as he was beaten only from short range by an Oliver Neuville volley.

---

[5] International Federation of Football History & Statistics; Wiesbaden, Germany. Website: www.iffhs.de.
[6] As of 17.04.06, Rogério Ceni of São Paulo FC has 58 goals, and is likely to soon surpass Chilavert's record.

In 1995 Chilavert became the only goalkeeper to date to receive the *South American Footballer of the Year* award (he also came in second in 1994, and third in 1996 and 1997).

  Awards: 1995 South American Footballer of the Year.
             1995, 1997, & 1998 Best Goalkeeper in the World.
             Six consecutive best South American goalkeeper awards (1994-1999).
             1996 Argentine League Player of the Year.
  International: 74 games with 8 goals.
  World Cup: 1986 (did not play), 1998, & 2002; 7 games with 2 shutouts.
  Clubs: Sportivo Luqueño, Guarani, San Lorenzo, Real Zaragoza, Vélez Sarsfield, Racing Strasbourg, Peñarol.

8 Pat Jennings   (Northern Ireland)   12.01.45

Pat Jennings kept goal for and captained Northern Ireland in their headiest World Cup days, as not even George Best had been able to guide them to a World Cup Finals qualification. Jennings made the penalty area his home, and if his perfect positioning failed him, his shot-stopping ability most often did not.

Jennings' greatest game for country was perhaps the 1-0 win over Spain in Valencia in the 1982 World Cup, which brought Ireland through to the second round. His last appearance for country came on his 41st birthday, in a loss to Brazil in the 1986 World Cup.

With Tottenham Hotspur he won the English League Cup in 1971 and 1973, and the initial UEFA Cup in 1972. He also scored a memorable "clearance" goal from free-play for Tottenham Hotspur in the 1967 Charity Shield match against Manchester United at Old Trafford (in Manchester), a match that ended 3-3.

  Awards: 1973 English Footballer of the Year Award.
             1976 Professional Footballers Association Player of the Year.
             France Football's World Cup Top-100 1930-1990.
  International: 119 games.
  World Cup: 1982 & 1986; 7 games with 2 shutouts.
  Clubs: Watford, Tottenham, Arsenal.

9 Walter Zenga   (Italy)   28.04.60

After Dino Zoff, Walter Zenga was Italy's best goalkeeper. Zenga is the only goalkeeper with under 0.5 goals per game average conceded in international games (his career average was a staggering 0.414 goals per game).

Zenga was Italy's goalkeeper as they opened the 1990 World Cup with five straight shutouts, and as a result, he holds the World Cup record for consecutive minutes (517 minutes) without conceding a goal. However, in the semi-final game, Italy lost a penalty kick competition to Argentina after the game had ended 1-1. Italy only won the bronze medal in the 1990 Cup, after winning six games and tying one on their home soil. Italy and Zenga gave up only two goals in seven games, which was tied by France in 1998 for the all-time low-goals record in seven games.

Capping a successful career with Inter Milan, Zenga won the Italian league championship in 1989, and the UEFA Cup in 1991 & 1994.

  Awards: 1989, 1990, & 1991 World's Best Goalkeeper.
             1987 Italian Footballer of the Year.
             France Football's World Cup Top-100 1930-1990.
  International: 58 games.
  World Cup: 1990; 7 games with 5 shutouts.
  Clubs: Inter Milan, Sampdoria, Padua, New England Revolution, National Bucharest.

10 Thomas N'kono   (Cameroon)   20.07.56

Thomas N'kono was a steady and often spectacular keeper who kept goal for the first impressive Sub-Saharan African World Cup team. N'kono kept another outstanding Cameroon keeper, Joseph Antoine Bell, on the sidelines as the second choice keeper for years.

Cameroon was the first African team to advance to the World Cup quarterfinals in 1990, where they lost 2-3 to England in overtime. N'kono could not be blamed, as the tying and winning England goals came on two penalty kicks by Gary Lineker.

N'kono won four league titles and two African Club Championships (1978 & 1980) with Canon Yaounde, and the 1984 African Nations Cup with Cameroon. He migrated to Spain after the 1982 World Cup, and subsequently played nearly a decade with Barcelona side Espanyol, where he became a club goalkeeping idol secondary only to the legendary Ricardo Zamora.

N'kono was the first goalkeeper to win the African Footballer of the Year award, and is the only keeper to win the award twice.

Awards: 1979 & 1982 African Player of the Year.
France Football's World Cup Top-100 1930-1990.
International: 112 games.
World Cup: 1982, 1990, & 1994 (did not play); 8 games with 3 shutouts.
Clubs: Canon Yaounde, Espanyol.

Goalkeeper Runner-ups
(Must have made first national team appearance by 1994)

Immediate runner-ups (considered for original list)
Rinat Dassaiev (Soviet Union), Gilmar (Brazil), Ronnie Hellström (Sweden), Jean-Marie Pfaff (Belgium), Peter Shilton (England) Jan Tomaszewski (Poland).

Complete runner-up list
Vitor Baia (Portugal), Fabien Barthez (France), Joel Bats (France), Joseph Antoine Bell (Cameroon), Jorge Campos (Mexico), Antonio Carbajal (Mexico), Hugo Gatti (Argentina), Sergio Goycoechea (Argentina), Bruce Grobbelaar (Zimbabwe), Michel Preud'homme (Belgium), Thomas Ravelli (Sweden), Reçber Rüstü (Turkey), Claudio Taffarel (Brazil), Badou Zaki (Morocco), Andoni Zubizarreta (Spain).

Best Defenders

Defense positions are called "backs", including center backs (traditionally called a "center-half" in England) and wingbacks, and include the *sweeper* or *libero* position. The old term of "full-back" has been largely abandoned.

1 Franz Beckenbauer (West Germany) 11.09.45

Franz Beckenbauer virtually invented the position of *libero*, the defensive sweeper position able to advance on offensive missions. Originally a midfielder on the 1966 West Germany team that lost to England in the World Cup Final, Beckenbauer had the ability to perform in any position. He could defend by anticipation (most years he played without shin guards, unthinkable for a defender today), create like a "number 10," and score important goals (he had 67 goals in 556 First Division games).

Beckenbauer played in some of the most incredible World Cup games ever. In 1966 he played in the Cup Final, won by England 4-2 in overtime. In the 1970 World Cup semi-final he participated in another thrilling overtime game against Italy, but West Germany lost again 4-3. Finally, in 1974 he captained West Germany to the World Cup Championship over the "total soccer" Dutch team led by Johan Cruyff.

Beckenbauer also led West Germany to the 1972 European Championship and to the 1976 European Championship Final, the latter of which was lost to Czechoslovakia on the first ever penalty kick shootout in a major championship. Beckenbauer elected not to participate in the 1978 World Cup Finals in Argentina, although his ultimate international game for West Germany was in 1981.

He directed his Bayern Munich club to three consecutive European Cup Championships from 1974-1976, a feat matched only by Johan Cruyff's Ajax and Alfredo Di Stéfano's Real Madrid. Beckenbauer also won the 1976 Intercontinental Cup and the 1967 Cup Winner's Cup with Bayern Munich. After leaving Bayern he signed with the New York Cosmos, where he played alongside Pelé, Carlos Alberto, Johan Neeskens, and Giorgio Chinaglia, and contributed to three championships (1977, 1978, and 1980).

After retiring, Beckenbauer coached the German national team to second place in the 1986 Mexico World Cup Finals, and to the 1990 World Cup championship in Italy. He also coached Bayern Munich to the German league and UEFA Cup titles in 1996.

  Awards: 1972 & 1976 European Footballer of the Year.
      1966, 1968, 1974, & 1976 West German Footballer of the Year.
      2002 FIFA World Cup Dream Team.
      1998 FIFA Century XI.
      Planète Foot (France) best 50 players of all time.
      World Soccer's 100 Greatest Footballers of all time.
      France Football's Footballer of the Century (# 6).
      France Football's World Cup Top-100 1930-1990.
      2004 Pelé/FIFA Best 125 Living Players.
  International: 103 games with 14 goals.
  World Cup: 1966, 1970, & 1974; 18 games with 4 goals.
  Clubs: Munich 1906, Bayern Munich, New York Cosmos, Hamburg.

1 Elías Figueroa (Chile) 25.10.46

Elías Figueroa (Elías Ricardo Figueroa Brander) was a central defender from Chile whose career spanned five teams in the Americas. Figueroa was a defensive marshal with a midfielder's technique and a scorer's ability.

Defenders rarely win Footballer of the Year trophies, but Figueroa was such an exceptional performer that he won the South American Footballer of the Year *three years in a row* from 1974-1975-1976 (the first three winners in 1971-1972-1973 were striking and midfield stars Tostão, Nene Cubillas, and Pelé). No defender won the award again until Argentine central defender Oscar Ruggeri in 1991 and Brazilian wing defender Cafú in 1994; no defenders have won since.

Figueroa had a stellar club career that spanned championship teams in three countries; in Uruguay with Peñarol in 1967 & 1968, in Brazil with Internacional of Porto Allegre in 1975, and in Chile with Palestino in 1978. He dominated the game and scored the only goal in Internacional's 1975 Brazilian championship.

Figueroa was the captain of Chile teams that participated in the World Cup Finals in 1966, 1974, and 1982, as his World Cup career spanned sixteen years (Chile did not qualify in 1970 and 1978). He also led Chile to second place in the 1979 Copa America.

> Awards: 1974, 1975, and 1976 South American Footballer of the Year.
> 1976 Brazil Footballer of the Year.
> IFFHS 50 World Players of the Century list.
> *Placar* (Brazil) best 100 players of all time.
> *Placar* (Brazil) Best Brazil League Foreign Footballer ever.
> 2004 Pelé/FIFA Best 125 Living Players.
>
> International: 47 games with 2 goals.
> World Cup: 1966, 1974, & 1982; 9 games.
> Clubs: Santiago Wanderers, Peñarol, Internacional, Palestino, Fort Lauderdale, Colo Colo.

1 Bobby Moore   (England)   17.04.41

Bobby Moore captained England to the 1966 World Cup championship at home, anchoring one of the best back lines ever. Four years later at the 1970 World Cup, none other than Pelé called him the world's finest defender.

Moore played defense mostly by his genius of positional play, as he had an uncanny intuitive sense for where the ball was headed. His timing in the tackle was unmatched, and he was rarely off of his feet while winning the ball back for his team.

He spent most of his English career at West Ham United, winning the European Cup Winners Cup in 1965. He finished off his career at Fulham alongside football iconoclasts George Best and Rodney Marsh, then accompanied them to the green pastures of the NASL in the USA.

> Awards: 1998 FIFA Century XI.
> 1964 English Footballer of the Year Award.
> *Planète Foot* (France) best 50 players of all time.
> *World Soccer's* 100 Greatest Footballers of all time.
> *France Football's* World Cup Top-100 1930-1990.
>
> International: 107 games with 2 goals.
> World Cup: 1962, 1966, & 1970 Cups; 14 games.
> Clubs: West Ham United, Fulham, Seattle Sounders.

4 Franco Baresi   (Italy)   08.05.60

Franco Baresi was the best sweeper back of the late 1980s and early 1990s. He was a football leader with excellent technique, vision, and courage on the pitch.

Baresi was a member of four Italy World Cup squads, and captained Italy to the 1994 World Cup Final against Brazil. Despite knee surgery two weeks before that game, he was still the best defender on the field. An exhausted Baresi probably shouldn't have taken one of the Italian penalty kicks that decided the winner of the tied Final match; he missed.

Baresi played his entire club career at AC Milan during their modern renaissance. Playing alongside Paolo Maldini and the Dutch triumvirate of Frank Rijkaard, Ruud Gullit, and Marco Van Basten, Baresi won the Champions Cup and Intercontinental Cups in 1989 & 1990, the European Super Cup, and six Italian league titles.

> Awards: 1990 Italian Footballer of the Year in 1990.
> Italian Sportsman of the Twentieth Century.
> 1989 European Footballer of the Year voting, 2nd place.
> *Planète Foot* (France) best 50 players of all time.
> *World Soccer's* 100 Greatest Footballers of all time.
> *France Football's* World Cup Top-100 1930-1990.
> 2004 Pelé/FIFA Best 125 Living Players.
>
> International: 81 games with 1 goal.
> World Cup: 1982, 1990, & 1994; 10 games.
> Clubs: AC Milan.

5 Carlos Alberto Torres   (Brazil)   17.07.44

Carlos Alberto Torres captained the 1970 World Cup Final winning Brazilian side, the greatest team of the Modern Era. He was a brilliant positional defender who performed in a composed and elegant style, and always seemed to know where the ball was going. He played both outside and inside defensive positions, and typically made forward runs to support the offense. Carlos Alberto could also score, as demonstrated by his *coup de grace* goal in the 1970 World Cup Final.

Carlos Alberto played for years on Pelé's Santos side, where he won four Paulista championships. Later he played with the New York Cosmos, where he supplanted Franz Beckenbauer from the sweeper position as Beckenbauer successfully returned to midfield. It was a rare treat to watch two such composed and skilled defensive players (and two World Cup-winning captains) perform on the same team. The Cosmos won three NASL championships (1978-1980-1982) with Carlos Alberto directing play from the back.

    Awards: 1998 FIFA Century XI.
                     France Football's World Cup Top-100 1930-1990.
                     Placar (Brazil) best 100 players of all time.
                     2004 Pelé/FIFA Best 125 Living Players.
    International: 58 games with 8 goals.
    World Cup: 1970; 6 games with 1 goal.
    Clubs: Fluminense, Santos, Botafogo, Flamengo, New York Cosmos.

6 Paolo Maldini   (Italy)   26.06.68

Paolo Maldini is a modern left wing and center back with considerable technique and vision. Solid defensively, quick, and with excellent recuperation skills, he often initiated offensive moves for both club and country. He is the son of Cesare Maldini, the coach of the 1998 Italian World Cup team and a former star at AC Milan.

Maldini had massive success in his one-club career with AC Milan. Starting in Serie A at 16 years of age, he subsequently won six Italian titles, four European Cups, and two Intercontinental Cups.

Maldini was captain of Italy for many years, but was unlucky to never lead them to a title. Italy lost the 2000 European Championship Final to France in overtime, and after being eliminated in three successive penalty kick competitions in the 1990, 1994, and 1998 World Cups, Italy lost in overtime to South Korea in the second round of the 2002 World Cup.

Maldini holds the World Cup record of twenty-three consecutive complete games played, as well as the record of 2,217 total minutes of World Cup performance. Although he retired from international competition in 2002, he was still performing at top level for Milan in 2006.

    Awards: 1994 *World Soccer* Footballer of the Year.
                     1994 European Footballer of the Year voting, 3rd place.
                     2002 FIFA World Cup Dream Team.
                     Planète Foot (France) best 50 players of all time.
                     World Soccer's 100 Greatest Footballers of all time.
                     France Football's World Cup Top-100 1930-1990.
                     2004 Pelé/FIFA Best 125 Living Players.
    International: 126 games with 7 goals.
    World Cup: 1990, 1994, 1998, & 2002; 23 games.
    Clubs: AC Milan.

7 Frank Rijkaard   (Netherlands)   30.09.62

Frank Rijkaard was a defenseman-midfielder who excelled all over the field. He played more midfield with his club teams, and was a bedrock defender for the Dutch national team.

Rijkaard possessed tremendous determination and excellent technique, both of which served him well in controlling the middle of the field. His vision and ability to advance forward also made him a formidable offensive force.

Rijkaard initially played for Ajax Amsterdam, and he participated in five league championships with them. He won two European Cups and two Intercontinental Cups in 1989 & 1990 with AC Milan. He also appeared in the 1993 European Final with Milan, losing to Marseille. He then returned to Ajax and guided a very young squad to European Cup victory in 1995, ironically over his old AC Milan team. The winning goal was supplied by his pass to Patrick Kluivert, while his old pals Baresi and Maldini attempted to defend.

Rijkaard was a formidable central defender with the Dutch national team, and he won the 1988 European Championships held in West Germany, Holland's first international championship.

After retiring Rijkaard had a stint as Holland's coach, and led a good Dutch team into the 2000 European Championship co-hosted by Holland-Belgium; Holland was unlucky to go out in the semi-final on penalties. He was coaching Barcelona in 2005.

Awards: *Placar* (Brazil) best 100 players of all time.
1992 Italy Footballer of the Year.
European Footballer of the Year, finished 3rd twice.
2004 Pelé/FIFA Best 125 Living Players.
International: 73 games with 10 goals.
World Cup: 1990 & 1994; 8 games.
Clubs: Ajax Amsterdam, Sporting Lisbon, Zaragoza, AC Milan.

8 Ruud Krol   (Netherlands)   24.03.49

Ruud Krol was the defensive stalwart for the "Orange Machine" that reached the 1974 and 1978 World Cup Finals, and for the Ajax team that won three European Cups in a row (1971-1973) and an Intercontinental Cup.

An intelligent, skillfully elegant, and yet physically commanding player, Krol played either outside or inside defense (or sweeper) with equal expertise for club and country.

Krol's play was emblematic of the "Total Football" or "Dutch Swirl" of Holland's national team. Who can forget Krol streaking into the left wing position against Brazil in the 1974 World Cup, centering with his left foot, only to have Cruyff fly-volley it home? After Johan Cruyff left the national team, Krol captained Holland at the 1978 World Cup, using his leadership skills to guide Holland to the Final again in host country Argentina. Playing for Napoli, Krol was the first foreign player to win the Italian Footballer of the Year award in 1981, a remarkable feat for a defender.

Awards: 1981 Italian Footballer of the Year.
1979 European Footballer of the Year voting, 3rd place.
International: 83 games with 4 goals.
World Cup: 1974, & 1978; 14 games with 1 goal.
Clubs: Ajax, Vancouver, Napoli, Cannes.

9 Lothar Matthäus   (W. Germany & Germany)   21.03.61

Matthäus was the "iron-man" of modern soccer, with an international career spanning an incredible 20 years (from June 14, 1980 to June 20, 2000, from age 19 to 39). He was a long-time captain of Germany, who played in a record twenty-five World Cup Final games spanning 2,048 minutes over five World Cups.

Like Franz Beckenbauer, Matthäus could play any midfield or defensive position, including libero. With great energy, movement, and vision for a defender, he excelled as sweeper for Bayern Munich and Germany. He had a total of six World Cup goals, four coming when playing as a midfielder in the 1990 West Germany World Cup winning team. He also participated in the 1980 European Championship win for West Germany. Matthäus was also successful at club level, winning seven top division titles, and the UEFA Cup twice.

Awards: 1990 European Footballer of the Year and *Onze d'Or* winner.
1991 FIFA Footballer of the Year (first year awarded).
France Football's World Cup Top-100 1930-1990
1990 & 1999 German Footballer of the Year.
Planète Foot (France) best 50 players of all time.
World Soccer's 100 Greatest Footballers of all time.
France Football's World Cup Top-100 1930-1990.
2004 Pelé/FIFA Best 125 Living Players.
International: 150 games with 23 goals.
World Cup: West Germany 1982, 1986, 1990; Germany 1994 & 1998: 25 matches and 6 goals.
Clubs: Borussia Mönchengladbach, Bayern Munich, Internazionale, NY/NJ Metrostars.

10 Daniel Passarella   (Argentina)   25.05.53

Daniel Passarella was captain of the Argentine team that won their first World Cup as host in 1978. He organized a first-rate defense as a central defender or libero, and was excellent in the air despite his medium height. Passarella also played on Argentina's 1982 World Cup team, but did not see any action on the 1986 World Cup winning team.

Passarella was a tenacious player defending, but was not afraid to advance and go for goal in the opposition's half. He is second on the list of First Division goals scored by defensive players, with 134 goals in 451 games.

Passarella was equally successful in club play, winning three league championships with River Plate.

His uncompromising characteristics as a player influenced his coaching style in his post-player career. He subsequently coached the Argentine and Uruguayan and national teams (including Argentina in the 1998 World Cup), and was at River Plate in 2006.

Awards: France Football's World Cup Top-100 1930-1990.
  1976 Argentine Player of the Year.
  World Soccer's 100 Greatest Footballers of all time.
  France Football's World Cup Top-100 1930-1990.
  2004 Pelé/FIFA Best 125 Living Players.
International: 70 games with 21 goals.
World Cup: 1978, 1982 & 1986 (did not play); 12 games with 3 goals.
Clubs: Sarmiento de Junin, River Plate, Fiorentina, Internazionale.

11 Paul Breitner   (West Germany)   05.09.51

Paul Breitner was a stellar defender-midfielder for West Germany and his club teams. One of few defenders to be converted to creative midfielder, he had outstanding technique, vision, and shooting ability.

Breitner had three goals for West Germany in their 1974 World Cup championship as a defender, and one in the 1982 World Cup as a midfielder. He is only the third player (after Brazilians Vavá and Pelé) to score a goal in two World Cup Final matches (1974 and 1982 Finals). He elected not to travel to the 1978 World Cup. Breitner was also on the 1972 West Germany European Championship team.

In club play, Breitner won a combined seven top division championships with Bayern Munich and Real Madrid, and one European Cup with Bayern in 1974. Breitner is fifth on the list of First Division goals scored by defensive players, with 103 goals in 369 games.

Awards: 1981 European Footballer of the Year voting, 2nd place.
  1981 West Germany Footballer of the Year.
  Planète Foot (France) best 50 players of all time.
  France Football's World Cup Top-100 1930-1990.
  2004 Pelé/FIFA Best 125 Living Players.
International: 48 games with 10 goals.
World Cup: 1974 & 1982; 14 games with 4 goals.
Clubs: Bayern Munich, Real Madrid, Eintracht Braunschweig.

12 Nílton Santos   (Brazil)   16.05.25

Nílton Santos (dos Reis Santos) was an attacking defenseman on four Brazil World Cup squads (1950, 1954, 1958, 1962) – the last two as World Cup champion. As an inside or outside defender on the Brazilian 4 – 2 – 4 system, he was one of the first defensemen to advance deep into opposition territory as a legitimate offensive weapon.

Santos anchored one of the all-Time World Cup defenses with Djalma Santos (no relation), Zito, and Gilmar for the 1958 & 1962 World Cup winners.

He also played on a stellar Botafogo squad that included Garrincha, with whom he was instrumental in arranging to sign for the team.

Awards: FIFA 1998 Century XI.
  World Soccer's 100 Greatest Footballers of all time.
  2004 Pelé/FIFA Best 125 Living Players.
International: 75 games with 3 goals.
World Cup: 1950, 1954, 1958, & 1962; 15 games with 1 goal.
Club: Botafogo.

13 Giacinto Facchetti (Italy) 18.07.42

Giacinto Facchetti was a physically impressive and mobile defender with excellent skills. Facchetti scored often for a defender, a rare act in the defense-minded world of Italian football, and he probably started the fashion of defensive backs making offensive runs in Europe.

Facchetti played for Italy in three World Cups, acting as captain of Italy in the 1970 Final against the peerless Brazil team. He also performed in Italy's 1968 European Championship triumph.

Facchetti scored 60 Italian League goals as a defenseman, getting 10 in the 1965-66 season alone. He scored a vital goal in the 1965 European Cup semifinal against Liverpool, which Internazionale won by one goal to qualify for the Final. He scored 78 goals over his career.

Facchetti won four Italian League titles, two European Cups and two Intercontinental Cups (1964 & 1965) with Internazionale.

Awards: 1965 European Footballer of the Year voting, 2nd place.
World Soccer's 100 Greatest Footballers of all time.
2004 Pelé/FIFA Best 125 Living Players.
International: 94 caps, 3 goals.
World Cup: 1966, 1970, & 1974; 12 games.
Clubs: Trevigliese, Internazionale.

14 Laurent Blanc (France) 19.11.65

Laurent Blanc began his career as an attacking midfielder for Montpellier in the French league. That experience was perhaps useful as he coaxed in the Golden Goal to beat Paraguay 1-0 in the critical 1998 World Cup second round match, and allowed France to continue their eventually successful World Cup campaign. Unfortunately, Blanc missed the World Cup Final through suspension, but was ably replaced by Frank Leboeuf. In addition to winning the 1998 World Cup with France, he was a 2000 European Championship winner.

Blanc was blessed with excellent anticipation and an elegant on-the-ball skill style. He was a threat to the opposition's goal from the air or from either foot. Blanc is number six on the list of First Division goals scored by defensive players, with 95 in 500 games.

Blanc was twice a top division champion during his extensive club career, with Auxerre and Manchester United.

Awards: French Player of the Century, 4th place after Platini, Zidane, and Kopa.
1990 French Player of the Year.
International: 97 games with 16 goals.
World Cup: 1998; 5 games with 1 goal.
Clubs: Montpellier, Napoli, Nimes, St. Etienne, Auxerre, Barcelona, Marseille, Internazionale, Manchester United.

15 Cafú (Brazil) 07.06.70

Cafú (Marcos Evangelista de Morais) is a wing defender with outstanding pace and technique, and a dynamic defensive and offensive force for Brazil and his club teams.

Cafú was captain of the victorious Brazil squad in the 2002 World Cup, and was the first player to appear in three straight World Cup Final matches (1994-1998-2002). He also played in Brazil's two Copa America winning squads in 1997 & 1999. Cafú is also due to play in the 2006 World Cup.

Also successful in club competitions, Cafú won the Copa Libertadores and Intercontinental Cup with São Paulo in 1992 & 1993, alongside major talents Raí, Muller, and Palhinha. He won the Italian league title with Roma in 2001, and the European Champion's League with AC Milan in 2003.

Cafú is the only other defensive back besides Elías Figueroa and Oscar Ruggeri to win the South American Footballer of Year.

Awards 1994 South American Footballer of the Year.
2004 Pelé/FIFA Best 125 Living Players.
International: 137 games with 5 goals.
World Cup: 1994, 1998, & 2002 (2006); 16 games.
Clubs: São Paulo, Zaragoza, Palmeiras, AS Roma, Yokohama, AC Milan.

16 **Ronald Koeman**   **(Netherlands)**   21.03.63

Ronald Koeman was a sweeper-back and free-kick specialist for both club and country. His intelligent play ensured an organized defense, and he provided excellent distribution from the back. His leadership abilities enabled him to excel as captain of the 1994 Holland World Cup team and his Barcelona club team.

Koeman won the 1988 European Championship with the Netherlands, and he captained the 1994 World Cup team to the quarterfinals, where the Dutch lost to Brazil in the best game of the tournament.

Koeman possessed a ferocious shot that provided many goals for club and country. Koeman is the World's Top Defensive First Division goal scorer, with 193 in 533 games. He had more career goals than most midfielders - or even strikers.

Koeman won the 1992 European Cup for Barcelona on a free kick, and was also a 1988 European Cup winner with PSV Eindhoven. He won eight top division championships with Ajax, PSV Eindhoven, and Barcelona.

    Awards: 1987 & 1988 Dutch Footballer of the Year.
    International: 78 caps, 14 goals.
    World Cup: 1990 & 1994; 9 games with 1 goal.
    Clubs: Groningen, Ajax, PSV Eindhoven, Barcelona, Feyenoord.

17 **Matthias Sammer**   **(East Germany & Germany)**   05.09.67

Matthias Sammer was the most successful player from East Germany to play for united Germany. He played both sweeper and creative midfield roles for nation and club, with impressive vision and technique.

Sammer had his most success with Borussia Dortmund, whom he guided to two German league championships, and the European Champions Cup and Intercontinental Cup in 1997. Sammer won five top division championships in total.

As a Germany national team member, Sammer contributed greatly to Germany's 1996 European Championship win, and subsequently won the European Footballer of the Year. He also played on the 1994 Germany World Cup team.

Sammer was always a threat on goal, having 39 goals for Dynamo Dresden in only 102 games over a four-year period.

    Awards: 1996 European Footballer of the Year.
                    1995 & 1996 German Footballer of the Year.
    International: 51 games with 8 goals for Germany; 23 games with 6 goals for East Germany. Total of 74 games with 14 goals.
    World Cup: 1994; 4 games.
    Clubs: Dynamo Dresden, Stuttgart, Internazionale, Borussia Dortmund.

18 **Marius Trésor**   **(France)**   15.06.50

Marius Trésor was a stopper and sweeper extraordinaire for France and his club teams. Originally from Guadeloupe in the West Indies, he had excellent marking ability and overall technique, and was also a threat on goal.

Trésor had a brilliant goal in the 1982 France - West Germany World Cup semi-final, spectacularly volleying home Alain Giresse's centering pass in overtime. His goal would have won the match and entered France in the Final if the *Golden Goal* setup had been used in that World Cup, but West Germany came from 3-1 down to tie and subsequently advance on the first ever World Cup penalty kick competition.

Trésor won the French league with Bordeaux and the French Cup with Marseille.

    Awards: 1972 French Footballer of the Year.
                    2004 Pelé/FIFA Best 125 Living Players.
    International: 65 games with 4 goals.
    World Cup: 1978 & 1982; 10 games with 1 goal.
    Clubs: Ajaccio, Marseille, Bordeaux.

19 Gaetano Scirea   (Italy)   25.05.53

Gaetano Scirea was Italy sweeper in their 1982 World Cup championship, and Italy captain in the 1986 World Cup. Scirea performed with impeccable technique and efficiency of movement, his sense of anticipation saving the Italian defense countless times.

Along with Franco Baresi, Scirea is considered the best ever Italian sweeper/libero. Scirea had a very successful club career with Juventus, winning seven Italian league championships, the 1977 UEFA Cup, the 1985 European Cup, and the 1985 Intercontinental Cup as best club team in the world.

Awards: *France Football's* World Cup Top-100 1930-1990
Venerdì (Italy) All-Time Top-100 Footballers (100 Magnifici).
International: 78 games with 2 goals.
World Cup: 1982 & 1986; 11 games.
Clubs: Atalanta, Juventus.

20 John Charles   (Wales)   27.12.31

John Charles was a spectacular athlete who was Great Britain's greatest-ever export footballer. He started out as a central defender, but his scoring technique was so solid that he was converted into a deadly striker at Leeds (150 goals in eight years, with 42 goals in 1953-54 alone). Still, once the game was in hand for club or country, he would fall back into a central defending role from which he had few contemporary peers.

With excellent technique, balance, and grace for a large man, Charles was a gentleman on and off the pitch, and was never booked in an international or First Division game in Italy or Great Britain.

Charles performed in the three group games for Wales in the 1958 World Cup, which were ties against eventual finalist Sweden, Hungary, and Mexico, then performed in the playoff win against Hungary. He was unfortunately absent through injury in the quarterfinal against Brazil, when a 17-year old named Pelé scored the lone goal to eliminate Wales. It is tempting to speculate what the outcome would have been if Wales' greatest-ever player had been available.

Charles had 93 goals in 155 games with Juventus, forming a wonderful partnership with Argentine striker Omar Sivori. He won the Italian Championship three times (1958, 1960, & 1961), the Italian Cup twice (1959 & 1960), and was Italy's Serie A *Capocannoniere* (top scorer) in 1958.

Awards: *World Soccer's* 100 Greatest Footballers of all time.
1958 Italian Footballer of the Year.
European Footballer of the Year voting, 3rd in 1959, and 4th in 1958.
International: 38 games with 15 goals.
World Cup: 1958; 4 games, 1 goal.
Clubs: Swansea, Leeds, Juventus, Roma, Cardiff City.

21 Oscar Ruggeri   (Argentina)   26.01.62

Oscar Ruggeri was a center back committed to marshalling a tight defense, skillful at marking and positioning, and excellent in the air. He played in three World Cups for Argentina, the first (1986) of which he played every minute of every game on the way to winning the Cup. The 1986 team gave up five goals in seven games, while the 1990 team topped that by allowing only four goals in seven games (but lost the Final to West Germany). Those figures are testimony to Ruggeri's abilities to organize a smothering defense.

Ruggeri also had a very successful club career, starting with a league win at Boca Juniors with Diego Maradona. At River Plate he won the league, Copa Libertadores, and Intercontinental Cup in 1986. He also won the league championship with Real Madrid and San Lorenzo.

Ruggeri is the only other defensive back besides Elías Figueroa and Cafú to win the South American Footballer of Year.

Awards: 1991 South American Footballer of the Year (El País - Uruguay).
International: 97 games with 7 goals.
World Cup: 1986, 1990,& 1994; 16 games with 1 goal.
Clubs: Boca Juniors, River Plate, Logroñés, Real Madrid, Velez Sarsfield, Ancona, América (Mexico), San Lorenzo, Lanús.

22 Alan Hansen   (Scotland)   13.06.55

Alan Hansen was a stylish central defender for Liverpool during their glory years. A stellar defensive organizer and technician, he had unprecedented success directing the Liverpool defense for fourteen years (1977-1990). During his Liverpool tenure he won seven English league titles, and the 1978, 1981, and 1984 European Cups.

Hansen was also a member of the 1985 Liverpool European Cup runner-up team, which participated in the infamous final at Heysel, Belgium where 39 fans were killed in a stadium collapse.

He appeared for the 1982 Scotland World Cup team that was eliminated in the first round, despite being equal on points with the Soviet Union. Hansen is currently a football commentator, and had a cameo playing himself in the movie "*Bend it Like Beckham.*"

    Awards: 1986 and 1990 English Footballer of the Year voting, 2nd place.
    International: 26 games.
    World Cup: 1982; 3 games.
    Clubs: Partick Thistle, Liverpool.

23 Fernando Hierro   (Spain)   23.03.68

Fernando Hierro was an excellent defender always looking to advance for a scoring opportunity. He dominated air battles in front of his goal, and his distribution from the back was technically impressive. He played with an intensity that served to motivate him and deflect the spotlight off the skill players.

As a defender, Hierro had a remarkable scoring record, and was an excellent free-kick taker and penalty-kick converter. He led Spain in total goals with 29 before being overtaken by striker Raúl Gonzalez in 2003, and in club play was fourth in the world for defensive player goals, with 105 goals in 497 First Division games.

Hierro had a long and successful career with Real Madrid, winning five Spanish league championships, three European Cups, and two Intercontinental Cups.

    Awards: 1997/98 UEFA Best Defender Award.
    International: 89 games with 29 goals.
    World Cup: 1994, 1998 & 2002; 12 games with 5 goals.
    Clubs: Real Valladolid, Real Madrid, Al-Rayyan, Bolton.

24 Marcel Desailly   (France)   07.09.68

Marcel Desailly was a stalwart central defender or defensive midfielder for France and several successful club teams. Born in Ghana but raised in France, he had excellent technique, dominated in the air, and radiated confidence and leadership.

Desailly represented France in the 1998 World Cup, performing well, but was sent off against Brazil in the Final. Fortunately, France was already firmly in control and even scored again to win 3-0. With France, he also won the 2000 European Championship, and the 2001 & 2003 Confederations Cups. Desailly captained France to the 2002 World Cup in Asia, and is currently France's leader in national team games played.

Desailly won the 1993 European Cup with Marseille, then moved to AC Milan where he won a consecutive European Cup in 1994. He appeared in his third European Cup Final in a row in 1995, but AC Milan lost to Ajax.

    Awards: All-Time France XI.
                         2004 Pelé/FIFA Best 125 Living Players.
    International: 116 games with 3 goals.
    World Cup: 1998 & 2002; 10 games.
    Clubs: Nantes, Marseille, Milan, Chelsea, Al Gharafa, Qatar Sports Club.

25 Andreas Brehme   (West Germany & Germany)   09.11.60

Andreas Brehme was a physical yet technical defender and midfielder for club and country. Able to operate in the middle or the left, Brehme was adaptable to the challenge, and had a good scoring rate in World Cups. He is most famous for slotting home the only goal on a penalty kick that won the 1990 World Cup 1-0 for West Germany against Maradona's Argentina.

Brehme also had a successful club career that took him to Italy and Spain – he even won the Italian Footballer of the Year in 1989, a rarity for both foreigners and defenders (Dutch defenders Ruud

Krol and Frank Rijkaard also won this award). He won the Bundesliga championship with both Bayern Munich and Kaiserslautern, and the UEFA Cup in 1991 with Internazionale.

Awards: *Venerdi's* All-Time Top-100 (100 Magnifici)
1989 Italy Footballer of the Year.
International: 86 games with 8 goals.
World Cup: 1986, 1990, & 1994; 16 games with 4 goals.
Clubs: Saarbrücken, Kaiserslautern, Bayern Munich, Internazionale, Real Zaragoza.

26 Carlos Gamarra (Paraguay) 17.02.71

Carlos Gamarra is Paraguay's best defender ever, and the current holder of the most national team appearances. A quick central defender with impeccable timing in the tackle, good positioning, and dominant in the air, most observers thought he was the best defender in the 1998 World Cup. Surprisingly, he did not commit one foul in the 1998 Cup despite marshalling an airtight defense (#10 best defense below).

Gamarra also captained Paraguay to second place in the 2004 Olympics.

After Gamarra won the third of three championships with home team Cerro Porteño in 1992, he performed with numerous top European and South American teams.

Awards: 1998 South American Footballer of the Year, 2nd place.
1997 & 1998 Paraguayan Footballer of the Year.
International: 104 games with 11 goals.
World Cup: 1998 & 2002 (2006); 8 games.
Clubs: Cerro Porteño, Internacional, Benfica, Corinthians, Atlético Madrid, Flamengo, AEK Athens, Internazionale, Palmeiras.

27 Bergomi, Giuseppe (Italy) 22.12.63

Giuseppe Bergomi broke into Internazionale's first team as a seventeen-year old, and made the 1982 World Cup winning squad at age eighteen. In the Final he kept Karl-Heinz Rummenigge quiet as Italy won 3-1.

Bergomi was captain of the 1990 Italy World Cup squad that won six games and only "lost" one on penalties to Argentina – the Best World Cup defense ever.

With his only club Internazionale, Bergomi won one Italian championship, two Italian Cups, and three UEFA championships.

Awards: 2004 Pelé/FIFA Best 125 Living Players.
International: 81 caps, 6 goals.
World Cup: 1982, 1986, 1990, 1998; 20 games.
Club: Internazionale Milan.

28 Roberto Carlos (Brazil) 10.04.73

Roberto Carlos (Roberto Carlos da Silva) continues the tradition of stellar Brazilian outside wingbacks such as Marinho, Josimar, Jorginho, Branco, and Cafú. Operating with Cafú as right wingback and Roberto Carlos as left wingback, recent Brazilian teams could play any formation from 3 to 5 defenders according to necessity.

Preferring to use his dominant left foot, Roberto Carlos' powerful free kicks are one of his trademarks, along with excellent technique, recuperation, and work rate through the left side of the field. With the Brazilian national team, Roberto Carlos won the 2002 World Cup, the 1997 & 1999 Copa America, and the 1997 Confederations Cup. He is due to appear in the 2006 World Cup.

He won two Brazilian championships with Palmeiras, and three Spanish league titles, three European Cups, and two Intercontinental Cups with Real Madrid.

Awards: 2002 FIFA World Cup Dream Team.
2001/2002 and 2002/2003 UEFA Best Defender Award.
2002 European Footballer of the Year, 2nd in voting.
2004 Pelé/FIFA Best 125 Living Players.
International: 119 games with 11 goals.
World Cup: 1998 & 2002 (2006); 13 games with 1 goal.
Clubs: Palmeiras, Internazionale, Real Madrid.

29 Hector Chumpitaz (Peru) 12.04.44

Hector Chumpitaz captained a successful Peru in the 1970 and 1978 World Cups, which saw them advance to the second round both times. A strong reader of the game with excellent ball skills and distribution, he marshaled a capable defense to support Peru's attack led by Teófilo Cubillas. In the 1978 Cup, Peru even finished top of their Group stage above Finalist Holland. Chumpitaz also captained Peru's Copa America winning side in 1975.

He served with several of the top teams in his domestic league in a long career, winning several national titles. The day after his transfer from Municipal to Universitario in 1966, he scored a rare goal as they beat Argentina giant River Plate.

Awards: *World Soccer's* 100 Greatest Footballers of all time.
Internationals: 105 games with 3 goals.
World Cup: 1970 & 1974; 10 games with 1 goal.
Clubs: Deportivo Municipal, Universitario, Sporting Cristal.

30 Berti Vogts (West Germany) 30.12.46

Hans Hubert "Berti" Vogts was a compact and quick defender who played in three World Cups for West Germany. He was able to mark the best strikers out of the game, effectively neutralizing Johan Cruyff for much of the 1974 World Cup Final, which West Germany won as host. Four years later, Vogts captained the 1978 West Germany team to a second round elimination in Argentina.

Vogts played his whole club career with Borussia Mönchengladbach, where he won five German championships, two UEFA Cups, and one Cup Winners Cup.

After retirement, Vogts coached the German national team, winning the European Championship in 1996, and later coached Scotland's national team.

Awards: 1971 & 1979 West German Footballer of the Year.
International: 96 caps, 1 goal.
World Cup: 1970, 1974, & 1978; 19 games.
Club: Borussia Mönchengladbach.

Defender Runner-ups
(Must have made first national team appearance by 1994)

Immediate runner-ups (players strongly considered for the original list)
Branco (Brazil), Frank de Boer (Netherlands), Karlheinz Förster (West Germany), Eric Gerets (Belgium), Emlyn Hughes (England), Jorginho (Brazil), Júnior (Leovegildo Lins da Gama - Brazil), Jürgen Kohler (West Germany), Danny McGrain (Scotland), Phil Neal (England), Kenny Sansom (England), Djalma Santos (Brazil), Wim Suurbier (Netherlands), Alberto Tarantini (Argentina), Lilian Thuram (France), Wladyslaw Zmuda (Poland).

Complete runner-up list
Tony Adams (England), Viv Anderson (England), Patrik Andersson (Sweden), Marcelo Balboa (USA), Maxime Bossis (France), Alain Geiger (Switzerland), Jerzy Gorgoń (Poland), Colin Hendry (Scotland), Manfred Kaltz (West Germany), Bülent Korkmaz (Turkey), Hong Myung-Bo (Korea Republic), Trifon Ivanov (Bulgaria), Robert Jarni (Croatia), Josimar (Brazil), Paul McGrath (Ireland), Nelinho (Brazil), Bjorn Nordqvist (Sweden), Luís Pereira (Brazil), Gheorghe Popescu (Romania), Jaap Stam (Netherlands), Phil Thompson (England), Claudio Suarez (Mexico).

Great Defenses
of the Modern Era World Cups 1958-2002

There is something about playing the World Cup at home that encourages a strong defensive performance. Many of the best World Cup defenses are represented by the host team, including (1) Italy 1990, (2) France 1998, (5) England 1966, (7b) West Germany 1974, and (8) Argentina 1978.

The team standing in the World Cup is noted after the team and year in parentheses, and the number of goals scored by each player is noted after their name in parentheses.

(1) Italy 1990 (third place)
Franco Baresi, Giuseppe Bergomi, Luigi de Agostini, Riccardo Ferri, Paolo Maldini, and goalkeeper Walter Zenga.

Italy's airtight defense opened with 5 straight shutouts, and allowed only 2 goals in 7 games. They finished the 1990 World Cup with six wins and one tie, winning only 3rd place after losing a semi-final penalty kick contest against Argentina.

Because of the 24-team competition with 16 qualifiers to the second round, Italy met Argentina in the semi-finals with a 5-0-0 record while Argentina was only 2-2-1. Argentina's loss in the Final left them with a .500 record in the Cup, going 2-3-2, with 5 goals for and 4 goals against (Italy scored 10 goals with 2 against). Something is horribly wrong in World Cup planning when a Finalist has a .500 record, while the 3rd place team has a 1.000 record.

(2) France 1998 (winners)
Laurent Blanc (1), Marcel Desailly, Lilian Thuram (2), Bixente Lizarazu (1), Frank Leboeuf, and goalkeeper Fabien Barthez.

France allowed only 2 goals in 7 games (with 5 shutouts) in the 1998 World Cup Finals; tying Italy's 1990 record for goal stinginess in Cup Finals.

France had the modern defense: intelligent, fast, courageous, and creative. Blanc (1), Lizarazu (1), and Thuram (2) scored critical goals for *the Bleus*, as their defense alone scored twice as many goals as their opponents. Their defense had to contend with Brazilian offensive powers Ronaldo, Rivaldo, Bebeto, Edmundo, and Denilson in the Cup Final, and shut them all down.

(3) Netherlands 1974 (second place)
Ruud Krol (1), Arie Haan, Wim Suurbier, Wim Rijsbergen, and goalkeeper Jan Jongbloed.

The Dutch had only 3 goals scored against in 7 games, including 5 shutouts. Only one of the goals against was from free-play; the other two were from a penalty kick and an own goal.

Holland entered the Final having scored 14 goals and allowing 1 (an own goal); against lesser competition West Germany had scored 11 and allowed 3. Holland, however, lost in the final on West Germany's home ground, with Gerd Müller's winning goal the only offensive goal from free-play that Holland allowed in the whole tournament.

(4) Brazil 1994 (winners)
Jorginho, Cafú, Marcio Santos (1), Aldair, Branco (1), and goalkeeper Taffarel.

Brazil allowed only 3 goals in 7 games, 2 of them against Holland; they also had 5 shutouts.

Cafú was 1994 South American Footballer of the Year, but Jorginho started the Final (Cafú replaced Jorginho after his injury). In addition to airtight defense, Cafú and Branco were serious offensive threats on the wings and goals. Marcio Santos and Branco both had goals – Branco's being the critical winning free kick that beat Holland in the quarterfinal.

(5) England 1966 (winners)
Jackie Charlton, George Cohen, Bobby Moore, Ray Wilson, Nobby Stiles, and goalkeeper Gordon Banks.

England allowed only 3 goals in 6 games, with 4 shutouts against Uruguay, Mexico, France, and Argentina.

Only the highest scoring teams of Portugal (17 goals) and West Germany (16 goals) scored against England, and the England defense prevailed in the overtime Final 4-2 against West Germany.

(6) West Germany 1974 (winners)
Franz Beckenbauer, Berti Vogts, Paul Breitner (3), Hans-Georg Schwarzenbeck, and goalkeeper Sepp Maier.

West Germany allowed only 4 goals in 7 games, including 4 shutouts. Breitner himself had 3 goals. West Germany lost one game to East Germany 1-0.

Beckenbauer and company held Johan Cruyff and high-scoring Holland to one penalty kick goal in the Final, prevailing 2-1.

(7a) Brazil 2002 (winners)
Cafú, Lúcio, Roque Júnior, Edmílson (1), Roberto Carlos (1), and goalkeeper Marcos.

Brazil allowed only 4 goals in 7 games, with 4 shutouts. With a dynamic offense featuring Ronaldo, Rivaldo, and Ronaldinho that scored 18 goals, the stingy defense highlights how much Brazil dominated the 2002 competition.

Cafú is the only player who qualified on two top-ten defensive teams.

(7b) West Germany 2002 (second place):
Thomas Linke (1), Carsten Ramelow, Torsten Frings, Christoph Metzelder and goalkeeper Oliver Kahn.

Germany allowed only 3 goals in 7 games, with 5 shutouts, to advance to the Final, where the Brazil offense finally broke down the German "no-name" defense.

With some of their firepower injured, Germany needed an exemplary defense to advance in the 2002 World Cup, and their defense delivered just that.

(8) Argentina 1978 (winners)
Daniel Passarella (1), Alberto Tarantini (1), Luis Adolfo Galvàn, Jorge Mario Olguin, and goalkeeper Ubaldo Fillol.

Argentina allowed only 4 goals in 7 games, with 3 shutouts (against Brazil, Poland, and Peru). Each of the five members of Argentina's defense played every minute of every game (660 minutes).

Against a great Dutch team in the Final, their defense held in overtime as they won the title on their home ground.

(9) Brazil 1958 and 1962 (both winners)
Djalma Santos, Nílton Santos (1), Zito (1), Bellini, Mauro, and goalkeeper Gilmar.

This Brazil team allowed only 4 goals in 6 games in each competition in those offensive-minded years, with 4 shutouts in 1958 and 2 shutouts in 1962. Mauro replaced Bellini in the 1962 starting squad, with no apparent downside.

(10a) Paraguay 1998 (second round)
Francisco Arce, Celso Ayala (1), Roberto Acuña, Carlos Gamarra, Pedro Sarabia and goalkeeper José Luis Chilavert.

Paraguay allowed only 2 goals in 4 games, one of them a "golden goal" in extra time against eventual winners and host France. Paraguay held Spain and Bulgaria scoreless, while beating group winners Nigeria 3-1.

(10b) England 1982 (second round)
Terry Butcher, Mick Mills, Phil Thompson, Kenny Sansom, and goalkeeper Peter Shilton.

England only allowed one goal in five undefeated games. They beat Czechoslovakia 2-0 and France 3-1, and tied West Germany and Spain at 0-0. Despite a great collective defense, England was eliminated from the Cup because they could not score in their last two games.

Best Midfielders

Also known as "link men" or "halfbacks", the midfield position is the most versatile on the field. While strikers and defenders traditionally have had discrete jobs (to score and to defend, respectively), the midfielders must be intimately involved in both offense and defense. Therefore, the list has some very offensive minded midfielders (Platini, Maradona, Di Stéfano, Baggio), and some all-rounders (Neeskens, Robson). Di Stéfano, Platini and Maradona are together selected the best midfielders.

Many of these midfield players wore the number "10", for they were their teams' creative talent who also could score goals. "Number 10" players are often referred to as *fantasistas* (literally "fantasy makers") in South America.

1 Alfredo Di Stéfano (Argentina/Spain) 24.07.26

Alfredo Di Stéfano is arguably the modern era's finest "all-rounder," a player who controlled games from all positions and angles. Perhaps his teams lined him up as a "forward" on a five-man striking line, but he could be found organizing the midfield or even the defense before advancing to assist or score himself. Because of his individual "total soccer" tendencies, he is placed at a midfield position.

Di Stéfano was born in Argentina to a father who had played for River Plate, and he debuted with River at age seventeen, on an attacking line called La Maquina (The Machine). After Argentine soccer players went on strike in 1949, Di Stéfano went to play for Millionarios of Bogotá in the "pirate" Columbian league that was operating outside of FIFA's control. Millionarios' dominating technical style was famously called the "Blue Ballet." Later, Real Madrid outmaneuvered Barcelona to sign him in Spain, and the rest is legend.

With Di Stéfano, Real Madrid won the first five European Cups in a row, from 1956 to 1960. He scored in each Final, including a hat trick in Real Madrid's 7-3 win against powerhouse Eintracht Frankfurt in Glasgow in 1960. Di Stéfano also won the inaugural Intercontinental Cup in 1960 with Real Madrid. He also played in the 1962 and 1964 European Cup Finals, but Real succumbed to Eusébio's Benfica and Facchetti's Internazionale, respectively. Di Stéfano scored a record total of 49 goals in 58 European matches, surpassed only in 2005 when Raúl scored his 50th goal in 97 games, and subsequently on 4 April 2006 when Andriy Shevchenko scored his 52nd.

Di Stéfano was the winner of five *Pichichis* (the Spanish league scoring leader), and finished with 227 goals in La Liga, 216 of them in 282 games with Real Madrid (he remains Real Madrid's leading scorer). Di Stéfano led his Top Division teams in scoring eight times, and he had 377 goals in 521 Top Division matches over his career.

Di Stéfano helped his club teams win championships in three countries: with River Plate in Argentina (1945, 1947), Millionarios in Colombia (1949, 1951, 1952, 1953), and Real Madrid in Spain (1954-58, 1961-64).

Di Stéfano won 37 caps for two countries. He had six goals in six games for Argentina as they won the 1947 Copa America held in Ecuador, but then had a ten-year international hiatus before winning 31 caps for Spain (with 23 goals scored) from 1957-1961.

Di Stéfano never played in a World Cup Finals match. He missed the 1958 World Cup with Argentina, as he was already playing for Spain (which did not qualify for the Cup Finals in Sweden). Di Stéfano helped Spain qualify for the 1962 World Cup in Chile, and was on Spain's World Cup roster at the age of 36, but he could not perform due to injury.

Awards: 1957 & 1959 European Footballer of the Year.
1998 FIFA Century XI.
World Soccer's 100 Greatest Footballers of All Time.
France Football's Football Player of the Century (# 4).
Planète Foot (France) best 50 players of all time.
World Soccer's 100 Greatest Footballers of all time.
2004 Pelé/FIFA Best 125 Living Players.
International: Argentina 6 goals in 6 games; Spain 31 games with 23 goals.
World Cup: 1962 (Spain); did not play due to injury.
Clubs: River Plate, Huracán, Millionarios, Real Madrid, Espanyol.

1 Diego Maradona　　　　(Argentina)　　　　　　　　30.10.60

Maradona was a ball wizard who had incredible touch and control of the *pelota*; he could have been world football juggling champion if he had so desired. Maradona's genius was as a creator of opportunities assisted by exceptional passing technique, which lifted good teams (Argentina in 1986 and Napoli in 1987) into a great class.

Maradona was a football phenomenon, leading Argentina to the sub-20 World Cup title in 1979 immediately after he was denied a place on the 1978 World Cup team. Maradona was never a straight-up striker as his passing talents were too prodigious. If played as striker, it was as a withdrawn forward, so he could advance the ball using his formidable dribbling skills. Later in his career (in the 1990 and 1994 World Cups), he was a creative midfielder with limited defensive duties in a 4-4-2 scheme.

Maradona essentially willed the Argentine team to World Cup victory in Mexico in 1986, scoring five goals along the way (including the famous "Goal of the Century" and the infamous "Hand of God" goal, both against England). He also helped bring the scudetto (Italian championship) to Napoli in 1987 and 1990, and won the UEFA Cup in 1989.

His strike rate of 34 goals in 91 national team games is deceptive, as he surely setup at least twice as many goals. Still an excellent rate for a midfielder, and his goals were often spectacular. In club play, he had 259 goals in 490 Top Division matches, and he led his top division leagues in scoring six times.

Exceptional on the field, Maradona could be just as extraordinary off the field. He was an acknowledged cocaine addict, had trouble staying at home, and got in serious trouble with tax officials. In his first book *Yo Soy el Diego de la Gente* ("*I am Diego of the People*"), he provides excuses and side stories rather than a true understanding of what made his career nosedive (mostly drug addiction and two long suspensions from the game). Fortunately, at the end of 2005 he appears to have conquered many of his demons and is well on his way to a second career just being Diego, a sensitive man who has not forgotten his roots in the streets of Argentina.

　　Awards:　　1979 & 1980 South American Footballer of the Year.
　　　　　　　　1986 *World Soccer's* Footballer of the Year.
　　　　　　　　1986 & 1987 *Onze d'Or* winner.
　　　　　　　　1979, 1980, 1981, & 1986 Argentine Footballer of the Year.
　　　　　　　　1985 Italian Footballer of the Year.
　　　　　　　　2002 FIFA World Cup Dream Team.
　　　　　　　　1998 FIFA Century XI.
　　　　　　　　France Football's Footballer of the Century (# 2).
　　　　　　　　Planète Foot (France) best 50 players of all time.
　　　　　　　　World Soccer's 100 Greatest Footballers of all time.
　　　　　　　　France Football's World Cup Top-100 1930-1990.
　　　　　　　　2004 Pelé/FIFA Best 125 Living Players.
　　International:　91 games with 34 goals.
　　World Cup:　　1982, 1986, 1990 & 1994; 21 games with 8 goals.
　　Clubs: Argentinos Juniors, Boca Juniors, Barcelona, Napoli, Seville, Newell's Old Boys.

1 Michel Platini　　　　(France)　　　　　　　　21.06.55

Michel Platini was the midfield schemer for France, Saint Etienne, and Juventus in the late 1970s and early 1980s, and was the most dominant player in the world between the 1982 and 1986 World Cups. He was a superlative passer, free kick specialist, and leader, and his technical ability and reading of the game were second to none. Platini was also a capable defender.

He was ruthless in front of the goal for France, having an outstanding strike rate for an attacking midfielder of 41 goals in 72 international games. He also had 68 goals in 147 league games for Juventus, and ended his career with 207 goals in 400 Top Division games.

Platini captained the French team to a 3rd and 4th place in the 1982 and 1986 World Cups, respectively. However, he got his World Cup Finals start in the 1978 World Cup, where he scored against the eventual host winners Argentina. Platini was critical to France qualifying for three successive World Cups, as he scored the definitive qualifying goals against Bulgaria, Holland, and Yugoslavia in 1977, 1981, and 1985, respectively.

Platini and France were to tragically exit the 1982 World Cup in an infamous semi-final match against West Germany. After a horrific injury to Patrick Battiston inflicted by German goalkeeper Schumacher (see Chapter 6), France rallied to go ahead 3-1 in overtime. Under the "golden goal" rule,

France would have won the game twice over, but West Germany came back to score two late goals to equalize at three goals apiece. The Germans then won the World Cup's first-ever penalty kick contest to advance to the Final against Italy.

Four years later France, having just defeated Brazil, was again in the semifinals in Mexico against Germany. This time, a hobbled Platini could not rally his team against a German team who had just beaten Mexico. Ironically, France and West Germany advanced to their 1986 meeting by winning their previous games on penalty kick shootouts.

Platini led France to the European Championship in 1984, himself scoring nine goals in only five games, including two pure "hat-tricks" (scoring with head, right and left feet in one game), in the most dominating individual European Championship performance ever.

Watching the French midfield (known as the *'carré magique'* or *'magic square'*) composed of Platini, Alain Giresse, Jean Tigana and Luis Fernandez, was to witness one of the most technically gifted midfields ever.

Platini was Italian league champion with Juventus three times, and also won the 1984 European Cup Winner's Cup, the 1985 European Cup, and 1985 Intercontinental Cup with the "Old Lady" team. He was Italy's Serie A *Capocannoniere* (top scorer) three years in a row (1983-1985).

Platini is still the only player to win three consecutive European Footballer of the Year awards (1983, 1984, and 1985), and one of a select group of three players to have won it three times (along with Dutchmen Johan Cruyff and Marco Van Basten). He remains France's all-time goal scorer.

Platini was France's national team coach from 1987-1992, and subsequently was a co-organizer of the 1998 World Cup held in France. He has been a member of FIFA's executive committee since 2002, and will likely run for the UEFA Presidency in 2007.

Awards: 1983, 1984, & 1985 European Footballer of the Year and *Onze d'Or* winner.
1984 & 1985 *World Soccer's* Footballer of the Year.
1976 & 1977 French Footballer of the Year.
1984 Italian Footballer of the Year.
2002 FIFA World Cup Dream Team.
1998 FIFA Century XI.
France Football's Footballer of the Century (# 5).
Planète Foot (France) best 50 players of all time.
World Soccer's 100 Greatest Footballers of all time.
2004 Pelé/FIFA Best 125 Living Players.

International: 72 games with 41 goals.
World Cup: 1978, 1982, & 1986 14 games with 5 goals.
Clubs: Nancy, Saint Etienne, Juventus.

4 Zinedine Zidane   (France)   23.06.72

Zinedine Zidane is the contemporary technical and creative midfield wizard, a true "fantasista." He is a goal scorer with his head (two goals in the 1998 World Cup Final) or either foot, and is a free-kick expert to boot.

Zidane was the midfield genius that helped France win the 1998 World Cup and the 2000 European Championship. Injured at the last minute before the 2002 World Cup, France was but a shadow of itself without Zidane.

Equally successful at club level, he won two league championships and an Intercontinental Cup (1996) with Juventus, and with Real Madrid a league championship, a European Cup (2002) and an Intercontinental Cup (2002).

Zidane clinched the crowning glory for a centenary Real Madrid side in 2002, as his spectacular left-footed volley found the upper left-hand corner of the net for the winning goal. Zidane returned from international retirement to lead France team into the 2006 Germany World Cup Finals.

Awards: 1998 European Footballer of the Year.
1998, 2000, &2001 *Onze d'Or* winner
1998, 2000, & 2003 FIFA World Footballer of the Year.
2002 FIFA World Cup Dream Team.
1998 & 2002 French Footballer of the Year.
World Soccer's 100 Greatest Footballers of all time.
2004 Pelé/FIFA Best 125 Living Players.

International: 98 games with 28 goals.

World Cup: 1998 & 2002 (2006); 6 games with 2 goals.
Clubs: Cannes, Bordeaux, Juventus, Real Madrid.

5 Didí   (Brazil)   08.10.28

Didí (Waldir Pereira) was the central midfielder who guided Brazil to their first two World Cup wins in 1958 and 1962. Didí had great technique and vision, and was responsible for many of the assists to Brazil's strikers of the era (Pelé, Váva, Zagallo, Amarildo, and Garrincha). Didí is also credited as the inventor of the unpredictable "dry leaf" or "banana" free kick technique.

Didí played on club teams in Brazil, Spain, and Peru. He also joined powerhouse Real Madrid as their first Brazilian star, but had difficulty settling into the Real style. After playing for Sporting Cristal in Peru, he later coached the Peruvian national team in the 1970 World Cup, thus helping to open up the possibilities for other ex-Brazil players to coach abroad.

Awards: *World Soccer's* 100 Greatest Footballers of all time.
France Football's World Cup Top-100 1930-1990.
Best 20 Players of Century list [Placar].
International: 68 games with 20 goals.
World Cup: 1954, 1958 & 1962; 15 games with 3 goals.
Clubs: Fluminense, Botafogo, Real Madrid, Sporting Cristal.

6 Bobby Charlton   (England)   11.10.37

Bobby Charlton was a speedy withdrawn striker or attacking midfielder with excellent close control, and he combined those attributes as a devastating dribbler in the open field. He packed considerable power with either foot, and used it to score many spectacular goals.

After winning the 1957 English championship with Manchester United, Charlton survived the February 6, 1958 airplane crash of Manchester United's "Busby Babes" team that killed many of his teammates, and continued to build a successful career as a central attacker.

Charlton won three English championships with Manchester United (1957, 1966 & 1967), and captained the 1968 European Cup winning team in their win against Eusébio's Benfica.

Charlton was instrumental for England when they won the 1966 World Cup on their own soil, as he scored the two goals in the 2-1 semi-final win against Portugal to gain the Final. He still holds the England scoring record with 49 goals.

Awards: 1966 European Footballer of the Year.
1966 English Footballer of the Year Award.
France Football's Football Player of the Century (# 16).
France Football's World Cup Top-100 1930-1990.
Planète Foot (France) best 50 players of all time.
World Soccer's 100 Greatest Footballers of all time.
2004 Pelé/FIFA Best 125 Living Players.
International: 105 games with 49 goals.
World Cup: 1962, 1966, & 1970; 14 games with 4 goals.
Clubs: Manchester United, Preston North End.

7 Ruud Gullit   (Holland)   01.09.62

Ruud Gullit was an offensive midfielder possessing all the technique and physique that were enhanced by superior vision on the field. An instinctive improviser on the pitch, he led the second generation of Dutch players after the 1970s successes of Cruyff & Company's "Orange Machine."

Gullit was the captain of the 1988 European Championship team that brought the first international soccer championship medal to the Netherlands, and he scored the first goal in the 2-0 Final win over the Soviet Union. He subsequently played in the 1990 World Cup, but declined to appear in the 1994 World Cup in the USA.

Gullit won six top division championships with Feyenoord, PSV Eindhoven, and AC Milan. With Milan he was most successful, winning both the European Champions Cup and Intercontinental Cup two years in a row (1989-1990). He finished with 161 goals in 429 top division matches.

Never afraid to voice his opinion, Gullit campaigned for the release of Nelson Mandela before it was fashionable.

Awards: 1987 European Footballer of the year.
1987 and 1989 *World Soccer* Footballer of the year.
1984 & 1986 Dutch Footballer of the Year.
Planète Foot (France) best 50 players of all time.
World Soccer's 100 Greatest Footballers of All Time.
Placar (Brazil) best 100 players of all time.
2004 Pelé/FIFA Best 125 Living Players.
International: 66 games with 17 goals.
World Cup: 1990; 4 games with 1 goal.
Clubs: Haarlem, Feyenoord, PSV Eindhoven, Milan, Sampdoria, Chelsea.

8 Teófilo Cubillas   (Peru)   08.03.49

Teófilo "Nene" Cubillas was a "number 10" creative midfielder who directed Peru's play in their second golden era of soccer in the 1970s (first golden era was the 1930's – see Chapter 13). Pelé said "After Cubillas there is nobody [comparable] in Peruvian soccer." Actually, there were not too many to compare to him globally as well – especially at the World Cup level.

Cubillas was quick, liked to run at defenses, and had excellent close control and a powerful shot. Cubillas played large on the world stage as he scored 10 goals in 10 games in the 1970 and 1978 World Cup tournaments (tied for fifth overall). He won the Silver Boot award in the 1978 World Cup, and remains the only player to score at least five goals in two separate World Cups.

Peru did not qualify for the 1974 World Cup, but one year later they conquered all in South America as they became Copa America champions. Cubillas scored the go-ahead goal in their shocking 3-1 first leg semifinal win over Brazil in Belo Horizonte, and he remains the all-time goal leader for Peru.

Cubillas began with local team Alianza Lima, and led the First Division in scoring at the age of 16. He joined Basel in 1973, and shortly thereafter settled into a midfield role for Porto. He was an Alianza player again when he helped Peru reach the second phase of the 1978 World Cup, and he won two league championships with Alianza in 1977-1978. He joined Fort Lauderdale after the 1978 World Cup, and in five seasons in the NASL Cubillas scored 59 goals in 120 games, including a hat trick in seven minutes against Los Angeles Aztecs in 1981. Overall, Cubillas had 268 goals in 469 top division games.

Cubillas was the second South American Footballer of the Year in 1972. Interestingly, two of the Peru World Cup teams Cubillas played for were coached by Brazilian World Cup stars – Didí (Waldir Pereira) was coach in 1970, and Tim (Elba Pádua Lima, 1938 World Cup) coached in 1982.

After Alianza Lima's team airplane crashed on December 8, 1987, Cubillas remarkably came out of retirement to help his original club recover from the immediate shock.

Awards: 1972 South American Footballer of the Year.
World Soccer's 100 Greatest Footballers of all time.
France Football's World Cup Top-100 1930-1990.
Placar (Brazil) best 100 players of all time.
2004 Pelé/FIFA Best 125 Living Players.
International: 81 and 26 goals.
World Cup: 1970, 1978, & 1982; 13 games with 10 goals.
Clubs: Alianza Lima, Basel, Porto, Fort Lauderdale.

9 Johan Neeskens   (Netherlands)   15.09.51

Johan Neeskens was a mercurial midfielder on the Ajax and Dutch teams of the 1970s who could fulfill any role – ball winner, creator, or scorer. Always one of the fittest players on the pitch, he nonetheless had excellent technique and vision, and was deadly on penalty kicks. Neeskens personified the "total football" style as well as Johan Cruyff.

Neeskens was a stellar World Cup performer, and was twice runner-up with the Netherlands, reaching the 1974 and 1978 World Cup Final in the host countries. He is one of three midfielders to score five goals in one World Cup, along with Teófilo Cubillas and Rivaldo.

Neeskens played on championship teams in three different countries: Ajax in Holland (1972 and 1973), Barcelona in Spain (1974), and the New York Cosmos in the USA (1980 and 1982). He was a critical part of Ajax's team, as they won three consecutive European Cup championships (1971, 1972, 1973) and the 1972 Intercontinental Cup.

Awards: 1976 Best Spanish League foreign player.
Planète Foot (France) best 50 players of all time.
Placar (Brazil) best 100 players of all time.
2004 Pelé/FIFA Best 125 Living Players.
International: 49 games with 17 goals.
World Cup: 1974 & 1978; 12 games with 5 goals.
Clubs: Haarlem, Ajax Amsterdam, Barcelona, New York Cosmos, Groningen.

10 Luis Suárez (Spain) 02.05.35

Luis Suárez was one of the great organizing and attacking midfielders of the modern era. Not content to direct from a distance, he helped modernize the forward-looking more free-ranging creative midfielder.

Suárez remains the only Spanish-born European Footballer of the Year, winning in 1960 while with Barcelona. He led Barcelona to two league titles and the 1958 and 1960 UEFA Cups. The following year Suárez led Barcelona to victory over Real Madrid in the 1961 European Cup quarterfinals, which was Real Madrid's first ever defeat in the European football competition. Later that year Internazionale brought him to the Italian league, in the process making him the world's most expensive footballer.

In Italy, Suárez led Internazionale to the Serie A title in 1963, 1965 and 1966, and the European Cup championship and Intercontinental Cup in 1964 and 1965.

Suárez led the Spanish national side in the 1962 & 1966 World Cups, and to the European Championship in 1964.

Awards: 1960 European Footballer of the Year.
1961 & 1964 European Footballer of the Year, 2nd place.
Venerdì's All-Time Top-100 (100 Magnifici).
Placar (Brazil) best 100 players of all time.
International: 32 games with 14 goals.
World Cup: 1962 & 1966; 4 games.
Clubs: Deportivo de La Coruña, Barcelona, Internazionale, Sampdoria.

11 Kazimierz Deyna (Poland) 23.10.47

Kazimierz Deyna was the indisputable organizer of the great Polish teams of the 1970s. He was a dynamic midfielder who could create, and excelled in precision passing and rushing up field to score with powerful and accurate shooting.

Deyna won the Olympic Gold medal with the Poland squad in 1972, and followed up by winning the World Cup bronze in 1974 (beating giants Brazil, Argentina, and Italy along the way). As captain in the 1978 World Cup, Poland advanced to the second round but could not duplicate their 1974 success.

After the 1974 World Cup, Real Madrid sought Deyna's services, but he was not allowed to leave Poland. He won the Polish championship twice with Legia Warsaw, then was one of the first East European players to play in the West, signing at age 31 with Manchester City. He then played with the San Diego Sockers of the NASL, where he scored 44 goals in 90 games as a midfielder. He also played professional indoor soccer where he again excelled.

Awards: 1974 European Footballer of the Year voting, 3rd after Cruyff and Beckenbauer.
France Football's World Cup Top-105 1930-1990.
International: 84 games with 33 goals.
World Cup: 1974 & 1978; 13 games with 4 goals.
Clubs: Legia Warsaw, Manchester City, San Diego Sockers.

12 Rivaldo (Brazil) 19.04.72

Rivaldo (Vito Borba Ferreira) is an all-rounder who can dribble, shoot, and pass with the best. Rivaldo could play either the creative "number 10" midfielder position, or in an out-and-out striker position. In the 1998 World Cup Final he played more of a creative midfielder role and was one of few decent Brazilian players in their 3-0 loss.

Rivaldo played a combined withdrawn position again in the 2002 World Cup, as central striker Ronaldo needed sophisticated service. Even so, he had goals in Brazil's first five World Cup games -- a feat even Ronaldo could not match. He was the 2002 World Cup's best performer (as evaluated by Brazil coach Scolari), although he officially finished only fourth (after Oliver Kahn, Ronaldo, and

Hong Myung Bo). He also won the 1997 & 1999 Copa America with Brazil, and was the 1999 World Player of the Year.

Rivaldo was twice league champion with Barcelona, and a European Cup winner with AC Milan. As of December 2005, he scored 202 goals in 402 top division matches. Rivaldo scored 125 goals with Barcelona; perhaps the three most memorable came in 2001 in one game and sealed a European Champions League qualification spot. The ultimate goal of that hat trick against Valencia was a wonderful bicycle kick goal from 20 yards.

    Awards: 1999 World Player of the Year.
                      1999 *Onze d'Or* winner.
                      1998 Best Spanish League foreign player.
                      2004 Pelé/FIFA Best 125 Living Players.
    International: 74 games with 34 goals.
    World Cup: 1998 & 2002; 14 games and 8 goals.
    Clubs: Corinthians, Palmeiras, Deportivo la Coruña, Barcelona, AC Milan, Cruzeiro, Olympiakos.

13 Enzo Francescoli   (Uruguay)   12.11.61

Enzo Francescoli was Uruguay's best modern footballer, a real "number 10" with excellent vision and scoring ability. He was much admired for his elegant play, including being Zinedine Zidane's boyhood idol, as he played for Zidane's hometown Marseille in the 1980s (Zidane even named his son after him).

Francescoli was a massive success with the Uruguay national team, as he led them to three Copa America titles (1983, 1987, 1995).

Francescoli also won top division championships with River Plate and Marseille, and the 1996 Copa Libertadores with River Plate.

    Awards: 1984 & 1995 South American Footballer of the Year.
                      1985 & 1995 Argentine Footballer of the Year.
                      1987 French League Foreign Player of the Year.
                      France Football's Footballer of the Century (# 12).
                      Planète Foot (France) best 50 players of all time.
                      World Soccer's 100 Greatest Footballers of all time.
                      Placar (Brazil) best 100 players of all time.
                      2004 Pelé/FIFA Best 125 Living Players.
    International: 72 games with 15 goals.
    World Cup: 1986 & 1990; 8 games with 1 goal.
    Clubs: Wanderers, River Plate, Racing Matra, Marseille, Cagliari, Torino.

14 Gheorghe Hagi   (Romania)   05.02.65

Gheorghe Hagi was Romania's best-ever footballer. He had excellent technique and vision, his passing abilities were unparalleled, and his shots often found the goal. He was very creative in the pass or the shot, as witnessed by his long-range goal against Colombia in the 1994 World Cup, which caught the keeper just off his line. His dribbling abilities were also formidable.

Hagi was instrumental in guiding Romania to their first three World Cups, bringing them to the quarterfinals in 1994 and the second round in 1998.

Hagi played for many big clubs, and helped bring first-ever European trophies to a Turkish team in 2000, when Galatasaray won the UEFA Cup and SuperCup. He had 227 goals in 485 Top Division matches over his career.

    Awards: 1994 European Footballer of the Year, 4th in voting.
                      1985, 1987, 1993, 1994, 1997, 1999 & 2000 Romania Footballer of the Year.
                      2004 Pelé/FIFA Best 125 Living Players.
    International: 125 caps with 35 goals for Romania.
    World Cup: 1990, 1994 & 1998; 12 games with 3 goals.
    Clubs: Steaua Bucharest, Real Madrid, Brescia, Barcelona, Galatasaray.

15 **Raymond Kopa** (France) 13.10.31

Raymond Kopa [born Kopaszewski] was the progeny of a Polish immigrant family who grew up to be France's greatest midfield influence until Michel Platini. A wonderfully creative dribbler and passer, most goal moves would pass through his feet until their successful execution.

Kopa guided France to a third-place finish in the 1958 World Cup, assisting on most of Just Fontaine's record (for one tournament) 13 goals.

Kopa also won six top division championships directing the midfields of Stade de Reims and Real Madrid, and three European Cups with Real Madrid.

- Awards: 1958 European Footballer of the Year.
  France Football's Footballer of the Century (# 18).
  Planète Foot (France) best 50 players of all time.
  World Soccer's 100 Greatest Footballers of all time.
  France Football's World Cup Top-100 1930-1990.
  2004 Pelé/FIFA Best 125 Living Players.
- International: 45 games with 18 goals.
- World Cup: 1954 & 1958; 8 games with 4 goals.
- Clubs: Angers, Stade de Reims, Real Madrid.

16 **Roberto Rivelino** (Brazil) 01.01.46

Roberto Rivelino was a ball wizard with his sole of the foot and stepover (now often referred to as "lollipop") moves, able to routinely extricate himself from three or four defenders. He also had magical passing and free kick skills. Rivelino was the *futbolista* Maradona admired most for his ball skill, which should vouch for his superlative abilities.

Rivelino was one of "*five number 10's*" in the 1970 Brazil team, playing a withdrawn left wing position. He later played the creative midfield role in the 1974 and 1978 Brazil World Cup teams, and served as Brazil captain.

Rivelino is credited with scoring the fastest goal in club play ever - 3 seconds after kickoff – a direct shot from the center circle after he noticed the keeper was not concentrating.

- Awards: Best 50 South American Players of the Century.
  Planète Foot (France) best 50 players of all time.
  World Soccer's 100 Greatest Footballers of all time.
  France Football's World Cup Top-100 1930-1990.
  Placar (Brazil) best 100 players of all time.
  2004 Pelé/FIFA Best 125 Living Players.
- International: 91 games with 25 goals.
- World Cup: 1970, 1974 & 1978; 15 games with 6 goals.
- Clubs: Corinthians, Fluminense, Al Hilal.

17 **Kenny Dalglish** (Scotland) 05.03.51

Kenny Dalglish was the quicksilver *fantasista* of the successful Liverpool teams of the late 1970s and 1980s. With tremendous ball skills, field awareness, incisive passing and lethal shooting – Dalglish could play any midfield or striker position.

Dalglish performed in three World Cups for Scotland, and shares Scotland's top goal scorer mantle with Denis Law.

Dalglish was a perennial winner in his club career. In total, he won thirteen top division championships with Celtic and Liverpool, and three European Cup championships with Liverpool (1978, 1981, and 1984). Dalglish scored 230 goals in 558 Top Division games over his career, and was the first to score 100 goals in the English and Scottish leagues.

- Awards: 1979 & 1983 English Footballer of the Year.
  1983 European Footballer of the Year, 2nd behind Platini.
  World Soccer's 100 Greatest Footballers of all time.
  2004 Pelé/FIFA Best 125 Living Players.
- International: 102 games with 30 goals.
- World Cup: 1974, 1978, & 1982; 8 games with 2 goals.
- Clubs: Celtic, Liverpool.

18 **Michael Laudrup** (Denmark) 15.06.64

Michael Laudrup was Denmark's top field player ever, an extremely quick attacking midfielder with exceptional technique and vision, remarkable on the dribble and a clinical finisher. Laudrup is Denmark's most capped outfield player, but he missed out on the greatest Danish football achievement of the 1992 European championship.

Laudrup was extremely successful on the club side, having the extraordinary experience of winning seven top division titles on four championship teams in three countries (Italy, Spain, and Holland). He won league titles with Juventus (1986), Barcelona (1991-1994), Real Madrid (1995), and Ajax (1998). Laudrup also won the European Cup with Barcelona in 1992. He finished with 117 goals in 464 top division matches.

Awards: 1992 Best foreign Footballer of Spanish league.
1989, 1992, 1995, & 1997 Danish Footballer of the Year.
1985 (4th) & 1993 (5th) European Footballer of the Year voting.
Placar (Brazil) best 100 players of all time.
2004 Pelé/FIFA Best 125 Living Players.

International: 104 games with 37 goals.
World Cup: 1986 & 1998. 9 games with 2 goals.
Clubs: Copenhagen, Brondby, Lazio, Juventus, Barcelona, Real Madrid, Vissel Kobe, Ajax.

19 **Gianni Rivera** (Italy) 18.08.43

Gianni Rivera was an advanced creative midfielder with offensive ideas, often at odds with the proponents of the classic Italian defensive schemes. Rivera had a classy elegant and aesthetic style, impeccable in the dribble and distribution.

Rivera won the European championship with Italy in 1968, and was a World Cup finalist in 1970, where he sometimes shared the creative duties with Sandro Mazzola. Overall he participated in four World Cup Finals competitions.

Rivera won two league Cups, two European Cups (1963 and 1969), and an Intercontinental Cup (1969) with Milan. He finished with 124 goals in 501 top division matches.

Awards: 1969 European Footballer of the Year.
1963 European Footballer of the Year voting, 2nd to Lev Yashin.
Venerdì's All-Time Top-100 (100 Magnifici).
France Football's World Cup Top-100 1930-1990.
Planète Foot (France) best 50 players of all time.
World Soccer's 100 Greatest Footballers of All Time.
France Football's World Cup Top-100 1930-1990.
2004 Pelé/FIFA Best 125 Living Players.

International: 60 games with 14 goals.
World Cup: 1962, 1966, 1970, & 1974; 9 games with 3 goals.
Clubs: Alessandria, AC Milan.

20 **Gérson** (Brazil) 11.01.41

Gérson (Gérson de Oliveira Nunes) was a left-footed complete midfielder who served thirteen years for Brazil. A tireless worker, he had excellent vision and distribution, and had the dribbling skills of a striker. He scored many important goals with long drives off his thundering left foot.

One of the 1970 Brazil team's *"five number 10's,"* he scored the winning goal for Brazil in the 1970 World Cup Final.

Gérson won several national competitions with his club teams Flamengo, Botafogo, and São Paulo.

Awards: *World Soccer's* 100 Greatest Footballers of all time.
Placar (Brazil) best 100 players of all time.
Brazil All-Time XI Team.

International: 69 games with 14 goals.
World Cup: 1966 & 1970; 5 games with 1 goal.
Clubs: Flamengo, Botafogo, São Paulo, Fluminense.

21 Josef Masopust (Czechoslovakia) 09.02.31

Josef Masopust was the midfield general of Dukla Prague and Czechoslovakia national team. Possessed with great stamina and vision, he was an incisive passer who liked to press forward. He won eight national championships with Dukla Prague, and helped them to advance to the semi-finals of the 1966 and 1967 European Cups.

With Masopust directing the play, Czechoslovakia faced Brazil twice in the 1962 World Cup. In the first match, in a show of exemplary sportsmanship, Masopust refused to take advantage of the injured Pelé, and the game ended 0-0. In the subsequent 1962 Cup Final, Masopust scored the game's initial goal and performed well against defending champions Brazil. However, Czechoslovakia eventually succumbed to Brazil 1-3. Based on his World Cup performances, he was voted European Footballer of the Year.

Awards: 1962 European Footballer of the Year.
Best Czech Footballer of the Century.
Planète Foot (France) best 50 players of all time.
World Soccer's 100 Greatest Footballers of all time.
France Football's World Cup Top-100 1930-1990.
2004 Pelé/FIFA Best 125 Living Players.
International: 63 games, 10 goals.
World Cup: 1958 & 1962. 10 games with 1 goal.
Clubs: Dukla Prague, Crossing Molenbeeck.

22 Falcão (Brazil) 16.10.53

Paulo Roberto Falcão was a Brazilian midfielder with great technical ability, vision, and shooting ability. He was part of the Brazil team of the 1980s who played with tremendous imagination, but failed to win a major championship. Falcão nevertheless thrilled the world with his performances in the 1982 Cup, including three wondrous goals from midfield.

Falcão was a three-time Brazilian champion with Internacional, before leaving for Roma. Falcão was a very successful import to Italian soccer, and won the 1983 Italian championship and the 1981 & 1984 Italian Cup with Roma, where the fans remember him fondly.

Awards: *Placar* (Brazil) best 100 players of all time.
Guerin' Sportivo's I 50 Grandi del Secolo.
IFFHS 50 South American Footballer of the Century list.
1978 & 1979 Brazil Footballer of the Year.
Onze Mondial Footballer of the Year, 2nd in 1983, 3rd in 1982.
Venerdì's All-Time Top-100 (100 Magnifici).
2004 Pelé/FIFA Best 125 Living Players.
International: 32 games with 9 goals.
World Cup: 1982 & 1986; 7 games with 3 goals.
Clubs: Internacional, Roma, São Paulo.

23 Sócrates (Brazil) 19.02.54

Sócrates (Sócrates Brasileiro Sampaio de Souza Vieira de Oliveira) had wonderful technique combined with the ability to inspire collective play at club and country level. Sócrates and Falcão controlled the Brazil midfield with pinpoint passing rather than pointless running after the ball. Long and lean, Sócrates was dominant on the ball – if challenged he would simply change direction and move or pass away. He spelled trouble for the opposition when he launched into attack, as he was a formidable goal scoring threat from midfield.

In club play, Sócrates won three championships with Corinthians, and one with Flamengo. He was also the founder of what was called the "Corinthian Democracy," a grassroots movement that empowered players to make their own decisions, and also challenged the Brazilian soccer authorities and military dictatorship.

Sócrates is trained as a pediatrician, but should take Johan Cruyff's medical advice and quit smoking cigarettes. A delightful interview of Sócrates is presented in Alex Bellos' book on Brazilian soccer.

Awards: 1983 South American Footballer of the Year.
Placar (Brazil) best 100 players of all time.
Venerdì's All-Time Top-100 (100 Magnifici).

2004 Pelé/FIFA Best 125 Living Players.
International: 60 games with 22 goals.
World Cup: 1982 & 1986; 10 games with 4 goals.
Clubs: Botafogo, Corinthians, Fiorentina, Flamengo, Santos.

24 Wolfgang Overath   (West Germany)   29.09.43

Wolfgang Overath was the midfield conductor for the West German teams in the 1960s and 1970s. He had excellent technique and vision, and operated as an organizing as well as a creative midfielder.

Overath's duties in the West German national team increased when Franz Beckenbauer moved from midfielder to sweeper, but he responded very well as West Germany won the World Cup at home in 1974. Overath also won the 1972 European Championship with West Germany.

Overath was Bundesliga champion once with FC Köln, and scored 84 goals in 409 games for his only club.

Awards: World Soccer's 100 Greatest Footballers of All Time.
International: 81 games with 17 goals.
World Cup: 1966, 1970 & 1974; 19 games with 3 goals.
Club: FC Köln.

25 Alessandro Mazzola   (Italy)   08.11.42

Sandro Mazzola was an attacking midfielder much in the mold of his soccer star father, Valentino Mazzola, who died in the *Superga* airplane disaster in 1949. Despite his personal tragedy, Mazzola grew into a true "number 10" like his father, with excellent vision and distribution, formidable dribbling skills, and a nose for the goal.

Mazzola won the European championship with Italy in 1968, and was a World Cup finalist in 1970, where he often shared the creative duties with Gianni Rivera. Mazzola participated in three World Cup Finals competitions.

Mazzola won four league championships (1963, 1965, 1966, & 1971), two European Cups (1964 and 1965), and two Intercontinental Cups (1964 & 1965) with Internazionale Milan. He scored the first and last goals as Inter beat Real Madrid 3-1 in their first European Championship Cup win in 1964. He finished with 157 goals in 561 top division matches.

Awards: 1971 European Footballer of the Year voting, 2nd to Johan Cruyff.
Venerdì's All-Time Top-100 (100 Magnifici)
World Soccer's 100 Greatest Footballers of All Time.
France Football's World Cup Top-100 1930-1990.
International: 70 games with 22 goals.
World Cup: 1966, 1970, & 1974; 12 games with 1 goal.
Clubs: Internazionale Milan.

26 Zbigniew Boniek   (Poland)   03.03.56

Zbigniew Boniek played in three World Cups for Poland, helping them reach the second round each time. A tireless attacking and creative midfielder, he helped engineer Poland's third place in the 1982 World Cup. At that Cup, he had a memorable hat trick against a good Belgian team. Unfortunately, he was suspended for the key game against Italy, which Poland lost.

Boniek joined Juventus in Italy after the 1982 World Cup, and formed an impressive attacking trio with Michel Platini and Paolo Rossi. With Juventus, he won the 1984 Cup Winners' Cup, and the European Champions Cup and Intercontinental Cup in 1985. He then won an Italian Cup medal with his next team, Roma.

Awards: *Planète Foot* (France) best 50 players of all time.
France Football's World Cup Top-100 1930-1990.
2004 Pelé/FIFA Best 125 Living Players.
International: 80 games with 24 goals.
World Cup: 1978, 1982, and 1986; 16 games with 6 goals.
Clubs: Widzew Lodz, Juventus, Roma.

27 **Bernd Schuster** (West Germany) 22.12.59

Bernd Schuster was a midfielder with flair, great technique and vision, who elected to spend much of his successful club career in the Spanish league. He was an excellent conductor of a team, and had potent shooting and heading abilities.

After he won the European Championship with West Germany in 1980, Schuster effectively retired from the national team at age 23. No doubt they could have used his creative abilities for the rest of the decade.

Schuster was very successful playing in the Spanish league, and he showed up on many Footballer of the Year lists. With Barcelona, he won the Spanish League once, the Spanish Cup three times, and the Cup Winners' Cup once, but lost the 1986 European Champion's Cup in 1986 in a penalty shootout to Steaua Bucharest. With Real Madrid he won the Spanish League twice and the Cup once. He later won the Spanish Cup twice more with Atletico Madrid.

Schuster ended with more than 100 goals in 445 First Division matches.

Awards: European Footballer of the Year, 2nd in 1980, 3rd in 1981 & 1985.
1985 & 1991 Best Foreign Footballer in Spanish League (with Barcelona and Atletico Madrid, respectively).
International: 21 games with 4 goals.
World Cup: No appearances.
Clubs: Augsburg, Köln, Barcelona, Real Madrid, Atletico Madrid, Bayer Leverkusen, UNAM.

28 **Osvaldo Ardiles** (Argentina) 03.08.52

Osvaldo "Ossie" Ardiles was the creative *mediocampista* of the 1978 World Cup winning Argentine home side. Small and slight, with excellent dribbling and passing skills, he was also an outstanding creator for Huracán and later for Tottenham in England.

Along with fellow compatriot Ricardo Villa, Ardiles helped Spurs win the 1981 English FA Cup. However, during the Argentina-England Malvinas-Falklands "war" in 1982, Ardiles was forced to avoid controversy and move temporarily to France and Paris Saint-Germain, where he won the French Cup. Ardiles returned to England and Tottenham after the conflict and helped them win the 1984 UEFA Cup.

Ardiles trained in law, and after retiring he made a career in coaching, including stints in England (Swindon Town, Newcastle, Tottenham), Japan (Yokohama), Croatia (Zagreb), and Argentina (Racing).

Awards: *Venerdì's* All-Time Top-100 (100 Magnifici).
All-Time Argentina XI.
International: 53 games with 8 goals.
World Cup: 1978 and 1982; 11 games with 1 goal.
Clubs: Huracán, Tottenham, Paris-Saint-Germain, Blackburn, Swindon Town.

29 **Raí** (Brazil) 15.05.65

Raí (Souza Vieira de Oliveira) was an offensive midfielder for clubs in Brazil and France, and for the Brazilian national team. He was a 1994 World Cup winner, although he did not see any action in the Final match (because Brazil opted for a more "defensive" midfield, and not surprisingly the Final ended 0-0).

Raí had a very successful club career, especially at São Paulo when they reigned supreme, winning two consecutive Copa Libertadores and Intercontinental Cups in 1992 & 1993. Raí scored both goals in the 1992 Intercontinental Cup as São Paulo defeated a superb Barcelona side 2-1. Raí also won the 1996 Cup Winners' Cup with Paris St. Germain.

Raí is the younger brother of Sócrates (#22 midfielder).

Awards: 1992 South American Footballer of the Year.
1992 Intercontinental Cup MVP.
1995 and 1997 French Foreign Footballer of the Year.
International: 49 games with 15 goals.
World Cup: 1994; 4 games with 1 goal.
Clubs: São Paulo, Paris St. Germain.

30 Luis Figo (Portugal) 04.11.72

Luis Figo is the best Portuguese player of the last decade, a wing-midfielder with outstanding ball skills, lightning change of pace and the ability to make pinpoint passes as well as being a regular goal-scorer. He also has a striker's ability to "take players on" and beat them one-on-one.

Figo was a member of the young Portuguese team that won the World Youth Cup U-20 in 1991, but despite high aspirations, this success was never repeated at the full national team level until host Portugal reached the Final of the 2004 European championships.

Figo was very successful in club play, winning league titles at Barcelona (1999) and Real Madrid (2001 & 2003). He also won the European Champions League and the Intercontinental Cup with Real Madrid in 2002.

Awards: 2000 European Footballer of the Year.
2001 FIFA World Footballer of the Year.
1995 – 2000 Portuguese Footballer of the Year awards.
2004 Pelé/FIFA Best 125 Living Players.
International: 117 caps, 31 goals.
World Cup: 2002 (2006); 3 games.
Clubs: Sporting Lisbon, Barcelona, Real Madrid.

31 Pavel Nedved (Czech Republic) 30.08.72

Pavel Nedved has been the midfield engine for the Czech Republic and his club teams for the last decade. Nedved's determined style of play and outstanding skills have at times allowed him to dominate games. Nedved is really a "total" midfielder, able to create, defend, score, and control the game tempo.

Nedved was instrumental in the Czech Republic's success at the European Championships in 1996 and 2004, when they lost in the Final and semi-final, respectively. Nedved came out of international retirement to help the Czech Republic qualify for the 2006 World Cup.

Making his name at Dukla and then Sparta Prague, he moved to Lazio where he won the 1998 Italian Cup and the final Cup Winner's Cup competition in 1999, when he scored the winning goal. Lazio also won the Italian championship (scudetto) in 2000. He then moved to Juventus to replace the departing Zinedine Zidane, and proceeded to help them win the scudetto in 2002 and 2003. When Juventus reached the 2003 Champions League Final, however, Nedved had been suspended, and Juventus lost on penalties to Milan.

Awards: 2004 European Footballer of the Year.
2003 Italy Footballer of the Year.
1998, 2000, 2003 & 2004 Czech Republic Player of the Year.
2004 Pelé/FIFA Best 125 Living Players.
International: 85 games and 17 goals.
World Cup: (2006).
Clubs: Dukla Prague, Sparta Prague, Lazio, Juventus.

32 Bryan Robson (England) 11.01.57

Bryan Robson was the inspiring midfield scoring engine for England in the 1980s. Robson had tremendous stamina, and ball-winning and passing abilities, but what set him apart from other midfielders was his ability to get to the goal. If he had managed to remain relatively injury-free, the public would have enjoyed him even more.

Robson played in three World Cups but only eight games, often playing injured. He scored a goal after only 27 seconds, in a losing effort in the 1982 England-France game (recently eclipsed for speed by Turkey's Hakan Sükür's 11-second effort in the 2002 World Cup 3rd place game against South Korea).

Robson was a long-time captain of Manchester United, where he won the top division championship twice (1993 & 1994). He also won the FA Cup in 1983, 1985, and 1990, and finished with 97 goals in 434 games for Manchester United. Robson finished with 163 goals in 748 matches for his career.

Awards: *France Football's* World Cup Top 100 1930-1990.
International: 90 games with 26 goals.
World Cup: 1982, 1986 & 1990; 8 games with 2 goals.
Clubs: West Bromwich Albion, Manchester United, Middlesbrough.

33 Julio César Romero   (Paraguay)   28.08.57

Julio César Romero Insfrán (widely known as *Romerito*) was a creative and attacking midfielder with extraordinary dribbling technique and field vision. He had early success with the Paraguayan national team, when he scored two goals in the home leg to help win the Copa America in 1979.

His impressive skills brought him to top club teams in the USA, Brazil, and Spain. He won three First division championships, including the Brazilian championship and three state titles with Fluminense, and two titles with the New York Cosmos (1980 & 1982).

Romero was the first Paraguayan to win the South American Footballer of the Year in 1985.

Awards: 1985 South American Footballer of the Year.
              2004 Pelé/FIFA Best 125 Living Players.
International: 32 caps, 13 goals.
World Cup: 1986; 4 games with 2 goals.
Clubs: Sportivo Luqueño, New York Cosmos, Fluminense, Barcelona, Puebla.

34 Fernando Redondo   (Argentina)   06.07.69

Fernando Redondo was a left-footed midfield maestro for Argentina and Real Madrid. With impressive technique, vision, and passing abilities, Redondo performed well in his only (by choice) World Cup in 1994. He was one of few players who could perform in either a defensive or creative midfielder role.

Redondo missed the 1990 World Cup because of his law studies and coach Carlos Bilardo's "safety first" approach (Argentina eventually arrived at the Final, but only after playing non-creative football for much of the tournament). Playing again for the national team, Redondo then helped Argentina win the 1993 Copa America. In the 1994 World Cup, he played superbly alongside Diego Maradona in his last international games. Argentina sorely missed Redondo in the 1998 World Cup because of coach Daniel Passarella's ludicrous hair-length requirements that excluded him.

Redondo won the 1998 and 2000 European Champions League and the 1998 Intercontinental Cup with Real Madrid, and the Champions League again in 2003 with Milan (but did not play due to injury). He was also 1995 & 1997 Spanish League champion with Real Madrid.

Awards: 1999/2000 UEFA Most Valuable Player award.
              1992 FIFA Confederation's Cup Golden Ball (Best Player) award.
International: 29 games with 1 goal.
World Cup: 1994; 4 games.
Clubs: Argentino Juniors, Tenerife, Real Madrid, AC Milan.

35 Liam Brady   (Ireland)   13.02.56

Liam Brady was Ireland's best player ever. The creative midfielder had one of the best left feet in history – a "most magical left peg" as they say in Britain. Brady had tremendous vision and exactness in his passing, and more than enough dribbling ability to get free for his incisive strikes.

Although Brady was the midfield general of the Irish national team, he alone was never able to engineer their qualification for the World Cup Finals.

Brady was an Arsenal legend, and there was much sadness when he left for Italy. However, Brady was one of the few successful British exports to Italian league soccer, and was twice league champion with Juventus just before the Platini era. Brady became as much admired for his abilities by Juventus fans as the Arsenal fans.

Awards: Europe's Best 100 Players of the Century by IFFHS.
International: 72 games with 9 goals.
World Cup: No appearances.
Clubs: Arsenal, Juventus, Sampdoria, Inter Milan, Ascoli, West Ham United.

36 Michel   (Spain)   23.03.63

Michel (José Miguel González) was an outstanding midfielder with the Spanish national team and Real Madrid. An organizational presence in the midfield, he could also create the play going forward, and track back well defensively.

Michel played in two World Cups (1986 and 1990), even getting three goals against South Korea in 1990. He scored 21 goals in 66 games for Spain, an outstanding rate for a midfielder.

Michel led Real Madrid to five straight Spanish League championships (1986-1990) and two UEFA Cups (1985 & 1986), on a team that also featured Hugo Sanchez and Emilio Butragueño. He had 97 goals in 404 matches for Real Madrid.

Awards: 1986 Spanish Footballer of the Year.
International: 66 games and 21 goals.
World Cup: 1986 & 1990; 9 games with 4 goals.
Clubs: Castilla, Real Madrid, Atlético Celayo.

37 Marco Etcheverry (Bolivia) 26.09.70

Marco Etcheverry is the best player to ever emerge from Bolivia. A creative midfielder with prodigious dribbling and passing talents, his nickname was El Diablo ("the Devil").

Etcheverry helped Bolivia qualify for their first World Cup in 1994, including beating Brazil 2-0 for their first ever qualifying loss. Unfortunately, due to injury and a red card, Etcheverry's World Cup time was limited to a few minutes of one game.

Etcheverry was a winner in club play, as he was an integral piece on championship teams in four different countries: Bolivar in Bolivia (1991-1992), Colo-Colo in Chile (1993), D.C. United in MLS-USA (1996, 1997, 1999), and Barcelona in Ecuador (1997).

Etcheverry joined D.C. United in the new MLS league in 1996, and in addition to leading them to three championships (in 1996, 1997, & 1999), he helped them win the 1996 USA Open Cup, the 1998 CONCACAF Champion's Cup (over Toluca of Mexico), and the 1998 Inter-American Cup (over Vasco da Gama of Brazil).

Awards: 1998 MLS (USA) Most Valuable Player (Footballer of the Year).
1996 MLS title game MVP.
Best MLS XI 1996-1999 (only player).
1993 South American Footballer of the Year, 2nd place.
International: 71 games with 13 goals.
World Cup: 1994; 1 game.
Clubs: Destroyers, Bolivar, Albacete, Colo Colo, América de Cali, Barcelona (Ecuador), Emelec, DC United.

38 Jan Ceulemans (Belgium) 28.02.57

Jan Ceulemans was a tall and lanky offensive midfielder who led the Belgian team during their impressive World Cup run during the 1980s. Ceulemans possessed great technique, could dribble at speed and take defenders on, and scored at an impressive rate for a midfielder. He was also the "lung" of club and country, able to cover tremendous ground in the midfield.

At the 1982 World Cup, he dribbled 80 yards before assisting on a goal against Hungary. As Belgium captain, he led the team to fourth place in the 1986 World Cup, scoring three goals in the process. He is still the all-time national team appearance leader for Belgium.

With his only club, Ceulemans won three league championships with Club Brugge. Over his career, Ceulemans scored 230 goals in 517 matches.

Awards: 1980, 1985 & 1986 Belgium Player of the Year.
1981 *Onze d'Or*, 3rd place.
1986 World Soccer Player of the Year, 5th place.
Voetbal International's "Great Fifty Footballers."
2004 Pelé/FIFA Best 125 Living Players.
International: 96 games and 23 goals.
World Cup: 1982, 1986, and 1990; 16 games with 4 goals.
Clubs: Club Brugge.

39 Carlos Valderrama (Columbia) 02.09.63

Carlos Valderrama, (known as *El Pibe* "the kid") was the midfield creative director for Colombia and numerous club teams in the 1980s and 1990s. Valderrama had an inimitable dribbling style and appeared deceptively slow, but he was nearly impossible to dispossess. Always ready to pass instead of shoot, he still had his share of goals in addition to many assists.

He was the long-time captain of Colombia, and his control of the Colombian midfield was the backbone that brought Colombia into three successive World Cups, where they advanced to the second round in 1990.

Valderrama won the League Cup with Montpellier, and was twice Colombian champion with Junior Barranquilla. He finished his career in the USA with several MLS teams, and played his last competitive game in 2004 at 40 years old.

He won his second South American Footballer of the Year award in 1993 on the strength of Colombia's first position in their World Cup qualifying group, which included a 5-0 demolition of Argentina in Buenos Aires.

Awards: 1987 & 1993 South American Footballer of the Year.
1996 MLS (USA) Player of the Year (MVP).
2004 Pelé/FIFA Best 125 Living Players.
International: 111 games with 11 goals.
World Cup: 1990, 1994, & 1998; 10 games with 1 goal.
Clubs: Unión Magdalena, Millionarios, Deportivo Cali, Montpellier, Real Valladolid, Independiente de Medellin, Junior Barranquilla, Tampa Bay Mutiny, Miami Fusion, Colorado Rapids.

40 David Platt   (England)   10.06.66

David Platt was a stellar attacking midfielder, and probably the most underrated English player in the modern era. He had excellent passing, dribbling and finishing skills, which were refined by his Italian experience. He served England well, with a strike rate that would make a forward envious.

Platt played in only one World Cup, but had the goal of the tournament. Platt took advantage of Paul Gascoigne's speculative free kick against Belgium in the final minute as he made a tremendous goal out of a scant chance – volleying the ball nearly blindly from behind and into the Belgian net – enabling England to advance to the next round. He had many more quality goals from midfield for club and country.

Platt was England captain for a time until injuries curtailed further contributions to the national side. He also played in the 1992 and 1996 European Championships, scoring three goals in seven games combined. Platt (like Roberto Baggio for Italy) won national team selection while playing for five club teams (Aston Villa, Bari, Juventus, Sampdoria, and Arsenal).

Platt was one of the few successful British players to perform in Italy, and won the UEFA Cup with Juventus in 1993. He finally transferred home to Arsenal, where he won the league and FA Cup double in 1998.

Awards: 1990 PFA Player of the Year.
International: 62 games with 27 goals.
World Cup: 1990; 6 games with 3 goals.
Clubs: Manchester United, Crewe, Aston Villa, Bari, Juventus, Sampdoria, Arsenal.

Midfielder Runner-ups
(Must have made first national team appearance by 1994)

Immediate runner-up list (players strongly considered for the original list):
Giancarlo Antognoni (Italy), John Barnes (England), Franz Beckenbauer (West Germany), Zvonimir Boban (Yugoslavia/Croatia), Vladislav Bogićević (Yugoslavia), Rainer Bonhof (West Germany), Mário Coluna (Portugal), Rui Costa (Portugal), Johan Cruyff (Netherlands), Cesar Cueto (Peru), Roberto Donadoni (Italy), Paul Gascoigne (England), Alain Giresse (France), Glenn Hoddle (England), Leonardo (Brazil), Jari Litmanen (Finland), Lothar Matthäus (Germany), Günther Netzer (West Germany), Pelé (Brazil), Abedi Ayew Pelé (Ghana), Robert Prosinecki (Yugoslavia & Croatia), Frank Rijkaard (Netherlands), Enzo Scifo (Belgium), Graeme Souness (Scotland), Marco Tardelli (Italy), Wim Van Hanegem (Netherlands), Zito (Brazil).

Complete runner-up list:
Alex Aguinaga (Ecuador), Lakhdar Belloumi (Algeria), Leonardo Cuellar (Mexico), Edgar Davids (Netherlands), Didier Deschamps (France), Youri Djorkaeff (France), Dunga (Brazil), Arie Haan (Netherlands), Uli Hoeness (West Germany), Thomas Hässler (Germany), Paul Ince (England), Christian Karembeu (France), Roy Keane (Ireland), Alan Kennedy (England), Tugay Kerimoglu (Turkey), Yordan Lechkov (Bulgaria), Pierre Littbarski (West Germany), Rabah Madjer (Algeria), Andreas Möller (West Germany & Germany), Jay Jay Okocha (Nigeria), Martin Peters (England), Emmanuel Petit (France), Karel Poborsky (Czech Republic), Claudio Reyna (USA), Freddy Rincon (Columbia), Erwin Sanchez (Bolivia), Diego Simeone (Argentina), António Simões (Portugal), Nolberto Solano (Peru), Alain Sutter (Switzerland), Jean Tigana (France), Zlatko Zahovič (Slovenia).

Great Midfields
of the Modern Era World Cups 1958-2002

The team standing in the World Cup is noted after the team and year in parentheses, and the number of goals scored by each player is noted after their name in parentheses. France's player totals are combined from the 1982 and 1986 World Cups.

(1) France 1982 (4th place) and 1986 (3rd place)
Michel Platini (4), Alain Giresse (3), Jean Tigana (1), Bernard Genghini (2), and Luis Fernandez (1).

This French midfield of the 1980s (the latter version that included Luis Fernandez) was called the *'carré magique'* or *'magic square,'* for their instinctive movement and passing.

Along with midfield substitutes Couriol (1), Girard (1), and Ferreri (1), this French midfield scored 9 of their 16 goals in the 1982 Cup, and 5 in the 1986 Cup. In between the two World Cups, this France team won the 1984 European championship.

(2) Brazil 1982 (second phase)
Falcão (3), Sócrates (2), Cerezo (and Zico).

When joined by "number 10" Zico (4), this Brazil midfield scored 9 of Brazil's 15 goals in 1982 World Cup. Led by offensive dynamo Zico and marshaled by Sócrates and Falcão, they were as sublime a ball-moving quartet as the 1980s French team.

(3a) West Germany 1974 (winners)
Wolfgang Overath (2), Rainer Bonhof (1), and Ulrich Hoeness (1).

This midfield had 4 of West Germany's total 13 goals in their title-wining effort, and was instrumental in controlling explosive Holland in the Final.

To emphasize the quality of this midfield; Günther Netzer - the stylish creative midfielder and hero of the West Germany's 1972 European Championship - was relegated to the bench by this trio for most of the competition.

(3b) Netherlands 1974 (second place) and 1978 (second place)
Johan Neeskens (5), Wim Van Hanegem, Wim Jansen, Arie Haan (2), Willie Van der Kerkhof (1).

Holland's midfield scored 5 (Neeskens' 5 goals) of their tournament high 15 goals in 1974, and 3 of their 13 goals in 1978. Van Hanegem was the creator, Haan scored from distance, and Neeskens was everywhere.

(5) France 1998 (winners)
Zinedine Zidane (2), Emmanuel Petit (2), Didier Deschamps, Christian Karembeu, and Youri Djorkaeff (1).

The same midfield (minus Christian Karembeu but plus Patrick Vieira) won the 2000 European Championships. Zidane was the creative force, although Djorkaeff and Petit were good defense penetrators as well.

(6) Italy: 1994 (second place on penalties)
Dino Baggio (2), Demetrio Albertini, Roberto Donadoni, and Nicola Berti.

Dino Baggio had two good goals, Donadoni provided the service, and the others prevented opposing teams from getting comfortable on the ball.

(7) West Germany 1990 (winners)
Lothar Matthäus (4), Thomas Hässler, Pierre Littbarski (1), and Thomas Berthold.

Lothar Matthäus was clearly the leader of this German team, but Hässler's and Littbarski's creative efforts were also critical to West Germany's World Cup-leading offense.

(8) Italy: 1982 (winners)
Marco Tardelli (2), Antonio Cabrini (1), Bruno Conti (1), Giancarlo Antognoni, Gabriele Oriali.

Antognoni provided the creativity, and the others the legs and the shooting for four goals from midfield to help Italy win their third World Cup title.

(9) England 1990 (4th place)
David Platt (3), Paul Gascoigne, Chris Waddle, Mark Wright (1), John Barnes, and Bryan Robson.

England had many of their skill positions locked up in this superb midfield, which although hampered by injury had a lot to do with their arrival in the semi-finals. But for bad luck in a post-game penalty competition against West Germany, they could have taken on Argentina in the Final.

(10) Turkey 2002 (3rd place)
Hasan Şaş (2), Ümit Davala (2), Emre Belözoğlu (1), and Yildiray Baştürk.

The best midfield of the 2002 World Cup, all of them dynamic two-way performers. All but Baştürk had great goals, and Baştürk had one shot cleared off the Senegalese goal line by Omar Daf in the defensive play of the tournament.

Best Strikers

1 Pelé (Brazil) 21.11.40

The player born Edson Arantes do Nascimento was from his youth known simply as Pelé. Compact and medium-sized, his explosive first step and feinting abilities gave defenses nightmares, and his football imagination was equal to his impressive finishing skills. Perhaps most significantly, audiences could witness the supreme joy that the expression of Pelé's talent gave him when he played "the beautiful game" (his own description of soccer, and the title of his autobiography "*Pelé, My Life and the Beautiful Game*").

Pelé played a withdrawn central striker and playmaker role, and defined the "number 10" position of a special creative player who can score. But Pelé's skills were not limited to one position, and once he played all eleven positions in a Brazilian league game. Pelé was a complete footballer that could have been a stellar defender like Passarella or Chumpitaz, or a Hugo Campos-style goalkeeper.

Pelé exploded onto the world scene at the age of seventeen, scoring six goals in the 1958 World Cup, including two against Sweden in the Final. He is the only player to have participated on three World Cup championship teams (1958, 1962, and 1970), and one of two players to score in four World Cups (record shared with Uwe Seeler of West Germany).

Pelé played for Santos from 1956-1974, shattering club and Brazilian league records. He led Santos to six Brazilian championships, two Copa Libertadores (South America championship) wins, and two world club championships (the Intercontinental Cup). The 1962 Intercontinental Cup win came against Eusébio's Benfica team only a few months after he had been injured in the 1962 World Cup; Pelé had five goals in the home and away series. The 1963 Intercontinental Cup success came against the great Milan team of Amarildo, Altafini, Rivera, Trapattoni, and Maldini.

Pelé came out of retirement in 1975 to perform with the New York Cosmos. He was the 1976 NASL MVP, and led the Cosmos to the 1977 Soccer Bowl league championship. To celebrate his permanent retirement in 1977, Pelé played in an emotional game between the Cosmos and Santos, performing one half for each team before a thundering sellout crowd of 76,000 at Giants Stadium and an international television audience. His last words to the crowd at the conclusion were "Love, Love, Love." A perfect end to an incredible career.

Pelé led the Brazil league in scoring eleven times, and had 541 goals in 560 league matches over his career. He had a total of 1,088 goals in 1,114 games for Santos, and 39 goals in 64 NASL games (55 in 105 total appearances) for the Cosmos. His career goal total of 1,280 in 1,324 games played (0.939 goals per game) is second only to his compatriot Arthur Friedenrich's total of 1,329 goals in the early 1900s (Pelé's goals came in an era of more difficult goal scoring).

Pelé's one season scoring record of 125 goals (in 1959) still stands; he scored 3 goals in a game 93 times, 4 goals in a game 31 times, 5 goals in a game 6 times, and 8 goals in a game once.

Surpassing soccer, Pelé was declared a Brazilian National Treasure in 1965, and he was named the Reuters Sports Personality of the 20th Century.

Awards: 2002 FIFA World Cup Dream Team.
1998 FIFA Century XI.
1973 South American Footballer of the Year (only the third year given).
France Football's Football Player of the Century (# 1).
Planète Foot (France) best 50 players of all time.
World Soccer's 100 Greatest Footballers of all time.
France Football's World Cup Top-100 1930-1990.
Reuters Sports Personality of the 20th Century.
2004 Pelé/FIFA Best 125 Living Players.
International: 92 games with 77 goals.
World Cup: 1958, 1962, 1966, & 1970; 14 games with 12 goals.
Club teams: Santos, New York Cosmos.

1 Johan Cruyff (Netherlands) 25.04.47

Johan Cruyff (also spelled Cruijff) was the key to the execution and refinement of *total football*, a tactical yet "non-tactical" style that Dutch coach Rinus Michels encouraged. Total football meant free-flow of players about the ball with defenders attacking and attackers defending depending on active opportunities. Cruyff could play any of the midfield or striker positions, and could defend as well, but he was best as the orchestrator of the "controlled chaos" of the *Orange Machine* (as that Dutch team was called).

Cruyff was the leader of the brilliant Ajax team that won three consecutive European Cups (1971, 1972, 1973), as well as the Dutch national team that that fell to West Germany 2-1 in the 1974 World Cup Final in Munich. Above all, Cruyff was an electrifying talent who performed the supernatural like it was natural. The flying goal against Brazil in the World Cup? The two-touch goal from the left sideline? One must witness a highlight video of Cruyff's career to see what this slender genius was capable of.

Cruyff did not elect to participate in the 1978 World Cup finals, where Holland could have used him even though they advanced to the Final and nearly won. Cruyff also won the 1972 Intercontinental Cup (also known as the World Club Championship) with Ajax Amsterdam, and the 1974 Spanish Championship with Barcelona. After leaving Barcelona, he played in the NASL before finishing his career in Holland with Ajax and Feyenoord, fortuitously nurturing future Holland stars Ruud Gullit, Marco Van Basten, and Frank Rijkaard. Cruyff had 291 goals in 520 Top Division matches over his career.

After retirement he went on to manage Barcelona, guiding them to four Spanish championships and the 1992 European Cup. Johan Cruyff was one of the game's greatest innovators, both as player and coach.

Awards: 2002 FIFA World Cup Dream Team.
1971, 1973 & 1974 European Footballer of the Year.
1977 & 1978 Best Foreign Footballer Spanish League
France Football's Football Footballer of the Century (# 3).
France Football's World Cup Top-100 1930-1990.
Planète Foot (France) best 50 players of all time.
World Soccer's 100 Greatest Footballers of all time.
2004 Pelé/FIFA Best 125 Living Players.
International: 48 games with 33 goals.
World Cup: 1974; 7 games with 3 goals.
Club teams: Ajax, Barcelona, Los Angeles Aztecs, Washington Diplomats, Levante, Feyenoord.

1 Eusébio   (Portugal)   25.01.42

Eusébio (Eusébio da Silva Ferreira) was the first African soccer superstar, having been born and raised in Mozambique. A striker in the center-forward mold, Eusébio was the possessor of one of the most fearsome shots to have graced the planet, and also had sublime dribbling and passing skills.

Eusébio led the great Portuguese team that earned the bronze medal in the 1966 World Cup, bowing out to eventual victor England. Eusébio was top scorer of that competition with nine goals, including four against the surprising North Korean team that had already beaten Italy.

Eusébio led Benfica to the European Cup championship in 1962, and to the Finals in 1963 and 1968. Benfica won a memorable 5-3 victory against Real Madrid in 1962, but lost the last two Finals to Milan and Manchester United. Eusébio scored in both the 1962 and 1963 European Cup Finals, and in both the 1961 and 1962 Intercontinental Cup losses against Peñarol in 1961 and Pelé's Santos in 1962.

Eusébio won 10 Portuguese championships with Benfica. He was the Portuguese League's top scorer seven times, and had 342 goals in 373 Top Division matches (294 goals in 316 matches at Benfica) over his career. He won the first Golden Boot award (for Europe's top scorer) in 1968, and repeated in 1973. Not surprisingly, a statue of Eusébio stands at the Estadio da Luz in Lisbon.

Eusébio could not get enough of the beautiful game and retired well after his prime, ending his playing days with battered knees in the Mexican and USA soccer leagues – even winning an NASL championship with Toronto in 1975.

Awards: 1965 European Footballer of the Year.
1970 & 1973 Portuguese Footballer of the Year (award began 1970).
France Football's World Cup Top-100 1930-1990.
Planète Foot (France) best 50 players of all time.
World Soccer's 100 Greatest Footballers of all time.
2004 Pelé/FIFA Best 125 Living Players.
International: 64 games with 41 goals.
World Cup: 1966; 6 games with 9 goals.
Clubs: Benfica, Toronto, Monterrey, Boston, New Jersey, Las Vegas, Beira Mar.

1 Garrincha (Brazil) 28.10.33

Garrincha (real name Manoel Francisco dos Santos; his nickname means "Little Bird") grew up in poverty with his right leg 6 centimeters shorter than the left. Rather than shying away from soccer after a childhood illness left his right leg bowing inward while the left bowed outward, he developed a devastating body swerve that mocked his body's special anatomy as well as the defenders attempting to mark him. Garrincha so befuddled expert defender Nílton Santos at his initial Botafogo tryout that Santos insisted that Garrincha be signed, as he did not relish marking him as an opponent in league play! Adding to his bag of tricks was close control, wonderful acceleration, and excellent crossing and shooting ability.

Garrincha was overlooked in the 1958 World Cup until team members pleaded with coach Vicente Feola to include him in the first team. Once Garrincha got into the field, Brazil became a golden team. He played on the 1958 World Cup winning team and was the leading figure in the 1962 World Cup championship after Pelé was injured. Of the 60 Brazil national team games Garrincha played in (only 50 are FIFA "official"), Brazil won 52, tied 7 and lost 1. The only game Garrincha lost with Brazil was to Hungary in the 1966 World Cup, and that was the last national team game he ever played. *Incredibly, Brazil never lost a game when Pelé and Garrincha were on the field together.*

Garrincha also had club success, winning three championships with Botafogo alongside quality players like Amarildo, Zagallo, Didí and Nílton Santos.

Garrincha's life was an inspiring story that ultimately ended in tragedy, as he died prematurely at age 49 from poverty and alcohol induced liver failure.

Awards: 1998 FIFA Century XI.
FIFA World Cup All-Time Team (1993/94).
France Football's Football Player of the Century (# 12).
France Football's World Cup Top-100 1930-1990.
Planète Foot (France) best 50 players of all time.
World Soccer's 100 Greatest Footballers of all time.

International: 50 games with 12 goals.
World Cup: 1958, 1962, & 1966; 12 games with 5 goals.
Clubs: Botafogo, Corinthians, Flamengo, Bangu, Portuguesa, Olaria.

5 George Best (Northern Ireland) 22.05.46

George Best was a tremendously skilled and innovative footballer, nearly as creative on defense as offense (he once stole the ball out of Gordon Banks' hands and scored, but the goal was annulled). Unsurpassed on the dribble and penetration, Best would often pass off for the score rather than take the goal himself. Best was one of few players with virtually ambidextrous ball control with both feet.

Best was part of Manchester United's triumvirate of European Footballer of the Year awardees (with Bobby Charlton and Denis Law); he earned his European Footballer of the Year award in 1968 when he was English league leading scorer and led Manchester United to the European Cup championship over Benfica. Overall, he had 185 goals in 465 matches for Manchester United, and 237 goals in 615 top division games.

A virtuoso player who was also one of soccer's first showmen, Best was the first European soccer superstar, a status that was perhaps due as much to his lifestyle as his ability. He was called the "*Soccer Beatle,*" living the fast life of women and cars off the football field. Eventually his football suffered, and he was relegated to the lower English divisions before traveling to the USA to dazzle the crowds at NASL venues.

Best was one of the most talented players never to play in the World Cup, as he played between the 1958 and 1982 World Cup qualifying Northern Ireland sides.

Awards: European Footballer of the Year in 1968.
English Footballer of the Year Award 1968.
France Football's Football Player of the Century (# 12).
Planète Foot (France) best 50 players of all time.
World Soccer's 100 Greatest Footballers of all time.
2004 Pelé/FIFA Best 125 Living Players.

International: 39 games with 9 goals.
World Cup: No appearances.
Clubs: Manchester United, Stockport County, Cork Celtics, Dunstable Town, Los Angeles Aztecs, Fulham, Fort Lauderdale Strikers, Hibernian, San Jose Earthquakes, Bournemouth, Brisbane Lions.

6 **Marco van Basten** (Netherlands) 31.10.64

Marco van Basten was the world's top striker for a five year stretch in the late 1980s and early 1990s. Two-footed grace with close control, quick on the turn and excellent in the air, he scored spectacular goals for club and country.

Raised in the Ajax system, he helped Ajax win three league championships and the Cup Winners' Cup in 1987 before leaving for AC Milan. He helped Holland win the 1988 European championship, scoring the second goal against the Soviet Union in the Final from a seemingly impossible angle. The shear audacity and technique of that strike showed his supreme class.

At AC Milan, van Basten won three league championships, the 1989 & 1990 European Cups, 1989 & 1990 European Super Cups, and 1989 & 1990 Intercontinental Cups. He played his last game in AC Milan's loss to Marseille in the 1993 European Cup Final. He was then forced to retire at 29 years old due to a chronic ankle injury.

Van Basten led his top division leagues in scoring six times, and had 218 goals in 280 Top Division matches over his career. He won the 1986 Golden Boot with 37 goals, and was European Footballer of the Year three times.

Van Basten was appointed coach of the Netherlands, and in his first coaching job led them to the 2006 World Cup Finals.

Awards: 1988, 1989, & 1992 European Footballer of the Year.
1988 & 1992 *World Soccer* Footballer of the Year.
1988 & 1989 *Onze d'Or* winner.
1992 FIFA World Footballer of the Year.
Planète Foot (France) best 50 players of all time.
World Soccer's 100 Greatest Footballers of all time.
France Football's Football Player of the Century (# 8).
2004 Pelé/FIFA Best 125 Living Players.
International: 58 games with 24 goals.
World Cup: 1990; 4 games.
Clubs: Ajax, AC Milan.

7 **Zico** (Brazil) 03.03.53

Zico (Arthur Antunes Coimbra) was an exceptional offensive-minded midfielder/striker, a real "number 10," and is Brazil's best player who never won a World Cup.

An excellent organizer and creator, but also a deadly dribbler on the run, Zico was an equally proficient finisher. Many of his goals were sudden and unexpected, but spectacular efforts.

Zico was most successful with his Flamengo club, as he led them to the Copa Libertadores and Intercontinental Cup championships in 1981, spanking Liverpool 3-0. Zico led his Top Division leagues in scoring eight times, and had 406 goals in 596 Top Division matches over his career.

A three-time South American Footballer of the Year, Zico turned to coaching at the end of his career. He was named Japan coach in 2004, and directed the Japanese national team to a 2006 World Cup appearance.

Awards: 1977, 1981 & 1982 South American Footballer of the Year.
1974 & 1982 Brazil Footballer of the Year.
France Football's Footballer of the Century (# 9).
Planète Foot (France) best 50 players of all time.
World Soccer's 100 Greatest Footballers of all time.
2004 Pelé/FIFA Best 125 Living Players.
International: 72 games with 52 goals.
World Cup: 1978, 1982, & 1986; 14 games with 5 goals.
Clubs: Flamengo, Udinese, Kashima Antlers.

8 Ronaldo   (Brazil)   22.09.76

Ronaldo (Ronaldo Luís Nazário de Lima) is a center-forward possessing great ball control and dribbling skills. With a powerful physique that can hold off most defenders, he proved himself a goal machine in the Brazilian, Dutch, Italian, and Spanish leagues.

Ronaldo's soccer abilities were recognized early on by Brazil soccer great Jairzinho. While at Cruzeiro, Ronaldo played for the Brazil national team and made the 1994 World Cup squad at age seventeen. Despite coach Carlos Alberto Parreira's mother imploring him to play "*the phenomenon*," Ronaldo did not see any action in Brazil's 1994 World Cup championship.

After winning the 1996 and 1997 FIFA World Player of the Year awards at PSV Eindhoven and Barcelona, and the 1998 UEFA Cup with Internazionale, Ronaldo looked set to be successful in the 1998 World Cup. He performed well until suffering a seizure before the 1998 championship match against host France, and his Final performance was understandably subdued. Winning the 1997 and 1999 Copa America with Brazil helped to keep his winning mentality focused.

Ronaldo disappeared from action for much of 2000 and 2001 due to rehabilitation for a serious knee injury. He came back with a vengeance to score eight goals to help Brazil win their *Penta* championship in the 2002 World Cup. As of 31.12.05, Ronaldo had 214 goals in 277 top division matches.

With the "champagne team" of Real Madrid, Ronaldo went back to top form and helped Real win the 2002 Intercontinental Cup and the 2003 Spanish league championship.

Awards: 1997 & 2002 European Footballer of the Year and *Onze d'Or* winner.
1996, 1997, and 2002 FIFA World Player of the Year.
1997 Spanish Foreign Footballer of the Year.
Placar (Brazil) best 100 players of all time.
2004 Pelé/FIFA Best 125 Living Players.
International: 91 games with 58 goals (as of 30 March 2006).
World Cup: 1994 (did not play), 1998, & 2002 (2006); 14 games with 12 goals.
Clubs: Sao Cristovao, Cruzeiro, PSV Eindhoven, Barcelona, Inter Milan, Real Madrid.

9 Gerd Müller   (West Germany)   03.11.45

Gerd Müller was the predominant center forward of the early 1970s. Deceptively quick and able to shoot with little wasted motion, Müller was a nightmare for opposing goalkeepers. "*Der Bomber*" was the forerunner to players such as Romário, Batistuta, and Lineker, whom given the slightest chance, could often find a way to put the ball in the goal that eluded other strikers' abilities.

Müller scored ten goals in the 1970 World Cup as West Germany won third place, and four goals when West Germany won the 1974 Cup at home. Appropriately, Müller scored the Cup Final winner against a great Dutch team. His 14 goals in 13 games make him the all-time leading World Cup goal scorer.

Müller scored 68 goals in 62 international games for West Germany, an incredible strike rate of 1.10 goals per match in international play. Müller is the *only player after 1959 with a strike rate of better than one goal per game in international games*, including World Cup matches.

Müller played for Bayern Munich alongside Franz Beckenbauer and Sepp Maier, and helped Bayern win three consecutive European Cups from 1974-1976. He led the German league in scoring seven times, and had 405 goals in 507 Top Division matches over his career.

Müller finished with the Fort Lauderdale Strikers of the NASL, ending his career demonstrating how finishing was properly done in the United States.

Awards: 1970 European Footballer of the Year.
1967 & 1969 West German Footballer of the Year.
France Football's Football Player of the Century (# 10).
France Football's World Cup Top-100 1930-1990.
Planète Foot (France) best 50 players of all time.
World Soccer's 100 Greatest Footballers of all time.
2004 Pelé/FIFA Best 125 Living Players.
International: 68 goals in 62 games.
World Cup: 1970 & 1974; 13 games with 14 goals.
Clubs: TSV Nordingen, Bayern Munich, Fort Lauderdale Strikers.

Best Players of the Modern Era 1958 – 2006 • 175

10 **Romário** (Brazil) 29.01.66

Romário (Romário de Souza Faria), one of the greatest first-touch goal-getters of all time, possessed great shooting and dribbling technique. While Romário was sometimes criticized for "disappearing" during games, he would then crop up and score one or more goals. A master of Zen-like "no-play," he would let the action sweep around him until it was his time to strike. When man-marked (which was usual) he often stopped moving, reasoning that his marker's natural tendency was to move rather than stand still. After his marker moved, he was off in the other direction for a pass or goal opportunity.

Romário supplied the goals (five) that led to Brazil claiming the 1994 World Cup, and was the MVP of that tournament. He was still scoring goals at the age of 35 for Brazil, and could have been a threat to Pelé's all-time Brazil goal record if not effectively ignored by selectors during the 1998 and 2002 World Cups.

Romário had a niggling thigh injury before the 1998 World Cup, but would likely have been fit to replace Ronaldo (who was ill) for the Final, making the game against France much more interesting. Incredibly, Romário could not secure a place for the 2002 World Cup team despite playing in the qualifiers and scoring eight goals in only five games! With Brazil, Romário also won the 1989 & 1997 Copa America, and the 1997 Confederations Cup.

Romário holds the world record in scoring titles, having led his Top Division teams in scoring *fourteen times* from 1986-2005 (the final time leading the Brazilian league in 2005 at 39 years old). As of December 2005 he had 485 goals in 603 Top Division matches over his career. He was leading scorer of the inaugural FIFA World Club Championship in 2000, where his Vasco da Gama team lost to Corinthians in an all-Brazil Final on penalty kicks. He also won five league championships at PSV Eindhoven and Barcelona.

    Awards: 2002 FIFA World Cup Dream Team.
                   2000 South American Footballer of the Year.
                   2000 Brazil Footballer of the Year.
                   1994 FIFA World Footballer of the Year.
                   France Football's Football Player of the Century (# 17).
                   Planète Foot (France) best 50 players of all time.
                   2004 Pelé/FIFA Best 125 Living Players.
    International: 70 games with 55 goals.
    World Cup: 1990 & 1994; 8 games with 5 goals.
    Clubs: Vasco da Gama, PSV Eindhoven, Barcelona, Flamengo, Valencia, Fluminense.

11 **Ferenc Puskas** (Hungary) 02.04.27

Ferenc Puskas had great striking technique and was a deadly goal finisher. Puskas was part of the great Honved and Hungarian teams before the Soviet Union crushed the Hungarian democracy movement in 1956. His Honved club team was traveling out of the country during the upheaval, and Puskas decided to defect. FIFA regrettably slapped a one-year ban preventing him from playing, and he signed with Real Madrid after the ban expired. Before his leaving Hungary, Puskas had played on the "Magical Magyar" teams that won the 1952 Olympic Gold, beat venerable England 6-3 and 7-1 in 1953-54, and unexpectedly lost to West Germany in the 1954 World Cup Final.

Puskas' "second career" with Real Madrid was equal to his first; he won the Spanish league scoring title (the *Pichichi*) four times, and played in all of Real Madrid's five consecutive European Cup championships from 1956-1960. Puskas had four goals in the last of those championships, a 7-3 Real Madrid win over Eintracht Frankfurt in Glasgow in 1960 (often called the "Game of the Century"). Puskas helped win the inaugural 1960 Intercontinental Cup with Real over Peñarol, getting two goals in the home game.

Puskas, then aged 35, also played in Real Madrid's 1962 European Cup Final loss against Benfica in 1962; he scored all three goals for Real as they lost 3-5! He also played in the 1964 European Cup Final loss to Internazionale at age 37. In 39 European matches for Real Madrid, Puskas scored an impressive 35 goals.

Puskas led Top Division leagues in scoring eight times, and had 511 goals in 533 Top Division matches over his career. He won nine top division championships in his career with Honved and Real Madrid. He will likely remain the all-time Hungary national team goal scorer with 83 goals.

    Awards: FIFA World Cup All-Time Team (1993/94).
                   France Football's Football Player of the Century (# 7).

     Planète Foot (France) best 50 players of all time.
     World Soccer's 100 Greatest Footballers of all time.
     2004 Pelé/FIFA Best 125 Living Players.
International: 84 games with 83 goals for Hungary; 4 games for Spain.
World Cup: 1954 (Hungary); 3 games with 4 goals. 1962 (with Spain); 3 games.
Clubs: Kisped, Honved, Real Madrid.

12 **Mario Kempes**   **(Argentina)**   15.07.54

  Mario Kempes had all the tools of a top-class striker, including a wonderful "change of rhythm" dribbling technique. His speed and exciting technique almost single-handedly grabbed the 1978 World Cup Final away from the visiting Dutch team, as he scored the initial and winning goals in Argentina's 3-1 overtime win.
  The 1978 World Cup was his best performance, and he dominated as thoroughly as Diego Maradona would eight years later. All of his World Cup leading six goals came after the initial group elimination stages, and in the Final.
  Kempes won a league championship with River Plate, and the 1979 Copa de España with the Valencia team coached by Alfredo Di Stéfano. He scored 276 goals in 494 Top Division matches over his career, and earned two *Pichichis* as the Spanish league top scorer.
  After retirement, Kempes went on to coach the national sides of Indonesia, Albania, and Venezuela.

  Awards: 1978 South American Footballer of the Year.
      1978 Argentine Footballer of the Year.
      1978 *Onze d'Or* winner.
      Planète Foot (France) best 50 players of all time.
      France Football's World Cup Top-100 1930-1990.
      2004 Pelé/FIFA Best 125 Living Players.
  International: 43 games with 20 goals.
  World Cup: 1974, 1978, 1982. 18 games with 6 goals.
  Clubs: Rosario Central, Valencia, River Plate, Hercules, Vienna, Austria Salzburg.

13 **Roberto Baggio**   **(Italy)**   18.02.67

  Roberto Baggio played either a creative midfield or a striker role, including a role the Italians call the *trequartista* (a creative player behind the strikers). An elegant player who was an excellent dribbler and defense infiltrator, he was also a free-kick specialist.
  Baggio played in three World Cups, especially excelling in 1994 when he scored five of Italy's eight goals. Unfortunately, Italy's advance was halted in all three World Cups by penalty kick competition losses.
  Baggio was looking to make the 2002 World Cup his fourth straight, and had made an incredible comeback after knee surgery for a serious knee ligament injury. However, Italy coach Trapattoni thought he had enough firepower with Totti, Del Piero, and Vieri (he was wrong).
  Baggio was most successful with his Juventus (1990-1995) and Milan (1995-1997) clubs, where he won the Serie A (1995, 1996), Italian Cup, and UEFA Cup.
  Baggio joined a select group of Silvio Piola (290 goals), Gunnar Nordahl (225), Giuseppe Meazza (220), and Jose Altafini (216) in scoring 200 Serie A goals, which he did in 2004 at age 37 (Altafini, the most recent of the four players, had retired 30 years earlier). Baggio finished his club career with 206 goals in 452 Top Italian league games.

  Awards: 1993 European Footballer of the Year and *Onze d'Or* winner.
      1993 World Footballer of the Year.
      2002 FIFA World Cup Dream Team.
      France Football's Footballer of the Century (# 18).
      Planète Foot (France) best 50 players of all time.
      World Soccer's 100 Greatest Footballers of all time.
      2004 Pelé/FIFA Best 125 Living Players.
  International: 56 caps with 27 goals.
  World Cup: 1990, 1994, & 1998; 16 games with 9 goals.
  Clubs: Vincenza, Fiorentina, Juventus, AC Milan, Bologna, Internazionale, Brescia.

14 Denis Law   (Scotland)   22.02.40

Denis Law was a rapid and intelligent goal maker and scorer. He was the first of the Manchester United triumvirate (including Bobby Charlton and George Best) to win the European Footballer of the Year. Some who saw all three play claim he had the best skills of the three.

Law led Manchester United to the English league championships in 1965 & 1967 and to the European Cup Final in 1968, which he was forced to miss through injury (Manchester United prevailed over Benfica in overtime).

Law had 236 goals in 393 games for Manchester United, and still holds the Manchester United season record with 46 goals. He ended his career back at Manchester City, where in his last club game he ironically scored the goal that temporarily relegated his former team Manchester United from the First Division.

While performing brilliantly for Scotland, it was only when he was on the verge of retirement that he made a World Cup appearance. Law scored 30 goals for Scotland, and shares the top goal scorer position with Kenny Dalglish.

    Awards: 1964 European Footballer of the Year.
                  Planète Foot (France) best 50 players of all time.
                  World Soccer's 100 Greatest Footballers of All Time.
    International: 55 games and 30 goals.
    World Cup: 1974; one game.
    Clubs: Huddersfield, Torino, Manchester United, Manchester City.

15 Just Fontaine   (France)   11.08.33

Just Fontaine was a classic center forward who had the most explosive goal scoring exploits in World Cup history. He started off the 1958 World Cup with a hat-trick against Paraguay, and finished with four against 1954 champions West Germany to help France earn the World Cup bronze medal. In between he had two goals against Yugoslavia, one against Scotland, two against Northern Ireland, and one against Brazil, for an incredible six-game total of thirteen goals. It is hard to imagine another player replicating this feat in a future World Cup, as Fontaine appeared to have a telepathic relationship with French midfield wizard Raymond Kopa.

Fontaine won the French league with Nice in 1956, then again with Reims in 1958 & 1960. He reached a then-record 160 goals in the French league, and had 200 goals in 213 top-division games. Fontaine retired in 1961 aged only 28 years old because of irreparable injury.

After his playing career, he managed Paris Saint-Germain, and the Moroccan and French national teams.

    Awards: *World Soccer's* 100 Greatest Footballers of All Time.
                  Venerdì (Italy) best 100 players of all-time.
                  France Football's World Cup Top-100 1930-1990.
                  France Football's Football Player of the Century (# 18).
                  Planète Foot (France) best 50 players of all time.
                  2004 Pelé/FIFA Best 125 Living Players.
    International: 21 games with 30 goals.
    World Cup: 1958; 6 games with 13 goals.
    Clubs: Casablanca, Nice, Reims.

16 Jairzinho   (Brazil)   25.12.44

Jairzinho (Jair Ventura Filho) was one of Brazil's *"5 number 10's"* in the 1970 World Cup, and he did much of the scoring in that Cup. Relegated to the outside striker positions by Pelé and Tostão, he never complained and performed his duties impeccably. His scintillating pace turned defenses inside out, exposing the opponents' goalkeepers to his powerful and accurate shooting.

Jairzinho is still the only player to have scored in *every round of the World Cup including the Final*; in 1970 he accomplished this feat with 7 goals in 6 games as Brazil won the Cup. Jairzinho had a chance to play briefly with his boyhood hero Garrincha in the 1966 World Cup Finals, and also performed in the 1974 World Cup. Despite being top scorer in the 1977 Brazilian championship, Jairzinho was controversially not picked for the 1978 Brazilian World Cup side.

Also successful in club play, Jairzinho scored the critical goal in Cruzeiro's 1976 Copa Libertadores championship win over River Plate.

Awards: World Soccer's 100 Greatest Footballers of All Time.
Planète Foot (France) best 50 players of all time.
Venerdì's (Italy) All-Time Top-100 ("100 Magnifici").
France Football's World Cup Top-100 1930-1990.
Top Twenty Brazil Footballers of the Century.
International: 80 games with 33 goals.
World Cup: 1966, 1970, 1974; 16 games with 9 goals.
Clubs: Botafogo, Marseille, Cruzeiro, Portuguesa (Venezuela), Noroeste, Fast Clube, Jorge Wilsterman (Bolivia).

17 Tostão   (Brazil)   25.01.47

Tostão (Eduardo Gonçalves de Andrade) was a dynamic center-forward that when his game was on, he could be as stellar and inventive as Pelé. Tostão had incredible technique, could turn and shoot on a dime, and had brilliant dribbling skills and cerebral distribution.

He had a short-lived career due to medical caution after suffering a retinal detachment in 1969. His eye recovered sufficiently enough to play in the 1970 World Cup, but he decided to retire from football in 1973 before sustaining more extensive eye damage.

He was instrumental in Brazil's 1970 World Cup championship, being one of the team's *"5 number 10's"*. He was subsequently elected the inaugural South American Footballer of the Year.

Tostão excelled for Cruzeiro as they won five Campeonato Mineiro competitions, and he was also the competition's leading scorer five times.

Tostão retired at age 26 to become an ophthalmologist, and is now a respected football commentator in Brazil.

Awards: 1971 South American Footballer of the Year (first year given).
Placar (Brazil) best 100 players of all time.
France Football's World Cup Top-100 1930-1990.
International: 53 games with 31 goals
World Cup: 1966 & 1970; 7 games with 3 goals.
Clubs: América (Brazil), Cruzeiro, Vasco da Gama.

18 George Weah   (Liberia)   01.10.66

George Weah was an elegant and rapid striker with great touch, balance, and heading ability, who migrated from clubs in Liberia and Cameroon to perform brilliantly on the European soccer stage.

Weah was brought in by Milan to replace Marco Van Basten, who had retired prematurely due to injury. Weah did so well in 1995, galvanizing Milan to the 1996 league championship with spectacular goals, that he was the first African to win the European Footballer of the Year award and the FIFA World Footballer of the Year.

Weah won league championships in three countries; with Tonnerre in Cameroon in 1988, with Paris Saint-Germain in France in 1994, and with Milan in Italy in 1996 and 1999. He also won the French Cup three times, and the English FA Cup with Chelsea.

Weah's World Cup experience was like none other. Coming from a small country with great players but little organization, Weah almost single-handedly willed Liberia into the 2002 World Cup. After Liberia led their group for much of the qualifying competition, powerhouse Nigeria beat out Liberia by a solitary point. Weah financed much of the Liberian World Cup team's expenses, as well as other charity works in Liberia. After retirement, Weah was an UNICEF goodwill ambassador and narrowly lost the Liberian presidential election in 2005.

Awards: 1995 European Footballer of the Year and *Onze d'Or* winner.
1995 FIFA World Footballer of the Year.
1989, 1994 & 1995 African Footballer of the Year.
1991 French League Foreign Player of the Year.
Planète Foot (France) best 50 players of all time.
Placar (Brazil) best 100 players of all time.
2004 Pelé/FIFA Best 125 Living Players.
International: Full record not available.
World Cup: No Finals appearances.
Clubs: Monrovia, Tonnerre, Mónaco, Paris Saint-Germain, Milan, Chelsea, Manchester City, Marseille.

Best Players of the Modern Era 1958 – 2006

19 Gabriel Batistuta   (Argentina)   01.02.69

Gabriel Batistuta (known in Italy and Argentina as "Batigol") was a crafty and courageous goal scorer, possessing a booming but accurate shot at the center forward position

Batistuta started at Newell's Old Boys, and at age 19 found himself in the Copa Libertadores Final, but his team lost to Nacional of Uruguay. He transferred to River Plate and won the Argentinean championship in 1990, but left after that one season for rivals Boca Juniors. He started a nine-year stint at Fiorentina in 1991, winning the Italian Cup and SuperCup, and moved to Roma in 2000 to help win the Italian league in 2001. For his long service at Fiorentina, he had a statue erected in his honor.

Despite his prodigious goal scoring exploits, Batistuta fell short of joining Roberto Baggio in scoring 200 Serie A goals, as he left for Qatar at the end of his career. Had he not loyally remained with relegated Fiorentina in *Serie B* in 1992, he would likely have joined the exclusive *Serie A* 200 goal quintet. He ended with 184 Serie A goals, and scored 233 goals in 415 Top Division games in his career.

On the national scene, Batistuta was the top scorer in the 1991 Copa America, which Argentina won for the first time in 32 years, and Argentina repeated as winners in 1993. Batistuta was also the primary goal threat for Argentina in the 1994, 1998, and 2002 World Cups, and he finished with 10 World Cup goals. Batistuta remains the all-time Argentine goal scorer with 56 goals.

    Awards: 1991 South American Footballer of the Year.
                     1998 Argentine Footballer of the Year.
                     Placar (Brazil) best 100 players of all time.
                     Guerin' Sportivo (Italy) top-50 of the 20th century.
                     2004 Pelé/FIFA Best 125 Living Players.
    International: 78 caps with 56 goals.
    World Cup: 1994, 1998, 2002; 12 games with 10 goals.
    Clubs: Newell's Old Boys, River Plate, Boca Juniors, Fiorentina, Roma, Internazionale, Al Arabi.

20 Hugo Sánchez   (Mexico)   11.07.58

Hugo Sánchez was the best Mexican and CONCACAF player ever, with excellent technique, athleticism, and enthusiasm for the game. He became famous worldwide for his bicycle kicks (with which he scored many goals) and somersaults (his standard goal celebration).

After starring for UNAM Pumas (Universidad Nacional Autónoma de México) in Mexico City, where he also received dentistry training, Sánchez played briefly in the NASL before launching a successful career in Spain. With Real Madrid he won five successive Spanish league titles and a UEFA Cup, and was a five time winner (1985-1988, 1990) of the *Pichichi* (top scorer of the Spanish league).

Sánchez finished with 164 goals in 207 games for Real Madrid, and a total of 234 goals in La Liga – second overall to Telmo Zarra and just ahead of Alfredo Di Stéfano. He had 394 goals in 662 Top Division matches over his career.

Sánchez was less lucky in national team play, although playing in three World Cups. Mexico's best performance came in 1986 at home, when they were eliminated on penalty kicks to eventual Finalist West Germany.

Sánchez is one of two footballers to play in both the NASL (which folded in 1984) and the MLS (began in 1996); the two professional leagues spanning a 12-year gap in North American professional soccer.[7] His NASL team was the San Diego Sockers and the MLS team was the Dallas Burn (now FC Dallas). He finished his career playing with Atlético Celaya alongside old Real Madrid mates Michel and Emilio Butragueño.

    Awards: 1987 & 1990 Best Foreign Footballer in the Spanish league.
                     Placar (Brazil) best 100 players of all time.
                     Venerdi's All-Time Top-100 (100 Magnifici).
                     World Soccer's 100 Greatest Footballers of All Time.
                     2004 Pelé/FIFA Best 125 Living Players.
    International: 58 games with 29 goals.
    World Cup: 1978, 1986, & 1994; 8 games with 1 goal.
    Clubs: UNAM, San Diego Sockers, Atletico Madrid, Real Madrid, América, Rayo Vallecano, Atlante, Linz, Dallas Burn, Atlético Celaya.

---

[7] The other is Roy Wegerle, who played for Tampa Bay (NASL), Colorado and DC United (both MLS).

21 Uwe Seeler (West Germany) 05.11.36

Uwe Seeler was the top West German forward for more than a decade. He was a technically gifted and effective goal scorer, working to score inside or outside the penalty area. He was also very creative, once back-heading a goal in a World Cup game.

Seeler led the West German league in scoring eight times in the decade 1954-1964, and he led his only club Hamburg to the West German title in 1960. Seeler scored an amazing 764 goals in 810 games.

Seeler was around a long time for the West German national team, playing a prominent role in four World Cups that unluckily spanned Pelé's and Brazil's dominance. He held the West German goal record until Gerd Müller broke it in 1972.

    Awards: 1960, 1964, & 1970 West German Footballer of the Year.
                  France Football's World Cup Top-100.
                  World Soccer's 100 Greatest Footballers of All Time.
                  IFFHS's Best 100 Footballers of the Century.
                  2004 Pelé/FIFA Best 125 Living Players.
    International: 72 games with 43 goals.
    World Cup: 1958, 1962, 1966, & 1970; 21 games with 9 goals.
    Club: Hamburg.

22 Gary Lineker (England) 30.11.60

Gary Lineker was a quick all-around center-forward with excellent technique, possessing goal-scoring prowess with both feet and head.

As an example of his abilities, in 1987 Lineker scored all four goals for England in a devastating 4-2 win against Spain in Madrid. He had an excellent goal ratio in World Cup play, scoring nearly a goal per game. His goals helped England advance to the 1990 World Cup semi-final, but eventual champion West Germany eliminated them by a penalty competition.

Lineker remarkably led the English First Division (now the Premier League) in scoring with three different clubs (1985 Leicester City, 1986 Everton, and 1990 Tottenham). He later left for Spain where he won the league and Copa de España with Barcelona, despite playing wide out of his natural position.

Lineker is currently a television football commentator, and had a cameo playing himself in the movie *"Bend it Like Beckham."*

    Awards: 1986 & 1992 English Footballer of the Year.
                  Venerdi's (Italy) All-Time Top-100 ("100 Magnifici").
                  France Football's World Cup Top-100 1930-1990.
                  1986 European Silver Ball
                  1986 *World Soccer's* 3rd best World Footballer.
                  2004 Pelé/FIFA Best 125 Living Players.
    International: 80 games with 48 goals.
    World Cup: 1986 & 1990; 12 games with 10 goals.
    Clubs: Leicester City, Everton, Barcelona, Tottenham, Nagoya Grampus

23 José João Altafini (Brazil and Italy) 24.07.38

José João Altafini (also known as "Mazzola") was born in Brazil but played much of his remarkable club career in Italy. He was a center-forward with excellent close control, passing, and shooting ability.

Altafini was a star at Palmeiras at 19 years old, and was the second youngest to Pelé (17 years old) on the 1958 Brazil World Cup team. He was Brazil's star of the first match, scoring two goals in the opener against Austria, and played three matches for Brazil. But against Wales, and in the semi-final and Final, he was substituted by Pelé, who scored six goals in those three games.

After the 1958 World Cup Altafini signed with AC Milan, and subsequently had 216 goals in 459 Serie A games (plus an undetermined number of goals and games in Brazil for Palmeiras). He is the only player in the Modern Era besides Roberto Baggio to score 200 Serie A goals.

Altafini also had an excellent goal scoring record in European Cup matches, scoring 20 goals in 19 games for AC Milan, 6 goals in 16 games for Napoli and 9 goals in 20 games for Juventus. He scored the two goals that beat Benfica 2-1 in the 1963 European Champions Cup, and played his last game of his career for Juventus in the 1973 European Champions Cup Final, losing 0-1 to Ajax. He also scored in the Intercontinental Cup series loss to Pelé's Santos in 1963.

Awards: Venerdì's All-Time Top-100 (100 Magnifici)
              Guerin' Sportivo's 50 Grandi del Secolo (#23 of 50).
              Voetbal International's Elftal van de Eeuw (# 2 behind Pelé').
International: Brazil, 11 games with 8 goals; 6 games with 5 goals for Italy.
World Cup: Brazil in 1958 – 3 games with 2 goals; Italy in 1962 – 2 games.
Clubs: Palmeiras, AC Milan, Napoli, Juventus.

24 Jimmy Greaves   (England)   20.02.40

Jimmy Greaves was a dribbler and goal finisher extraordinaire for both club and country, and still holds the modern record of 357 English First Division goals scored in 517 games. Including 9 goals scored in 10 games for Milan, he had a total of 366 goals in 527 Top Division matches over his career. Greaves led the English First Division in scoring six times, and was European Top Scorer in 1964.

Greaves was on the 1966 England World Cup team but did not quite fit in with the work-rate squad that coach Alf Ramsey desired. Geoff Hurst acquired his striker position and went on to score a hat-trick in the Final.

After retiring from football, Greaves went on to become a successful soccer journalist.

Awards: *Voetbal International's* (Holland) Top 100 Footballers of the Century.
             Venerdì's (Italy) All-Time Top-100 ("100 Magnifici").
International: 56 games with 43 goals.
World Cup: 1962 & 1966; 7 games with 1 goal.
Clubs: Chelsea, Milan, Tottenham, West Ham United.

25 Paolo Rossi   (Italy)   23.09.56

Paolo Rossi was a prototype speedy center-forward, able to penetrate at will and deadly in front of goal. His goal-opportunism came at the best time for Italy, as he fully contributed to Italy's 1982 World Cup championship, especially in the semi-final against Brazil. His hat-trick against the best Brazil team never to win a World Cup contributed to the entertainment value of one of the best World Cup games ever. In fact, Rossi titled his autobiography (published 2002) *"I Made Brazil Cry."* He justifiably won multiple 1982 Footballer of the Year awards.

Also successful in club play, he was *Serie A* top scorer in 1978 with Lanerossi Vincenza, and won the 1982 and 1984 League championship and 1985 European Cup with Juventus.

Despite tremendous successes on the pitch, his reputation was damaged from a two-year playing ban after being implicated in a match-fixing scheme. Fortunately for victorious Italy, the ban finished shortly before the 1982 Cup.

Awards: 1982 World Soccer's Footballer of the Year (first year awarded).
             1982 European Footballer of the Year and *Onze d'Or* winner.
             Venerdì's (Italy) All-Time Top-100 ("100 Magnifici").
             Planète Foot (France) best 50 players of all time.
             France Football's World Cup Top-100 1930-1990.
             2004 Pelé/FIFA Best 125 Living Players.
International: 48 games with 20 goals.
World Cup: 1978, 1982, & 1986 (did not play); 14 games with 9 goals.
Clubs: Juventus, Como, Lanerossi Vincenza, Perugia, Milan, Verona.

26 Kevin Keegan   (England)   14.02.51

Kevin Keegan was one of the few lights in the dark 1970s soccer decade for England. A work-horse center-forward with excellent technique, he was a natural leader for Liverpool, Hamburg, and England.

Keegan captained England in an altogether unsuccessful period for the founders of the modern game, only playing part of a World Cup game in 1982. He was however, top scorer of the 1980 European Championships in which England finished out of the medals.

Keegan won his first division league three times with Liverpool and once with Hamburg. He won the European Cup with Liverpool in 1977, but lost the Final with Hamburg in 1980.

After Keegan returned from Hamburg in 1982, he signed for unfashionable Southampton, where he immediately became English First Division top scorer. After retiring, Keegan managed several clubs and the England national team.

 Awards: 1978 & 1979 European Footballer of the Year.
      1977 & 1979 *Onze d'Or* winner.
      1976 English Footballer of the Year.
      1982 PFA Player of the Year (England).
      Planète Foot (France) best 50 players of all time.
      2004 Pelé/FIFA Best 125 Living Players.
 International: 63 games with 21 goals.
 World Cup: 1982; 1 game.
 Clubs: Scunthorpe, Liverpool, Hamburg, Southampton, Newcastle.

27 Hristo Stoichkov (Bulgaria) 08.02.66

Hristo Stoichkov was a striker with prodigious dribbling and shooting skills, and also able to perform in the withdrawn creative role. He was Bulgaria's best player ever, and was the major force that carried Bulgaria into the 1994 and 1998 World Cups.

Stoichkov shared the European Golden Boot Award in 1990 with Hugo Sanchez; both scored 38 goals. He then shared the 1994 World Cup Golden Boot award with Oleg Salenko; both had 6 goals.

With Barcelona, Stoichkov won four Spanish championships, the 1992 European Cup, and the 1997 Cup Winners' Cup. He scored 208 goals in 434 Top division games.

 Awards: 1994 European Footballer of the Year.
      1992 *Onze d'Or* winner.
      Planète Foot (France) best 50 players of all time.
      Placar (Brazil) best 100 players of all time.
      IFFHS's best 100 European Footballers of the Century.
      2004 Pelé/FIFA Best 125 Living Players.
 International: 83 games with 37 goals.
 World Cup: 1994 & 1998; 10 games with 6 goals.
 Clubs: CSKA Sofia, Barcelona, Parma, Kashiwa Reysol, Chicago Fire, DC United.

28 Jürgen Klinsmann (West Germany & Germany) 30.07.64

Jürgen Klinsmann was a mobile central striker who roamed all along the forward line probing for weaknesses and opportunities, and finding them with a consistent scoring record. Always in shape, he could punish the defenses' lapses, and his excellent technique with both feet and head ensured his efforts were rewarded.

Klinsmann performed in three World Cups, including West Germany's championship in 1990. He also played for Germany's European Championship winning team in 1996.

With his club teams, Klinsmann won the UEFA Cup in 1991 with Internazionale and with Bayern Munich in 1996. He signed twice with Tottenham Hotspurs, the second time saving them from Premiership relegation in 1998 with four goals against Wimbledon on the last day of the season.

Klinsmann was somewhat of a Renaissance man, serving as his own agent and playing in France, Italy, and England for the language and cultural experiences. He became German team coach in 2004, leading them into the World Cup as host in 2006.

 Awards: 1995 English Footballer of the Year.
      1988 and 1994 (West) German Footballer of the Year.
      Placar (Brazil) list of the best 100 players of all time.
      2004 Pelé/FIFA Best 125 Living Players.
 International: 108 games with 47 goals.
 World Cup: 1990, 1994, & 1998; 17 games with 11 goals.
 Clubs: Stuttgarter Kickers, VFB Stuttgart, Internazionale, Monaco, Tottenham, Bayern Munich, Sampdoria.

29 Roger Milla (Cameroon) 20.05.52

Roger Milla was an elegant and skillful center forward, and was one of the pioneers from the African continent that succeeded professionally in Europe. Milla had a high technical level, and was always attuned to chances in his refined waste-no-movement style.

Milla led Cameroon to the World Cup Finals for the first time in 1982, scoring 6 goals in the qualifiers. In the 1990 World Cup, he was 38 years old and scored four goals. He famously stole the ball away from Colombia keeper Rene Higuita and scored, thereby dooming Colombia's progress in that Cup. Milla was 42 years and 39 days old when he scored against Russia in the 1994 World Cup, making him the oldest goal scorer ever in the competition.

Milla played for a succession of teams in his home country and France, winning French Cups with both Monaco and Bastia (twice). He had 220 goals in 422 Top Division matches over his career.

Milla was the first to win the African Footballer of the Year award twice, with an incredible 14 year span between the major honors.

    Awards: 1976 and 1990 African Footballer of the Year.
                  World Soccer's 100 Greatest Footballers of All Time.
                  Placar (Brazil) best 100 players of all time.
                  Venerdì's *All-Time Top-100 (100 Magnifici)*.
                  France Football's Football Player of the Century (# 24).
                  France Football's World Cup Top-100 1930-1990.
                  2004 Pelé/FIFA Best 125 Living Players.
    International: Full record not available.
    World Cup: 1982, 1990, & 1994; 10 games with 5 goals.
    Clubs: Leopard Douala, Tonnerre Yaounde, Valenciennes, Monaco, Bastia, Saint Etienne, Montpellier.

30 **Grzegorz Lato**   (Poland)   08.08.5

Grzegorz Lato played as a wing or withdrawn striker on Poland's best-ever teams in the 1970s. His style was of relentless running on and off the ball with excellent ball domination, for which he created many goal chances.

Lato was on Poland's Olympic Gold-winning soccer team in 1972, and in 1973 helped eliminate England from qualifying for the 1974 World Cup.

Lato was the top scorer (with seven goals) at the 1974 World Cup, when Poland won the bronze medal, besting favorites Argentina, Brazil, and Italy, and losing only to eventual winners West Germany 0-1. In the 1982 World Cup he was once again an instrumental player for Poland, as they won the bronze medal for a second time.

Lato is Poland's second leading career scorer after Wlodzimierz Lubanski. Lato won a few national championships with Stal Mielec, but had little success in international club Cup play.

    Awards: *Venerdì* (Italy) best 100 players of all-time.
                  France Football's World Cup Top-100 1930-1990.
                  IFFHS best 100 European Footballers of the Century.
    International: 95 games with 42 goals.
    World Cup: 1974, 1978, & 1982; 20 games with 10 goals.
    Clubs: Stal Mielec, Lokeren, Atlante.

31 **Davor Šuker**   (Croatia)   01.01.68

Davor Šuker was a stylish center-forward with exceptional technique. Šuker had all of France trembling when he put Croatia ahead 1-0 in the second-half of the 1998 semi-final, but host France eventually won the game 2-1. Šuker also scored in the third-place play-off against Holland, finishing with six goals and the tournament top-scorer Golden Boot award.

Šuker initially played for Yugoslavia before Croatia broke away, winning the under-21 World Cup in Chile in 1987.

Šuker is Croatia's all-time leading scorer with 45 goals (his closest team mate has only 15 goals). He was the European Championship all-time leading goal scorer with 18 goals.

Šuker was most successful at club level with Real Madrid, where he won the Spanish league and SuperCup in 1997, and the Champions League and Intercontinental Cup in 1998.

    Awards: *Placar* (Brazil) best 100 players of all time.
                  1998 European Footballer of the Year voting, second to Zidane.
                  2004 Pelé/FIFA Best 125 Living Players.
    International: 69 games with 45 goals.
    World Cup: 1998 & 2002; 8 games with 6 goals.
    Clubs: Osijek, FC Zagreb, Seville, Real Madrid, Arsenal, West Ham United, 1860 Munich.

32 Careca   (Brazil)   05.10.60

Careca (Antônio de Oliveira Filho) was the greatest modern-era Brazilian striker not to win a World Cup. An archetypal center-forward, Careca had the technique and courage to score many goals from all angles in the penalty box. He had an excellent World Cup goal record on Brazilian teams that finished just short of greatness.

At Napoli in the Italian league, Careca set up a successful relationship with Diego Maradona, with his goals helping to win two *scudettos* and the UEFA Cup. Prior to that, Careca had won two Brazilian championships with Guarani (the only championship of this small interior team) and São Paulo. Careca scored over 300 top division goals in his career.

    Awards: 1986 Brazilian Footballer of the Year.
                      Placar (Brazil) best 100 players of all time.
    International: 60 games with 29 goals.
    World Cup: 1982 (did not play), 1986 & 1990; 9 games with 7 goals.
    Clubs: Guarani, São Paulo, Napoli, Kashiwa Reysol, Santos.

33 Oleg Blokhin   (Soviet Union)   05.11.52

Oleg Blokhin (also spelled Blochin or Bloklin) was a striker with a sprinter's speed, technically excellent, and with an exceptional work rate. He is so far the best player ever from Ukraine.

A five-time goal leader of the Soviet league, he had 217 goals in 471 Top Division matches over his career. He was an eight-time Soviet champion with Dynamo Kiev, with whom he won the Cup Winners' Cup in 1975.

Blokhin was the 1975 European Footballer of the Year, and is the all-time Soviet Union goal scorer. After retiring, Blokhin became the head coach of the Ukrainian National Team.

    Awards: 1975 European Footballer of the Year.
                      1973, 1974, & 1975 USSR Footballer of the Year.
                      France Football's Football Player of the Century (# 18).
                      Planète Foot (France) best 50 players of all time.
                      World Soccer's 100 Greatest Footballers of All Time.
    International: 101 games with 35 goals.
    World Cup: 1982 & 1986; 7 games with 2 goals.
    Clubs: Dynamo Kiev, Vorvaerts Stayr, Aris de Salónica.

34 Flórián Albert   (Hungary)   15.09.41

Flórián Albert was the best Hungarian player in the 1960s, emerging after the great Puskas-inspired Hungarian teams of the 1950s. Albert not only had an excellent record as a marksman, but could create and play the "number 10" position. Albert was outstanding in the 1966 World Cup, especially in Hungary's 3-1 win over Brazil (which was Garrincha's last game for Brazil).

Albert won the 1965 Fair's Cup (which evolved into the UEFA Cup in 1971) with Ferencváros, the only team he ever played for. Albert had 256 goals in 351 Top Division matches over his career.

    Awards: 1967 European Footballer of the Year.
                      France Football's World Cup Top-100 (1930-1990).
                      Venerdì (Italy) best 100 players of all-time.
    International: 75 games with 31 goals
    World Cup: 1962 & 1966; 7 games with 4 goals.
    Club: Ferencváros.

35 Karl-Heinz Rummenigge   (West Germany)   25.09.55

Karl-Heinz Rummenigge was an athletic central striker who beat opposing defenses with speed, power, and technique. His never-say-die attitude made him a natural captain for his country as 1982 and 1986 World Cup Finalists, and West Germany's 1980 European Championship win.

Rummenigge's character showed when he came on as an injured substitute against France in the 1982 semi-final overtime, and willed in a goal that led to a tie, with West Germany going through to the Final on penalty kicks. Even injured, Rummenigge converted one of the penalty kicks.

Rummenigge won the European Cup twice with Bayern Munich in 1975 and 1976, and the Intercontinental Cup in 1976. He had 220 goals in 424 Top Division matches over his career.

    Awards: 1980 & 1981 European Footballer of the Year and *Onze d'Or* winner.
                      1980 West German Footballer of the Year.

World Soccer's 100 Greatest Footballers of All Time.
Placar (Brazil) list of the best 100 players of all time.
Planète Foot (France) best 50 players of all time.
France Football's World Cup Top-100 1930-1990.
2004 Pelé/FIFA Best 125 Living Players.
International: 95 caps with 45 goals.
World Cup: 1978, 1982, 1986. 19 games with 9 goals.
Clubs: Bayern Munich, Internazionale, Servette.

36 Luigi Riva   (Italy)   07.11.44

Luigi Riva was an opportunistic center-forward on Italy's national teams of the 1960s. Surrounded by the creative talents of Rivera and Mazzola, Riva was the superb technician to ram the ball home for valuable points.

Riva was a critical cog in Italy's European Championship in 1968, and he subsequently had seven goals in only four games in Italy's qualifying for the 1970 World Cup. In the 1970 World Cup, Riva had a combined three goals in the quarterfinal and semi-final game. Riva remains the Italian top scorer with 35 goals.

In 1970 Riva led unfashionable Cagliari from the island of Sardinia to their only Italian League championship (*scudetto*) in the 20th century.

Awards: 1969 European Footballer of the Year, finished 2nd to Gianni Rivera by four votes.
                Placar (Brazil) best 100 players of all time.
                France Football's World Cup Top-100 1930-1990.
International: 42 games with 35 goals.
World Cup: 1970 & 1974; 8 games with 3 goals.
Clubs: Legnano, Cagliari.

37 Bebeto   (Brazil)   16.02.64

Bebeto (José Roberto Gama de Oliveira) was a striker of slight stature, which did not prevent him from being a deadly dribbler, passer, and goal scorer. Bebeto was often relegated to the wings with Brazil while playing with Romário or Ronaldo, but he still grabbed his share of goals. For example, Bebeto topped the goal scoring list with 6 goals as Brazil won the 1989 Copa America.

Bebeto had 283 goals in 536 Top Division matches over his career, and won the 1993 *Pichichi* for Spanish league top scorer. Bebeto also played a prominent part in the emergence of Deportivo la Coruña as a viable creative soccer force in La Liga in Spain.

Awards: 1989 South American Footballer of the Year.
International: 75 games with 39 goals.
World Cup: 1990, 1994 & 1998; 15 games with 6 goals.
Clubs: Flamengo, Vasco da Gama, Deportivo la Coruña, Vitoria Bahia, Gremio, Botafogo, Jubilo Cerezo.

38 Rob Rensenbrink   (Netherlands)   03.07.47

Rob Rensenbrink was a skillful striker who graced the forward lines of Holland, Brugge, and Anderlecht. Rensenbrink often operated on the left, yet was a capable creator as well as defensive infiltrator. He embraced the total football of the Dutch national team and starred in two World Cup Finals, only to lose to the host team each time. In 1978, Rensenbrink's shot that hit the post against host Argentina in the final minutes was as close as Holland got to winning the Cup.

Rensenbrink played many years for top Belgian team Anderlecht, winning several league titles. He also won the Cup Winners' Cup in 1976 and 1978, scoring two goals in each Final. He was a prolific scorer at European level, scoring 37 goals in 62 games.

Awards: 1976 Onze d'Or winner (first year given), 3rd place in 1978 & 1979.
                Planète Foot (France) best 50 players of all time.
                1976 European Footballer of the Year, 2nd place (3rd in 1978).
                1976 Belgian Footballer of the Year.
                2004 Pelé/FIFA Best 125 Living Players.
International: 46 games with 14 goals.
World Cup: 1974 & 1978; 13 games with 6 goals.
Clubs: D.W.S Amsterdam, Brugge, Anderlecht, Portland, Toulouse.

39 Vavá   (Brazil)   12.11.34

Vavá (Edvaldo Izidio Neto) was the center striker of the Brazil 1958 and 1962 teams, with Pelé and Amarildo in more supporting roles. He played his role excellently, scoring in the World Cups at a rate of almost one goal per game, often assisted by Garrincha.

Vavá had wonderful off the ball movement, control and one-time striking abilities, which enabled him to conquer the most durable defenses. He is one of only three players to have scored in two World Cup Final matches (along with Pelé and Paul Breitner), and the only one to have done it in consecutive Finals.

On the club side, he won several Brazil national tournaments with Vasco da Gama and Palmeiras.

Awards: *France Football's* World Cup Top-100 1930-1990.
International: 25 games with 15 goals.
World Cup: 1958 & 1962; 10 games with 9 goals.
Clubs: Vasco da Gama, Atlético de Madrid, Palmeiras.

40 Eric Cantona   (France)   24.05.66

Eric Cantona was a flexible striker who could drop back and play a "number 10" role. He was masterly in front of the goal, and could pass like the best *fantasistas*. He led his teams by superb skills and confidence, thereby motivating both by deed and idea.

Cantona found club success both in France and England, really making an impact when he went to Leeds United and won the last English First Division title in 1992. He was then transferred to Manchester United, where he led them to an incredible four Premiership titles in five seasons, scoring 81 goals in 180 matches. He was subsequently voted the Premiership Player of Decade.

Cantona also had a good international career that was only marred by France missing the 1994 World Cup. He made 45 national team appearances and scored 20 goals, but seven of his goals came in only eleven World Cup qualifying matches.

Cantona was both a football talisman and iconoclast, and therefore perhaps unsurprisingly had some disciplinary problems in his career. He retired twice – once from French football, and ultimately from football altogether one week before his 31st birthday. However, even that retirement was short-lived, as he went on to be the player-coach of the French team that won the inaugural FIFA Beach Soccer World Cup in 2005.

Awards: 1994 PFA Player of the Year (England).
            1996 *Onze d'Or* winner.
            1996 England Footballer of the Year.
            Fan's Awards: 2005 Premiership Player of Decade.
                            2001 Manchester United Player of the Century.
            2002 Only non-British inaugural inductee into National Football Museum Hall of Fame.
            2004 Pelé/FIFA Best 125 Living Players.
International: 45 games with 20 goals.
World Cup: No appearances.
Clubs: Auxerre, Martigues, Marseilles, Bordeaux, Montpellier, Nimes, Leeds United, Manchester United.

41 Dennis Bergkamp   (Netherlands)   10.05.69

Dennis Bergkamp was the best Dutch forward of the 1990s, possessed with uncanny imagination for a central striker. He was not only a threat to score with either foot or head, but could create chances along the front line for his team mates. He was cool under pressure, as his astounding goal that put Argentina out of the 1998 World Cup attests.

Bergkamp would have had more appearances (and goals) for Holland, had he not had an aversion to flying to away matches.

With Ajax, Bergkamp led the Dutch league in scoring three consecutive years. Bergkamp won the UEFA Cup with Ajax and Internazionale, and with Arsenal he won the League and Cup double in 1998 & 2002. He helped Arsenal to the Premier League championship again in 2004, when Arsenal went undefeated in 38 matches, the first time an English Premiership side went a season undefeated.

Awards: 1998 English Footballer of the Year.
            1991 & 1992 Dutch Footballer of the Year.
            IFFHS's best 100 European Footballers of the Century.
            2004 Pelé/FIFA Best 125 Living Players.

International: 79 games with 37 Goals.
World Cup: 1994 & 1998; 12 games with 6 goals.
Clubs: Ajax, Internazionale, Arsenal.

42 Jean-Pierre Papin (France) 05.11.63
Jean-Pierre Papin was a fast and lethal striker who made goal scoring his signature for club and country.

Papin appeared in only one World Cup, as France failed to qualify in 1990 and 1994. He helped France to a fourth-place finish in 1986.

Papin was a five-time consecutive goal leader in the French league, and was a regular scorer for France. He won six league championships with Marseille and Milan, and was in the European Cup Finals twice (1991 with Marseille and 1993 with Milan), but failed to win the championship. However, Papin did win the 1996 UEFA Cup with Bayern Munich.

Awards: 1991 European Footballer of the Year and *Onze d'Or* winner.
1991 *World Soccer* Footballer of the Year.
2004 Pelé/FIFA Best 125 Living Players.
International: 54 games with 30 goals.
World Cup: 1986; 4 games with 2 goals.
Clubs: Valenciennes, Bruges, Marseille, AC Milan, Bayern Munich, Bordeaux.

43 Rudi Völler (West Germany & Germany) 13.04.60
Rudi Völler was an agile and determined forward who scored many important goals for West Germany and Germany. He scored in the 1986 World Cup Final that was lost 2-3 to Maradona's Argentina, but became a World Cup winner in 1990 against the same team. Völler first teamed up with Karl-Heinz Rummenigge in the 1986 World Cup, and subsequently partnered with Jürgen Klinsmann in the 1990 and 1994 World Cups.

Völler also had a very successful club career, including seven successful years in France and Italy. He reached the UEFA Cup Final in 1991 with Roma, and won the European Champions League in 1993 with Olympique Marseille. Völler was Bundesliga scoring champion at age 23, and finished with 132 goals in 232 matches over eight years in the German First division.

Awards: 1983 West Germany Footballer of the Year.
International: 90 games with 47 goals.
World Cup: 1986, 1990, and 1994; 15 games with 8 goals.
Clubs: 1860 Munich, Werder Bremen, Roma, Marseille, Bayer Leverkusen.

44 Geoff Hurst (England) 08.12.41
Geoff Hurst was a center forward with a powerful physique, able to destroy defenses with a headed goal or by a potent shot from either foot.

Hurst was a footballer in the right place and time with the English national team in the 1966 World Cup. He replaced prolific league goal scorer Jimmy Greaves in the quarterfinal against Argentina, and scored the only goal of the game. He then had three goals in the 1966 World Cup Final as England beat West Germany. Hurst remains the only player to score a hat-trick in the World Cup Final.

Hurst had 227 goals in 554 Top Division matches over his career, and won the 1965 Cup Winners Cup with West Ham.

Awards: *France Football's* World Cup Top-100 (1930-1990).
International: 49 games with 24 goals.
World Cup: 1966 & 1970; 6 games with 5 goals.
Clubs: West Ham, Stoke City, West Bromwich Albion.

45 Salvatore Schillaci (Italy) 01.12.64
Salvatore "Toto" Schillaci was perhaps the biggest World Cup surprise since a 17-year old Pelé took over the 1958 Cup. If "timing is everything," it went perfectly for "Toto" at Juventus in 1989-90 and for Italy in 1990. An energetic forward in constant motion, his skills brought him 21 goals for Juventus as he earned his way onto the 1990 Italian team, albeit as a substitute.

Schillaci scored his first World Cup goal two minutes after coming on as a substitute to win Italy's initial game against Austria. By the third game he was a starter for Italy, and he ended up scoring 6 of

Italy's 10 goals (four of them game-winning goals). Italy won six games and tied one, but only finished third (because of losing a penalty kick contest after the Argentina semifinal tie).

The six goals made him the 1990 World Cup's top goal scorer, and his goal against Uruguay, a superb volley over the goalkeeper, was one of the goals of the competition. It was the only World Cup Schillaci would be selected, and he only earned Italy selection in 1990 and 1991.

His most successful club stint was with Juventus, with which he won the UEFA and Italian Cup in 1990.

Awards: *France Football's* World Cup Top-100 1930-1990.
1990 *France Football* Footballer of the Year, 2nd place.
International: 16 games with 7 goals.
World Cup: 1990; 7 games with 6 goals.
Clubs: Messina, Juventus, Inter Milan, Jubilo Iwata.

Striker Runner-ups
(Must have made first national team appearance by 1994)

Immediate runner-up list (players strongly considered for the original list):
Alessandro Altobelli (Italy), Amarildo (Brazil), Igor Belanov (USSR), Hristo Bonev (Bulgaria), Kalusha Bwalya (Zambia), John Charles (Wales), Alfredo Di Stéfano (Argentina/Spain), Roberto Dinamite (Brazil), Preben Elkjær-Larsen (Denmark), Klaus Fischer (Germany), Trevor Francis (England), Francisco Gento (Spain), Jimmy Johnstone (Scotland), Hans Krankl (Austria), Henrik Larsson (Sweden), Wlodzimierz Lubanski (Poland), Johnny Rep (Netherlands), Ian Rush (Wales), Alan Shearer (England), Alan Simonsen (Denmark), Omar Sívori (Argentina/Italy), Hakan Sükür (Turkey), Jorge Valdano (Argentina), Paul Van Himst (Belgium), Gianluca Vialli (Italy), Mark Wilmots (Belgium), Ivan Zamorano (Chile).

Complete runner-up list:
Carlos Aguilera (Uruguay), Shota Arveladze (Georgia), Ferenc Bene (Hungary), Carlos Bianchi (Argentina), Oliver Bierhoff (Germany), Alan Boksic (Croatia), Tomas Brolin (Sweden), Emilio Butragueño (Spain), Claudio Caniggia (Argentina), José Cardozo (Paraguay), Bum-Kun Cha (South Korea), Stéphane Chapuisat (Switzerland), Giorgio Chinaglia (Italy), Martin Dahlin (Sweden), Ali Daei (Iran), Dragen Dzajic (Yugoslavia), Ralf Edström (Sweden), Ryan Giggs (Wales), David Ginola (France), Fernando Gomes (Portugal), Hossam Hassan (Egypt), Luis Hernandez (Mexico), Carlos Hermosillo (Mexico), Josef Heynckes (West Germany), Salif Keita (Mali), Patrick Kluivert (Netherlands), Sándor Kocsis (Hungary), Brian Laudrup (Denmark), Savo Milosevic (Yugoslavia/Serbia and Montenegro), Kazuyoshi Miura (Japan), Zdénék Nehoda (Czechoslovakia), Tibor Nyilasi (Hungary), Luboslav Penev (Bulgaria), Toni Polster (Austria), Marcelo Salas (Chile), Leonel Sánchez (Chile), Emmanuel Sanon (Haiti), Andrzej Szarmach (Poland), Hugo Sotil (Peru), Kubilay Türkyilmaz (Switzerland), Rashidi Yekini (Nigeria), Mario Zagallo (Brazil), Gianfranco Zola (Italy).

Great Offenses
of the Modern Era World Cups 1958-2002

The team standing in the World Cup is noted after the team and year in parentheses, and the number of goals scored by each player is noted after their name in parentheses.

The number of career World Cup goals of the team forwards are then noted in the order of the players presented. For example, for Brazil 1970: Pelé had 12 *career* World Cup goals, Tostão 5 goals, Rivelino 4 goals, Jairzinho 9 goals, and Gérson had 1 career World Cup goal.

(1) Brazil 1970 (winners)
Pelé (4), Tostão (2), Rivelino (3), Jairzinho (7), and Gérson (1).
The team with the famed *"five number 10's"* – each a deserving member of the 125 greatest footballers of the modern era. This quintet had seventeen of Brazil's nineteen 1970 goals, and has a total of 31 World Cup goals between them. **12 5 4 9 1**

(2) Brazil 2002 (winners)
Rivaldo (5), Ronaldo (8), and Ronaldinho (2).
The "Three R's" exuded technique, speed, power, and panache; and they had 15 of Brazil's 18 goals in the 2002 World Cup. They have a total of 22 goals between them in only two World Cups, and Ronaldo and Ronaldinho are obviously not yet finished. **8 12 2**

(3) France 1958
Just Fontaine (13), Roger Piantoni (3), Maryan Wisniewski (2), Jean Vincent (1), Raymond Kopa (3).
This quintet was responsible for 22 of France's 23 goals, as France earned 3rd place. They have a total of 24 total World Cup goals between them. **13 3 2 2 4**

(4) Brazil 1958 & 1962 (combined)
Pelé (7), Vavá (9), Garrincha (4), Zagallo (2), and Amarildo (3).
This quintet provided Brazil scoring power for two World Cup Final wins. They have a total of 31 World Cup goals amongst them, the same as the 1970 quintet. **12 9 5 2 3**

(5) Portugal 1966
Eusébio (9), Jose Torres (3), Antonio Simões (1).
These three forwards had 13 of Portugal 17 goals in six games, as they won 3rd place in 1966. As Portugal did not soon qualify again, the 13 goals were the final tally of this trio. **9 3 1**

(6) Netherlands 1974
Johan Cruyff (3), Johnny Rep (4), and Rob Rensenbrink (1).
A trio of complete forwards, performing total football on the front line. The individuals of this group ripped through European club ranks as well as World Cup competition, as Cruyff, Rep, and Piet Keizer was the Ajax front line that won their third European Champions Cup in a row in 1973, and Rensenbrink was the goal scorer during Anderlecht's European successes. This trio has a total of 16 World Cup goals between them. **3 7 6**

(7a) Argentina 1978
Mario Kempes (6), Leopoldo Luqué (4), Daniel Bertoni (2), and Rene Houseman (1).
Mario Kempes led this quartet that had 13 of Argentina's 15 goals in the 1978 tournament, and they have a total of 18 World Cup goals between them. **6 4 4 4**

(7b) West Germany 1970
Gerd Müller (10) and Uwe Seeler (3)
Gerd Müller and Uwe Seeler had 13 goals in the 1970 Cup – the only other forward to score for West Germany in this Cup was Libuda (1 goal). Müller and Seeler together have a total of 23 World Cup goals, the highest total for two players who performed on the same team. **14 9**

(8) Poland 1974
Grzegorz Lato (7), Andrzej Szarmach (5), Robert Gadocha.
This trio scored 12 of Poland's tournament high 16 goals, as Poland finished 3rd in 1974. They have a total of 17 World Cup goals between them. **10 7**

(9a) Argentina 1986
Diego Maradona (5), Jorge Valdano (4), Jorge Burruchaga (2).
This trio had 11 of Argentina's 14 goals in the 1986 tournament, and have 15 career World Cup goals between them. **8 4 3**

(9b) Netherlands 1978
Rob Rensenbrink (5), Johnny Rep (3), Rene van de Kerkhof (1), Dick Nanninga (1).
This forward quartet had 10 of Holland's 15 goals in the 1978 Cup, and they have a total of 15 goals in World Cup play. **6 7 1 1**

(10) Brazil 1994
Romário (5), Bebeto (3).
This striker duo had 8 of Brazil's 11 goals in the 1994 Cup, and finished with 11 World Cup goals between them. **5 6**

Represented Countries[8] and Number of Players Selected As Best Modern Era Footballers 1958-2006[9]

SOUTH AMERICA [40]

Brazil	22[10]
Argentina	9
Paraguay	3
Peru	2
Bolivia	1
Chile	1
Colombia	1
Uruguay	1

EUROPE [81]

Germany[11]	14
Italy	13
England	9
France	9
Netherlands	9
Scotland	3
Spain	3
Poland	3
Czech Republic[12]	2
Denmark	2
Hungary	2
Northern Ireland	2
Portugal	2
Soviet Union	2
Belgium	1
Bulgaria	1
Croatia	1
Ireland	1
Romania	1
Wales	1

AFRICA [3]

Cameroon	2
Liberia	1

CENTRAL AMERICA [1]

Mexico	1

---

[8] Thirty-one countries represented [South America 8, Europe 20, Africa 2, Central America 1].
[9] South American teams won 7 of the 12 World Cups from 1958-2002
 [Brazil 5, Argentina 2; West Germany 2, England 1, France 1].
[10] Brazil's 22 players are composed of 4 defenders, 7 midfielders, and 11 strikers.
[11] Includes West Germany, East Germany and (unified) Germany players.
[12] Includes one player from former Czechoslovakia.

World Football Dream Teams 1958-2002

First Team

Cruyff	Pelé	Eusébio	Garrincha	**Substitutes**
				Best
				Van Basten
Maradona	Di Stéfano	Platini		Zico
				Didí
				Zidane
Figueroa	Beckenbauer	Moore		Charlton
				Baresi
				Carlos Alberto
Yashin				Zoff

Second Team

Puskas	Müller	Romário	Ronaldo	**Substitutes**
				Kempes
				Baggio
Gullit	Neeskens	Cubillas		Law
				Suárez
				Deyna
Maldini	Rijkaard	Krol		Rivaldo
				Passarella
				Matthäus
Banks				Fillol

Countries	Players	World Cup Wins in Modern Era (1958-2002)
Brazil	8	5
Netherlands	6	Twice Finalist in host country
Argentina	5	2
Italy	4	1
Germany	3	2
England	3	1
France	2	1

Chile, Hungary, Northern Ireland, Peru, Poland, Portugal, Scotland, Soviet Union, and Spain: 1 each

Summary:
16 countries: 12 European countries (25 players)
4 South American countries (15 players)

40 players 12 World Cup championships

Final Notes

Fantasy Footballers from other Sports or Arts

It is intriguing to ponder which athlete in another art or sport would have made the best soccer player – had he made soccer his career. He would have had to be an all-round great athlete, flexible and adaptable, one that could literally do anything within the human athletic realm.

Would it be basketball great Michael Jordan, ice hockey superstar Wayne Gretzky, USA-football legend Walter Payton, or diving gold medalist Greg Louganis? No doubt all of them could have been good to excellent players, but there are three more obvious candidates:

(1) **Mikhail Baryshnikov**, the dancer from the Soviet Union, who came to the West and changed the face of ballet, and

(2) **Bruce Lee**, the kung-fu master from Hong Kong, who revolutionized modern martial arts.

Both men excelled in arts that required the mastery of whole body movement, similar to the requirements of a master soccer player. Baryshnikov could have been a whirling dervish of a center forward in the mold of Tostão or Hugo Sánchez. Lee would have made a bicycle kick look mundane, and had power galore in both legs. Both would have been able to feint a defender out of his boots.

To confirm their athleticism would be transferable to soccer, one can view a copy of the films *White Nights* co-starring Baryshnikov and Gregory Hines, and *Enter the Dragon* starring Lee and his over-the-head kicks.

(3) **Jim Thorpe** was an all-history athlete that cannot be ignored. Winner of the 1912 pentathlon and decathlon, he also played professional baseball and USA-football. A Native American, Thorpe was voted the best USA athlete of the 20th century, and could have been a central defender or goalkeeper of the highest caliber.

Just some wishful thoughts of chances that world soccer missed out on.

Chapter Eight

Best Teams of the Modern Era 1958-2006

"A football team is like a piano. You need eight men to carry it and three who can play the damn thing."
Bill Shankly[1]

I consider football to be a very simple game. You will win as long as you don't always play in the same way. You have got to add some variations to make your game more dynamic. There has to be room for improvisation outside of classical tactics. Modern football must be above all a team game.
Valentino Mazzola[2]

What makes a soccer team one of the best of their era? Certainly it is somewhat measurable by the actual championships they have won, but accountable for those victories are essential intangibles such as the skills and imagination of the footballers, and how successfully a coach inspires his players. Then there are always some tactics involved (usually separated simply into "attacking" or "counter-attacking" strategies), which are most often less important than the inherent cohesiveness and attitude of the team.

The "Natural Ability" Theory versus Soccer Team-Work Ethic

Certain countries are assumed to have "natural abilities" for soccer, similar to how some players are purported to have "natural soccer talents" (see Chapter 7). This conjecture is most often applied to Brazil, the most successful national team ever, and Holland, the most successful small country team in the Modern Era. The suppositions are the Brazilian ability to create salsa music and rhythmic dance translates to soccer, while the Dutch liberal-mindedness leads to creativity on the field. However innocently these theories are presented, they are seriously flawed because (1) both Brazil and Holland have made tremendous efforts at developing quality soccer players in the Modern Era, and (2) both have at times failed to produce beautiful football (such as Brazil failing to qualify for the 2004 Olympic Football tournament, and Holland failing to qualify for the 2002 World Cup).

---

[1] Legendary manager of Liverpool FC.
[2] Quote from the last interview of the legendary Italian midfielder Valentino Mazzola, aged 30, shortly before he perished in the 1949 Superga plane crash.

Brazilians have created many different non-traditional soccer games (e.g., beach soccer, soccer volleyball), with *futebol de salão* (commonly called *futsal* outside of Brazil) the most important. *Futebol de salão* is a five versus five player game played on a small field or court with a smaller and heavier ball filled with foam – a format that is excellent for developing football skills. The game revisits the creativity of street soccer, even approximating the rag-filled ball that Brazilian children (such as a young Pelé) used in lieu of a proper ball. Brazil has been so successful at developing quality soccer players by grounding them in *futebol de salão* that it exports far more players than any other country. In 2005, Brazil sent more than 700 footballers abroad, and Brazilian footballers are in such demand that they also lead the world in naturalized players for other countries in international tournaments (see Chapter 3).

In Holland, the Ajax Amsterdam team method has been copied both within and outside Holland. The Dutch perfected "total football" with the Ajax Amsterdam and national teams of the 1970s, and that is the foundation of their success. Total football requires that each player learn all the soccer skills so they can smoothly switch duties on the field, so it is not uncommon to see a defenseman in Holland make moves like a forward, or a forward running back on defense to cover an overlapping wing back. The other Dutch precept is "the ball should do the running."

It is perhaps no accident that "defensive players" from Brazil (e.g., Branco, Roberto Carlos) and Holland (e.g., Ronald Koeman, Frank de Boer) have had the best skills to be the free kick experts for their club and national teams.

Nigeria is the latest team to bear the burden of the "natural abilities" label, notwithstanding an impressive football work ethic demonstrated by their players. Despite formidable management and logistical difficulties, Nigeria has so far accounted well for itself in international competitions, capped by their 1996 Olympic win (when they bested both Brazil and Argentina). To claim that Nigeria's successes are due to their "natural abilities," and not due to their practiced and inventive abilities and capacity to unite and work as a team, is a form of xenophobia that does not give full respect to their efforts.

Soccer Internationalism

Both national team and club team personnel structure have changed radically over the last 40 years, as many national teams have welcomed players from newly-immigrant backgrounds into their countries' side. This has changed some national teams (such as Holland, Sweden, Portugal and England) from essentially uni-ethnic into multi-ethnic squads, and many other European teams are following suit. The French team has been multi-ethnic the longest in Europe, and across the Atlantic Ocean some teams (Brazil, Peru, Uruguay, and other Latin American teams) have been multi-ethnic for nearly a century.

Some European club teams were determined to bring the best players together in the 1950s and 1960s, and imported stars from South America. Many talented Brazilians (Altafini, Amarildo, Didí) and Argentines (Sívori, Di Stéfano) found their way to significant success at top European teams. In those days of erratic trans-Atlantic flights, their exodus to Europe usually meant retiring from their national team, and playing for their adopted country of Italy or Spain. Didí was a notable exception, as he returned to Brazilian club football from Real Madrid, and won his second World Cup in 1962.

BEST NATIONAL TEAMS

There have been quite a few stellar national teams in the Modern Era, and it is difficult to compare the 20 excellent teams below (7 South American and 13 European). The top national team of all time is generally acknowledged to be the 1970 Brazil World Cup-winning team, although virtually any team on the list could have given them a scare on a particular day. That potential equity contributes to the passion and splendor of international soccer.

(1) Brazil 1970

The 1970 Brazil team had six of the best modern era players: Pelé, Jairzinho, Tostão, Rivelino, Gérson, and Carlos Alberto. The attack line composed of the first four is rated to be the best in the modern era. This was the team said to play with "*five number 10s* " (Pelé, Tostão, Rivelino, Jairzinho, and Gérson).[3]

The full lineup was: Félix; Carlos Alberto (captain), Brito, Piazza, Everaldo; Clodoaldo, Gérson; Jairzinho, Tostão, Pelé, and Rivelino. Although the formation was technically a 4-2-4, both Everaldo and Carlos Alberto could overlap in attack, and any of the forwards (usually Rivelino) could drop back to cover in midfield. Still, the midfielders in a 4-2-4 system must be very fit and technically superior, qualities that both Clodoaldo and Gérson exhibited.

The way Brazil played in the final could be construed as the independent development of "total soccer" in the South American realm. However, this was due less to their 4-2-4/4-3-3 system than the remarkable flexibility and skills of the players themselves.

#[4]	Name[5]	D.O.B.[6]	Club	Games/Minutes/Goals[7]
1	FÉLIX Mielli Venerando	24.12.37	Fluminense	6 (540)
2	Hércules de BRITO Ruas	09.08.39	Flamengo	6 (540)
3	Wilson da Silva PIAZZA	25.02.43	Cruzeiro	6 (537)
4	CARLOS ALBERTO Torres	17.07.44	Santos FC	6 (540) 1
5	CLODOALDO Tavares de Santana	25.09.49	Santos FC	6 (523) 1
6	MARCO ANTÔNIO Feliciano	06.02.51	Fluminense	2 (125)
7	JAIRZINHO -Jair Ventura Filho	25.12.44	Botafogo	6 (529) 7
8	GÉRSON de Oliveira Nunes	11.01.41	São Paulo	4 (319) 1
9	TOSTÃO - Eduardo Gonçalves de Andrade	25.01.47	Cruzeiro	6 (517) 2
10	PELÉ -Édson Arantes do Nascimento	23.10.40	Santos FC	6 (540) 4
11	Roberto RIVELINO	01.01.46	Corinthians	5 (450) 3
13	ROBERTO Lopes Miranda	31.07.43	Botafogo	2 (34)
15	José de Anchieta FONTANA	31.12.40	Cruzeiro	2 (93)
16	EVERALDO Marques da Silva	11.09.44	Grêmio	5 (415)
18	Paulo César LIMA	16.06.49	Botafogo	4 (221)
19	EDU -Jonas Eduardo Américo	06.08.49	Santos FC	1 (17)
	Coach: Mário Jorge Lobo ZAGALLO[8]	09.08.31		

The scoring sheet in the Final against Italy read two goals for the forwards, (Pelé, Jairzinho), one for midfielder maestro Gérson, and one for defenseman Carlos Alberto. Pelé thus became the second player (after his 1958-1962 team mate Vavá) to score in two World

---

[3] A "number 10" is a "creator (usually an attacking midfielder or withdrawn forward) who can score."
[4] Shirt number. Players who did not perform are not listed, so certain shirt numbers are missing.
[5] Brazilian soccer players use abbreviated names, which may be part of their first name (CARLOS ALBERTO), a diminutive of their first name (JAIRZINHO), their last name (RIVELINO), or a nickname (PELÉ).
[6] Date of birth (day, month, year).
[7] Games played, total minutes in all games, and goals scored in that particular World Cup.
[8] Previously Zagallo was spelled Zagalo, a wrong spelling in historical documents.

Cup Finals. For the tournament, Brazil scored 19 goals and allowed 7. Brazil scorers were: Jairzinho with 7 goals, Pelé with 4, Rivelino with 3, Tostão with 2, and Carlos Alberto, Clodoaldo, and Gérson with one each. Tostão had done the yeoman's work in qualifying, having scored ten goals. Jairzinho still remains the only player to score in every round of one World Cup (with 7 goals over 6 consecutive games) including the championship match.

Both Pelé and Uwe Seeler of Germany scored in their fourth World Cup, a record unlikely to be equaled soon. Pelé won his third World Cup victory as a player, being the lone Brazil survivor from the 1958 and 1962 World Cups. Three World Cup victories is a record unlikely to ever be equaled because of increasing parity among national teams, and the increased number of teams at the World Cup (from 16 to 32). Mario Zagallo also won his third World Cup, but this time as the coach of the Brazil team.

All Brazil teams are in effect "world teams", as the ancestral mixture of the population includes African, European, and Asian contributions in a Latin American country.

(2a) West Germany 1974

West Germany was above all a great disciplined team, able to beat the iconoclastic Dutch team in a thrilling Final on Bayern Munich's home ground. This team had the third best midfield and the sixth best defense, and possessed six of the greatest modern-era players: Franz Beckenbauer, Berti Vogts, Gerd Müller, Wolfgang Overath, Paul Breitner, and keeper Sepp Maier.

West Germany scored 13 goals and allowed 4. While the 1970 West Germany goal machine was mostly Müller who scored 10 goals, the 1974 squad was more balanced with Müller getting four, including the winning goal in the Final.

#	Name	D.O.B.	Club	Games/Minutes/Goals	
1	Josef Dieter "Sepp" MAIER	08.02.44	Bayern München	7 (630)	
2	Hans-Hubert "Berti" VOGTS	30.12.46	Borussia MG	7 (630)	
3	Paul BREITNER	05.09.51	Bayern München	7 (630)	3
4	Hans-Georg SCHWARZENBECK	03.04.48	Bayern München	7 (608)	
5	Franz BECKENBAUER	11.09.45	Bayern München	7 (630)	
6	Horst-Dieter HÖTTGES	10.09.43	Werder Bremen	1 (22)	
7	Herbert WIMMER	09.11.44	Borussia MG	2 (96)	
8	Bernhard CULLMANN	01.11.49	1.FC Köln	3 (247)	1
9	Jürgen GRABOWSKI	07.07.44	Eintracht Frankfurt	6 (475)	1
10	Günther NETZER	14.09.44	Real Madrid	1 (21)	
11	Josef HEYNCKES	09.05.45	Borussia MG	2 (135)	
12	Wolfgang OVERATH	29.09.43	1.FC Köln	7 (594)	2
13	Gerhard "Gerd" MÜLLER	11.11.45	Bayern München	7 (630)	4
14	Ulrich "Uli" HOENESS	05.01.52	Bayern München	7 (557)	1
15	Heinz FLOHE	28.01.48	1.FC Köln	3 (110)	
16	Rainer BONHOF	29.03.52	Borussia MG	4 (360)	1
17	Bernd HÖLZENBEIN	09.03.46	Eintracht Frankfurt	6 (400)	
18	Dieter HERZOG	15.07.46	Fortuna Düsseldorf	2 (155)	
Coach: Helmut SCHÖN		15.09.15			

West Germany had already won the 1972 European championship, and went on to tie Czechoslovakia in the same competition in 1976, but lost on penalties (in the first ever major championship determined by a penalty contest). West Germany followed up their World Cup success with many of their players winning three consecutive European Cups with Bayern Munich (Bayern München).

Gerd Müller still holds the record of 14 career World Cup goals. Paul Breitner scored in the 1974 and 1982 Finals, thereby equaling Pelé and Vavá with two Final match goals.

(2b) Netherlands 1974

This wonderful Dutch team had four of the best modern-era players; Johan Cruyff, Johan Neeskens, Rob Rensenbrink, and Ruud Krol. This team had the third-best defense, fourth-best midfield, and sixth-best offense as they played "Total Football" nearly to perfection. They had the misfortune of playing the ultimate "away game" – matched against the host team in their favorite stadium – in both the 1974 and 1978 Finals. The Dutch would likely have fared better if there had been a "home and away" series.

Holland scored 15 goals and allowed only 3 in the 1974 competition, a better goal difference than winners West Germany. Incredibly, the Dutch *allowed no offensive goals before the Final* (the only goal before the Final was an own goal). The *Orange Machine* had a fantastic tournament, only failing to win the Final.

This team jumps near the top of the list because of its sustained excellence as they earned a consecutive World Cup Final in 1978 (see 10c).

#	Name	D.O.B. Club	Games/Minutes/Goals	
2	Arie HAAN	16.11.48 Ajax	7 (630)	
3	Wim van HANEGEM	20.02.44 Feyenoord	7 (569)	
5	Rinus ISRAËL	19.03.42 Feyenoord	3 (55)	
6	Wim JANSEN	28.10.46 Feyenoord	7 (630)	
7	Theo de JONG	11.08.47 Feyenoord	4 (73)	1
8	Jan JONGBLOED	25.11.40 FC Amsterdam	7 (630)	
9	Piet KEIZER	14.06.43 Ajax	1 (90)	
10	Rene van de KERKHOF	16.09.51 PSV Eindhoven	1 (44)	
12	Ruud KROL	24.03.49 Ajax	7 (630)	1
13	Johan NEESKENS	15.09.51 Ajax	7 (614)	5
14	Johan CRUYFF	25.04.47 Barcelona	7 (630)	3
15	Rob RENSENBRINK	03.07.47 Anderlecht	6 (473)	1
16	Johnny REP	25.11.51 Ajax	7 (630)	4
17	Wim RIJSBERGEN	18.01.52 Feyenoord	7 (608)	
20	Wim SUURBIER	16.01.45 Ajax	7 (624)	
Coach: Rinus MICHELS		09.02.28		

Holland shirt numbers were given out alphabetically, with the exception of Johan Cruyff wearing his usual number 14.

This ethnic "All-Dutch" team was the last in Holland, antedating the integration of that country's formerly colonial populations, which brought in Caribbean, South American, Asian, and African talent into the team in the 1980s, 1990s and 2000+ teams.

(3) Brazil 2002

The Brazil 2002 team scored 16 goals and allowed only 4, as they won seven straight games to win the championship. They required a little luck in their first meeting with Turkey, which was sealed by a dubious Brazil penalty kick.

This team contained four of the best modern era players: wingbacks Cafú and Roberto Carlos, center forward Ronaldo, and "number 10" Rivaldo. They had the seventh best defense, and the second best offense.

This team is most notable for being the second team to win the World Cup out of their hemisphere and for winning all their games, both of which only the 1970 Brazil team had accomplished. Further coverage of this team is located in Chapter 9.

#	Name	D.O.B.	Club	Games/Minutes/Goals
1	MARCOS Roberto Silveira Reis	04.08.73	Palmeiras	7 (630)
2	CAFÚ Marcos Evangelista de Moraes	07.06.70	AS Roma	7 (630)
3	LÚCIO Lucimar da Silva Ferreira	08.05.78	Bayer Leverkusen	7 (630)
4	José Vítor ROQUE JÚNIOR	31.08.76	AC Milan	6 (540)
5	EDMÍLSON José Gomes de Moraes	10.07.76	Lyon	6 (540) 1
6	ROBERTO CARLOS da Silva	10.04.73	Real Madrid	6 (540) 1
7	RICARDINHO Luís Pozzi Rodrigues	23.05.76	Corinthians	3 (52)
8	GILBERTO Aparecido da SILVA	07.10.76	Atletico Mineiro	7 (630)
9	RONALDO Luís Nazário de Lima	22.09.76	Inter Milan	7 (548) 8
10	RIVALDO Vítor Borba Ferreira	19.04.72	Barcelona	7 (610) 5
11	RONALDINHO de Assis Moreira	21.03.80	Paris St-Germain	5 (331) 2
13	Juliano Haus BELLETTI	20.06.76	Sao Paulo	1 (6)
14	ÂNDERSON Corrêa POLGA	09.02.79	Gremio	2 (180)
15	José KLÉBERSON Pereira	19.06.79	Atletico Paranaense	5 (308)
16	JÚNIOR Jenílson Ângelo de Souza	20.06.73	Parma	1 (90)
17	DENÍLSON de Oliveira	24.08.77	Real Betis	5 (120)
18	VAMPETA Marcos André Batista dos Santos	13.03.74	Corinthians	1 (19)
19	JUNINHO PAULISTA Oswaldo Giroldo Júnior	22.02.73	Flamengo	5 (262)
20	LUIZÃO Luiz Carlos Goulart	14.11.75	Gremio	2 (41)
22	KAKÁ Ricardo Izecson dos Santos Leite	22.04.82	Sao Paulo	1 (19)
	Coach: Luiz Felipe SCOLARI	09.11.48		

(4) France 1998

In 1998, France had the second best-rated defense and the fifth-rated midfield ever. This team had three of the best modern era players: (Zidane, Desailly, and Blanc) but as they were still young, they could add more for the next century.

#	Name	D.O.B.	Club	Games/Minutes/Goals
2	Vincent CANDELA	24.10.73	AS Roma	1 (90)
3	Bixente V. LIZARAZU	09.12.69	Bayern München	6 (594) 1
4	Patrick VIEIRA	23.06.76	Arsenal	2 (106)
5	Laurent BLANC	19.11.65	Olympique Marseille	5 (487) 1
6	Youri DJORKAEFF	09.03.68	Internazionale	7 (585) 1
7	Didier DESCHAMPS	15.10.68	Juventus	6 (594)
8	Marcel DESAILLY	07.09.68	AC Milan	7 (661)
9	Stéphane GUIVARC'H	06.09.70	AJ Auxerre	6 (267)
10	Zinedine ZIDANE	23.06.72	Juventus	5 (459) 2
11	Robert PIRES	29.01.73	FC Metz	3 (134)
12	Thierry HENRY	17.08.77	AS Monaco	6 (367) 3
13	Bernard DIOMÈDE	23.01.74	AJ Auxerre	3 (222)
14	Alain BOGHOSSIAN	27.10.70	Sampdoria	5 (216)
15	Lilian THURAM	01.01.72	AC Parma	6 (594) 2
16	Fabien BARTHEZ	28.06.71	AS Monaco	7 (684)
17	Emmanuel PETIT	22.09.70	Arsenal	6 (502) 2
18	Franck LEBOEUF	22.01.68	Chelsea	3 (197)
19	Christian KAREMBEU	03.12.70	Real Madrid	4 (239)
20	David TRÉZEGUET	15.10.77	AS Monaco	6 (347) 1
21	Christophe DUGARRY	24.03.72	Olympique Marseille	3 (118) 1
	Coach: Aimé JACQUET	27.11.41		

France's full lineup was: Barthéz; Desailly, Lizarazu, Thuram, Blanc (Leboeuf, Candela); Deschamps (captain), Karembeu, Zidane, Petit, (Boghossian, Vieira, Pires,

Dioméde); Djorkaeff, Henry or Trezuguet (Dugarry, Guivarc'h). Coach Aimé Jacquet picked his squad to perfection around injury and suspensions of key players (such as Zidane for two games and Blanc for the Final).

France scored 14 goals and allowed only 2, a defensive World Cup record for a team reaching the Final. The French allowed the 2 goals in 7 games, recording 5 shutouts. The goals allowed came from best modern players Davor Šuker (Croatia) and Michael Laudrup (Denmark), so those scoring were top class. France shut out four of the best modern era players: Ronaldo, Rivaldo, Bebeto, and Roberto Baggio, as well as two more top attackers in the final, Edmundo and Denilson. In a remarkable display of unselfish team play, nine players combined for France's 14 goals. Henry was France's leading scorer with three goals.

This French team is famous for beating Brazil by the score of 3-0 in the 1998 World Cup Final. Until this game, Brazil had never lost by more than two goals in any World Cup qualifying or Finals competition dating back to 1930.

France beat Paraguay and one of the best goalkeepers in the modern-era (José Luis Chilavert) 1-0 in an extra time golden goal by Blanc. However, France was fortunate to squeeze by an excellent Italian team on penalty kicks in the quarterfinals.

To further demonstrate their quality, France won the 2000 European Championship (beating Italy 2-1 in the Final), and the 2001 and 2003 Confederations Cups.

France has always been the European leader in soccer cultural diversity. By encouraging all French talent to develop, they have used their increasingly multiethnic nation to their advantage in football. Besides ethnic French, this French team had other European (Italian, Basque, Armenian), North African (Berber), Caribbean (Guadeloupe), Sub-Saharan African (Ghana, Senegal), South American (Argentina), and Oceanic (New Caledonia) contributions. France 1998 was truly a "world team."

(5) Argentina 1986

The 1986 World Cup winning Argentina team starring Diego Maradona was a completely different team to the 1978 World Cup winning team starring Mario Kempes and Daniel Passarella. Former captain Passarella was the only repeat player on the 1986 team (he wore # 6), but he did not participate in any of the games.

Argentina scored 14 goals and allowed 5 in the 1986 World Cup, as they won six games and tied one (1-1 to Italy). They had the ninth best offense and three of the modern era's best players in Diego Maradona, Oscar Ruggeri, and Passarella. The 1986 team was Diego Maradona's – famous and infamous for his "Goal of the Century" and "Hand of God" goals scored in the quarterfinal game against England. Argentina then defeated a tough West German side in the Final, earning the win with Burruchaga's late goal in the 88th minute.

The Argentine shirt numbers were given out alphabetically, with the exception of Maradona (10), Jorge Valdano (11), and Passarella (6). The Argentine lineup was: Pumpido; Brown, Cuciuffo, Ruggeri, Olarticoechea; Giusti, Batista, Maradona (captain), Enrique; Burruchaga, Valdano. This was a typical Argentine team made up of Spanish, Italian, German, English, Basque, and indigenous Argentine contributions.

Although Argentina reached the World Cup Final again in 1990, they scored only 5 goals and allowed 4 in the whole tournament; the worst goal difference (+1) of any team ever reaching the Final. West Germany got revenge for 1986, as they defeated Argentina 1-0 in the Final from an Andreas Brehme penalty kick.

#	Name	D.O.B. Club	Games/Minutes/Goals
2	Sergio Daniel BATISTA	09.11.62 Argentinos Juniors	7 (534)
3	Ricardo BOCHINI	25.01.54 Independiente	1 (5)
4	Claudio BORGHI	28.09.64 Argentinos Juniors	2 (119)
5	José Luis BROWN	10.11.56 CD Español BA	7 (630) 1
7	Jorge Luis BURRUCHAGA	09.10.62 FC Nantes	7 (608) 2
8	Néstor CLAUSEN	29.09.62 Independiente BA	1 (90)
9	José Luis CUCIUFFO	01.02.61 Velez Sarsfield BA	6 (540)
10	Diego Armando MARADONA	30.10.60 Napoli SSC	7 (630) 5
11	Jorge Alberto VALDANO	04.10.55 Real Madrid	7 (630) 4
12	Héctor Adolfo ENRIQUE	26.04.62 River Plate BA	5 (331)
13	Oscar GARRE	09.12.56 Ferro Carril Oeste BA	4 (360)
14	Ricardo Ornar GIUSTI	11.12.56 Independiente BA	7 (630)
16	Julio Jorge OLARTICOECHEA	18.10.58 Boca Juniors BA	7 (366)
17	Pedro Pablo PASCULLI	17.05.60 US Lecce	2 (163) 1
18	Nery Alberto PUMPIDO	30.07.57 River Plate BA	7 (630)
19	Oscar Alfredo RUGGERI	26.01.62 River Plate BA	7 (630) 1
20	Carlos Daniel TAPIA	20.08.62 Boca Juniors BA	2 (32)
21	Marcelo TROBBIANI	17.02.55 Elche CF	1 (2)
Coach: Carlos Salvador BILARDO		16.03.38	

(6) Brazil 1958-1962

Brazil was the only team to win the World Cup out of their hemisphere in the 20th century (in 1958), and it remains the only team to win two World Cups consecutively. It had one of the best forward lines ever, fielding the four exquisite strikers Garrincha, Vavá, Pelé, and Zagallo, ably supported by superlative creative midfielder Didí. Nilton Santos organized the defense superbly at the age of 37 (in 1962), with tremendous help from the non-related Djalma Santos.

This Brazil team had five of the best modern era players (Garrincha, Vavá, Pelé, Didí, and Nilton Santos), and the fourth rated offense with the ninth best defense.

#	Name	D.O.B. Club	Games/Minutes/Goals
1958 Brazil			
2	Hideraldo Luiz BELLINI	07.06.30 Vasco da Gama RJ	6(540)
3	GILMAR dos Santos Neves	22.08.30 Corinthians SP	6 (540)
4	DJALMA dos SANTOS	27.02.29 Portuguesa SP	1 (90)
5	DINO Sani	23.05.32 São Paulo FC	2 (180)
6	DIDI - Waldir Pereira	08.10.28 Botafogo RJ	6 (540) 1
7	Mário Jorge Lobo ZAGALLO	09.08.31 Flamengo RJ	6 (540) 1
10	PELÉ - Édson Arantes do Nascimento	23.10.40 Santos FC	4 (360) 6
11	GARRINCHA Manoel Francisco dos Santos	28.10.33 Botafogo RJ	4 (360)
12	NÍLTON Reis dos SANTOS	16.05.25 Botafogo RJ	6 (540) 1
14	Newton DE SORDI	14.02.31 São Paulo FC	5 (450)
15	ORLANDO Peçanha de Carvalho	20.09.35 Vasco da Gama RJ	6 (540)
17	JOEL Antônio Martins	23.11.31 Flamengo RJ	2 (180)
18	MAZZOLA - José João Altafini	24.07.38 Palmeiras SP	3 (270) 2
19	ZITO - José Ely de Miranda	08.08.32 Santos FC	4 (360)
20	VAVÁ - Edvaldo Izídio Neto	12.11.34 Vasco da Gama RJ	4 (360) 5
21	DIDA - Edvaldo Alves de Santa Rosa	16.03.34 Flamengo RJ	1 (90)
Coach: Vicente Ítalo FEOLA		01.11.09	

1962 Brazil

#	Name	D.O.B. Club	Games/Minutes/Goals
1	GILMAR dos Santos Neves	22.08.30 Santos FC	6 (540)
2	DJALMA dos SANTOS	27.02.29 Palmeiras SP	6 (540)
3	MAURO Ramos de Oliveira	30.08.30 Santos FC	6 (540)
4	ZITO - José Ely de Miranda	08.08.32 Santos FC	6 (540) 1
5	ZÓZIMO Alves Calazans	19.06.32 Bangu RJ	6 (540)
6	NÍLTON Reis dos SANTOS	16.05.25 Botafogo RJ	6 (540)
7	GARRINCHA Manoel Francisco dos Santos	28.10.33 Botafogo RJ	6 (532) 4
8	DIDI - Waldir Pereira	08.10.28 Botafogo RJ	6 (540)
10	PELÉ - Édson Arantes do Nascimento	23.10.40 Santos FC	2 (180) 1
19	VAVÁ - Edvaldo Izídio Neto	12.11.34 Palmeiras SP	6 (540) 4
20	AMARILDO Tavares da Silveira	29.07.39 Botafogo RJ	4 (360) 3
21	Mário Jorge Lobo ZAGALLO	09.08.31 Botafogo RJ	6 (540) 1
Coach: Aimoré MOREIRA		24.04.12	

In the 1958 tournament Brazil scored 16 goals and allowed 4, winning five games and tying one (0-0 to England).

Much of the same team was retained in 1962, including all their best modern era players. Pelé – a sensation in Sweden in 1958 – was expected to be even more impressive in 1962 as the acknowledged world's best player. However, he could not perform further after suffering an injury after scoring one goal. With Pelé hurt, Amarildo came on and finished the central striking role beautifully. In an inconceivable player rotation today, Brazil used only 12 players for the whole 1962 tournament, with Amarildo being the only new player used. Brazil scored 14 goals and allowed 5 in their repeat championship, again winning five games and tying one (to Czechoslovakia 0-0 in their first game, but Brazil beat them 3-1 in their second meeting in the Final).

Vavá scored in both Finals, becoming the first to score in two Final matches (Pelé was second in 1970 and Paul Breitner of West Germany the third in 1982).

(7a) Italy 1982

#	Name	D.O.B. Club	Games/Minutes/Goals
1	Dino ZOFF	28.02.42 Juventus	7 (630)
3	Giuseppe BERGOMI	22.12.63 Internazionale	3 (237)
4	Antonio CABRINI	08.10.57 Juventus	7 (630) 1
5	Fulvio COLLOVATI	09.05.57 Internazionale	7 (573)
6	Claudio GENTILE	27.09.53 Juventus	6 (540)
7	Gaetano SCIREA	25.05.53 Juventus	7 (630)
9	Giancarlo ANTOGNONI	01.04.54 Fiorentina	6 (477)
11	Giampiero MARINI	25.02.51 Internazionale	5 (273)
13	Gabriele ORIALI	25.12.52 Internazionale	5 (435)
14	Marco TARDELLI	24.09.54 Juventus	7 (615) 2
15	Franco CAUSIO	01.02.49 Udinese	2 (48)
16	Bruno CONTI	13.03.55 AS Roma	7 (630) 1
18	Alessandro ALTOBELLI	28.11.55 Internazionale	3 (111) 1
19	Francesco GRAZIANI	16.12.52 Fiorentina AC	7 (526) 1
20	Paolo ROSSI	23.09.56 Juventus	7 (575) 6
Coach: Vincenzo BEARZOT		26.09.27	

Italy scored 12 goals while giving up 5 in seven games, as they won away the 1982 Spain World Cup. This team contained four of the best modern era players: goalkeeper Dino Zoff, defenders Gaetano Scirea, striker Paolo Rossi, and defender Franco Baresi (#2 - he was an unused reserve on this team). They made a cohesive team effort with the eighth-best rated midfield.

This team is probably as famous for beating a tremendous Brazilian team (with Zico, Socrates, and Falção) in the second phase as winning the Final against a Rummenigge-led West Germany. Paolo Rossi had just finished off a two-year suspension for financial chicanery, but he found his goal-scoring knack just in time for Italy, as he scored the only hat trick ever against Brazil in a World Cup, and had six goals in the last three games.

(7b) Argentina 1978

Argentina scored 15 goals and allowed only 4, as they took advantage of delirious fan support and won the World Cup on home soil. This team contained four of the best modern era players: goalkeeper Ubaldo Fillol, defender Daniel Passarella, midfielder Osvaldo Ardiles, and striker Mario Kempes. They had the seventh best-rated offense and the eighth best defense.

They won a controversial 6-0 victory over Peru (which on video review appears to have been legitimate), the Argentines dominating after Peru hit the post early on. Argentina won the Final with two goals in overtime against Holland, after the Dutch just missed winning in regular time on a Rensenbrink shot that hit the post.

#	Name	D.O.B.	Club	Games/Minutes/Goals
1	Norberto ALONSO	04.01.53	River Plate	3 (85)
2	Osvaldo César ARDILES	03.08.52	Huracán	6 (470)
4	Ricardo BERTONI	14.03.55	Independiente	6 (478) 2
5	Ubaldo Manido FILLOL	21.07.50	River Plate	7 (660)
6	Américo Rubén GALLEGO	25.04.55	Newell's Old Boys	7 (655)
7	Luis Adolfo GALVÀN	24.02.48	A. Talleres Córdoba	7 (660)
9	Rene Orlando HOUSEMAN	19.07.53	Huracán	6 (328) 1
10	Mario Alberto KEMPES	15.07.54	Valencia	7 (660) 6
12	Rubén Ornar LAROSSA	18.11.47	Independiente	2 (145)
14	Leopoldo LUOUE	03.05.49	River Plate	5 (480) 4
15	Jorge Mario OLGUIN	17.05.52	SL de Almagro	7 (660)
16	Oscar Alberto ORTIZ	08.04.53	River Plate	6 (293)
17	Miguel Angel OVIEDO	12.10.50	Tal. Rem. de Escalada	1 (5)
19	Daniel PASSARELLA	25.05.53	River Plate	7 (660) 1
20	Alberto César TARANTINI	03.12.55	Boca Juniors	7 (660) 1
21	José Daniel VALENCIA	03.10.55	A. Talleres Córdoba	4 (271)
22	Julio Ricardo VILLA	18.08.52	Racing C. Avellaneda	2 (90)
Coach: César Luis MENOTTI		05.11.38		

Anybody that witnessed the 1978 Final will not forget the massive *Albiceleste* (sky blue and white) outpouring of the fans, in the most emotional home stadium display until the 1998 Final in France. Most of the Argentine spectators were able to temporarily drown out their life sorrows under the military dictatorship by witnessing their team win at home.

In the same pattern as 1978, the Argentina shirt numbers were assigned alphabetically according to last name. By skipping number 8, Kempes was able to wear the coveted number 10 jersey.

(8a) France 1984

Best modern era player Michel Platini led this 1984 European Championship winning team, which triumphed in the middle of their excellent performances in the 1982 (4th place and top scoring team with 16 goals) and 1986 (3rd place) World Cups.

Platini was the star of the 1984 tournament, as he scored 9 goals in only 5 games, including two pure (left foot, right foot, and headed goals) hat tricks. This French midfield is ranked the best of the Modern Era (Chapter 7).

France scored 14 goals and allowed only 4 goals as they won their last five tournament matches.

France lineup: Joel Bats; Patrick Battiston (Manuel Amoros), Yvon Le Roux, Maxime Bossis, Jean François Domergue; Alain Giresse, Jean Tigana, Luis Fernandez, Michel Platini; Bernard Lacombe, Bernard Genghini (Bruno Bellone).
Coach: Michel Hidalgo.

(8b) Netherlands 1988

This team contained four of the best modern era players; defenders Frank Rijkaard and Ronald Koeman, and strikers Ruud Gullit and Marco Van Basten.

The Dutch exorcised their German ghosts in the semi-final, as they beat host West Germany 2-1 in Hamburg, after initially losing 1-0.

In the Final the Dutch avenged their only loss in thirteen games of the competition (0-1 to Soviet Union), as they beat the Soviets convincingly 2-0. Gullit scored the first, then Van Basten scored from a seemingly impossible angle over excellent keeper Rinat Dassaiev.

A similar Dutch team advanced to the next 1992 European Championship semi-final where they tied eventual winner Denmark 2-2, but the Netherlands lost on penalties to miss qualifying for two European Finals in a row (see Chapter 15).

Holland lineup: Hans van Breukelen; Berry van Aerle, Frank Rijkaard, Ronald Koeman, Adrie van Tiggelen; Gerald Vanenburg, Jan Wouters, Arnold Mühren, Erwin Koeman; Ruud Gullit, Marco van Basten.
Coach: Rinus Michels.

(9) England 1966

England scored 11 goals and allowed only 3 while winning the 1966 World Cup at home. This team contained four of the best modern era players: goalkeeper Gordon Banks, defender Bobby Moore, and strikers Bobby Charlton and Geoff Hurst, and they had the fifth-best rated defense. Coach Alf Ramsey's team was called the "wingless wonders", as they effectively played a 4-4-2 tactical scheme.

During the Cup a striker dilemma evolved concerning domestically prolific goal scorer Jimmy Greaves and the larger and more physical Geoff Hurst. Greaves played three full matches without scoring; Hurst played the last three games and scored four goals, and England entered the history books.

England won the Final 4-2 in overtime against West Germany. Hurst scored the two overtime goals; the first is still debated whether it crossed the goal line. Nevertheless, Hurst's third strike left no doubt as to the winner, and he remains the only player to score three goals in the Final match.

#	Name	D.O.B. Club	Games/Minutes/Goals
1	Gordon BANKS	30.12.37 Leicester City	6 (570)
2	George R. COHEN	22.10.39 Fulham	6 (570)
3	Ramon WILSON	17.12.34 Everton FC	6 (570)
4	Norbert Peter STILES	18.05.42 Manchester United	6 (570)
5	John CHARLTON	08.05.35 Leeds United	6 (570)
6	Robert F. C. MOORE	12.04.41 West Ham United	6 (570)
7	Alan James BALL	12.05.45 Blackpool	4 (390)
8	James Peter GREAVES	20.02.40 Tottenham Hotspur	3 (270)
9	Robert CHARLTON	11.10.37 Manchester United	6 (570) 3
10	Geoffrey C. HURST	08.12.41 West Ham United	3 (300) 4
11	John Michael CONNELLY	18.07.38 Manchester United	1 (90)
16	Martin S. PETERS	08.11.43 West Ham United	5 (480) 1
19	Terence Lionel PAINE	23.03.39 Southampton	1 (90)
20	Ian Robert CALLAGHAN	10.04.42 Liverpool FC	1 (90)
21	Roger HUNT	20.07.38 Liverpool FC	6 (570) 3
	Coach: Alfred Ernest RAMSEY	22.01.20	

(10a) Brazil 1994

Brazil scored only 11 goals and allowed 3 in the 1994 Cup. This team contained five of the best modern era players: defender Cafú, midfielder Raí, and strikers Romário and Bebeto; teenager Ronaldo (Luiz Nazário de Lima) was an unused substitute (#20). Brazil 1994 had the fourth best-rated defense and the tenth best offense.

#	Name	D.O.B. Club	Games/Minutes/Goals
1	Cláudio André Morgen TAFFAREL	08.05.66 Reggiana	7 (660)
2	JORGINHO-Jorge José de Amorim Campos	17.08.64 Bayern München	7 (559)
3	RICARDO Roberto Barreto da ROCHA	11.09.62 Vasco da Gama	1 (67)
5	MAURO da SILVA Gomes	12.01.68 Deportivo La Coruña	7 (615)
6	BRANCO - Cláudio Ibrahim Vaz Leal	04.04.64 Fluminense RJ	3 (298) 1
7	BEBETO José Roberto Gama de Oliveira	16.02.64 Deportivo La Coruña	7 (660) 3
8	DUNGA - Carlos Caetano Bledorn Verri	31.10.63 VfB Stuttgart	7 (648)
9	ZINHO - Crizam César de Oliveira Jr	17.06.67 Palmeiras SP	7 (605)
10	RAÍ Souza Vieira de Oliveira	15.05.65 Paris SG	5 (304) 1
11	ROMÁRIO de Souza Faria	29.01.66 FC Barcelona	7 (660) 5
13	ALDAIR Santos	30.11.65 AS Roma	7 (593)
14	CAFU - Marcos Evangelista de Moraes	19.06.70 São Paulo FC	3 (125)
15	MÁRCIO Roberto dos SANTOS	15.09.69 Girondins Bordeaux	7 (660) 1
16	LEONARDO Nascimento de Araújo	05.09.69 São Paulo FC	4 (312)
17	MAZINHO - Lomar do Nascimento	08.04.66 Palmeiras SP	6 (392)
18	PAULO SÉRGIO Silvestre Nascimento	02.06.69 Bayer 04 Leverkusen	2 (27)
19	MÜLLER - Luiz Antônio Corrêa da Costa	31.01.66 São Paulo FC	1 (11)
21	VIOLA - Paulo Sérgio Rosa	01.01.69 Corinthians SP	1 (16)
	Coach: Carlos Alberto Gomes PARREIRA	25.03.43	

Uncharacteristically for Brazilian teams, they had no goals in two consecutive World Cup finals (1994 & 1998), although they won the 1994 Cup against Italy on penalties. Brazil's overall dominance was shown by their Copa America wins in 1997 and 1999. Brazil was also in the 1995 Copa America final, but lost on penalties to Uruguay.

(10b) Brazil 1982

This team contained three of the best modern era players: midfielders Socrates and Falcão, and striker Zico.

Brazil won their first four games, scoring thirteen goals and allowing only two. Unfortunately, in the quarterfinals they met a superb Italian team, and only one nation could proceed in the tournament. Brazil threw caution to the wind and played openly, allowing Paulo Rossi to score an excellent hat trick (the only time Brazil has allowed 3 goals from an opposition player in World Cup play). Brazil finished with 15 goals in only 5 games, and allowed only six goals, but three of them were to Italy in the 3-2 loss.

Brazil 1982 is the only modern era World Cup team to have *five players score two or more goals*, which was accomplished in only five games.

#	Name	D.O.B.	Club	Games/Minutes/Goals
1	Valdir PERES	02.01.51	São Paulo	5 (450)
2	José LEANDRO Souza Ferreira	17.03.59	Flamengo	5 (450)
3	OSCAR - José Oscar Bernardi	20.06.54	São Paulo	5 (435) 1
4	LUIZINHO - Luiz Carlos Ferreira	22.10.58	Atlético - MG	5 (450)
5	Antônio Carlos CEREZO	21.04.55	Atlético - MG	4 (360)
6	Leovegildo Lins Gama JÚNIOR	29.06.54	Flamengo	5 (450) 1
7	PAULO ISIDORO de Jesus	03.08.53	Grêmio	4 (90)
8	SÓCRATES Brasileiro Sampaio Vieira de Oliveira	19.02.54	Corinthians	5 (450) 2
9	SERGINHO - Sérgio Bernardino	23.12.53	São Paulo	5 (404) 2
10	ZICO - Arthur Antunes Coimbra	03.03.55	Flamengo	5 (443) 4
11	ÉDER Aleixo de Assis	25.05.57	Atlético - MG	5 (450) 2
13	EDEVALDO de Freitas	28.01.58	Internacional	2 (8)
15	Paulo Roberto FALCÃO	16.10.53	Roma	5 (450) 3
16	EDINHO - Edino Nazareth Filho	05.06.55	Fluminense	1 (15)
21	DIRCEU José Guimarães	15.06.52	Atlético Madrid	1 (45)
Coach: Telê SANTANA DA SILVA		26.07.31		

(10c) Netherlands 1978

Retained its core group of players from 1974 – except Cruyff and Van Hanegem, who both helped Holland qualify but declined to travel to Argentina – this Dutch team narrowly lost the 1978 World Cup final to host Argentina in overtime.

#	Name	D.O.B.	Club	Games/Minutes/Goals
1	Piet SCHRIJVERS	15.12.46	Ajax	3 (201)
2	Jan POORTVLIET	15.09.55	PSV Eindhoven	6 (570)
3	Dick SCHOENAKER	30.11.52	Ajax	1 (30)
4	Adrie van KRAAY	01.07.53	PSV Eindhoven	2 (51)
5	Ruud KROL	24.03.49	Ajax	7 (660)
6	Wim JANSEN	28.10.46	Feyenoord	7 (612)
7	Piet WILDSCHUT	25.10.57	FC Twente	3 (213)
8	Jan JONGBLOED	25.11.40	Roda JC	5 (459)
9	Arie HAAN	16.11.48	Anderlecht	6 (570) 2
10	Rene van de KERKHOF	16.09.51	PSV Eindhoven	7 (616) 1
11	Willie van de KERKHOF	16.09.51	PSV Eindhoven	7 (630) 1
12	Rob RENSENBRINK	03.07.47	Anderlecht	7 (660) 5
13	Johan NEESKENS	15.09.51	Barcelona	5 (378)
14	Jan BOSKAMP	21.10.48	RWD Molenbeek	1 (80)
16	Johnny REP	25.11.51	Bastia	7 (528) 3
17	Wim RIJSBERGEN	18.01.52	Feyenoord	3 (226)
18	Dick NANNINGA	17.01.49	Roda JC	3 (92) 1
20	Wim CUURBIER	16.01.45	Schalke 04	4 (318)
22	Ernie BRANDTS	03.02.56	PSV Eindhoven	4 (366) 2
Coach: Ernst HAPPEL		29.06.25		

This team contained three of the best modern era players: defender Ruud Krol, midfielder Johan Neeskens, and striker Rob Rensenbrink; and had the ninth best rated offense.

Incredibly, this Dutch team had a good chance to win the Final in Buenos Aries, as Rensenbrink agonizingly hit the post in the dying minutes in regulation time. Fifteen minutes into overtime, tournament MVP Mario Kempes put the hosts ahead for good.

Not as pretty a team as the 1974 Holland edition, as they missed Johan Cruyff and Wim Van Hanegem's creative talents. Holland's offense still scored 15 goals, but their more porous defense allowed 10 goals in seven games.

(10d) Italy 1990

This team contained five of the best modern era players: goalkeeper Walter Zenga, defenders Paolo Maldini and Franco Baresi, and strikers Roberto Baggio and Salvatore Schillaci.

As the host team, they won six games and tied one, scoring ten goals and allowing only two to rate the number one defense. However, Italy only finished third after losing the semi-final to Argentina on a penalty kick competition. Salvatore Schillaci was the revelation and star of the Cup, along with Lothar Matthäus of West Germany.

#	Name	D.O.B.	Club	Games/Minutes/Goals
1	Walter ZENGA	28.04.60	Internazionale	7 (660)
2	Franco BARESI	08.05.60	AC Milan	3 (259)
3	Giuseppe BERGOMI	22.12.63	Internazionale	7 (660)
4	Luigi De AGOSTINI	07.04.61	Juventus	6 (450)
5	Ciro FERRARA	11.02.67	Napoli	1 (90)
6	Riccardo FERRI	20.08.63	Internazionale	7 (570)
7	Paolo MALDINI	26.06.68	AC Milan	7 (660)
8	Pietro VIERCHOWOD	06.04.59	Sampdoria	3 (126)
9	Carlo ANCELOTTI	06.10.59	AC Milan	3 (164)
10	Nicola BERTI	14.04.67	Internazionale	4 (255)
11	Fernando DE NAPOLI	15.03.64	Napoli	6 (545)
13	Giuseppe GIANNINI	20.08.64	AS Roma	7 (585) 1
15	Roberto BAGGIO	18.02.67	AC Fiorentina	5 (376) 2
16	Andrea CARNEVALE	12.01.61	Napoli	2 (125)
17	Roberto DONADONI	09.09.63	AC Milan	5 (441)
19	Salvatore SCHILLACI	01.12.64	Juventus	7 (535) 6
20	Aldo SERENA	25.06.60	Internazionale	3 (108) 1
21	Gianluca VIALLI	09.07.64	Sampdoria	3 (250)
Coach: Azeglio VICINI		20.03.33		

(10e) Italy 1994

This team contained three of the best modern era players: defenders Paolo Maldini and Franco Baresi, and midfielder Roberto Baggio.

Italy won four games, tied one, and lost two as they scored 8 goals and allowed 5. They lost the 1994 World Cup Final on penalty kicks to Brazil, after a scoreless regulation and overtime. This Italian team was one of the toughest teams in any World Cup, as both Franco Baresi and Roberto Baggio played the Final injured.

#	Name	D.O.B. Club	Games/Minutes/Goals	
1	Gianluca PAGLIUCA	18.12.66 Sampdoria	5 (411)	
2	Luigi APOLLONI	02.05.67 Parma	3 (216)	
3	Antonio BENARRIVO	21.08.68 Parma	6 (600)	
4	Alessandro COSTACURTA	24.04.66 AC Milan	6 (570)	
5	Paolo MALDINI	26.06.68 AC Milan	7 (690)	
6	Franco BARESI	08.05.60 AC Milan	3 (259)	
8	Roberto MUSSI	28.08.63 Torino	3 (245)	
9	Mauro TASSOTTI	19.01.60 AC Milan	2 (180)	
10	Roberto BAGGIO	18.02.67 Juventus	7 (603)	5
11	Demetrio ALBERTINI	23.08.71 AC Milan	7 (646)	
12	Luca MARCHEGIANI	22.02.66 Lazio	3 (279)	
13	Dino BAGGIO	24.07.71 Juventus	7 (560)	2
14	Nicola BERTI	14.04.67 Internazionale	7 (466)	
15	Antonio CONTE	31.07.69 Juventus	2 (100)	
16	Roberto DONADONI	09.09.63 AC Milan	6 (535)	
17	Alberigo EVANI	01.01.63 Sampdoria	2 (71)	
18	Pierluigi CASIRAGHI	04.03.69 Lazio	3 (205)	
19	Daniele MASSARO	23.05.61 AC Milan	6 (439)	1
20	Giuseppe SIGNORI	17.02.68 Lazio	6 (392)	
21	Gianfranco ZOLA	07.05.66 Parma	1 (10)	
Coach: Arrigo SAACHI		01.04.46		

(10f) Italy 1970

This team contained four of the best modern era players: defender Giacinto Facchetti, midfielders Gianni Rivera and Sandro Mazzola, and striker Luigi Riva.

Italy was European Championship winners in 1968. In the 1970 World Cup, Italy won 3 games, tied two, and only lost the Final. They scored 10 goals and gave up 8 (4 of which came in the Final to Brazil).

#	Name	D.O.B. Club	Games/Minutes/Goals	
1	Enrico ALBERTOSI	02.11.39 Cagliari	6 (570)	
2	Tarcisio BURGNICH	25.04.39 Internazionale	6 (570)	1
3	Giacinto FACCHETTI	18.07.42 Internazionale	6 (570)	
4	Fabrizio POLETTI	13.07.43 Torino	1 (29)	
5	Pierluigi CERA	25.02.41 Cagliari	6 (570)	
7	Comunardo NICCOLAI	15.12.46 Cagliari	1 (37)	
8	Roberto ROSATO	18.08.43 Milan	6 (504)	
10	Mario BERTINI	07.01.44 Internazionale	6 (554)	
11	Luigi RIVA	07.11.44 Cagliari	6 (570)	3
13	Angelo DOMENGHINI	25.08.41 Cagliari	6 (476)	1
14	Gianni RIVERA	18.08.43 AC Milan	4 (168)	2
15	Alessandro MAZZOLA	08.11.42 Internazionale	6 (452)	
16	Giancarlo DE SISTI	13.03.43 Fiorentina	6 (570)	
18	Antonio JULIANO	01.01.43 Napoli	1 (16)	
19	Sergio GORI	24.02.46 Cagliari	1 (6)	
20	Roberto BONINSEGNA	13.11.43 Internazionale	6 (564)	2
21	Giuseppe FURINO	05.07.46 Juventus	1 (44)	
Coach: Ferruccio VALCAREGGI		12.02.19		

(10g) Poland 1974

This team contained two of the best modern era players: midfielder Kazimierz Deyna and striker Grzegorz Lato. They had a stellar attack with Lato, Szarmach, and Gadocha, and a resolute defense of Zmuda, Gorgon, Szymanowski, and Musial. Excellent goalkeeper Tomaszewski saved two penalties in regulation time in the tournament.

Poland won six games and lost only one, to host and eventual winner West Germany 0-1. They scored 16 goals and allowed only 5, and finished 3rd after beating powerhouses Brazil, Argentina, and Italy in the tournament.

With seven goals, Lato had the most goals in the tournament, and won the Golden Boot award.

#	Name	D.O.B.	Club	Games/Minutes/Goals	
2	Jan TOMASZEWSKI	01.09.48	LKS Lodz	7 (630)	
4	Antoni SZYMANOWSKI	01.13.51	Wisla Krakow	7 (630)	
5	Zbigniew GUT	04.17.49	Odra Opole	2 (109)	
6	Jerzy GORGON	07.18.49	Górnik Zabrze	7 (630)	1
9	Wladyslaw ZMUDA	06.06.54	Gwardia Warszawa	7 (630)	
10	Adam MUSIAL	12.18.48	Wisla Krakow	6 (521)	
11	Leslaw CMIKIEWICZ	08.25.48	Legia Warszawa	6 (102)	
12	Kazimierz DEYNA	10.23.47	Legia Warszawa	7 (620)	3
13	Henryk KASPERCZAK	07.10.46	Stal Mielec	7 (603)	
14	Zygmunt MASZCZYK	05.03.45	Ruch Chorzow	7 (595)	
16	Grzegorz LATO	04.08.50	Stal Mielec	7 (630)	7
17	Andrzej SZARMACH	10.03.50	Górnik Zabrze	6 (430)	5
18	Robert GADOCHA	01.10.46	Legia Warszawa	7 (625)	
19	Jan DOMARSKI	10.28.46	Stal Mielec	3 (120)	
20	Zdzislaw KAPKA	12.07.54	Wisla Krakow	1 (15)	
21	Kazimierz KMIECIK	09.19.51	Wisla Krakow	2 (40)	
Coach: Kazimierz GORSKI		02.03.21			

(10h) West Germany 1990

#	Name	D.O.B.	Club	Games/Minutes/Goals	
1	Bodo ILLGNER	07.04.67	1.FC Köln	7 (660)	
2	Stefan REUTER	16.10.66	Bayern München	6 (429)	
3	Andreas BREHME	09.11.60	Internazionale	6 (570)	3
4	Jürgen KOHLER	06.10.65	Bayern München	4 (390)	
5	Klaus AUGENTHALER	26.09.57	Bayern München	7 (660)	
6	Guido BUCHWALD	24.01.61	VfB Stuttgart	7 (660)	
7	Pierre LITTBARSKI	16.04.60	1.FC Köln	6 (376)	1
8	Thomas HÄSSLER	30.05.66	1.FC Köln	5 (408)	
9	Rudolf VÖLLER	13.04.60	AS Roma	6 (418)	3
10	Lothar H. MATTHÄUS	21.03.61	Internazionale	7 (660)	4
13	Karl-Heinz RIEDLE	16.09.65	Werder Bremen	4 (204)	
14	Thomas BERTHOLD	12.11.64	AS Roma	7 (599)	
15	Uwe BEIN	26.09.60	Eintracht Frankfurt	4 (292)	1
17	Andreas MÖLLER	02.09.67	Borussia Dortmund	2 (23)	
18	Jürgen KLINSMANN	30.07.64	Internazionale	7 (629)	3
19	Hans PFLÜGLER	27.03.60	Bayern München	1 (90)	
20	Olaf THON	01.05.66	Bayern München	2 (123)	
Coach: Franz BECKENBAUER		11.09.45			

This West Germany team contained four of the best modern era players: defenders Andreas Brehme and Lothar Matthäus (although Matthäus played midfield in this Cup), and strikers Jürgen Klinsmann and Rudi Völler. West Germany 1990 had the seventh best-rated midfield.

West Germany had built on momentum and ambition from two consecutive Final losses in 1982 and 1986 to Italy and Argentina, respectively. They won the 1990 Final 1-0 on Andreas Brehme's penalty kick against Argentina.

West Germany scored 15 goals to 5 against, and beat Argentina, which scored only 5 goals with 4 against (the best Final would have been West Germany versus Italy, which had lost the semi-final penalty kicks to Argentina). Matthäus had 4 goals as midfielder and was star of the tournament along with Italy's Toto Schillaci.

Franz Beckenbauer became the second person (after Mário Zagallo of Brazil) to win a World Cup as a player and as a coach.

BEST CLUB TEAMS 1958-2006

	Abbreviations for Common Continental and International Competitions
EC	European Champions Cup or European Champion's League.[9] This tournament is the European Club Championship.
CL	Copa Libertadores. This tournament is the South American Club Championship.
ICC	Intercontinental Club Cup (known unofficially as the World Club Cup). Comprised of a game(s)[10] between the winners of the EC (Europe) and CL (South America); the winner is acclaimed to be the Best Club Team in the World. Since 2005 the ICC has been supplanted by the Club CWC.
CWC	New tournament invites club champions from all six Confederations to play for the Club World Championship, the effective World Club Champion.

Club teams of a more recent era have to deal with much more changeover in personnel, so even if successful, they are less likely to keep the "core" of their team together.

For example, after Dutch club Ajax won the biggest trophies in 1995 (the European Champions Cup and the Intercontinental Cup), and was European Champions Cup Finalist again in 1996, nearly all their starting players left for the so-called "big clubs." Similarly, in 2004, after Porto won the Champion's League, many crucial players and the coach left for greener pastures - more money. There is now much less loyalty to a club, and players and coaches often gravitate to where the most money is offered.

Unlike the national team rankings, it is pointless to discuss which was the number one club team was in the Modern Era. Four superlative teams stand out and define the football of their time, and they are presented in alphabetical order. Twenty-one other excellent teams follow the best four.

(1a) Ajax Amsterdam (Netherlands) 1971-1973
Ajax won three consecutive ECs from 1971-1973, and won the only ICC they contested in this period, against Independiente of Argentina in 1972 by a 4-1 aggregate score.

For the first EC triumph Ajax was coached by Rinus Michels, who was assisted by his on-field protégé Johan Cruyff. With a supporting cast that included Dutch World Cup players Johan Neeskens, Wim Suurbier, Ruud Krol, Arie Haan, and Johnny Rep, Ajax provided the backbone of the 1974 Holland World Cup team that placed second to West Germany.

The Ajax style was called "total soccer," or the "Dutch whirl," which when transplanted to the national side became the "Orange Machine" (Sp. *Naranja Mecánica*). This style required that all players possess the skills to play every position, and they would switch back and forth freely as opportunities arose. Ajax's collective football philosophy was to "let the ball do the running."

This Ajax team broke up in 1974, as first Cruyff and then Neeskens followed Michels to FC Barcelona. If the team had remained in place, they would likely have challenged Bayern Munich for the 1974 European Cup.

LINEUP: Heinz Stuy; Wim Suurbier, Barry Hulshoff, Horst Blankenburg, Ruud Krol; Johan Neeskens, Gerry Mühren, Arie Haan; Johnny Rep, Johan Cruyff, Piet Keizer.
Coaches: Rinus Michels (1971) and Stefán Kovács (1972-1973).

---

[9] Known as the European Champions' Cup from 1955-1998, and the UEFA Champion's League from late 1998-present.
[10] Was played as a home-and-away series from 1960-1979, then changed to a single game format in Tokyo from 1980-2004. FIFA introduced the Club World Championship in 2000 that was supposed to supplant any future ICCs, but the 2001-2004 versions were cancelled, and it was re-introduced in 2005.

(1b) AC Milan (Italy) 1989-1990

AC Milan won two consecutive ECs and ICCs in 1989-1990. Milan also demonstrated complete domestic dominance as they won the Italian Serie A in 1991/1992 undefeated (22 won and 12 tied). AC Milan still holds the world record run of consecutive top division matches without defeat; 58 games from 1991-1993.

AC Milan combined the best Dutch and Italian players and styles, including Ruud Gullit, Marco Van Basten, and Frank Rijkaard from Holland, and Franco Baresi, Roberto Donadoni, and Paulo Maldini from Italy, forming a sparkling creative and resolute unit that was second to none.

LINEUP: Giovanni Galli; Mauro Tassotti, Alessandro Costacurta, Franco Baresi, Paolo Maldini; Angelo Colombo, Frank Rijkaard, Carlo Ancelotti, Roberto Donadoni; Ruud Gullit, Marco Van Basten.
Coach: Arrigo Saachi.

(1c) Real Madrid (Spain) 1956-1960

This Real Madrid team featured an attacking line including Alfredo Di Stéfano, Ferenc Puskas, and Paco Gento, with Raymond Kopa at the creative midfield slot.

In an outrageous show of European dominance, Real Madrid won the first five ECs from 1956-1960, with Di Stéfano scoring in each final (a total of 7 goals in 5 finals). Puskas scored seven goals in the last two Finals (1959-1960). These three feats are unlikely to be duplicated.

Real Madrid's most dominant championship was their last, and their 7-3 win over Eintracht Frankfurt in Glasgow in 1960 is often referred to as the "Game of the Century."

Real Madrid also won the inaugural ICC in 1960 against Peñarol of Uruguay.

LINEUP: Rogelio Dominguez (Alonso); Ángel Atienza (Marquitos), José Santamaria, Rafael Lesmes, Juan Santisteban; José María Zárraga, Raymond Kopa; Enrique Mateos, Alfredo Di Stéfano, Héctor Rial (or Ferenc Puskás), Francisco Gento.
Coaches: Pepe Villalonga (1956-1957), Luis Carniglia (1958-1959), Miguel Múñoz (1960).

(1d) Santos (Brazil) 1962-1963

Santos was Pelé's team throughout his Brazilian career. Pelé led Santos to two consecutive CL wins in 1962-1963, against Peñarol of Uruguay and Boca Juniors of Argentina. Santos won both ICCs they played. In 1962, they beat Benfica 3-2 in Rio de Janeiro and 5-2 away in Lisbon; Pelé had five goals in the home-and-away series. Benfica featured Eusébio, Mário Coluna, and António Simões; all would star for Portugal in the 1966 World Cup. In 1963, Santos beat Milan in a playoff, with Pelé getting two goals in the three games. That Milan team had two future Italy national team coaches anchoring the defense (Cesare Maldini and Giovanni Trapattoni), and their scintillating offense included Gianni Rivera, 1958 ex-Brazilian World Cup player Jose Altafini (who switched to play for Italy in the 1962 World Cup), and Brazilian Amarildo, who had starred in the 1962 World Cup after Pelé had been injured.

Pelé had a marvelous relationship with national midfielder Zito, as well as fellow strikers Coutinho and Pepe, two forwards who could never quite break into the regular Brazil starting lineup. World Cup defenseman Mauro and goalkeeper Gilmar anchored the Santos defense.

Brazilian journalist Odir Cunha persuasively argues in his 2003 book *Time dos Sonhos* ("Dream Team") why he believes Santos was the best club team of all time.

LINEUP: Gilmar; Lima, Mauro, Calvet, Dalmo; Mengalvio, Zito; Dorval, Coutinho, Pelé, Pepe.
Coach: Luiz Alonso "Lula."

(2) Bayern Munich (Germany) 1974-1976

Bayern Munich won three consecutive ECs from 1974-1976. Because of a 1-1 tie with Atlético Madrid, they had to replay the 1974 final, which they won convincingly 4-0. Bayern also won the only ICC they contested in this period, by a 2-0 aggregate score against Cruzeiro of Brazil (featuring Jairzinho and Ze Carlos) in 1976.

Stars of the Bayern team were captain Franz Beckenbauer, Paul Breitner, Gerd Müller, Georg Schwarzenbeck, Uli Hoeness, goalkeeper Sepp Maier and a young Karl-Heinz Rummenigge. Six of them (all but Rummenigge) lined up for the World Cup winning West German side in 1974, but Breitner left for Real Madrid after the World Cup.

LINEUP: Sepp Maier; Johnny Hansen, Georg Schwarzenbeck, Franz Beckenbauer, Rainer Zobel; Franz Roth, Bernd Dürnberger, Jupp Kapellman, Ulrich Hoeness; Karl-Heinz Rummenigge, Gerd Müller.
Coach: Udo Lattek (1974), Dettmar Cramer (1975-1976).

(3a) Liverpool (England) 1977-1978

Liverpool won two consecutive ECs in 1977 and 1978, but did not contest the ICC either year. Kevin Keegan led the team in 1977, but promptly left for Hamburg after the championship. Fellow top modern-era player Kenny Dalglish seamlessly replaced him for the 1978 team. Liverpool was a team of great will and skill, with stellar teamwork anchored by Alan Hansen's back line.

From this Liverpool club, only Neal and Kennedy won both years 1977-1978 and also won the 1981 and 1984 European Cups with Liverpool – winning an amazing four ECs in only eight years. Clemence, Dalglish, Hansen, McDermott, and Souness each won three ECs in that period.

LINEUP: Ray Clemence; Phil Neal, Peter Thompson, Alan Hansen, Emlyn Hughes; Terry McDermott, Alan Kennedy, Graeme Souness; Steve Heighway, David Fairclough, Kenny Dalglish (1978 - or Kevin Keegan 1977).
Coach: Bob Paisley.

(3b) São Paulo (Brazil) 1992-1993

This Sao Paulo team won two CL's & two IC's in 1992-1993. They bested two of the most powerful European teams in the modern era, winning ICCs against Barcelona in 1992 and AC Milan in 1993.

Cafú anchored the back line, Raí and Leonardo provided the midfield creativity, and Müller and Palinha provided the scoring offense. All except Palinha were Brazil 1994 World Cup team players.

LINEUP: Zetti; Cafú, Válber, Ronaldo, André; Raí, Dinho, Toninho Cerezo, Leonardo; Palhinha, Müller.
Coach: Telé Santana.

(4a) Real Madrid (Spain) 1998, 2000, 2002

This Real Madrid team won three ECs in five years, 1998, 2000, & 2002, and won the ICC in 1998 and 2002.

All three teams contained strikers Raúl and Fernando Morrientes, wingback Roberto Carlos, and central defender Fernando Hierro. The first two teams had Fernando Redondo as the dominant midfielder, while the last team had both Luis Figo and Zinedine Zidane as creative forces.

No wonder after the 2002 Cup, the Real Madrid director said, "There are no more stars (which are called *galacticos* in Spain) to buy." He was wrong, as after the 2002 World Cup they acquired Ronaldo from Internazionale, and he duly contributed a goal in the 2002 ICC win against fellow centenarians Olympia of Paraguay.

Coach del Bosque and captain Hierro were sacked after the 2003 campaign, and Morrientes was sent packing to Monaco on loan. The moves backfired as Real's defense faltered, and Morrientes scored two critical goals that helped Monaco eliminate them from the 2004 European Champion's League.

LINEUP: Bodo Illgner or Iker Casillas; Michel Salgado, Fernando Hierro, Iván Helguera, Roberto Carlos; Luis Figo or Iván Campo, Claude Makélélé or Steve McManaman, Fernando Redondo or Zinedine Zidane, Santiago Solari; Raúl González, Fernando Morrientes.
Coach: Jupp Heynckes (1998) and Vicente del Bosque (2000 & 2002).

(4b) Boca Juniors (Argentina) 1977-1978

This pre-Maradona Boca team accomplished much more than when Maradona was at the club. Boca Juniors won two consecutive CLs in 1977 and 1978, and won their only ICC they contested, against Borussia Mönchengladbach in 1977.

Incredibly, Argentina's 1978 World Cup winning squad used only one player from this very successful squad – defender Alberto Tarantini.

LINEUP: Hugo Gatti; Vincente Pernía, Roberto Mouzo, Alberto Tarantini, J.J. Benitez, Daniel Pavón, Rubén Suñé, Mario Zanabria, Ernesto Mastrángelo, Carlos Veglio, Darío Felman.
Coach: Juan Carlos Lorenzo.

(5a) Independiente (Argentina) 1972-1975

Independiente won the Copa Libertadores four years in a row (1972-1975), a record unlikely to be equaled. They lost the 1972 ICC to Ajax, won the 1973 ICC against Juventus, and lost the 1974 ICC against Atlético Madrid.

Francisco Sá later played in the dual-Copa winning Boca Juniors squad, while striker Daniel Bertoni was an integral part of the 1978 Argentine World Cup-winning team, scoring their final goal in overtime in the Final against Holland.

LINEUP: Miguel Ángel Santoro, Miguel Ángel López, Ricardo Elbio Pavoni, Eduardo Comisso, Miguel Ángel Raimondo, Francisco Sá, Agustín Alberto Balbuena, Rubén Galván, Eduardo Andrés Magglioni, Ricardo Enrique Bochini, Ricardo Daniel Bertoni.
Coaches: Pedro Dellacha (1972 & 1975), Humberto Maschio (1973), Roberto Ferreiro (1974).

(5b) Benfica (Portugal) 1961-1962

Benfica made it to the European Cup Final five times (1961, 1962, 1963, 1965, 1968) in the 1960s. Consecutive winners in 1961-1962, they beat two very strong Spanish squads in Barcelona (1961) and Real Madrid (1962). They were the first team to win the European Cup after Real Madrid's dominance, but lost the two ICCs they contested, to Peñarol and Pelé's Santos.

Benfica's power emanated from midfielder and captain Mário Coluna and center forward and future European Footballer of the Year Eusébio. António Simões was the creative midfielder who set up many of Benfica's goals. Their coach was the legendary Hungarian Bela Guttman.

LINEUP: Costa Pereira; João, Germano, Angelo; Domiciano Cavem, Cruz; José Augusto, Eusébio, José Águas, Mário Coluna, António Simões.
Coach: Bela Guttman.

(6a) Internazionale (Italy) 1964-1965

Internazionale won two consecutive ECs in 1964-1965 (against 37-year old Di Stéfano's Real Madrid and Eusébio's Benfica), and won both ICCs they played against Independiente of Argentina.

Inter was led by Giacinto Facchetti in defense and Sandro Mazzola in offense, while the midfield was marshaled by Luis Suárez, the only Spanish player thus far to have won the European Footballer of the Year award.

LINEUP: Giuliano Sarti; Tarcisio Burgnich, Aristide Guarneri, Giacinto Facchetti; Gianfranco Bedin, Armando Picchi, Jair Da Costa; Sandro Mazzola, Joaquin Peiro, Luis Suárez, Mario Corso.
Coach: Helenio Herrera.

(6b) Nottingham Forest (England) 1979-1980

Nottingham Forest showed complete domestic dominance in 1978, when they played a record 42 consecutive games without loss in the English First Division (a run surpassed only in 2004 by Arsenal's 49 undefeated match streak).

Forest won the 1979 EC over Malmö and the 1980 EC over Kevin Keegan's Hamburg, but lost the only ICC they contested in 1980 to Nacional.

Their lineup featured England goalkeeper Peter Shilton, defensemen Viv Anderson and Kenny Burns, midfielders John McGovern and John Robertson, and quicksilver strikers Tony Woodcock and Trevor Francis.

LINEUP: Peter Shilton; Viv Anderson, Larry Lloyd, Kenny Burns, Frank Clark; Trevor Francis, John McGovern, Ian Bowyer, John Robertson, Tony Woodcock, Gary Birtles.
Coach: Brian Clough.

(7a) Ajax (Netherlands) 1995-1996

Ajax won the 1995 EC by beating Milan 1-0 on 18-year old Patrick Kluivert's goal. The reached the 1996 Final as well, but lost on penalties to Zidane's Juventus. Ajax won the 1995 ICC on penalties, besting Gremio of Brazil.

Ajax fielded a young team guided by veteran Frank Rijkaard's leadership. However, this outstanding team was dismantled after the Bosman ruling (Chapter 5), losing no fewer than twelve players within a few months.

LINEUP: Edwin van der Sar, Michael Reiziger, Danny Blind, Frank Rijkaard, Frank de Boer, Finidi George, Clarence Seedorf (Nwankwo Kanu), Jari Litmanen (Patrick Kluivert), Edgar Davids, Marc Overmars, Ronald de Boer.
Coach: Louis van Gaal.

(7b) AC Milan (Italy) 1993-1994

This Milan team lost the 1993 EC Cup Final 0-1 to Marseille, but bounced back and annihilated Barcelona 4-0 in the 1994 EC Final in one of the most dominant European title performances ever. However, they lost both ICCs they contested to Sao Paulo (#4) and Velez Sarsfield.

Maldini and Donadoni were left over from the great 1989-1990 Milan side, and they added Boban and Desailly in midfield and Savicevic and Massaro in offense.

LINEUP: Sebastiano Rossi; Mauro Tassotti, Christian Panucci, Demetrio Albertini, Filippo Galli, Paulo Maldini, Roberto Donadoni, Marcel Desailly, Zvonimir Boban, Dejan Savicevic, Daniele Massaro.
Coach: Fabio Capello.

(8a) <u>Manchester United (England) 1968 and 1999</u>

Manchester United won the EC thirty-one years apart – in 1968 and 1999 – with very dynamic teams.

The Red Devils were league champion and FA Cup winner in 1967, and won the EC with a 4-1 defeat of Eusébio's Benfica in overtime. European Footballer of the Year (1968) George Best was one of the heroes as he scored the winning goal, and Bobby Charlton had a brace.

Manchester United won "the treble" in 1999, winning the English Premiership, FA Cup, and the EC. They won the EC 2-1 with two goals in injury time against a shocked Bayern Munich, and the 1999 ICC against Palmeiras 1-0. The 1999 team contained international players from England, Ireland, Denmark, Norway, Wales, the Netherlands, and Trinidad & Tobago.

LINEUP 1968: Alex Stepney; Shay Brennan, Nobby Stiles, Bill Foulkes, Tony Dunne; Pat Crerand, Bobby Charlton, David Sadler; George Best, Brian Kidd, Denis Law (John Aston). Coach: Matt Busby.

LINEUP 1999: Peter Schmeichel; Gary Neville, Ronny Johnsen, Jaap Stam, Denis Irwin; David Beckham, Nicky Butt (Roy Keane), Ryan Giggs, Jesper Blomqvist (Teddy Sheringham), Dwight Yorke, Andy Cole (Ole Gunnar Solskjær). Coach: Alex Ferguson.

(8b) <u>Flamengo (Brazil) 1981</u>

Zico's dynamic Flamengo team won the CL against Cobreloa, and then spanked Liverpool 3-0 in the ICC. Flamengo's flamboyant attack started from the back, with nominal defenders Marinho and Junior advancing far up field. Zico was both the creative and scoring force for Flamengo, and the centerpiece of the best Brazil team never to win a World Cup (1982).

LINEUP: Raul, Leandro, Mozer, Junior, Marinho, Amdrade, Tita, Adilio, Zico, Lice, Nunes. Coach: Paulo Cesar Carpeggiani.

(9a) <u>Independiente (Argentina) 1964-1965</u>

Independiente beat the two top Uruguayan teams, Nacional and Peñarol, winning consecutive Copa Libertadores tournaments. However, they could not beat the EC winners, falling twice to Internazionale in the ICC.

LINEUP: Miguel Ángel Santoro; Juan Carlos Guzmán, Tomás Rolan; Roberto Oscar Ferreiro, David Acevedo, Jorge Alberto Maldonado; Raúl Emilio Bernao, Osvaldo Luis Mura, Pedro Prospitti, Mario Rodríguez, Raúl Armando Savoy. Coach: Manuel Giudice.

(9b) <u>Peñarol (Uruguay) 1960-1961</u>

This Peñarol team won the first two Copa Libertadores competitions, beating Olimpia of Paraguay and Palmeiras of Brazil in the Finals. They lost the first ICC in 1960 to Real Madrid (after a scoreless tie at home they lost 5-1 in Madrid), but won the 1961 ICC 2-1 against Eusébio's Benfica. They finally got their revenge when they beat Real Madrid 2-0 in the 1966 ICC Final after winning the CL for the third time in the decade.

LINEUP: L.M. Maidana; W.R. Martínez, D.N. Cano, E. González, N. Gonçálvez, W. Aguerre, L.A. Cubilla, E. Ledesma, J.F. Sasía, P.A. Spencer, J.V. Joya. Coach: Roberto Scarone.

(10a) **Barcelona (Spain) 1992**

Barcelona was in the midst of a four year Spanish championship run when they won the 1992 EC over Vialli's Sampdoria in overtime. They arrived at the EC Final again two years later, but lost to AC Milan.

After going ahead early on Stoichkov's goal, Barcelona lost the 1993 ICC 2-1 to São Paulo on Raí's two strikes.

Barcelona's strength was up the middle, with Ronald Koeman in defense, Michael Laudrup in midfield, and Hristo Stoichkov as striker. Their coach was legendary Dutch *fantasista* Johan Cruyff.

LINEUP: Andoni Zubizarreta; Eusebio Sacristán, Albert Ferrer, Ronald Koeman, Nando Munoz, Juan Carlos, José María Bakero, Josep Guardiola, Michael Laudrup, Julio Salinas, Hristo Stoichkov.
Coach: Johan Cruyff.

(10b) **Boca Juniors (Argentina) 2000-2004**

Boca Juniors won the Copa Libertadores three out of four years (twice by the penalty kick competitions in 2000 and 2001), and in the year they failed (2002), they were eliminated by eventual champions Olimpia of Paraguay. In addition, they lost the Copa Libertadores Final in 2004 on penalty kicks to upstart Once Caldas of Colombia. All of these teams were coached by Carlos Bianchi, himself an ex-national team player who had a very successful career as a striker in France in the 1970s.

Juan Román Riquelme (2001) and Carlos Tévez (2003-2005) were two South American Footballer of the Year awardees who directed their respective Boca teams. The only players who participated in all three winning Finals for Boca were Hugo Ibarra (6 games) and Sebastián Battaglia (5 games).

Boca also won the 2000 and 2003 ICC beating Real Madrid 2-1 in 2000 and AC Milan in 2003 (on penalties), and the 2004 Copa Sudamericana against Bolivar of Bolivia.

2000-2001 LINEUP: Oscar Córdoba; Hugo Ibarra, Jorge Bermúdez, Walter Samuel (Anibal Matellán), Rodolfo Arruabarrena (Clemente Rodriguez); Sebastián Battaglia (Mauricio Serna), Cristian Traverso, José Basualdo, Juan Román Riquelme; Guillermo Barros Schelotto (Walter Gaitán), Martín Palermo (Marcelo Delgado).

2003 LINEUP: Roberto Abbondanzieri; Hugo Ibarra, Rolando Schiavi, Nicolás Burdisso, Clemente Rodríguez; Sebastián Battaglia, Raúl Cascini, Javier Villarreal, Diego Cagna; Carlos Tévez, Marcelo Delgado (Guillermo Barros Schelotto).
Coach: Carlos Bianchi.

(10c) **Borussia Dortmund 1997**

This Borussia Dortmund team had Best Modern Era player Matthias Sammer and runner-ups Jürgen Kohler and Andreas Möller. They had won the Bundesliga two years running, and easily sailed through to the EC final after dispatching Manchester United in the semi-finals by winning both the home and away matches. Borussia Dortmund then won the 1997 EC 3-1 over Zidane's 1996 EC winner Juventus, and the ICC by 2-0 over Bebeto's Cruzeiro.

LINEUP: Stefan Klos; Stefan Reuter, Matthias Sammer, Jürgen Kohler, Martin Kree; Jörg Heinrich, Paul Lambert, Paulo Sousa, Andreas Möller; Karlheinz Riedle, Stéphane Chapuisat.

(10d) Feyenoord (Netherlands) 1970

It was the Feyenoord club (also spelled Feijenoord) – not Ajax – that started the Dutch international soccer success. Feyenoord won the 1970 EC against 1967 winners Celtic, and subsequently the IC against Estudiantes de la Plata.

Midfielders Wim van Hanegem and Wim Jansen also figured prominently in the Dutch success at the 1974 World Cup.

LINEUP: Eddy Pieters Graafland; Piet Romeijn (Guus Haak), Theo Laseroms, Rinus Israël, Theo van Duivenbode; Franz Hasil, Wim Jansen, Wim van Hanegem; Henk Wery, Ove Kindvall, Coen Moulijn.
Coach: Ernst Happel.

(10e) Juventus (Italy) 1985

Five of Juventus' players had been stars of their 1982 World Cup teams (Scirea, Tardelli, Rossi for Italy, Platini for France, and Boniek for Poland). Juventus met Dalglish's Liverpool side in the tragic 1985 EC Final in Heysel, Belgium, where they won on Platini's penalty (after 39 spectators had already died when a stadium wall collapsed and a stampede ensued).

Juventus then won the 1985 ICC against Argentinos Juniors on penalties.

LINEUP: Stefano Tacconi; Luciano Favero, Antonio Cabrini, Sergio Brio, Gaetano Scirea; Massimo Bonini, Michel Platini, Marco Tardelli; Massimo Briaschi (Prandelli), Paolo Rossi (Vignola), Zbigniew Boniek.
Coach: Giovanni Trapattoni.

(10f) Estudiantes de la Plata (Argentina) 1968-1970

The Estudiantes de la Plata club won three CLs in a row, defeating Palmeiras, Nacional, and Peñarol. They fared less well in the ICC, beating only Manchester United 2-1 on aggregate in 1968, while falling to Gianni Rivera's AC Milan and Wim van Hanegem's Feyenoord in the 1969 and 1970 ICC, respectively.

Although they were dominant in South America for a few years, their persistently negative and violent play drops them down considerably on this list. Incredibly, the neo-fascist Argentine President Juan Carlos Onganía rebuked them for their negative style of play, and even had them arrested after the 1969 Intercontinental Cup match against Milan.[11]

LINEUP: Alberto José Poletti; Eduardo Luján Manera, Ramón Alberto Aguirre Suárez, Raúl Horacio Madero, Oscar Miguel Malbernat; Carlos Salvador Bilardo, Daniel Romero, Néstor Togneri; Marcos Norberto Conigliaro, Juan Alberto Taverna, Juan Ramón Verón.
Coach: Osvaldo Juan Zubeldía.

---

[11] An irony is that President Onganía (1966-70) came to power in a military junta, which would be the political equivalent of "destroyer tactics" and "negative style of play." But attractive football was evidently more important to Onganía than the human rights suppressed by his military dictatorship. Onganía was himself later jailed in 1981 for challenging the military junta government of Roberto Viola. In a further irony, Estudiantes players Carlos Bilardo and Raúl Madero were both graduated physicians, but apparently made no efforts to prevent the destruction wreaked on their opponent's physiques in the name of "football." Later, Bilardo coached the exciting 1986 Argentina World Cup winning side, as well as the sluggish 1990 World Cup team that lost the Final to West Germany – Madero was team physician both years. For greater detail see Chapter 15 in *Treacheries and Traditions in Argentinian Football Styles: The Story of Estudiantes de la Plata* by Pablo Alabarces, Ramiro Coelho and Juan Sanguinetti in Armstrong, G. & Giulianotti, R, eds. *Fear and Loathing in World Football*. Berg, Oxford. 2001.

Best 2006 Clubs Honorable Mention:

Both Arsenal and Barcelona have recently dominated their domestic league, but will still have to win international silverware to break into the top 25 club team ranking. They meet in the 2006 UEFA Champions League Final in Paris on 17 May 2006.

Arsenal (England) 2004-2006:

Arsenal won the English Premiership in 2003-2004, going undefeated in 38 games, and later extended their English record of consecutive undefeated top division games to 49. Although Preston North End was the only prior English team to finish a season undefeated (they played only 22 games in the 1888 campaign 116 years previously), a modern team going undefeated in a top division playing more matches is a superior accomplishment.

The modern Arsenal squad is heavily international. On 14 February 2005 – for the first time in English football history – they fielded a 16-man squad without any English players.

LINEUP: Jens Lehmann; Lauren (Emmanuel Eboué), Philippe Senderos (Sol Campbell), Kolo Touré, Mattieu Flamini (Ashley Cole); Robert Pirès, Freddie Ljungberg (Gilberto), Cesc Fábregas, Alexander Hleb (José Antonio Reyes); Dennis Bergkamp (Robin van Persie), Thierry Henry.
Coach: Arsene Wenger.

Barcelona (Spain) 2004-2006:

Barcelona was the 2005 and 2006 Spanish league champions, dominating with a creative style orchestrated by Brazilian 2004 and 2005 World Player of the Year Ronaldinho.

Barcelona's style is to place players with superior technical abilities at every position – even if this means fielding two, three, or four "*fantasistas*" (such as Brazilian-Portuguese Deco, Argentine Lionel Messi, Spain's Xavi, and Brazil's Ronaldinho). Cameroon's Samuel Eto'o leads the scoring line, and Mexico's Rafael Márquez and Catalan Carles Puyol lead the stalwart defensive line.

LINEUP: Victor Valdes; Giovanni van Bronckhorst, Carles Puyol, Oleguer Presas, Beletti; Rafael Márquez, Edmílson (Xavi), Deco (Lionel Messi), Ronaldinho, Ludovic Giuly (Henrik Larsson), Samuel Eto'o.

Chapter Nine

World Cup 2002

We can win this game, and the way we are going to go about it is quite simple. When we have the ball, we attack – and when we don't, we defend.

Luiz Felipe Scolari[1]

2002 World Cup Preparations

The 17th FIFA World Cup co-hosted by Japan and South Korea in 2002 made soccer history, as it was the initial World Cup competition in Asia, and the first World Cup shared between two nations. Problems of this unique co-host arrangement were minimal, probably because of the earlier "practice" co-hosting of the 2001 Confederations Cup by the same nations. European neighbors Holland and Belgium had paved the way for this bi-national format by successfully co-hosting the 2000 European Championships.

Prior to the 2002 World Cup, only the 1958 Brazil team had won a World Cup outside of their continent and hemisphere. The odds were formidable for one of the two hosting Asian nations or the other two qualified Asian nations to triumph in their continent at the 2002 World Cup. Entering the 2002 Cup, Japan and South Korea were still searching for their first World Cup Final wins, China had never before appeared in the World Cup Finals, and Saudi Arabia had reached the second round only once before. Therefore, it seemed inevitable that another team would duplicate the 1958 Brazil squad's achievement of winning the World Cup in a continent other than their own.

The Road to the 2002 World Cup

The 2002 World Cup was the second Cup competition (after the 1998 World Cup in France) to enter thirty-two countries. Each of the thirty-two qualifying countries had 23 players on their roster, for a total of 736 players competing in the world's most prestigious soccer tournament. In a continuity achievement, only nine of the thirty-two qualifying teams were making their *fourth consecutive* World Cup appearance in the 2002 World Cup (having participated in 1990, 1994, 1998, and 2002). The teams that accomplished that feat were Argentina, Belgium, Brazil, Cameroon, Italy, Germany, Spain, South Korea, and the USA.

The hotly contested qualifying rounds started in 2000, two years before the Finals competition itself. Most surprising was the quality of some teams that failed to qualify for the World Cup. According to FIFA rankings reported just before (May 15, 2002) the World Cup began, three of the top ten ranked teams and five of the top twenty did not reach the World

---

[1] 2002 World Cup winning Brazil coach Luiz Felipe Scolari's advice to his "Rest of the World" team before confronting Real Madrid in their centenary celebration game, December 18, 2002. The game ended 3-3.

Cup Finals. These nations were Columbia (4)[2], Netherlands (9), Yugoslavia (10), Romania (14), and Czech Republic (15) [FIFA rankings in parentheses]. Thus, 25% of the world's top 20 teams did not qualify for the 2002 Cup, a serious omission of some of the most attractive teams.

Most disturbing was the absence of Holland (the Netherlands), one of the best and most creative teams of the last thirty years. Holland is the home of the "the Orange Machine," the "Naranja Mecánica," the "Dutch whirl," and ultimately, "Total Football," the system where each soccer player has the skill to seamlessly interchange positions. The Dutch could only blame themselves, as they played the initial qualifying rounds in 2000 poorly and found themselves trailing Portugal and Ireland in Europe's toughest qualifying group. Diehard Dutch fans would be forced to endure another four-year wait for their nation to qualify (some fans could not bear to wait and organized "The Other Final," a story at the end of this chapter).

FIFA Confederations — Qualifying Number of Teams

Europe – UEFA [Union European Football Association]   15

Europe had fifteen World Cup positions including 1998 World Cup holder France; these countries made up nearly half of the thirty-two World Cup spots. The countries participating from UEFA were: Belgium (11), Croatia (2), Denmark (3), France (11), England (11), Germany (15), Ireland (3), Italy (15), Poland (6), Portugal (3), Russia (9), Slovenia (1), Spain (11), Sweden (9), and Turkey (3) [Finals appearances appear after country in parentheses]. France was also the reigning 2000 European champion.

Slovenia was the only World Cup Final virgin, although Turkey had not appeared in the Finals for 48 years since the 1954 Switzerland World Cup.

South America – CONMEBOL [Confederación Sudamericana de Fútbol]   5

South America qualified five countries (in order of placement): Argentina (13), Ecuador (1), Brazil (17), Paraguay (6), and Uruguay (10) [Finals appearances appear after country in parentheses]. Colombia, the reigning 2001 South American champion, ended even on points with Uruguay, but Uruguay qualified for the Oceania playoff by only one goal difference over Colombia.

South America was allocated four or five qualifying positions; the fifth finisher in the CONMEBOL competition would meet the Oceania qualifying champion in a playoff for the winner to progress to the World Cup. Uruguay beat Australia convincingly in the playoff (0-1, 3-0) to advance as the fifth South American team.

CONMEBOL has only ten members, but fully deserved its five spots in the 2002 World Cup. South America is the home of more quality soccer players per capita than any other geographic zone, and its World Cup soccer history is nothing short of amazing. After all, only three South American countries (Brazil [4], Argentina [2] and Uruguay [2]) had won a total of eight of the previous sixteen World Cups.

Ecuador was the only World Cup novice of the group. Rapidly improving Venezuela remains the lone Spanish-speaking South American country not to have qualified for any World Cup.

---

[2] Columbia's ranking of 4th in the world was inflated, as five other South American nations qualified for the World Cup above them in the CONMEBOL region. Although Columbia had won the 2001 Copa America (the South American championship) as the host country, many of the other teams sent novice squads to gain experience. Powerhouse Argentina did not even send a team, ostensibly for security reasons (this excuse from a country who hosted the 1978 World Cup during a military dictatorship). Argentina's lack of participation sacrificed valuable international experience for its young players that would have been useful in the 2002 World Cup competition.

Africa – CAF [Confederacion Africaine de Football] 5

Africa was allocated five positions, which went to regional group winners Cameroon (5), Nigeria (3), Senegal (1), South Africa (2), and Tunisia (3) [Finals appearances appear after country in parentheses]. Cameroon was the reigning 2002 African champion, having beaten Senegal on penalty kicks. Senegal was the lone African novice in the World Cup competition, and the only team to qualify by goal difference (over four-time Cup Finalist Morocco).

Many African teams have a unique problem; they develop great players but sometimes lack cohesive team play because of a shortage of practice time. Their top players perform in different countries and rarely convene for proper practice sessions. As a result, African teams have never ventured beyond the quarterfinals of the World Cup. These poor resources and logistics are a legitimate excuse, but not one that African fans will tolerate much longer.

Nigeria was in the toughest African group, and almost did not qualify due to the tenacious play of Liberia. Former World Player of the Year George Weah bankrolled and led the Liberian national team to within a whisker of qualifying over Nigeria, but they faltered in the critical game against Ghana.

Asia – AFC [Asian Football Confederation] 4

China (1) and Saudi Arabia (3) joined hosts Japan (2) and South Korea (6) as Asian representatives in 2002 [Finals appearances appear after country in parentheses]. It was China's initial World Cup Finals competition, a welcome event for the world's most populous country.

Japan was the reigning 2000 Asian champion, and had impressively finished second to France in the 2001 Confederations Cup competition.

South Korea made an effort to include their ethnic brethren to the north, offering to place at least one North Korean player on their squad. The organizers also tried to arrange one of the World Cup matches to be played in a North Korean venue. Because of North Korean intransigence neither of these objectives was realized, and the 2002 Cup ultimately failed to improve the volatile politics of the Korean peninsula.

North and Central America and Caribbean – CONCACAF 3
[Confederation of North, Central American & Caribbean Association Football]

The CONCACAF group finished with Costa Rica (2), USA (7), and Mexico (12) as representatives [Finals appearances appear after country in parentheses]. Mexico was lucky to scrape through, as a dynamic Honduras squad appeared certain to qualify until a disastrous home loss to Trinidad & Tobago. Honduran striker Carlos Pavón was the second highest scorer in the entire World Cup qualifying tournament with 15 goals (Archie Thompson of Australia was first with 16 goals in qualifying, but 13 came in one match against hapless American Samoa).

The USA won the 2002 CONCACAF Championship, also called the Gold Cup.

Oceania – OFC [Oceania Football Confederation] 0

The OFC, like CONMEBOL, has only ten members. But only Australia (1) and New Zealand (1) had ever qualified for the World Cup Finals before and still remain a serious threat to qualify again.

Australia won their Oceania four-game qualifying group with a ridiculous 66 goals scored and zero against; the weak competition was Fiji, Tonga, Samoa, and American Samoa. Australian Archie Thompson scored a record 13 goals in the 31-0 demolition of American Samoa (both individual and team scoring records of World Cup qualifying matches). However, Australia could not get by Uruguay in the playoff, and therefore did not qualify for the 2002 Finals.

World Cup Preparation: Other Aspects
No Sex, Please: We're Belgian, Croatian, Nigerian…Italian?…Brazilian??

The question of bringing along wives and partners before and during competition arises at every World Cup. For the 2002 World Cup the coaching staffs of Belgium, Croatia, and Nigeria all warned against or forbid such contact during the Cup. Two additional surprises for advocating celibacy were Italy and Brazil – normally nations that ooze sensuality.

Coach "Big Phil" Scolari imposed forty days of celibacy on his Brazil players. Ronaldo did not object, saying, "I'm not saying that sex is not special," but making clear that the World Cup only comes around every four years and he was prepared to sacrifice.

Poland's Coach Jerzy Engel placed no restrictions on his players. He must have read the 1999 *New Scientist* article, which reported that sexual activity the night prior to competition is just as likely to improve an athlete's performance.

Odds of Winning at the Start of the 2002 World Cup

Before the World Cup began, odds makers divided the thirty-two teams into nine groups with similar betting odds.

Argentina 7/2   France 7/2

The first group was comprised of top favorites Argentina and France. However, neither team with the best odds in the 2002 World Cup would enter the second round!

Brazil 11/2   Italy 6/1   England 8/1   Spain 8/1

The second group included Brazil, Italy, England and Spain. Italy crashed out in the second round, while England and Spain lost in the quarterfinals (England lost to Brazil). Brazil made it to the Final and became World Champion once again.

Germany 10/1   Portugal 12/1

The third group included Germany, which made it to the Final, and Portugal, which was surprisingly eliminated in the first round.

Poland 33/1   Paraguay 40/1   Russia 40/1

The fourth group included two Eastern European teams, Poland and Russia, which were eliminated after the first round. Paraguay went to the second round group of 16, where they lost to Germany 0-1.

Cameroon 50/1   Croatia 50/1   Ireland 50/1   Turkey 50/1   Uruguay 50/1

The fifth group included five teams at 50/1 odds. Ireland and Turkey went through to the second round, where Ireland lost to Spain on penalty kicks. Turkey defeated Japan and Senegal to go through to the semifinals where they lost to Brazil. Uruguay just missed going to the second round in a thrilling game against Senegal.

Belgium 66/1   Denmark 66/1   Japan 66/1   Nigeria 66/1   Sweden 66/1

The sixth group included five teams at 66/1 odds. Nigeria was eliminated in the first round, but the other four advanced and lost in the round of 16.

Mexico 70/1   Ecuador 90/1   USA 90/1

The seventh group had two CONCACAF teams (Mexico and the USA), and the surprising runner-up in the South America qualifying (Ecuador). The USA and Mexico went through to the round of 16, the USA beating Mexico 2-0 to advance to the quarterfinals, where they lost 0-1 to eventual Cup Finalist Germany.

Costa Rica 100/1   Slovenia 100/1   South Africa 100/1   South Korea 100/1

The eighth group had four teams at 100/1 odds. Only the host team South Korea made it past the first round games, going all the way to the semi-finals.

China 150/1   Tunisia 150/1   Saudi Arabia 200/1   Senegal 200/1

The ninth group had four teams at 150-200 to 1 odds. Senegal was the revelation of the tournament; beating France and Uruguay in the opening round, Sweden in the round of 16, and reaching the quarterfinals where they lost to Turkey. The other three teams had a combined 26 goals against and only one scored.

World Cup 2002 Teams in their Assigned Groups
[Seeded teams are at Left in each Group]

Group A:	France	Senegal	Uruguay	Denmark
Group B:	Spain	Slovenia	Paraguay	South Africa
Group C:	Brazil	Turkey	China PR	Costa Rica
Group D:	Korea Republic	Poland	USA	Portugal
Group E:	Germany	Saudi Arabia	Ireland	Cameroon
Group F:	Argentina	Nigeria	England	Sweden
Group G:	Italy	Ecuador	Croatia	Mexico
Group H:	Japan	Belgium	Russia	Tunisia

First Round Group Strength

The 2002 World Cup teams are summarized in Group context below. The letter/number combination before the country name is the designated FIFA country code for the 2002 Cup. The last FIFA country ranking before the World Cup (from May 2002) is listed after each nations names.

The combined team ranks of all four members in each group give a *group rank* that is used to assess group strength. Group F – containing Argentina, England, Nigeria and Sweden – was the strongest and thereby informally named the "Group of Death." Group H, with co-host Japan, was the weakest. Eventual champion Brazil landed in the second weakest group despite being comprehensibly beaten by Argentina in the CONMEBOL qualifying competition.

GROUP	TEAMS	GROUP RANK
Group F:	Argentina (2), Nigeria (27), England (12), Sweden (19)	60
Group G:	Italy (6), Ecuador (35), Croatia (21), Mexico (7)	69
Group E:	Germany (11), Saudi Arabia (34), Ireland (15), Cameroon (17)	77
Group A:	France (1), Senegal (42), Uruguay (24) , Denmark (20)	87
Group B:	Spain (8), Slovenia (25), Paraguay (18), South Africa (37)	88
Group D:	Korea Republic (40), Poland (38), United States (13), Portugal (5)	96
Group C:	Brazil (2), Turkey (22), China PR (50), Costa Rica (29)	103
Group H:	Japan (32), Belgium (23), Russia (27), Tunisia (30)	112

All of the 2002 World Cup games are summarized in the rest of the chapter. Each game lists the FIFA match number (from 01 to 64, indicating the temporal order it was played in), the teams playing, the venue, and a headline that characterizes the game.

All final games in each Group were played simultaneously in order to avoid teams "packing it in" if they knew their selection was guaranteed from the results of a previous Group game that day. This is to avoid future embarrassments such as the West Germany-Austria game in 1982 when both teams played not to win, but just enough for both teams to advance (at the expense of Algeria, which had already beaten West Germany).

First Round Scheduling Inequities

There were 48 first round games in eight groups of four teams each. The first (Game 01 – France vs. Senegal played 31.05.02) and the last (Game 16 – USA vs. Portugal 05.06.02) teams to play their initial games were involved in huge upsets. Game 01 saw 2002 Africa Nations Cup runner-up Senegal deservedly defeat World Cup defenders France 1-0, while Game 16 saw the USA beat World Cup favorite Portugal 3-2, surprisingly leading 3-0 after the first 36 minutes.

However, the above two games detail poor match planning for the first round of the 2002 World Cup, as the amount of time between games varied dramatically for different teams. For example, USA and Portugal were at a distinct disadvantage to France, Senegal, Germany, and Ireland. France and Senegal played their first game 5 days before USA and Portugal, meaning that they would play 7 games in 31 days (one game per 4.4 days) if they reached the Final. USA and Portugal would have to play 7 games in 26 days (one game per 3.7 days), a decided handicap amounting to 16% less recovery time, in a tournament where players need to recover from top physical action.

Germany and Ireland played their second game on the same day as the USA, Portugal, Tunisia, and Russia played their first game. This kind of inequitable scheduling is not good for the tournament. An alternative schedule could have the first set of games spread out over three days, with four on the first day and six on days 2 & 3. Then everybody (including the fans) would rest for the two days in between games. All teams would then have 4 or mostly 5 days rest in between games until the final.

When the USA met Germany on June 21[st,] the USA was playing their fifth game in 17 days, while Germany was playing in their fifth game in 21 days; nearly an extra day off per match. Teams playing in the quarterfinals on June 22nd played in the semi-finals with only 72 hours rest on June 25th. This is unfair for the team without an extra day of recovery (a 25% recovery time advantage for the semi-finals).

Group A: France, Senegal, Uruguay, Denmark

Total group score: 87   [4th hardest group by cumulative rankings]

Group A was composed of defending World Cup Champions France, first-timer Senegal, old-timer Uruguay (won two previous World Cups in 1930 & 1950), and Denmark (which qualified top of European Group 3). Although ranked only the fourth hardest group, this was a deceptively strong group of teams with ability to play 90 minutes or more.

A1: (FIFA team number)   Country [1] (FIFA rank before World Cup)

A1. France [1]

As the 1998 champions, France qualified automatically for the 2002 World Cup, their eleventh World Cup appearance. The French *équipe tricolore* finally received the FIFA world top-ranked team notice as of May 2001, nearly three years after beating Brazil in the 1998 World Cup! France had so much success after the World Cup they almost could be excused for being overconfident. After all, the reigning 1998 World Champions were also the 2000 European champions and the 2001 Confederations Cup champions.

Coach Roger Lemerre brought a team with many faces from the 1998 model; their defense was experienced but old with an average age of nearly 33 years old. The team would be tested early by injuries just before the Cup to critical midfielders Robert Pires (ruling him out of the Cup) and Zinedine Zidane (ruling him out of the first two games). A natural replacement for Zidane would have been 2001 French League Player of the Year Eric Carrière, who filled Zidane's role when France won the 2001 Confederations Cup.

A2. Senegal [42]

Senegal qualified for their first World Cup Finals from Africa's Group 3 only by goal difference over Morocco, but Coach Bruno Metsu had also guided Senegal to the 2002 African Nations Cup Final, only to lose on penalty kicks to Cameroon.

African Player of the Year 2001 & 2002 El Hadji Diouf led the technically talented team that was nearly all French-clubs based. The Senegalese were therefore very familiar with the French league and style, which made for a surprising (to some) result against defending champion France in the first World Cup Finals match in Senegal's history.

A3. Uruguay [24]

Uruguay squeezed into the 2002 World Cup from the tough CONMEBOL group. Uruguay tied for fifth with Colombia, but a goal difference of only 1 earned them the right to play the Oceania winner Australia. Uruguay then qualified as the fifth team from South America after beating Australia in a home and away series by a 3-1 aggregate score.

This was Uruguay's tenth World Cup Finals appearance; their first two historic appearances in 1930 and 1950 resulted in them winning the World Cup.

Uruguay and Coach Victor Pua's star was left-footed Alvaro Recoba from Internazionale Milan; quicksilver Recoba was such a talent he commanded the largest salary of Inter's star triad that also included Christian Vieri and Ronaldo.

A4. Denmark [20]

Denmark qualified for the Cup by finishing at the top of Europe Group 3, ahead of the Czech Republic and Bulgaria. Only their third appearance in the Cup (1986, 1998, 2002), they had made it to the second round in their first two appearances.

Always strong on the ball and with good technique, Denmark had more steady team players than stars. Even so, Denmark rarely embarrasses and spectacularly won the 1992 European Championship, entering only after Yugoslavia was forced to withdraw because of their civil war. Denmark and Coach Morten Olsen's new star was Feyenoord forward Jon Dahl Tomasson, who complemented established striker Ebbe Sand.

OPENING GAME for the Entire 2002 World Cup
[Staged in South Korea]

01 France 0 – 1 Senegal: The Bleus get the Blues

May 31: Seoul, South Korea

The opening game of the 2002 World Cup was held in South Korea, and matched *current World Cup champion* France against their former colony Senegal, *which was playing their first World Cup Finals match ever.* France had many of their aging stars back, but missed star midfielder Zinedine Zidane for the first two Group games after he had strained a thigh muscle in a meaningless pre-Cup game against host South Korea.

The first-half Senegal score started as Omar Daf stripped Djorkaeff of the ball at midfield and immediately passed to El Hadji Diouf on the left flank. Diouf nonchalantly streaked past LeBoeuf, darted into the left corner of the box, and centered the ball creating a nightmare for the French defense. Midfielder Emmanuel Petit and goalkeeper Fabien Barthez tried to clear, but the ball bounced off Barthez to Pape Bouba Diop, who did well to scramble it on goal from three yards out while sliding on his backside.

The "Bleus" often looked sluggish and old, while Senegal had fresh legs and ideas. France's high-powered strike force of David Trezeguet (Juventus) and Thierry Henry (Arsenal) each hit the woodwork, but Senegal also hit the woodwork through Khalilou Fadiga. Tony Sylva performed immaculately in the Senegal goal.

This result shocked defending world champion France and provided two lessons: (1) Do not depend on older stars of the past to win everything again, and (2) Do not underestimate the creative power and technique of African football.

Senegal had won their first World Cup match ever on their first try.

France: Fabien Barthez, Bixente Lizarazu, Marcel Desailly, Lilian Thuram, Frank Leboeuf, Patrick Vieira, Youri Djorkaeff (Christophe Dugarry, 60), Emmanuel Petit, Sylvain Wiltord (Djibril Cisse, 81), Thierry Henry, David Trezeguet.

Senegal: Tony Sylva, Omar Daf, Pape Malick Diop, Aliou Cisse, Lamine Diatta, Ferdinand Coly, Khalilou Fadiga, Moussa Ndiaye, Salif Diao, Pape Bouba Diop, El Hadji Diouf.

Goals: Senegal; Pape Bouba Diop 30.

Referee: Ali Bujsaim (UAE).

Men of the Match: Pape Bouba Diop for his concentration in finishing the goal move, and El Hadji Diouf for setting up the lone goal and creating constant havoc amongst the experienced French defense.

03 Uruguay 1 – 2 Denmark :   Denmark's "finishing" beats Uruguay's passion

June 1: Ulsan, South Korea

The last World Cup encounter between these two teams was in 1986 and ended in a 6-1 Danish win. Denmark would win again, but not so convincingly.

This was a very skillful and entertaining end-to-end match from two lesser-appreciated teams. Uruguay's Alvaro Recoba looked dangerous throughout the first half and just missed a goal off a 30-yard free kick. Dario Silva took a lot of punishment worrying the Danish defense with his dangerous runs.

Danish persistence paid off shortly before half-time as Jesper Gronkjaer set up Jon Dahl Tomasson who slotted a shot in from eight yards out.

Just after half time, Dario Rodriguez scored one of the best goals of the World Cup as he left-foot volleyed a floating square pass into the left top corner from 23 yards to equalize.

Further chances from both teams lacked providence until the last ten minutes of the game when substitute Martin Jorgensen laid the ball up for Tomasson to perfectly head the ball off the crossbar from nine yards out for his second goal of the game.

A more even game than the final score, as the cool Danes prevailed.

Uruguay Fabian Carini, Gustavo Mendez, Gonzalo Sorondo, Paolo Montero, Dario Rodriguez (Federico Magallanes 87), Gianni Guigou, Pablo Garcia, Gustavo Varela, Alvaro Recoba (Mario Reguiero 80), Dario Silva, Sebastian Abreu (Richard Morales 89).

Denmark Thomas Sorensen, Thomas Helveg, Rene Henriksen, Martin Laursen, Jan Heintze (Niclas Jensen 58), Thomas Gravesen, Stig Tofting, Jon Dahl Tomasson, Ebbe Sand (Christian Poulsen 89), Jesper Gronkjaer (Martin Jorgensen 70), Dennis Rommedahl.

Goals: Uruguay - Rodriguez 47; **Denmark** -Tomasson 45, 83.

Referee: Saad Mane (Kuwait).
Man of the Match: Jon Dahl Tomasson, for his two well-taken goals.

18 France 0 – 0 Uruguay : Cautious and scoreless tie
June 6: Busan, South Korea

The first 0 : 0 draw in the 2002 World Cup, this game was a strangely cautious affair pitting two capable teams shadow-boxing to avoid another catastrophic loss (as both had lost their initial game).

Vibrant counter-attacking provoked enough interest, and both teams wasted several excellent chances. Alvaro Recoba for Uruguay and Sylvain Wiltord of France missed early chances after they were clear through on goal. France played with only ten men after the 26th minute, as France forward Thierry Henry was sent off after making a dangerous studs-up tackle.

Barthez made an excellent kick-save on a Recoba deflection in the early going, but France had the early momentum until Henry's sending off deflated them. Petit unluckily hit the post on a free kick in the 35th minute, and after the half Recoba dribbled past Barthez but somehow could not steer the ball into the beckoning net. Barthez made several saves in the second half to ensure at least one point for the World Cup holders.

The nil-nil result determined that in order to advance to the second round Uruguay would have to beat Senegal by one goal, and France would need to surpass Denmark by two goals.

France: Fabien Barthez, Lilian Thuram, Frank Leboeuf (Vincent Candela 16), Marcel Desailly, Bixente Lizarazu, Patrick Vieira, Emmanuel Petit, Johan Micoud, Sylvain Wiltord (Christophe Dugarry 90), Thierry Henry, David Trezeguet (Djibril Cisse 81).
Uruguay: Fabian Carini, Alejandro Lembo, Gonzalo Sorondo, Paolo Montero, Marcelo Romero (Gonzalo De Los Santos 70), Pablo Garcia, Gustavo Varela, Dario Rodriguez (Gianni Guigou 72), Alvaro Recoba, Dario Silva (Federico Magallanes 59), Sebastian Abreu.
Referee: Felipe Ramos Rizo (Mexico).
Men of the Match: The two fabulous Fab goalkeepers: Fabien Barthez for keeping France alive with several spectacular saves, and Fabian Carini for covering everything France could launch at him.

20 Denmark 1 – 1 Senegal : Senegal superior but both teams receive a point
June 6: Daegu, South Korea

Senegal came out ready to win and qualify for the next round, but their early energy turned aggressive, as Khalilou Fadiga was booked for an ugly tackle. Another rude tackle by midfielder Salif Diao brought Jon Dahl Tomasson down in the penalty box, and Tomasson scored the resulting penalty in the lower left-hand corner past Senegal keeper Tony Sylva.

The rest of the game swung in Senegal's favor, but they had to wait until the second half to equalize. After another superb Omar Daf tackle on Jon Dahl Tomasson deep in his own end, Senegal rapidly advanced the ball through an intricate series of accurate passes that Diao, redeeming himself, stylishly finished off with the outside right of his foot from eight yards. This Senegal goal was the prettiest quick team buildup for goal in the entire World Cup; Denmark never even touched the ball.

Senegal had many more good chances but could not convert. Diao was again in focus after being sent off in the 80th minute for another dangerous tackle. The draw was then played out, as both teams would only need to tie their last game to advance to the second round.

Denmark: Thomas Sorensen, Rene Henriksen, Martin Laursen, Jan Heintze, Thomas Helveg, Stig Tofting, Thomas Gravesen (Christian Poulsen, 62), Jesper Gronkjaer (Martin Jorgensen, 50), Jon Dahl Tomasson, Ebbe Sand, Dennis Rommedahl (Peter Lovenkrands, 89).
Senegal: Tony Sylva, Omar Daf, Pape Malick Diop, Lamine Diatta, Ferdinand Coly, Pape Sarr (Souleymane Camara, 46, (Habib Beye, 83), Khalilou Fadiga, Moussa Ndiaye (Henri Camara, 46), Salif Diao, Pape Bouba Diop, El Hadji Diouf.
Goals: Denmark - Jon Dahl Tomasson 16 (penalty); **Senegal** - Salif Diao 52.
Referee: Carlos Batres (Guatemala).
Man of the Match: Salif Diao, for his two touches in the goal sequence including his well-taken goal.

33 Denmark 2 – 0 France : Denmark advances over Defending Champion France
June 11: Incheon, South Korea

Even Zinedine Zidane's return from injury could not rescue France from early elimination, as the Danes successfully clogged the midfield and inhibited the smooth French passing game. Despite the best movement of France's three games, when pushing forward the Bleus' defense often left wide gaps for the patient Danes to plunder. The Danes scored a vital goal early after a poor French clearance, as

Stig Tofting lofted a ball to Dennis Rommedahl who one-timed the ball past helpless French keeper Fabien Barthez from eight yards out.

France continued to attack and hit the crossbar twice – first by Desailly's header from Zidane's corner kick, and then by Trezeguet's blast near the end of the match.

Jon Dahl Tomasson added a second goal from seven yards in the second half after a beautiful buildup on the left side from Thomas Gravesen to Jesper Gronkjaer, who centered perfectly ahead of the defense to Tomasson. France's defense again faltered leaving Barthez all alone with no chance to save from Tomasson.

With this defeat, France was only the third titleholder to be eliminated in the first round of the World Cup. At least the other two titleholders, Italy in 1950 and Brazil in 1966, scored goals and earned victories before being eliminated. France could not manage even one goal, an embarrassment shared only with China and Saudi Arabia in the 2002 World Cup. The Bleus ended up singing the Blues in the 2002 World Cup.

Denmark: Thomas Sorensen, Rene Henriksen, Martin Laursen, Thomas Helveg, Niclas Jensen, Stig Tofting (Brian Nielsen, 79), Thomas Gravesen, Martin Jorgensen (Jesper Gronkjaer, 46), Christian Poulsen (Kasper Bogelund, 76), Jon Dahl Tomasson, Dennis Rommedahl.

France: Fabien Barthez, Vincent Candela, Bixente Lizarazu, Marcel Desailly, Lilian Thuram, Patrick Vieira (Johan Micoud, 71), Claude Makélélé, Zinedine Zidane, Sylvain Wiltord (Youri Djorkaeff, 83), David Trezeguet, Christophe Dugarry (Djibril Cisse, 54).

Goals: Denmark - Dennis Rommedahl 22, Jon Dahl Tomasson 67.

Referee: Vitor Melo Pereira (Portugal).

Man of the Match: Dennis Rommedahl for expert finishing that set the tone for the match.

34 Senegal 3 – 3 Uruguay Both teams win one half, and Senegal advances
June 11: Suwon, South Korea

This game was one of the most exciting matches of the World Cup. Requiring a win to advance, Uruguay pushed forward early but instead was caught back badly by Senegal, who scored three unanswered goals in the first 38 minutes.

El Hadji Diouf engineered a penalty kick in the 20th minute, leaping over diving keeper Fabian Carini. Video showed Diouf was "diving," as Carini never touched him – the penalty kick was an erroneous referee call. Khalilou Fadiga duly converted the penalty inside the left post. Senegal then counter-attacked with Henri Camara advancing down the left side and locating Papa Bouba Diop, who fired a shot from 18 yards into the top right corner for the second goal. Fadiga then floated a ball over the back line for Diop who touched the ball over Carini on the volley from ten yards, the ball bouncing off the underside of the crossbar into the net. Senegal could do no wrong as they led 3-0 at the half against the stunned Uruguayans.

Uruguay came out firing in the second half as Dario Silva's shot pressured Senegal keeper Tony Sylva, and new substitute Richard Morales scored on the rebound on his first touch of the game. Diego Forlan then chested down a clearance of an Alvaro Recoba free kick, and impressively volleyed into the far-side netting from 24 yards, narrowing the difference to 2-3. After a whirlwind second half, Morales was fouled in the penalty area a few minutes before stoppage time. The ever-dangerous Recoba scored the equalizing penalty into the left corner.

Uruguay had one more chance after a desperate Senegalese clearance of a long shot, but Morales mistimed an uncontested header from only four yards out. The wild scramble in front of the Senegalese goal terminated the match with the fans standing, and Senegal hanging on to advance to the 2nd round.

Senegal: Tony Sylva, Omar Daf, Pape Malick Diop, Alassane Ndour (Amdy Moustapha Faye, 76), Aliou Cisse, Lamine Diatta, Ferdinand Coly (Habib Beye, 63), Khalilou Fadiga, Pape Bouba Diop, Henri Camara (Moussa Ndiaye, 67), El Hadji Diouf.

Uruguay: Fabian Carini, Alejandro Lembo, Paolo Montero, Dario Rodriguez, Gonzalo Sorondo (Mario Regueiro, 32), Garcia Pablo, Gustavo Varela, Marcelo Romero (Diego Forlan, 46), Alvaro Recoba, Dario Silva, Sebastian Abreu (Richard Morales, 46).

Goals: **Senegal** - Khalilou Fadiga 20 (penalty), Pape Bouba Diop 26, 38;

Uruguay - Richard Morales 46, Diego Forlan 69, Alvaro Recoba 88 (penalty).

Referee: Jan Wegereef (Netherlands).

Men of the Match: Papa Bouba Diop for two superbly taken goals for Senegal, and Richard Morales for helping rally Uruguay back through his goal and run into the box for a penalty.

Group B: Spain, Slovenia, Paraguay, South Africa

Total group score: 88 [4th easiest group by cumulative rankings]

Spain is a soccer enigma – it likely has the best professional football league in the world, but has been perennial underachievers in the World Cup. Paraguay would probably be the second strongest team in this group because of captain José Luis Chilavert's organizational leadership. South Africa had tremendous talent and won their African group easily, but lacked international experience. Slovenia surprisingly qualified for their first World Cup in a playoff over favored Romania.

B1. Spain [8]

Spain had won the weak European Group 7 rather easily, and the nation expected quality play from Raúl, Mendieta, Hierro, and the rest of the team despite past failures. This was Spain's eleventh World Cup Finals appearance, but they had never progressed past the quarterfinals.

Coach Jose Camacho favored a 4-4-2 option, but the central defenders Hierro and Nadal averaged 34 years old and were susceptible to strikers with pace.

Number one goalkeeper Santiago Canizares had injured himself just before the World Cup, but Real Madrid keeper Iker Casillas was a capable substitute at just 21 years of age.

B2. Slovenia [25]

Slovenia finished second to Russia in Europe Group 1, nipping Yugoslavia by one point. Slovenia then beat Romania in a home-and-away playoff to qualify for their first World Cup Finals.

Slovenia emerged from Yugoslavia in 1991, and was the country with the least population in the 2002 World Cup (about 2 million). Coach Srečko Katanec had done an amazing organizing job as Slovenia qualified for their first World Cup only eleven years after becoming an independent country. Katanec was the only Slovenian on the 1990 Yugoslavian World Cup squad.

Zlatko Zahovič was the creative "number 10" midfielder of the team, and was the most recognizable Slovenian in the soccer world.

B3. Paraguay [18]

Paraguay was near the top of the CONMEBOL group in the beginning of qualifying, but later tailed off and tied in points with Brazil. Brazil came in third on goal difference, with Paraguay winning the fourth and last guaranteed spot. This was Paraguay's sixth World Cup, and they had progressed to the second round in their last two Cups (in 1986 and 1998).

Iconoclastic goalkeeper Jose Chilavert was the undisputed leader of the team, and it would be his last World Cup. Home to a solid defense, Paraguay also had several clinical attackers.

Paraguay's coach was ex-Italy player and manager Cesare Maldini, hired after the yeoman work of qualifying was finished by Sergio Markarian.

B4. South Africa [37]

South Africa topped their Africa Group 5 easily, but continuity was sacrificed as player legend Jomo Sono came in to coach the team in place of Carlos Quieroz. This was South Africa's second World Cup Finals appearance, having failed to progress past the first round in 1998.

A nation liberated from apartheid for just a decade, the "Bafana Bafana" fielded a multi-ethnic team of players with ancestries from Africa, Europe, and Asia.

Many of their players had valuable experience performing overseas for club teams, but the national team frequently had difficulty coordinating their foreign-based players.

06 Paraguay 2 – 2 South Africa   Paraguay misses Chilavert presence
June 2: Busan, South Korea.

Paraguay set out to win the game even though team captain Jose Luis Chilavert was on suspension. The opening goal came on a charging 4-yard header from Roque Santa Cruz off a right-sided Francisco Arce cross in the 39th minute. The first half ended 1-0 to Paraguay.

In the 55th minute, defender Arce fired an amazing free-kick from the left corner of the 18-yard box into the upper-left hand corner to beat South African keeper Andre Arendse to the near post for a 2-0 lead.

Tebogo Mokoena had a shot deflected into the net by Estanislao Struway in the 63rd minute for South Africa's first goal, and thereafter the "Bafana Bafana" continued to pressure the Paraguayan goal. Ricardo Tavarelli, Chilavert's replacement in goal, brought down Sibusiso Zuma unnecessarily on a challenge on the side of the penalty box in the 90th minute, and Quinton Fortune thumped the penalty ball into the upper right corner for the tie.

Paraguay: Ricardo Tavarelli, Francisco Arce, Carlos Gamarra, Celso Ayala, Julio Cesar Caceres, Denis Caniza, Estanislao Struway (Juan Carlos Franco, 86), Guido Alvarenga (Diego Gavilan, 66), Roberto Acuna, Roque Santa Cruz, Jorge Campos (Gustavo Moringo, 73).

South-Africa: Andre Arendse, Cyril Nzama, Bradley Carnell, Aaron Mokoena, Pierre Issa (McDonald Mukansi, 27), Lucas Radebe, Macbeth Sibaya, Quinton Fortune, Tebogo Mokoena, Sibusiso Zuma, Benni McCarthy (George Koumantarakis, 78).

Goals: **Paraguay -** Roque Santa Cruz 39, Francisco Arce 55.
             South Africa - Estanislao Struway 63, (own goal), Quinton Fortune 90 (penalty).

Referee: Lubos Michel (Slovakia).

Men of the Match: Francisco Arce for setting up the first and scoring the second Paraguayan goal, and Sibusiso Zuma for creating havoc in the Paraguayan defense all game and forcing the tying penalty kick.

08 Spain 3 – 1 Slovenia :   Spain dominates after late start
June 2: Gwangju

Spain often starts tournaments slowly, and this opening game was no different. Fortunately for Spain, Raúl González scored just before half time after Luis Enrique's mazy run was interrupted. It was a typically skillful opportunistic goal after a loose ball came to Raúl; surrounded by five defenders, he coolly slotted the ball into the right corner of the goal from 16 yards.

The Spanish scored a spectacular goal after Fernando Morientes over-head kicked a pass to Francisco De Pedro, who launched a cross-field pass from the left side that snaked behind three defenders. Juan Carlos Valeron met the pass on the right side of the penalty box and one-timed it into the left-hand corner from 8 yards out.

Slovenia got on the scoreboard as second-half substitutes Sebastjan Cimirotič and Milenko Ačimovič exchanged a 1-2 pass in the Spanish penalty area, and Cimirotič pushed the ball past Spanish keeper Iker Casillas from 15 yards to close the gap to 2-1.

In the final minutes of the game, Spain won a dubious penalty as Morientes fell over after a fair challenge for the ball. Captain Fernando Hierro slotted into the right hand corner to temporarily remain Spain's career goal leader with 29 goals – a remarkable feat for a defender (Raúl later surpassed his total after the World Cup to become Spain's leading goal scorer at age 26).

Slovenia star playmaker Zlatko Zahovič was later dismissed from the team after a disagreement over his being substituted for Ačimovič.

Spain: Iker Casillas, Carlos Puyol, Fernando Hierro, Miguel Nadal, Juanfran (Enrique Romero 82), Luis Enrique (Ivan Helguera 74), Ruben Baraja, Francisco De Pedro, Juan Carlos Valeron, Raul Gonzalez, Diego Tristan (Fernando Morientes 67).

Slovenia: Marko Simeunovic, Zeljko Milinovic, Marinko Galic, Aleksander Knavs, Doni Novak (Sasa Gajser 77), Ales Ceh, Miran Pavlin, Amir Karic, Mladen Rudonja, Zlatko Zahovic (Milenko Acimovic 62), Milan Osterc (Sebastjan Cimirotič 56).

Goals: **Spain** Raúl González 44, Juan Carlos Valeron 74, Fernando Hierro 87 (penalty);
             Slovenia Sebastjan Cimirotič 82.

Referee: Mohammed Guezzaz (Morocco).

Man of the Match: Raúl González for getting Spain started right.

22 Spain 3 – 1 Paraguay: Spain snuff Chilavert bluff
Jeonju, South Korea

The Spanish had not won their first two World Cup matches since 1950. Paraguay captain and goalkeeper Jose Luis Chilavert, in a futile effort to unnerve young Spanish keeper Iker Casillas, had stated that he wanted to score twice against Spain. But it was Spain's half-time substitute Fernando Morientes who scored two goals, making Spain the first team to qualify for the second round of the competition.

Paraguay controlled possession early, and the Spanish cleared poorly when off-suspension Chilavert punted a ball into the opposite penalty area. The clearance went to defender Francisco Arce at the right side of the penalty box; Arce took a powerful shot that Casillas managed to stop, but the rebound bounced off defender Carlos Puyol and into the net for an own goal. The half ended with Paraguay leading 1-0.

The Spanish striking pair of Francisco De Pedro and Fernando Morrientes saved Spain in the second half. After De Pedro served up a left-sided corner kick, Morrientes rose above the defense to head past Chilavert. Sixteen minutes later it was De Pedro again streaking to the left touchline, faking the cross once, then delivering close to goal whereupon Morrientes kneed it in after Chilavert uncharacteristically missed the ball.

Chilavert had a chance on a free kick from 30 meters, but Casillas called Chilavert's bluff and made the save.

De Pedro also had a hand in creating the third goal, as he made a long throw-in that found Raúl at the penalty spot, whose twisting shot was saved. But referee Al-Ghandour ruled a penalty which Fernando Hierro converted to the right-hand corner past Chilavert. Video showed that Raúl was impeded at the shoulder and the leg, and the penalty call was justified despite his impressive shooting effort. By beating Paraguay, Spain booked their qualification for the second round.

Spain: Iker Casillas, Carlos Puyol, Fernando Hierro, Miguel Angel Nadal, Juanfran, Enrique Romero (Ivan Helguera 46), Ruben Baraja, Juan Carlos Valeron (Xavi Hernandez 85), Francisco De Pedro, Raul Gonzalez, Diego Tristan (Fernando Morientes 46).

Paraguay: Jose Luis Chilavert, Francisco Arce, Carlos Gamarra, Celso Ayala, Julio Cesar Caceres, Denis Caniza, Carlos Paredes, Diego Gavilan, Roberto Acuña, Roque Santa Cruz, Jose Cardozo (Jorge Campos 63)

Goals: **Spain**: Fernando Morientes 53, 69, Fernando Hierro 83 (penalty).
  Paraguay Carlos Puyol 10 (own goal).
Referee: Gamal Al-Ghandour (Egypt).
Men of the Match: Fernando Morrientes and Francisco De Pedro for two well positioned goals and assists.

24 South Africa 1 – 0 Slovenia :   South Africa first ever World Cup Finals win
June 8: Daegu, South Korea

This game was the first time the "Bafana Bafana" had taken a lead in five previous World Cup games, and the first South African win ever at the World Cup.

South Africa scored an unusual goal in the fourth minute when a Quinton Fortune free kick from the left side found Siyabonga Nomvethe in front of the 6-yard goal box. Nomvethe missed the header but luckily made legal contact with his thigh, and the ball sneaked into the right corner of the net.

South Africa controlled the match and had most of the chances, but could not add to their early goal. Benni McCarthy had two glorious chances in the second half; he unluckily hit the post on a cross from Fortune, and Slovenia keeper Simeunovič well saved his next effort.

South Africa: Andre Arendse, Cyril Nzama, Lucas Radebe, Aaron Mokoena, Bradley Carnell, Sibusiso Zuma, MacBeth Sibaya, Tebeho Mokoena, Quinton Fortune (Jabu Pule 84), Siyabonga Nomvethe (Delron Buckley 71), Benni McCarthy (George Koumantarakis 80).

Slovenia: Marko Simeunovic, Zelijko Milinovic, Muamer Vugdalic, Aleksander Knavs (Spasoje Bulajic 60), Djoni Novak, Ales Ceh, Miran Pavlin, Amir Karic, Milenko Acimovic (Nastja Ceh 60), Mladen Rudonja, Sebastjan Cimirotič (Milan Osterc 41).

Referee: Angel Sanchez (Argentina).
Goal: South Africa – Siyabonga Nomvethe 4.
Man of the Match: Quinton Fortune, for creating many goal chances including the one that Siyabonga Nomvethe converted.

39 South Africa 2 – 3 Spain : Spain gets maximum nine points
June 12: Daejeon, South Korea

Raúl Gonzalez put Spain on the scoreboard in the fourth minute by stripping South African keeper Andre Arendse after he had bobbled an errant pass, and then walked into goal unmolested. Gaizka Mendieta nearly made it 2-0 in the thirteenth minute after his shot inside the box beat the goalkeeper, but it was cleared off the line by Aaron Mokoena.

Benni McCarthy pulled South Africa level when after receiving a head pass from Siyabonga Nomvethe, he jump volleyed past advancing Spain keeper Iker Casillas from 5 yards.

Mendieta did not waste his next chance for goal before half-time, as his 22-yard free-kick outside the left side of the penalty area was expertly curled inside the far right post, leaving Arendse little chance.

After the break South Africa again equalized following a poor Spanish clearance from a corner kick; defender Lucas Radebe headed the ball inside the near post from 8 yards.

Three minutes later, Spain scored the decisive goal as Raúl slipped past Radebe to meet Joaquin Sanchez's cross, and nodded the ball past Arendse from 8 yards out. The last 34 minutes were hotly contested, but neither team could create another goal.

Spain finished at the top of Group B with a maximum nine points, but South Africa missed out on the second round by scoring one less goal than Paraguay.

Spain: Iker Casillas, Curro Torres, Ivan Helguera, Miguel Angel Nadal, Enrique Romero, Gaizka Mendieta, Xavi Hernandez, David Albelda (Sergio 53), Joaquin Sanchez, Raul Gonzalez (Luis Enrique 82), Fernando Morientes (Albert Luque 76).

South Africa: Andre Arendse, Cyril Nzama, Aaron Mokoena, Lucas Radebe (Thabang Molefe 80), Bradley Carnell, MacBeth Sibaya, Teboho Mokoena, Quinton Fortune (Jacob Lekgetho 83), Sibusiso Zuma, Siyabonga Nomvethe (George Koumantarakis 74), Benni McCarthy.

Goals: **Spain** - Raul Gonzalez 4, 56, Gaizka Mendieta 45.
South Africa – Benni McCarthy 31, Lucas Radebe 53.

Referee: Saad Mane (Kuwait).

Men of the Match: Raúl and Gaizka Mendieta for getting the Spain goals.

40 Slovenia 1 – 3 Paraguay : Paraguay squeaks through to second round
June 12: Seogwipo, South Korea

Paraguay needed to beat Slovenia and make up three goals of difference in order to secure a second round position from South Africa, and did just that in beating Slovenia 3-1.

Paraguay had an inauspicious start as Carlos Paredes received a red card in the 22nd minute; Paraguay used only ten men for the rest of the game. Then Milenko Acimovic scored from a nearly impossible angle one yard on the right byline, as his off-goal shot was directed into the net by Chilavert's foot. The situation looked grim for Paraguay entering the break playing with one man down and losing 0-1.

Slovenia looked dangerous after the break as Acimovic hit the crossbar in the 52nd minute, but Paraguay finally got back in the game after Nelson Cuevas entered in the 61st minute, and he had his first international goal five minutes later. Cuevas dribbled to find space in the area, beat three defenders, and fired a low left-footed shot from 15 yards past keeper Mladen Dabanovic.

The Paraguayans were energized by the goal and seven minutes later another substitute, Jorge Campos, shot another low ball past Dabanovic from 24 yards just inside the far post. Paraguayan keeper Chilavert got into the offensive action when his 35-yard free kick tested Dabanovic who could only push over for a corner. Minutes later it was a "ten versus ten man" game as Nastja Ceh was red-carded for a rough tackle.

Cuevas showed his brilliance on the dribble again as he beat three defenders on the border of the penalty area, and blasted a ball from 18 yards off the underside of the crossbar that defied gravity as it bounced inside the goal and stretched the upper netting. Thus Paraguay, through three substitutes' goals and by one goal difference, passed through to face Germany in the second round.

Slovenia: Mladen Dabanovic, Zeljko Milinovic, Spasoje Bulajic, Dzoni Novak, Ales Ceh, Miran Pavlin (Mladen Rudonja, 40), Rajko Tavcar, Milenko Acimovic (Nastja Ceh, 63), Amir Karic, Milan Osterc (Senad Tiganj, 78), Sebastjan Cimirotič.

Paraguay: Jose Luis Chilavert, Francisco Arce, Carlos Gamarra, Celso Ayala, Julio Cesar Caceres, Denis Caniza, Guido Alvarenga (Jorge Campos 54) Roberto Acuña, Carlos Paredes, Roque Santa Cruz, Jose Cardozo (Nelson Cuevas 61).

Goals: **Slovenia** - Milenko Acimovic 45.
Paraguay - Nelson Cuevas 66, 84, Jorge Campos 74.

Referee: Felipe Ramos Rizo (Mexico).
Man of the Match: Nelson Cuevas, for his dynamic 30 minutes of play and two goals on the pitch, paradoxically his only substantial appearance in the World Cup.

Group C: Brazil, Turkey, China PR, Costa Rica
Total group score: 103   [2nd easiest group by cumulative rankings]

The year 2001 was easily the worst in Brazilian soccer. Brazil was still ranked number three in the world even as they lost games to South Korea, Ecuador, Bolivia, Australia and Honduras – none of them world powers. Brazil had lost *six games in qualifying* for the 2002 World Cup, when previously it had *only lost once before in its history in qualifying* from 1930-1998. That loss was a 2-0 defeat to Bolivia in 1993 at 3700 meters above sea level in La Paz; a chastened Brazil had subsequently demolished Bolivia 6-0 in the return match.

Group C might well have seemed like a vacation to Brazil after a terrible time qualifying in the tough South American CONMEBOL competition, and there was some merit to this prediction. China was a newcomer to the World Cup, and Turkey appeared improved but was making its first World Cup appearance since the 1954 Switzerland World Cup. Costa Rica however, had a well organized and dynamic team, and had easily won the CONCACAF group.

Brazil couldn't have been happier with the draw as it seemed the weakest of the groups, and was the 2nd easiest group by cumulative rankings. Turkey and Costa Rica however, stretched Brazil to the limit, and Turkey was to follow Brazil into the semi-finals with a very attractive side.

C1. Brazil [2]

What to say about Brazil? Their football pedigree included: World Cup winners in 1958, 1962, 1970, and 1994, World Cup runners-up in 1950 and 1998, winners of the FIFA U-20 World Cup in 1983, 1985 and 1993, and winners of the FIFA U-17 World Cup in 1997, 1999, and 2003. Even so, Brazil qualified only third in the CONMEBOL group, the first time they had not finished first. This was their seventeenth World Cup Finals appearance, and they had progressed to the second round in all but three.

Brazil is the only country that can afford to leave a multitude of quality offensive players at home that it is simply scandalous. These included Romário, whose credentials included: Phillips Best-11 Dream team member, second on the Brazil scoring list after Pelé, and scorer of eight Brazil goals in the 2002 World Cup qualifying – *in only four qualifying games* (Rivaldo also led the team with eight goals). Brazil also left behind 1999 and 2002 European Golden Boot award winner Mario Jardel, and 1999 Serie A and 2002 Bundesliga leading scorer Marcio Amoroso. Any other country would have loved to have this mothballed attacking talent.

Brazil went through three coaches during their worst ever CONMEBOL qualifying tournament. Brazil's third coach Luis Felipe ("Big Phil") Scolari did not have immediate success, as Brazil opened up the 2001 Copa America by losing 1-0 to Mexico. It was Brazil's fourth straight loss, the worst Brazil losing streak since 1921.

Scolari brought a squad of players that was either very experienced or completely naïve at the World Cup level. Cafú had already played ten World Cup matches while Ronaldo, Rivaldo, Denilson and Roberto Carlos had played in eight. The rest of the team prepared to play in their first World Cup matches. Brazil's captain and midfield "destroyer" Emerson dislocated his shoulder in a freak training accident just before the first game, which left the possibility of an unsettled midfield.

Many said Rivaldo (a "number 10" who likes to be the center of attention as he justifiably was at Barcelona) could not play alongside Ronaldo, a straight-up center forward. Rivaldo adapted his game, and was arguably Brazil's most valuable weapon.

C2. Turkey [22]

Coach Şenol Güneş had guided Turkey to finish second to Sweden in Europe Group 4, and Turkey subsequently demolished Austria 6-0 on aggregate to qualify for the Cup. That should have woken some people up.

Turkey had not appeared in a World Cup for 48 years, yet had a very promising squad as team members were from top European and Turkish teams. Many of the Turkish players perform in the German Bundesliga, and seven were even born in Germany! The German-Turkish football connection started in 1984 when Jupp Derwall coached Galatasaray, and subsequently German coaches managed big Turkish clubs Fenerbahce, Besiktas and Trabzonspor. These Germans inspired Turkish team discipline that complemented their prodigious football technique.

Three Turkish players (Emre Belözoglu, Okan Buruk, and Hakan Şükür) were Inter Milan club teammates of Brazilian star Ronaldo. Therefore, Brazil and Turkey were no strangers to their respective styles.

C3. China PR [50]

China lost only once in the weak Asia Group B qualifying group to qualify for their first World Cup Finals ever.

China hired the globetrotting coach Bora Milutinovic, who had previously coached four different teams to the second round in consecutive World Cups - Mexico (1986), Costa Rica (1990), USA (1994), and Nigeria (1998). Still, China had only a nascent professional soccer atmosphere, and was very inexperienced at the international level. It would take a miracle for Bora to lead China into the second round against established Group C competition.

C4. Costa Rica [29]

Costa Rica was CONCACAF's uncontested top team in the World Cup qualifiers, even breaking Mexico's 20-year home-unbeaten streak when they bested Mexico 2-1 in the Azteca Stadium. This was Costa Rica's second World Cup Finals appearance; their first appearance in 1990 resulted in their advancing to the second round.

Costa Rica was rated the "Best Mover of the Year" for 2001 as their world rank jumped from 60 to 30. Paulo Wanchope and Rolando Fonseca's goals led them in qualifying.

Coach Alexandre Guimaraes should be given credit for Costa Rica playing the wide open, skillful, and entertaining soccer they exhibited in the 2001 Copa America. Guimaraes, Brazil-born but an ex-Costa Rica player in the 1990 World Cup, would meet his ex-coach Bora's China team in the same group.

10 Brazil 2 – 1 Turkey: Brazil's "beautiful game" versus "win at any cost"
June 3: Ulsan, South Korea

Turkey proved to be more than a handful for Brazil, with just as much skill and creativity on the ball. Shortly before half-time Hasan Şaş received a perfect lob through ball from Yildiray Baştürk, and expertly blasted it from 6 yards inside the near post past Brazil keeper Marcos. Brazil had conceded at least one goal in their last six World Cup matches, and Turkey continued this trend.

Shortly after the second half started, Rivaldo lasered in an ambitious cross from the left side to Ronaldo who was streaking in between three Turkish defenders. Somehow Ronaldo was able to extend his body and direct the ball into the net on a bounce to equalize; a spectacular goal in which Turkish keeper Rüştü Reçber had no chance.

Turkey and Brazil continued to battle with equal technique and invention. At one point, flamboyant substitute İlhan Mansiz pulled a "rainbow" move over Roberto Carlos' head (see Chapter 2 – a "rainbow" is a "sombrero" move played from behind the body with both feet, very difficult and unheard of in big matches)! Roberto Carlos was so beaten that he had to foul Mansiz from behind to stop his advance.

The game came to a late climax in the 87th minute. After a poor clearance by Reçber, Ronaldo's substitute Luizao was pulled down by Turkish defender Alpay Özalan just outside the 18-yard box. Although the foul occurred outside the penalty box, Brazil was gifted a penalty kick by referee Kim Young Joo. Rivaldo duly converted a quality shot to the lower right-hand corner that Reçber almost got a touch on.

During the next Brazilian corner kick, the frustrated Hakan Ünsal was red-carded after he kicked the ball at Rivaldo's knees. Rivaldo faked the severity of the foul, and ultimately received a token fine by FIFA (the fine of 11,250 Swiss francs was not a credible deterrent to preventing future bad behavior). After the game, both Rivaldo and Luizao admitted faking the foul and/or injury. In Brazil, the advantage brought by faking is called "*malandragem*," and is unfortunately accepted in some countries as being a "smart play".

Besides the wrong penalty kick decision, the referee allowed the Brazil defense to creep up to less than 10 yards on Turkish free kicks around the goal. This negated any free-kick equality for Turkey to equalize from a dead-ball situation, as Brazil was stuffing the ball from 5 yards. Brazil defenders deserved a yellow and/or red card for persistent cheating. Perhaps this was the "win-at-any-cost" football that coach Scolari had brought to the Brazil national team. It remained to be seen whether Brazil could demonstrate their technique and the "beautiful game" they were famous for in future games, as well as fair play.

The attractive Turks came away from the equally played game with nine men and no points, from a game that would justifiably have ended tied had it not been for an erroneous referee decision for Brazil.

Brazil: Marcos, Cafu, Lúcio, Roque Junior, Carlos, Edmílson, Juninho Paulista (Vampeta 72), Gilberto, Ronaldinho (Denilson 67), Rivaldo, Ronaldo (Luizao 73).
Turkey: Rüstü Reçber, Bülent Korkmaz (Ilhan Mansiz 66), Fatih Akyel, Alpay Özalan, Hakan Unsal, Umit Özat, Yildiray Bastürk (Umit Davala 65), Emre Belözoglu, Tugay Kerimoglu (Arif Erdem 88), Hakan Sükür, Hakan Sas.
Goals: Turkey: Hakan Şaş 45. **Brazil:** Ronaldo 50, Rivaldo 87 (penalty).
Ref: Kim Young-Joo (South Korea).
Men of the Match: Hasan Şaş for his clinical strike and creative play, and Ronaldo for getting Brazil started on a beautiful flying re-direction goal.

12 China 0 – 2 Costa Rica : Newcomers meet Central American flair
June 4: Gwangju, South Korea

China's first ever World Cup match ended in a loss as they could not match Costa Rican ball skill and finishing. The evenly played first half ended tied 0-0, and the match was decided in a four-minute stretch in the second half by Ronald Gomez and Mauricio Wright goals.

Ronald Gomez was the protagonist in both Costa Rican goals. The first goal sequence started when he tapped a risky back-heel to Paulo Wanchope whose subsequent shot was stuffed by the Chinese defense. But Gomez was still advancing and won the loose ball, which he slotted past giant Chinese keeper Jiang Jin into the upper left corner from 16 yards out. Four minutes later Gomez received a short corner kick on the left end line, wheeled and made a short cross that found Mauricio Wright at the near post. Wright was able to angle his head shot into the opposite corner from a mere three yards out.

China showed plenty of energy but their attacks lacked finishing skills.

China: Jiang Jin, Wu Chengying, Fan Zhiyi (Yu Genwei 74), Sun Jihai (Qu Bo 23), Li Tie, Ma Mingyu, Hao Haidong, Li Weifeng, Li Xiaopeng, Yang Chen, Xu Yunlong.
Costa Rica: Erick Lonnis, Luis Marin, Mauricio Wright, Gilberto Martinez, Rolando Fonseca (Hernan Medford 57), Mauricio Solis, Paulo Wanchope (Wilmer Lopez 80), Walter Centeno, Ronaldo Gomez, Harold Wallace (Steven Bryce 70), Carlos Castro.
Goals. Costa Rica: Ronald Gomez 61, Mauricio Wright 65.
Referee: Kyros Vassaras (Greece).
Man of the Match: Ronald Gomez for his superb creative and finishing display.

26 Brazil 4 – 0 China: "Beautiful game" sloppy but improving
June 8: Seogwipo, South Korea

The Brazilians came to this game still searching for their best form. On paper they far outclassed China, but China was very active and made a game of it.

In the 15th minute Roberto Carlos scored his first long range Brazil free kick since his 1997 wonder goal against France. Taken from 26 meters out on the right, he lasered his left-footed shot into the top left hand corner, leaving 198 cm tall (6 foot 6 inch) keeper Jiang Jin with no chance.

In the 32nd minute Ronaldinho cleverly crossed from the left side to Rivaldo's left foot; Brazil's number 10 unerringly slotted the ball into the right side of the goal from 4 yards out. Two famous left feet, and two goals.

Just before halftime Ronaldo was brought down near the penalty spot, and his diminutive (in name only) Ronaldinho duly converted the penalty kick into the lower left corner. At halftime it was all Brazil 3-0.

All game Roberto Carlos and Brazil captain Cafu were active on the wings, acting as the most offensive outside back pair in history. In the 55th minute Cafu found himself in front of the goal, but instead of shooting, he centered from right to left for Ronaldo to tap-in the fourth from four yards.

To their credit China didn't give up, and hit the right post on a fine shot from Zhao Junzhe at the top of the penalty box. Substitute Shao Jiayi then uncorked a clever free kick from the right corner of the 18-yard box that drew a superb save from Marcos.

China's efforts revealed some of Brazil's weaknesses at the back, as a more experienced team could have had some goals. China however, was eliminated from the second round with this defeat, while Brazil qualified for the next round.

Brazil: Marcos, Cafu, Lúcio, Roque Junior, Roberto Carlos, Gilberto Silva, Juninho (Ricardinho 71), Anderson Polga, Ronaldinho (Denilson 46), Ronaldo (Edilson 72), Rivaldo.
China: Jiang Jin, Wu Chenying, Li Tie, Ma Mingyu (Pu Yang 62), Hao Haidong (Qu Bo 75), Li Weifeng, Zhao Junzhe, Du Wei, Li Xiaopeng, Qi Hong (Shao Jiayi 67), Xu Yunlong.
Referee: Anders Frisk (Sweden).
Goals: Brazil: Roberto Carlos 15, Rivaldo 32, Ronaldinho 45 (penalty), Ronaldo 55.
Men of the Match: Wingbacks Roberto Carlos, for getting Brazil started with his 25-yard laser shot, and Cafú, who had a hand in two of Brazil's goals.

28 Costa Rica 1 –1 Turkey   Turkey equals Costa Rica skills
June 9: Incheon, South Korea

An entertaining game between two evenly matched sides, Turkey was without suspended starters Alpay Özalan and Hakan Ünsal, and keeper Rüştü Reçber was hampered by a leg injury.

In a first half that saw Paulo Wanchope and Ümit Özat come close to scoring, Hakan Şükür also missed a header and Ronald Gomez blasted over after a dribbling exhibition.

Emre Belözoglu scored on a nice move in the 55th minute. His first shot was stuffed after receiving a chest pass from Hasan Şaş in the middle of the penalty box, but the enterprising playmaker then made a 180-degree turn to push the ball into the right side of the goal from 8 yards away.

Costa Rica stepped up the pressure, and in the 86th minute Reynaldo Parks left-footed into the net unchallenged from 6 yards, after an overhead kick flick-on that fooled the defense and beat Reçber. Costa Rica then searched for the winner, with Parks shooting wide on an empty net from an acute angle after he had already beaten Reçber.

Costa Rica probably had the better chances, but it was a fair result between two superbly skilled squads seeking the second advancement berth of the group.

Costa Rica: Erick Lonnis, Luis Marin, Mauricio Wright, Gilberto Martinez, Harold Wallace (Steven Bryce 77), Carlos Castro, Wilmer Lopez (Reynaldo Parks 77), Mauricio Solis, Walter Centeno (Hernan Medford 67), Ronald Gomez, Paulo Wanchope.
Turkey: Rüştü Reçber, Emre Asik, Fatih Akyel, Umit Özat, Tugay Kerimoglu (Arif Erdem 88), Yildiray Bastürk (Nihat Kahveci 79), Ergun Penbe, Emre Belözoglu, Umit Davala, Hakan Sükür (Ilhan Mansiz 75), Hasan Sas.
Goals. Costa Rica - Reynaldo Parks 86. **Turkey** - Emre Belözoglu 56.
Referee: Coffi Codjia (Benin).
Man of the Match: Emre Belözoglu for his goal and Paulo Wanchope for his offensive activity all game.

41 Costa Rica 2 – 5 Brazil: Two Teams Play Samba Soccer
June 13: Suwon, South Korea

Costa Rica needed just one point to qualify, but that would have to be gained against Brazil. The Ticos missed some excellent chances in this exciting and skilled Latin match up which brought seven goals, and the score could have been closer.

The first goal came in the 10th minute from Ronaldo's effort to steer an Edmílson pass into the net from 6 yards. The replay showed that the ball would have missed the goal had Luis Marin not deflected it into his own net. Initially marked as an own goal, it was later credited to Ronaldo.

Ronaldo had a second goal three minutes later as he controlled a corner kick to the near post, and surrounded by three defenders, did some nifty sole-of-the-foot work to create just enough space to put the ball between keeper Erick Lonnis and the near post from six yards out.

The game looked over when defender Edmílson scored one of the goals of the tournament. Edmílson himself started the move from the Brazilian half, passing to Rivaldo who returned the ball back to the advancing defender, who then passed to Roberto Carlos' stand-in Junior on the left flank. Junior's cross was partially blocked, but the onrushing Edmílson instantly adjusted by spectacularly bicycle-kicking the ball past the astonished Lonnis from 6 yards out.

Costa Rica finally got on the score sheet when Mauricio Wright gave Paulo Wanchope a return pass in the penalty box, and Wanchope shot past Marcos from 11 yards. Rivaldo's free-kick hit the left post as the first half expired 3-1 to Brazil.

Costa Rica scored first in the second half as they continued their all-out attack; Walter Centeno crossed from the right side and Ronald Gomez's flying header from three yards out flashed past a helpless Marcos.

Rivaldo finally scored when he converted a pass from Junior and first-timed it pass Lonnis with his favored left foot from nine yards out. Junior himself then scored as he got free and beat Lonnis from eight yards at the near post.

The skillful and entertaining Costa Ricans lost out on second-round advancement to Turkey, who advanced on equal points but superior goal difference.

Costa Rica: Erick Lonnis, Luis Marin, Mauricio Wright, Gilberto Martinez, (Winston Parks, 74), Harold Wallace (Steven Bryce, 46), Carlos Castro, Wilmer Lopez, Mauricio Solis (Rolando Fonseca, 65), Walter Centeno, Paulo Cesar Wanchope, Ronald Gomez.
Brazil: Marcos, Cafú, Lúcio, Edmílson, Anderson Polga, Junior, Gilberto Silva, Rivaldo (Kaka, 72), Paulista Juninho (Ricardinho, 61), Ronaldo, Edilson (Kleberson, 57).
Goals: Costa Rica - Paulo Cesar Wanchope 40; Ronald Gomez 56. **Brazil** Ronaldo 10, 13; Edmílson 38; Rivaldo 62; Junior 64.
Referee: Gamal Al-Ghandour (Egypt).
Man of the Match: Edmílson for his wonderfully opportunistic overhead kick goal.

42 Turkey 3 – 0 China   Hasan Şaş sparks Turkey win to advance
June 13: Seoul, South Korea

Coach Bora had already ended his streak of four teams progressing to the second stage, but his China team had plenty of energy left and wanted to impress in their last match of the World Cup. Turkey, knowing it needed goals to advance past Costa Rica, foiled their ambitions by grabbing two goals within the first 10 minutes.

In the 6th minute a rampant Hasan Şaş liberated the ball after a mix-up between two Chinese defenders, and shot over Chinese keeper Jiang Jin from 15 yards on the right side. Three minutes later Şaş crossed from the left side and Bülent Korkmaz out jumped the defense to score at the far left post.

China kept attacking and almost scored their first goal in the 28th minute as Yang Chen's shot hammered off the left post. However, after the half China was forced to be more defensive after they lost red-carded Shao Jiayi to a clumsy tackle on Emre Belözoglu.

In the second half it was Şaş once again who expertly crossed from the left side to the right, where Ümit Davala volleyed from eight yards off the far (left) post into the net. Turkey therefore progressed to the second round on a three-goal difference over Costa Rica.

Turkey: Rüstü Reçber (Omer Catkic, 35), Emre Asik, Bülent Korkmaz, Fatih Akyel, Tugay Kerimoglu (Tayfur Havutcu, 84), Yildiray Bastürk (Mansiz Ilhan, 70), Hakan Unsal, Emre Belözoglu, Umit Davala, Hakan Sükür, Hasan Sas.
China : Jiang Jin, Yang Pu, Wu Chengying (Shao Jiayi, 46), Li Weifeng, Du Wei, Xu Yunlong, Li Tie, Zhao Junzhe, Li Xiaopeng, Hao Haidong (Qu Bo, 73), Yang Chen (Genwei Yu, 73).
Goals: Turkey – Hasan Sas 6, Bülent Korkmaz 9, Umit Davala 85.
Referee: Oscar Ruiz (Colombia)
Man of the Match: Hasan Şaş for his goal and prominent role in the other two goals.

Group D: Korea, Poland, United States, Portugal

Total group score: 96   [3rd easiest group by cumulative rankings]

As a co-hosting country, South Korea was sky-high for the World Cup. Both South Korea and the United States qualified for their fourth consecutive World Cups (1990-1994-1998-2002), bringing some young stars supported by a cadre of seasoned veterans. Poland and Portugal were both back in their first World Cup since 1986, when Poland beat Portugal 1-0.

Portugal was thought to be the real danger team, and by reputation and previous experience was expected to come in first. Full of international stars, they had dumped powerhouse Holland out of the World Cup and qualified ahead of Ireland.

D1. Korea Republic [40]

South Korea (also known as Korea Republic) qualified as a result of being the co-host along with Japan. This was South Korea's sixth World Cup Finals appearance, but they had never advanced to the second phase.

South Korea had hired Gus Hiddink, the 1998 Dutch World Cup coach who just missed going to the 1998 World Cup Final by an after time penalty-kick loss to Brazil. The team was led by four-time World Cup veteran (1990-1994-1998-2002) defender Hong Myung Bo, and Italy Serie A player Ahn Jung Hwan.

In an effort to try and establish more cordial relations between South Korea and North Korea, a remarkable attempt was made to include a North Korean player on the South Korean team, and to stage at least one game in North Korea. Both these efforts failed as the North was not ready to cooperate with the South. North Korea had entered the World Cup once before in 1966, where they passed the first round, surprisingly beat favored Italy, and finally lost to a Eusébio-led Portugal.

D2. Poland [38]

Poland finished top of Europe Group 5, and was in their first World Cup since 1986. Of their six previous World Cup Final appearances, they had failed to reach the second phase only once before. But pre-World Cup losses to Japan and Romania at home fueled worries about their readiness.

With no international stars, Poland relied on team unity. Coach Jerzy Engel played a 4-4-2 system that featured Emmanuel Olisadebe and Paweł Kryszałowicz as strike partners. Olisadebe is the first Polish national team member of African ancestry, and supplied many of the goals essential for qualifying.

D3. United States [13]

The United States qualified third and last in the CONACAF group, even on points but behind on goal difference to Mexico. This was the USA's seventh World Cup Finals appearance, and their fourth in a row. Their previous best was reaching the semi-finals way back in 1930.

The team had a significant skill level to do well in the World Cup, but it is likely that the final piece of the puzzle was new coach Bruce Arena. Arena had already won five university titles at Virginia, and the first two MLS titles with D.C. United, which established him as the premier homegrown soccer mind and motivator.

The USA brought in new stars Landon Donovan and DaMarcus Beasley to spice up seasoned veterans such as Jeff Agoos, Eddie Pope, Cobi Jones, Earnie Stewart, and captain Claudio Reyna. One of Arena's toughest but most pleasant task was to choose between two world-class goalkeepers playing in the English Premier Division, Brad Friedel (Blackburn) and Kasey Keller (Tottenham).

D4. Portugal [5]

Portugal finished top of the toughest European qualifying group 2, edging out Ireland on goal difference and booting powerful Holland out of the competition. This was to be Portugal's Cup, with many of the generation that won the World Youth Cup (U-20) in 1989 and 1991 fully matured. Still, this was only Portugal's third World Cup ever, so it was a relatively new experience for all involved. Portugal's previous World Cup experience was highlighted by Eusébio's third-placed team in 1966.

Coach Antonio Oliveira could depend on his stars performing in the Italian, Spanish, Portuguese, and French leagues. The team leader in accomplishments was 2001 World Player of the Year Luis Figo, midfielder for 2002 European Champion's League winners Real Madrid. The expectation for this team was to sail through to the second round, and at least reach the quarterfinals, with a possible chance to win it all.

14 South Korea 2 – 0 Poland: South Korea reveals its quality
June 4: Busan, South Korea

A hosting nation had never lost their opening match in the World Cup, and South Korea was not about to change that pattern. Both teams came out attacking, but South Korea got the crucial first goal in the 26th minute. Lee Eul Yong's low cross from the left side found unmarked Hwang Sun Hong, who brilliantly volleyed the ball to the near post to beat Polish keeper Jerzy Dudek from 12 yards.

The Koreans thought they had another goal in the first half after Park Ji Sung scored, but the goal was disallowed for offside. South Korea carried a one-goal lead into the halftime interval.

Dudek was kept busy after halftime, and his desperate touch on Yoo Sang Chul's clinical 23-yard strike in the 53rd minute could not keep the ball out of the net. By that time the home crowd was delirious at the certainty of South Korea's first ever World Cup win on their 15th try, which was accomplished as the Korean defense completed their shutout.

South Korea: Lee Woon Jae, Choi Jin Chul, Kim Tae Young, Hong Myung Bo, Yoo Sang-Chul (Chun Soo Lee, 62) , Kim Nam Il, Lee Eul Yong, Park Ji Sung, Seol Ki Hyeon (Du-Ri Cha, 90) , Hwang Sun Hong (Ahn Jung Hwan, 50) , Song Chong Gug.
Poland: Jerzy Dudek, Michal Zewlakow, Tomasz Hajto, Tomasz Waldoch, Jacek Bak (Tomasz Klos, 51) , Piotr Swierczewski, Radoslaw Kaluzny (Marcin Zewlakow, 65) , Jacek Krzynowek, Marek Kozminski, Emmanuel Olisadebe, Maciej Zurawski (Pawel Kryszalowicz, 46).
Goals: South Korea Hwang Sun Hong 26, Yoo Sang-Chul 53.
Referee: Oscar Ruiz (Colombia).
Man of the Match: Yoo Sang Chul for his individual effort and goal to clinch victory.

16 United States 3 – 2 Portugal: USA shocks Portugal
June 5: Suwon, South Korea

USA supporters were pinching themselves as their team was beating Portugal 3-0 after only 36 minutes gone, and subsequently held on to win. Although the improving USA team had beaten Germany, England, Brazil, and Argentina in the previous eight years, it was the USA's first win against a top quality team in a World Cup since 1950, when they had beaten England 1-0 in the biggest World Cup upset ever. The modern USA team's previous top win in an international competition was the 3-0 win against Argentina in the 1995 Copa America.

Coach Arena's tactical masterstroke was placing Pablo Mastroeni as the defensive midfielder in front of Eddie Pope and Jeff Agoos. His effective work gave the USA offense freedom to create without undue defensive concerns.

The USA stunned Portugal in the fourth minute as Brian McBride won a corner kick from Earnie Stewart and headed it towards the far post. Goalkeeper Vítor Baía managed to stop the shot but John O'Brien blasted the rebound from 3 yards past him and two other defenders at the near post.

After both teams traded numerous attacking runs, pressure from Tony Sanneh led to a Portuguese defensive breakdown that sent the ball to Landon Donovan on the right wing. Donovan's seemingly innocent cross deflected off defender Jorge Costa's shoulder, and incredibly flew past a diving Baía at the near post, for a very improbable Portuguese own-goal in the 30th minute.

Six minutes later the more confident USA squad got their third unanswered goal as Donovan passed the ball to an overlapping Sanneh, who sent a perfect cross to McBride in the box. McBride extended perfectly and his diving header beat the diving Baía at the far post from 6 yards out.

A poor clearance of Beto's header from Luis Figo's corner kick gave hope to Portugal before the half ended. Beto himself picked up the loose ball and slotted past Brad Friedel inside the near post from 9 yards out. The half ended with the USA leading 3-1.

The teams traded chances by Costa and Donovan after the half, but increased Portuguese pressure took its toll in the 71st minute as Pauleta's cross was steered into the USA goal by an airborne Jeff Agoos. The two own-goals in this game were so improbable that if either team had tried them in practice they would have been unable to duplicate them.

The USA defense was able to withstand further Portuguese incursions and close out the match. The USA was off to an optimistic start, as their three goals in one game were the equal to their 1994 World Cup Finals total, and their combined Italy 1990 and France 1998 goal totals.

Portugal: Vitor Baia, Jorge Costa (Jorge Andrade 74), Fernando Couto, Luis Figo, Joao Pinto, Pauleta, Rui Costa (Nuno Gomes 80), Sergio Conceição, Petit, Beto, Rui Jorge (Paulo Bento 69).

USA: Brad Friedel, Anthony Sanneh, Eddie Pope (Carlos Llamosa 80), Jeff Agoos, Frankie Hejduk, Earnie Stewart (Cobi Jones 46), Pablo Mastroeni, John O'Brien, DaMarcus Beasley, Brian McBride, Landon Donovan (Joe-Max Moore 75).

Goals: **United States**: O'Brien 4, Costa 29 (own goal), McBride 36.

Portugal: Beto 39, Agoos 71 (own goal).

Referee: Byron Moreno (Ecuador).

Man of the Match: Brian McBride, whose opportunistic header enabled O'Brien's crucial initial goal, and for his diving header, the third and eventual winning goal.

30 South Korea 1 – 1 USA   USA holds off South Korea

June 10: Daegu, South Korea

A fortuitous first-half USA goal and penalty save were enough to tie the talented host Koreans.

In the 26th minute John O'Brien made a classy run from his own half and beautifully chipped in to Clint Mathis near the 18-yard line. Mathis one-touch controlled and expertly left-footed the ball into the right-hand corner from 15 yards.

Thereafter the Koreans put the USA under steady pressure, but the defense and especially Brad Friedel was mostly equal to the task. An exception was when Jeff Agoos brought down Hwang Sun-Hong in the area for a penalty kick. Friedel swatted away the good penalty kick from Lee Eul Yong (headed for the upper left corner), and South Korea could not take advantage of the favorable rebound to Kim Nam Il, either. The USA would exit the half leading 1-0 and breathing a sigh of relief.

Friedel was retested immediately after the break, when he was forced to make a spectacular right-handed save from Seol Ki Hyeon from close range. The inevitable Korean goal came in the 78th minute as Lee Eul Yong's free kick from mid-field found a leaping Ahn Jung Hwan who head-flicked the ball from 7 yards out into the right-side netting. The Italians should have taken note of this move: a nearly identical disguised head-flick by Ahn won the South Korea-Italy game in the second round.

South Korea went for the win as Lee skillfully dribbled along the left end line and pulled the ball back for Choi Yong Soo, who lifted the ball too high due to the velocity of the pass. The hosts had to settle for one point in a match that they probably had the better chances.

South Korea: Lee Woon Jae, Choi Jin Chul, Kim Tae Young, Bo Hong Myung, Kim Nam Il, Yoo Sang Chul (Choi Yong Soo, 70), Lee Eul Yong, Park Ji Sung (Chun Soo Lee, 38), Seol Ki Hyeon, Hwang Sun Hong (Ahn Jung Hwan, 56), Song Chong Gug.

United States: Brad Friedel, Anthony Sanneh, Jeff Agoos, Eddie Pope, Frankie Hejduk, John O'Brien, Claudio Reyna, DaMarcus Beasley (Eddie Lewis, 75), Landon Donovan, Clint Mathis (Josh Wolff, 82), Brian Mc Bride.

Goals: South Korea - Ahn Jung Hwan 78; **United States** - Clint Mathis 24.

Referee: Urs Meier (Switzerland).

Men of the Match: Ahn Jung Hwan and Clint Mathis for not wasting their chances, and Brad Friedel for the penalty save and solid job in the net.

32 Portugal 4 – 0 Poland   Portugal outclass Poland

June 10: Jeonju, South Korea

Portuguese striker Pauleta was the matchmaker with a well-taken hat trick over Poland in a Korean rainstorm. Pauleta had some good looks at goal before he was able to capitalize on a Joao Pinto pass in the penalty box in the 14th minute; cutting to his right he powered a shot from 12 yards past Polish keeper Jerzy Dudek at the near post.

The Portuguese offense was productive again after a 60th minute substitution that brought Rui Costa in the game; he started the move that led to Luis Figo centering the ball for Pauleta to tap in from

4 yards in the 65th minute. In the 77th minute Rui Costa again threaded a pass to Pauleta who after disengaging his marker, left-footed past Dudek from 12 yards.

Rui Costa scored at the end with a sliding re-direction of Nuno Capucho's cross from 6 yards out, capping an impressive Portuguese win in difficult climatic conditions.

Portugal: Vitor Baia, Jorge Costa, Fernando Couto, Rui Jorge, Luis Figo, Sergio Conceição (Nuno Capucho, 69), Paulo Bento, Nuno Frechaut (Beto, 64), Armando Petit, Joao Pinto (Rui Costa, 60), Pedro Pauleta.

Poland: Jerzy Dudek, Michal Zewlakow (Tomasz Rzasa, 71), Tomasz Hajto, Tomasz Waldoch, Piotr Swierczewski, Radoslaw Kaluzny (Arkadiusz Bak, 16), Jacek Krzynowek, Marek Kozminski, Pawel Kryszalowicz, Emmanuel Olisadebe, Maciej Zurawski (Marcin Zewlakow, 56).

Goals: Portugal - Pedro Pauleta 14, 65, 77, Rui Costa 87.

Referee: Hugh Dallas (Scotland).

Man of the Match: Pedro Pauleta was the hat-trick hero for Portugal.

47 Portugal 0 – 1 South Korea: Portugal shocked and eliminated
June 14: Incheon, South Korea

Portugal needed to win this match to control their own destiny and guarantee advancement to the next round, but South Korea came out full of vigor. Hustling the ball quickly around the field, they were able to keep Portugal's potent offense back on their heels.

In the 27th minute, João Pinto threw a near-crippling double-leg tackle from behind on Park Ji Sung, and was justifiably sent off by Argentine referee Angel Sanchez. Portugal protested the red-card vigorously, to the point where team captain Fernando Couto took the referee's face in his hands, and Pinto got a parting shot to the referee's stomach. Couto was very lucky not to join Pinto on the sidelines after manhandling the referee, and Pinto later received a six-month suspension from FIFA for his violence. The send-off hampered Portugal's efforts further, and soon after, Pauleta's good chance was wasted as he lofted the ball over the goal from 22 yards after breaking in on goal alone. Seol Ki Hyeon came close twice for South Korea in the first half.

By half time both teams surely had heard that the United States was losing 2-0 to Poland. If that result stood and Portugal and South Korea tied, both would go through to the second round at the expense of the USA.

After half-time, however, it was clear that South Korea would play to win in front of their fans. With a massive crowd roaring them on, they began to create better chances. In the 66th minute Beto was dismissed for a second yellow card for a foul on Lee Young Pyo, leaving Portugal with only nine men on the field. South Korea pressed forward, and success finally came in the 70th minute. Park Ji Sung received a left-sided cross-field pass in the right side of the penalty box, trapped it on his chest, saw Sérgio Conceição coming from his left, looped it past Conceição with a right-footed juggle, then volleyed with his left through Vítor Baía's legs from 6 yards out. This spectacular piece of dynamic ball-juggling skill put the Koreans up 1-0. It was one of the best goals of the 2002 World Cup, and somewhat reminiscent of Dennis Bergcamp's superb strike against Argentina in the 1998 World Cup.

Portugal was now desperate, and went on the attack as much as possible – and almost succeeded! First Figo came close to the left post on a 20-yard free kick (75th minute), then substitute Nuno Gomes missed a redirection from 6 yards in the 85th minute. In the 90th minute, Sérgio Conceição beat the keeper and hit the left post on a superb right-footed volley from 15 yards, and then tested keeper Lee Woon Jae after a perfect cutback move at the left side of the 6-yard box.

Where had the Portuguese been hiding all this brilliance? They could have used it when the teams were at even-strength. In the meantime, Vitor Baia was kept busy by South Korean forays in a thrilling finish. But then time was up and South Korea had won Group D with two wins and a draw.

By South Korea beating Portugal, one of the pre-tournament favorites was finished.

South Korea: Lee Woon-Jae, Choi Jin-Cheul, Kim Nam-il, Yoo Sang-Chul, Kim Tae-Young, Seol Ki-Hyeon, Lee Young-Pyo, Ahn Jung-Hwan (Lee Chun-Soo 90), Hong Myung-Bo, Park Ji-Sung, Song Chong-Gug.

Portugal: Vitor Baia, Jorge Costa, Fernando Couto, Luis Figo, Joao Pinto, Pauleta (Jorge Andrade 68), Paulo Bento, Sergio Conceição, Petit (Nuno Gomes 77), Beto, Rui Jorge (Abel Xavier 73).

Goals: South Korea: Park Ji-Sung 70.

Referee: Angel Sanchez (Argentina).

Man of the Match: Park Ji Sung for getting the superbly inventive and finished goal.

48 Poland 3 – 1 USA: Poland's quality shows too late
June 14: Daejeon, South Korea

Poland only had pride to win in this game as they had already been eliminated from the second round, having lost their first two games by conceding six goals and scoring none. They made six changes in their starting lineup and came out in blazing form.

Emmanuel Olisadebe headed a corner kick to the near post in the 3rd minute, tracked his own rebound as his marker fell down, and slammed the ball in off the crossbar near the right corner from 6 yards out.

The USA came right back with Landon Donovan nodding in from 4 yards after a rebound in the 4th minute, but the goal was disallowed for a push which appeared to have been legal shoulder to shoulder contact. Buoyed by their good fortune, Poland again attacked the soft central defense and immediately scored on a low cross from the left that Paweł Kryszałowicz converted cleverly to the near post. The game was five minutes old and the USA was already down 0-2.

This game could have gotten much uglier for the United States, as in the 29th minute Maciej Żurawski shot from the middle of the box and Friedel could only redirect onto the left post. Meanwhile, the USA wasn't getting the same quality chances as Poland.

After the half, Friedel again had to make a point blank save, this time on Cezary Kucharski running in from the left. Then new substitute Marcin Żewłakow scored on his first touch, as his header from 4 yards out flashed by Friedel in the 66th minute. In the 77th minute, Tony Sanneh gave up a contested ball for a penalty, which Friedel incredibly saved to make him 2 for 2 saved penalty kicks in the first round.

Finally, in the 83rd minute, Landon Donovan took a head flick-on from Clint Mathis and expertly side-foot volleyed into the right corner of the goal from 12 yards out to salvage some pride in a game in which the USA was outplayed. The USA was fortunate to progress to the second round because of South Korea's surprise win over Portugal.

Poland: Radoslaw Majdan, Tomasz Klos (Tomasz Waldoch, 89), Jacek Zielinski, Arkadiusz Glowacki, Maciej Murawski, Jacek Krzynowek, Marek Kozminski, Cezary Kucharski (Marcin Zewlakow, 65), Pawel Kryszalowicz, Emmanuel Olisadebe (Pawel Sibik, 86), Maciej Zurawski.

United States: Brad Friedel, Frankie Hejduk, Jeff Agoos (DaMarcus Beasley, 36), Eddie Pope, John O'Brien, Earnie Stewart (Cobi Jones, 68), Claudio Reyna, Landon Donovan, Anthony Sanneh, Clint Mathis, Brian Mc Bride (Joe-Max Moore, 58).

Goals: **Poland** Emmanuel Olisadebe 3, Pawel Kryszalowicz 5, Marcin Zewlakow 66.
 United States Landon Donovan 83.

Referee: Lu Jun (China PR)

Man of the Match: Jacek Krzynówek, for creating the midfield runs and setting up the goals.

Group E: Germany, Saudi Arabia, Ireland, Cameroon

Total score: 77   [3rd hardest group by cumulative rankings]

Germany was very lucky that after qualifying behind England in Europe's Group 9, they had a much easier World Cup Group draw than England (who was in Group F, the "Group of Death"). Ireland managed to finish behind Portugal but over Holland in Europe Group 2, and then beat Iran in a home-and-away series to qualify.

Saudi Arabia was the best of their weak Asian group comprising Vietnam, Bangladesh, and Mongolia, (scoring 30 goals and allowing none), and in the second round qualified over Iran.

African champions Cameroon won their African Group 1 easily to qualify. Cameroon had also won the Olympic championship in 2000, and had a good group of young players with experience.

E1. Germany [11]

Germany finished second behind England in qualifying on goal difference, but then beat Ukraine in a playoff to qualify for their fifteenth World Cup Finals appearance.

Three time winners of the World Cup (1954, 1974, 1990 as West Germany), Germany had been going through a low period in their football history. Germany was unsettled after being pasted at home 5-1 by England in the qualifiers, and their pre-Cup ranking of 11th in the world was a very low ranking for this perennial world power. Still, given the German presence in world football history, underestimating the German potential could be fatal.

Germany's coach was Rudi Völler, the ex-Germany striker with eight World Cup goals in three World Cup competitions. Völler brought a physically imposing team, as ten players were 188 cm (6'2" – six feet and two inches) or taller, making them the tallest team at the World Cup. Most of Völler's starting team was home-league based, a rarity for any European team.

E2. Saudi Arabia [34]

Saudi Arabia qualified in the tougher Asia Group A over Iran and Iraq. This was their third World Cup Finals appearance, having reached the second round in their first World Cup in 1994, but lacking the same success in 1998. The Saudis had had some success in pre-Cup friendlies against Uruguay and South Africa.

Coach Al-Johar fielded only Saudi-based players, as none were featured in any European league. Therefore, international experience was limited, which would be tested in the white-hot cauldron of the international World Cup.

As the lowest ranked team in Group E, Saudi Arabia would have difficulty achieving what they did in 1994.

E3. Ireland [15]

Ireland finished below Portugal (on goal difference only) but above Holland in Europe qualifying Group 2, then had to defeat Iran in a home-and-away series to qualify for the Cup. This was their third World Cup Finals appearance, and they aimed to match their 1990 quarterfinals accomplishment.

Coach Mick McCarthy fielded an all-English club based team that was to be led by Manchester United midfielder Roy Keane, but Keane left the team before the first game, allegedly because of poor team logistics. Ireland was not permitted to replace Keane, as it was too close to the World Cup matches, and as a result Ireland was allowed only 22 players.

Ireland's team morale remained steadfast and they were eager to demonstrate to the world their football skills, and showcase budding stars such as Robbie Keane (no relation to Roy Keane) and Damien Duff.

E4. Cameroon [17]

Cameroon qualified for their fifth World Cup Finals by easily winning Africa Group 1. They, like Ireland, were also aiming to match their 1990 quarterfinals achievement (their only advancement to the second phase).

Cameroon had just come off winning their second African Nations Cup in a row (by penalties over Senegal), and had a long unbeaten string after losing to Japan in the 2001 Confederations Cup in Niigata. Cameroon coincidentally would start their 2002 World Cup adventure against Ireland in the same city.

Coach Winifred Schafer drew on a large talent pool of Europe based players for Cameroon's team. Still, Cameroon would have to overcome either Ireland or their ex-colonial rulers Germany to pass onto the next round. Heading their attack were the experienced and powerful Patrick Mboma (who should have been 2002 African Player of the Year) and the young and fleet Samuel Eto'o.

OPENING GAME of the Japan-Hosted Matches of the 2002 World Cup

02 Ireland 1 – 1 Cameroon: Ireland and Cameroon earn a point

June 1: Niigata, Japan

This was the opening match of the thirty-two games of the 2002 World Cup played in Japan. Cameroon was making their fourth consecutive World Cup appearance, one of only nine teams that accomplished that in the 2002 World Cup.

With Irish captain Roy Keane sent home for insubordination to manager Mick McCarthy, Ireland was presumably at a mental disadvantage against the soccer stylists of the African continent. Indeed, Cameroon dominated the first half, with Eto'o a constant threat out on the right flank, exposing the defense several times for pace and cleverness. After two close attempts, another Eto'o move led to the Indomitable Lions' goal; he raced to the right end line, nutmegged his defender, and pulled back for Mboma, who twisted his body from right to left to control the pass and then left-foot it home from 8 yards in the 39th minute.

Ireland recovered well after the break and had the better of the play in the second half. Ireland's goal came in the 52nd minute on a counterattack as Kilbane's cross was weakly cleared by the defense, and Matt Holland superbly one-timed the ball into the left corner of the goal from 25 yards.

Cameroon goalkeeper Alioum Boukar was kept busy in the second half, and was stretched when Robbie Keane's drive bounced off the far post in the 84th minute. Both teams earned a fair point in an entertaining match.

Ireland: Shay Given, Gary Kelly, Steve Staunton, Ian Harte (Stephen Reid, 78), Gary Breen, Jason McAteer (Steve Finnan, 46), Matt Holland, Kevin Kilbane, Mark Kinsella, Damien Duff, Robbie Keane.
Cameroon: Alioum Boukar, Raymond Kalla, Rigobert Song, Bill Tchato, Geremi Njitap, Pierra Wome, Marc-Vivien Foe, Salomon Olembe, Lauren Etame Mayer, Samuel Eto'o, Patrick Mboma (Patrick Suffo, 69).
Goals: Ireland - Matt Holland 52, **Cameroon** - Patrick Mboma 39.
Referee: Toru Kamikawa (Japan).
Man of the Match: Ireland – Matt Holland for his ambitious strike, and Cameroon – Alioum Boukar, who made several spectacular saves to keep the game safe.

04 Germany 8 – 0 Saudi Arabia: Professionals versus Amateurs

June 1: Sapporo, Japan

The final score was 8-0, but tragically for Saudi Arabia it could have been more. This game was the largest German victory in World Cup history, as they scored four goals in each half.

The first German goal originated with Michael Ballack's cross from the left flank. Carsten Jancker only got part of the ball on an attempted bicycle kick, but Miroslav Klose thrust himself forward like a hungry egret, nodding the ball to the far post.

The second goal was similar, again Ballack crossing and Klose powering over the defense to head in. The third came from the left side again, this time Christian Ziege crossing and Ballack heading home. The fourth came from the right, with a neat ball-heel flick from Klose serving up Jancker in front of the goal where he converted. All four goals came from 8 yards out, as Saudi Arabia defended that space poorly.

After the half, Klose again headed in from 8 yards for an *all-header hat trick*, but this time from a right-sided cross. Defender Linke got the sixth goal, rising to head a corner kick in from the right side from 4 yards out. Substitute Oliver Bierhoff fired an opportunistic left-footed shot from 27 yards out for the seventh, and Bernd Schneider closed the scoring in injury-time with a 23 meter free-kick banana shot into the upper-right corner.

A useful first game for Germany to find their rhythm, but Saudi Arabia looked more like an amateur side than a World Cup team.

Germany: Oliver Kahn, Thomas Linke, Christoph Metzelder, Carsten Ramelow, (Jens Jeremies, 46), Christian Ziege, Dietmar Hamann, Michael Ballack, Bernd Schneider, Torsten Frings, Carsten Jancker, (Oliver Bierhoff, 67), Miroslav Klose (Oliver Neuville, 77).

Saudi Arabia: Mohammed Al Deayea, Redha Tukar, Abdullah Sulaiman Zubromawi, Ahmed Dukhi Al Dossary, Hussein Sulimani, Mohammed Noor, Khamis Alowairan Al Dosari, (Ibrahim Al Shahrani, 46), Abdullah Alwaked Al Shahrani, Nawaf Al Temyat , (Abdulaziz Al Khathran, 46), Sami Al Jaber, Al Hassan Al Yami (Abdullah Jumaan Al Dosary, 77).

Goals: Germany: Miroslav Klose 20, 25, 69, Michael Ballack 40, Carsten Jancker 45, Thomas Linke 73, Oliver Bierhoff 84, Bernd Schneider 90.

Referee: Ubaldo Aquino (Paraguay).

Man of the Match: Miroslav Klose for his remarkable triple-header game and neat back-heel assist to Jancker.

17 Germany 1 – 1 Ireland: German grief and Irish relief
June 5: Ibaraki, Japan

Miroslav Klose headed in a cross from the penalty spot delivered by playmaker Michael Ballack to stake the Germans to an early lead in the 19th minute. Meanwhile, Ireland was threatening through Damien Duff and Matt Holland, the latter making a long-range shot reminiscent of his strike against Cameroon that skipped just wide of the German goal.

The Germans had another good chance before half time as Dietmar Hamann had his shot kick-saved by Irish keeper Shay Given, who left a rebound to Carsten Jancker. Jancker was offside, but Given still got up and stopped Jancker's shot.

German keeper Oliver Kahn made one of the saves of the tournament after the half, as Kevin Kilbane's clever head-pass put Duff through one-on-one with the keeper. Duff shot towards the far post, but Kahn somehow advanced rapidly and the well-hit ball was redirected away from goal by the keeper's body.

Jancker broke into the penalty area alone, and similar to Kahn's save Given charged out and forced Jancker to chip just wide of goal. Klose wasted a chance to score from a Torsten Frings cross as his header sailed over the bar.

Robbie Keane threatened twice with swift run-ins on goal before the end of the match. In his first action in the 84th minute, he was only able to get his toe on the ball and Kahn saved. The second opportunity came in injury-time as Germany tried to run out the clock for the win. Niall Quinn laid the ball on for Keane again with a head-flick off a long pass, but this time Keane was able to power the ball off Kahn's arms into goal from six yards out.

Germany could not hold their early lead into injury time, and both teams earned a well-deserved point.

Germany: Oliver Kahn, Thomas Linke, Christoph Metzelder, Carsten Ramelow, Christian Ziege, Dietmar Hamann, Michael Ballack, Bernd Schneider (Jens Jeremies, 90), Torsten Frings, Carsten Jancker (Oliver Bierhoff, 75), Miroslav Klose (Marco Bode, 85).

Ireland: Shay Given, Steve Finnan, Ian Harte (Stephen Reid, 73), Steve Staunton (Kenny Cunningham, 88) , Gary Breen, Gary Kelly (Niall Quinn, 73), Matt Holland, Kevin Kilbane, Mark Kinsella, Damien Duff, Robbie Keane.

Goals: Germany - Miroslav Klose 19, **Ireland** - Robbie Keane 90.

Referee: Kim Milton Nielsen (Denmark).

Men of the Match: Robby Keane and Miroslav Klose for their expertly taken chances.

19 Cameroon 1 – 0 Saudi Arabia   Cameroon wins on Eto'o strike
June 6: Saitama, Japan

A more organized and resilient Saudi Arabian team turned up to play against Cameroon than had performed against Germany.

Cameroon was surprised when Saudi forward Obaid Al Dosari nearly headed in an Abdullah Alwaked Al Shahrani cross in the 9th minute, but the ball went over the crossbar.

Newly alerted Cameroon then scored twice, as Patrick Mboma dribbled the goalkeeper in the 12th minute and Lauren headed in during the 43rd minute, only to have them both annulled for offside.

After the half-time break Samuel Eto'o had two chances to break the scoreless tie. In the 52nd minute substitute Salomon Olembe broke through the Saudi Arabia defense and unselfishly passed to Eto'o whose over struck shot missed the goal. Thirteen minutes later Eto'o got it right when he controlled a cross, brought Al Deayea off his line, and pushed the ball past him into the goal with the outside of his right foot from 16 yards out.

Just before Eto'o's goal Saudi Arabia's Al Temyat made a nice move and forced Cameroon keeper Alioum to dive to his left to save. Saudi Arabia continued to push forward as best they could, but with this second loss they were eliminated after the first round for the second successive World Cup.

Cameroon: Alioum Boukar; Bill Tchato, Pierre Wome (Pierre Njanka 84), Rigobert Song, Raymond Kalla, Geremi Njitap; Lauren, Marc-Vivien Foe, Daniel Ngom Kome (Salomon Olembe 46), Samuel Eto'o, Patrick Mboma (Pius Ndiefi 74).

Saudi Arabia: Mohammed Al-Deayea; Mohammed Al-Jahani, Redha Tukar, Abdullah Sulaiman Zubromawi (Abdullah Gaman Al-Dosary 72), Fouzi Al-Shehri, Hussein Sulimani; Ibrahim Al Shahrani, Abdulaziz Al-Khathran (Mohammed Noor 87), Abdullah Alwaked Al-Shahrani, Nawaf Al-Temyat, Obaid Al Dosari (Al Hasan Al-Yami 35).

Cameroon: Samuel Eto'o, 65.

Referee: Terje Hauge (Nor).

Man of the Match: Samuel Eto'o for his constant attacks leading to the lone goal.

35 Cameroon 0 – 2 Germany   Fouls obscure good football
June 11: Shizuoka, Japan

Reigning Olympic and African champions Cameroon needed to tie to have a chance to go through to the second round.

Both of these ambitious teams went all-out to win, but the match ended up a foul-plagued affair that the referee attempted to control by freely handing out disciplinary cards. Each team received eight (!) yellow cards and had one man dismissed, a new World Cup disciplinary card record.

The first half produced good chances from both teams. Michael Ballack had the first serious effort, but his shot wandered wide of Boukar Alioum's goal. Oliver Kahn continued to save nearly every one-on-one situation as he robbed Salomon Olembe's initial shot and rebound. Cameroon followed this opportunity with Pierre Wome's 25-yard free kick being punched clear by Kahn, and Rigobert Song's close-in header going just wide at the near post.

Alioum then turned Christian Ziege's free kick destined for the upper left-hand corner over the crossbar, and the Germans became frustrated at their inability to score. Carsten Ramelow received his second yellow card in the 40th minute and was sent off to leave Germany with ten men. The half ended scoreless.

Five minutes after the break, Miroslav Klose showed that he was a creator as well as a scorer. On the right side of the pitch he took on four defenders and slipped a perfect pass for substitute Marco Bode to left-foot into the right side netting from 11 yards out.

Cameroon's momentum seemed affected by the goal occurring when they had a one-man advantage. They finally were able to challenge again in the 73rd minute when Geremi's free kick found Lauren, whose 12-yard header bounced off the left post. Patrick Mboma desperately put the rebound on goal but it was aimed directly at the relieved Kahn.

Referee Lopez kept producing yellow cards, and in the 77th minute Patrick Suffo was sent off, severely damaging Cameroon's final attempts to tie and qualify. Indeed, Germany was energized to be on equal terms, and earned a second goal as Ballack crossed to an unmarked Klose who made no mistake with his fifth headed goal of the first round from 5 yards out.

Alioum had no chance on Klose's goal, but he made nice saves on Ballack and Jeremies to keep the score respectable. Once again Germany found a way to beat a quality opponent, even being a man down for much of the match.

Cameroon: Boukar Alioum, Bill Tchato (Patrick Suffo, 53), Rigobert Song, Raymond Kalla, Lauren Etame Mayer, Pierre Wome, Geremi Njitap, Marc-Vivien Foe, Salomon Olembe (Daniel Ngom Kome, 64), Samuel Eto'o, Patrick Mboma.
Germany: Oliver Kahn, Thomas Linke, Christoph Metzelder, Carsten Ramelow, Christian Ziege, Dietmar Hamann, Michael Ballack, Bernd Schneider (Jens Jeremies, 80), Torsten Frings, Carsten Jancker (Marco Bode, 46), Miroslav Klose (Oliver Neuville, 84).
Goals: Germany - Marco Bode 50, Miroslav Klose 79.
Referee: Antonio Lopez (Spain).
Man of the Match: Miroslav Klose for assisting on the first goal and netting the second.

36 Saudi Arabia 0 – 3 IrelandIreland pass to second round as usual
June 11: Yokohama, Japan

Ireland had never failed at the Group stage in the World Cup, always going through to the next round. At the same time, Ireland had incredibly never scored *more than one goal* in a World Cup Finals match. They would be aiming for multiple goals in this game, for if Cameroon tied Germany then advancement from the Group would come down to goal difference between Cameroon and Ireland.

Ireland started out with an intense effort to score the vital first goal in rainy conditions. The pressure paid off in the 7th minute as Matt Holland's floating cross from the left found Robbie Keane, whose impressive volley from 15 yards zoomed past Saudi Arabia goalkeeper Mohammed Al Deayea. The match evened out soon thereafter and the Saudis created some credible chances, the best of which was when Mohammed Al Jahani had a clear shot that Ireland goalkeeper Shay Given covered well.

Ireland refocused and continued searching for their second goal after the half. They were successful in the 67th minute when Steve Staunton's cross from the left was remarkably redirected into the goal by an extended Gary Breen from 9 yards out.

Damian Duff finally made his energetic runs pay off in the 87th minute when he rocketed a shot at Al Deayea from 14 yards, but the keeper could not hold on in the wet conditions. Duff ran to the sidelines and clasped his hands together in a prayerful salute that Ireland had found the path to multiple goals and entered the second round.

Saudi Arabia: Mohammed Al Deayea, Mohammed Al Jahani (Ahmed Dukhi Al Dossary 79), Redha Tukar, Abdullah Sulaiman Zubromawi (Abdullah Jumaan Al Dosary, 68), Fouzi Al Shehri, Hussein Sulimani, Ibrahim Al Shahrani, Abdulaziz Al Khathran (Mohammad Al Shlhoub, 67), Khamis Alowairan Al Dosari, Nawaf Al Temyat, Al Hassan Al Yami.
Republic of Ireland: Shay Given, Steve Finnan, Ian Harte (Niall Quinn, 46), Steve Staunton, Gary Breen, Gary Kelly (Jason McAteer, 80), Matt Holland, Kevin Kilbane, Mark Kinsella (Lee Carsley, 89), Damien Duff, Robbie Keane.
Goals: Republic of Ireland - Robbie Keane 7, Gary Breen 62, Damien Duff 87.
Referee: Ndoye Falla (Senegal).
Man of the Match: Robbie Keane for his wonderful early strike.

Group F: Argentina, Nigeria, England, Sweden
Total score: 60   [Hardest group by cumulative rankings]

This group contained the "best" teams as assessed by FIFA rankings, and came to be known as the "Group of Death." Despite proclamations by the four participating teams of "wanting to play the best," it would obviously be better to play "the best" in the second round after already qualifying from the first round.

It was especially bad luck for Argentina and England. Argentina had far outperformed Brazil in the qualifiers, and England qualified over Germany, even beating them 5-1 in Germany, but both had a much more difficult draw than either of their vanquished competitors.

Sweden was rebuilding but is always disciplined and dangerous, and qualified over emerging power Turkey in Europe's Group 4.

Nigeria has tremendous players, but the problems are usually preparation and organization of their overseas players, and a coherent game plan by a settled coach. But Nigeria was Olympic champion in 1996, and those players had now had six years of professional seasoning in top leagues.

Argentina was playing at such a level that they ran away with the South American CONMEBOL qualifying, the first time ever that Brazil did not win the group. Their depth was so strong that Argentina's goal leader Gabriel Batistuta didn't make the starting eleven for most of the qualifiers.

England was just starting to jell under Swedish coach Sven-Göran Eriksson, but this was a nightmare group for them. England had not beaten Sweden since 1968, and many of the Nigerian stars played in England and were familiar with the English style of football. Argentina was England's biggest nemesis ever in World Cup play, for both political and football reasons.[3]

F1. Argentina [2]

Argentina qualified top of the CONMEBOL region for the first time, easily outdistancing their archrival Brazil by thirteen (43 to 30) points. This was Argentina's thirteenth World Cup Finals, having twice been champions (1978 and 1986) and twice runner-ups (1930 and 1990). Only three times had they failed to pass through to the second phase.

This would be a nightmare Argentina team for 1998 World Cup coach Daniel Passarella, as ten players had Sampson-sized hair of the type sported by Pascrell's ex-teammate and 1978 World Cup hero Mario Kempes. German Burgos, Diego Placente, Juan Pablo Sorin, Mauricio Pochettino, Matias Almeyda, Gabriel Batistuta, Ariel Ortega, Claudio Husain, Hernan Crespo, and old-timer Claudio Caniggia (1990 & 1994 World Cups) all had the rock-star hair styles that would have failed Pascrell's 1998 "short-hair" test (Chapter 3).

In contrast to Brazil, whose players often use a diminutive or adopted "stage-name" on the back of their shirts, Argentine players have colorful nicknames. Batistuta is "Batigol", Veron is "Bruja" (The Witch), Lopez is "Piojo" (The Flea), and Simeone is "Cholo" (somebody with mixed Spanish-indigenous heritage).

One big story for Argentina was whether goalmeister Gabriel Batistuta or his protégé Hernan Crespo would see more playing time, as coach Marcelo Bielsa was convinced that the two greatest modern Argentine strikers were incompatible on the field. Too much was

---

[3] The Argentina – England rivalry has been a passionate affair. The 1966 World Cup match won by England resulted in bad feelings after English coach Ramsey called the Argentineans "animals," the 1986 match was won by Argentina after Maradona's "Hand of God" cheat goal followed by his "Goal of the Century" (and was seen as vindication by some for Argentina's loss of the 1982 Falkland/Malvinas War to England), and the 1998 Cup match resulted in David Beckham's dismissal and Argentina "winning" on penalty kicks after extra time.

made of this unproven negative, whereas Brazil made a positive by playing their two great offensive weapons Ronaldo and Rivaldo together. If Argentina made a poor showing, this might be the biggest personnel mistake since Brazil left Romário home for the 1998 World Cup Final.

Bielsa also left two young and potent offensive weapons at home: striker Javier Saviola (Barcelona) and midfield wizard Juan Roman Riquelme (Boca Juniors). Both had recently won the South American Player of the Year award; Saviola was the 1999 recipient and Riquelme the 2001 winner. The emphasis on older players at the expense of quality younger players left the Argentine squad with less talent and energy.

F2. Nigeria [27]

Nigeria had a tough time qualifying for this Cup, as they pipped an excellent George Weah led Liberian team by only one point. This was their third consecutive World Cup Finals appearance, and they had reached the second round in each of their first two appearances.

Nigeria usually has a wealth of talent but often lacks direction by the national team administration. By changing coaches mere months before the World Cup, some established players were forced out while newcomers were given a quick chance.

Back in control after 18 years, recycled national team coach Adegboye Onigbinde used the few preparatory pre-World Cup matches to test new players instead of consolidating the team. The result was a more defensive and less adventurous and skillful team than prior versions. One only hopes to see a fully prepped and manned Nigeria squad in a future World Cup.

F3. England [12]

England qualified by finishing at the top of Europe Group 9 on goal difference over Germany. This was their eleventh World Cup, having advanced to the second phase in all but two Finals. England was World Cup champion at home in 1966.

Swedish coach Sven-Göran Eriksson was the first non-British coach of England, and the hopes of a nation rested on his ability to mold the players into a formidable team. As former coach of Lazio in Italy, he would be facing some of his former players, notably Diego Simeone and Juan Sebastián Verón of Argentina.

Eriksson claimed he would have England attacking, and it was therefore strange that he chose eight defenders at the expense of some experienced creative and offensive midfielders; Steve McManaman of Real Madrid would have added much-needed link talent. Veteran striker Alan Shearer came off a superb year with 23 goals but had ruled himself out of the World Cup; Eriksson should have convinced him that England needed his stellar form if the oft-fragile Michael Owen was off the pitch.

F4. Sweden [19]

Sweden finished unbeaten and at the top of Europe Group 4 to qualify for the Cup Finals. This was Sweden's tenth World Cup Finals appearance, having advanced to the second phase in all but three. Sweden was World Cup runner-up at home in 1958, and third-place in 1950 and 1994.

Many people assumed Sweden was an inferior football team when compared to England. Actually, England had not beaten Sweden *in thirty-four years*, going 0-3-6 in their last nine meetings. Perhaps England thought hiring a Swedish coach would do the trick?

Sweden usually has a combination of spectacular and dependable talent. Defender Patrik Andersson, midfielder Fredrik Ljungberg, and Golden Boot winner striker Henrik Larsson represented the spectacular. Andersson was unfortunately ruled out of the Cup with injury, and Ljungberg played hurt. Still, Sweden had good depth and technique, and most importantly a cohesive team spirit instilled by co-coaches Lars Lagerback and Tommy Soderberg.

05 England 1 – 1 Sweden: England fails to break their Swedish curse
June 2: Saitama, Japan

England would not break their thirty-four year Swedish no-win streak. Although England controlled more play in the first half, Sweden dominated in the second.

Sol Campbell chose an opportune time to score his first England goal, as he headed home a David Beckham corner kick from 6 yards in the 24th minute. Ashley Cole then tested Swedish keeper Magnus Hedman, while Henrik Larsson and Marcus Allbäck worried English netman David Seaman.

After the half, a poor English clearance allowed Niclas Alexandersson to dribble into the penalty arc and launch a left-footed rocket, which zipped past Seaman's touch to equalize from 22 yards.

Teddy Lucic tested Seaman twice later in the second half, while Emile Heskey had two chances late for England that were unsuccessful.

England was hoping to finally snatch a win against Sweden, but once again the Swedes proved their equals.

England: David Seaman, Danny Mills, Rio Ferdinand, Sol Campbell, Ashley Cole, David Beckham (Kieron Dyer 64), Owen Hargreaves, Paul Scholes, Emile Heskey, Darius Vassell (Joe Cole 74), Michael Owen

Sweden: Magnus Hedman, Olof Mellberg, Andreas Jakobsson, Johan Mjallby, Teddy Lucic, Niclas Alexandersson, Tobias Linderoth, Magnus Svensson (Anders Svensson , Freddie Ljungberg, Henrik Larsson, Marcus Allbäck (Andreas Andersson 80).

Goals: England - Campbell 24; **Sweden** - Alexandersson 59.

Referee: Carlos Simon (Brazil).

Men of the Match: Sol Campbell and Niclas Alexandersson for their fine finishing.

07 Argentina 1 – 0 Nigeria: Batigol heads lone goal
June 2: Ibaraki, Japan

This was the first World Cup match between these teams since the 1994 World Cup, when Argentina won 2-1 with both Claudio Caniggia goals assisted by Diego Maradona. That was Maradona's last international for Argentina, as he was subsequently suspended from international play for a drug violation. Caniggia never played a minute for Argentina in the 2002 tournament, but he did manage to get red carded from the bench during the Sweden game.

Like the 1994 game there was a lot of covering in midfield precluding many serious goal chances. With Gabriel Batistuta, Ariel Ortega, and Juan Sorin getting the best Argentine chances, Jay Jay Okocha came the closest for Nigeria.

An ambitious second half header from a near impossible angle one yard from the end line by Gabriel Batistuta was the winner, "Batigol" meeting Juan Veron's corner kick as it arrived beyond the far post. That was Batistuta's tenth World Cup Final goal in his third World Cup Finals competition. With this win, Argentina was able to approach their big game against England with confidence.

Argentina: Pablo Cavallero, Mauricio Pochettino, Walter Samuel, Diego Placente, Juan Pablo Sorin, Javier Zanetti, Ariel Ortega, Juan Sebastian Veron, (Pablo Aimar, 78'), Diego Simeone, Claudio Lopez, (Cristian Gonzalez, 46'), Gabriel Batistuta, (Hernan Crespo, 81').

Nigeria: Ike Shorunmu, Joseph Yobo, Celestine Babayaro, Isaac Okoronkwo, Taribo West, Efetobore Sodje, (Justice Christopher, 73'), Austin 'Jay Jay' Okocha, Garba Lawal, Nwankwo Kanu, (Pius Ikedia, 48'), Bartholomew Ogbeche, Julius Aghahowa.

Goals: Argentina - Gabriel Batistuta 63.

Referee: Gilles Veissiere (France).

Man of the Match: Gabriel Batistuta for his opportunistic headed goal from an improbable angle.

21 Sweden 2 – 1 Nigeria Sweden escapes with a win
June 7: Kobe, Japan

Henrik Larsson had debuted in the 1994 World Cup with long blonde dreadlocks. Now bald-headed and fresh from several stellar seasons with Scottish champions Celtic (including a 50 goal *Golden Boot* season), he continued his world-class performances scoring both of Sweden's goals.

Sweden had several good chances early, and although Johan Mjallby's header beat Nigerian keeper Ike Shorunmu it was cleared by defender Justice Christopher.

Nigeria came at Sweden on the other end as Julius Aghahowa scored a remarkable leaping header from 6 yards after an ambitious right-sided cross from Joseph Yobo in the 27th minute. His goal celebration was just as entertaining, as he executed six successive handsprings rounded off by a full flip.

Sweden leveled the score eight minutes later as midfield creator Freddie Ljungberg threaded a pass to Larsson, who managed to maneuver and toe-poke home his goal from 12 yards surrounded by three defenders.

Sweden almost gave up a goal in the 40th minute on a freak clearance by Teddy Lucic who hit Mjallby in error, and the ball crashed off the Swedish post. The half ended tied 1-1.

After the break Larsson was pulled down by Ifeanyi Udeze in the 18-yard box for a penalty in the 63rd minute. Larsson made a good shot to the upper left-hand corner that Shorunmu almost made a tremendous save on, but the ball ran through his hands for the winning score.

Nigeria still fought for the tie in the remaining time, and almost succeeded. John Utaka rounded keeper Magnus Hedman but his shot was cleared off by Mjallby. Finally, Yobo had his low shot come off the left post.

Nigeria was terribly unlucky to come away without a point after hitting two posts and forcing two clearances off the Swedish line.

Sweden: Magnus Hedman, Olof Mellberg, Johan Mjallby, Andreas Jakobsson, Teddy Lukic, Tobias Linderoth, Niclas Alexandersson, Anders Svensson (Magnus Svensson, 84), Fredrik Ljungberg, Markus Allbäck (Andreas Andersson, 64), Henrik Larsson.

Nigeria: Ike Shorunmu, Ifeanyi Udeze, Taribo West, Isaac Okoronkwo, Celestine Babayaro (Nwankwo Kanu 65), Joseph Yobo, Jay Jay Okocha, Justice Christopher, Bartholomew Ogbeche (Pius Ikedia 71), Julius Aghahowa, John Utaka.

Goals: Sweden Henrik Larsson 35, 63 (penalty), **Nigeria** Julius Aghahowa 27.

Referee: Rene Ortube (Bolivia).

Man of the Match: Henrik Larsson for his goal scoring exploits.

23 Argentina 0 – 1 England: England exacts some revenge
June 7: Sapporo, Japan

This match was probably the most anticipated game of the first round. Previous World Cup history from 1966 (won by England 1-0), 1986 (won by Argentina 2-1), and 1998 (tied 2-2 but won by Argentina on penalties) weighed on both teams. Argentina especially felt the weight of a nation due to their favorite status and the crumbling economy back home. The Argentine people were counting on their team to lift their depressed spirits as they did in the 1978 World Cup during the oppressive military regime.

Each team had made one change from their opening starting lineups: England had replaced quicksilver Darius Vassell with defensive midfielder Nicky Butt, and Argentina had sidelined 'Piojo' Lopez for Kily Gonzales. Both teams were equally matched but the forwards had difficulty getting served, particularly well-covered Gabriel Batistuta. Michael Owen, however, made several dangerous runs, and hit the post after shooting through defender Walter Samuel's legs. Finally, Mauricio Pochettino was forced to foul Owen in the box just before the first half ended. David Beckham badly wanted the penalty kick, and stepped up to power the ball just to the left side of the keeper Pablo Cavellero. Not great placement, but Beckham disguised it enough to fool Cavellero and score.

Argentina had much of the possession for the second half, but they could not make a successful challenge to the rapidly improving English defense. England also had some chances, especially substitute Teddy Sheringham's superb volley from the right side that forced a punch-save from Cavellero. Pochettino almost redeemed himself with a late goal, but a desperate David Seaman save cleared his strong header off the line.

Beckham and England finally had some revenge for the 1998 World Cup match, when Beckham was ejected after striking out at Diego Simeone. However, it was not equivalent circumstances, as the 1998 game prevented England from reaching the quarterfinals. This match was just a first round match and did not immediately knock Argentina out of the tournament.

Argentina: Pablo Cavallero, Mauricio Pochettino, Walter Samuel, Diego Placente, Juan Pablo Sorin, Javier Zanetti, Ariel Ortega, Juan Sebastian Veron (Pablo Aimar, 46), Diego Simeone, Gabriel Batistuta (Hernan Crespo, 60), Cristian Gonzalez Claudio Lopez, 64).

England: David Seaman, Danny Mills, Ashley Cole, Rio Ferdinand, Sol Campbell, David Beckham, Paul Scholes, Owen Hargreaves (Trevor Sinclair, 19), Nicky Butt, Michael Owen (Wayne Bridge, 80), Emile Heskey (Teddy Sheringham, 56).

Goals: England David Beckham 44 (penalty).

Referee: Pierluigi Collina (Italy).

Man of the Match: Michael Owen, who hit the post and created the penalty opportunity.

37 Sweden 1 – 1 Argentina   First round Argentina elimination
June 12: Miyagi, Japan

Argentina had not been eliminated in the first round of the World Cup since 1962, but they needed a win against Sweden to go through to the second round.

Argentina dominated possession for most of the match, but was let down by poor finishing and a tough Swedish defense. Juan Pablo Sorin had two good headed chances early, but Claudio Lopez missed the whole goal on three clear first half chances.

Sweden finally had a good chance in the second half with a tremendous 30-yard curling Anders Svensson free kick that found the upper-left corner in the 59th minute. Argentina then pushed everybody forward and brought in attacking options Hernan Crespo (with Batistuta exiting), "Piojo" Lopez, and Kily Gonzalez. Pablo Aimar's eight yard shot beat keeper Hedman but was cleared off the line by the defense.

Argentina was nearly caught behind as Andreas Andersson hit the crossbar in the 85th minute, but then Ariel Ortega was awarded a penalty in the 88th minute. Ortega tried the over-rated delayed penalty-kick method, which Hedman saved but gave up a rebound for Crespo to score. However, video showed that Crespo had crept almost 4 yards into the penalty box before Ortega struck the ball; the referee should have annulled the goal.

Argentina, one of the World Cup favorites to win the 2002 championship, would have to wait until 2006 for their chance at redemption.

Sweden: Magnus Hedman, Olof Mellberg, Johan Mjallby, Andreas Jakobsson, Teddy Lukic, Tobias Linderoth, Niclas Alexandersson, Anders Svensson (Mattias Jonson 68), Magnus Svensson, Henrik Larsson (Zlatan Ibrahimovic 88), Markus Allback (Andreas Andersson, 45).

Argentina: Pablo Cavallero, Javier Zanetti, Walter Samuel, Mauricio Pochettino, Jose Chamot, Ariel Ortega, Matias Almeyda (Juan Sebastian Veron 63), Juan Pablo Sorin (Cristian Gonzalez), Pablo Aimar, Claudio Lopez, Gabriel Batistuta (Hernan Crespo, 58).

Goals: Sweden - Anders Svensson; **Argentina** - Hernan Crespo.
Referee: Ali Bujsaim (United Arab Emirates).
Man of the Match: Anders Svensson for a superbly struck free kick.

38 Nigeria 0 – 0 England   Scoreless game puts England through
June 12: Osaka, Japan

Nigeria was already out of the Cup, but the Super Eagles still wanted to leave a good impression on the fans; England needed only to tie to advance to the second round. Although the match was well contested, the finishing was suspect and the goalkeeping spotless on both sides.

New Nigerian goalkeeper Vincent Enyeama (youngest keeper in the World Cup at 19 years old) was tested by strikers Emile Heskey and Michael Owen, but Paul Scholes came the closest when his blistering shot was tipped off the right post by Enyeama just before half-time. After the half Ashley Cole struck the top of the crossbar with a cross, but it bounced harmlessly into foul territory.

Nigeria went out with their heads high, as they competed well but could not break the stranglehold of the "Group of Death."

England: David Seaman, Danny Mills, Rio Ferdinand, Sol Campbell, Ashley Cole (Wayne Bridge 84), David Beckham, Nicky Butt, Paul Scholes, Trevor Sinclair, Emile Heskey (Teddy Sheringham 68), Michael Owen (Darius Vassell 77).

Nigeria: Vincent Enyeama, Joseph Yobo, Isaac Okoronkwo, Ifeanyi Udeze, Efetobore Sodje, Justice Christopher, Jay-Jay Okocha, James Obiorah, Julius Aghahowa, Benedict Akwuegbu, Femi Opabunmi (Pius Ikedia 86).

Referee: Brian Hall (USA).
Man of the Match: Vincent Enyeama for turning back all of England's efforts.

Group G: Italy, Ecuador, Croatia, Mexico
Total score: 69   [2nd hardest group by cumulative rankings]

Italy was the favorite to top this group, but Mexico was ranked only one place behind despite being lucky to have qualified past a dynamic Honduran team. Ecuador qualified second in South America and had their best team ever, but was a World Cup virgin. Croatia was a top European team, talented and disciplined but with aging stars.

G1. Italy [6]

Italy easily qualified at the top of Europe Group 8 to make their fifteenth World Cup appearance. The three-time World Cup champions had last won 20 years prior in the 1982 Spain Cup. They had also finished runner-up in 1970 and 1994.

Starting in 1990, Italy had a most unfortunate run, being eliminated in three successive World Cups (1990, 1994, 1998) on penalty kick competitions. Captain Paolo Maldini was the only survivor of all three of those disappointing Cups.

Coach Giovanni Trapattoni had world-class players at every position, but elected not to take Italy legend Roberto Baggio as a backup "number 10." With Christian Vieri, Francesco Totti, and Alessandro del Piero, along with a defense marshaled by Maldini, the Italians seemed a sure bet for the semi-finals. They only hoped to avoid another penalty kick fiasco.

G2. Ecuador [35]

Ecuador was a surprising second behind Argentina in the marathon CONMEBOL qualifying group, finishing above fellow qualifiers Brazil, Paraguay and Uruguay. They had a solid team led by aging superstar midfielder, Alex Aguinaga, and the impressive striker Agustin Delgado. This was Ecuador's first ever World Cup appearance.

Ecuador played their home qualifying games in the capital of Quito at 2811 meters above sea level (9222 feet), so they had a significant home altitude advantage. Colombian Coach Hernan Dario Gomez recovered from a gunshot wound to direct Ecuador's first ever participation in a World Cup.

G3. Croatia [21]

Croatia finished at the top of Europe's Group 6, ahead of Belgium and Scotland. Croatia had a tremendous first World Cup in 1998, coming in third with forward Davor Šuker taking the Golden Boot with 6 goals.

Šuker had a remarkable 44 goals in 66 internationals with Croatia, but was out of form and would have to defer to Alen Bokšić in the central striking role in 2002. Croatia once played free-flowing football, but with Zvonimir Boban retired the team turned ultra-defensive, and coach Mirko Jozić even played a 5-3-2 formation at times. It was hard to see how Croatia could match their 1998 success if they could not get forward enough to score.

G4. Mexico [7]

Mexico had a difficult time in the CONCACAF qualifiers as Costa Rica beat them at home, and they waited until the last qualifying match against Honduras to qualify. This was Mexico's twelfth World Cup appearance, with their previous highlight being reaching the quarterfinals in the 1970 and 1986 Cups held in Mexico.

Team symbol and the world's most capped male player Claudio Suarez (170 national games) pulled up lame before the Cup and Mexico would miss his leadership. Still, coach Javier Aguirre had a lot of quality young players, almost all playing in the Mexican league because of the highest salaries in Latin America.

09 Croatia 0 – 1 Mexico   Penalty and red card bury Croatia

June 3: Niigata, Japan

Mexico and Croatia were two evenly matched teams that played a cautious match decided by a Cuauhtémoc Blanco penalty kick.

Croatian legend Davor Šuker tested Mexico keeper Oscar Perez early with a header, but Perez was able to parry it away.

After the half Croatia had a good chance from Zvonimir Soldo's header, but again Perez was up to the task.

Jared Borgetti released a beautifully laid-on back heel to Blanco that completely fooled the defense in the 60th minute. As Blanco was controlling it he was hacked down in the penalty area by defender Boris Živković, who was immediately red-carded (for the first dismissal of the World Cup). Blanco was slow getting to his feet but took the penalty himself, and struck a masterful shot into the upper left of the goal for the winning score. The Mexican defense held on for the shutout.

Croatia: Stipe Pletikosa, Boris Zivkovic, Robert Kovac, Josip Simunic, Robert Jarni, Stjepan Tomas, Zvonimir Soldo, Niko Kovac, Robert Prosinecki (Milan Rapaic 46), Davor Suker (Daniel Saric 64), Alen Boksic (Mario Stanic 67).

Mexico: Oscar Perez, Manuel Vidrio, Rafael Marquez, Salvador Carmona, Ramon Morales, Gabriel Caballero, Gerardo Torrado, Braulio Luna, Sigifredo Mercado, Cuauhtémoc Blanco, Jared Borgetti (Luis Hernandez 68).

Goals: Mexico – Cuauhtémoc Blanco 61.

Referee: Lu Jun (China)

Man of the Match: Oscar Perez for his clean sheet of a good Croatian team.

11 Italy 2 – 0 Ecuador   Italy controls their opener

June 3: Sapporo, Japan

Italy scored in the seventh minute as Francesco Totti streaked down the right side to the end line and clairvoyantly centered behind to pursuing strike mate Christian Vieri. Vieri slammed the ball into the upper-right corner in a remarkable first-time touch; Ecuador keeper Jose Cevallos had no chance to save the 15-yard blast.

Vieri got his second goal in the 27th minute when he chest-controlled a long ball from Luigi de Biaggio at the top of the penalty box, evaded his defender, and left-footed from 12 yards. Cevallos got his feet on the ball, but it bounced behind him, leaving Vieri an easy tap-in.

After the half, Italy searched for a third goal as Damiano Tommasi first tested Cevallos from long-range, then Cristiano Doni volleyed a shot off the crossbar.

Italian keeper Gianluigi Buffon kept his shutout in the last minute of regulation, as he dove to stop an excellent turn and shot by Agustin Delgado.

Italy: Gianluigi Buffon, Christian Panucci, Fabio Cannavaro, Alessandro Nesta, Paolo Maldini, Gianluca Zambrotta, Damiano Tommasi, Luigi Di Biaggio (Gennaro Gattuso 68), Cristiano Doni (Di Livio 65), Francesco Totti (Alessandro Del Piero 73), Christian Vieri.

Ecuador: Jose Cevallos, Ulises De la Cruz, Ivan Hurtado, Augusto Poroso, Raul Guerron, Edison Mendez, Alfonso Obregon, Alex Aguinaga (Carlos Tenorio 46), Edwin Tenorio (Marlon Ayovi 59), Cleber Chala (Nicolas Ascencio 84), Agustin Delgado.

Goals. Italy – Christian Vieri 7, 27.

Referee: Brian Hall (USA).

Man of the Match: Christian Vieri for his well-taken brace (two goals).

25 Italy 1 – 2 Croatia: Italy's non-losing streak ends amid referee errors

June 8: Ibaraki, Japan

The Croatian team came out with a new-look after dropping aging astros Robert Prosinečki and Davor Šuker from the starting lineup. Paolo Maldini was battling an ankle injury, but showed up to tie Uwe Seeler's record of 21 complete World Cup games without missing a minute (with Maldini having logged more minutes due to overtimes).

The game commenced with Croatia showing none of the sluggishness they displayed in their opener. Both sides came ever so close to scoring in the first half; Italy in the 15th minute through Cristiano Doni as he burst through the center only to be denied by Croatian keeper Stipe Pletikosa, and Croatia in the 26th through Davor Vugrinec whose effort had to be cleared off the goal line by the Italian defense.

After the break in the 50th minute, Christian Vieri scored on a header from Gianluca Zambrotta's flick-on from a Cristiano Doni cross, but the goal was called back for offside. Video of the play confirmed a gross referee and lineman error, as neither Vieri nor Zambrotta were close to being offside.

Italy came back from this unlucky break in the 56th minute, as Vieri scored on a header from the left side of the 6 yard box that ended in the right hand corner.

Croatia persisted and in the 73rd minute, Ivica Olić met a cross from the left side and steered it past Buffon into the right side of the goal from 4 yards out. A scant four minutes later Milan Rapaić scored an unusual goal from 16 yards out. An opportunistic header was floated into the penalty box, Rapaić one-touched it and then executed an extended side-volley that was partially blocked by Marco Materazzi, but the ball ended up in the upper left-hand corner.

Italy was not done fighting. In the 87th minute, Francesco Totti made a beautiful 25-yard free kick that left keeper Pletikosa for dead, but *rebounded off the inside left post and passed along the goal-line behind the keeper and out the right side of the goal!* Totti came as close as one could come to scoring without success.

In the 90th minute substitute Filippo Inzaghi burst into the box meeting a long pass from Materazzi; he was able to dummy it past the onrushing Croatian keeper and the ball entered the goal. But once again Italy was out of luck as Inzaghi was penalized for shirt pulling and the goal was annulled. Video showed that Inzaghi himself had his progress impeded by shirt pulling from the Croatian defense. Interestingly, if the goal had stood, it would have been awarded to Materazzi as it was not touched by either team; as Materazzi passed from his own half, it would have been the longest goal ever in World Cup play.

Italy had been unbeaten in regulation for twelve consecutive World Cup matches from 1994 thru 2002 (they had lost the Final in 1994 on a penalty shootout, and went out on penalties again in 1998 to France). They were very unlucky to lose this match, as Vieri's first goal was legitimate, and Inzaghi's goal appeared to be annulled for a phantom foul.

By Croatia defeating Italy, Italy failed to equal the all-time World Cup record of 13 unbeaten matches held by Brazil between 1958 and 1966. Still, a great feat by the most consistent country of recent times, and an incrimination of the penalty lottery system that an unbeaten team such as Italy could not progress in previous tournaments.

Italy: Gianluigi Buffon, Christian Panucci, Fabio Cannavaro, Alessandro Nesta (Marco Materazzi 24), Paolo Maldini, Damiano Tommasi, Cristiano Doni (Filippo Inzaghi 79), Cristiano Zanetti, Gianluca Zambrotta, Francesco Totti, Christian Vieri.
Croatia: Stipe Pletikosa, Josip Simunic, Stjepan Tomas, Niko Kovac, Robert Jarni, Davor Vugrinec (Ivica Olic 57), Daniel Saric, Robert Kovac, Zvonimir Soldo (Jurica Vranjes 63), Milan Rapaic (Dario Simic 79), Alen Boksic.
Goals: Italy 1 (Vieri 55), **Croatia** 2 (Olic 72, Rapaic 76).
Referee: Graham Poll (Eng).
Man of the Match: Croatia: Milan Rapaić for his opportunistic winning strike. Italy: Christian Vieri for scoring two legal goals, but only one was allowed.

27 Mexico 2 – 1 Ecuador   Mexico qualifies for second round
June 9: Miyagi, Japan

Ecuador went ahead early as striker Agustin Delgado headed a goal off the crossbar after meeting a right-sided cross from Ulises de la Cruz in the 5th minute.

Mexico equalized in the 28th minute as Ramon Morales crossed for Jared Borgetti who scored a superb left-foot volley goal from 10 yards that Jose Cevallos could only get a hand on. The half ended 1-1, but Mexico was earning most of the chances.

Mexico finally got the winner in the 57th minute when Geraldo Torrado was given too much room outside the penalty box and flashed a left-footer into the right side of the goal from 23 yards. Keeper Cevallos appeared to be screened by his defenders and reacted too late.

Despite the possession advantage, Mexico almost lost the win when Ecuador substitute Carlos Tenorio forced a desperation kick-save from Mexico keeper Oscar Perez. But Mexico held on to get their second win and qualify for the second round.

Mexico: Oscar Perez, Rafael Marquez (c), Manuel Vidrio, Gerardo Torrado, Ramon Morales, Jared Borgetti (Luis Hernandez 77), Cuauhtémoc Blanco (Sigifredo Mercado 90), Braulio Luna, Salvador Carmona, Johan Rodriguez (Gabriel Caballero 87), Jesus Arellano.
Ecuador: Jose Cevallos, Augusto Poroso, Ivan Hurtado (c), Ulises De la Cruz, Alfonso Obregon (Alex Aguinaga 58), Raul Guerron, Ivan Kaviedes (Carlos Tenorio 53), Agustin Delgado, Cleber Chala, Edison Mendez, Edwin Tenorio (Marlon Ayovi 35).

Goals: Mexico - Borgetti 28, Torrado 57; **Ecuador -** Delgado 5.
Referee: Mourad Daami (Tunisia).
Man of the Match: Carlos Torrado for scoring the enterprising winner.

43 Mexico 1 – 1 Italy: Del Piero saves Italy's ambitions
June 13: Oita, Japan

Italy kept one eye on the Ecuador-Croatia game, as both Italy and Croatia had three points with Italy holding a one-goal cumulative advantage. If both teams tied, Italy would go through to the second round.

Italy came out with their offense clicking and creating chance after chance. Fillippo Inzaghi caused major headaches for the Mexican defense; he first tested Mexican keeper Oscar Perez with a 25-yard shot, then beat Perez from the top of the penalty area but the goal was called back for an offside violation. Inzaghi then passed to Francesco Totti whose curled shot went wide of the far post with only Perez to beat. Perez then saved Vieri's quality volley from 18 yards in the 22nd minute. The game was only 25% gone and Perez had already earned a full day's pay.

But it was Mexico that opened the scoring with excellent ball movement in the 34th minute. Braulio Luna ran into the left end line area, but instead of centering the ball he cut it way back to Cuauhtémoc Blanco. Blanco made an ambitious chip to Jared Borgetti in the corner of the penalty area, guarded by Paolo Maldini. Borgetti then scored the most creative headed goal of the tournament, as he blindly flicked the ball from the left side of the six-yard box over Italy keeper Buffon into the right side of the net. Neither Maldini nor Buffon had any chance to stop the wonder goal. The lack of direct eyesight to the goal made his goal the header equivalent of a bicycle kick. The half ended 1-0 to Mexico.

Inzaghi almost dribbled around goalkeeper Oscar Perez at the start of the second half, but Perez was just able to get a hand on the ball. Mexico then had a chance to get their second goal, as Blanco got the ball to Jesus Arellano; Buffon touched his 6-yard shot, and the Italian defense was left to clear the rebound as Borgetti lurked nearby.

Italy's Vincenzo Montella then lobbed Perez from 15 yards off a beautiful chip from Francesco Totti in the 64th minute, but Italy was once again called for offside to annul the goal. Video showed that Montello was even with the last defender, not offside.

Italy finally scored in the 85th minute when Montella centered from the right side for new substitute Alessandro del Piero to rush in and head past Perez from 6 yards out.

Italy had tied the match and gone through to the second round with Mexico. Because Croatia lost to Ecuador by one goal, Italy would have advanced even without Del Piero's goal. Lost in the excitement was Paolo Maldini's 22nd consecutive full (90 minutes or more) World Cup match, breaking his and Uwe Seeler's record of twenty-one.

Mexico: Oscar Perez, Rafael Marquez, Manuel Vidrio, Salvador Carmona, Gerardo Torrado, Ramon Morales (Rafael Garcia, 76), Braulio Luna, Joahan Rodriguez (Gabriel Caballero, 76), Jared Borgetti (Francisco Palencia, 80), Cuauhtémoc Blanco, Jesus Arellano.
Italy: Gianluigi Buffon, Christian Panucci (Francesco Coco, 63), Paolo Maldini, Fabio Cannavaro, Alessandro Nesta, Christian Zanetti, Francesco Totti (Alessandro Del Piero, 78), Damiano Tommasi, Gianluca Zambrotta, Filippo Inzaghi (Vincenzo Montella, 56), Christian Vieri.
Goals: Mexico: Jared Borgetti 34; **Italy**: Alessandro Del-Piero 85.
Referee: Carlos Simon (Brazil).
Men of the Match: Mexico's Cuauhtémoc Blanco and Italy's Francesco Totti; the creative forces who helped make this match a spectacle. Blanco also executed his signature "Cuauhtémoc hop" move (or "Cuauhtémiña") against the Italian defense, a move where he picks up the ball with both feet and carries it over an oncoming tackle.

44 Ecuador 1 – 0 Croatia   Ecuador's first win ruins Croatia's chance
June 13: Yokohama, Japan

Croatia needed to win to go through to the second round; Ecuador was looking for their first-ever World Cup win.

Croatian Alan Boksic had two great chances at goal in the first half. First he made a turn and shot off the left post from 16 yards, then he beat keeper Jose Cevallos only to see the ball cleared by a defender.

Ecuador had their first real chance after the half, and they took full advantage. Agustin Delgado headed back to Edison Mendez, who half-volleyed from 12 yards away. Croatian keeper Stipe Pletikosa could only touch the ball on its way into the net.

Once again the Ecuador defense had to clear off the line in the second half, as a Mario Stanic header off a corner kick was goal bound.

Ecuador had gained a measure of respect with their play and first World Cup win in their initial World Cup Finals. The teams played their last game as they both were eliminated on points.

Ecuador: Jose Cevallos, Ulises De la Cruz, Ivan Hurtado, Raul Guerron, Marlon Ayovi, Edison Mendez, Alfonso Obregon (Alex Aguinaga 40), Augusto Poroso, Carlos Tenorio (Ivan Kaviedes 76), Cleber Chala, Agustin Delgado.

Croatia: Stipe Pletikosa, Josip Simunic, Stjepan Tomas, Dario Simic (Davor Vugrinec 52), Robert Kovac, Robert Jarni, Niko Kovac (Jurica Vranjes 59), Daniel Saric (Mario Stanic 67) Milan Rapaic, Ivica Olic, Alen Boksic.

Goals: Ecuador - Mendez 48.
Referee: William Mattus Vega (Costa Rica).
Man of the Match: Edison Mendez for his well-taken goal.

Group H: Japan, Belgium, Russia, Tunisia
Total score: 112   [Easiest group by cumulative rankings]

Japan had jumped over Korea to be the best-ranked Asian team, and as co-hosts they were expected to be very motivated. Belgium, Russia, and Tunisia all had strong and disciplined teams that would compete to go through to the second round, and the group was essentially a toss-up as to which team would go through.

H1. Japan [32]

Japan qualified for their second World Cup by virtue of being a co-host. Japan had disappointed in the 1998 World Cup as they lost all three games, including to a talented Jamaican team (but a country with $1/50^{th}$ their population).

The Japanese soccer community gained confidence in the last decade, as they established the professional J-league and had better results in internationals. Japan finished second in the 2001 Confederations Cup, losing to champions France 1-0 in the final. French coach Philippe Troussier had Japan playing better than ever.

Once out of the J-league, despite their talents top Japanese players had a hard time finding regular football. Midfielder Hidetoshi Nakata was part of Roma's champion Serie A team in 2001, but because of the limited foreigner rule he often sat on the bench in lieu of Roma's other *fantasista* ("number 10"), Francesco Totti. Junichi Inamoto had a similar problem with Arsenal; only Shinji Ono was playing regularly with Feyenoord Rotterdam.

Although Japan was ranked last by FIFA in this group, they had a home advantage that could prove crucial.

H2. Belgium [23]

Belgium came second to Croatia in Europe Group 6, and beat the strong Czech Republic in a home-and-away playoff to book their eleventh World Cup Finals appearance. Belgium had progressed to the second phase in four of their first ten appearances.

Belgium had a mediocre run up to the Cup, losing or tying games against several lesser opponents. They also lost key striker Emile Mpenza shortly before the Cup started.

Belgium tied all three of their games in the 1998 World Cup, and was looking to improve on that result. Coach Robert Wasiege finally had creative midfielders Marc Wilmots and Johan Walem healthy, and this boded well for a sometimes suspect Belgian attack.

H3. Russia [27]

Russia qualified first in Europe Group 1 over Slovenia, to make their ninth World Cup Finals appearance. While Russia (part of the Soviet Union until 1991) made it into the second round in their first six World Cups, they had failed to reach the second round in 1990 and 1994, and did not appear in 1998.

National team coach Oleg Romantsev brought an experienced team of mostly current or former Moscow Spartak players, perhaps a natural occurrence since he was also the coach of Spartak. Included in his lineup were important foreign league players including sweeper Victor Onopko of Real Oviedo and the Celtic Vigo midfield dynamic duo of Alexander Mostovoi and Valery Karpin.

Teenage sensations midfielder Marat Izmailov and striker Dmitri Sychev also figured to play in the Russian team mix.

H4. Tunisia [30]

Tunisia qualified by virtue of finishing top of Africa's Group 4. This was Tunisia's third World Cup, but since their first ever Finals game and victory against Mexico in 1978, they had not won another Cup game.

Henri Michel, ex-coach of France, Cameroon, and Morocco in the 1986, 1994, and 1998 World Cups, respectively, resigned as Tunisian coach in March 2002 after just five months in charge. Two local coaches, Ammar Souayeh and Khaies Laabidi, were recruited to try and organize Tunisia's Cup effort. They would use a blend of local and overseas players in an attempt to create enough team unity for improved results in this Cup.

13 Japan 2 – 2 Belgium   Belgium and Japan equally excellent
June 4: Saitama, Japan

Despite assumptions that these were two pedestrian teams of lesser quality, the second half was one of the best 45 minutes of the World Cup. Four superb goals were scored, and eventually both teams deservedly went on to the second round.

The first half ended scoreless, but was highlighted by Japan keeper Seigo Narazaki's superb save on Mark Wilmots' header from 11 yards out.

Belgium finally got on the scoreboard in the 57th minute when a weak defensive clearance came to Eric van Meir, who lobbed the ball into the penalty area where Wilmots spectacularly converted a bicycle kick from 12 yards past Narazaki.

Takayuki Suzuki equalized two minutes later in as nearly a spectacular manner, as he caught up with a long pass and threw his body forward getting a toe-poke past advancing goalkeeper Geert de Vlieger to score from 16 yards.

Japan then went ahead for the first time ever in their World Cup history, as Junichi Inamoto stole the ball at midfield, received a return pass, and proceeded to take three Belgium defenders on a solo run ending in his left-footed rocket past de Vlieger from 13 yards.

Peter van der Heyden pulled Belgium level after he beat the offside trap and successfully lobbed Narazaki from 14 yards despite the keeper's attempted parry.

Inamoto was looking for his second goal as he chipped over de Vlieger near the end, but the goal was annulled for a foul prior to the goal. A hosting nation had never lost their opening match in the World Cup, and Japan was able to continue that tradition with this quality tie.

Japan: Seigo Narazaki, Naoki Matsuda, Ryuzo Morioka (Tsuneyasu Miyamoto 72), Koji Nakata, Junichi Inamoto, Hidetoshi Nakata, Shinji Ono (Alessandro Santos 63), Kazuyuki Toda, Daisuke Ichikawa, Takayuki Suzuki, Atsushi Yanagisawa.
Belgium: Geert De Vlieger, Eric Van Meir, Peter Van Der Heyden, Jacky Peeters, Daniel Van Buyten, Timmy Simons Bart Goor, Johan Walem (Wesley Sonck 70), Gert Verheyen (Branko Strupar 83), Yves Vanderhaeghe, (Wesley Sonck 46), Marc Wilmots.
Goals: Japan Takayuki Suzuki 59, Junichi Inamoto 68 , **Belgium** Marc Wilmots 57, Peter Van Der Heyden 75.
Referee: William Mattus Vega (Costa Rica).
Men of the Match: Japan: Junichi Inamoto for his spectacular scoring run and almost getting a second. Belgium: Marc Wilmots for his sparkling bicycle kick and other close chances.

15 Russia 2 – 0 Tunisia: Russia finally solves Tunisian keeper
June 5: Kobe, Japan

Russia created most of the chances in the first half, but could not capitalize on their 5-1 edge in shots, as Tunisian keeper Ali Boumnijel made some classy saves.

A Tunisian defensive breakdown in the 59th minute allowed Yegor Titov to shoot into the lower-left corner, although Boumnijel got a touch on the ball.

Four minutes later, substitute Dmitri Sychev was fouled in the penalty box after running onto a long ball, and Valery Karpin put the penalty kick low in the left-hand corner. The Russian technique was too clinical for the Tunisians.

Russia: Ruslan Nigmatullin, Yuri Kovtun, Yury Nikiforov , Andrey Solomatin, Viktor Onopko, Igor Semshov (Dmitry Khohlov, 46), Valery Karpin, Yegor Titov, Marat Izmailov (Dmitry Alenichev, 78), Vladimir Beschastnykh (Dmitri Sychev, 55), Ruslan Pimenov.

Tunisia: Ali Boumnijel, Khaled Badra (Ali Zitouni, 84), Mohamed Mkacher, Hatem Trabelsi, Raouf Bouazaiene, Radhi Jaidi, Hassen Gabsi (Imed Mhedhebi, 67), Riadh Bouazizi, Slim Ben Achour, Ziàd Jaziri, Adel Sellimi (Zoubeir Baya, 67).

Goals: Russia - Yegor Titov 59; Valery Karpin 64 (penalty).

Referee: Peter Prendergast (Jamaica).

Man of the Match: Valery Karpin for his midfield energy and leadership.

29 Japan 1 – 0 Russia   Japan wins their first ever World Cup match
June 9: Yokohama, Japan.

This game marked Japan's first ever World Cup win, after losing all three games in 1998 and tying their initial game against Belgium in 2002. The first half went at full speed, with both teams seeking velocity and possession advantages, but no score was forthcoming.

The second half brought the second goal in two games from Junichi Inamoto. A teammate found him in the penalty area in the 51st minute, and he maintained his composure for his 10-yard shot past Russian keeper Ruslan Nigmatullin into the upper right-hand corner.

Substitute Vladimir Beschastnykh rounded the Japanese keeper Seigo Narazaki in the 58th minute, but strangely failed to put the ball on goal. Hidetoshi Nakata just missed a goal in the 71st minute as his 25-yard free kick smashed off the crossbar, for the last serious goal chance of the game.

Japan: Seigo Narazaki, Naoki Matsuda, Koji Nakata, Tsuneyasu Miyamoto, Junichi Inamoto (Takashi Fukunishi, 85), Hidetoshi Nakata, Shinji Ono (Toshihiro Hattori, 75), Tomokazu Myojin, Kazuyuki Toda, Takayuki Suzuki (Masashi Nakayama, 72), Atsushi Yanagisawa.

Russia: Ruslan Nigmatullin, Yuri Kovtun, Yury Nikiforov, Andrey Solomatin, Viktor Onopko, Alexei Smertin (Vladimir Beschastnykh, 57), Igor Semshov, Valery Karpin, Yegor Titov, Marat Izmailov (Dmitry Khohlov, 52), Ruslan Pimenov (Dmitri Sychev, 46) .

Goals: Japan - Junichi Inamoto 51.

Referee: Markus Merk (Germany).

Man of the Match: Junichi Inamoto for coolly converting his chance in the penalty area.

31 Tunisia 1 – 1 Belgium   Tunisians hold Belgians level
June 10: Oita, Japan.

Belgian captain Marc Wilmots again opened the scoring in the 13th minute, as he slotted home a leading head pass from Gert Verheyen. Belgium was helpless to protect their lead four minutes later from an immaculate Raouf Bouzaiene 26-yard free kick that tucked just inside the left post.

The Tunisians more than held their own in the first half, and even intensified Belgian efforts for a go-ahead score in the second half were unsuccessful

Tunisia: Ali Boumnijel, Khaled Badra, Ziad Jaziri (Ali Zitouni 78), Hatem Trabelsi, Hassen Gabsi (Adel Sellimi 67) , Kaies Ghodhbane, Raouf Bouazaiene, Riadh Bouazizi, Radhi Jaidi, Slim Ben Achour, Mourad Melki.

Belgium: Geert De Vlieger, Eric Deflandre, Glen De Boeck, Timmy Simons (Mbo Mpenza 74), Marc Wilmots, Bart Goor, Gert Verheyen (Sven Vermant 46), Peter Van Der Heyden, Daniel Van Buyten, Yves Vanderhaeghe, Branko Strupar (Wesley Sonck 46).

Goals: Tunisia – Raouf Bouazaiene 17. **Belgium** – Marc Wilmots 13.

Referee: Mark Shield (Australia).

Men of the Match: Goal scorers Raouf Bouzaiene and Marc Wilmots for expert finishing.

45 Tunisia 0 – 2 Japan — Japan eases into second round

June 14: Osaka, Japan

The first half of this match was a defensive struggle as the two teams probed for any opponent weakness.

Shortly after the half break, the Tunisia defense cracked and the ball fell to half-time substitute Hiroaki Morishima inside the penalty area. Morishima's 14-yard shot flew past Tunisia keeper Ali Boumnijel into the left-side netting.

A few minutes later Morishima almost had another goal as his header from a Daisuke Ichikawa cross hit the left post. Another Ichikawa cross figured in the second Japanese goal, as Hidetoshi Nakata's header from 8 yards nutmegged Boumnijel on its way into the net.

Tunisia did not give up as Ali Zitouni hit the bar from 18 yards, and later he just missed with a bicycle kick shot. A valiant try by the Tunisians, but the Japanese went through to the second round.

Tunisia: Ali Boumnijel, Khaled Badra, Hatem Trabelsi, Raouf Bouazaine (Ali Zitouni, 79), Radhi Jaidi, Jose Clayton (Imed Mhedhebi, 61), Kaies Ghodhbane, Riadh Bouazizi, Slim Ben Achour, Mourad Melki (Zoubeir Baya, 46), Ziàd Jaziri.

Japan: Seigo Narazaki, Naoki Matsuda, Koji Nakata, Tsuneyasu Miyamoto, Junichi Inamoto (Daisuke Ichikawa, 46), Hidetoshi Nakata (Mitsuo Ogasawara, 84), Shinji Ono, Tomokazu Myojin, Kazuyuki Toda, Takayuki Suzuki, Atsushi Yanagisawa (Hiroaki Morishima, 46).

Japan Hiroaki Morishima 48, Hidetoshi Nakata 75.

Referee: Gilles Veissiere (France).

Man of the Match: Hidetoshi Nakata for his goal and stellar midfield play.

46 Belgium 3 – 2 Russia — Belgium over Russia to second round

June 14: Shizuoka, Japan

Belgium required three points to go through to the second round, Russia only a tie. These team requirements produced a match that was fast-paced with end-to-end action, as both teams sought the goals to put them through.

Johan Walem put the Belgians ahead early with a superlative left-footed free kick from 26 yards, curling the ball around a defensive wall into the upper-right corner in the 7th minute. The first half ended 1-0.

Russia answered shortly after half time as Vladimir Beschastnykh scored from 9 yards on a rebound of Dmitri Sychev's shot in the penalty area. If the score stood at 1-1, Russia would advance over Belgium.

But in the 78th minute, substitute Wesley Sonck headed in Walem's corner kick from 8 yards to reverse the team advancement possibilities. Belgium scored again four minutes later with Marc Wilmots' shot deflected in from 19 yards, giving Russian keeper Ruslan Nigmatullin no chance.

Wilmots' strike gave Belgium the needed insurance to go through to the second round, because shortly before regulation time expired Sychev burst through the defense and beat onrushing Belgian keeper de Vlieger from near the penalty spot.

Despite last-minute jitters, Belgium advanced to the second round and Russia ended their World Cup adventure.

Belgium: Geert De Vlieger, Glen De Boeck (Eric Van Meir 89), Niko Van Kerckhoven, Jacky Peeters, Daniel Van Buyten, Bart Goor, Johan Walem, Gert Verheyen (Timmy Simons 77), Yves Vanderhaeghe, Marc Wilmots, Mbo Mpenza (Wesley Sonck, 70).

Russia: Ruslan Nigmatullin, Yuri Kovtun, Yury Nikiforov (Dmitri Sennikov), Andrey Solomatin, Viktor Onopko, Alexei Smertin (Dmitri Sychev 33), Valery Karpin (Alexander Kerzhakov 81), Yegor Titov, Dmitry Alenichev, Dmitry Khohlov, Vladimir Beschastnykh.

Goals: Belgium - Johan Walem 7, Wesley Sonck 78, Marc Wilmots 82; **Russia** - Vladimir Beschastnykh 52, Dmitri Sychev 89.

Referee: Kim Nielsen (Denmark).

Man of the Match: Johan Walem for his initial goal and assist on Sonck's goal.

First Round Summary

First Two Teams Eliminated

Two teams had already been eliminated from second round advancement by June 8th. The teams happened to be the least (Slovenia - 2 million) and most (China - 1.2 billion) populous countries represented in the 2002 World Cup – demonstrating that finding the right eleven players is more important than the size of the home population.

China's team played some attractive attacking soccer, a departure from the usual defensive emphasis for Bora Milutinovic's previous four teams (Mexico, Costa Rica, USA, Nigeria) that he coached in the World Cup. Perhaps as a result, China was frequently caught at the back, and ultimately did not score. Outplayed by Costa Rica, they played valiantly against Brazil creating some good chances and hitting a post. If China sends their strikers to "finishing school," they could be dangerous at future World Cups.

Slovenia never got untracked; after the 3-1 loss to Spain in their opener resulted in their star Zlatko Zahovic being substituted and sent home early, they were distracted and disheartened (unlike Ireland which was able to overcome all the noise surrounding captain Roy Keane's departure before the World Cup).

Surprise Teams Eliminated

Argentina, France, and Portugal? They were all favorites to progress deep into the Finals, and were even favorites to win the whole tournament! It was a massive shock to see these quality teams failing to reach the second round.

Overconfidence, failure to bring younger in-form players, players used for sentimental reasons, and coaching and selection errors were some of the reasons these teams failed to progress.

France gained a measure of pride back when they won the 2003 Confederation's Cup, as did Portugal when they reached the Final of the 2004 European Championships. Argentina later reached the Final of the 2004 Copa America, which they lost on penalty kicks to Brazil.

Competitive Teams Eliminated

Costa Rica, Cameroon, Uruguay, Russia, Croatia, Poland, South Africa, and Ecuador all won at least one game but did not progress in the tournament; all left a positive impression. Although Nigeria did not win a game, they played attractive football in the toughest group.

Teams to Try Again (No Wins)

Saudi Arabia and Tunisia had no wins and were at times out of their league in the 2002 World Cup (especially Saudi Arabia being walloped by Germany 8-0). They needed to improve significantly in order to be competitive, which they accomplished by again qualifying for Germany 2006.

Goal Leaders

After the first round, Miroslav Klose of Germany was the goal leader with five goals – all by headers. This was the first time any player had headed five consecutive goals in a single World Cup competition. There were 18 players with two goals or more:

5 goals Miroslav Klose (GER).
4 goals Ronaldo (BRA) and Jon Dahl Tomasson (DEN).
3 goals Pape Bouba Diop (SEN), Pauleta (POR), Raúl (SPA), Rivaldo (BRA), Christian Vieri (ITA), Marc Wilmots (BEL).
2 goals Jared Borgetti (MEX), Nelson Cuevas (PAR), Ronald Gomez (CRC), Hasan Sas (TUR), Fernando Hierro (SPA), Junichi Inamoto (JPN), Robbie Keane (IRL), Henrik Larsson (SWE), Fernando Morientes (SPA).

The world would get to watch more skills from sixteen of these scorers, as only Pauleta and Ronald Gomez saw their teams (Portugal and Costa Rica) exit in the first round.

SECOND ROUND GAMES

49 Germany 1 – 0 Paraguay — Germany finally beats Chilavert
June 15: Seogwipo, South Korea

This first game of the second round turned out to be a pedestrian affair between a shorthanded Germany and a subdued Paraguay. Because of the previous match against Cameroon, which brought a superfluous 16 yellow cards from the referee, the Germans were without the services of Carsten Ramelow, Christian Ziege and Dietmar Hamann. And when young Paraguayan star Roque Santa Cruz was hobbled by injury and left after 29 minutes, Paraguay looked short on attacking options. Still, Paraguay had the best of the chances of the first half, as Francisco Arce tested Kahn from long-range in the 22nd minute. In the 37th minute Jorge Campos also stretched Oliver Kahn from the left 18-yard line, on a shot destined for the upper left hand corner. Campos nearly duplicated the shot in the 49th minute.

As the second half wore on, Germany gained confidence and created good run-ins and shots on Paraguay captain and keeper Jose Luis Chilavert, whose positioning was impeccable. Neuville had a superb shot heading for the near post saved by Chilavert in the 62nd minute.

Chilavert trotted up to take a free kick from 24 yards in the 74th minute, but gave Kahn no challenge as he harmlessly floated the ball over. Just to be sure, Kahn had a defender stand on the line with him; Chilavert could have taken advantage of this rash defensive tactic and passed the ball to give a teammate a better chance on goal.

Just as the game looked sure to enter overtime, Oliver Neuville poached a goal off a right cross in the 88th minute, blasting a half-volley from 7 yards to the near post, leaving Chilavert no chance to save. Previous game two-goal hero Nelson Cuevas was not inserted into the game by Coach Cesare Maldini until the 90th minute, which was strange as he could have given Germany serious trouble at the back with his pace and technique. Neuville took his opportunistic chance; Cuevas never had a chance.

As it was, a sub-par Germany survived a difficult match with Neuville's first World Cup Final goal, a memorable piece of skill past one of the all-time best goalkeepers in his last important international.

Germany: Oliver Kahn, Thomas Linke, Marko Rehmer (Sebastian Kehl, 46), Christoph Metzelder (Frank Baumann, 60), Michael Ballack, Jens Jeremies, Bernd Schneider, Torsten Frings, Oliver Neuville (Gerald Asamoah, 90), Miroslav Klose, Marco Bode.
Paraguay: Jose Luis Chilavert, Francisco Arce, Carlos Gamarra, Celso Ayala, Julio Cesar Caceres, Denis Caniza, Estanislao Struway (Nelson Cuevas, 90), Roberto Acuna, Carlos Bonet (Diego Gavilan, 84), Roque Santa Cruz (Jorge Campos, 29), Jose Cardozo.
Goals. Germany - Oliver Neuville 88.
Referee: Carlos Batres (Guatemala).
Man of the Match: Oliver Neuville, for making the effort to sprint in and finish a deadly half-volley at the end of the game.

50 Denmark 0 – 3 England — England take advantage of keeper woes
June 15: Niigata, Japan

History was on the side of England, as they had previously only been beaten (Uruguay 1954, Brazil 1962, West Germany 1970 and 1990, and Argentina in 1986 and 1998) or eliminated (1982 by West Germany) in the second phase of the World Cup (second round or better) by another World Cup winner. Denmark was not a World Cup winner, nor did they look to threaten this time.

In the fifth minute Danish keeper Thomas Sorenstam bundled a Rio Ferdinand header off a left-sided corner right into his goal. A nice gift from Sorenstam (really an own-goal from the keeper), who plied his trade in the English Premier league.

In the 22nd minute Michael Owen took an opportunistic strike after a loose ball from 8 yards in the center, deftly stroking just inside the right post.

Owen's Liverpool strike mate Emile Heskey got on the score sheet in the 44th minute, as Sorenstam could not get down quick enough on his powerful drive from 21 yards out. The game was effectively finished by half time.

The game would have been more competitive if Sorenstam had been more on-form as he had been until this match. The Danish offense was also to blame; incredibly, it was the first time Denmark had ever failed to score in a World Cup Finals match (it was Denmark's thirteenth World Cup Finals match).

Denmark: Thomas Sorensen, Rene Henriksen, Martin Laursen, Thomas Helveg (Kasper Bogelund, 7), Niclas Jensen, Stig Tofting (Claus Jensen, 58), Thomas Gravesen, Jesper Gronkjaer, Jon Dahl Tomasson, Ebbe Sand, Dennis Rommedahl.
England: David Seaman, Danny Mills, Ashley Cole, Rio Ferdinand, Sol Campbell, Trevor Sinclair, David Beckham, Paul Scholes (Kieron Dyer, 49), Nicky Butt, Michael Owen (Robbie Fowler, 46), Emile Heskey (Teddy Sheringham, 69).
Goals: England - Rio Ferdinand 5; Michael Owen 22; Emile Heskey 44.
Referee: Markus Merk (Germany).
Man of the Match: Rio Ferdinand: for "scoring" the initial goal and marshalling the central defense.

51 Sweden 1 – 2 Senegal (aet)   Soccer lovers delight
June 16: Oita, Japan

Sweden had emerged the victor of the "Group of Death," but Senegal was riding a 16-game unbeaten streak when they met (Senegal had lost to Cameroon in the Africa Cup Final on penalties which does not count as a full-game loss).

This was one of the most entertaining games of the 2002 World Cup. Either team could have won, as both produced multiple forays into enemy territory, constantly threatening their opponent's goal. The Senegalese produced beautiful touches on the ball, but Swedish skill was not lacking either.

Sweden showed they were all business, as Olof Mellberg's blast from the right side of the box in the 4th minute drew a kick save from focused Senegalese keeper Tony Sylva. The rebound went to Magnus Svennson who couldn't manage a shot on goal. Golden Boot 2001 winner Henrik Larsson opened the scoring for Sweden from a left-sided Anders Svensson corner kick, heading past an advancing Sylva from 5 yards away to inside the near post in the 11th minute.

Senegal was not discouraged, and both teams were unlucky not to draw penalty kicks in the first half after hard challenges in the penalty area. Despite these developments, the game never became overly physical. El Hadji Diouf should have earned a clear penalty after his clever run through two defenders; he was brought down by a third who the videotape showed had no chance for the ball. Shortly thereafter Diouf's left-foot shot was re-directed on goal by Papa Bouba Diop, but the linesman raised the flag for offside canceling out the goal.

In the 37th minute, Henri Camara shifted right between three Swedish defenders at the 22-yard line, then shot across his body to squeeze in a shot at the left post that tied the game. Four minutes later he had a golden opportunity to double the advantage, but his glancing header flew wide of the goal.

In the 42nd minute, Anders Svensson had a glorious 26-yard free kick destined for the upper right-hand corner denied by a flying Sylva.

After the half, Marcus Allback and El Hadji Diouf tested the opposing keepers from a volley and free kick, respectively. Substitute Zlatan Ibrahimovic beat two defenders at the right side of the box, and his shot drew a superb save from Sylva at the near post. Larsson was lurking in the middle waiting for a rebound that never came.

After ninety entertaining minutes of a creative offensive game, both teams entered the overtime prepared to risk defeat in pursuit of victory. Sweden almost got the Golden Goal in the 95th minute, as Anders Svensson did a pirouetted double-foot/double pullback move near the penalty spot, completely disengaging his marker, but his subsequent fluid shot rattled off the right upright.

Senegal got the Golden Goal in the 104th minute, as Camara took a back-heel pass from Pape Thiaw on the right side of the penalty box, swept left, and shot with his left foot. His shot was not clean as he over hit above the ball's center, but it rolled forward with bumping topspin past Hedman to kick in off the left post. Senegal could celebrate, but Sweden could be proud at their excellent effort.

Sweden: Magnus Hedman, Andreas Jakobsson, Olof Mellberg, Johan Mjallby, Teddy Lucic, Niclas Alexandersson (Zlatan Ibrahimovic 76), Magnus Svensson (Mattias Jonson 100), Anders Svensson, Tobias Linderoth, Henrik Larsson, Marcus Allback (Andreas Andersson 64).
Senegal: Tony Sylva, Omar Daf, Ferdinand Coly, Pape Malick Diop (Habib Beye 66), Henri Camara, Papa Bouba Diop, Aliou Cisse, Amdy Faye, Lamine Diatta, Pape Thiaw, El Hadji Diouf.
Goals: Sweden: Larsson 11. **Senegal:** Camara 37, 103 (Golden Goal).
Referee: Ubaldo Aquino (Paraguay).
Man of the Match: Henri Camara for superb setup and finishing on both goals.

52 Spain 1 – 1 Ireland (3:2 penalties)   Spain sweats through penalty lottery
June 16: Suwon, South Korea

Spain proved it was more than the "Raúl-Show," after going to the mat in overtime with 10 men, and then winning a poorly performed penalty series by both teams. Raúl had been substituted in the 80th minute, and therefore missed one-third of the game (40 of the total 120 minutes including overtime).

Spain started the game in excellent form, with crisp passing and dominating play. Robbie Keane interrupted this briefly in the 3rd minute with a good run that featured a nutmeg of defender Carlos Puyol, but his shot went wide of the far post. Puyol got his revenge in the 8th minute as he crossed from the right side to the near post finding Fernando Morrientes, who nodded the ball down to the far post past Ireland keeper Shay Givens.

In the 25th minute, Luis Enrique poached an opportunistic goal from 6 yards out, but it was disallowed for offside. Thereafter Spain seemed content with ball possession and protecting their one-goal lead.

After half time, Ireland came out with new purpose and began to dominate possession and generate better scoring chances. They did get sloppy at the back in the 47th minute, however, as Givens had to come out and stuff a Morientes strike from 17 yards.

Ireland then really threatened to score as Casillas dropped an Irish cross to Kilbane's feet in the 50th minute; Kilbane did well to volley it to goal where it was cleared off the line by Fernando Hierro. Damien Duff, who was constantly beating the Spanish defense, was brought down in the area for a penalty kick by Juanfran in the 63rd minute. Ian Harte struck the penalty at Casillas who punch-saved to Kilbane, who also muffed his chance to equalize.

Raúl got his best chance in the 72nd minute, chesting a ball down beautifully to his left foot, but once again Givens smartly rushed out to cut down the angle and made a brave save.

Duff then went on a run from the right touchline into the center of the 18-yard line, where his left-foot laser passed the left post by a fraction. Ireland kept up the pressure, and in the last minute of regulation (90th) Hierro manhandled and almost disrobed Niall Quinn off the ball in the penalty area. Hierro had Quinn's shirt halfway off before a penalty was called, as referee Frisk demonstrated that he would not tolerate this kind of off-the-ball defensive mugging in the penalty area. Robbie Keane made no mistake on Ireland's second penalty chance of the night, stroking the ball into the left corner after his body language spoke right corner. Casillas was frozen with no chance to save this penalty.

The overtime featured more Irish energy and control, with Spain attempting to stop them in the midfield and back. Spain was forced to play with only ten men after losing Albelda through injury after using all three substitutions. Ireland's best chance was a volley by Gary Breen in the 99th minute that Casillas handled well. In the 111th minute, Baraja shot from 24 yards forcing Givens to make an excellent punch save on a ball headed to the left corner. Then it was on to the penalty kick lottery.

After Finnan converted the first Irish penalty, there were no four-leaf clovers to be found. Holland struck the crossbar to miss, then Casillas saved from Connolly and Kilbane, leaving Ireland with only one penalty converted after four tries. Robbie Keane expertly converted their last, but clever midfielder Gaizka Mendieta scored the third penalty for Spain, sending them into the next round.

After an entertaining game between two equals, the Spanish were lucky to have survived to advance to the quarterfinals and meet host South Korea.

Spain: Iker Casillas, Juanfran, Carlos Puyol, Fernando Hierro, Ivan Helguera, Ruben Baraja, Javi De Pedro (Gaizka Mendieta, 66), Juan Valeron, Luis Enrique, Raul Gonzalez (Albert Luque, 80), Fernando Morientes (David Albelda, 72).
Ireland: Shay Given, Steve Finnan, Ian Harte (David Connolly, 82), Steve Staunton (Kenny Cunningham, 50), Gary Breen, Gary Kelly (Niall Quinn, 55), Matt Holland, Kevin Kilbane, Mark Kinsella, Damien Duff, Robbie Keane.
Goals: Spain Fernando Morientes 8. **Ireland** Robbie Keane 90 (penalty).
Spain wins on penalties:3-2.
Spain penalty scorers: Fernando Hierro , Ruben Baraja , Gaizka Mendieta.
Spain penalty misses: Juanfran, Juan Valeron.
Ireland penalty scorers: Steve Finnan, Robbie Keane.
Ireland penalty misses: Matt Holland, David Connolly, Kevin Kilbane.
Referee: Anders Frisk (Sweden).
Men of the Match: **Spain:** Iker Casillas, for keeping his head and stopping three penalties in all.
Ireland: Damien Duff, for creating all sorts of havoc all game long.

53 Mexico 0 – 2 USA   USA wins CONCACAF showdown
June 17: Jeonju, South Korea

These two CONCACAF teams met in the Round of 16, leaving the possibility of only one advancing from the region to the quarterfinals. Although the United States record against Mexico was 0-21-3 from 1930 to 1980, since 1990 they became competitive and had a good record of 9-6-5. This match was the first meeting of the neighboring countries in World Cup Finals competition.

Mexico had been playing very well, winning Group G with two wins, and a tie (against venerable Italy). The USA started off shocking Portugal, fended off hosts Korea, and then went down in poor form to Poland.

USA coach Bruce Arena decided to play a three center-back formation of Tony Sanneh, Eddie Pope, and Gregg Berhalter in an effort to cut down on defensive breakdowns, especially in the air against dangerous center forward Jared Borgetti. Captain Claudio Reyna played the right wingback position and Eddie Lewis the left. Pablo Mastroeni took the center midfield position with John O'Brien and Landon Donovan just ahead on opposite flanks. *Kopfmeister* (headmaster) Brian McBride and speed-merchant Josh Wolff (who had a goal and assist in a 2-0 win against Mexico in the qualifiers in 2001) would start as strikers. Mexico coach Javier Aguirre elected to use the same starting eleven that was successful against their vanquished Group G opponents.

USA team captain Claudio Reyna took a quick direct kick from Brian McBride in the 8th minute, then rounded one defender and worked another down the right side to the end line, centering to Josh Wolff at the near post. Wolff cleverly touched the ball back to Brian McBride, who calmly threaded his shot through three diving Mexican defenders and the goalkeeper into the left side of the net. The USA had accomplished their first objectives – score the first goal and upset the Mexican rhythm.

Ramon Morales made his only dangerous run of the game in the 15th minute, just shooting wide left from 19 yards. He was soon substituted in the 28th minute for Luis Hernandez (who had four goals in 1998 World Cup) after not being able to solve Claudio Reyna. Mexico kept up the pressure, and after a poor clearance by keeper Friedel in the 35th minute, Cuauhtémoc Blanco forced a reaction save by Friedel to get a corner kick. Friedel was lucky to escape so easily.

In the 37th minute, Donovan head-flicked on to Wolff who executed a good left-footed volley that was well saved by keeper Oscar Perez.

In the 52nd minute, Braulio Luna tested Friedel with a curling free kick from the right penalty-box corner that the keeper parried against the crossbar and out of bounds. Another close call for the USA.

The 57th minute was another critical moment in the game. Off a corner kick, John O'Brien punched out the centering pass. This could have resulted in a penalty kick that would have brought Mexico back into the game, but the referee did not notice the infraction. Eight minutes later Lewis took a perfect release pass from O'Brien, ran down the left sideline and flashed a center to the far post. A streaking Donovan was there to head it in from 5 yards for a decisive 2-0 lead in the 65th minute. Soon after, in the 72nd minute, Ernie Stewart hit the left post after a volley from in close. The Mexicans were demoralized, as thereafter the game became very physical with the referee attempting to control the violence. In the 88th minute, Mexican center back and captain Rafael Marquez committed a cowardly head-butt on a defenseless Cobi Jones and was immediately sent off – Jones was lucky not to sustain a broken jaw and/or neck.

With this loss, Mexico was eliminated in the second round of the 1994, 1998, and 2002 World Cups. But the USA had solved their defensive problems, and continued with their inventive and opportunistic scoring. With a lucky non-call on O'Brien's handball, they were able to overcome a very good Mexican team. The USA—Mexico derby has now evolved into a memorable international rivalry.

Mexico: Oscar Perez, Rafael Marquez, Manuel Vidrio (Sigifredo Mercado, 46), Salvador Carmona, Gerardo Torrado (Alberto Garcia Aspe, 78), Ramon Morales (Luis Hernandez, 28), Braulio Luna, Joahan Rodriguez, Jared Borgetti, Cuauhtémoc Blanco, Jesus Arellano.
United States: Brad Friedel, Gregg Berhalter, Pablo Mastroeni (Carlos Llamosa, 90), Eddie Pope, John O'Brien, Eddie Lewis, Claudio Reyna, Landon Donovan, Anthony Sanneh, Josh Wolff (Earnie Stewart, 59), Brian Mc Bride (Cobi Jones, 79).
Goals: United States; Brian McBride 8, Landon Donovan 65.
Referee: Vitor Melo Pereira (Portugal)
Man of the Match: Claudio Reyna for his stellar controlling play, and making the chance for the first goal out of nothing.

54 Brazil 2 – 0 Belgium — Brazil beat excellent Belgian squad
June 17: Kobe, Japan

Brazil faced a very skillful and disciplined European side in Belgium. Mbo Mpenza forewarned the Brazilians with a superb 22-yard running shot from outside the right corner of the penalty box that was heading to the left upper corner. Marcos produced an equally superb save as he leapt and swatted it away. For a stretch after it was all Brazil, as Juninho and Ronaldo shot wide, and Rivaldo tried an unsuccessful overhead kick in front of goal.

But in the 35th minute, Marc Wilmots received a cross from the right side and headed it past a beaten Marcos into the left hand corner. However, this skillful goal was waved off by referee Prendergast for a suspected push on Roque Junior. Brazil kept attacking as Ronaldo had two more chances and Roberto Carlos one before the half, all of which went wide.

After the half, Wilmots continued his brilliance with a blast from 23 yards that fully extended Marcos in the 53rd minute, and a shot from 16 yards in the 63rd minute that again required a diving save from "Saint Marcos."

Brazil got back to business, and in the 67th minute Rivaldo received a pretty outside-of-the-right pass from Ronaldinho and (1) chested, (2) foot controlled (left of course), (3) let the ball bounce, and (4) blasted the ball toward goal from 19 yards out. Belgium defender Timmy Simons got a slight touch on the ball just redirecting it past the helpless Geert de Vlieger for the Brazil goal.

With Belgium pushing forward for the equalizer, Brazil substitute Kleberson ran up the right side and made a perfect center to Ronaldo; the center-forward was fortunate to nutmeg the keeper from 15 yards when he had the whole goal to shoot at. That goal sealed the result for Brazil.

Brazil continued their good fortune to have Belgium's goal disallowed, as that would have changed the whole character of the game. Brazil succeeded with their relentless attacking, and Marcos was in-form to deny Wilmots again and again.

At the end of this game, Rivaldo had four goals in the tournament and Ronaldo five; Wilmots ended his World Cup with three for his impressive efforts. This match marked the *first time in World Cup Finals play that two teammates each scored a goal in their first four matches*. Brazil's offense certainly was clicking, but more ominous for future opponents, Brazil's defense was also improving game by game.

Brazil: Marcos, Cafú, Lúcio, Roque Junior, Edmílson, Roberto Carlos, Gilberto Silva, Ronaldinho (Kleberson 81), Juninho Paulista (Denilson 57), Rivaldo, Ronaldo (Ricardinho 90).
Belgium: Geert De Vlieger, Jacky Peeters (Wesley Sonck 73), Timmy Simons, Daniel van Buyten, Nico van Kerckhoven, Mbo Mpenza, Johan Walem, Yves Vanderhaeghe, Bart Goor, Marc Wilmots, Gert Verheyen.
Goals: Brazil - Rivaldo 67, Ronaldo 87.
Referee: Peter Prendergast (Jamaica).
Men of the Match: Rivaldo with his riveting opening goal, and Marcos for his saves.

55 Japan 0 – 1 Turkey: — Turkey prevails over co-hosts Japan
June 18: Miyagi, Japan

This match was the initial second round World Cup experience for both Japan and Turkey. Turkey held the edge in players performing for top European teams who were tested and experienced in major European competitions, but the 1997 friendly between the two teams had ended 1-0 for Japan.

This game started out as a lively affair despite rainy conditions that made the pitch very slick. The Japanese crowd was not as boisterous as the Korean crowd at the Italy game, and after Ümit Davala leaped above the crowd and scored on a header from 7 yards off a Ergün Penbe right-sided corner kick in the 12th minute, they became less of a factor. Once Turkey scored, they set about protecting that lead.

Both teams had good technique on the ball, and with furious covering in midfield neither team could maintain possession for long periods. The midfield engines for Turkey were Baştürk and Şaş, and for Japan Nakata and Ono.

The closest Japan came in the game was late in the first half when Brazilian-born Alessandro Santos ("Alex") took a splendid 19 yard free-kick from the left just outside the box, curled it over the wall and struck the junction of the crossbar and left upright. A few inches were enough to end the co-host's dream of progressing in the 2002 World Cup.

Japan: Seigo Narazaki, Naoki Matsuda, Koji Nakata, Tsuneyasu Miyamoto, Junichi Inamoto (Daisuke Ichikawa, 46), Hiroaki Morishima, 86), Hidetoshi Nakata, Alessandro Santos (Takayuki Suzuki 46), Shinji Ono, Tomokazu Myojin, Kazuyuki Toda, Akinori Nishizawa.

Turkey: Rüstü Reçber, Bülent Korkmaz, Fatih Akyel, Alpay Özalan, Tugay Kerimoglu, Yildiray Bastürk (Mansiz Ilhan, 90), Ergun Penbe, Hakan Unsal, Umit Davala (Nihat Kahveci, 74), Hakan Sükür, Hasan Sas (Tayfur Havutcu, 85).
Goals: Turkey - Umit Davala 12.
Referee: Pierluigi Collina (Italy).
Man of the Match: Ümit Davala for his leaping header that put Turkey through.

56 South Korea 2 – 1 Italy: Home team South Korea stuns Italy
June 18: Daejeon, South Korea

Italy faced a less experienced but dangerous team that had knocked out favorite Portugal and won Group D. In a historical note, the Italians had experienced their most embarrassing World Cup loss against North Korea (making their only appearance ever in the World Cup) in the 1966 World Cup. The Italians again faced a Korean team, this time in front of a rabid South Korean home crowd.

Both Italy and South Korea played this match at a high physical and technical level. Italy was in trouble early, as Christian Panucci was called for mugging Seol Ki Hyeon off the ball in the penalty area in the 5th minute. Ahn Jung-Hwan's penalty kick went towards the left corner, but Italian keeper Gianluigi Buffon anticipated and saved the shot. This was the second South Korean penalty kick saved in regular time in the Cup (their previous penalty kick was denied by USA keeper Brad Friedel).

The Italians came back in the 18th minute when Totti centered a corner kick from the left side to the near post, where Vieri headed into the left corner of the net from 3 yards out for the opening goal.

Ahn then tried to equalize after his Cruyff-turn in the box disengaged his defender, but his 9-yard shot flew just wide of the upper-left corner. Francesco Totti gave a lead pass to Damiano Tommasi whose 14-yard shot was brilliantly stuffed by keeper Lee, with the defense making the final clearance.

The second half was full of chances for the Italians, and few for South Korea. Regulation time was coming to a close, but the Koreans were still running hard for an equalizer. South Korean ball movement worked the ball into the middle of the box in the 88th minute, and defender Panucci failed to clear (and committed a handball as well). The ball fell to the feet of Seol Ki-Hyeon who swiftly punched the ball into the right corner with a left-footed volley. Pandemonium ensued in the stadium after the late tying goal. Overtime beckoned, but Italy was not through as Vieri just missed a 6 yard sitter centered in from the left side that he attempted with his weaker right foot. South Korea came back with a Cha Du Ri bicycle kick that fortuitously went straight at Buffon, and Park shot just wide as regular time expired.

In extra-time South Korea took the initiative. Italy keeper Buffon barely stopped a low-roller by Hwang Sun Hong in the 99th minute on a clever 26-yard free kick that *went under* the jumping Italians. In the 103rd minute (first overtime), Francesco Totti dribbled his way into the penalty area and was seemingly tripped up before he could shoot. The referee saw it differently, and gave the incredulous Totti a yellow card for diving ("*simulazione*" in Italy). That being Totti's second yellow card of the game, he was then shown the red card and dismissed. Slow-motion video showed that although contact between the players had been made, Totti did not initiate it, and defender Song Chong-Gug had actually touched the ball. Therefore, there should have been neither a penalty nor a dive call made, and Totti should not have been dismissed.

A few days later, the FIFA head Sepp Blatter shared his thoughts of the call, "Totti's sending off against Korea was neither a penalty nor a dive," and "A referee with a feeling…..would not have shown him the card, bearing in mind the same player had already been booked." He then added, "The refereeing has been the only negative aspect of this World Cup magnificently organized by two countries."

After Totti was banished, Tommasi was released for a one-on-one with Lee, but was called offside when he rounded the keeper and scored what would have been the winning Golden Goal – video replay showed that Tommasi was onsides. Gattuso then intercepted a misplay by Park but shot right at keeper Lee Woon-Jae who made an incredible reaction save on the 6-yard blast.

Italy had had their chances to win, but the Koreans kept coming On a cross from Lee Young Pyo from the middle left of the field, Ahn Jung Hwan out jumped Maldini and guided a glancing header from 7 yards to the far post past Buffon for the Golden Goal in the 117th minute. USA keeper Brad Friedel had been victimized by a nearly identical goal from Ahn in the group games. Ahn, the only Korean player in Serie A in Italy (Perugia) had buried his club team's homeland in the World Cup.

Italy's coach Trapattoni was incensed about the refereeing decisions, especially about Totti's dismissal but also about the callback of Damiano Tommasi's goal (Italy had 5 goals called back in 3 games). Some Italians did not take kindly to those whom have performed well against them in World

Cup play. Even supernova Diego Maradona faced fan repercussions that numbered his days with Napoli after he helped eliminate host country Italy in the 1990 World Cup.

Within days of his historic goal, Perugia announced that Ahn would not continue playing for them. In a fit of petulant xenophobia, Perugia's chairman Luciano Gaucci said he had no intention of "paying a salary to someone who has ruined Italian soccer." Italy already has many problems concerning racism against foreign stars ("*stranieri*"), and Perugia's actions against Ahn could only fan the flames – a worrisome development for Italian soccer.

What to say about Italy? The Totti ejection was unjustified, but there was no disgrace in their actual performance. However, this was the fourth straight World Cup in which Italy was defeated after regulation time (in 1990, 1994, 1998 Italy was eliminated in penalty kick lotteries), but this match was perhaps the hardest blow. In a cruel irony Paolo Maldini, who was beaten on Ahn's header, was a member of all four of these teams. It was also Maldini's 23rd consecutive full World Cup match, an individual record that may not be broken for a very long time.

And South Korea? They had never won a World Cup match before the 2002 World Cup, going 0-10-4. Now they had won three, tied one, defeated giants Portugal and Italy, and were in the quarterfinals. The whole country remained in a dream state, as Ahn seemingly floated around the field after his goal.

South Korea: Lee Woon-Jae, Choi Jin Chul, Kim Tae Young (Hwang Sun Hong, 63), Bo Hong Myung (Du-Ri Cha, 83), Kim Nam Il (Chun Soo Lee, 68), Yoo Sang Chul, Lee Young Pyo, Ahn Jung Hwan, Park Ji Sung, Seol Ki Hyeon, Song Chong Gug.
Italy: Gianluigi Buffon, Christian Panucci, Paolo Maldini, Francesco Coco, Mark Iuliano, Christian Zanetti, Francesco Totti, Damiano Tommasi, Gianluca Zambrotta (Angelo Di Livio, 72), Alessandro Del-Piero (Gennaro Ivan Gattuso, 61), Christian Vieri.
Goals: South Korea - Seol Ki Hyeon 88, Ahn Jung Hwan 117 (Golden Goal). **Italy -** Christian Vieri 18.
Referee: Byron Moreno (Ecuador).
Man of the Match: Ahn Jung Hwan for never giving up after his failed penalty, beating one of the greats of the game (Maldini) to get the Golden Goal.

QUARTERFINALS

Most pundits would never have predicted four of the eight countries advancing to the quarterfinals. While the betting odds had been favorable for Brazil (7/2), England (8/1), Spain (8/1), and Germany (10/1), they were distinctly unfavorable for Turkey (50/1), USA (90/1), South Korea (100/1), and Senegal (200/1).

Brazil, England, Germany, and Spain advancing to the quarterfinals was no surprise, although Spain was lucky to advance past Ireland on penalty kicks. Unfancied USA and Turkey won their games in regulation against Mexico and Japan, but spoilers Senegal and South Korea needed Golden Goals against Sweden and Italy, respectively. All eight teams were of high quality and deserving of the quarterfinals.

The new odds of winning the Cup at the start of the quarterfinals were (in decreasing order):

Country	Odds	FIFA ranking
Brazil	12/5	2
Spain	11/4	8
England	10/3	12
Germany	4/1	11
Senegal	16/1	42
Korea Republic	16/1	40
Turkey	18/1	22
United States	25/1	13

Strangely, the USA received the worst odds despite their higher FIFA ranking than three other teams (Senegal, Korea, and Turkey). The British bookmakers may have been skeptical of the presence of quality footballers "across the pond" but that attitude would start to change after the USA's fine performance in the 2002 World Cup.

57 England 1 – 2 Brazil: The Ronaldinho and Blue-Brazil Show
June 21: Shizuoka, Japan

England and Brazil had met three times before in the World Cup Finals; the 1958 game ended in a 0-0 tie, but Brazil had won 3-1 in 1962 and 1-0 in 1970. Brazil was the only country ever to beat England more than once in World Cup Final play.

Brazil entered the stadium in their new royal blue kit, and started in their typical attacking form. England resisted and actually scored first in the 23rd minute, the move beginning when Emile Heskey sent a searching through ball that defender Lúcio should have easily cleared. Instead, he trapped the ball directly to Michael Owen's feet, and the speedy striker merrily one-touched it away and lifted a goal-bound shot from just above the penalty spot over Brazil's charging keeper Marcos.

Brazil was surprised but not disconsolate at the goal, and went back to work attacking. Just before the half, Beckham ducked out of contesting a 50-50 ball and Ronaldinho gathered the ball in his own half. He decided to take matters into his own hands, going on a 40-yard run featuring a tremendous high speed step-over that totally wrong-footed defender Ashley Cole. After Ronaldinho had done the penetrating work he calmly laid the ball off to Rivaldo on the right side of the box, who neatly one-timed with his left foot past keeper David Seaman into the left corner from 16 yards. A few moments later the half whistle blew. Brazil had managed to equalize before the half time break – an ominous sign for England.

Brazil's second half attacks came to fruition in the 50th minute as Ronaldinho took a 35-yard free kick from the right side. He lofted what appeared to be a crossing-style pass that ended up sneaking into the upper left hand corner of the goal. Seaman, who was not out of position but slow-of-foot, could only wave helplessly as the ball tucked in perfectly. One of the great goals of any World Cup, it was similar in distance and location to a strike made on the run by Brazil defenseman Josimar in the 1986 World Cup. Goalkeeper Seaman must have had *déjà vu* harking back to the 1995 Cup Winners Cup Final when he was Arsenal's keeper against Real Zaragoza. In that game he misjudged another long shot as Nayim (who had played for arch-Arsenal rivals Tottenham) put a 50-yard volley over his head in extra-time to win it for the Spanish club team.

Shortly after Ronaldinho had engineered the Brazil comeback, he was shown a straight red-card for a modest challenge on a loose ball. In a remarkable display of "no feel for the game" the referee booted him from the rest of the England game and the semi-final as well.

The Brazil defense was typically porous after the goal, and the pesky Heskey got several crosses over in the box that none of his teammates could locate. Both Michael Owen and Ronaldo were eventually substituted. Rivaldo had scored in five straight games, but Ronaldo's four game goal streak was broken upon substitution.

With two of the "R's" off the field, and the Brazil defense shaky, Rivaldo soldiered on as the torchbearer of Brazilian technical excellence. Clearly exhausted, Rivaldo held his own controlling clearances, making space, and marking time. England could not develop any more offensive capabilities with a one-man advantage, even when Darius Vassel and Teddy Sheringham were brought on as extra firepower.

The game result was just, as Brazil outplayed England and displayed a growing maturity in defense and teamwork in adverse conditions.

England: David Seaman, Danny Mills, Rio Ferdinand, Sol Campbell, Ashley Cole (Teddy Sheringham 79), David Beckham, Nicky Butt, Paul Scholes, Trevor Sinclair (Kieron Dyer 56), Michael Owen (Darius Vassell 79), Emile Heskey.
Brazil: Marcos, Cafu, Lúcio, Roque Junior, Edmílson, Roberto Carlos, Gilberto Silva, Ronaldinho, Kleberson, Rivaldo, Ronaldo (Edilson 70).
Goals: England - Owen 23. **Brazil -** Rivaldo 45, Ronaldinho 50.
Referee: Felipe Rizo Ramos (Mexico).
Man of the Match: Ronaldinho, for his brilliant setup of Rivaldo's initial goal, and spectacular imagination and execution for the second.

58 Germany 1 – 0 USA: German set-piece beats quality USA effort
June 21: Ulsan, South Korea

The German and USA teams knew each other's playing styles, as many USA World Cup players had experience playing on German club teams. The USA had lost to Germany 2-0 in the 1998 World Cup Finals, but subsequently beat Germany in two out of three friendly games (by 2-0 and 3-0 scores in 1999, but lost 4-2 in a final warm-up in Germany in 2002).

This game exposed the inherently unequal and flawed World Cup match schedule. Germany had played their second match on the same day that the USA had played their first game, meaning that the USA was playing its 5th game in 16 days, while the Germans had played only four games in the same time period. Immediately before this quarterfinal match, the Germans had five days rest while the USA had only three days, or 67% more time to recuperate; this significant recuperation advantage should not be ignored in future World Cups.

The game started evenly but the USA developed the best chances in the first half. A right-sided slalom run by Landon Donovan that included a cheeky nutmeg of his defender resulted in a left-footed shot headed for the left hand corner; keeper Oliver Kahn was just able to tip the ball around the far post. Claudio Reyna then lifted a fine pass over the defense on the left side to Donovan who was attacking from all sides; his left-footed shot was saved once again by Kahn.

The German breakthrough came on a ball similar to the Ahn headed goals for Korea against the USA and Italy. An in-swinging free kick from the right side from Christian Ziege resulted in Michael Ballack heading a goal from only 7 yards, as keeper Brad Friedel remained on his line and had little chance as the ball flashed by on his right.

With the USA one goal down, Germany kept attacking. Miroslav Klose failed to extend his record of five consecutively headed goals when his header from a left-sided cross hit the base of the right post.

After the half, Donovan had yet another fine chance turned around the post, but Kahn was not so fortunate on the resultant corner that concluded the game's most controversial moment. USA defender Greg Berhalter left-foot volleyed a Claudio Reyna corner kick on goal from 5 yards out, and Kahn was only able to slow the ball's progression into goal. Torsten Frings was guarding the far post and the ball ricocheted off his bare arm directly preventing the ball's entrance into goal; an apparent handball infraction giving a penalty kick. The referee did not think so, and the game tape probably supported this view. Video replay showed that Frings did not move his hand towards the ball, and therefore the handball was unintentional. A dose of bad luck for the USA.

The USA kept pressuring as Kahn was forced to head clear from outside the box; Reyna's distance volley from Kahn's desperate defensive maneuver went just wide. Finally, a cross from Clint Mathis on the right found a pouncing Tony Sanneh whose fierce header beat Kahn and found the netting; only it was the harmless side netting as Sanneh rued his last-ditch chance.

Three USA players who had played in Germany (Donovan, Berhalter, and Sanneh) came the closest to equalizing against Germany, but Kahn and the German defense was good and lucky enough to live another day. Michael Ballack was able to take a half-chance and steer Germany into the semi-finals with his goal off Friedel's hand. The USA would leave the 2002 World Cup with heads held high, knowing they had knocked off one of the favorites (Portugal), beaten their biggest rival (Mexico), and had made a good show in the quarterfinals against perennial power Germany.

Germany: Oliver Kahn, Thomas Linke, Christian Ziege, Christoph Metzelder, Torsten Frings, Dietmar Hamann, Michael Ballack, Sebastien Kehl, Bernd Schneider (Jens Jeremies 60), Miroslav Klose (Oliver Bierhoff 88), Oliver Neuville (Marco Bode 79).
United States: Brad Friedel, Frankie Hejduk (Cobi Jones 65), Gregg Berhalter, Tony Sanneh, Pablo Mastroeni, Eddie Pope, John O'Brien, Eddie Lewis, Claudio Reyna, Landon Donovan, Brian McBride (Clint Mathis 58).
Goals: Germany – Michael Ballack 39.
Referee: Hugh Dallas (Scotland).
Man of the Match: Michael Ballack for his goal above the USA defense.

59 Spain 0 – 0 (aet) [3-5 penalties] South Korea Host Team has Home Luck
June 22: Gwangju, South Korea

Because of the forgiving architecture of the Gwanju Stadium, Spain was subjected to less crowd noise than co-host South Korea's former opponents. A larger problem was that Spain was Raúl-less, as their star striker was out injured.

The game started with both sides feeling each other out at a lesser pace than had been demonstrated in South Korea's previous games. Although first half-play was equally distributed, the goal chances were nearly all Spain's.

In the 18th minute Baraja received a throw-in from Puyol and tried an overhead kick from 15 yards that went wide right. In the 25th minute, Morrientes went high to head a ball going to the right upper corner, which was well saved by goalkeeper Lee Woon-Jae. Just before the half in the 45th minute Spain had two good chances: De Pedro shot wide right from 22 yards, and Hierro headed just over from inside the 6-yard box.

In the second half South Korea had their best opportunity of the game in a scramble on both sides of the Spanish 6-yard box in the 67th minute. Park Ji-Sung received a deflected shot on the left side just outside the box, chested down and right-footed a blast headed for the upper left-hand corner if not for Spain keeper Iker Casillas' lightning right-handed parry.

Joaquin hit the right side netting from 18 yards in the 72nd minute, while Lee Chun-Soo had his 20-yard shot saved by Casillas in the 90th minute.

In the overtime period, Joaquin beat his man to the right end line and beautifully centered to Morrientes who nodded it in for goal. Keeper Lee Woon-Jae may have stopped at the referee's whistle at the last second but was likely beaten anyway. However, the goal was disallowed for the linesman's judgment of the ball being out of play before Joaquin kicked it. Video replays showed the ball had been in-play by half the circumference of the ball; a massive refereeing error. An almost certain Golden Goal for Spain had been wrongly disallowed.

Spain was disheartened, but still Morrientes took a right-footed volley from 10 yards off Joaquin's bouncing throw-in from the right side in the 100th minute; Spain watched helplessly as the ball ricocheted off the left post. The rest of the game was less active as both fatigued teams seemed resigned to penalties.

In the penalty shootout, Joaquin tried a stutter-step penalty-kick made famous by Brazilian Sócrates, but his intention was "telegraphed" and the kick saved by the keeper Lee Woon-Jae. Skipper Hong Myung-Bo sealed Spain's fate with a well-placed kick to the right side that fooled Casillas.

Although Spain had probably scored a legitimate Golden Goal, it was erroneously disallowed and they eventually lost on penalties. The South Koreans, although industrious and with good technique, only seriously threatened the Spanish goal once.

Morrientes' goal would be discussed at length – whose fault was it – linesman and/or referee? Did referee blow his whistle before he nodded in? Was the Korean goalkeeper and defender still attempting to prevent the score after a whistle had been blown? The Koreans certainly should have been trying in a packed stadium with all sorts of unofficial whistles going off. It would be foolish to stop one's effort when the other team is in the act of scoring, unless the play is stopped with a dead ball (which it was not).

The match circumstances illustrate perfectly why instant video replay is necessary for World Cup Games. Spain had formerly underachieved in the World Cup; in the 2002 Cup they had competed fairly in the host country, only for their historical misfortune to continue. As for history, South Korea was the first Asian team to reach the semi-final level of the World Cup.

Spain: Iker Casillas, Carlos Puyol, Fernando Hierro, Ivan Helguera (Xavi 93), Enrique Romero, Joaquin Sanchez, Ruben Baraja, Francisco De Pedro (Gaizka Mendieta 70), Juan Carlos Valeron (Luis Enrique 80), Miguel Nadal, Fernando Morrientes.
South Korea: Lee Woon Jae, Choi Jin Cheul, Kim Nam Il (Lee Eul Yong 32), Yoo Sang Chul (Lee Chun Soo 61), Kim Tae Young (Hwang Sun Hong 90), Seol Ki Hyeon, Lee Young Pyo, Ahn Jung Hwan, Hong Myung Bo, Park Ji Sung, Song Chong Gug
Goals: No goals scored in regular time or overtime.
Spain penalty scorers: Fernando Hierro, Ruben Baraja, Xavi. **Spain penalty miss**: Joaquin.
Korea penalty scorers: Hwang Sun Hong, Park Ji Sung, Seol Ki Hyeon, Ahn Jung Hwan, Hong Myung Bo.
Referee: Gamal Al-Ghandour (Egypt).
Men of the Match: **South Korea:** Keeper Lee Woon-Jae kept Korea in the game with several superb saves and excellent positioning. **Spain:** Joaquin was the best field player, making several long runs and setting up Morrientes' Golden Goal header chance that was annulled.

60 Senegal 0 – 1 (aet) Turkey: Golden Goal wins it for Turkey
June 22: Osaka, Japan

Neither of these well-skilled sides conceded any advantage in this match. The driving and creative forces were Hasan Şaş and El Hadji Diouf for Turkey and Senegal, respectively.

The first great chance on goal came in the 19th minute when Khalilou Fadiga's shot from the left side beat Turkish defense and keeper Rüştü Reçber, but his certain goal was unluckily stopped by teammate Henri Camara, who was actually behind the keeper. Camara's subsequent shot into the net was justifiably annulled for offside.

Turkey's all-time leading goal scorer Hakan Šükür had not yet scored in the World Cup, and his touch still needed sharpening as he missed two gilded chances from very close in the 28th and 39th minutes.

Just before halftime, Şaş lofted a clever ball that Yildiray Bastürk headed past Senegal keeper Tony Sylva, only to have a sure goal saved by Omar Daf's miraculous sliding clearance off the line, in the defensive play of the tournament.

After the half Diouf's 25-yard free kick sailed just over the upper-right hand corner. Turkey then had several near chances that were either defused by the Senegalese defense or by poor Turkish play decisions.

Henri Camara made a bid to be the Senegalese hero the second game running, but Reçber saved his fine 18-yard shot in injury-time.

The buildup to the Golden Goal in the 94th minute was sublime. Turkish keeper Reçber broke up a Senegalese attack and quickly distributed to Arif Erdem, who cleanly pushed the ball to one side of Omar Daf, ran around and collected it. Daf was not happy about these events and tackled Erdem some steps later, but referee Oscar Ruiz wisely played the possession rule and let play continue. The ball ran on to Ümit Davala sprinting down the right touchline, and he centered before Daf could contest the ball again. Davala's speculative pass found substitute striker İlhan Mansiz in the right side of the penalty area, and he one-touched an inspired half-volley from 11 yards past a stunned Tony Sylva who had no chance to save. The Turks started celebrating as the ball tucked into the left-side netting.

One could not ask for a more beautiful Golden Goal to end a well-played scoreless World Cup tie by two of the world's emerging football powers.

Even after losing to Turkey, the gallant Senegalese equaled Cameroon's 1990 feat of an African team advancing to the quarterfinals.

Senegal: Tony Sylva, Omar Daf, Pape Malick Diop, Aliou Cisse, Lamine Diatta, Ferdinand Coly, Khalilou Fadiga, Salif Diao, Pape Bouba Diop, Henri Camara, El Hadji Diouf.
Turkey: Rüştü Reçber, Bülent Korkmaz, Fatih Akyel, Alpay Özalan, Tugay Kerimoğlu, Yildiray Bastürk, Ergün Penbe, Emre Belözoglu (Arif Erdem 91'), Ümit Davala. Hakan Şükür (İlhan Mansiz 67'), Hasan Şaş.
Goals: Turkey - Ilhan Mansiz 94'.
Referee: Oscar Ruiz (Colombia).

Man of the Match: Ümit Davala for creating several dangerous chances including the opportunity for Ilhan Mansiz to deflect the ball past keeper Sylva to win the game.

SEMIFINALS

The odds of winning the Cup at the start of the semifinals were recalculated for the four countries involved. Presumably Turkey was ranked lower because of the Korean home advantage.

Country	Odds	FIFA ranking
Brazil	8/13	2
Germany	3/1	11
Korea Republic	6/1	40
Turkey	8/1	22

61 Germany 1 – 0 South Korea — Ballack to the rescue
June 25: Seoul, South Korea

Korea started the game promisingly with Cha Du Ri crossing the ball for Lee Chun Soo to redirect to the far post; keeper Oliver Kahn responded with a full length one-hand diving save to turn the ball around the post. Cha again created a chance down the right wing that ended with striker Park Ji Sung in excellent position, but his left-footed shot was directly at Kahn. Bernd Schneider volleyed from 20 yards at Lee Woon Jae but the keeper's positioning was exact enough to make the stop.

The second half brought more scoring chances than the first. Miroslav Klose tried for his sixth headed goal, but his weak *Kopfball* was captured by Lee. Ahn Jung Hwan then had a chance in the box but fired high and wide. On the other end, Klose wasted Ramelow's useful chip pass well wide.

In the most controversial play of the game, Lee Chun Soo made a skillful dribbling run through the German defense that was cut short by a dangerous Michael Ballack tackle from behind. Ballack was fortunate not to receive a straight red card, but the yellow card given meant Ballack would miss the Final, a negative outcome surely not worth the unsportsmanlike foul. The resulting free kick came to naught as the German wall deflected Lee Chun Soo's shot.

Minutes later Oliver Neuville picked up a pass from a poor clearance from Kim Tae Young, scampered down the right side and centered for the onrushing Ballack. Lee saved the German midfielder's right-footed shot but Ballack immediately slotted in the rebound with his left for Germany to go up 1-0 in the 75th minute. Marco Bode then tried to expeditiously double the lead with a free kick, but Lee dove and punch-saved cleanly.

South Korea's last chance fell to Park Ji Sung who received a hurried pass at the top of the box; under pressure from Thomas Linke he missed the goal.

South Korea had over-achieved to get to the semi-finals, but could not crack the German defense. Nevertheless, they brought an attractive and skilled brand of soccer that resulted in the best Asian team finish ever at a World Cup.

Germany: Oliver Kahn. Torsten Frings, Thomas Linke, Carsten Ramelow, Christoph Metzelder, Bernd Schneider (Jens Jeremies 85), Michael Ballack, Dietmar Hamann, Marco Bode, Miroslav Klose (Oliver Bierhoff 70), Oliver Neuville (Gerald Asamoah 88).
South Korea: Lee Woon Jae, Song Chong Gug, Choi Jin Cheul (Lee Ming Sung 56), Hong Myung Bo (cap.) (Seol Ki Hyeon 80), Kim Tae Young, Yoo Sang Chul, Lee Chun Soo, Lee Young Pyo, Park Ji Sung, Hwang Sun Hong (Ahn Jung Hwan 54), Cha Doo Ri.
Referee: Urs Meier (Switzerland).
Goals: Germany - Michael Ballack 75.
Man of the Match: Michael Ballack for calmly putting in his own rebound to win the game.

62 Brazil 1 – 0 Turkey   Ronaldo's remarkable toe-poke wins
June 26: Saitama, Japan

This was the second meeting of Brazil and Turkey in the 2002 World Cup. The only reason *two teams from the same Group could meet before the Final* was because the 2002 World Cup was *co-hosted*, and South Korea had the right to play all games at home unless they reached the Final (to be played in Yokohama, Japan). Normally, it would be impossible for two teams advancing from the same Group to meet *until the Final match*.

There were two modern examples of two teams meeting twice in the World Cup Group stages and the Final match. In the 1954 World Cup in Switzerland, a half-strength Germany was crushed 8-3 by Hungary in the first round, but a full-strength Fritz Walters-led German squad rebounded to beat Ferenc Puskas' Hungarian team 3-2 in the Final. Brazil met Czechoslovakia twice in the 1962 World Cup, once in the Group stage (a 0 – 0 draw), and later in the Final match (a 3-1 win for Brazil).

With Ronaldinho sitting out his one-game suspension, it was imperative for Ronaldo and Rivaldo to elevate their games in order for Brazil to advance.

Brazil keeper Marcos was kept busy in the opening moments of the game as Emre Belözoglu and Alpay Özalan threatened Brazil's goal. Marcos only just got a hand on Özalan header destined for the far corner.

Brazilian wing defender Cafú decided to emulate defender Özalan and was put through by Ronaldo, but Turkish keeper Rüstü Reçber just got down to deflect Cafú's bullet-shot. Rivaldo then whipped in a shot that Reçber could not hold, but Reçber somehow saved Ronaldo's point-blank rebound shot (this sequence was repeated in the Final, but Ronaldo then scored on the rebound from Kahn).

Rivaldo fired in two more dipping and swinging shots; the first from 24 yards forced a diving save from Reçber, and the second shaved the right upright so closely that the video replay revealed the ball shadow on the post. Reçber finished the first half with a good save from an offensive foray by Roberto Carlos.

After the half Ronaldo ran onto a pass from Gilberto Silva on the left side and took on four defenders on the way to the goal. Surrounded by three of them, he let loose with an unstoppable toe-poke that Reçber parried but could not prevent from nestling in the side netting by the far post. Brazil led 1-0 and was looking confident.

Ronaldo then centered to Kleberson who shot firmly to Reçber from the penalty spot. Once again Cafú went to the end line to center for substitute Luizão (who had come in the 67th minute for Ronaldo); the striker got off a pretty bicycle kick that bounced spectacularly over the crossbar.

Turkey had two chances to equalize near the end of the match. Substitute İlhan Mansiz tried an ambitious shot from outside the left corner of the penalty box that Marcos just finger-tipped over the right-upper corner of the goal. Then a memory was stirred of England's Paul Gascoigne's free kick to set up David Platt's unsighted goal in the 1990 World Cup, as Hasan Şaş put in a cross that Hakan Šükür turned on blindly to brilliantly redirect to the near post. However, Marcos was immaculately positioned to make the save.

Even without the ever-dangerous Ronaldinho, Brazil had created enough magic to earn their 7th World Cup Final appearance.

Brazil: Marcos, Cafú, Lúcio, Roque Junior, Edmílson, Roberto Carlos, Gilberto Silva, Ronaldo (Luizão 67), Rivaldo, Kleberson (Belleti 85), Edilson (Denilson 75).
Turkey: Rüstü Reçber, Bülent Korkmaz, Fatih Akyel, Alpay Özalan, Tugay Kerimoglu, Hakan Šükür (captain), Yildiray Bastürk (Arif Erdem 88), Hasan Sas, Ergun Penbe, Emre Belözoglu (Ilhan Mansiz 61), Umit Davala (Muzzy Izzet 73).
Goal: Brazil - Ronaldo 49.
Referee: Kim Milton Nielsen (Denmark).

Man of the Match: Ronaldo for conjuring up a goal out of a half-chance.

3rd Place Match

63 South Korea 2 – 3 Turkey   Outstanding action in 3rd place match
June 29: Daegu, South Korea

Third-place consolation matches are often a tepid affair between two spent teams going through the motions after they have been denied the glory of the Final. But South Korea and Turkey endeavored to finish the World Cup leaving a positive impression on the soccer world, by competing fairly in a stylish and creative contest.

The teams had played a 0 – 0 tie match in Germany in 2002, so were somewhat familiar with their opponent's form – Turkey's half-Brazilian/half-European style and South Korea's nouveau-Dutch approach. In their only previous World Cup match in 1954, Turkey had defeated South Korea 7-0, but there would be no mismatch this time. As red is the dominant color for both countries, the all-crimson spectacle of the Korean crowd in Daegu stadium did not appear to affect Turkey's composure.

This was one of the best-played matches of the 2002 World Cup, as both South Korea and Turkey exhibited their newly developed strengths.

Turkey opened with a goal in a new World Cup record eleven seconds after kickoff (the old record was 27 seconds by England's Bryan Robson against France in 1982). New starting forward İlhan Mansiz immediately harassed South Korea captain Hong Myung Bo and forced the ball to Hakan Šükür; Šükür slotted home his first World Cup goal with a 17-yard left-footed shot past Lee Woon Jae. For four-time World Cup veteran Hong, it was virtually his first error of the competition.

After the goal, Emre Belözoglu had a free kick that was encroached upon by the Korean wall – a basic referee error that had been repeated throughout the World Cup. In the ninth minute, the Koreans won a free kick from the right side of the penalty box. Lee Eul Yong's left-footed strike perfectly touched off the upper right post from 24 yards; Turkish keeper Rüstü Reçber had no chance. Before ten minutes were gone, the score stood 1 – 1, and the game was wide open with speed and skill.

Another Šükür-Mansiz counter-attack sequence led to a second "give-and-go-goal" in the 13th minute, this time Mansiz stroking the ball under the defender into the right corner from 10 yards out. Turkey led 2-1.

On the other side of the pitch Ahn Jung Hwan confused the defense with two Cruyff turns in succession before blasting at the upper right hand corner; Reçber miraculously raised up to fingertip away the shot. Reçber was then kept under fire the rest of the first half, as he made many fine controlling efforts in the box that did not count for saves.

In the 32nd minute, the Mansiz-and-Šükür-show succeeded in another give-and-go play, with Mansiz neatly chipping over an on-rushing Lee from 15 yards, and Turkey led 3 – 1. Turkish legend Šükür was now playing freely after spending most of the World Cup looking stiff and missing chances. He ventured down the left end line, casually popped a *"sombrero"* over his defender, but lost the ball after the next touch. He then jumped sky-high on a corner kick from Belözoglu and hammered a header down that required a lightning kick-save from keeper Lee.

Belözoglu nutmegged an opponent at midfield but was injured for his efforts, and limped off for defensive substitute Hakan Ünsal. To close the half, keeper Reçber drove a clearance kick eighty yards to Šükür who forced a save from Lee.

The second half featured more free-flowing fair play soccer, delightful to watch. Song Chong Gug had two good chances erased, and Lee Chun Soo was saved in the box by Reçber as the Turkish goal remained under assault. Ahn had a shot saved by a defender's backside, followed by his unsuccessful bicycle kick in the 6-yard box.

In the final minute of play, Song Chong Gug right-footed a blast from outside the penalty area headed for the right corner that was deflected off teammate Cha Doo Ri's backside, and the ball ended up in the left corner. Reçber had no chance on the accidental redirection. Cha's football legend father Cha Bum Kun must have been proud.

Then there was no more time for the hosts to equalize. Both teams had given their all, a superb showing of high quality and fair soccer that placed them in the new hierarchy of football nations. Both teams embraced, then walked a solidarity and thank-you lap of the stadium. That was good stuff, a perfect ending to a brave World Cup from both of these teams that exceeded pre-tournament expectations from the experts, and earned all football fans' admiration.

South Korea: Lee Woon Jae, Song Chong Gug, Lee Min Sung, Hong Myung Bo, (Kim Tae Young 46), Lee Eul Yong (Cha Doo Ri 65), Yoo Sang Chul, Lee Chun Soo, Lee Young Pyo, Park Ji Sung, Ahn Jung Hwan, Seol Ki Hyeon (Choi Tae Uk 79).
Turkey: Rüstü Reçber, Fatih Akyel, Bülent Korkmaz, Alpay Özalan, Ergun Penbe, Umit Davala (Okan Buruk 76), Tugay, Yildiray Bastürk (Tayfur Havutcu , Emre Belözoglu (Hakan Unsal 41), Ilhan Mansiz, Hakan Şükür.
Goals: **South Korea -** Lee Eul Yong 9, Song Chong Gug 90;
     Turkey - Hakan Sükür 1, Ilhan Mansiz 13, 32.
Referee: Saad Mane (Kuwait).

Man of the Match: İlhan Mansiz for two well-taken goals.

2002 World Cup FINAL:
Brazilian brilliance vs. German resilience

Brazil and Germany had appeared in a combined total of 170 World Cup matches over the World Cup's 72 years (World Cups from 1930 to 2002), yet this was the *first World Cup meeting EVER for these two soccer giants.*[4] Either Brazil or Germany (or West Germany before 1991) had participated in 12 of the last 13 World Cup Final Matches; this included every World Cup Final since World War II except for the 1978 Cup Final between Argentina and Holland. Brazil and Germany's first meeting in World Cup history would be for the ultimate prize in football - the gold FIFA World Cup™ trophy.

Brazil and Germany had already appeared in six Finals each; the 2002 edition was the seventh Cup Final for both. Brazil had lost the 1950 World Cup Final as host country but won the next four Finals they contested in 1958, 1962, 1970, and 1994. They then lost the 1998 Cup Final to host France. Germany had won the World Cup in 1954, 1974 (as host country), and 1990, and lost in 1966, 1982, and 1986.

This was the third consecutive World Cup Final that Brazil participated in (1994-1998-2002), equaling the record already set by West Germany (1982-1986-1990). Brazil went into the Final as 4/5 odds-on favorites, while Germany was rated at 10/3 (odds valid only for regulation time). The odds for a draw were 2/1.

Statistical analysis of previous Brazil-Germany games favored the Brazilians. In their previous 18 matches played (all outside of the World Cup), Brazil had won 11, tied 4, and lost only 3 times. The most recent Brazil vs. Germany game had taken place in the FIFA Confederations Cup on July 24, 1999, when Brazil beat an off-form Germany 4-0.

Brazil had won all six of their 2002 World Cup games coming into the Final. Prior to this Cup competition, the 1970 World Cup was the only time a nation had a 100% record when they played at least six games including the Final. That nation was the Pelé-led Brazil team, with Jairzinho scoring in all six games including the Final (still a record).

The 2002 World Cup was the fifth World Cup tournament that Brazil won all three Group matches. Strangely, in only one of their previous four World Cup wins did they have a perfect Group record (in 1970).

Brazilian wing-defender Cafú was the first player to participate in each of three consecutive Final games. He replaced the injured Jorginho in the 22nd minute of the 1994 World Cup Final, and started the 1998 and 2002 Finals. Lothar Matthäus and Pierre Littbarski were on the three German teams from 1982-1986-1990, but Matthäus did not play in the 1982 Final, and Littbarski did not play in the 1986 Final.

Ronaldo was also on the three consecutive Brazil Final teams, but he did not play in the 1994 Final. In fact, Ronaldo did not play a minute in the 1994 USA World Cup, even though Brazilian Coach Carlos Alberto Parreira's mother scolded her son for ignoring the then teenage prodigy.

Until early 2002, it appeared that Ronaldo might not make the Brazil squad due to fitness problems. He had played only a handful of matches for Inter Milan the two previous seasons, suffering through multiple knee operations and extensive physical rehabilitation. Yet he appeared in the Final having already scored six goals, and completely fit.

Taking away from the Final's star power, Germany's star midfielder Michael Ballack was forced to miss the Final due to his yellow card in the semi-final.

Finally, this Final matched the best offense (Brazil – 16 goals) against the best defense (Germany – 1 goal allowed) in the 2002 World Cup.

---

[4] Brazil had defeated only East Germany 1-0 in the 1974 FIFA World Cup tournament.

64 Germany 0 – 2 Brazil   Brazil Earns the Penta
June 30: Yokohama, Japan

Brazil's starting lineup included players performing in the Brazilian, French, German, Italian, and Spanish leagues; all Germany's starters performed in the German Bundesliga with the lone exception of midfielder Dieter Hamann (Liverpool, English Premiership).

Germany started the game brightly, with Neuville and Klose attempting to create some offensive pressure on the Brazilians. Simultaneously, the German midfield and defense prevented the Brazil attack from developing a rhythm by close man-marking and aggressive tackling. Several tackles were of borderline legality, as the Germans explored the infraction limits of Italian referee Pierluigi Collina.

Brazil probed the opposition defense as Kleberson broke down the right side, but he should have passed to the poorly marked Ronaldinho. The active Kleberson then stole the ball but wasted his shot wide. Meanwhile, Brazil was living dangerously with less than optimal passing and poor clearances, allowing the Germans to create more dangerous positions, as Edmílson had to sprint back to clear a dangerous cross before it was allowed to run on to Klose.

In the 19th minute Ronaldinho smartly passed with perfect weight to a cutting Ronaldo, who from 8 yards out on the right side of goal curiously used the outside of his left foot to shoot wide left. He likely would have done better with his dominant right foot. In the 30th minute Ronaldo was again put through by Ronaldinho for a one-on-one with Oliver Kahn, but he was not able to optimally control the ball, and his weak toe shot fell at the fortunate keeper's feet.

Kleberson had a chance from 18 yards in the 42nd minute but pushed his kick wide right. The Brazilians were creating, but would have to start testing Kahn instead of gifting the goalkeeper the ball or shooting wide.

Brazil did just that before the break. In the 45th minute, Ronaldinho passed from left to right – as Ronaldo dummied (laid off) the ball it ran to Kleberson who curled a shot from 23 yards that beat Kahn but rebounded back off the crossbar. In injury time Roberto Carlos' laser cross from the left side found Ronaldo in the penalty area, and he superbly one-timed to goal with his left foot from near the penalty spot. Kahn just got his body to the ball and made a spectacular leg save.

By half time the Germans had achieved their first objective – to enter the break at least tied with Brazil. They had not succeeded in their second objective, which was to score on the Brazilians.

Germany came out attacking after the interval as Jens Jeremies' header off a corner gave an early scare to Brazil. The game then almost turned on a spectacular long-range free kick by forward Oliver Neuville in the 49th minute. Neuville struck a 36-yard direct kick with the outside of his right foot, and the ball first flew *inside* of the two-man defensive wall and *curved out again* destined for the Brazil goal's right upper corner. Marcos flung himself across the goal to fingertip the ball away against the right post. A brilliant shot from Neuville that drew a world-class save, with Marcos getting a little help from the woodwork.

In the 61st minute, wingback captain Cafú found himself 40 yards forward in the German penalty box where he unselfishly centered, but no compatriot was there to do any damage. He might have done well to shoot.

In the 68th minute, Ronaldo rudely dispossessed Dietmar Hamann before he could clear from his defensive end, and touched to Rivaldo who took a blistering left-footed shot from 24 yards. Rivaldo's dipping shot handcuffed Kahn and caused him to give up a rare rebound. Ronaldo, who had continued running off the ball, scooped up the freebie from the usually immaculate keeper and side-footed it into the right corner for the opening goal. Kahn was devastated by his error, but many a goalkeeper has been fooled by Rivaldo's left footed cannon-shots that seem to defy the laws of physics. Ronaldo did his usual trot and "Number

One" finger wave before being mobbed by teammates. No Pelé-type jump and punch after scoring for this still recovering athlete – Ronaldo would save his legs for the game.

Brazil earned their second goal in the 79th minute, two minutes after German coach Rudi Völler had made an odd substitution, placing newly entered Gerald Asamoah in a defensive position (Asamoah is normally a striker). Kleberson started the move as he made a clever run and pass from the right towards Rivaldo at the top of the penalty box. Rivaldo ducked his shoulder dummying defender Thomas Linke, and the ball ran on to an unmarked Ronaldo. Inexperienced defender Asamoah was also fooled by Rivaldo's dummy and remained a step behind Ronaldo, who one-touch controlled and neatly slotted the ball into the extreme lower right hand corner from 16 yards.

Germany, although outplayed much of the second half, was not yet finished. Veteran substitute Oliver Bierhoff made an excellent turn and shot from 12 yards in the box, forcing a left-handed reaction save from Marcos to maintain his scoreless outing. A mix-up in the Brazil box on a cross from the right gave defender Christoph Metzelder a last chance to touch the ball into the goal with his left foot, but he mis-timed with his right and the ball was left wide.

Then it was over, referee Collina blew his whistle and Brazil began the glorious celebration of their PENTA – the first team to win the World Cup five times.

Brazil: (3-5-2): Marcos, Lúcio, Roque Junior, Edmílson, Cafu, Ronaldinho (Juninho Paulista 85), Gilberto Silva, Kleberson, Roberto Carlos, Rivaldo, Ronaldo (Denilson 90).
Germany: (4-4-2): Oliver Kahn, Torsten Frings, Thomas Linke, Carsten Ramelow, Christoph Metzelder, Bernd Schneider, Jens Jeremies (Gerald Asamoah 78), Dietmar Hamann, Marco Bode (Christian Ziege 84), Oliver Neuville, Miroslav Klose (Oliver Bierhoff 74).
Goals: Brazil Ronaldo 67, 79.
Referee: Pierluigi Collina (Italy).

Men of the Match: Ronaldo and Rivaldo. Ronaldo, for converting both goals, and Rivaldo, for hammering the initial shot that Kahn could not handle and stylishly dummying to give Ronaldo space to convert for the second.

2002 WORLD CUP FINAL SUMMARY

The 2002 Final was the best contested World Cup Final since the 1986 World Cup Final. Compared to the boring 1990 Final (Germany 1 – 0 Argentina by a penalty kick), the exhausting and ultimately uninspiring overtime-penalty kicks 1994 Final (Brazil 0 – 0 Italy), and the blowout over-by-halftime 1998 Final (France 3 – 0 Brazil), this game was competitive until the last minute. In addition, Brazil was the first team since Diego Maradona's 1986 Argentina squad to become world champions without requiring extra-time or penalty shoot-outs in any game.

Although Germany was outplayed by Brazil, the players did everything Coach Rudi Völler could have asked. Having lost several key players before the Cup started, and with star Michael Ballack forced to miss the Final on suspension, it is arguable that Germany had over-achieved with the personnel they used. By now the world knows the German resolve on the soccer field can never be underestimated – worth remembering for 2006 Germany.

Brazil's World Cup Accomplishments

Brazil's "Three R's" – Rivaldo, Ronaldinho, and Ronaldo – scored 15 of Brazil's tournament-topping 18 goals; Ronaldo with eight, Rivaldo five and Ronaldinho two. Not since Gerd Müller's ten goals in the 1970 World Cup had a striker been as prolific as Ronaldo. Both Rivaldo and Ronaldo scored in the first four of Brazil's games (first time ever in World Cup Finals play), but only Rivaldo was able to find the net against England.

Only a select group has scored in five consecutive Modern Era (1958-2002) World Cup Finals games besides Rivaldo – Hristo Stoichkov for Bulgaria in 1994, Toto Schillaci for Italy in 1990, Jairzinho for Brazil and Gerd Müller for West Germany in 1970, Eusébio for Portugal in 1966, and Just Fontaine in 1958. Two players hold the modern World Cup record for six consecutive games; Jairzinho for Brazil in 1970, and Just Fontaine for France in 1958, but only Jairzinho included the Final match as part of his streak.

Brazil's 2002 World Cup win added to their existing record established by Pelé's 1958 Brazil team – a team winning the World Cup outside of it's own geographic zone (in Brazil's case the Americas). All other World Cup Finals had been won by a team from the same host area (Europe or the Americas). The 1958 Brazil team (adjudged to be the 6th best team in the modern era - see Chapter 8) won the Final against the host nation of Sweden. In one of football's enduring images, the Brazilian team paraded the Swedish flag around the grounds in a wonderful show of appreciation for the hospitality shown by their hosts. With the 2002 World Cup win Brazil could now claim two World Cup Championships away from their home zone. Finally, *the 2002 Brazil team was the first to win the World Cup by winning seven straight games without tie or loss.*

Added to his total of four in 1998 World Cup, Ronaldo's World Cup goal total stood at twelve after the 2002 World Cup – the same as Pelé's total in the same amount of matches (fourteen matches). Rivaldo had three goals in 1998, so his World Cup total is eight, an impressive total for a player with such a prominent creative role. Gerd Müller is the career World Cup goal leader with fourteen goals over two World Cups (1970, 1974) and thirteen matches, while Just Fontaine of France scored an incredible thirteen goals in only six matches in the 1958 World Cup.

At the conclusion of the 2002 World Cup, Ronaldo had 45 international goals and trailed only Pelé (77), Romário (54) and Zico (48) in Brazilian international goals. Over the next four years Ronaldo scored 13 goals to surpass Romario and Zico with 58 goals, and if he remains healthy during the 2006 World Cup he will have a chance to break Gerd Müller's all-time World Cup scoring record.

World Cup MVP Golden Ball

The Golden Ball Award is presented for the best performance in the World Cup. The first ten players receiving votes for the 2002 Golden Ball were (highest votes first): Oliver Kahn (Germany), Ronaldo (Brazil), Myung Bo Hong (South Korea), Rivaldo (Brazil), Ronaldinho (Brazil), Hasan Sas (Turkey), El Hadji Diouf (Senegal), Roberto Carlos (Brazil), Michael Ballack (Germany), and Fernando Hierro (Spain). Oliver Kahn was the first goalkeeper to win the Golden Ball, Ronaldo received the Silver Ball, and Myung Bo Hong the Bronze Ball.

Some do not believe a goalkeeper is deserving of the award because he is not an "outfield" player. Kahn did play well, but arguably no better than position-mates Rüstü (Turkey), Marcos (Brazil), or even Lee (South Korea). A strange award particularly in Kahn's case, because of his glaring error in the Final. One would have expected Michael Ballack to be higher up the list, as his overall performance as a creative and scoring "number 10" should have ranked him at least as high as his compatriot Kahn. Although Ronaldo had double the goals in the 2002 Cup than he had in the 1998 World Cup, some were of the tap-in version.

Previous Golden Ball awards were not necessarily given to the best player and/or MVP of previous tournaments. Ronaldo won the Golden Ball in 1998 when he had four goals prior to the Final, but was practically non-existent against France in the Final match itself. France's midfield inspiration Zinedine Zidane scored two goals in the Final and merited the 1998 Golden Ball award.

Discriminating fans that watched every 2002 World Cup games know Rivaldo could justifiably have been awarded the 2002 Golden Ball. Rivaldo shouldered much of the creative and scoring weight for Brazil, his five goals were well taken, and his non-scoring shots set up other goals for Brazil. He logged 610 out a possible 630 minutes, finishing out games that were in doubt while Ronaldo was being rested and Ronaldinho was sitting out his ejection against England and suspension against Turkey. One image of Rivaldo, totally exhausted and soldiering up front alone, chest-trapping the ball down with perfect control from a long 50-50 clearance from Marcos – literally holding England at bay solo as the clock ticked down – is enough for Rivaldo to clinch the Golden Ball.

In the Final, again it was Rivaldo's magic left foot that stymied Oliver Kahn, the sheer torque of his long-range shot forcing Kahn to misjudge and gift Ronaldo the all-important first goal. His stylish and unselfish "dummy" – a move of a certifiable football wizard supremely aware of the dynamic environment – created space for Ronaldo's second goal. For his all-around effort and excellence, Rivaldo was most deserving of the Golden Ball.

Brazil coach Luiz Felipe Scolari waited until the end of 2002 to confirm Rivaldo's superiority in the World Cup when he stated, "Rivaldo, for me, was the best player in the World Cup. Tactically, as well as in his shots, he was very strong." Scolari intimated that Rivaldo was the only irreplaceable Brazil player when he referred to Ronaldo saying "A team is not a man. There were other solutions in his position." Indeed, Ronaldo had a great World Cup, but in the shadows could have been Romário, Marcio Amoroso, or Mario Jardel – all prolific goal scorers who did not even make the Brazil team. Rivaldo, however, was a unique "number 10" who had a spectacular Cup and would likely have been irreplaceable in his position.

Having said that, when one important individual is missing a team can sometimes make up his absence. Brazil became 1962 World Cup champion again despite Pelé's injury, and Holland reached the 1978 World Cup Final even without their talismanic captain Johan Cruyff. Soccer remains a team game, and only when individuals are integrated into the group concept may they reach their full potential as an individual within their team.

All-Star Teams of the 2002 World Cup*

BEST ELEVEN of 2002

Oliver Kahn

Cafú   Rio Ferdinand   Hong Myung Bo   Roberto Carlos

Pape Bouba Diop   Michael Ballack   Ronaldinho   Hasan Şaş

Ronaldo   Rivaldo

NEXT THIRTY-FIVE BEST PLAYERS

Rüştü Reçber
Marcos
Lee Woon Jae

Fernando Hierro
Francisco Arce   Alpay Özalan   Edmílson   Christoph Metzelder
Omar Daf   Sol Campbell   Thomas Linke   Bülent Korkmaz

Francesco Totti
Junichi Inamoto   Anders Svensson   Khalilou Fadiga
Yoo Sang Chul   Ümit Davala   El Hadji Diouf
Landon Donovan   Claudio Reyna   Hidetoshi Nakata

Marc Wilmots
Henri Camara   Jared Borgetti   Brian McBride   Fernando Morientes
Robbie Keane   Miroslav Klose   Jon Dahl Tomasson   İlhan Mansız
Ahn Jung Hwan   Henrik Larsson   Christian Vieri   Raúl Gonzalez

Numbers of players per nation:
Brazil (7), Turkey (6), Germany (5), Senegal (5), Korea Republic (4), Spain (3), USA (3), England (2), Italy (2), Japan (2), Sweden (2), Belgium (1), Denmark (1), Ireland (1), Mexico (1), Paraguay (1).
*The forty-six players chosen represent two full teams of 23 players each, or 6.25% of the total players in the World Cup.

BEST SIXTEEN YOUNG PLAYERS of 2002 WORLD CUP

                             Iker Casillas

                         Christoph Metzelder

Henri Camara   Landon Donovan   Lee Chun Soo   Emre Belözoglu

Dmitri Sychev   El Hadji Diouf   Ronaldinho   Joaquin Sanchez

Park Ji Sung   Julius Aghahowa   Roque Santa Cruz Robbie Keane

                  Samuel Eto'o   Nelson Cuevas

A "young player" was defined as being born in 1980 or later, making the player 22 years old or less at the 2002 World Cup. This would be a formidable 2002 World Cup team of young players, except that Metzelder and Casillas would be all alone in defense.

Magic Moments of the 2002 World Cup

Best free play goal
(1) Ronaldo (Brazil) throwing his body and volleying in the first goal against Turkey on a laser assist from Rivaldo from the left side. This athletic goal was typical of Rivaldo's adventurous passing, and signaled that Ronaldo had returned with full powers, which was critical against super-skilled opponent Turkey.
(2) İlhan Mansiz's (Turkey) half-volley off a half-chance from Ümit Davala for the Golden Goal against Senegal in the quarterfinals.
(3) Oliver Neuville's (Germany) half-volley past keeper Jose Luis Chilavert, ending a tense second round game with Paraguay.

Best headed goal
(1) Jared Borgetti's (Mexico) "blind" header off a great feed from Cuauhtémoc Blanco against Italy. The sheer imagination of this goal was special, and "world best" keeper Buffon had no chance.
(2) Henrik Larsson's (Sweden) power header against Senegal, going one-on-one successfully against keeper Tony Sylva.
(3) Ahn Jung Hwan's (South Korea) flick header against Italy beating Paolo Maldini and Buffon to the far corner.

Best diving header goal
(1) Ronald Gomez (Costa Rica) in full extension against Brazil.
(2) Brian McBride (USA) from Tony Sanneh's cross against Portugal.
(3) Miroslav Klose's (Germany) lunging header for his first goal against Saudi Arabia. Not strictly a diving header, but a magnificent piece of heading skill.

Best driven goal
(1) Roberto Carlos' (Brazil) left-footed direct kick against China.
(2) Matt Holland's (Ireland) 24-yard shot against Cameroon.
(3) Henri Camara's (Senegal) first goal against Sweden.

Best volleyed goals
(1) Rivaldo (Brazil) controlled a ball with his back to goal, then wheeled and blasted past Belgium keeper De Vlieger.
(2) Ümit Davala (Turkey) off a cross from Hasan Sas against China; arriving at the right side of the goal Davala met the left-sided cross and volleyed into the lower left corner.
(3) Gary Breen (Ireland) scored with the outside of his right foot across his body into the corner of the goal against South Africa.
(4) Benni McCarthy (South Africa) beat Iker Casillas (Spain) with a jumping volley in the 6-yard box off a half-chance corner kick.

Best free kick goal
(1) Lee Eul Yong (South Korea) against Turkey, which temporarily tied the third place match.
(2) John Walem's (Belgium) free-kick goal against Russia.
(3) Anders Svensson's (Sweden) long-distance free kick into the upper left-hand corner that sealed Argentina's fate.
(4) Francisco Arce's (Paraguay) long free kick beat the South African keeper to the near post.
(5) Ronaldinho's (Brazil) speculative longest distance shot which beat England keeper David Seaman to the upper-left corner – giving Seaman *déjà vu all over again* (appropriate but idiosyncratic phrase borrowed from Yogi Berra).

Best free kick from distance (> 30 yards)
(1) Oliver Neuville against Brazil. From 36 yards it was spectacularly saved by keeper Marcos.
(2) Ronaldinho (Brazil) against England. Lucky or not, he was apparently trying for goal.

Best outside of the foot goal
(1) Diego Forlan's (Uruguay) right-footed score against Senegal
(2) Dario Rodriguez's (Uruguay) left-footed score against Denmark
(3) Salif Diao's (Senegal) right-footed score against Denmark.

Best bicycle kick for goal
(1) Edmílson's (Brazil) mid-air adjustment bicycle goal against Costa Rica. And by a defender no less....
(2) Marc Wilmots (Belgium) against Japan.
(3) Cha Doo Ri's (South Korea) lightning bicycle kick against Italy did not score as it went right at keeper Buffon, but what a superb piece of imaginative athletic skill!

Quickest and prettiest end-to-end team goals
(1) <u>Senegal against Sweden</u>. Daf tackles Jorgensen deep in the right side of the Senegalese half, and immediately passes to Diouf who back heels to Diao. Diao passes cross-field to Fadiga who dribbles down the left side and finds Diao again in the middle; Diao slots the ball into the lower right corner with the outside of his right foot. Denmark never touches the ball.
(2) <u>Turkey against Senegal</u>. Keeper Rüştü Reçber releases to Arif Erdem who pushes the ball around Omar Daf, runs around him and again collects the ball. Daf roughly tackles Erdem but the ball squirts to Ümit Davala anyway. Davala dribbles down the right side and speculatively centers to İlhan Mansız, who with his right leg sweeps the ball into the far left corner in one fluid motion. The Golden Goal puts Turkey into the semi-finals.
(3) <u>Brazil against England</u>: David Beckham pulled out of a challenge that is won on the left touch line by Brazil's Roque Júnior. Scholes contends the ensuing pass to the center of the field but Gilberto touched the ball ahead to Ronaldinho just inside Brazil's half-line. Ronaldinho burst up the field with frightening dribbling speed, and when challenged by Ashley Cole on his left shoulder, executed a stepover at high speed that leaves the defender floundering. With England's central defense straining to stop him, Ronaldinho rolled a pass to the onrushing Rivaldo at the right side of the penalty box. Rivaldo uses his lethal left foot to rifle in a goal past Sol Campbell's desperate lunge and keeper Seaman's reach.

Best assists
(1) Ronaldinho (Brazil) running half the pitch and drawing the defense, thereby setting up Rivaldo's magic left foot for Brazil's first goal against England (see above).
(2) Yildiray Baştürk's (Turkey) leading cross-field chip to Hasan Şaş, which he one-time lashed into the back of the Brazil net. The commentator's remark perfectly summed up the service and delivery of the goal, "a delicate touch from Baştürk, and rather less delicate from Hasan Şaş."
(3) Francesco Totti's (Italy) run down the right side, only to clairvoyantly center backwards for a trailing Christian Vieri to slot home.

Best dribble
(1) Nelson Cuevas (Paraguay) winding his way through the Slovenian defense to score in two separate dribbling exhibitions.
(2) El-Hadji Diouf (Senegal) slaloming through the Swedish defense, only to be mugged for an obvious penalty kick which was not called.
(3) Miroslav Klose (Germany) taking on four Cameroon defenders, passing between them perfectly for Marco Bode to score.

Best defensive play
(1) Omar Daf (Senegal) somehow clearing Yildiray Baştürk's (Turkey) headed shot off the line from a position behind the ball in the quarterfinal.
(2) Lamine Diatta (Senegal) headed a blistering shot from Uruguay's Paolo Montero off the goal line, preserving a 3-3 draw that saw Senegal through to the second round.
(3) Carsten Ramelow tracking and tackling Denilson in the Final after he had just embarrassed two German defenders, putting them on their backs.

Best save
(1) Marcos' critical save in the Cup Final to deny Neuville's superb long-distance blast (Brazil vs. Germany).
(2) Rüştü Reçber denying Ronaldo a freebie after saving Rivaldo's laser shot (Turkey vs. Brazil in semi-final).
(3) Oliver Kahn denying Damien Duff from close range with a hip save (Germany vs. Ireland).
(4) Gianluigi Buffon (Italy) saving from Hwang Sun Hong (South Korea) after his clever 25-yard free kick beat the defensive wall by *going under it*. Somehow Buffon went the length of the goal to parry the ball with his left hand just before it went over the line.

Best skill move
(1) Park Ji Sung's (South Korea) triple air juggle and shot for goal against Portugal.
(2) Anders Svensson's double pullback move in the penalty box that resulted in a shot rocketing off the upright against Senegal.
(3) Denilson's running Cruyff-turn at speed, which misdirected and upended Torsten Frings (Brazil vs. Germany in the Final).
(4) Ahn Jung Hwan's rapid double Cruyff-turns to disorient the Turkish defense and set up his shot; his blast was saved well by keeper Rüştü Reçber (Turkey vs. South Korea 3rd place match).

Unluckiest play
(1) Henri Camera (Senegal) stopping a certain goal (the shot had passed all Turkish players) from his teammate Khalilou Fadiga against Turkey. His follow-up goal was justifiably called back for offside.

Cheekiest nutmeg awards
The first three nutmegs were performed just outside the penalty area as a setup for a shot on goal; all three were good efforts but did not result in a score. Larsson's reverse nutmeg did not result in a shot. Eto'o's nutmeg led to a goal by Patrick Mboma.
(1) Landon Donovan against Germany.
(2) El Hadji Diouf against Sweden.
(3) Robbie Keane against Spain.
(4) Henrik Larsson's reverse nutmeg (his back to the defender, he dragged the ball back through the defender's legs) against Senegal.
(5) Samuel Eto'o (Cameroon) nutmeg of Ireland's Steve Staunton on the touchline, just prior to passing the ball for Patrick Mboma to score.

Most audacious move
(1) İlhan Mansız's (Turkey) "rainbow" reverse flick-over pulled successfully over Brazil's Roberto Carlos -- an outrageous skill move to pull in a World Cup on a world-class defender. The beaten Roberto Carlos was forced to crudely foul from behind in order to stop Mansız's advance, which should have merited a yellow card.

Not So Magic Moments of the 2002 World Cup

Eleven Refereeing Errors Disallowing or Allowing Goals in the 2002 FIFA World Cup

Disallowing

(1) Christian Vieri's (Italy) first goal against Croatia was disallowed for offside; video replay showed that he was well onsides.

(2) Vincenzo Montella's (Italy) goal against Mexico was annulled for offside; video showed he was onsides.

(3) Fernando Morrientes' (Spain) Golden Goal header against South Korea was annulled when Joaquin's pass was erroneously ruled out-of-bounds.

(4) Landon Donovan's (USA) first goal against Poland was disallowed for a phantom foul.

(5) Marc Wilmots' (Belgium) headed goal against Brazil was annulled for a phantom foul after he had out-hustled Roque Junior.

(6) Damiano Tommasi's (Italy) Golden Goal against South Korea was disallowed by an erroneous offside decision.

Allowing

(1) Hernan Crespo (Argentina vs. Sweden) was three meters over the 18-yard line before Ariel Ortega kicked from the penalty spot. Crespo put in the rebound despite the gross infraction – and the goal counted.

(2) Jon Dahl Tomasson (Denmark versus France) pulled down Marcel Desailly in the penalty area before he shot the second goal against France.

Penalties that were really not penalties

(1) El Hadji Diouf (Senegal) and (2) Richard Morales (Uruguay); both dove for penalties in the same game (Senegal vs. Uruguay). Diouf was not touched by the Uruguay keeper and Morales was fairly beaten by the Senegalese defender. Both should not have been penalties.

Other refereeing error

(1) Not calling an obvious penalty for El Hadji Diouf (Senegal) against Sweden.

WORLD CUP 2002 Notes

There was a better offensive mindset for many of the teams in this World Cup, perhaps because some teams adopted a 3-5-2 formation with the two outside wingbacks used effectively as offensive weapons. The best examples of this style were Cafú and Roberto Carlos for Brazil.

Also important was the quality of the many spectacular goals scored. Who can forget Ronaldinho's and Rivaldo's goals against England, Mansiz's against Senegal, Ahn's against Italy? Near misses such as Neuville's against Brazil were just as entertaining.

There were also freak goals, such as Ronaldo's against Costa Rica that was deflected off a defender for a seeming own-goal, but was tallied for the striker. Perhaps the most unusual goal was the own-goal in the USA-Portugal game, when an innocent cross by Landon Donovan went into the goal from the shoulder of defender Jorge Costa. Also unusual was the Croatian goal that beat Italy, being unpredictably deflected off a defender's foot past keeper Buffon.

Any dissatisfaction from the 2002 World Cup (for both fans and teams) clearly derived from refereeing and linesman errors. Some of the refereeing was of such poor quality that it affected the outcome of important games, and if not corrected by the 2006 World Cup may threaten the integrity of the competition itself.

# World Cup Team Summary
[Win= 3 points;   Tie= 1 point;   Loss= 0 points]

(1) Brazil: 21 points (7 games; 7 wins)

This Brazil team was comparable to other Brazil World Cup winners, and certainly superior to the 1994 winners. Still, there was uncertainty of how Brazil would perform until Ronaldo scored his first and best goal in the initial game against Turkey. Throwing his body at Rivaldo's laser cross, he redirected the ball into Rüştü Reçber's goal. After that spectacular goal, Ronaldo had more confidence in his body's resilience after his long layoff.

But if Ronaldo had been injured, Brazil would likely not have had the center-forward firepower available to win, as many second-choice star strikers were left home. It would have been more entertaining for the crowds to see world-class goal scorers Romário, Jardel, or Amoroso finish up games, since Ronaldo needed to be rested frequently.

Before the World Cup Coach Scolari had infuriated Brazil supporters by saying that "the beautiful game is dead," but Scolari finally abandoned his overly defensive ways and generally went with the flow of Brazil talent and technique. If Brazil had played defensively, they would have given several teams (especially England) the chance to get back in the game, and likely would not have had the success they did.

The beautiful game is very much alive, thanks to the individual Brazil players who refused to play a style incompatible with their soccer upbringing.

MVP: *Rivaldo.*

(2) Germany: 16 points (7 games; 5 wins, 1 tie, 1 loss)

Germany played their usual efficient and hard style to maximum effect, and because of pre-Cup injury losses they performed above their level. Although Franz Beckenbauer was critical of their technique, nobody could criticize the heart of this over-achieving team.

The most pleasant surprise was the stellar play of Michael Ballack and Oliver Kahn, and emerging stars Christian Metzelder and Miroslav Klose. A major disappointment was Germany MVP Ballack missing the Final due to suspension. Germany would have been a much more interesting and dangerous opponent with Ballack on the field, despite their strong play in the Final.

If Germany can field a more creative and attacking team with a quality creative midfielder to help Ballack, they will emerge as one of the favorites to win the World Cup at home in 2006.

MVP: *Michael Ballack.*

(3) Turkey: 13 points (7 games; 4 wins, 1 tie, 2 losses)

Turkey gave 2002 World Cup winners Brazil all the competition they could handle, losing two close games by one goal each. With the victory over South Korea, Turkey became the first team to defeat each of a World Cup's co-hosts, as it had also defeated Japan in the Round of 16.

Turkey appeared ready to become a soccer power with an enviable base from two soccer-rich nations, as soccer-mad Turkey is welcoming many German-born Turks to play for their ancestral land. Moreover, Turkey has a delightful soccer style that is as close to the South American style as European. It would have been very interesting to see Turkey in Germany 2006 as many players would effectively be "playing at home," but they lost to Switzerland in a contentious qualifying playoff.

MVP: *Hasan Şaş.*

(4) South Korea: 13 points (7 games; 4 wins, 1 tie, 2 losses)

The Koreans performed brilliantly as they finished in fourth place, and they won the FIFA World Cup "Most Entertaining Team" prize.

The question is whether they can continue the excellence shown in 2002 away from a home-field advantage. The 2002 World Cup showcased their soccer technique, which is at the top in Asia. Most of their players were homegrown, but more Koreans are going abroad to showcase their talents in European leagues. If the South Korean team is able to adjust to a new coach and improve their finishing, they will be able to compete with any nation in 2006.

MVP: *Hong Myung Bo.*

(5) Spain: 12 points (5 games; 4 wins, 1 loss)

Spain usually under-performs at the World Cup, but they looked to leave that impression behind after steamrolling through Group B with three wins and maximum points. Only when Spain lost clever striker Raúl in the Ireland game, did they get untracked once again.

Spain would again be said to have underachieved, even with bad luck in the South Korea game. But to pass through on two consecutive shootouts would have been too much luck to receive, as Spain barely got past Ireland on penalties. Raúl's injury hurt Spain badly, as his presence on the pitch could not be replaced. Still, Spain qualified for the 2006 World Cup in Germany for their next chance at advancing their formidable skills.

MVP: *Raúl Gonzalez.*

(6) England: 8 points (5 games; 2 wins, 2 ties, 1 loss)

England arrived with a team not completely set due to indecision and injuries, and left some good attacking midfield players home. Still, their defensive opulence did not prevent Brazil from beating them after being one goal down after Lúcio's defensive error gifted a goal to Michael Owen.

England still has a fairly young team, and if they develop their offense and consolidate their defense, they may succeed in 2006 or 2010. However, England will likely impress in the 2006 World Cup only if they eventually manage to risk the offensive flair they potentially possess – maybe they should consider hiring a Brazilian coach.

MVP: *Rio Ferdinand.*

(7) Senegal: 8 points (5 games; 2 wins, 2 ties, 1 loss)

Very impressive debut for this debut African nation. Senegal's pipeline of players in the French league ensured quality for their World Cup team – provided their national team organization supports them (the Achilles heel of many African nations).

Many Senegalese players made high profile club moves after the Cup, and popular coach Bruno Metsu also left. Team cohesiveness did not survive his departure, as Senegal failed to qualify for 2006.

MVPs: *Pape Bouba Diop* and *El-Hadji Diouf.*

(8) USA: 7 points (5 games; 2 wins, 1 tie, 2 losses)

USA made their best showing since the 1930 World Cup, when the USA advanced to the semi-finals in the first World Cup. Coach Arena used his players to perfection, and gave the Germans a most competitive game.

Brad Friedel performed admirably in goal even saving two World Cup penalty shots, which was last accomplished by Poland's Jan Tomaszewski in the 1974 World Cup.

Captain Claudio Reyna was the rock of the team, but if Landon Donovan continues to develop he has a chance to be the USA's best modern player. As the MLS (Major League Soccer) is still a league in development, it would behoove US Soccer to guide some of their top players to further develop in European or South American leagues, in order to fully realize national team potential.

MVPs: *Claudio Reyna* and heir apparent *Landon Donovan.*

(9) Japan: 7 points (4 games; 2 wins, 1 tie, 1 loss)

In only their second World Cup, Japan made their mark as they went through to the second round, only to lose to a superbly trained Turkey team.

Two midfield players who could rarely get a game for their European clubs – Junichi Inamoto at Arsenal and Hidetoshi Nakata at Roma – ended up outperforming many of their more touted teammates. Nakata was the bedrock of the team but Inamoto was the revelation.

MVP: *Hidetoshi Nakata* and *Junichi Inamoto.*

(10) Mexico: 7 points (4 games; 2 wins, 1 tie, 1 loss)

Mexico was formerly the top CONACAF region team, but has recently found that space shared with the USA and Costa Rica. They still played some very classy football, finishing on top of their group ahead of Italy. Their stars were the creative midfielder Cuauhtémoc Blanco and striker Jared Borgetti, with Oscar Perez performing impressively in goal.

Mexico was slightly unlucky in the second round against archrivals USA, but came up against two sterling USA goals, and despite several close calls could not beat goalkeeper Brad Friedel. Mexico is a guaranteed CONACAF World Cup qualifier for the foreseeable future.

MVP: *Cuauhtémoc Blanco* and *Jared Borgetti.*

(11) Denmark: 7 points (4 games; 2 wins, 1 tie, 1 loss)

Denmark sparkled in winning their Group with France and Senegal, but faltered badly in the round of 16 against England when their keeper Tomas Sorensen was off-form.

Jon Dahl Tomasson was in scintillating form as the Danish point man with four goals in the Group stage. Having knocked off defending World Cup champions France and ex-champions Uruguay, Denmark could not defeat ex-champions England, down 3-0 in the only bad half they played in the World Cup.

Ironically, Denmark gained some revenge by defeating England 4-1 in 2005 in a friendly match, but they ultimately failed to qualify for the 2006 World Cup.

MVP: *Jon Dahl Tomasson.*

(12) Ireland: 5 points (4 games; 1 win, 2 ties, 1 loss)

Ireland performed passionately and with quality, despite not advancing beyond the round of 16 with their penalty lottery loss to Spain. Team players did not seem to miss Roy Keane's departure; indeed, the players abilities may have been freed up by his absence.

New stars Robbie Keane, Damien Duff and keeper Shay Given will likely form the backbone of the team for years to come. With a fairly young and talented team, it was a surprise when Ireland missed out on qualifying for the 2006 World Cup.

MVP: *Robbie Keane.*

(13) Sweden: 5 points (4 games; 1 win, 2 ties, 1 loss)

Sweden was very impressive winning the Group of Death, as they were undefeated against England, Argentina, and Nigeria. They put up a good fight before going out to Senegal on a Golden Goal. But this was Sweden's 10th World Cup experience, and they always seem to play quality soccer.

Henrik Larsson's efforts were impressive, and he has extended his international career through the 2006 World Cup. With Anders Svensson and Freddie Ljungberg, Sweden has a solid middle, and Zlatan Ibrahimovic has a chance to be another great Swedish striker in the tradition of Ralf Edström and Larsson. Sweden qualified for the 2006 World Cup and was once again selected for England's group.

MVP: *Henrik Larsson.*

(14) Belgium: 5 points (4 games; 1 win, 2 ties, 1 loss)

Belgium started tentatively, drawing their first two matches (establishing a record for consecutive draws in World Cup play with five, as they drew their three matches in 1998) before beating Russia. The Belgians saved their best for last, as they gave the Brazilians a run for their money in the second round. Brazil was very lucky to have Marc Wilmots' apparently legitimate opening headed goal disallowed – it would have been a different game if it had stood.

This Cup marked the end of the Wilmots era – Belgium's 6th straight and 11th total visit to the Finals. However, they failed to qualify for Germany 2006.

MVP: *Marc Wilmots.*

(15) Italy: 4 points (4 games; 1 win, 1 tie, 2 losses)

Christian Vieri was both the hero (with his four goals) and the goat (missing an open goal at the end of the South Korea game with his less-favored right foot) for Italy. That was the kind of World Cup that three-time champion Italy had.

Bad luck is when you have as many goals annulled as you score (five each), as Italy experienced in this World Cup. Italy played well in spots, but was the recipient of some very poor refereeing decisions that likely affected game outcomes (matches against Croatia and South Korea).

The study of these errors will hopefully serve as examples for improving the refereeing process for future international competitions. Still, that does not ameliorate the feeling of sadness – and in some quarters anger – at the early Italy exit. This was the fourth World Cup that Italy was eliminated after regulation time (the first three were penalty kick losses in 1990, 1994, and 1998).

Italy qualified for the 2006 World Cup and should be aiming to win each game outright.

MVP: *Christian Vieri.*

(16) Paraguay: 4 points (4 games; 1 win, 1 tie, 2 losses)

A typical Paraguay team with a tough defense and solid goaltending by José Luis Chilavert, offset by an erratic offense that was sometimes brilliant.

Paraguay was eliminated by a last-minute goal to runner-ups Germany. Why Nelson Cuevas was withheld from most of the Germany game after his sparkling brace scored against Slovenia was a mystery.

Chilavert's leadership would be difficult to replace, but Paraguay again qualified for Germany 2006 with a solid performance in the South American qualifiers.

MVPs: *Francisco Arce, José Luis Chilavert, and Nelson Cuevas.*

(17) Argentina: 4 points (3 games; 1 win, 1 tie, 1 loss)

Were it not for France – the biggest bust in the tournament – Argentina would have been the biggest disappointment. The Argentine nation suffered much more, as the populace had pinned hopes of a third World Cup win lifting their spirits in an economic recession.

Coach Bielsa's refusal to play Gabriel Batistuta and Hernan Crespo up front together was an unnecessary negative hanging over the team, and always kept one great goal scorer on the bench. Argentina also missed the young energy and creativity from recent South American Footballers of the Year Javier Saviola and Juan Roman Riquelme – both inexplicably left off the roster.

Incredibly, Bielsa stayed on as coach after Argentina's most ignominious World Cup elimination ever, and led Argentina to the 2004 Copa America Final, which Argentina lost to Brazil only by penalties.

MVP: *Gabriel Batistuta.*

(18) South Africa: 4 points (3 games; 1 win, 1 tie, 1 loss)

South Africa exited in the first round for the second time in two World Cups, but they made it closer this time, as only a miraculous comeback from Paraguay over Slovenia edged them from the second round. Their inspired performance against Spain might have resulted in a win had their keeper not had an off day.

But that is what comes from experience, which South Africa is quickly obtaining. With the likes of Quinton Fortune, Sibusiso Zuma, Benni McCarthy, and Steven Pienaar, one expected to see South Africa again qualifying for the 2006 Finals, but it was not to be. But in 2010, South Africa will return as host of the first African World Cup.

MVP: *Quinton Fortune.*

(19) Costa Rica: 4 points (3 games; 1 win, 1 tie, 1 loss)

The Ticos competed extremely well with attractive and creative football, but perhaps played too wide-open in the Brazil game. They were losing to Turkey by one goal, but pulled a tie out with dominating play in the second half. Turkey ended up going through to the second round over Costa Rica on a goal difference of three, and went all the way to the semi-finals of the 2002 World Cup.

Costa Rica had the talent available to qualify again from the CONACAF region for the 2006 World Cup, which they did without difficulty.

MVP: *Ronald Gomez.*

(20) Cameroon: 4 points (3 games; 1 win, 1 tie, 1 loss)

Cameroon showed some power in tying Ireland in the first game, and winning their second game against Saudi Arabia. But Cameroon was not able to overcome their former colonial rulers Germany in the last game, and subsequently failed to qualify for the second round.

With three-time African Player of the Year (2003-2005) Samuel Eto'o heading the squad, the two-time defending African Cup champions Cameroon (2000 and 2002) were favored to qualify for the 2006 Finals, but just missed out. Their future challenge will be to emulate the 1990 Cameroon team that reached the quarterfinals – the other four Finals Cameroon has contested (1982, 1994, 1998, 2002) have ended first round and out.

MVP: *Samuel Eto'o.*

(21) Portugal: 3 points (3 games; 1 win, 2 losses)

Portugal was a great favorite but inexperienced at World Cup play, as the 2002 Cup was only their third World Cup ever (1966, 1986, 2002).

Portugal gave an uneven performance – outplayed by the USA in the first game, they destroyed Poland in the second. But in the decisive game, Portugal came up short to an inspired South Korea, and lost 1-0 on a spectacular goal by Park Ji Sung.

Nearly the end of the "Future Generation" that won both the 1989 and 1991 Youth World Cups, only Luis Figo extended his international career for the 2006 World Cup.

2002 World Cup-winning Brazil coach Felipe "Big Phil" Scolari accepted the Portuguese national team coaching position after the World Cup. He guided Portugal to the Final of the 2004 European Championships (only to fall 1-0 to unheralded Greece), and also to 2006 World Cup qualification.

MVP: *Pauleta.*

(22) Russia: 3 points (3 games; 1 win, 2 losses)

Although Russia was the second highest FIFA ranked team of Group H, they failed to qualify for the second round. After an opening win against Tunisia, Russia crashed to two losses against Japan and Belgium.

Teenager Dmitri Sychev was one of Russia's best players, and was the fifth youngest World Cup scorer ever (and the youngest at the 2002 World Cup). Russia failed to qualify for the 2006 World Cup.

MVP: *Valery Karpin.*

(23) Croatia: 3 points (3 games; 1 win, 2 losses)

Croatia beat venerable Italy with some luck from the referee, but also lost to Mexico and Ecuador. The older generation of Davor Šuker and Robert Prosinečki could not recreate the 1998 magic in this Cup, but once newer players were inserted Croatia became more competitive. Robert Jarni was the exception, as he was the lone player to perform in all 10 World Cup Finals matches for Croatia.

Croatia continued to look to their new generation and qualified for the 2006 World Cup.

MVP: *Robert Jarni.*

(24) Ecuador: 3 points (3 games; 1 win, 2 losses)

After losing to Italy and Mexico without being outclassed, Ecuador played their best match against Croatia, triumphing for their first World Cup win in their first Cup ever. The win denied Croatia passage through to the second round.

This Cup marked the end of international play for Alex Aguinaga, Ecuador's greatest ever player. But Ecuador still has several excellent players that made them competitive for the 2006 World Cup. Playing their home matches in Quito at 2811 meters above sea level gives them a definite psychological home advantage, and they played well to qualify for the 2006 World Cup.

MVP: *Austin Delgado.*

(25) Poland: 3 points (3 games; 1 win, 2 losses)

This was Poland's sixth visit to the World Cup, and surprisingly their first exit without advancing to the second phase.

After performing poorly in the first two Group games against South Korea and Portugal, the Poles outclassed the USA in their last game, nearly denying them passage to the second round. That game salvaged Polish pride, which satisfied until they qualified for Germany 2006.

MVP: *Jacek Krzynowek.*

(26) Uruguay: 2 points (3 games; 2 ties, 1 loss)

In their 10th World Cup, this was only the third time Uruguay had failed to progress to the second phase. There is no better demonstration on why the South American region deserves a playoff for a 5th World Cup spot, as Uruguay showed off their passionate and intelligent play. With Alvaro Recoba one of the world's top performers, the team seemed to get better by the game.

The 3-3 match against Senegal was one of the best games of the tournament, and Uruguay almost pipped the eventual quarterfinalists for the second round position. Uruguay will remain strong contenders to qualify for future World Cups from CONMEBOL, although they failed to qualify for Germany 2006 by losing on penalty kicks to Australia.

MVP: *Alvaro Recoba.*

(27) Nigeria: 1 point (3 games; 1 tie, 2 losses)

This was Nigeria's third consecutive World Cup (1994, 1998, 2002), and the first time they did not reach the second phase. Perhaps the draw did them no favors, as they came bottom of the "Group of Death" with Argentina, England, and Sweden.

Nigeria has great players that unfortunately do not have enough practice time together. Some have called them "the Spain of Africa" after promising much but delivering little, an unfair comparison because of their inherent logistical problems with getting their Europe-based players prepared for African qualifying. Still, they competed well and kept the games close, with Julius Aghahowa's soaring headed goal the highlight of their tournament.

Nigeria again had preparation difficulties and failed to qualify for Germany 2006.

MVP: *Joseph Yobo.*

(28) France: 1 point (3 games; 1 tie, 2 losses)

C'est la vie. France made the worst defense by a World Cup champion in tournament history. France peaked too early, and appeared burned out and starved for ideas without the injured Zinedine Zidane.

Although France's match results just before the Cup were unimpressive, coach Lemerre lacked the flexibility he showed in engineering France's European Cup win in 2000. Perhaps France's biggest planning error was leaving Eric Carrière home – the creative midfielder had filled in well for Zidane as France won the Confederation's Cup in Japan/Korea in 2001. Also missing was quality young defenseman William Gallas.

France later won the 2003 Confederations Cup again, but failed to impress in the 2004 European Championships despite having Zidane healthy. France qualified for the 2006 World Cup, but it remains to be seen whether this era of French soccer excellence is in decline.

MVP: *Fabien Barthez.*

(29) Tunisia: 1 point (3 games; 1 tie, 2 losses)

Losing by two goals each to Russia and Japan, Tunisia tied a strong Belgian team thanks to Raouf Bouzaiene's excellent free kick. Not a brilliant campaign for Tunisia, which was drawn in a seemingly favorable group for their abilities.

Tunisia later won the 2004 African Nation's Cup and qualified for the 2006 World Cup.

MVP: *Raouf Bouzaiene.*

(30) Slovenia: 0 points (3 games; 3 losses)

Somewhat of a surprise to make the World Cup Finals, the Slovenians failed to impress once they lost their star player Zlatko Zahovic. They were outclassed in all three games as they lost to Spain, South Africa, and even after a good start, to a desperate Paraguay. Slovenia will be hard-pressed to soon qualify again for the World Cup from the tough European groups.

MVP: *Milenko Acimovic.*

(31) China: 0 points (3 games; 3 losses)

Newcomers China competed fairly but fared poorly as their defense and offense both needed refinement. They also were a bit unlucky, hitting the post against Brazil and Turkey in vain efforts to score their first World Cup goal. While competitive in the weak Asian field, the world's most populous nation needs to provide more international experience for its best players.

Coach Bora Milutinovic ran out of luck, as the last of his five successive World Cup teams failed to make it to the second round (his first four teams did pass through).

MVP: *Yang Chen.*

(32) Saudi Arabia: 0 points (3 games; 3 losses)

This was not one of Saudi Arabia's better World Cups. Initially stunned into submission by Germany, they eventually gave up twelve goals and scored none. Their closest game was 0-1 to Cameroon, but the game was not as close as the score indicated.

With the Asian competition improving, Saudi Arabia was still able to qualify for Germany 2006.

MVP: *Nawaf Al-Temyat.*

"THE OTHER FINAL"

A game billed as "The Other Final" was held in Thimphu, Bhutan on the same day as the FIFA World Cup™ Final (June 30, 2002). The match was played in the spirit of friendship and football sportsmanship between the two lowest FIFA ranked teams in the world – the Himalayan kingdom of Bhutan and the Caribbean island of Montserrat. Bhutan is located between China and India in a relatively unspoiled area of the Himalayas, while Montserrat is located in the Leeward Island chain in the West Indies.

Bhutan was the newest member of FIFA – joining in 2000 – and was ranked number 202 in the world. Montserrat was ranked number 203 – dead last in the FIFA rankings. The game was dreamed up by Netherlands communications firm KesselsKramer, whose members were perhaps upset that their own *Oranje* team had failed to qualify for the Finals. The match was meant to showcase the global significance of football, and to demonstrate that even at the lowest ranks of the football world, quality footballers playing the beautiful game would emerge to entertain the crowds.

Thimphu is the capital of Bhutan and is 7,600 feet (2316 meters) above sea level. Even with several days acclimation to the mountain conditions, the typical Montserrat team fitness was lacking.

Bhutan's captain Wangyel Dorji scored early in the 4th minute on a header, to the delight of the overflow crowd in Changlimithang Stadium. The Montserrat team was able to hold off further goals and the first half ended 1-0. The second half was action-packed with Bhutan scoring three more times, and Dorji completing a hat trick including a free-kick goal. Although Montserrat threatened Bhutan's goal several times they could not score. Perhaps the altitude was too radical a change for the seafaring islanders. For fairness, a return match should be scheduled in the Caribbean.

Some might think that Montserrat lost the game and won the title of "The World's Worst Football Team," but this was not the point of the game. The British protectorate has only 4,000 people left after the Soufriere volcano became active again in 1995, and therefore has only 150 amateur football players. Even after the evacuation of two-thirds of the population, Montserrat still had an active football federation and league, and was therefore entitled to field a national team and participate in FIFA tournaments.

Even though Montserrat lost the match they really were winners. The organizers of the match had the good sense to saw the "Cup" trophy exactly in half, each nation receiving part of the trophy in a ceremony after the game. Just participating in this historic game was a victory in itself.

Bhutan rose to number 199 in the FIFA rankings after the game; Montserrat was still at 203 but with dreams of rising from the ashes of Soufriere with future victories.

Distinct from the stars of the "Real" FIFA 2002 World Cup, both teams had an acclaimed documentary movie made about their game. It was called the "The Other Final" and directed by Johan Kramer (see www.theotherfinal.com). Beautifully made, the movie is as much about the diverse cultures of Montserrat and Bhutan as it is about football.

Chapter 10

World Cup 2006

¡Fútbol es pasión! [Soccer is passion!]   *Billions of soccer players and fans*

Soccer World Cup as the Most Important Global Sports Event
Soccer Popularity
The soccer World Cup may be the single most watched and followed *event of any type* in modern human society – more popular than the crowning of monarchs or religious figures, and more monitored than many political events.[1] Millions of people travel to witness the spectacle of the World Cup, ranging from international tourists watching the games in person to poor villagers seeking basic television access.[2]

The World Cup is definitely the world's most popular *sporting competition of any type*. Doubters of soccer's popularity propose that the Olympic games are more popular, as nearly every nation participates and there are dozens of sports in addition to a soccer competition. But global popularity can now be objectively measured by counting Internet visits and page views of representative websites such as the official websites of the 2002 Olympic Games and the 2002 FIFA World Cup. By the middle of the competition, the 2002 World Cup website had recorded more than one billion visits – three times more than the 350 million visits for the entire 2002 Olympic competition. The 2002 FIFA World Cup website eventually totaled 2.4 billion visits, thereby erasing any doubt of which global sporting competition is more popular.

World Cup Soccer as a Study of Everything
Because soccer is integrated into many facets of life, soccer in general and the World Cup in particular provide a generous supply of sociological, cultural, linguistic, political, and historical data for investigations of the modern world. A recent example of soccer sociology and politics on an international scale occurred when 2002 World Cup newcomer China asked FIFA – because of the unfortunate historical mistrust between China and Japan – *not* to be placed in a first round 2002 World Cup Group that would play in Japan. FIFA acquiesced to China's request, and China happily played all their matches in the Korea Republic.

Many excellent histories of previous FIFA World Cups are available to assist those interested in comprehensive coverage; recommended books are by Paul Gardner and Brian Glanville (see Chapter 17). The FIFA World Cup website www.fifaworldcup.com is another valuable resource.

---

[1] The soccer World Cup is held every four years – the official name is the 2006 FIFA World Cup™ Germany.
[2] *The Cup* (2000), a football-culture movie by writer/director Khyentse Norbu, was about Tibetan Buddhist monk refugees who became fanatics for the 1998 World Cup, and arranged to watch the spectacle on television.

Previous World Cup Appearance by World's Countries

Nearly all of FIFA's 207 represented countries and states took part in the 2006 World Cup qualifying tournament. Many of the world's countries have already made an appearance in the World Cup Finals – a total of 77 countries qualified for the eighteen World Cup Finals from 1930—2006. Eight countries – four of them African – made their first trip to the World Cup Finals in 2006. The newcomers include Angola, the Czech Republic, Ghana, Ivory Coast, Serbia & Montenegro, Togo, Trinidad & Tobago, and the Ukraine.

Brazil is the only country to have qualified for all eighteen Final competitions from 1930-2006 (1942 and 1946 were canceled due to World War II). The complete list of national appearances appears in Table 1 at the end of the chapter.

Previous World Cup Winner Trends

All of the previous seventeen World Cup winners, *except the 1958 and 2002 Brazil teams*, had been World Cup Champions within their home hemisphere (Brazil beat host Sweden in the 1958 Final, and won in Korea/Japan in 2002). The 2006 World Cup edition would then seem to favor a European champion, but Brazil has defied those odds before.

Six countries have won the World Cup that they were hosting, including: Uruguay in 1930, Italy in 1934, England in 1966, Germany in 1974, Argentina in 1978, and France in 1998 (ironically Brazil failed to win their only hosted World Cup in 1950, as they lost the Final to Uruguay). Three-time Cup winner Germany (1954, 1974, 1990) tries to add to their championship total on their home turf in 2006.

The importance of a successful start in the World Cup cannot be overstated. None of the seventeen World Cup Final champions ever lost their first match. Fifteen of the seventeen won their opening matches; only England in 1966 (Uruguay 0-0) and Italy in 1982 (Poland 0-0) earned a draw in their opening games. None of the sixteen teams that advanced to the second round of 1998 World Cup in France lost their opening match; their cumulative record for first round games was eleven wins and five draws. A similar pattern emerged in the 2002 World Cup, where nine of the sixteen advancers won their first game, while six earned a draw. The only team to advance after losing their opener was Turkey, which lost to eventual champion Brazil 1-2. Turkey bounced back to reach the semi-finals, only to be tamed by Brazil again 0-1.

The Road to the 2006 World Cup

The 2006 FIFA World Cup Finals was the third consecutive World Cup competition to qualify thirty-two countries. Thirty-two teams appears to be the maximum number of qualifying World Cup teams for the foreseeable future, although there was official discussion of entering an asymmetric thirty-six teams for the 2006 Cup. This discussion came as FIFA was considering decreasing the number of qualifying South American teams from a possible five to four; a foolish idea considering South American teams have dominated the World Cup competition, winning nine of the first seventeen World Cup tournaments (1930-2002). The South American decrease was later rescinded, and the super-competitive region still had a chance at five qualifying teams when Uruguay met Australia in a home-and-away series in 2005. In a replay of the 2002 Cup Final qualifying playoff when Uruguay beat Australia 3-1 on aggregate, Uruguay lost out on qualifying for the 2006 Cup after falling to Australia on penalty kicks (the first time a team qualified for the World Cup on penalty kicks – see Chapter 15).

FIFA changed its rule regarding title defense after the 2002 World Cup, and for the first time mandated that the defending champion progress through World Cup qualifying rounds to enter the Finals. For that reason Brazil had to enter the qualifying competition, and showed their quality by coming in first place in the CONMEBOL region.

Only seven of the thirty-two qualifying teams were making their fifth consecutive World Cup appearance in the 2006 World Cup (participating in 1990, 1994, 1998, 2002 and 2006). Those teams were Argentina, Brazil, Italy, Germany, Spain, South Korea, and the USA.

All of the top ten countries in the December 2005 FIFA rankings qualified for the Finals (Brazil, Czech Republic, Holland, Argentina, Mexico, Spain, France, USA, England, and Portugal). Still, four of the top twenty nations did not reach the World Cup Finals; these were Turkey (11), Denmark (13), Greece (16), and Uruguay (18) [FIFA rankings in parentheses]. Thus, 20% of the world's top 20 teams did not qualify for the 2006 Cup. Also surprising was the absence of Africa's top rated nations Cameroon (23) and Nigeria (25), the best African teams of the last thirty years.

World Cup 2006 Germany Special Historical Significance to 1936 & 1974

The 18th FIFA World Cup is hosted by Germany, which unified previously divided East and West Germany in 1991. Unified Germany rehearsed their 2006 World Cup logistics by hosting the 2005 Confederations Cup event, which was won by Brazil over Argentina 4-1.

West Germany previously hosted the World Cup in 1974, and even after losing to their neighbors East Germany in the first round, they emerged as champions after beating the fancied Dutch "Orange Machine" team.

The 18th World Cup is the first international soccer competition in unified Germany since the 1936 Olympics. The refurbished Berlin Olympiastadion – built especially for the 1936 "Nazi" Olympics and the site of the Italy-Austria 1936 Olympic Soccer Final – is also scheduled to host the 2006 FIFA World Cup Final.

The 2006 World Cup in Germany is also special because of two other historical soccer events that occurred in Berlin and West Germany:

(1). The 1936 Olympic Soccer tournament held in unified Nazi Germany – sponsored by FIFA – allowed Peru to be unfairly eliminated after winning all their matches. This gross error can never be rectified; however, it should be officially recognized as a xenophobic event that should never again recur in organized soccer (see Chapter 13). An official tribute to the 1936 Peru Olympic team at the World Cup in Germany would be long overdue, but certainly welcome.

(2). The 1974 World Cup in West Germany featured the first players participating in a World Cup that later died of AIDS – the most catastrophic illness of the 20th (and possibly 21st) century (see Chapter 6). One envisions a special commemoration and dedication to soccer taking a primary role in the global education and prevention of HIV/AIDS at World Cup Germany 2006 (see Chapters 6 & 16). Some players (such as Ronaldo – Brazil, Claudio Pizarro – Peru, Cobi Jones – USA) have already made themselves available for hosting HIV/AIDS education events, but many more soccer players and institutions are needed to participate in targeted health campaigns in their own countries. Therefore, the 2006 World Cup provides an unprecedented opportunity to advance HIV/AIDS prevention and treatment awareness that must not be missed.

Both of the above events should be recognized at Germany 2006 – not only to honor the memory of the 1936 Peru team and the suffering of the 1974 World Cup players – but to harness the full power of international soccer for global health and human rights.

2006 World Cup Specifics

I. FIFA Confederations   Qualifying number of teams

Europe – UEFA [Union European Football Association]   14

Europe had fourteen World Cup positions in 2006. The countries participating from UEFA were: Croatia (3), Czech Republic (1), France (12), England (12), Germany (16), Holland (8), Italy (16), Poland (7), Portugal (4), Serbia & Montenegro (1), Spain (12), Sweden (10), Switzerland (8), and Ukraine (1) [number of total Finals appearances follows each country in parentheses].

The Ukraine was the first team to qualify for the 2006 World Cup after host Germany (who had an automatic placement), and did so from the toughest European group that included Denmark, Turkey, and Greece. Surprisingly absent from the Finals were 2004 European champion Greece and 2002 World Cup third-place team Turkey.

The Czech Republic, Serbia & Montenegro and Ukraine were first-time entrants to the World Cup Finals, although all had participated before as units of Czechoslovakia, Yugoslavia, and the Soviet Union, respectively.

The four European countries of Germany (3), Italy (3), England (1), and France (1) had won eight of the previous seventeen World Cups.

South America – CONMEBOL [Confederación Sudamericana de Fútbol]   4

South America qualified four countries (in order of placement): Brazil (18), Argentina (14), Ecuador (2), and Paraguay (7). [Finals appearances appear after country in parentheses]. Brazil and Argentina finished equal on 34 points, as did Ecuador and Paraguay with 28 points. However, Brazil finished above Argentina on goal difference, while Ecuador finished above Paraguay because of a better head-to-head record.

South America was allocated four or five qualifying positions. Fifth-placed CONMEBOL team Uruguay met Oceania qualifying champion Australia in a home-and-away playoff for the winner to progress to the World Cup, but Uruguay eventually lost on penalty kicks (1-0, 0-1, penalties 2-4).

Two-time World Cup winner Uruguay (1930, 1950) was the only previous winner that failed to qualify for the 2006 Finals. The three South American countries of Brazil (5), Argentina (2), and Uruguay (2) had won a total of nine of the previous seventeen World Cups.

North and Central America and Caribbean – CONCACAF   4

[Confederation of North, Central American & Caribbean Association Football]

The CONCACAF group finished with the USA (8), Mexico (13), Costa Rica (3), and Trinidad & Tobago (1) qualifying [Finals appearances appear after country in parentheses]. The USA and Mexico finished level on 22 points, but the USA won first place by virtue of a better head-to-head record.

Trinidad & Tobago qualified for their first World Cup Finals ever by defeating Bahrain in a CONCACAF-AFC playoff; first tying them at home, then surprisingly beating them 1-0 in Bahrain.

Mexico won the 2003 and the USA the 2005 CONCACAF Championship (also called the Gold Cup).

Africa – CAF [Confederacion Africaine de Football]   5

Africa was allocated five positions, which went to regional group winners Togo (1), Ghana (1), Ivory Coast (1), Angola (1), and Tunisia (4). [Finals appearances appear after country in parentheses]. A major surprise was that four of the five qualifiers were first-time entrants. Angola had the same amount of points as Nigeria in Group 4, but qualified on the basis of a better head-to-head record.

Tunisia was the 2004 African Nation's Cup champion and lost in the 2006 quarterfinals to Nigeria only on penalties. Ivory Coast progressed to the 2006 African's Nations Cup championship game, only to lose on penalties to host Egypt. However, Ghana, Angola, and Togo did not progress to the quarterfinals in the 2006 African Nation's Cup, possibly an ominous sign for their World Cup prospects.

Ivory Coast prevailed in the toughest African Group 3, qualifying over World Cup experienced teams Cameroon and Egypt. Ghana finally made it to the World Cup Finals after posting several fine performances in the youth versions of the World Cup.[3]

Asia – AFC [Asian Football Confederation][4]   4

The four Asia qualifiers were Iran (3) Japan (3), Saudi Arabia (4), and South Korea (7) [Finals appearances appear after country in parentheses].

Japan was the reigning 2000 and 2004 Asian champions, and had impressively finished second to France in the 2001 Confederations Cup competition. South Korea finished fourth at the 2002 World Cup.

Oceania – OFC [Oceania Football Confederation]   1

Australia won the OFC group, and then qualified for their second World Cup Finals ever by beating Uruguay on penalty kicks (4-2) after trading 1-0 wins at the home venues. Australia thus became the *first team ever to qualify for a World Cup Final on penalties.*

In 2005, Australia applied for an unusual confederation switch from the OFC to the AFC. This was apparently an effort to avoid meeting the 5th-placed South American team again in order to qualify for the Cup, as they think they have a better chance of qualifying from Asia than Oceania. As they just qualified for the 2006 competition on penalty kicks, they may be correct.

FIFA debated whether to guarantee the Oceania region a place for the 2006 World Cup in Germany at the apparent expense of a South American team. It was finally decided that the OFC representative should defeat another confederation's team in a home-and-away series in order to qualify for the World Cup.

---

[3] Ghana won the FIFA U-17 Championship in 1991 and 1995 (and was runner-up in 1993 and 1997), won second place in the 1993 and 2001 U-20 Championship. Ghana has also won the Africa Nations Cup four times (1963, 1965, 1978, 1982) with their full national team.

[4] The forty-five member AFC represents nearly 60% of the world's soccer playing population, as Asia's population of 3.7 billion contributes 6 of every 10 people on the planet (total of 6.1 billion).

II. World Cup 2006 Teams in Assigned Groups

[Seeded teams at left in each Group; Teams assigned sequentially from left to right]

Group A	Germany	Costa Rica	Poland	Ecuador
Group B	England	Paraguay	Trinidad & Tobago	Sweden
Group C	Argentina	Ivory Coast	Serbia & Montenegro	Netherlands
Group D	Mexico	Iran	Angola	Portugal
Group E	Italy	Ghana	USA	Czech Republic
Group F	Brazil	Croatia	Australia	Japan
Group G	France	Switzerland	Korea Republic	Togo
Group H	Spain	Ukraine	Tunisia	Saudi Arabia

III. World Cup Groups by Difficulty of Competition

[By Combined Team Ranks from December 2005 FIFA World Rankings in parentheses ( )]

GROUP	TEAMS	COMBINED TEAM RANKS
Group E	Italy (12), Ghana (50), USA (8), Czech Republic (2)	72
Group F	Brazil (1), Croatia (20), Australia (49), Japan (15)	85
Group C	Argentina (4), Ivory Coast (41), Serbia & Montenegro (47), Netherlands (3)	95
Group A	Germany (16), Costa Rica (21), Poland (23), Ecuador (37)	97
Group D	Mexico (7), Iran (19), Angola (62), Portugal (10)	98
Group B	England (9), Paraguay (30), Trinidad & Tobago (51), Sweden (14)	104
Group H	Spain (6), Ukraine (40), Tunisia (28), Saudi Arabia (32)	106
Group G	France (5), Switzerland (36), Korea Republic (29), Togo (56)	126

Despite the final group rankings above, there are really two "Groups of Death" (Groups E and C are the most difficult groups) in the 2006 World Cup.

Group E has three teams ranked within the top twelve teams in the world, even accounting for Italy's under-ranking. Ghana is also one of the strongest African teams. Group C contains the number 3 and 4 teams in the world, and both Ivory Coast and Serbia & Montenegro are grossly under-ranked. It is impossible to determine beforehand which two teams will emerge from these groups to qualify for the second round, but the two African teams may be at a disadvantage because it is their first trip to a World Cup.

Although Group F is ranked more difficult than Group C, Brazil and Croatia are the favorites to emerge from this group and therefore it does not qualify as a "Group of Death."

IV. Odds of Winning the World Cup at the Start of the 2006 World Cup
Team odds of winning the 18th World Cup were posted just after the 2006 World Cup draw in December 2005. Odds makers divided the thirty-two teams into ten groups with similar betting odds.

Brazil 11/4 - England 11/2 - Germany 13/2 - Argentina 7/1
The top four teams included two from Europe and two from South America – all of them previous World Cup winners (Brazil 1958, 1962, 1970, 1994, 2002; Germany 1954, 1974, 1990; Argentina 1978, 1986; England 1966). Brazil was the clear favorite at odds of 2¾ to 1, while England followed at exactly double the odds at 5½ to 1. Germany and Argentina were pegged slightly behind at 6 ½ and 7 to 1 odds, respectively.

France 10/1 - Italy 11/1 - Holland 12/1 - Spain 12/1
Four European soccer powers made up the second group. Both Italy (1934, 1938, 1982) and France (1998) were previous World Cup winners; Holland was a two-time finalist (1974, 1978). Spain has underachieved in previous World Cups despite having one of the highest quality leagues (La Liga) and dozens of quality players.

Portugal 25/1 - Czech Republic 33/1 - Sweden 33/1
Three European teams made up the third group. Both Sweden (1958) and the Czech Republic were previous Finalists (if one counts Czechoslovakia in 1962), while Portugal narrowly lost the European championship Final in 2004.

Mexico 50/1 - Ukraine 66/1 - Croatia 80/1
The fourth group at medium odds included perennial CONCACAF power Mexico, debutante Ukraine, and three-time consecutive qualifier Croatia.

Poland 100/1 - USA 100/1 - Ivory Coast 100/1
Despite reaching the 2002 World Cup quarterfinals and beating Mexico, the USA paradoxically received worse odds than they did at the 2002 World Cup (90/1). Ivory Coast debuted as the top ranked African team, while Poland made their second consecutive Finals.

Australia 125/1 - Serbia & Montenegro 125/1 - Switzerland 125/1
These are generous odds for Australia and Serbia & Montenegro, but probably just right for Switzerland, which qualified over 2002 third-place country Turkey.

Ghana 200/1 - Korea Republic 200/1 - Paraguay 250/1
Three good teams have fairly long odds reflecting the difficulty of advancing from their difficult Group stages.

Ecuador 300/1 - Japan 300/1 - Togo 300/1 - Tunisia 300/1
These odds are likely a bit too long for Ecuador, Japan, and Tunisia, but are adequate for newcomer Togo.

Angola 400/1 - Costa Rica 500/1 - Iran 500/1
Costa Rica is severely short-changed in these odds, as newcomers Angola and returning Iran do not have the soccer pedigree that the Central American nation does. Iran and Angola are both in Group D, and therefore group-mates Portugal and Mexico felt very confident with the draw.

Saudi Arabia 1000/1 - Trinidad & Tobago 1000/1
Despite Saudi Arabia's three previous World Cup appearances, they shared the most distant odds with newcomers Trinidad & Tobago.

V. GROUP OVERVIEW: [Updated information to 25 April 2006]

A1: FIFA team number [1] FIFA rank before World Cup

GROUP A   Germany, Costa Rica, Poland, Ecuador

2002 World Cup Finalist Germany is favored to top this group, as the other three countries exited the 2002 World Cup after the group stages. Still, Costa Rica and Ecuador are both World Cup experienced and could spring a surprise – especially since Germany has never played them before.

Each of these group teams lost their preliminary friendly match on 1 March 2006: Costa Rica lost to Iran 2-3, Poland lost to the USA 0-1, Ecuador lost to the Netherlands 0-1, and Germany lost 1-4 to Italy in a shocking result. However, Germany redeemed themselves in a 4-1 win against a substandard USA on 22 March 2006, thereby taking some pressure off the team and coach Klinsmann.

A1. Germany [16]

2006 FIFA World Cup host Germany qualified automatically, and therefore only had friendly games to prepare for Cup action. Although the Bundesliga is a strong league, none of its teams had won a European title since Bayern Munich won the 2001 European Championship on penalties.

Die Nationalelf (National Eleven) final lineup will likely be flexible as perhaps only star midfielder Michael Ballack and striker Miroslav Klose are certain of their starting spots. Creative midfielder Sebastien Deisler was injured shortly before the Finals, and will likely miss his second consecutive Cup due to injury. Current coach Jürgen Klinsmann (see Chapter 7) has tried several different lineups in order to introduce some flair into what is normally a power-soccer team, but the disturbing result against Italy prior to the Cup gives doubt as to whether Germany can compete with other top teams. But with the home crowd behind them, Germany is certainly favored to advance from the group stages.

Possible lineup: Jens Lehmann (Oliver Kahn); Patrick Owomoyela, Robert Huth, Christoph Metzelder, Per Mertesacker (Christian Worns); Bernd Schneider (Tim Borowski), Torsten Frings, Bastian Schweinsteiger, Michael Ballack; Kevin Kuranyi (Lukas Podolski), Miroslav Klose.
Coach: Jürgen Klinsmann.

A2. Costa Rica [21]

Costa Rica qualified comfortably in third place in the CONCACAF region, but not quite as impressively as in 2002 when they qualified in first place.

Los Ticos have several players back from the 2002 team that finished tied on points at the group stage with eventual third-place winner Turkey (Costa Rica did not advance because of inferior goal difference). Perhaps the most important are midfielder Walter Centeno, and strikers Paulo Wanchope (Costa Rica all-time top scorer with 43 goals) and Ronald Gómez.

Possible lineup: Alvaro Mesen; Harold Wallace, Luis Marin, Gilberto Martinez, Leonardo Gonzalez; Jose Luis Lopez, Alonso Solis, Carlos Hernandez, Walter Centeno; Paulo Wanchope, Ronald Gómez.
Coach: Alexandre Guimaraes.

A3. Poland [23]

Poland qualified only one point behind Europe Group 6 leaders England, but had a better goal difference (18 to 12) than the English. The only points they dropped were to England, so they must be vigilant when confronting another big team such as Germany.

The *Białо-czerwoni* (The White and Red) have a solid goalkeeper in 2005 European Champions League winner Jerzy Dudek (Liverpool), while captain Tomasz Hajto and striker Maciej Zurawski are other key players. Poland will look to better their 2002 World Cup experience, when they were eliminated after the group stage (the first time in six World Cup qualifications they failed to progress to the second round).

Possible lineup: Jerzy Dudek; Sebastian Mila, Tomasz Rzasa, Jacek Bak, Michal Zewlakow; Arkadiusz Glowacki, Damian Gorowski, Jacek Krzynowek, Mariusz Lewandowski, Maciej Zurawski, Piotr Wlodarczyk.
Coach: Pawel Janas.

A4. Ecuador [37]

Ecuador qualified third in the hyper-competitive CONMEBOL region for their second consecutive World Cup appearance. With their talismanic number 10 Alex Aguinaga retired, Ecuador must rely on other 2002 returnees.

La Tri (nickname meaning *tricolor*) must improve on their international performances, as they passed the first round of the Copa America only once in five tries in the last decade. A recent tie against Italy may indicate they are ready to prove their abilities.

Possible lineup: Edwin Villafuerte; Ulises de la Cruz, Ivan Hurtado, Giovanny Espinoza, Paul Ambrossi; Edwin Tenorio, Marlon Ayovi, Edison Mendez, Antonio Valencia; Agustin Delgado, Ivan Kaviedes.
Coach: Luis Suárez.

SCHEDULE TEMPLATE
Match number   "Home" Team v. "Away" Team
Date: Venue & Kickoff time

01 Germany v. Costa Rica
    June 9: Munich 18:00

02 Poland v. Ecuador
    June 9: Gelsenkirchen 21:00

17 Germany v. Poland
    June 14: Dortmund 21:00

18 Ecuador v. Costa Rica
    June 15: Hamburg 15:00

33 Ecuador v. Germany
    June 20: Berlin 16:00

34 Costa Rica v. Poland
    June 20: Hanover 16:00

GROUP B — England, Paraguay, Trinidad & Tobago, Sweden

England and Sweden are favored to qualify from Group B, but it is far from guaranteed. In the 1 March 2006 friendly matches England nipped Uruguay 2-1 in the last minute in Liverpool, Sweden lost 0-3 to Ireland in Dublin, Paraguay tied Wales 0-0 in Cardiff, and Trinidad & Tobago beat Iceland 2-0 in London.

B1. England [9]

England qualified top of their World Cup qualifying group, despite two disappointing losses away to Denmark and Northern Ireland in 2005. England boasts quality at every position, but has lacked seamless teamwork when facing quality opposition (such as when England was one man up yet could not avoid defeat to Brazil in the 2002 World Cup). This applies to the four-man midfield setup of Cole, Gerrard, Lampard, and Beckham, which some critics doubt is fully compatible. Some also question if recent distractions involving coach Sven-Goran Eriksson will affect team performance.[5]

The Three Lions' wild-card is *enfant terrible* Wayne Rooney, a 20-year old creative striker/midfielder who can dominate a game. Also figuring in is quicksilver winger Shaun Wright-Phillips, who many think should displace Beckham from the starting lineup.

Man-for-man, England (along with Argentina, Italy, and Czech Republic) match up best against favorite Brazil. England's starting eleven account for 86 international goals (Owen 35, Beckham 16, Rooney 11, Lampard 11, Gerrard 6, Cole 5, Ferdinand 1, Campbell 1, others 0); a great total until one realizes that the Brazil team is just as young as England (and assuming that Owen has fully recovered from his broken foot suffered in January 2006). Still, it would be a massive collapse for England not to progress from this group, and many experts predict England will get to the semi-final against Brazil.[6] If so, it will then require a massive effort to disprove the modern soccer cliché, "Football: the English invented it, the Brazilians perfected it."

Possible lineup: Paul Robinson; Gary Neville, Rio Ferdinand (Ledley King), John Terry (Sol Campbell), Ashley Cole (Jaime Carragher); David Beckham (Shaun Wright-Phillips), Frank Lampard, Steven Gerrard, Joe Cole; Michael Owen, Wayne Rooney.
Coach: Sven-Goran Eriksson.

B2. Paraguay [30]

Paraguay has a potentially potent attack trio of Cuevas, Santa Cruz, and Cardozo, but despite the seemingly endless career of stellar defender and captain Carlos Gamarra, their defense may be suspect after the retirements of keeper José Luis Chilavert and defenders Francisco Arce and Celso Ayala. One potentially exciting newcomer is striker Nelson Haedo Valdez.

Paraguay won the football silver medal at the 2004 Athens Olympics, losing 0-1 to Argentina. The *Guaranies* reached the second round of the 1998 and 2002 World Cups, and will be working to reach that far or even farther in 2006.

Possible lineup: Justo Villar; Denis Caniza, Julio Cesar Caceres, Carlos Gamarra, Paulo da Silva; Angel Ortiz, Diego Gavilan, Carlos Paredes; Nelson Cuevas (Valdez), Roque Santa Cruz, Jose Cardozo.
Coach: Aníbal Ruiz.

---

[5] Eriksson had two personal affairs made public, and he explored future soccer opportunities while England coach – including a fake sheikh meeting arranged by the *News of the World* newspaper that also was made public.
[6] If England and Brazil both win their respective groups OR both come in second they could meet in a semifinal match, but if one team finishes first and the other second they could meet in the Final.

B3. Trinidad & Tobago [51]

Trinidad & Tobago is the smallest country by population and size to ever have claimed a place in a FIFA World Cup. It is also the fourth Caribbean island-country to qualify for the World Cup (the others are Cuba 1938, Haiti 1974, and Jamaica 1998).

The *Soca Warriors* are led by experienced strikers Dwight Yorke and Stern John, creative midfielder Russell Latapy, and quality goalkeeper Shaka Hislop. Yorke was a star with Manchester United, while prior to the World Cup John had scored 64 goals in his 89 internationals. The match with their former colonial rulers England will be eagerly awaited.

Possible lineup: Shaka Hislop; Brent Sancho, Nigel Henry, Leslie Fitzpatrick, Anton Pierre; Angus Eve, Carlos Edwards, Dennis Lawrence, Kenwyne Jones; Dwight Yorke, Stern John.
Coach: Leo Beenhakker.

B4. Sweden [14]

Sweden has not lost to England since 1968 – a fact that should concern the English. Sweden's *enfant terrible* is Zlatan Ibrahimovic (Juventus), who is capable of stunning passing and goals. Fortunately for Sweden, their skilled goal scorer Henrik Larsson opted to play in one last World Cup after recovery from an injured knee at Barcelona.

The *Blågult* (Blue and Gold) finished second in the 1958 World Cup, and third in the 1950 and 1994 competitions. With many of their talented players returning from the 2002 World Cup squad they could be capable of pushing far into the 2006 Cup.

Possible lineup: Andreas Isaksson; Alexander Ostlund, Olof Mellberg, Teddy Lucic, Erik Edman; Tobias Linderoth, Niclas Alexandersson, Anders Svensson, Fredrik Ljungberg; Zlatan Ibrahimovic, Henrik Larsson.
Coach: Lars Lagerbäck.

03 England v. Paraguay
    June 10: Frankfurt 15:00

04 Trinidad & Tobago v. Sweden
    June 10: Dortmund 18:00

19 England v. Trinidad & Tobago
    June 15: Nuremberg 18:00

20 Sweden v. Paraguay
    June 15: Berlin 21:00

35 Sweden v. England
    June 20: Cologne 21:00

36 Paraguay v. Trinidad & Tobago
    June 20: Kaiserslautern 21:00

GROUP C — Argentina, Ivory Coast, Serbia & Montenegro, Netherlands

One of the two "Groups of Death," along with Group E, it is impossible to predict which teams will advance. In the friendly matches on 1 March 2006 Argentina lost to Croatia 2-3, Ivory Coast lost to Spain 2-3, Serbia & Montenegro beat Tunisia 1-0, and the Netherlands beat Ecuador 1-0.

C1. Argentina [4]

Argentina finished tied with leaders Brazil in the 2006 South American qualifying, once again proving their top quality football. They have routinely won youth world championships in the last decade (1995, 1997, 2001 and 2005) – a performance superior to any other team, including Brazil. Argentina also won the 2004 Athens Olympic Football tournament, scoring eighteen goals while allowing none. The *Albicelestes* (White and Sky Blues) will be aiming to best their 2004 Copa America experience, when they lost the Final to Brazil in a penalty competition, and the 2005 Confederations Cup, when they lost to Brazil 1-4.

Argentina is the only other team in the World Cup capable of fielding five quality "number 10's" like the current Brazil team – Riquelme, D'Alessandro, Aimar, Gonzalez, and Messi. Hernan Crespo is their center forward "number 9" with 29 national team goals, and Carlos Tévez is a three-time South American Player of the Year. Eighteen-year old Lionel Messi stellar play has recently drawn comparisons to Diego Maradona, but this can only serve to overshadow his own unique footballing qualities. If Argentina can improve their defensive play they will have all the qualities to reach the semi-final and beyond.

Possible lineup: Roberto Abbondanzieri (Germán Lux); Javier Zanetti, Roberto Ayala, Walter Samuel (Fabricio Coloccini), Juan Pablo Sorin; Javier Mascherano (Andres D'Alessandro), Luis Gonzalez (Pablo Aimar), Juan Roman Riquelme, Esteban Cambiasso (Lionel Messi); Hernan Crespo, Carlos Tévez (Javier Saviola).
Coach: José Pekerman.

C2. Ivory Coast [41]

Ivory Coast is the only country that qualified for the 2006 World Cup that is at civil war. Although the rebel-held north is battling the government south, the national team players hail from all areas of the country and as such the team is potentially a symbol of national unity.

Still, many people are despairing at the senseless violence. Jacques Anouma, the president of the Ivory Coast Football Federation has said, "What cause does it serve to go to the World Cup without peace in our country? Without peace there is no glory. We ask all the protagonists to put down their arms and talk peace." Captain Didier Drogba led a prayer of peace immediately after the Ivorians had qualified for their first World Cup in 2005, saying "Ivorians we beg your forgiveness. Let us come together and put this war behind us." There is active talk of Ivory Coast pulling out of the World Cup if the violence does not abate – an absolutely unprecedented but potentially powerful protest against the war.

Les Éléphants performed well in the 2006 African Nation's Cup, losing in the Final to host Egypt only on a penalty kick competition. Otherwise, Ivory Coast players apparently have nerves of steel in penalty kick competitions – they won the 1992 African Nation's Cup against Ghana 11-10, and defeated Cameroon in the 2006 quarterfinals by 12-11 (12 rounds or 24 shots in each competition).

Coach Henri Michel has spent many years abroad coaching Cameroon, Morocco, the UAE, and Tunisia after coaching his native France in the 1980s, and his experience at international level can only help the Ivory Coast team.

Possible lineup: Jean-Jacques Tizie; Arthur Boka, Cyril Domoraud, Kolo Toure, Marc Zoro (Eboue); Didier Zokora, Emerse Fae (Kouassi), Gilles Yapi Yapo, Tchiressoa Guel; Bonaventure Kalou (Akale), Didier Drogba.
Coach: Henri Michel.

C3. Serbia & Montenegro [47]

Although the country broke away from greater Yugoslavia in 1992, it changed its name to Serbia & Montenegro only in 2003. It qualified for the 1998 World Cup under the name of Yugoslavia (making it to the second round), so the 2006 Cup marks the second Cup appearance for some of the current players.

Team captain Dejan Stanković controls the midfield, while national appearance and goal leader Savo Milošević (35 goals) and Mateja Kežman are the likely strikers. Defender Nemanja Vidić signed for Manchester United in 2006.

Serbia & Montenegro finished undefeated and top of their World Cup qualifying group, ahead of vastly experienced Spain and Belgium. The *Blue* (Плави) allowed only one goal in ten qualifying games – it would be a mistake to underestimate this team.

Possible lineup: Dragoslav Jevric; Mladen Krstajic, Nemanja Vidić, Goran Gavrancic, Ivica Dragutinovic; Igor Duljaj, Milos Maric, Dejan Stanković, Zvonimir Vukic; Savo Milošević, Mateja Kežman (Jestrovic).
Coach: Ilija Petković.

C4. Netherlands [3]

The Dutch must be wanting badly to make up for their absence in the 2002 World Cup – the first World Cup it had missed since 1986. The *Oranje* have been playing well, reaching the semi-finals of the 2004 European championship, but losing 1-2 in an excellent Portuguese performance. They also finished undefeated in their 2006 World Cup qualifying group with 10 wins and two draws, thereby forcing world number two team Czech Republic into a playoff qualifier.

Coach Marco van Basten (Chapter 7) has allowed many younger players to perform in lieu of more famous matured players, and has been successful doing it (the experienced Clarence Seedorf and Roy Makaay will likely not be picked by van Basten). Still, the Netherlands could be favored to advance to the semi-finals as they did in 1998.

Possible lineup: Edwin van der Sar; Khalid Boulahrouz, Jan Kromkamp, Andre Ooijer, Giovanni van Bronckhorst; Wesley Sneijder, Mark van Bommel, Phillip Cocu (Edgar Davids), Rafael van der Vaart; Ruud van Nistelrooy (Arjen Robben), Dirk Kuyt.
Coach: Marco van Basten.

05 Argentina v. Ivory Coast
    June 10: Hamburg 21:00

06 Serbia & Montenegro v. Netherlands
    June 11: Leipzig 15:00

21 Argentina v. Serbia & Montenegro
    June 16: Gelsenkirchen 15:00

22 Netherlands v. Ivory Coast
    June 16: Stuttgart 18:00

37 Netherlands v. Argentina
    June 21: Frankfurt 21:00

38 Ivory Coast v. Serbia & Montenegro
    June 21: Munich 21:00

GROUP D — Mexico, Iran, Angola, Portugal

Mexico and Portugal are the favorites to progress from this group, but Iran is also a threat. In the friendly matches on 1 March 2006 Portugal beat Saudi Arabia 3-0, Angola fell to Korea Republic 1-0, and Iran beat Costa Rica 3-2. Unfortunately, in the last match at Azadi Stadium in Tehran, the Iran government enforced a ban on women watching their national team (see Chapters 16). Mexico beat Ghana 1-0 in Dallas on 2 March 2006.

D1. Mexico [7]

Mexico was the seeded team of this group – the first time a CONCACAF team was seeded when not hosting the event. *Los Tricolores* moved up in the FIFA World rankings in February 2006, sharing the 6th world spot with Spain and their CONCACAF nemesis USA.

Normally football-insular Mexico has internationalized a bit. Most of the players still perform in the Mexican league, with two notable exceptions of Rafael Marquez (Barcelona) and Jared Borghetti (Bolton). Additionally, coach Ricardo Lavolpe is an Argentine and Mexico will likely play two naturalized players, Brazil-born playmaker Antonio Naelson (known as "Zinha") and Argentine-born striker Guillermo Franco (now at Villarreal in Spain). Partly because of a feud with Lavolpe, striker Cuauhtémoc Blanco not play in 2006.

Mexico won the 1999 Confederations Cup against Brazil, and recently defeated Brazil again (in the 2005 Confederations Cup) and Argentina (in the 2004 Copa America). They will likely top this group with Portugal, and should be dangerous in later rounds.

Possible lineup: Oswaldo Sanchez; Salvador Carmona, Rafael Marquez, Ricardo Osorio, Carlos Salcido; Pavel Pardo, Zinha, Jaime Lozano, Gerardo Torrado; Jose Fonseca, Jared Borgetti (Guillermo Franco).
Coach: Ricardo Lavolpe.

D2. Iran [19]

In their two previous World Cup appearances Iran won only one game – against the USA in 1998. More recently, Iran came third in the 2004 Asian Nations Cup (after winners Japan and runner-up China), having last won that competition in 1976.

Team Melli (National Team) has three players who either formerly (Ali Daei and Vahid Hashemian) or currently (Ali Karimi) play for Bayern Munich (Daei was 1999 Asian Player of the Year and Karimi won the 2004 award). Daei is finishing his career in Iran but Hashemian has moved to Hannover 96. Midfielder and 2003 Asian Player of the Year Mehdi Mahdavikia also plays in the Bundesliga for Hamburg. Captain Daei has 108 goals in 144 appearances for Iran, and is set to retire after the 2006 Cup.

Most of the team is still Iran-based, which could be an advantage for team cohesiveness. However, the lack of international exposure against top-ranked teams makes it a challenge for Iran to advance against Portugal and Mexico. In a positive sign, Iran beat a skilled Costa Rican team 3-2 in a friendly match in Tehran on 01 March 2006.

Possible lineup: Ebrahim Mirzapour; Hossein Kaebi, Yahya Golmohammadi (Taghipour), Rahman Rezaei, Mohammad Nosrati; Javad Nekounam, Mehdi Mahdavikia, Ali Karimi, Alireza Vahedi; Ali Daei, Vahid Hashemian.
Coach: Branko Ivankovic.

D3. Angola [62]

After impressively winning a World Cup qualifying group that included Nigeria, Angola failed to advance from the group stages at the 2006 African Nations Cup.

The *Palancas Negras* (Black Impalas) have managed to lure several Portugal-based players for their team, including midfield maestro Figueredo and defenders Pedro Emanuel and Rui Marques. Still, the professional experience of the Angola team is way below the rest of the group, and it would be a major surprise if they earn more than one point from this group.

Possible lineup: Joao Ricardo (Goliath); Pedro Emanuel, Kali, Jamba (Loco), Rui Marques; Figueredo, Medonca, Ze Kalanga, Andre Macanga; Flavio (Maurito), Akwa (Love Kabungula).
Coach: Luis Oliveira Gonçalves.

D4. Portugal [10]

Portugal has performed well in Europe, finishing second in the 2004 European Championships and progressing to the semi-finals of the 2000 edition (losing to eventual champion France). Despite their potential brilliance, the *Selecção das Quinas* (nickname refers to the five shields [escutcheons] or five dots [bezants] that used to grace the Portuguese shirts) can be wildly erratic at times. In 2004 they tied lowly Liechtenstein (population 34,000) 2-2, but only four days later hammered Russia (population 144,000,000) 7-1. Veteran defender Jorge Andrade was injured shortly before the World Cup.

Captain Luis Figo is the last member of the "golden generation" that won two U-20 World Youth Championships (1989 & 1991) to still play with the national team. The best Portuguese player of his generation, Figo will be looking to create just a little more magic in 2006.

Possible lineup: Ricardo Pereira; Luis Monteiro, Nuno Valente, Ricardo Carvalho, Paulo Ferreira; Luis Figo (Tiago Mendes), Francisco Costinha, Deco Souza, Maniche Ribeiro; Cristiano Ronaldo (Simao Sabrosa), Pedro Pauleta (Nuno Gomes).
Coach: Luiz Felipe Scolari.

07 Mexico v. Iran
     June 11: Nuremberg 18:00

08 Angola v. Portugal
     June 11: Cologne 21:00

23 Mexico v. Angola
     June 16: Hanover 21:00

24 Portugal v. Iran
     June 17: Frankfurt 15:00

39 Portugal v. Mexico
     June 21: Gelsenkirchen 16:00

40 Iran v. Angola
     June 21: Leipzig 16:00

GROUP E   Italy, Ghana, USA, Czech Republic

One of the two "Groups of Death" along with Group C, it is impossible to predict which teams will advance. Despite Italy being ranked lower than the Czech Republic and the USA they are playing superbly – especially after they thrashed Germany 4-1 in a World Cup friendly on 1 March 2006. In other matches that day the USA beat Poland 1-0, and the Czech Republic drew 2-2 with Turkey. Ghana lost to Mexico 0-1 on 2 March 2006.

The second-placed team from this group will likely face Brazil in the eight-finals, so each team must strive to be first.

E1. Italy [12]

Italy is one of the few teams that matches up well with Brazil, and possesses several brilliant players of their own. If Andrea Pirlo, Francesco Totti, and Alessandro Del Piero play to their level, and Gilardino and Toni get the goals, Italy will be in contention for the title. But Totti suffered a broken ankle (from an illegal tackle from the back with no ball contact) in mid-February 2006, so he is doubtful to be 100% fit. Del Piero is fast approaching 200 Serie A goals, a feat only accomplished by two men in the last 35 years (José João Altafini and Roberto Baggio – see Chapter 7).

The *Azzurri* (Sky Blues) defense is typically strong, and despite the retirement of in-form Milan defenseman Paolo Maldini, stellar goalkeeper Buffon should marshal an impressive defense that still includes Alessandro Nesta and Marco Materazzi. All-in-all, Italy possesses an explosive team that has the potential to get to the semi-finals and beyond.

<u>Possible lineup</u>: Gianluigi Buffon; Gianluca Zambrotta, Alessandro Nesta, Fabio Cannavaro (Materazzi), Fabio Grosso; Gennaro Gattuso, Andrea Pirlo, Francesco Totti; Alberto Gilardino (Alessandro Del Piero), Luca Toni (Filippo Inzaghi).
Coach: Marcello Lippi.

E2. Ghana [50]

Ghana finally qualified for the FIFA World Cup after twice winning the U-17 World Championship and twice finishing second at the U-20 Youth World Championships. Although Ghana has won the African Nation's Cup four times, their last such victory was in 1982 and they failed to progress past the first round in the 2006 edition.

Ghana has several established European stars such as defenseman Samuel Kuffour and midfielders Michael Essien and captain Stephen Appiah, and the team has many other European based players. Still, they have yet to show consistency outside the Cup qualifying matches.

<u>Possible lineup</u>: Sammy Adjei; Issa Ahmed, Dan Quaye, Samuel Kuffour, John Mensah; Michael Essien, Sulley Ali Muntari, Stephen Appiah, Anthony Obodai; Matthew Amoah, Asamoah Gyan (Frimpong).
Coach: Ratomir Dujkovic.

E3. USA [8]

Coach Bruce Arena has more internationally experienced USA players than ever, but his secret of success has been in obtaining the right mix of players. Kasey Keller, Gregg Berhalter, Carlos Bocanegra, Claudio Reyna, DaMarcus Beasley, and Brian McBride have all been tested in top divisions in Europe, although top talents Eddie Johnson, Landon Donovan have dominated the domestic MLS. Teen sensation Freddy Adu tried to make the 2006 USA World Cup squad after turning down World Cup-bound Ghana, his country of birth (Adu would just be seventeen years old at the start of the 2006 Cup).

The USA moved up in the FIFA World rankings in April 2006, being ranked an incredible 4th. The USA defeated neighbors Mexico 2-0 in September 2005 after losing to them 1-2 in March 2005. A 1-4 loss to Germany on 22 March 2006 in Dortmund left some uncertainty before the Cup, even though half the starting lineup was absent. The main worry is that the USA has historically not performed well in Europe; in fact, the USA has lost the last nine games played in Europe against England, Germany, Italy, France, and Spain. Arena will have to find a way to reverse this trend if the USA has any chance of advancing.

Possible lineup: Kasey Keller; Steve Cherundolo, Eddie Pope (Oguchi Onyewu), Gregg Berhalter, Carlos Bocanegra (Jonathan Spector); Pablo Mastroeni, Claudio Reyna (Bobby Convey), Landon Donovan, DaMarcus Beasley (Eddie Lewis); Brian McBride (Taylor Twellman), Eddie Johnson (Josh Wolff).
Coach: Bruce Arena.

E4. Czech Republic [2]

This is the first World Cup appearance for the Czech Republic, which became independent in 1993 after peaceably splitting from Czechoslovakia. The team has since performed well, finishing second in the 1996 European Championship and reaching the quarterfinals of the 2004 edition. Despite ranking second in the world, they have not won any titles yet save the 2002 U-21 European championship.

The team is driven by midfielder Pavel Nedved (Chapter 7) and anchored by stellar goalkeeper Petr Cech. Also vital are midfielders Tomas Rosicky, Vladimir Smicer, and Karel Poborsky, and the offensive duo of Jan Koller (top Czech scorer with 40 goals) and Milan Baroš (26 goals). The Czechs have a dynamic team and like to score a lot: the seven starters of Koller (40 goals), Baroš (26), Smicer (27), Nedved (17), Rosicky (15), Poborsky (8), and Jankulovski (7) have a massive 140 goals between them – a total that rivals only Brazil's firepower.

Possible lineup: Petr Cech; Zdenek Gygera (Jiranek), David Rozehnal (Bolf), Tomas Ujfalusi, Marek Jankulovski; Tomas Galasek (Jarosik), Pavel Nedved, Tomas Rosicky, Karel Poborsky (Vladimir Smicer); Jan Koller, Milan Baroš.
Coach: Karel Brückner.

09 Italy v. Ghana
    June 12: Hanover 21:00

10 USA v. Czech Republic
    June 12: Gelsenkirchen 18:00

25 Italy v. USA
    June 17: Kaiserslautern 21:00

26 Czech Republic v. Ghana
    June 17: Cologne 18:00

41 Czech Republic v. Italy
    June 22: Hamburg 16:00

42 Ghana v. USA
    June 22: Nuremberg 16:00

GROUP F Brazil, Croatia, Australia, Japan

In the friendly matches on 1 March 2006 Brazil beat Russia 1-0 in frigid Moscow and Croatia beat Argentina 3-2, and they will be the favorites to advance from this group. Japan tied Bosnia-Herzegovina 2-2 on 2 March 2006 in Dortmund.

F1. Brazil [1]

Brazil won the 2002 FIFA World Cup, the 2004 Copa America (their continental championship), and the 2005 Confederations Cup – the first time a nation held all three titles simultaneously. Brazilian players grace the soccer stage throughout the world, and the country possesses such player depth that a third-string *Seleção* (Brazil selection) could probably compete for the World Cup title.

Perhaps not since the 1970 Brazil team of the "five number 10s" (Pelé, Rivelino, Tostão, Gérson and Jairzinho) has the main World Cup story been whether any other team could beat one nation. Of course that nation is once again Brazil, but the formidable five are now Ronaldinho (2004 and 2005 FIFA World Player of the Year), Ronaldo (1997, 1999, and 2002 FIFA World Player of the Year), Kaká, Adriano and Robinho. One question is whether coach Carlos Alberto Parreira has the audacity to field all five at once, accompanying four defenders and only one defensive midfielder.

At the 2005 Confederations Cup Brazil lost only in the preliminaries 0-1 to Mexico's suffocating defensive marking and Jared Borgetti's superbly headed goal. Mexico's approach appears to be the only method of defeating Brazil – not necessarily a pretty strategy but it could be effective if Brazil has a bad day. However, Brazil recovered and had a superb Final as they dominated archrivals Argentina 4-1 in a match that could have had a more lopsided score. The fourth goal – in which the ball was worked around the entire field for Adriano to head his second goal – was distinctly reminiscent of Brazil's fourth goal against Italy in the 1970 Final, a match Brazil also won 4-1.

Brazil is so good that they cannot find time to play their other outstanding players, such as Cafú's deputy Cicinho who had a hand in all four Brazil goals against Argentina. A raw fact is that Brazil's substitutes are just as good or better than other nation's starters, and the common wisdom for 2006 is *only Brazil can beat Brazil*, i.e., only by playing poorly will they lose the championship.

The starting Brazil eleven has 152 international goals between them (Ronaldo 58, Ronaldinho 27, Adriano 22, Kaká 11, Roberto Carlos 11, Emerson 6, Ze Roberto 5, Cafú 5, Robinho 4, Lúcio 2, Edmílson 1). For the reasons above, the *Verde-amarela* (Green and Yellow) or *Os Canarinhos* (Little Canaries) are the favorites to become the second country after the 1958-1962 Brazil teams to retain their championship.[7]

Possible lineup: Dida; Cafú (Cicinho), Lúcio (Roque Junior), Juan (Edmílson), Roberto Carlos; Emerson, (Gilberto), Ze Roberto (Robinho), Kaká (Juninho Pernambucano), Ronaldinho; Adriano, Ronaldo.
Coach: Carlos Alberto Parreira.

---

[7] A significant change for Brazil's 2006 World Cup experience is that they will likely have a much stronger schedule than the 2002 Cup. In the 2002 World Cup, from the second round onwards, Brazil met Belgium (23), England (12), Turkey (22), and Germany (11) – not one team in the top 10 on their way to the championship [country rankings in parentheses].

This fortuitous lineup will not materialize in 2006 for Brazil. Conversely, from the second round onwards they are likely to meet the Czech Republic (2), Netherlands (3), Argentina (4), Spain (6), England (9), and/or Italy (12). Italy is grossly under-rated, but all the other teams are Top 10 teams, making it a harder road to the 2006 world title.

F2. Croatia [20]

The 2006 World Cup is Croatia's third consecutive Cup appearance after declaring their independence in 1991. They finished an amazing third in 1998 but were outplayed by Mexico and Italy in 2002 and failed to pass to the second round.

The Kovac brothers are pivotal players in defense and midfield for the *Vatreni* (Fiery), while Stipe Pletikosa is excellent in goal. Klasnic, Srna and Prso are responsible for scoring the goals. Croatia has shown it has the technique to play with South American teams by their 3-2 win over Argentina, so their match with Brazil will be a fascinating one.

Possible lineup: Stipe Pletikosa; Dario Simic, Robert Kovac, Igor Tudor (Josip Simunic), Ivan Leko; Darijo Srna, Jurica Vranjes, Niko Kovac, Marko Babic (Niko Kranjčar); Ivan Klasnic (Olic), Dado Prso.
Coach: Zlatko Kranjčar.

F3. Australia [49]

Australia has their most talented lineup ever, but still qualified only on a penalty kick competition over talented Uruguay. The *Socceroos* defeated England (in England) 3-1 in 2003, and have many successful players in the English Premiership.

Particularly important will be the performances of Harry Kewell, a creative midfielder with pace and guile, and goal scorers Mark Viduka and Brett Emerton. Tim Cahill provides energy in the midfield and the defense is fairly solid from goalkeeper Schwarzer.

Despite qualifying for the 2006 World Cup from Oceania, Australia has now joined the Asian Football Confederation (AFC) and will challenge current holders Japan for the next Asian Nations Cup in 2007, and seek to qualify for future World Cups from Asia.

Possible lineup: Mark Schwarzer; Lucas Neill, Ljubo Milicevic, Tony Popovic, Tony Vidmar; Brett Emerton, Tim Cahill, Stan Lazaridis, Marco Bresciano (Josip Skoko); Harry Kewell, Mark Viduka (Archie Thompson).
Coach: Guus Hiddink.

F4. Japan [15]

Japan has won three out of the last four Asian Nations Cups (1992, 2000, 2004), and went to the eight-finals in the 2002 World Cup (where they lost to Turkey).

Japan has an established midfield with Ono, Nakata, Nakamura, and Inamoto, but their defense may be suspect against top teams. Although they are ranked higher than Croatia or Australia, both teams should give the *Blues* a difficult match.

Possible lineup: Yoshikatsu Kawaguchi; Makoto Tanaka, Tsuneyasu Miyamoto, Yuji Nakazawa, Alessandro dos Santos (Koji Nakata); Shinji Ono, Hidetoshi Nakata, Shunsuke Nakamura, Junichi Inamoto; Naohiro Takahara, Atsushi Yanagisawa.
Coach: Zico.

11 Brazil v. Croatia
    June 13: Berlin 21:00

12 Australia v. Japan
    June 12: Kaiserslautern 15:00

27 Brazil v. Australia
    June 18: Munich 18:00

28 Japan v. Croatia
    June 18: Nuremberg 15:00

43 Japan v. Brazil
    June 22: Dortmund 21:00

44 Croatia v. Australia
    June 22: Stuttgart 21:00

GROUP G — France, Switzerland, Korea Republic, Togo

France and Switzerland qualified for the Cup from the same Europe Group 4 and were coincidentally drawn into the same Cup Group G.

In the friendly matches on 1 March 2006, France surprisingly lost to Slovakia 1-2 in Paris, but Switzerland won away in Scotland 3-1, and Korea Republic beat Angola 1-0.

G1. France [5]

France has great players (Thuram, Zidane, Viera, Henry) but has had recent trouble fielding a team that can play together. *Les Bleus* played the (Jazz) Blues again when they lost to Slovakia at home prior to the World Cup – a result that left many wondering if their 2006 Cup fate would be similar to their ignominious 2002 Cup exit.

Outstanding Lyon goalkeeper Gregory Coupet is awaiting his chance to claim the starting keeper position from Fabien Barthez, and in-form Johan Micoud is just waiting to be picked for the team. Otherwise, France needs to find some team cohesion and motivation to perform up to their potential and qualify from the easiest Cup group.

Possible lineup: Gregory Coupet (Barthez); Willy Sagnol, Lilian Thuram (Sebastien Squillaci), William Gallas, Patrice Evra (Mikael Silvestre); Claude Makelele (Vikash Dhorasoo), Zinedine Zidane (Johan Micoud), Patrick Vieira, Bruno Pedretti (Robert Pires); Thierry Henry (Sidney Govou), David Trezuguet (Sylvain Wiltord).
Coach: Raymond Domenech.

G2. Switzerland [36]

Switzerland has been playing well and should be ranked higher than 36th. They qualified for the Cup by beating a quality Turkey team on away goals, and will likely give France a battle for first in this group. The Swiss will be looking to avenge their 3-1 loss to France in the 2004 European Championships.

Coach Jakob "Kobi" Kuhn has developed a fairly young team that has matured well through qualifying, and responds well to difficult challenges.

Possible lineup: Pascal Zuberbuehler; Philip Degen, Patrick Mueller, Philippe Senderos, Ludovic Magnin (Spycher); Ricardo Cabanas (Hakan Yakin), Tranquillo Barnetta, Johann Vogel, Raphael Wicky; Daniel Gygax (Lustrinelli), Alexander Frei (Streller).
Coach: Kobi Kuhn.

G3. Korea Republic [29]

South Korea is Asia's most successful national team, having qualified for seven World Cup Finals. The *Asian Tigers* have many experienced players back from the fourth-placed 2002 Cup team.

Park Ji-Sung has successfully adapted to the Premiership, and 2002 striking hero Ahn Jung-Hwan will be back for likely his last Cup appearance.

Possible lineup: Lee Woon-Jae; Choi Jin-Cheul, Kim Young-Chul, Song Chong-Gug (Kim Dong-Jin), You Kyoung-Youl; Lee Young-Pyo, Park Ji-Sung, Kim Do-Heon, Lee Eul-Yong (Cha Du-Ri); Ahn Jung-Hwan (Lee Chun-Soo), Park Chu-Young (Seol Ki-Hyun).
Coach: Dick Advocaat.

G4. Togo [56]

Togo fired their CAF 2005 Coach of the Year Stephen Keshi in February 2006, after Togo's poor showing in the 2006 African Nations Cup. This was not a popular move with the players, and *Les Eperviers* (The Sparrow Hawks) need to resolve this emotional issue before they travel to the World Cup. African soccer experienced coach Otto Pfister was hired in Keshi's place – although Togo's equipment supplier Puma apparently recommended soccer traveler Bora Milutinovic.

Togo has a good strike team in Olufade (Lille) and Adebayor (Arsenal). Souleymane Mamam (midfielder on loan from Manchester United) was said to have been the youngest player in the world to play a World Cup qualifier when he appeared against Zambia at age thirteen and 310 days (information verified from FIFA website). If his birth date is correct, he would turn 18 during the 2006 World Cup.

<u>Possible lineup</u>: Kossi Agassa; Zanzan Atte-Oudeyi, Eric Akoto, Jean-Paul Yaovi Abalo, Emmanuel Mathias; Jacques Romao, Mamam Sherif-Toure, Souleymane Mamam, Yao Aziawonou; Adekanmi Olufade, Emmanuel Adebayor.
Coach: Otto Pfister.

13 <u>France v. Switzerland</u>
     June 13: Stuttgart 18:00

14 <u>Korea Republic v. Togo</u>
     June 13: Frankfurt 15:00

29 <u>France v. Korea Republic</u>
     June 18: Leipzig 21:00

30 <u>Togo v. Switzerland</u>
     June 19: Dortmund 15:00

45 <u>Togo v. France</u>
     June 23: Cologne 21:00

46 <u>Switzerland v Korea Republic</u>
     June 23: Hanover 21:00

GROUP H   Spain, Ukraine, Tunisia, Saudi Arabia

In the friendly matches on 1 March 2006 Spain beat Ivory Coast 3-2, but Tunisia lost 0-1 to Serbia & Montenegro and Saudi Arabia lost 0-3 to Portugal.

H1. Spain [6]

Despite Spain's injury woes to crucial team member Xavi Hernandez, *La Furia* (The Fury) is still playing well. There are still plenty of creative and technical players on Spain's bench – Joaquín, Fernando Torres, and José Antonio Reyes would start on almost any other team. Coach Luis Aragonés focused unwanted attention on the team by foolishly making idiotic ethnic remarks, which went relatively unpunished by similarly intolerant soccer authorities.

Notorious for not playing to its potential, Spain did perform well in the 2002 World Cup, only to unluckily exit on penalties to host South Korea. If most of their players remain healthy, Spain should qualify for the second round and pose a serious threat for the semifinals.

<u>Possible lineup</u>: Iker Casillas; Michel Salgado, Carlos Puyol, Pablo Ibanez (Carlos Marchena), Asier del Horno; Ruben Baraja, Luis Garcia, Xabi Alonso (David Albelda), Xavi Hernández (Joaquín); Raúl (José Reyes), Fernando Morientes (Fernando Torres).
Coach: Luis Aragonés.

H2. Ukraine [40]

The 2006 World Cup marks the first time since Ukraine's independence in 1992 (after the Soviet Union dissolved) that they will appear in a World Cup. Ukraine often supplied quality players who were integral to the old Soviet Union teams – including current coach Oleg Blokhin (Chapter 7).

Ukraine's talisman is 2004 European Player of the Year Andriy Shevchenko (AC Milan), who survived evacuating his home after the 1986 Chernobyl nuclear disaster. 2005 Ukrainian Player of the Year Oleh Husev is charged with running the midfield.

<u>Possible lineup</u>: Olexander Shovkovsky; Andriy Nesmachny, Andriy Rusol, Serhiy Fedorov, Vladimir Yezersky; Anatoliy Tymoshchuk, Oleg Shelayev, Oleh Gusev, Serhiy Nazarenko; Andrey Voronin, (Andriy Vorobey), Andriy Shevchenko.
Coach: Oleg Blokhin.

H3. Tunisia [28]

Germany 2006 is Tunisia's fourth World Cup, and their aim will be to advance to the second round for the first time. They were the first African team to win a game in the World Cup when they beat Mexico 3-1 in 1978, but have not won since.

Les Aigles de Carthage (The Eagles of Carthage) will rely on several successful overseas based players and a couple of naturalized Brazilians (Clayton, dos Santos). Experienced goalkeeper Ali Boumnijel will be 40 years old at the World Cup.

<u>Possible lineup</u>: Ali Boumnijel; Hatem Trabelsi, José Clayton, Radhi Jaidi, Wissem Abdi; Hamed Namouchi, Kaies Ghodhbane, Jawhar Mnari (Anis Ayari), Slim Benachour (Imed Mhadhebi); Ziad Jaziri (Haikel Gmamdia), Francileudo Silva dos Santos.
Coach: Roger Lemerre.

H4. Saudi Arabia [32]

Saudi Arabia is led from the back by 2005 Asian Player of the Year Hamad Al Montashari, and many other players have previous World Cup Finals experience.

However, Saudi Arabia has been shut out five of six games in the last two World Cups (1998 & 2002), scoring only two goals while giving up seventeen. It will likely be tough going again for the *Sons Of The Desert*.

<u>Possible lineup</u>: Mabrouk Zaid; Ahmad Al Bahri, Hamad Al Montashari, Naif Al Qadi, Hussein Sulimani; Khaled Aziz, Saud Ali Khariri, Nawaf Al Temyat (Mohammad Al Shalhoub), Mohammad Noor; Yasser Al Qahtani, Sami Al-Jaber.
Coach: Marcos Paquetá.

15 Spain v. Ukraine
    June 14: Leipzig 15:00

16 Tunisia v. Saudi Arabia
    June 14: Munich 18:00

31 Spain v. Tunisia
    June 19: Stuttgart 21:00

32 Saudi Arabia v. Ukraine
    June 19: Hamburg 18:00

47 Saudi Arabia v. Spain
    June 23: Kaiserslautern 16:00

48 Ukraine v. Tunisia
    June 23: Berlin 16:00

Second Round Matches

49 Winner A v. Runner-up B
    June 24: Munich 17:00

50 Winner C v. Runner-up D
    June 24: Leipzig 21:00

51 Winner B v. Runner-up A
    June 25: Stuttgart 17:00

52 Winner D v. Runner-up C
    June 25: Nuremberg 21:00

53 Winner E v. Runner-up F
    June 26: Kaiserslautern 17:00

54 Winner G v. Runner-up H
    June 26: Cologne 21:00

55 Winner F v. Runner-up E
    June 27: Dortmund 17:00

56 Winner H v. Runner-up G
    June 27: Hanover 21:00

Quarterfinals

57 Winner 49 v. Winner 50
    June 30: Berlin 17:00

58 Winner 53 v. Winner 54
    June 30: Hamburg 21:00

59 Winner 51 v. Winner 52
    July 1: Gelsenkirchen 17:00

60 Winner 55 v. Winner 56
    July 1: Frankfurt 21:00

Semifinals

61 Winner 57 v. Winner 58
    July 4: Dortmund 21:00

62 Winner 59 v. Winner 60
    July 5: Munich 21:00

Third Place Match

63 Runner-up 61 v. Runner-up 62
    July 8: Stuttgart 21:00

FINAL

64 Winner 61 v. Winner 62
    July 9: Berlin 20:00

World Cup Final Appearances 1930-2006 by Country
[77 Countries]

Multiple Appearances

#	Country	Appearances
1.	Brazil	18
2.	Germany/West Germany	16
	Italy	16
4.	Argentina	14
5.	Mexico	13
6.	England	12
	France	12
	Spain	12
9.	Belgium	11
10.	Uruguay	10
	Sweden	10
12.	Hungary	9
	Scotland	9
	Russia/Soviet Union	9
	Yugoslavia	9
16.	Austria	8
	Czechoslovakia	8
	Netherlands	8
	Switzerland	8
	USA	8
21.	Bulgaria	7
	Chile	7
	Romania	7
	Paraguay	7
	Poland	7
	Korea Republic	7
27.	Cameroon	5
28.	Colombia	4
	Morocco	4
	Peru	4
	Portugal	4
	Saudi Arabia	4
	Tunisia	4
34.	Bolivia	3
	Costa Rica	3
	Croatia	3
	Denmark	3
	Ireland (Republic)	3
	Nigeria	3
	Northern Ireland	3
	Norway	3
	Turkey	3
	Iran	3
	Japan	3
45.	Algeria	2
	Egypt	2
	El Salvador	2
	South Africa	2
	Australia	2
	Ecuador	2

One Appearance

- Angola
- Canada
- China
- Cuba
- Czech Republic
- Dutch Indies (inc. Indonesia)
- East Germany
- Ghana
- Greece
- Haiti
- Honduras
- Iraq
- Israel
- Ivory Coast
- Jamaica
- Kuwait
- New Zealand
- North Korea
- Togo
- Trinidad & Tobago
- Senegal
- Serbia & Montenegro
- Slovenia
- Ukraine
- United Arab Emirates
- Wales
- Zaire (DR Congo)

Soccer Chronicles

Chapter 11

Soccer at the Top of the World

Football is the most important of things that do not matter.
[Also translated as: "Soccer is the most important phenomenon, of those things in life that have little importance."] *Anonymous*

As football is the global game, matches are located in many different environments throughout the world. Teams perform in the dry desert heat of Africa, the wet tropical heat of Asia, the temperate climes of Europe, and at high altitude in South America. This chapter (and Chapter 12) explores soccer activities in diverse environments, all of which happen to be contained in the geologically and ecologically diverse country of Peru.

Three Distinct Geographic Zones for Soccer in Peru

The South American country of Peru is unique in that it has three natural geographical zones where top division soccer teams are based: the desert-like coastal region at sea level, the Amazon tropical rainforest region that ranges from 100 to 1500 meters, and the Andean mountain region that peaks at an altitude of 6800 meters. Peru has more soccer teams at high altitude than any other country in the world, and its sister Andean countries of Bolivia, Ecuador and Colombia also share its high-altitude soccer culture.

Most of the preeminent Peruvian soccer teams are based in the coastal capital of Lima near sea level (population 7 million). The largest and most successful clubs in Lima are Alianza Lima, Universitario, and Sporting Cristal. Alianza Lima has the longest football pedigree, having celebrated their centenary in 2001 with a national championship. Sporting Cristal was the best team in Peru in the mid-1990s, advancing all the way to the Copa Libertadores (South American championship) Final in 1997, where they lost 0-1 to Cruzeiro of Brazil. Universitario won three consecutive championships from 1998-2000. Other "sea level" first division clubs have been based in the coastal cities of Trujillo, Ica, Sullana, Chimbote, Chiclayo or Tacna.

The Peruvian football clubs located in the Amazon zone are smaller and poorer. The two best-known clubs are *La Loretana* and *Colegio Nacional de Iquitos* (CNI), located in the Amazon cities of Pucallpa and Iquitos, respectively. Both of these clubs have participated in the Peruvian First Division in the past, but as of 2006 are re-competing to enter again.

In the year 2000, Peru had three top division teams playing in cities above 3000 meters. These were *Deportivo Wanka* in Huancayo at 3200 meters, *Club Cienciano* in Cusco at 3360 meters, and *Unión de Minas* in the mining town of Cerro de Pasco, which is located at a mind-boggling 4340 meters above sea level. *Club Unión de Minas*, playing at the Daniel Alcides Carrión Stadium, had the distinction of being the highest altitude top division club in the world.[1] *Unión de Minas* dropped out of the top division after 2001, but in 2004 *Deportivo Wanka* scheduled most of their Clausura matches in Cerro de Pasco. In addition, Puno club *Alfonso Ugarte* plays matches near Lake Titicaca at 3827 meters, but have long dropped out of Peru's top division (last appearing in 1988). However, *Sport Ancash* joined the top division in 2005 and plays their home games at 3090 meters in Huaraz, often called the "Switzerland of Peru" because of its picturesque mountain scenery.

Cienciano from Cusco, along with legendary Lima club *Alianza Lima*, is the oldest soccer club in Peru (both clubs were founded in 1901 and celebrated their centenaries in 2001). This chapter addresses soccer activities at high altitude - specifically in the Andean mountains – and includes the dramatic story of *Cienciano*, a small provincial team successful in their centenary year that subsequently went on to win a continental championship.

Justification of Athletics at High Altitude – the Top of the World

The subject of competitive sport at high altitude was seriously debated as early as the 1974 World Congress of Sports Medicine in Melbourne, Australia. It was suggested at the meeting that physical sporting events at greater than 2600 meters (8530 feet) above sea level should be undertaken with extreme caution, with competition restricted above 3000 meters (9842 ft).

Playing soccer at altitude is largely an American phenomenon, as European teams are not required to prepare for this contingency. For example, the highest soccer league stadium in England is *West Bromwich Albion's* stadium The Hawthorns, located only 168 meters (551 feet) above sea level.

In North America, the USA's highest large city is Denver, also known as the "Mile High City" at 5280 feet high (1609 meters). In Central America, Mexico City, at 2286 meters (7500 feet) above sea level, hosted the 1968 Olympics and the 1970 and 1986 FIFA World Cups. Denver and Mexico City would therefore be exempt from altitude concerns for sporting events.

In South America, the Melbourne congress recommendations would classify the cities of Cajamarca in Peru, Quito in Ecuador, and Sucre in Bolivia as "sport danger zones" (between 2600-3000 meters); and Huaraz, Huancayo, Cusco, Juliaca, Puno, and Cerro de Pasco in Peru and La Paz and Potosí in Bolivia off limits to competitive sport. That conclusion would limit sport to lower cities around the coast and jungle, thus depriving much of the Andean population of competitive soccer.

It should be noted however, that the 1993 *South American women's volleyball championships* were held in Cusco, with Brazil winning without incident. Therefore, women athletes have already competed in continental competitions without evident harm at the Cusco elevation.

---

[1] The Cerro de Pasco stadium is named in honor of Daniel Alcides Carrión, a San Marcos University (Lima) medical student who died in 1885 after injecting himself with the microbe *Bartonella bacilliformis*, in an attempt to prove that the Verruga Peruana condition was the same disease as Oroyo Fever. At the time, Oroyo Fever was ravaging the highlands around Cerro de Pasco causing thousands of rail workers' deaths. Carrión's scientific attempt was successful, but his clinical outcome was extreme – death from medical investigation in a supreme sacrifice made to gain knowledge for control of an epidemic disease. *Bartonellosis* (comprising both Verruga Peruana and Oroyo Fever*)* is also called *Carrion's disease*, and is still common in some mountainous areas of Peru.

Performing at Altitude

Soccer clubs depend on local spectator support, but geographical and climate experience are major contributors to the "home team advantage." If a team routinely performs at a higher altitude, they will likely carry a significant physical and mental edge on their home fields because of their physical acclimatization and mental preparation. Therefore, to sustain athletic performance at higher altitude is the greatest physiological and emotional challenge for visiting soccer teams.

Imagine having to run ninety minutes at high altitude in a soccer game! Even though soccer is rated the most physically demanding team sport that is much to ask from the ordinary soccer player.[2] So when top teams from Lima visit the mountain teams in Peru they can be at a distinct disadvantage, and are often lucky to come away with a draw.

The best international example of high altitude advantage (or preparation) is the 1993 Brazil - Bolivia World Cup qualifying match in La Paz. Until that game, Brazil had the amazing record of *never having lost a World Cup qualifying game since the beginning of the competition in 1930*. Bolivia had previously played many home matches in the jungle city of Santa Cruz at 416 meters (1350 feet), but had lobbied hard to play the World Cup qualifiers at 3636 meters at the Estadio Hernan Siles Suazo in La Paz, the highest capital city in the world. The Brazil team prepared poorly for the La Paz altitude, were subsequently outmatched, and lost 2-0. Up until that game, *Brazil had only lost by two goals once before in the World Cup Final competition*. That was the 4-2 "Battle of Bern" loss in the 1954 World Cup against Hungary, arguably the greatest team of the early 1950s.[3] But in La Paz, Brazil lost against the best ever Bolivian team, including their "number 10" Marco Etcheverry, nicknamed *El Diablo* ("the Devil") for his prodigious dribbling and passing skills (see Chapter 7).[4] Brazil had to be content with embarrassing Bolivia 6-0 later at their home sea level venue in Recife.

Another successful example of home team advantage at altitude is the experience of the Mexican national team, which had a streak of *20 unbeaten years* in the Azteca stadium in Mexico City before they lost to Costa Rica in the 2001 World Cup qualifiers. In addition to the altitude of 2240 meters above sea level, visiting teams have to contend with the asthma-inducing Mexico City smog.

National teams have the right to play World Cup games in their capital cities. Bolivia uses La Paz's altitude advantage, as Ecuador did in qualifying for the 2002 and 2006 FIFA World Cup Finals using their Quito venue at 2811 meters above sea level. Previously, Ecuador had played some international games less successfully at sea level in the coastal city of Guayaquil. Colombia's capital of Bogotá is also located at an impressive altitude of 2556 meters above sea level.

Peru's capital of Lima is near sea level (only 130 meters above sea level), so they have not yet exploited their high altitude club experience in international home games. But after the 2003 Copa Sudamericana and Recopa victories of the Cienciano team (see below), there is discussion of using Cusco as a future venue for Peru's World Cup qualifying matches. However, during the 2004 Copa America tournament in Peru, the only match allowed to take place in Cusco was the consolation third-place match (Uruguay beat Colombia 2-1), and the 2005 FIFA U-17 World Cup in Peru did not utilize any venues over 150 meters above sea level. Peru did not use any high altitude site (such as Cusco or Arequipa) in its 2006 FIFA World Cup qualifying campaign, and failed to advance to the Finals in Germany.

---

[2] As judged by an ESPN forty-sport survey, soccer scored the highest for endurance and agility, and tied for the highest analytic aptitude required. [www.sports.espn.go.com/espn/page2/sportSkills].

[3] Since that match in Bolivia, Brazil lost 3-0 to France in the 1998 FIFA World Cup Final, and 3-1 to Argentina in a 2006 World Cup qualifying match played in 2005. However, Brazil beat Argentina 4-1 a few weeks later to win the 2005 Confederations Cup; the first time a team held the World Cup, Confederations Cup and continental (Copa America) championships concurrently.

[4] Etcheverry played for championship teams in four countries and won the MLS 1998 MVP award.

Altitude Physics and Physiology

As altitude increases, the atmospheric pressure decreases and there is less atmospheric gas to breathe in (the air is "thinner"), which means less of the critical life-sustaining gas of oxygen. Since all the atmospheric gases decrease proportionately with increasing altitude, oxygen still makes up 21% of the available air; *only there is less air and therefore less oxygen.*

At sea level the atmospheric pressure is 760 torr (torr = mmHg), while in La Paz it is only 497 torr, a decrease in air pressure of 34.6 % (the La Paz air is 34.6 % "thinner" than in New York). One can also accurately say the New York air is 53% "thicker" than La Paz air, so that one would need to breathe 53% more air in La Paz to receive the same oxygen in New York (not accounting for smog levels in either city). As a result of this environmental difference, some people start to hyperventilate upon descending an airplane ramp in cities at higher altitudes.

Below is a chart of the altitudes of cities where there has been professional soccer competition (with the exception of Mount Sajama), the atmospheric pressures at those city altitudes, and percentage of oxygen available in the air (using the sea level standard of 100%).

Oxygen Availability at Altitude

City	Meters	Feet	Atm. P.[a]	O_2%[b]
New York City[1]	0	0	760	100
Denver[1]	1609	5250	633	83.3
Mexico City[2]	2240	7350	588	77.4
Quito[3]	2811	9222	549	72.2
Huaraz[4]	3090	10138	531	69.9
Huancayo[4]	3261	10699	520	68.4
Cusco[4]	3360	11024	514	67.6
La Paz[5]	3636	11929	497	65.4
Puno[4]	3827	12556	487	64.1
Potosí[5]	4090	13419	470	61.8
Cerro de Pasco[4]	4340	14239	456	60.0
Mount Sajama[5]	6542	21463	344	45.3

[1] USA, [2] Mexico, [3] Ecuador, [4] Peru, [5] Bolivia.

[a] Atmospheric pressure (Atm. P.: measured in torr, or mmHg), decreases as altitude increases. Altitude data adapted from "The Physiologic Basis of High-Altitude Diseases" by Professor John West (*Annals of Internal Medicine*, 2004; 141:789-800), and the conversion chart available at: www.medicine.ucsd.edu/phys/convert.html.

[b] Percent O_2 availability at altitude compared to sea level atmospheric pressure of 760 torr (the standard comparison at 100%). In Cusco only about two-thirds of the oxygen is available when compared to sea level, and in Cerro de Pasco, only 60% of the oxygen is available when compared to sea level. This means there is nearly 50% more oxygen available at sea level than in Cusco, and 66.7% more oxygen available at sea level than in Cerro de Pasco. No wonder teams fear playing at extreme altitude!

Professional Teams Playing at Altitude	
Denver	Colorado Rapids
Mexico City	América, Cruz Azul, Atlante, Necaxa, and UNAM (Universidad Nacional Autónoma de México)
Quito	LDU Quito, Deportivo Quito, and El Nacional
Huaraz	Sport Ancash
Huancayo	Deportivo Wanka
Cusco	Cienciano
La Paz	Bolívar, La Paz FC, The Strongest
Puno	Alfonso Ugarte
Potosí	Real Potosí
Cerro de Pasco	Unión Minas

Preparation for Soccer at Altitude

How much does altitude affect players? The simple answer is that it affects players to different degrees, depending on their mental and physical attributes and preparation.

Teófilo "Nene" Cubillas played at locations above 3000 meters numerous times in his career, and for him altitude was "the great equalizer" physically (meaning one had to arrive in peak physical condition in order to compete successfully). Still, for Cubillas, up to a certain altitude level, "the difference was mainly mental," and the *attitude* the player brings into *altitude* is a critical factor to performance. Cubillas said he never had a problem in Huancayo or even Cusco; at those altitudes he could prepare mentally and physically by flying up to Andean altitude the morning of the matches.

But even Cubillas, a top player used to adapting to altitude, had a limit that he could not exclusively mentally adjust to and physically overcome. According to Cubillas, La Paz at 3636 meters, Puno at 3900 meters, and especially Cerro de Pasco at 4340 meters, were brutal environments to perform in unless significant acclimatization training had been planned and executed. At those extreme altitudes, mental preparation is inevitably subordinate to physical acclimatization. The body simply cannot get enough oxygen, and players may develop tachycardia (a rapid heart beat) after jogging for only a few minutes, which can be frightening for the mentally unprepared. Therefore, performing at altitudes above 3000 meters is the supreme test of both physical and mental conditioning for players and teams, and there are only two ways to adequately prepare for competition: (1) arrive at the game site the morning of the game, or (2) allow 2-3 weeks acclimatization and practice time at altitude.

Teams coming into game sites at higher altitudes (above 2600 meters) should *ideally* arrange for a period of acclimatization. This acclimatization option is the more desirable but more logistically difficult plan of preparation. In smog areas such as Mexico City, it is advisable to train players at altitude in a pollution-free zone elsewhere, as there is no acclimatization regimen for smog.

Most teams do not have the time for full acclimatization, and arrive to the match venue on the same day as the game. Therefore, their players have only a few hours to adjust to altitude before game time. Since it is impossible to fully adapt physically, players must be mentally prepared to play in a lower oxygen environment. Some teams employ a psychologist to help prepare their players for various situations, including those at extreme altitude.

For two reasons, it is *not advisable* that teams arrive the night before the game: (1) altitude sickness may worsen by the next day (game day), and (2) players may sleep badly, having a negative psychological effect on players by game time.

There is always a slight danger that a very fit player may not feel well because of altitude sickness. This is unpredictable and likely has to do with the individual physiology of the player. Even a few Cienciano players would get altitude sickness when they came back to Cusco from their month-long vacations at sea level, and would need several weeks to successfully acclimatize once again.

Home teams training at higher than 2600 meters adapt their play to altitude, and are likely fitter as a result. They also know the temperature and humidity levels of the match field, and how the soccer ball plays in their particular climate. But ultimately, all the players on the field must perform in the same environment, and after an initial rush of adrenaline, any home crowd advantage may wear off if the visiting team is physically fit and mentally prepared to play in the thinner zones of human habitation.

Altitude Sicknesses: Benign and Severe

Traveling to matches located at 2000, 3000, or even more than 4000 thousand meters above sea level complicates any sport preparation. Just flying to higher heights results in labored breathing while walking, let alone running and performing in a competitive sport! Occasionally individuals (mostly the elderly and/or infirm) have died just arriving at altitudes above 2600 meters from sea level.

Traveling over 2600 meters (8530 feet) above sea level leaves one at risk for *altitude sickness*, which is known as *soroche* in Peru. Altitude sickness was first described in the Peruvian Andes in 1590 by the Jesuit priest Joseph de Acosta, and consists of a constellation of symptoms including headache, shortness of breath, sleeplessness, and involuntary sighing. The cure for routine altitude sickness is rest and certain teas or medications. If symptoms do not improve, supplementary oxygen must be immediately supplied or the individual descended to a lower altitude. For most individuals, benign altitude sickness lasts no longer than 24-48 hours.

A traditional preventive measure for altitude sickness is the pleasant coca tea (called *mate de coca* and made from leaves of the *Erythroxylum coca* bush), a staple drink in the Andes for millennia.[5] The diuretic medication acetazolamide (Diamox) is an alternate prophylactic against altitude sickness. However, soccer players may not use this drug as a preventive measure against altitude sickness because it is on the FIFA prohibited drug list.

Typical *soroche* can occasionally progress to severe forms of altitude sicknesses such as *high altitude pulmonary edema* (HAPE - water in the lungs) or *cerebral edema* (swollen brain). The symptoms of these critical conditions are respiratory distress and mental confusion resulting from lack of oxygen and resultant brain swelling. The treatment for both conditions is 100% oxygen (and/or immediately descend the individual down from high altitude) and consult expert medical care (other medications such as steroids and/or nifedipine are often necessary). Very rarely does a player have a physical collapse during or after a game at altitude (but it has happened in Cusco). Those players likely have an undiagnosed heart and/or lung condition, or are predisposed to HAPE or cerebral edema.

---

[5] There is a minuscule amount of cocaine in coca tea, and players may test positive if the urine drug assay is sensitive enough. This happened to two players after the 1993 Brazil loss to Bolivia in La Paz. Fortunately for them, the cause for the positive tests was ascertained to be the otherwise harmless and non-addictive coca tea, and they were not suspended from future play.

One-Off at the Top of the World

On 2 August 2001, two Bolivian teams comprised of experienced mountain climbers played an extraordinary soccer game on the flat top of Mount Sajama, 6542 meters (21,463 feet) above sea level in the Bolivian Andes. The game was sponsored by two institutions from the capital city La Paz, the Club Andino Boliviano and the High Altitude Pathology Institute. Each team had seven players, and the match was composed of two 20-minute halves and played on a 35 meter by 50-meter field covered completely by snow and ice. The game ended tied at 3-3, but fortunately it was a friendly match and overtime was not scheduled!

The air on Mount Sajama is less than half at thick as air at sea level; one would need to breathe more than twice as much air to get the same oxygen as sea level. One of the organizers boasted "We can beat any team in the world at this altitude," and nobody could seriously doubt that claim.

Top Division Soccer at the Top of the World: Cienciano of Cusco

The Biblioteca Municipal (Municipal Library) in Cusco is an awe-inspiring place to write about local professional soccer club *Cienciano*. Constructed of original Inca stonework, the library is a place for Cusqueños to investigate their ancient traditions and invent the new. The library's stone blocks fit precisely without mortar, and the walls have withstood tons of pressure over more than five centuries without moving. Even devastating earthquakes have not budged the Inca walls – the 21 May 1950 Cusco earthquake severely damaged the colonial cathedral built by the Spanish, except for the structural base designed by Inca architects, which remained undisturbed.

Cusco (also spelled Cuzco, Qosqo, and Qusqu) is the most important archeological city in the Americas. Five hundred years ago, Cusco was the capital of the Inca Empire that stretched from Bolivia to Peru to Ecuador to Columbia, which boasted the largest indigenous civilization ever in South America. Nowhere else in the Americas has indigenous antiquity been so well preserved despite impressive colonial efforts to destroy it. Today, Cusco remains the center of the ancient Inca Empire, and the gateway to the spectacular preserved ruins of Macchu Picchu and Vilcabamba.

Cusco is located in an Andean mountain valley at an elevation of 3360 meters (11,024 feet, or more than two miles above sea level). At this altitude the barometric pressure is only 514 torr in comparison to the sea level of 760 torr, indicating that the Andean air is more than 30% thinner. Some people develop signs of altitude sickness after arrival at the airport in Cusco; it is in this place that *Cienciano* calls home.

The name Cienciano is derived from the Colegio Nacional de Ciencias (National College of Sciences), a famed secondary school in Cusco that was founded by El Libertador Simón Bolivar in 1825. The thousands of graduated students from the high school form part of the club's fervent Cusco fan base.

The college (a "high school" in South American terminology) was the original owner of the soccer club, a state of affairs that is inconceivable in the modern sports world. Cienciano is now a private club run by a President and fourteen board members, albeit with strong ties to the school.

Other Latin American sport clubs have taken their name from universities – prominent examples include UNAM *(Universidad Nacional Autónoma de México)* in Mexico, *Estudiantes de la Plata* in Argentina, *Universidad Catolica* in Chile, and *Estudiantes de Medicina* in Ica, Peru. But a sport club name from a secondary or high school is quite extraordinary (ex-top division team *Colegio Nacional de Iquitos* is another Peru team name derived from a high school).

The *Cienciano* club was founded in 1901, after a national directive in January 1900 dictated that Peruvian schools include sport training as part of the curriculum, The Director of the Colegio Nacional de Ciencias, Dr. Zenón Ochoa, contracted Englishman William H. Newell in order to teach the boys the "English sports."[6] Newell must have made quite an impression amongst his Peruvian students, for within 18 months (on July 8, 1901) the Club Sportivo Cienciano was dedicated in Cusco, and Newell was unanimously elected president and trainer of the club. The first game the new club played was against the "Athletic Club," a team of English expatriates. The *Cienciano* team contained ten Peruvians, with Newell himself playing at center forward. *Cienciano* won their inaugural game with a 2-3-5 lineup.[7]

During the 20th century *Cienciano* routinely won the Cusco league, but in 1973 became the only Cusco team to enter the professional ranks in the Peruvian top division (participating in the Decentralized League from 1973-1977). With the exception of the years 1978-1983, *Cienciano* has participated in top-flight soccer (Zona Sur 1984-1985, 1989, 1990-1991; Second Phase 1986; Decentralized League 1987; Regional Final 1988) and the professional First Division (1992-2006).

The team plays in the public stadium *Estadio Inca Garcilaso de la Vega*, which is owned by the Instituto Peruano del Deporte (IPD), the public institución responsible for all sport in Peru. The Garcilaso stadium is remarkably named after Inca Garcilaso de la Vega, the son of an Inca princess and a Spanish soldier, and the greatest of Inca historians.[8] Construction in 2001 at Estadio Garcilaso allowed for more than 30,000 spectators at games, and further construction in 2004 raised capacity to 42,056 fans (a spectator level allowing for South American Finals competitions).

Cienciano Centenary Celebrations

Cienciano presented their centenary *Furia Roja*[9] team before the start of the 2001 season on February 1, 2001, which preceded the actual 100th anniversary date of the club on July 8, 2001. The Don Antonio restaurant in old Cusco hosted the presentation dinner, with music provided by the excellent Cusco folklore band *Arco Iris* (Spanish for "rainbow"). The club administration spoke of their expectations for the new season, which included a hoped for but unprecedented Copa Libertadores (South American club championship) qualification. After the introduction of the coaching staff, the team members entered through a red tunnel escorted by two *Cusqueña* beer representatives.[10]

Cienciano's coach was Freddy Ternero, a defenseman for *Universitario* and the Peruvian national team in the 1980s, and formerly coach of the Peru national team that performed in the 1997 Copa America in Bolivia (Ternero became Peru national team coach again in 2005). His domestic players came from all over Peru – the coast cities of Lima and Talara, the jungle city of Pucallpa, and from Cusco and the mountain regions.

The *Cienciano* squad has often been in constant flux, as the established richer clubs from coastal Lima frequently snap up quality players that were finely developed in the mountains. Despite the constant raiding of players in the past decade, *Cienciano* has been the best club in the provinces competing with the big three clubs from Lima (*Alianza Lima, Universitario and Sporting Cristal*).

---

[6] William Newell was unrelated to fellow Englishman Isaac Newell, who founded the Newell's Old Boys club in Rosario, Argentina in 1903.
[7] The 2-3-5 tactical system stayed in general favor until the 1950s. The lineup for Cienciano's first game was: Augusto Ochoa (goalkeeper), Eduardo Cáceres (right fullback), Juan Samanez (left fullback), Luis Alberto Arguedas (right halfback), Juan J. Loayza (center halfback), Luis Alberto Aranibar (left halfback), Mateo Morán (inside right), Bonifacio Monteagudo (inside left), Humberto de la Soto (right wing), William H. Newell (center forward), Miguel del Castillo (left wing).
[8] Inca Garcilaso de la Vega wrote *Commentarios Reales de los Incas* (The Royal Commentaries of the Incas) in 1609, the seminal work of the Spanish invasion in Peru.
[9] The *Furia Roja* ("Red Fury") is the nickname of the Cienciano club.
[10] Longtime *Cienciano* sponsor *Cusqueña* produces an excellent Peruvian beer, exported even to beer connoisseur country Germany.

Cienciano finished in third place in the league at the end of the 2000 season, perfectly positioned for success in 2001. Still, *Cienciano* lost five of their best players over the holiday break to other teams, and had to present new players. The Centenary Team was comprised of Peruvians from throughout the country with some *extranjeros* from Argentina, Brazil and Uruguay. Their playmaker was Argentine Gabriel Rodriguez, and their strike force was Brazilian Roggiero Da Silva and Uruguayan Mauricio Martinez. The best-known Peruvians were midfielder Carlos Cumapa from the Amazon town of Pucallpa and goalkeeper Maurinho Mendoza.

A tribute was made to *Cienciano's* oldest living player, an octogenarian who had performed for *Cienciano* in the 1930s. He was with his wife in the invited section, an animated man possessed with a quick smile that was bent-over from age-induced scoliosis. It was clearly an important moment for everybody when he once again donned the red *camiseta* of *Cienciano*, and embraced club president Juvenal Silva and several others. A connection to the past is very important in Cusco, especially in modern times when club loyalty is fleeting.

Informal questioning from the press followed. The reporters were a cheery lot, but naturally tinged with pessimism because of *Cienciano's* difficult circumstances and previous failure to win a Peruvian championship. One reporter jokingly asked if the Estadio Garcilaso would be ready to use since it was undergoing remodeling, or would the club have to play in Urcos or Urubamba, two very small mountain towns.[11] Another asked how the club could promise good results, as in the euphoria of their centenary the club had practically guaranteed an entrance into the Copa Libertadores competition.

Finally, a prize was awarded to the 2001 *Cienciano* centenary shirt designer. The front of the 2001 jersey had an Inca sundial in relief with "100 Años" (100 Years) written in Inca stone within, and the years 1901-2001 inscribed at the top [Figure 11C]. The previous year, the 2000 *Cienciano* shirt had included an impression of Macchu Picchu – perhaps the only professional soccer jersey to model a world archeological monument.[12]

2001 Peruvian Championship

The 2001 Peruvian professional soccer league schedule was divided into two equal halves of twenty-two games; the Apertura (opening competition) and the Clausura (closing competition). The winner of each half-year schedule qualified for the Copa Libertadores, the South American Club Championship competition. The team that had the next highest point total also qualified for the Copa, giving Peru three entrants into the competition. While the Lima teams have dominated the Peruvian Copa Libertadores qualifying, an occasional smaller town team has squeezed into the competition, such as *Melgar* from Peru's second largest city of Arequipa. Before their centenary year, small town *Cienciano* had never come close to qualifying for the Copa.

Not having their own training facilities, *Cienciano* practiced in several locales near to Cusco. Tactical sessions took place in Huaro, a remote mountain village 43 kilometers south of Cusco, and occasionally at "El Hueco" ("The Hole"), a small enclosed field within Cusco city. *Cienciano's* physical training sessions took place on the plateau above Cusco city at an altitude of 3555 meters, directly in front of the massive stone artwork of the ancient sacred Inca parade ground of Sacsayhuamán. Half a millennia after its construction, the massive stones of Sacsayhuamán still fit together precisely without mortar. The walls are constructed of huge boulders that were transported from a distant quarry by mysterious means, with one boulder weighing in at more than 140 tons! Each year on June 24th, *Inti-Raymi* – the Inca Festival of the Sun – is re-created on the Sacsayhuamán plateau. With the monolithic

---

[11] *Cienciano* actually played several matches in smaller towns between Cusco and Urubamba in the Sacred Valley of the Incas (Valle Sagrado) when the Estadio Garcilaso was under renovations in 2003 and 2004.
[12] Importantly, the 2005 U-17 World Cup held in Peru also had a silhouette of Macchu Picchu incorporated into the official FIFA logo.

monument conspicuous during morning training sessions, *Cienciano* players are continually conscious of those thousands of tons of archeological and cultural history present at Sacsayhuamán [Figures 11A & B].[13]

Cienciano players also ingested *maca* (*Lepidium meyenii*), an indigenous Peruvian root grown at extremely high altitudes (up to 4400 meters) that is claimed to improve physical and mental capabilities.[14] The Cienciano team thereby derives some nutritional strength from their high altitude physical environment, in addition to spiritual enhancement from training at the world archeological site of Sacsayhuamán.

Cienciano started off the 2001 Apertura well, as they occupied the top half of the division. Early in the season Da Silva and Martinez dyed their hair red, apparently to demonstrate their commitment to *Cienciano* and their "Furia Roja" ("Red Fury") fans. It seemed to work as they led the team in scoring, with Martinez even getting four goals in one game after he came off suspension for the crime of "referee touching."

Cienciano faded a bit at the end of the Apertura, as the two Lima giants *Sporting Cristal* and *Alianza Lima* tied for the session title. They also shuffled their lineup, as striker Da Silva was replaced by Uruguayan Ernesto Zapata and Mexican Hector Hernandez, and creative midfielder Rodriguez was supplanted by Mexican Oscar Olvera. Uruguayan coach Carlos Daniel Jurado substituted for Ternero.

Cienciano needed to win the Clausura outright in order to qualify for the Copa Libertadores. They started out hot, and at the end of the session they were tied with the equally surprising *Estudiantes de Medicina - Ica* team ("Medical Students from Ica"); it was the first time ever that two provincial clubs tied for a Peruvian session title. In the compromise city of Arequipa - halfway in geography and altitude between Cusco and Ica - *Cienciano* beat *Estudiantes de Medicina* 2-1 in the playoff for the Clausura title.

Clausura winner *Cienciano* had earned the right to play for the 2001 Peruvian Championship in a home and away series against Apertura winner and fellow centenary celebrators *Alianza Lima* (1901-2001). *Alianza* won 2-1 in Lima, but *Cienciano* won 2-1 in Cusco, leaving a net tie result. In front of more than twenty thousand fans in Cusco, *Cienciano* lost the definitive penalty kick competition, five to three. *Cienciano* had lost the 2001 Peruvian Championship only on penalty kicks, but Cusco residents were still in pandemonium; their "small-town" team had qualified for the Copa Libertadores in their 100th anniversary year!

2003 Copa Libertadores Campaign

Cienciano was grouped with perennial great *Gremio* from Brazil, a two-time previous Copa Libertadores winner (1983 and 1995); the other group teams were *Oriente Petrolero* from Bolivia and *12 de Octubre* from Paraguay. The highlight match of the group was *Cienciano* beating *Gremio* 2-1 in Cusco, and by finishing second to *Gremio* in the group they passed into the second round. The other two Peruvian teams in the competition, *Alianza Lima* and *Sporting Cristal*, were eliminated from the competition after failing to win a game in their respective groups.

Cienciano's centenary year Copa Libertadores experience came to an end in the second round, when they lost a home and away series to Mexico's excellent *Club América*. *Olimpia* of Paraguay went on to win the 2002 Copa Libertadores against *São Caetano* of Brazil; fittingly, it was *Olimpia's* centenary year as well.

---

[13] Like the ancient pyramids in Egypt, it is still debated how the massive stones were transported and constructed to such exact proportions at Sacsayhuamán, in order to create the timeless rock monument of significant spiritual value to the Inca civilization.

[14] Cienciano even had an advertisement for MACA on the right front of their shorts in the 2004 Recopa match against Boca Juniors.

2003 Copa Sudamericana Championship

In 2003, *Cienciano* had the opportunity to compete in a recently introduced South American competition. The *Copa Sudamericana* competition was inaugurated in 2002 with *San Lorenzo* of Argentina winning the initial championship. In 2003, thirty-five South American teams were entered, including twelve teams from Brazil and seven from Argentina. Peru was allotted only two places and represented by *Cienciano* and *Alianza Lima*. By this time, Freddy Ternero was *Cienciano* coach again.

Cienciano began the competition by eliminating *Alianza*, winning 1-0 in both the home and away games. The *Furia Roja* then beat *Universidad Católica* of Chile, thanks to a convincing 4-0 win at home in Cusco. *Universidad Católica* player Cristian Álvarez inadvertently aided *Cienciano*'s advancement with an own-goal in each game.

Many gave *Cienciano* no chance as they then faced powerful *Santos* of Brazil in the quarterfinals. After all, *Santos* was Pelé's old team, with a dated history of two Copa Libertadores championships and Intercontinental Cups (1961-1962), but a very recent history of reaching the Copa Libertadores championship game again in July 2003 (losing the championship to *Boca Juniors* of Argentina). *Santos* also boasted the most sought after young superstars of Brazilian soccer, Diego and Robinho, and Brazil national team central defender Alex.

Cienciano "scored" first in the away leg, as *Santos'* Alex headed in a bizarre own goal. Robinho equaled on a brilliant strike from 22 yards, and the game ended 1-1. The Peruvians were content but cautious as they prepared for the second leg at home. Surrounded by two defenders in Cusco, Germán Carty opened the scoring in the eleventh minute on a quick 19-yard shot after some brilliant work by Julio García to supply him the ball. The lead was short-lived as Elano equalized two minutes later, his 17-yard shot finding the net after a mazy dribbling run. Carty then sealed *Santos'* fate when he rose above Alex and headed in from 8 yards in the 34th minute, and *Cienciano* hung on to win 3-2 on aggregate. The ancient Inca stronghold of Cusco rocked with celebrations, and the headlines blared the *double entendre* headline "*Ni los santos pudieron con Cienciano*" ["not even the saints could [beat] *Cienciano*"].

The semi-final drew dangerous *Atlético Nacional* of Colombia, also a former Copa Libertadores champion (1989). *Cienciano* won both games, 2-1 and 1-0, with Carty getting two goals and Paolo Maldonado one. Maldonado's goal in Medellin started out with a pretty *sombrerito* (literally a "hat play," popping the ball over the defender's head) at the left corner of the penalty box; he then raced around to collect the ball and placed it into the uppermost right hand corner. The headlines read "*Cienciano hace vibrar a todo el Perú*" ["*Cienciano* vibrates all of Peru"].

Cienciano's foe in the Final was *River Plate* of Buenos Aires, Argentina; twice-winners of the Copa Libertadores (1986 and 1996) and a giant of South American football. *River Plate's* regulars included Argentine midfielder Marcelo Gallardo and Chilean star forward Marcelo "*El Matador*" Salas. It was truly a *David versus Goliath* match up.

The first match was held in the Monumental stadium in Buenos Aires, and was a classic of modern soccer. *Cienciano* stunned the crowd as they opened the scoring when wing defender Giuliano Portilla scored from a rebound from fellow defender Santiago Acasiete's headed shot, which had come off *River Plate's* left post. *River Plate* wasted no time, as they equalized two minutes later on an eight-yard shot from Maxi López that knocked in off the right post. The first half ended 1-1, and the wide-open skillful play of both teams continued in the second half. The home crowd began to relax as Lopez scored his second goal on a *Cienciano* defensive breakdown in the 50th minute, and the dangerous Salas ominously entered the game in the 61st minute. Nevertheless, Germán Carty popped up to equalize on a headed shot from 12 yards in the 67th minute, and the *River Plate* players must have been thinking, "What do we do to keep this team down?"

Portilla scored his second goal in the 79th minute to put *Cienciano* ahead again, on a short-range header from a clever Maldonado free kick from the right side. The impossible – beating *River Plate* on their home ground – was becoming possible. But *River* finally leveled again in the 85th minute, as Salas courageously headed home a dangerous free ball at personal risk from 4 yards. After some frantic moments by both sides, including Salas being denied at short range by *Cienciano* keeper Oscar Ibáñez, the game ended 3-3, a good away result for the Cusqueños. The headlines read "*Cienciano enmudece a todo Sudamérica*" ["*Cienciano* silences all of South America"]. The lineup from the Buenos Aires match:

River Plate: Franco Costanzo; Luis Lobo, Cristian Tula, Ricardo Rojas, Kilian Virviescas; Eduardo Coudet (73' Alejandro Domínguez), Oscar Ahumada, Luis González (70' Daniel Ludueña); Marcelo Gallardo; Daniel Montenegro (62' Marcelo Salas), Maximiliano López. Coach: Manuel Pellegrini.
Cienciano: Oscar Ibáñez; Santiago Acasiete, Miguel Llanos (Abel Lobatón 87'), Carlos Lugo, Giuliano Portilla; Alessandro Morán, Juan Carlos La Rosa, Juan Carlos Bazalar, Julio César García; Rodrigo Saraz (Paolo Maldonado 46', Cesar Ccahuantico 91'); Germán Carty. Coach: Freddy Ternero.
Goals: **River Plate:** López 28', 50', Salas 85'.
  Cienciano: Portilla 26', Carty 67', Portilla 79'.
Site: Estadio Monumental de River Plate, Buenos Aires, Argentina.

The second leg was played in Arequipa (Peru) because Cusco's Estadio Garcilaso lacked the minimum capacity of 40,000 spectators required for CONMEBOL championship matches. Arequipa provided their UNSA (Universidad Nacional de San Agustín de Arequipa) university stadium, located at a still formidable 2,525 meters above sea level.

This was a tighter game than the first, as each team was loath to give up any advantage. *River Plate* attacked from the start, with Gallardo's shot hitting the right post in the 23rd minute. The expulsion of Juan Carlos La Rosa in the 51st minute for a seemingly innocuous kick threatened to eliminate any chance *Cienciano* had of winning. But *Cienciano* continued attacking with only ten men, and in the 77th minute, *Cienciano's* Paraguayan defender Carlos Lugo put a 26-yard free kick through the defensive wall and out of keeper Franco Costanzo's reach (Costanzo is also Paraguayan). The UNSA stadium crowd was in ecstasy as *Cienciano's* "David" had scored against "Goliath" *River Plate* with only ten men. *Cienciano* would then go two men down, as creative midfielder Julio García was expelled for a foul in the 86th minute. With only nine men *Cienciano* held their ground, won the game 1-0, and the series and championship with a 4-3 net score. Germán Carty was the goal leader of the competition with six goals, and Carlos Lugo won the Copa Sudamericana MVP award. The lineup from the Arequipa match:

Cienciano: Oscar Ibañez; Santiago Acasiete, Carlos Lugo, Giuliano Portilla; Alessandro Morán, Juan Carlos Bazalar (Miguel Llanos 92'), Juan Carlos La Rosa, Julio César García, Paolo Maldonado (Cesar Ccahuantico 58'); Rodrigo Saraz (Martín García 83'), Germán Carty. Coach: Freddy Ternero.
River Plate: Franco Costanzo; Oscar Ahumada (85' Daniel Ludueña), Horacio Ameli, Eduardo Tuzzio, Ricardo Rojas; Eduardo Coudet, Javier Mascherano, Luis González (76' Alejandro Domínguez), Marcelo Gallardo; Maximiliano López, Marcelo Salas (16' Daniel Montenegro). Coach: Manuel Pellegrini.
Goals: **Cienciano:** Lugo 78'.
Site: Estadio Universidad Nacional de San Agustín, Arequipa, Peru.

Cienciano, a modest club with a long history, had become the second *Copa Sudamericana* champion, and the first Peruvian club team ever to win a continental competition.[15] Many of the players were ex-stars or "rejects" from the more famous Lima teams; Juan Carlos Bazalar (ex-*Alianza*), Paolo Maldonado (ex-*Universitario*), Germán Carty (ex-*Sporting Cristal*), and Oscar Ibañez (ex-*Universitario*) were all aging players (midfielder Bazalar and striker Carty were both 35 years old and Ibañez was 36) who had made their name elsewhere. But the headlines now read *CIENCIANO CAMPEON!!!*, and "*Cienciano ya es parte de la historia*" ["*Cienciano* is now part of history"].

Cienciano was subsequently voted the *December 2003 World Club Team of the Month* (*El Club del Mes del Mundo, Welt-Club-Team des Monats, La Équipe Mondiale de Club du Mois*) by the International Federation of Football History and Statistics (IFFHS at www.iffhs.de). In the 2004 voting, *Cienciano* rose as high as the 17th best club in the world. However, the IFFHS curiously did not anoint *Cienciano* one of the twenty-five best clubs in the world in 2003, despite them beating the number 3 (*Santos*) and 12 (*River Plate*) teams.

Advertising notes of the 2003 Copa Sudamericana Final

The contrast in uniform advertising between a massive team like *River Plate* and a "provincial team" such as *Cienciano* was fascinating.

River Plate's kit was sponsored by multinational *Adidas*; *Cienciano's* kit was sponsored by local Peruvian sportswear firm *Walon*, which did not even have an Internet website.

Cienciano had *five sponsors* on their shirts and shorts: their longtime *Cusqueña* beer sponsor on the front of their shirts, *Aero Continente* and *PERURAIL* on the back, *Nazaro* (sneakers) on the sleeves, and *MiBalon* (*ball maker*) on their shorts. *River Plate* received enough money from a single sponsor, that of USA-based Budweiser beer. *River's* jersey had *Budweiser* printed on the front of the shirt, and *Bud* on the back, as if anybody missed the obvious message on the front.

Ironically, small-town Peruvian *Cusqueña* beer is a far superior beer than average-tasting colossus *Budweiser*. Perhaps *River Plate* would have done better promoting one of their better-tasting local beers.

2003 Recopa Match to Determine the "Real South American Champion"

The *Recopa* is a championship match between teams that have won a South American *Copa*, or continental championship. The 2003 *Recopa* matched up the 2003 Copa Libertadores winner *Boca Juniors* and the 2003 Copa Sudamericana winner *Cienciano*. After dispatching of *River Plate* in the *Copa Sudamericana* Final, *Cienciano* would confront *Boca Juniors*, the other giant of Buenos Aires and Argentine football.

The 2003 *Recopa* was initially scheduled for Los Angeles, and was delayed several times during early 2004 for lack of a date agreement. It was finally scheduled for 6 September 2004 at Lockhart Stadium in Fort Lauderdale, Florida.[16] Both *Cienciano* and *Boca Juniors* arrived in southern Florida just as the *Category 2 hurricane Frances* battered south Florida, and ultimately the *Recopa* was delayed until 7 September 2004.

Boca felt confident with the Final match site in Fort Lauderdale, as the game would be in the evening at sea level with acceptable humidity and temperature. *Boca* also had geographical soccer history on their side, as they had won the 1989 Recopa against *Atlético Nacional* (Medellin, Colombia) in Miami. There would be no altitude, cold, rain, or history advantages for Cienciano in this Final.

---

[15] Another Andean team, *Bolivar* from Bolivia, made it to the 2004 Copa Sudamericana Final, which was the first continental final for a Bolivian team. *Bolivar* beat *Boca Juniors* 1-0 in the La Paz altitude, but succumbed 0-2 in the return match at the Bonbonera stadium in Buenos Aires – thereby losing the Final on aggregate score.

[16] Lockhart Stadium was the first professional soccer-specific stadium created in the USA, and was completely renovated in 1998 for a capacity of 20,450. Lockhart was the former home of the defunct MLS Miami Fusion team, which was in operation for only seven years (1996-2002).

Boca's star striker Carlos Tévez had just performed on Argentina's stunning gold-winning 2004 Olympic soccer team, where he had scored eight goals in six matches and was acknowledged to be the star of the tournament (Argentina scored a fantastic seventeen goals and allowed none in winning all six of their Olympic games).

Cienciano arrived on September 4th, just two days before the match was scheduled, and only 12 hours before *Frances* made landfall north of Fort Lauderdale. Even so, two members from each team (goalkeeper Oscar Ibañez and defender Santiago Acasiete for *Cienciano,* and goalkeeper Roberto Abbondanzieri and Tévez for *Boca Juniors*) arrived in Miami on September 5th, all having appeared in the Peru-Argentina World Cup qualifying match in Lima on September 4th (Argentina won 3-1). Many flights were cancelled on September 4th and 5th due to the impending hurricane, and the last players were lucky to arrive on time.

Tickets for the *Recopa* were impossible to find anywhere – unavailable on the Internet, ticket services, or even at the stadium venue. Wild rumors before the game of no tickets for sale at Lockhart Stadium were correct; the ticket booths never opened for business.[17] People lacking tickets provided by the teams were foolishly denied entry, and it was very peculiar how *Boca Juniors* had received many more tickets than *Cienciano*.

Why were tickets not sold like any conventional championship game? The *Recopa* should have been an easy sellout in Miami, but advertising was nonexistent even though the match was scheduled long before the hurricane *Frances* was in the vicinity. Was there a ticket scam, and/or were television revenues the guarantor of both teams' monies, making a live audience superfluous? In an age when fewer spectators are showing up at games, it is never wise to turn away those who wish to be involved.

The *Recopa* spectators were generously estimated at seven thousand, with about 85% signaling their *Boca Juniors* affiliation by wearing their blue and yellow colors. The *Cienciano* fans showed up with more red-and-white Peru jerseys than scarce red *Cienciano* shirts. Several Peru fans showed up with inventive custom-made shirts composed of ½ of the *Cienciano* shirt and either ½ of the Peru national shirt or ½ of the *Boca Juniors* shirt [Figures 11D & E].

Cienciano arrived late to the Lockhart Stadium because their scheduled motor coach never arrived at their hotel, and the team had to hurry to the stadium in private vehicles. It was not an auspicious way to organize a team for a Final. The last *Cienciano* player arrived at the stadium at 8:25 pm, only five minutes before the official kickoff. Impressively, the *Furia Roja* remained calm and focused before entering the field several minutes after the *Boca* squad had already appeared.

Several celebrities were at the match, most notably Argentine rock star Charly García. Although the Argentine spectators heavily outnumbered the Peruvians, the Peru spectators remained vocal throughout the match.

The Lockhart field was in great shape, a soft and bouncy pitch despite the heavy rains supplied by the hurricane in the previous days. The match began evenly as both teams searched for their rhythm and probed the opposition defense. *Boca's* play progressed to a slight possession advantage in the first half, and in the 33rd minute Carlos Tévez broke through the defense on the left side, only to be confronted by Oscar Ibañez, *Cienciano's* advancing keeper [Recopa action Figures 11F, G, & H]. Ibañez dove to his right and thought he had the ball in his possession, but Tévez kicked the ball out of his grasp, and after the ball took a favorable bounce for Tévez, he slotted it into the back of the net.

The *Cienciano* team was incensed, including the normally poised Ibañez, who earned a yellow card for protests that held up the match for several minutes. With that contested goal on the score sheet, *Boca* entered the half time period leading 1-0.

---

[17] The author entered the stadium with a player agent driving two *Cienciano* players to the game – the only available access to the stadium with no tickets being sold.

Cienciano controlled the second half as they patiently sought to score the equalizing goal. The *Furia Roja* crowd cheered on their team louder than seemed possible, considering their small numbers. Coach Freddy Ternero went for broke, bringing on two offensive players at sixty minutes, and another at seventy-three minutes. Finally, with two minutes to go in regulation, Rodrigo Saraz rose to meet a 30-yard free kick from Daniel Gamarra, heading the ball into the corner of the goal to the right of helpless *Boca* keeper Abbondanzieri. The red *Cienciano* sections of the stadium crowd went berserk with celebrations, as their "small-time" team had equaled the great *Boca Juniors*.

The last few minutes in regulation and injury time were frantic, as both teams sought the winner. After full time the match was decided by penalty kicks, and *Cienciano* did not fail. Tévez made a tepid kick that Ibáñez anticipated, and for good measure Ibáñez also stopped Vargas' kick. Defender Santiago Acasiete sealed the win with a coolly placed fourth successful kick[18], and *Cienciano* and their fans could at last celebrate its second international championship [Figure 11I].

There was a quick award ceremony in the center of the field where *Cienciano* picked up their medals. Thereafter, the *Cienciano* players attempted to circle the field in an "Olympic style" celebratory lap, but were rudely and physically interrupted by the USA security personnel, which were clearly unfamiliar with standard soccer celebrations and traditions. The sorry Fort Lauderdale security spectacle would have been unthinkable had the match been played in South America [Figure 11J].

Peru newspaper headlines read "*Cienciano se baña de gloria, nuevamente*" ["Cienciano is once again bathed in glory"] and "*Todo el Perú celebra triunfo histórico de Cienciano*" ["All Peru celebrates the historic triumph of Cienciano"].

Team Lineups for the *Recopa*:

Boca Juniors: Roberto Abbondanzieri; José Calvo, Rolando Schiavi, Cristian Traverso, Claudio Morel; Alfredo Cascini, Diego Cagna, Andrés Guglielmipietro (Fabián Vargas 67), Pablo Ledesma, (Aníbal Matellán 80); Martín Palermo, Carlos Tévez.
Coach: Miguel Angel Brindisi.

Cienciano: Oscar Ibañez; Paolo De la Haza, Santiago Acasiete, Manuel Arboleda, Giuliano Portilla; Alessandro Morán (Carlos Lobatón 60), Juan Carlos Bazalar, Juan Carlos La Rosa, Daniel Gamarra; Miguel Mostto (Rodrigo Saraz 60), Germán Carty (Sergio Ibarra 73).
Coach: Freddy Ternero.

Goals: **Boca Juniors** - Carlos Tévez 33. **Cienciano** - Rodrigo Saraz 88.

Cienciano wins on penalties 4-2.
Cienciano: Ibarra 1-0; Lobatón 2-1; Portilla 3-1; Acasiete 4-2.
Boca Juniors: Schiavi 1-1; Tévez 2-1; Palermo 3-2; Vargas 4-2.

Site: Lockhart Stadium, Fort Lauderdale, Florida, USA.

---

[18] Acasiete, also a regular central defender for the Peru national team, was oddly transferred after the Recopa triumph to Spanish Second Division side *UD Almería* for only US $140,000. This shows how difficult it is for a quality Peruvian to play in Europe, despite the fact that the Peru league was rated the 10th best in the world by the IFFHS in 2004, just behind the Dutch league. After Acasiete's displays in the Copa Sudamericana and Recopa, he surely could have commanded a higher price for a higher Division team in Spain. As a comparison, Tévez was sold to *Corinthians* of Brazil for nearly US $20 million.

Cienciano Campeón Postscript

After they won the *Recopa*, *Cienciano* was scheduled to play their first match of the 2004 Clausura against *Deportivo Wanka* only four days later (on September 11, 2004). To make matters worse, *Wanka* had arranged for most of their matches in the 2004 Clausura to be played in Cerro de Pasco at 4340 meters above sea level! To play professional soccer traveling from sea level in Fort Lauderdale to the highest top division stadium in the world is the toughest physical assignment in any sport. Perhaps not surprisingly, *Cienciano* lost that match 1-0 after an international flight and virtually no preparation.

Despite that loss at extreme altitude while exhausted, *Cienciano* earned the most points in the Peru First Division during the 2004 season, with a record of 30 wins, 13 draws, and 9 losses in 52 matches (total 103 points). Apertura winner *Alianza Lima* finished four points behind and Clausura winner *Sporting Cristal* eight points behind *Cienciano*. In most soccer leagues in the world, *Cienciano* would have won the season title outright on total points, but because the Peru league had copied the Argentine Apertura-Clausura system, *Cienciano* was denied the title.

Cienciano also started out strong in 2005 winning the Apertura, thus ensuring their participation in the 2006 Copa Libertadores competition. Cienciano finished 2005 by winning more first division games than any other Peruvian team.

Could *Cienciano* lead Peru into their third golden age of football? Peru is certainly due for another golden age, as the 31-year period between the first (1933-39) and the second (1970-1978) golden eras will arrive again in 2009 – immediately before the 2010 World Cup.

Perhaps the Peruvian public will be seeing more *Cienciano* players donning the red and white shirt of their homeland. Freddy Ternero was recently the Peru national team coach and knows better than anybody what skilled, motivated, and altitude-experienced players can accomplish. There would be none more deserved to wear their national team colors.

Chapter Twelve

Soccer at the End of the World

Our love for the game began when we were children. It's beautiful to be part of the football world.
Frank Rijkaard[1]

Dónde diablos jugarán los pobres Nenes? En dónde jugarán? Se esta pudriendo el mundo, Ya no hay lugar. [Where will the poor children play? In where will they play? If the world is rotting, there no longer is a place.]
Maná[2]

    The "End of the World," a place so remote as to be nearly hidden from mankind, was usually imagined to be associated with water. That body of water was an apparently limitless ocean into which explorers sailed away into, not knowing if they would ever reach land again. The literary scenario of the end of the world is epitomized by the mythical underwater world of Atlantis.
    Although there are precious few unexplored parts of the planet today, the "End of the World" is still associated with water. With all oceans conquered, among the most inaccessible areas of the planet are now some black-water rivers of the Amazon basin that drain from hidden swamplands, and inhabited only by hardy rainforest dwellers who have endured centuries of relative isolation.
    In the concrete jungle of the 21st century, primary rainforest at the lowland origins of the Amazon river system can justly be characterized as the "End of the World." Even now there exist unexplored and seemingly impenetrable regions of this massive and wondrous – yet increasingly endangered – Amazon river and jungle system. Therein are contained small tribal groups not yet well described by anthropologists, which have created their own self-sufficient cultures enduring for centuries. The few persevering groups know nature well, as they must depend on their wits to survive in this extraordinary corner of the world.[3]

---

[1] Frank Rijkaard is one of the Modern Era's Top Players (Chapter 7), and current coach of FC Barcelona.
[2] From Mexican group Maná song *Dónde Jugarán Los Niños?* [Where Will the Children Play?].
[3] The Amazon basin is often correctly labeled the "Lung of the World" ("Pulmon del Mundo"), as it provides more vital oxygen per square kilometer than any other land mass in the world. However, the targeting of the mass destruction of much of the Amazon by weak governments and avaricious logging and oil companies is threatening not only the environment, but many forms of life on earth. Without the preservation of the miraculous Amazon rainforest biodiversity and oxygen generation, mammals and eventually humans will be at increased risk of species extinction (see www.earthrenewal.org/rainless.htm).

Peru Amazon Jungle

The city of Iquitos is the entry point into the northwest Peruvian department of Loreto, which is comprised of a rainforest area nearly as vast as California.[4] The massive Amazon River, still more than one kilometer wide, is adjacent to and dominates every facet of life in Iquitos. This Amazon city is reachable only by air or by water, and the lack of accessibility by land lends an authentic aura of being at the doorstep of one of the most secluded places in the world. It is sobering to realize that despite being situated 3,600 kilometers (2,250 miles) upstream from the mouth of the Amazon river in northeastern Brazil, Iquitos lies at an altitude of only 120 meters (394 feet) above sea level.[5]

Today, Iquitos is a bustling river city of 330,000 people, and many Iquiteños[6] make a living from river trade and jungle products. Many of its inhabitants are descendants of converted rainforest dwellers who adopted the Peruvian way of life after the heyday of the rubber boom in the early 20th century. Land reform in the late 1960s attracted additional migrants from coastal and mountain cities to try their luck in what they imagined to be a jungle "El Dorado."

An additional 450,000 individuals live in the jungle areas outside of Iquitos. Some are members of tribal groups that are to various degrees assimilated to Peruvian society, living in small villages by the rivers. Others live deep in the jungle, and one must travel for a week or more by motorboat before arriving at these destinations – if they can be reached at all.[7] Many isolated indigenous villages are weeks or even months away from industrialized society by canoe, if they are so inclined to visit.

To the Amazon novice, the geography of the world's largest river basin appears as an indistinguishable and unremitting wall of green and brown. This illusory jungle (green) and river (brown) semblance can create headaches for amateur explorers, as travel days on the river are often wasted going around in circles. Traveling on the Amazon River without an experienced guide is dangerous and may result in getting lost – or worse.

Soccer in Iquitos

Soccer arrived in Iquitos in the early 20th century and became organized in the 1960s. The two main soccer clubs in Iquitos are *Colegio Nacional de Iquitos* (CNI - pronounced *say-enna-ee*) and *Hungaritos* ("the Hungarians"). Hungaritos was obviously impressed by and named for the powerful Hungarian national squad in the 1950s, but it has now ceased to be a first level team. CNI remains the dominant Iquitos club and the city's only prospect for soccer in Peru's top soccer division.

The CNI club developed from a secondary school (the equivalent of a high school), similar to Cienciano of Cusco (see Chapter 11). But instead of being located in an Andean mountain valley at more than 3,300 meters above sea level like Cienciano, CNI is located next to the largest river in the world.[8] The Colegio Nacional de Iquitos school was founded on May 20, 1926, shortly after the Iquitos rubber boom went bust after the lucrative indigenous rubber business was displaced from the Amazon region to Asia. The school is now located in the suburb of San Juan on the busy two-lane road that runs between the

---

[4] Peru is more than three times as large as California: Peru is 1,283,092 km^2, Loreto has an area of 368,852 km^2 and California is 424,001 km^2.
[5] The Amazon river elevation drop is only 0.0033 centimeters (120 m/3600 km) or 0.0013 inches *per kilometer* for its length through eastern Peru and Brazil until it meets the Atlantic Ocean.
[6] Iquiteños (inhabitants of Iquitos) are often affectionately referred to as *charapas* (a type of Amazon turtle) by their compatriots.
[7] During the Amazon dry season when the rivers are lower, many distant villages are unreachable by the usual water route.
[8] As measured by water volume, the Amazon river is larger than the Mississippi, Nile and Yangtze rivers put together.

international airport and the city. Composed of a large group of cinderblock buildings, CNI educates children from Iquitos and its adjacent suburbs.

CNI's soccer training ground is located in the city center near the old abandoned airport, several kilometers away from the school itself. The two practice fields consist of sandy soil bordered by patchwork grass, conditions more suitable for beach soccer than the professional eleven a side version [Figure 12A]. Because the Amazon soil and rainy conditions are too oppressive to maintain proper natural grass, field conditions are often poor in Iquitos. Therefore, many adolescents escape both the equatorial heat and poor field conditions by playing soccer under the streetlights in the evenings.

CNI joined the Peruvian First Division in 1973 and they remained there for the next twenty years. Although not possessing the most talented squads, CNI was surprisingly competitive and resolutely represented the Amazon region. CNI's and Iquitos' most famous indigenous player is Marcial Salazar, who also represented the Peruvian national team in the 1990s. CNI finally exited the First Division at the end of 1992 and have not yet returned. CNI's best hope to revisit the Peruvian First Division is to win the Copa Peru, a competition open to all clubs not in the Peruvian First or Second Divisions.

Part of CNI's success in persevering in the top division may have been the local climate. When coastal clubs from Lima, Chiclayo, or Trujillo would arrive by plane from their 30% humidity environment, they would immediately be forced to embrace the nearly 100% humidity of the Amazon jungle. While descending the ramp from the plane the players would start to sweat, and they would need to replenish their bodily fluids just because of the exertion of walking around. These jungle conditions likely led to a short psychological and physiological edge for the home team, long enough to create a "home-climate" advantage unless the visitors were mentally and physically prepared for the Amazon conditions.

CNI was determined to stay in the First Division and perform well, and would therefore occasionally bring top-class players to help them compete. One of the more colorful players they signed during their first decade in the First Division was goalkeeper Ramón Quiroga in 1983. Originally from Rosario, Argentina, Quiroga performed for the Peru national team in the 1978 and 1982 World Cups after gaining Peruvian citizenship. Less than two years after Quiroga defended the Peru goal in the 1982 World Cup in Spain, he found himself defending goal for a jungle team named after a high school on the edge of the Amazon River [Figure 12B]!

While performing well in the early matches in the 1978 Cup, Quiroga was Peru goalkeeper for one of the World Cup's most contentious matches ever, the 6-0 defeat to host and eventual winner Argentina. This World Cup match, in which Argentina was obligated to beat Peru by four goals in order to advance to the Final, was coincidentally played in Quiroga's hometown of Rosario, Argentina. Because of the landslide Argentina-Peru result, Argentina advanced to the Final match while Brazil was relegated to the third place game.[9]

Quiroga was called "El Loco" (The Crazy) because of his forays away from goal, which were probably inspired by Argentine goalkeeping great Hugo Gatti (who was also called "El Loco"). This "open" goalkeeping style was later favored to different degrees by Hugo Campos (Mexico), Rene Higuita (Colombia), and Fabien Barthez (France). Quiroga still holds the dubious World Cup record of being the *only goalkeeper in World Cup Finals history to commit a foul in his opponents half of the field*. Quiroga later coached a series of top division teams in Peru, including Cienciano in the mid-90s, and Universitario in 2003.

In the 1980s CNI's sponsor was Peruvian soda-maker Inca Kola, which since 1935 successfully marketed a soda drink named after their Inca ancestors (Inca Kola was the

---

[9] Brazil completed their last 1978 World Cup group game before the Argentina-Peru match, so the Argentines knew exactly how many goals (four) they needed to score to eliminate Brazil. Since that World Cup, the last games of the group stages are played at the exact same time, in order to prevent such an unfair advantage to any team again.

largest local soda company in South America). Although a trade secret, Inca Kola was rumored to be a carbonated mix of *chamomile* and *hierba luisa* plant extracts.[10]

CNI played its matches at Max Augustin Stadium, a concrete monstrosity that packed in 8,000 spectators for one of their final first division appearances in 1992 matching them against Leon de Huánaco (the "Lions from Huánaco"). A relentless Amazon rain preceded the match, and the field was still soggy and slippery. Nevertheless, there was good action going on up and down the field for the duration of the game, with Leon's longhaired "number 10" continually penetrating and threatening to score. Finally, a CNI midfielder swept into the corner of the goal area, and from an acute angle scored the only goal of the game. The home fans spilled out of the stadium satisfied with the victory, fully able to enjoy their *inchicapi* dinner from the street vendors – made from chicken, rice, peanuts, cilantro and manioc.

After CNI exited the first division in 1993, two other Amazon teams, Yurimaguas and Pucallpa, briefly graced the Peru top division. But since 1998 there has been no representative soccer club from the Amazon region in the Peruvian First Division. Despite the local situation, Iquiteños remain certifiably soccer-mad. Many follow one of the Big Three Lima clubs of Alianza Lima, Universitario or Sporting Cristal, or the successful Cusco team Cienciano. When one of those teams wins, there is sure to be a flotilla of the legendary Iquitos *motocars* (three-wheeled motorcycle-taxis) riding around the city, showing off the colors of their adopted team.

There are several amateur leagues in Iquitos; the Punchana League is the most prestigious, with hard-fought and skillful games played on sandy Amazon pitches. Outside league play, boys and young men play street soccer, often in the evenings. Compared to pickup soccer farther downstream in Brazil where the Amazon is wider and conducive to play on its beaches, street soccer on concrete or asphalt is standard in Iquitos.[11] Iquiteños rise early in the morning to escape the equatorial heat, but more often games take place under the streetlights after the evening meal has finished. Goal posts are most often scrap pieces of concrete or iron, and a goal is scored if it passes through the posts at knee-level or lower. Depending on the quantity and zeal of the participants, the matches may last one, two or more hours. If a good game is in progress, it will not matter if there is an hour-long Amazon downpour, as the boys will play soaking wet right through the rain. Sometimes the game continues past midnight – the steady tap, tap, tap of the rubber ball on the wet pavement echoing for blocks in the still Amazon night [Figure 1C].

---

[10] In an attempt to gain soda market share in Peru in 1999, multinational soda behemoth Coca-Cola bought 50% of Inca Kola.

[11] See Alex Bellos' book for full description of the Brazilian Amazon beach soccer experience. The only Iquitos beach suitable for soccer is the field at Bellevista-Nanay, near to where the Nanay River flows into the Amazon.

Iquitos Hosts 2005 U-17 World Championship Matches

Peru hosted the 2005 edition of the FIFA U-17 World Championship in five cities. Four were coastal cities located on the west side of the Andes mountains: Lima, Chiclayo, Trujillo, and Piura (named from south to north). The fifth city was Iquitos, the only participating city from the eastern side of the Andes.

The Max Augustin stadium in Iquitos was completely renovated for the competition, nearly rebuilding the stadium from scratch. New stands were constructed allowing for a larger spectator capacity of 25,000, a roof placed over the seats, and an artificial turf field installed that allows quality soccer play during the Amazon rainy season.[12]

Barely had the concrete dried when the new Max Augustin stadium was host for three matches in the competition. The first round match between hosts Peru and Costa Rica was a crowd success (but Costa Rica prevailed over the hosts 2-0); and the two quarterfinal matches (Turkey beat China 5-1 and Brazil beat North Korea 3-1) were superb examples of youth soccer at the highest level. The only interruption was a huge earthquake that affected much of northern Peru during near the end of the Turkey-China match, which shook the stadium slightly. The earthquake confirmed the structural integrity of the rebuilt Max Augustin stadium.

All of the Iquitos matches were sold out, and the spectators offered the most vocal and energetic group of spectators in the whole competition. FIFA recognized the Iquiteños' enthusiastic response to the U-17 World Championship by awarding the city the 2005 FIFA Fair Play award. In light of the sparkling public reaction in Iquitos, the future of soccer in the Peruvian Amazon seems secure.

Soccer in Amazon River Communities Outside Iquitos

The Amazon villages outside Iquitos city have their own soccer traditions, as soccer fields are usually in a central area and may even double as the village square. A soccer game against a neighboring village is often the most important social event until the next match.[13]

Upriver from Iquitos, Santa Rita de Castilla (population 2,000) is a typical example of a larger Amazon town with a central soccer field lined by homemade spectator stands. But the Santa Rita field stands directly on the riverbank and is being eroded by the strong currents of the Marañon river.[14] In the not too distant future, pieces of the *cancha* (field) will drop into the river, and the inhabitants of Santa Rita will need to mark out a new soccer field. That is the course and force of nature; the mighty Amazon river system is forever changing and unforgiving, and in time, formerly habitable areas disappear into the swirling waters.

The village fields are composed of Amazonian mud with grass, and are naturally bumpy since the rains constantly alter the pitch consistency. In the rainy season, the grass is worn away in the most frequently used areas, exposing mud flats in the center. Because Amazon soil is made up of the finest silt brought down from the Andes Mountains, playing soccer on Amazon mud is akin to playing on ice. Matches in the rainy season feature a lot of slipping and sliding, with frequent and spectacular "wipe-outs" resulting. All players finish the game covered with mud, and afterwards clean off with a bath in the Amazon River.

---

[12] FIFA insisted that this would be the first world soccer competition completely played on artificial turf, as each of the five stadiums had a new artificial field installed.

[13] Between Iquitos and the Brazil border lays the island of San Pablo, which formerly housed a leprosarium where Che Guevara played village soccer with leprosy patients and medical staff in 1952.

[14] The Marañon and the Ucayali are the two rivers that join to form the mighty Amazon River in Peru. Although the Ucayali is longer and therefore leads to the "source" of the Amazon, the Marañon transports far more water by volume.

Soccer and the Urarina Indigenous Group

Isolated indigenous groups (sometimes called tribes) still exist that until recently had not been exposed to the soccer as played in the outside world. The Urarina are one such relatively sheltered tribe in the Peruvian Amazon, living between the *aguajals* (swamps) and black rivers that lie north of the Marañon river.[15] They are a semi-nomadic and peaceful people of more than four thousand individuals who still hunt by blowgun, and possess a language so distinct that it forms its own language family.

Along with the Matses (Mayorunas) and the Piros, the Urarina are among the most isolated and self-sufficient native group in Peru. Although they have been contacted on and off for eighty years, there are many Urarina villages not easily accessible by boat, and therefore remain very secluded.

The Urarina are quite environmentally flexible as they have adapted to both rainforest and riverine lifestyles (most Amazonian groups prefer one or the other). The word "Urarina" likely originated from the Inca language of Quechua, whose root words "ura" (below) and "runa" (people) would mean "people from below." To the highland Incas they would indeed be the rainforest "people from below." The most remarkable aspects of the Urarina are their peaceful demeanor, their cultural and linguistic integrity, and their harmonious existence in the challenging jungle environment.

Urarina reflexes are kept sharp by constant avoidance of numerous natural hazards present in the rainforest. On land this includes jaguars, snakes, (especially the dreaded and toxic *fer de lance*), scorpions and stinging ants, or being cornered by a pack of *sahinos* (ferocious wild pigs which roam in herds and have been known to kill men with their razor sharp teeth). In the water, they must carefully avoid the river hazards of freshwater stingrays, venomous swimming snakes, electric eels, pirañas (piranha fish) and crocodiles (named in the order of decreasing danger). Not least of all, avoiding the candirú fish (*Vandellia cirrhosa*), an accidental human parasite known to crawl up the urethra and lodge there (surgery is usually necessary for survival).

Although many skills in the jungle require exquisite use of hand movements, many require specialized use of the hips, legs, and feet. These include such daily activities as maneuvering a tiny canoe, chasing animals barefoot through dense jungle, and climbing up a tree without a ladder.

When soccer balls were provided to the Urarina in 1992, they immediately took to the game, dribbling with their feet and knees through unkempt jungle grass fields. Passing often took place at waist height, as that was more effective than weaving through the jungle grass [Figure 12C]. Goalkeeping was often spectacular, as they often used their knees and feet to save the ball.

The first soccer balls the Urarina used were the same durable rubber balls utilized by street soccer crews in Iquitos. The balls doubled as aquatic play toys for children when launched into the river during their daily bathing. As tough as those balls are, they were worn down after months of constant sun and water exposure, invariably bursting on contact after a hard shot. This inevitable event always produced unconstrained laughter from both teams.

The first Urarina soccer fields were constructed in the social areas between their clan houses. Soccer goalposts are built with ease by these humble people, who routinely build solid jungle dwellings out of a combination of twenty different species of rainforest trees – taking from nature only what is necessary. However, goal nets are usually unavailable, as any available netting is reserved for *net-fishing*, which along with the natural plant fish poison *barbasco*, brings in fish protein during the scarce dry season.

Games were held in the afternoons, after the men returned from their hunting activities and daily chores were finished. There were only a few spectators, as everybody wanted to

---

[15] "Black" rivers arise from swamps in the lower Amazon region, while "white" rivers drain into the Amazon after carrying silt from the Andes mountains for hundreds of miles.

play. Women would watch from the longhouses surrounding the field and join in the laughter after one of the men failed to execute a move, such as missing the ball completely. After the game everybody would wash off in the river and retreat to their evening meal, the Urarina specialty being smoked venison or stewed monkey meat. Sunset occurs at 6:00-6:30 PM in the Amazon, so except for the men venturing out night-hunting, everybody was usually asleep by 8 pm. Wakeup time is between 4 and 5 am.

Each village had several men whose evolved soccer skills were above the rest. Some could dribble well, some anticipate and defend well, and some could shoot hard. Even so, some techniques they employed may never have been used elsewhere in the world, as some were fond of trapping the ball between their knees and hopping forward. They sought to improve their skills spontaneously, even playing in the jungle mud after a rainstorm. There was no need for soccer boots (or shoes of any type), as their feet were already coarsened and widened over a lifetime of walking through the jungle, constantly exposed to the terrestrial nuisances that nature provides.

Some of the boys twelve or older would join in and play with the men. After all, they were approaching marrying age, and playing soccer with the men was emerging as a new rite of passage into manhood. Still, one boy named Kookuri ("armadillo") was already a standout player at age eight. A good dribbler with superior visual skills and distribution, he became a little "number 10." Kookuri later moved deep into the jungle with his family, but given his passion for the game, he is likely still playing some form of football today [Figure 12D].

Younger children would often play soccer at lunchtime, before the adults finished their communal duties. Even a thunderstorm was no excuse to cancel their noontime soccer respites from their household chores.

Soccer became a unifying force within the villages, with men even crossing clan lines to play with one another. It also brought more of a focus for primary health efforts in the river villages, especially when one village would journey to play another in friendly games. Often the traveling villages would participate in a cooperative *minga* in the host village, a form of donated community work to help their neighbors [Figure 12E].[16] Often the minga consisted of grooming the field before the game, or helping erect a dwelling. After the game the players would be offered food and *masato*, a natural beer made from cassava. Thereafter, the visiting players could make the several hours canoe trip back home with a full stomach.

The Healing Passion and Power of Soccer

On one occasion soccer directly helped to save the life of an Urarina child. A father had strangely been denying the illness of his five-month old infant girl, who was suffering from fever and diarrhea. As she lay dying from dehydration due to one of the frequent *Shigella* diarrhea epidemics in the Amazon, I explained that the baby would need intramuscular antibiotics and interosseous rehydration.[17] The father said the injection was acceptable, but not the rehydration therapy. His friends encouraged him to change his mind but they could not. The father was reluctant to allow such novel treatment, although by then the Urarina had accepted the rare but occasionally necessary injection treatment. Being expert blowgun hunters, they realized the power of poison-tipped needles, and were initially "needle phobic" until medicine injections were demonstrated to be of benefit.

I had witnessed the baby's birthing ceremony five months earlier, and was not keen to see her needlessly die. The family had already named the baby, which was unusual for the Urarina because she was so young. Similar to some other Amazon groups, the Urarina usually do not name their children before walking age, simply because walking is an auspicious sign the baby survived the hazardous first year of life. Because the jungle infant

---

[16] The Amazon *minga* is derived from the Inca *minka,* which also means collective community effort.
[17] Interosseous rehydration is a delicate procedure involving the insertion of a needle into the tibia bone in the lower leg in order to deliver replacement fluids to small children without necessity of an intravenous line.

mortality rate is so high and it is probably more emotionally traumatic to lose a child that is already named, the Urarina typically delay the naming ceremony until their children have demonstrated a good chance of survival.

As they did many afternoons the father and his friends went to play soccer around 4 o'clock. When they invited me, I declined the invitation and elected to watch from the sidelines. One of his friends asked me why I was not playing. I explained to him that I could not in good conscience enjoy myself while a child's life was in danger, and since the father was neglecting his daughter's condition, she would surely die if she was not properly attended. This was an unexpected development, as nobody had ever refused an invitation to play soccer before.

After nearly an hour of discussion that eventually involved his powerful mother-in-law, the father acquiesced and the infant girl was treated. After attending to the girl, I made an appearance before the end of the session to ensure the social continuity of the game. The little girl made an uneventful recovery and is alive today, no doubt running about kicking a ball.

Soccer Future in the Amazon

It is a given that once exposed to metal pots and cotton clothing, Amazon indigenous groups rapidly incorporate these commodities into their culture, and refuse to abandon them if they remain available. Still, some Urarina in the high rivers are so isolated that some do not always have cotton clothing or metal pots, but instead wear tree bark clothes and cast their own fine earthenware pots. But having seen the enthusiastic experience of the Urarina with the round ball, it is doubtful they will ever give up football either.

But that assessment assumes that the Urarina have a future, when in reality they are currently under attack from exploiters of all types – including multinational oil companies.[18] As mentioned at the start, the integrity of the Amazon is critical to everybody on the planet – especially to rain forest stewardship groups such as the Urarina. For if the Amazon is continued to be poisoned by loggers, oil companies, and ranchers, there will indeed be "no place to play" for anybody's children.[19]

---

[18] More Urarina information can be found in this article by Richard Witzig & Massiel Ascencios: *The Road to Indigenous Extinction: Case Study of Resource Exportation, Disease Importation, and Human Rights Violations against the Urarina in the Peruvian Amazon*, from the Harvard journal *Health and Human Rights*.1999;4(1):60-81. Harvard University has unfortunately not allowed this journal's articles to be circulated freely on the Internet – a ludicrous state of affairs for an international human rights publication. Readers can email fxbcenter@igc.apc.org to petition the journal to be given public status (see: www.hsph.harvard.edu/fxbcenter/V4N1.htm).

[19] The author thanks Bauti, Bidiûche, Fuan, Kiriná, Iguana, Kookuri, Nichatachunga, Santos, Shanti, Tabuina, Ufquasiri and dozens of others Urarina for the memorable life and soccer experiences at the "End of the World," as well as my friends and colleagues at German medical NGO Freundeskreis Indianerhilfe (www.indianerhilfe.de), who continue to work with the Urarina with FAAN (Fundación Alemana de Ayuda al Nativos).

Chapter Thirteen

Soccer Dishonor

The gods use us mortals as footballs. [Di nos quasi pilas homines habent.]
                        Titus Maccius Plautus (254-184 B.C.) in *Captivi*, Prologus, 22.[1]

He who is victorious should remember the instability of all things.   *Buddha*

The tenets of *Soccer Fair Play* – both on the playing field and in the structural integrity of competitions – can never be compromised, because if undermined, those actions may affect human societal dynamics.[2] For that reason, the importance of the events documented below cannot be overemphasized – that the inappropriate, unfair, and ultimately xenophobic actions of FIFA and the IOC in the 1936 Berlin "Nazi" Olympics served both the world sport and human dynamics poorly.[3]

Why bring these heretofore unexamined events to the forefront now, and why are they important to modern soccer history? Two reasons are that these critical events have never been explored in such detail, and heretofore only parts have been published in Spanish. The third reason is because world soccer returns to a unified Berlin and Germany for the first time in seventy years at the 2006 FIFA World Cup in Germany – from a time when the 1936 Olympics glorified Hitler's murderous Nazi regime to a world still struggling with its essential human diversity. Now is the time to reflect on these past events in order to secure the future integrity of organized soccer by ensuring that this type of shameful action – be it as large as 1936 or smaller – will blight neither the game nor humanity again.

Soccer and the Missed Opportunity of Human Understanding in 1936

The public fascination with soccer and the potential power resulting from control of "the people's game" did not escape the notice of Europe's fascist rulers in the 1930's. Adolf Hitler in Germany, Benito Mussolini in Italy and Francisco Franco in Spain all sought to manipulate soccer's impact on the masses in order to solidify their national popularity and politics.

---

[1] Plautus was certainly referring to the Roman football game of *haspartum* in this 2200-year-old quotation. Note the similarity between Plautus' quotation and Shakespeare's *Comedy of Errors* in Chapter One, wherein they both describe a condition in which a person is treated like a football, i.e. kicked around, in a sense that is inevitable or even designed by the gods. Plautus was a dramatist who wrote comedies, and Shakespeare actually based his *Comedy of Errors* on Plautus' *Menaechmi*. Plautus is also credited with coining the phrases "No smoke without fire," and "You can lead a horse to water but you cannot make him drink."
[2] FIFA Fair Play doctrine is located at http://images.fifa.com/fifa/fairplay/fairplayday98.html.
[3] This chapter is the only section that deals with events in the pre-1958 "Legends Era" of soccer, as the critical events described herein have never been adequately explored or explained.

Political influence in the game by fascist leaders had both a domestic and extra-national intent.[4] Franco's favoritism of Real Madrid was consistent with the dictator's policies of suppressing nationalist activities in the Basque (País Vasco) and Catalonia regions, home to the Athletic Bilbao and Barcelona football clubs, respectively. The San Mamés (Athletic Bilbao) and Camp Nou (Barcelona) football stadiums were the ultimate refuge for cultural and linguistic freedom in the four decades of the Franco dictatorship (1936-1975), as they were the only public places individuals could converse in their native language without fear of oppression.[5]

Fascist influence morphed into national team glorification, as illustrated by Mussolini and Hitler's personal interests in their Italian and German national team successes. The pressures were intense – for example, the Italian team members were instructed to win the 1938 World Cup in France or "don't come back."

However, the most important example of political manipulation of soccer occurred at the 1936 Berlin Olympics held in Nazi Germany. This long-forgotten event was a history-turning moment – not just for soccer – but also for humanity.

World Cups and Olympic Soccer Tournaments Prior to 1936

The Olympic Games had included a soccer tournament since 1908. Early soccer power England won both the 1908 London and the 1912 Stockholm tournaments, but the 1916 Games were cancelled due to World War I. Belgium won at home in the 1920 Antwerp Olympics, and Uruguay then impressively won both the 1924 and 1928 titles in Paris and Amsterdam. The Uruguayans followed their Olympic successes by winning the first World Cup at home in Montevideo in 1930. The 1932 Los Angeles Olympics did not host a soccer tournament due to disagreement over the *amateur* soccer player status, as international soccer was then undergoing the growing pains of professionalism.

By the early 1930's, South American soccer teams had made tremendous progress in skills and team play, best exemplified by Uruguay's successes. In the first World Cup, won by host Uruguay 4-2 over Argentina, three of the four semi-finalists were from the Americas, including the USA, which won its first two games against Paraguay and Belgium by 3-0 scores The lone European semi-finalist was Yugoslavia, which was humbled 6-1 by Uruguay.

The 1934 World Cup was hosted and won by Italy, with Germany placing third after beating fourth-placed Austria. Italy had poached organizing halfback Luisito Monti, the best Argentine player from the 1930 Final squad, as well as Argentine-born forwards Raimundo Orsi and Enrique Guaita. They were eligible to play for Italy as *oriundi* (foreign players of Italian ancestry). Italian coach Vittorio Pozzo, a psychologist by profession, justified their transfer of national allegiance "because if they can die for Italy, they can play for Italy" – a reference to their citizen eligibility for national military service. Some players did not agree with Pozzo's opinion; after the 1936 Olympic Games, Guaita and two other oriundi were caught sneaking over the border after they had been summoned for their army physicals.

Mussolini had a personal interest in football's World Cup, and an insatiable desire for Italian national team success, especially since his favored Lazio club team never won the *scudetto* (the Italian championship) when he was in power. Mussolini pushed the construction of massive sporting stadiums and arenas, and affixed his name to the stadium

---

[4] In *The Football World* Stephen Wagg sums up the fascist attitude towards national soccer teams: "The claim that the Mussolini regime had ever valued sport for its own sake was of course absurd and, indeed, it was the recognition by even the most politically illiterate football correspondent that no major power any longer saw sport in this way....In Germany, as England were to find in the famous Berlin international of 1938, little expense was spared by the Nazi government in the preparation of the national football team, a win for whom was claimed as a vindication of Nazism and Strength through Joy Movement."

[5] Basque (Euskara) in País Vasco and Catalan in Catalonia.

built in Turin.[6] Italian athletic arenas had idealized marble figures representing various sports, including a nude marble soccer player in sandals, complete with soccer ball. At the 1934 World Cup games, the Italian team made the fascist salute directly to Mussolini, and some visiting teams such as Czechoslovakia did the same to honor him. One World Cup poster even featured Hercules with his hand raised in the Fascist salute.

As traversing the Atlantic Ocean took three weeks in this era, the forced ship living resulted in limited physical training for the traveling teams in the 3-4 weeks of travel before the competition. Only three of the sixteen teams in the 1934 Games were from the Americas (Brazil, Argentina, USA). However, all semifinalists were from European nations.

The 1936 Olympic Games; Fascist Victory over Justice and Diversity

The 1936 Olympic Games were held in Berlin in Nazi-ruled Germany; these Games bisected the 1934 and 1938 World Cups won by fascist Italy. For the Berlin Olympics, Hitler had boasted that the German "Aryan race" would demonstrate its innate sporting superiority.

Even before the 1936 Olympic Games began in August, world politics were in a very precarious state of affairs. Germany had already invaded and taken control of the Rhineland from France, Italy had invaded Ethiopia, and Franco's fascist army was fighting a civil war against the Republicans. These "pre-Olympic events" were in fact the preliminaries of the Second World War. As a result of that massive war, the 1936 Olympics would be the last Games until 1948, and all World Cups after 1938 until 1950 were cancelled.

Of course, the 1936 Olympics should never have been held in Nazi Germany, as the regime had long shattered Olympic rules forbidding discrimination based on religion and ethnicity. By 1936, Nazi Germany already had in place strict laws restricting the human rights of Jews, Gypsies and other "undesirables." There was furious global debate concerning a boycott of the Games, but Nazi Germany's supporters eventually won the argument in the USA, and soon after, other countries fell into line and committed to the Games. A "counter-Olympiad" was planned in Barcelona to compete with the official Berlin Games, but these alternative Games had to be abandoned with the outbreak of the Spanish Civil War in July 1936, just as the alternative athletes were arriving to compete.

Just before the Games opened, eight hundred Roma (often called "Gypsies") were forcibly removed from their homes in Berlin and sent to the Marzahn concentration camp. Although the IOC (International Olympic Committee) knew these facts beforehand, the Games went on as scheduled.

According to the International Federation of Football History and Statistics (IFFHS), Nazi Germany "used the event as a political propaganda weapon...the swastikas were more conspicuous than the flags of the IOC and the participating nations. The Nazis misused the Games to glorify the "New Germany."[7]

The Undefeated 1936 Peru Soccer Team

Peru alone represented South American soccer in the 1936 Olympics. The 1930's represented the first golden era of Peruvian soccer; Peru's second golden age would come 40 years later in the 1970s teams led by Teófilo "Nene" Cubillas.

Peru's 1936 Olympic soccer team was led by three soccer legends – Alejandro Villanueva, Juan Valdivieso and Teodoro "Lolo" Fernández – that formed a soccer triumvirate unsurpassed in the world at that time.

---

[6] Built in 1933 for the 1934 World Cup in Italy, the stadium was originally called *Stadio Mussolini*, but after World War II it was changed to the Stadio Comunale di Torino and was home to Juventus and Torino Calcio until 1990. Recently it was renamed Stadio Olimpico, and it hosted the opening ceremony and the closing ceremonies of the 2006 Winter Olimpics in Turin. It is now again renamed Stadio Grande Torino, and will remain a football ground.
[7] *Olympic Football Tournaments [2] 1928 & 1936*. International Federation of Football History and Statistics. Wiesbaden, 2002.

Peru's undisputed leader was Alejandro Villanueva, slim and 190 centimeters tall (6 feet 3 inches). Even at a comparatively tall height, Villanueva was technically the most superior player on the team, and one of the most talented players in the world. Villanueva was commonly called "*El Maestro*" ("the master") – his other nickname *Manguera* ("tube") mimicked his slim physique. Villanueva either invented or brought into prominence many new moves in Peru, including the "*matada*" fake shot, back heel pass, the nutmeg (*el tunél*), and the dummy (*el callejón*). He was a master of ball control with any part of his body, and would leave his opponents gasping with his magical fakes, keen vision and adept passing ability. Villanueva also had great leadership skills, with a demeanor that was always cool and collected, even under the incredible pressure encountered in the Berlin games. He had led Peru's national team in their first ever-international game in 1927, their first World Cup in Uruguay in 1930 (losing to eventual champions Uruguay by only 1-0), and his club team Alianza Lima to Peruvian championships in 1927, 1928, 1931, 1932, and 1933. Villanueva was at the same time the "Father" of Peruvian football as well as its primary innovator [Figure 13A, B, & D].

Juan Valdivieso is still considered the best Peruvian goalkeeper ever, nicknamed *El Mago* (the magician) for his all-around skills [Figures 13A, B, C, E, F & G]. Valdivieso had an impeccable sense of timing and balance, as well as phenomenal athletic ability and courage in goal. He was also a specialist in stopping penalty kicks, and was a good field player and goal scorer; he once scored four goals in a game for his club Alianza Lima. In an interview in January 2003, Valdivieso credited a meeting in Lima with the legendary Spanish goalkeeper Ricardo Zamora as contributing to his driving inspiration to be the best.

Teodoro "Lolo" Fernández was a young center forward nicknamed "*El Cañonero*" ("cannon shot") for his fearsome shooting ability. Fernández was as solid as Villanueva was slim; a pure goal scorer who would take on entire defenses, it was said that "*su remate era sinónimo de gol*" (his shot was synonymous to a goal). Fernández was the best player for the Universitario team, which won Peruvian championships in 1939, 1941, 1945 and 1946 in the post-Villanueva/Valdivieso period [Figure 13A, B, & H].

The remainder of the Peru team was composed of lesser legends Arturo Fernández (Lolo's brother) and Victor Lavalle in defense, Segundo Castillo, Orestes Jordán and Carlos Tovar in midfield, and Jorge Alcalde, Adelfo Magallanes and José Morales accompanying Fernandes and Villanueva in attack. Villanueva, Valdivieso and Lavalle had played for Peru in the first World Cup in Uruguay in 1930, and most of the 1936 Olympic team had participated in the Peruvian "Equipo Pacifico" team tour of Europe in 1933. The Equipo Pacifico tour was a grueling autumn/winter Europe tour of 33 games in 55 days, and the team had a respectable away record of 11 games won, 11 tied and 11 games lost [Figure 13A].

Peru's rock-solid team reflected the multi-ethnicity of their nation. Peruvian journalist Guillermo Thorndike described the team as "*mestizos, apenas blancos, tambíen mandingas y coromantos. Y todos mezclados con quechua.*" ["Mixed, almost white, also black and brown. And all mixed with quechua."][8] The double significance of "all mixed with quechua" referred to the Inca ancestry carried by team members, and that above all they were authentic Peruvians.

The IFFHS described the 1936 Peru team as "well prepared, a technically excellent and strong attacking side, creative and temperamental yet fair," even commenting that "Peru had everything to be a finalist."

The Peruvian team left from Lima for Europe on the steamship *Orazio* on June 13th, arriving in Genoa, Italy on July 8th, an overseas trip of 25 days duration. After traveling to Germany by train, they had only a few weeks to lose their "sea legs" and prepare to represent all of South American soccer in the 1936 Olympic Games [Figure 13B].

---

[8] Thorndike, Guillermo. *El Reves de Morir*. [The Reverse of Dying]. Mosca Azul, Lima. 1978.

Peru Soccer Success at the 1936 Games

Peru started off their Olympic Games by destroying Finland 7-3. By half time, Fernandes had a hat trick, and Finland could only answer with a penalty kick. In the second half, Villanueva scored, then Fernández incredibly with two more goals (for a one game total of five), then Villanueva again with his second goal. As the game outcome had already been determined, Peru gave up two late goals, losing their concentration and saving their strength. There was not much time for celebrating because their next opponents were the Austrian *"Wunderteam"* ("Wonder Team," developed by legendary coach Hugo Meisl) that had finished fourth in the 1934 World Cup, losing 1-0 to eventual winners Italy. Only three months earlier on May 6, 1936, Austria had beaten venerable England 2-1 in Vienna.

In the meantime, Jesse Owens had already produced a heroic four gold medal performance by winning the sprints and long jump, humiliating the Nazis and their philosophy of Aryan dominance [Figure 13C]. Nazi "damage control" propaganda subsequently sought to brainwash their own population, explaining away Owens' feats as "mere physical events" conferring advantage to the "animalistic tendencies" of "inferior races."

Hitler and the Nazis were depending on their football team to perform well at the *world's most popular team game*, thereby demonstrating their claims of Aryan superiority of physique, ball skill (technique), and intelligent tactics. But Hitler was shocked as he watched Norway eliminate Germany by a 2-0 score in Berlin's Poststadion, stomping out after Norway's second goal. Hitler would not personally attend any more soccer games, but instead sent Josef Goebbels, his infamous propaganda minister. Goebbels' job was to watch over the Austrians – the last hope of the Germanic "Aryans" – in the Olympic soccer tournament.

The Peru-Austria game was played on August 8th 1936, and was refereed by three Europeans. With Goebbels watching,[9] the Hertha Berlin stadium was packed full of German spectators sympathizing with the Austrian team. Peru started out nervously in the intimidating atmosphere, and gave up two goals in the first half. Norwegian referee Kristiansen did not seem to see the fouls, many violent, committed by the over-aggressive Austrians. Villanueva calmed down his forces at half time, and in the second half Peru controlled the game with their short-passing technique. Shortly thereafter, Alcalde was scythed down by a terrible Austrian foul from a foot to his stomach, and from this incident the Peruvians drew their ultimate courage. Incredibly, the crowd began to warm to the beauty of the Peruvian style, as cheers were heard from the partisan crowd. Dominating play, the goals finally came for Peru – in the 75th minute by Alcalde, and the 81st minute by Villanueva.

After the two Peru goals, some fans streamed out of the stands past the Nazi soldiers (whose main job was crowd control) and onto the pitch to salute the players. The spectators were later claimed by some to be South Americans; this accusation was never proven. FIFA documents refute any speculation of their identity, and the true identity of the pitch-invaders remains unknown.[10] The referee shooed them off after a few minutes, and the last nine minutes of regular play resumed.

---

[9] Goebbels was quite a football fan; he also attended the Germany-England match on May 14, 1938 in Berlin, only to see Germany fall 6-3 to the English. Before that game, he even convinced British ambassador Sir Neville Henderson to instruct the English team to give the Nazi salute. With English Football Association Secretary Stanley Rous's support, the English players performed the Nazi raised arm salute to the German national anthem, as Nazi leaders Goebbels, Göring, Hess and von Ribbentrop watched with satisfaction. This ill-advised salute to Nazi power took place just 16 months before England and Nazi Germany went to war. Stanley Rous later became the President of FIFA from 1961 to 1974.

[10] FIFA document from 10 August 1936 in French denies any knowledge of spectator nationality: *"LE JURY D'APPEL DE LA F.I.F.A."*

In the 90th minute the referee called a phantom penalty foul against the Peruvians. It was unbelievable that the game would be decided in such an unfair manner, but Valdivieso was ready; he had saved six penalty kicks on a recent trip to Chile. The Austrian penalty taker tried to put the ball in the left corner, but "El Mago" dived and turned the ball around the post before it could enter the net.

A 30-minute extra time period loomed. The Austrians breathed oxygen from high-tech tanks during the interim, while the Peruvians took in the natural Berlin air and waited confidently for their chance to win. As overtime started, the Austrians knew their skill was overmatched and fell back in a defensive formation. Three times the Peruvians scored; first Magallanes, then Alcalde and Villanueva, but all their goals were annulled by the referee's dubious offside rulings. Villanueva called out to his teammates not to worry, that they had the Austrians where they wanted them, and the referee could not nullify all their goals.

In the 114th minute Peru could not be denied as Villanueva broke the tie with a goal off a cross that had no chance of being ruled offside. Peruvians listening at home by way of a Berlin-London-Lima radio connection exploded in joy. Peru did not cease attacking, and in the 119th minute Fernández put a ferocious shot past a ten-man Austrian wall for the final score of 4-2, resulting in more rapture in Lima as the news arrived.[11]

Jules Rimet reportedly came into the Peruvian dressing room afterwards and shook hands with Jordan and Fernández, saying "Congratulations. You won like lions."[12] Peru had won against all odds, and had earned the right to go into the semi-finals against Poland. The winner of that match would play in the final against Italy.

FIFA Dishonors Peru and the Beautiful Game

Peru would never play Poland. Hitler and Goebbels could not let Austria lose, even after the Austrians had been more than fairly beaten by Peru. The Nazis were already planning to annex Austria and viewed the Austrian soccer team as a natural extension of the German *Ubermensch* ("superior-man").[13]

Within 48 hours FIFA, which was coordinating the soccer tournament for the International Olympic Committee (IOC), announced that the game had to be replayed in an empty stadium. The Austrians had cried foul after they had lost, claiming their concentration had been broken after the second Peruvian goal when a fan had come onto the pitch. FIFA declared a replay despite: (1) the Nazi soldiers were negligent of their duty in preventing a pitch invasion, (2) the game was played in an overwhelmingly negative atmosphere for the Peruvians, (3) the refereeing was shameful in advantage for the Austrians, (4) the Austrians had multiple chances with a phantom penalty foul, extra-time, and three goals against them called back, and (5) the invading fans were never identified. Further, (6) it is against sports protocol that a *visiting team* (which Peru effectively was) would ever be penalized for any pitch invasion. It is always the responsibility of the hosts for crowd control.

As a final point, how many Peruvian fans could have possibly made the long ocean crossing, made their way to the game, and forced their way onto the pitch at the same time in 1936? Another possibility never investigated was that if the Austrian team was in danger

---

[11] FIFA Peru-Austria Match Report from 8 August 1936 in German, documenting Peru's 4:2 win: "*Ergebnisliste für Spiele: Peru gegen Österreich; Sieger - Peru. 2. Verlängerung 4:2.*"
[12] Rimet was the active President of FIFA from 1921 to 1954 (from 48 to 81 years of age), and had the first World Cup trophy named after him (The Jules Rimet Trophy).
[13] Nazi Germany annexed Austria in March 1938 shortly before the 1938 World Cup in France, and the "ex-Austrians" were forced to play under Germany's Nazi banner. Austria's best player Matias Sindelar (called "The Man of Paper" for his slimness and silky moves) was distraught at the turn of events, and begged off from playing in the 1938 World Cup for Germany. However, Sindelar led an "Ostmark" team of ex-Austrians to a famous 2-0 win over the occupying Germans on 3 April 1938 in a game purporting to celebrate the "Anschluss." Sindelar died from carbon monoxide poisoning (it was suspected but not proven to be a suicide) in January 1939, one month before his 36th birthday. Legendary Austrian coach Hugo Meisl, a Jew, died in 1937 before the annexation, but this did not prevent the Nazis from prominently desecrating his gravesite.

against Peru, disguised Nazi soldiers would stage a pitch invasion in a planned strategy to force a replay.

The Peruvian players discussed the unjust situation amongst themselves. All the players said since they had come so far, they would have to play and beat Austria again. Thorndike quotes Valdivieso on that fateful day as saying "*Jugamos? Sí, por supuesto que sí. Hemos llegado tan lejos. No será para volver sin medallas.*" [Do we play? Yes, of course yes. We have come so far. It won't do to return without medals.]

But the Peruvian Olympic delegation led by Claudio Martinez was at full alarm. Peru had already beaten Austria fairly, but FIFA was now ordering them to play the game over in a vacant stadium with only Nazi soldiers as witnesses. Additionally, the referees and linemen nominated for the repeat game were all from fascist-ruled Italy. The match setup would not only remove all spectator testimony and objective judges of fairness, but would include a refereeing team from the country that would be the winner's opponent for the title.

At the same time, Norwegian referee Kristiansen (the referee of the Peru-Austria match) finally acknowledged that the Peruvians had won fair and square and there was no need for a replay. Even German newspapers indicated that the 4-2 Peru-Austria result was a fair outcome. But FIFA would overrule all of these external professional judgments.

Martinez received no settlement from his protests to FIFA. The notorious Goebbels attempted to invite him to dinner, ostensibly to show him that the Nazis had nothing to do with the FIFA decision. When the FIFA decision appeared final, Martinez sent an elegant letter refuting each point of the FIFA complaint.[14]

The Peru contingent refused a replay after concluding that the new match was a setup, which the "Aryan" Austrians were predetermined to win at any cost. FIFA then informed Peru that they would forfeit to Austria if they did not show up for the game. After consultation with Peruvian President Oscar Benavides' administration in Lima, the Peru Olympic Committee decided that in protest of the total absence of basic sportsmanship and fairness (of what was supposed to be the most sporting of competitions – the Olympics), Peru *would immediately withdraw all its athletes in all Olympic sports*. Martinez also announced that Peru would retire from FIFA.

Even though they did not field soccer teams in the 1936 Games, other Latin American nations were incensed by the manipulation of the soccer tournament. The delegations of Mexico, Argentina, Uruguay and Chile, with the support of their governments, offered to join a general boycott and withdraw from the Games. Goebbels was panicking now, for that would place a bigger stain on the Games that the Nazis fervently wanted to avoid. The proud Peru delegation advised the other countries to remain in the Games; Peru would remonstrate alone. Peru then withdrew their athletes and prepared to leave. On the trip home, they heard a report in Paris that Colombia had also withdrawn from FIFA in protest of the fiasco. In September 1936, after a long sea voyage, the Peru Olympic squad arrived home to massive support from their aggrieved nation.

In a street poll done in 2003 by the author, all Peruvians who were familiar with the events at the 1936 Olympics offered that the annulment of the Peru win over Austria was the consequence of racism. Racist ideology was an underlying tenet of Nazi Germany and to fascism in general; this 1936 Olympics event demonstrates that the fascists were successful in putting their ideology into practice, even before firing a shot in World War II.

---

[14] Martinez's letter (in Spanish) from the Comite Olimpico Peruano on 11 August 1936 to FIFA Presidente Senor (sic) Jules Rimet was in response to two FIFA documents. The first was a press release (in German): *Olympisches Fussballturnier Pressestelle: Oesterreich/Peru wird wiederholt* ("Austria/Peru will be replayed"). This document has no date but was presumably released on 10 August 1936 – it also incorrectly states the final score was 5:4 for Peru. The second document was a hastily written letter (in French) from FIFA to the *Monsieur le Président de la Federacion Peruana de Football*; dated 9 August 1936 and signed only "President." The Peru delegation may have received this letter later on 10 August 1936.

The Impact of the FIFA-IOC Decision

The above events showed that soccer is more than a simple game with little impact on the greater society. On the contrary, soccer is an integral and dynamic part of society, culture and even politics. As the world's most popular sport, soccer affects society more than any other sport (examining a good history of the game such as Bill Murray's *The World's Game* or Paul Gardner's *The Simplest Game* will prove this contention). In the aftermath of the events detailed above, the Peru-Austria Olympic fiasco may have changed world history, and most certainly for the worse.

How could history have been changed? Peru had their greatest team at that time, equal to the best European national teams. Against tremendous odds and pressure, they had fairly beaten the "Wunderteam" Austrians, whose land and people the Nazis coveted. Peru had a superb leader, innovator and true "number 10" in Villanueva, an unstoppable goal scorer in Fernández, and a top goalkeeper in Valdivieso. The rest of the team was unshakable. It is very probable that Peru would have first beaten Poland, and then had an excellent chance to beat Italy in the Final. That would have broken the "*Ubermensch*" theory that a "superior race" must win team sports based on physique, intelligence, team play and tactics, as well as disrupting the fascist hold on soccer titles.

But instead of Peru, *Austria was given a free pass* to play in the semi-finals, and easily beat Poland 3-1. Austria then lost to Italy 2-1 in a close final settled in extra time. The two fascist countries - Germany and Italy - felt satisfied that they had accomplished their goal, as both Italy and the German surrogates Austria reached the final.

The 1936 Berlin soccer tournament held the Olympic soccer attendance record until 1984, documenting its temporal societal importance (the Italy-Norway semi-final drew 95,000 spectators while the Italy-Austria final drew 85,000 spectators). And despite Jesse Owens' heroics, Nazi Germany "won" the Olympics with a medal total of 89, far above the USA's 56 medals (Italy was third with 23 medals).

Two years later, the 1938 World Cup took place in soon-to-be-invaded France, and fascist-ruled Italy triumphed again, this time against Hungary 4-2 (Italy had made the impressive Uruguayan halfback Miguel Andreolo eligible as an *oriundi* in this Cup). By that time, Germany had already annexed Austria and incorporated a "Wunderteam" player, but was subsequently eliminated by the Swiss team in a historic match still remembered in Switzerland (the first game was tied 1-1, the replay was won 4-2 by Switzerland).

The 1934 and 1938 World Cups, and the 1936 Olympics in Berlin, were all won by fascist Italy, but with Austria a finalist or semifinalist, and Nazi Germany a prominent participant. There is little doubt these results, in the world's most popular sport, served to bolster public acceptance of the superiority of fascist ideology in the Axis countries. Indeed, the Aryan dominance theory of sport remained vigorous until well after World War II, not only in fascist countries but also in the USA, which forbade "black" players to enter professional team sports.

What would have happened if Peru had won the soccer gold in the 1936 Olympics, and/or Brazil the 1938 World Cup? It was certainly possible, as both Peru and Brazil were acknowledged to have been the most attractive sides in these two tournaments held in Europe. An overconfident Brazil had left star players Leonidas and Tim off the roster against Italy "to rest them for the final," and surprisingly lost to Italy in the 1938 World Cup semi-final. That was Brazil's error, which was speculated by some to have been perpetrated by the racist influence of some members of the Brazil soccer entourage. Peru, however, failed to advance in 1936 due to sinister circumstances beyond their control.

The evolving cordiality of the Berlin crowd to the Peruvian talent, intelligence and courage in the game against Austria confirms that even the most biased aficionados appreciate quality soccer from any source. The Nazi propaganda machine would have had to work overtime to clarify the Peru victory, which could not be explained simply by "animalistic" tendencies as they disparaged Jesse Owens' incredible feats.

The philosophical stranglehold of the "superior man" would have been severely damaged, leaving the designers of that doctrine with less credibility and power in the fascist nations. Many people living in the fascist countries would have come to the realization earlier that the *Ubermensch* theory was merely a hoax perpetrated upon them by Hitler and his henchmen. The societal dynamics supporting Nazism and fascism would have been unsettled, a good thing for a world facing a "war to end all wars." If a world war could not have been averted in the face of Hitler's vain insanity, the Nazi resolve might have been vanquished earlier, thereby saving lives in many countries.

Responsibility for the Peru-Austria Fiasco

Both FIFA and the IOC are culpable for the 1936 Peru-Austria replay fiasco. FIFA ran the soccer tournament in the 1936 Olympics, made the decision to cancel the already completed Peru-Austria game, and ordered a Nazi-controlled replay. However, the Olympic Charter, Chapter 3, Rule 30:1.5 states "The role of the international federation [in this case FIFA] is to assume the responsibility for the technical control and direction of their sports at the Olympic Games *under the patronage of the IOC*" (italics author). In other words, the IOC as patron had veto power, and could have overruled the replay order by FIFA. The IOC had surely been informed of the commotion surrounding the replay decision and the threat of nations withdrawing from the Games. Therefore, the IOC also must share some of the blame for the debacle of the 1936 Olympic Games soccer tournament.

Did Nazi intimidation contribute to the bizarre FIFA-IOC replay decision? After all, FIFA President Jules Rimet had witnessed the game, and had reportedly gone into the Peruvian dressing room to enthusiastically congratulate the winners. Even the Norwegian referee denied the need for a replay, and recognized the result as legitimate. What exactly helped change Rimet's and the FIFA administration's minds to the necessity of replaying the game in an empty stadium with only Nazi guards for a crowd? Perhaps that will never be known, as Rimet died in 1955.

What is known is on May 10, 1940, Rimet's beloved France was invaded by Nazi Germany, and the resultant Nazi occupation would lead to the deaths of more than half a million French citizens. If there was a deal made, it certainly did not help the future of Rimet's own people. The decision to annul the Peru-Austria game was probably the worst judgment FIFA, Rimet and the IOC was to ever make, and likely had negative repercussions for the world at large.

Peru Soccer Postscript

The high quality of the Peruvian team in the 1936 Olympics was no fluke. Peru maintained its superlative level in 1938, as they proceeded to win the first Bolivar Games in Colombia, prevailing in all four games by scoring 18 goals and conceding only 4. The trio of Valdivieso, Villanueva and Fernández was still intact, although the first two would retire after that competition. Peru then won the Copa America (South American championship) held in Lima in 1939, where they won all four games with 13 goals scored and only four conceded. In addition to Lolo Fernández, the defenders Arturo Fernández and Raúl Chappel, the midfielders Segundo Castillo, Carlos Tovar and Orestes Jordán, and the forward Jorge Alcalde played in all three tournaments. It was a time of Peruvian soccer excellence not to be repeated until the Cubillas era in the 1970s.

The architect of Peru's soccer success, Alejandro Villanueva, had a difficult situation arise immediately after the 1936 Olympic debacle. After being away in Europe for three months, a telegram addressed to him reached the team in Paris during the team's trip home. Fortunately his friend Juan Valdivieso intercepted the telegram before he could read it, as it simply stated, "Your wife has died." Valdivieso immediately recognized the dilemma: Villanueva had an ex-wife and a current wife, but the telegram did not specify which woman had died. Valdivieso did not want Villanueva agonizing over which wife had died during the sea voyage back to Peru, so he withheld the news until they were to pull into port in Callao outside Lima. Villanueva then found out his ex-wife had died, leaving their twins (son and daughter) waiting for him. A few years later, his only son contracted tuberculosis and died. Finally, on 11 April 1944, Alejandro Villanueva succumbed to tuberculosis at the tender age of thirty-five. The Matute stadium in Lima, where his club Alianza Lima still plays, is formally named the Alejandro Villanueva Stadium.

Lolo Fernández had a long career and life, scoring goals and winning championships. His club Universitario used to play in the Lolo Fernández Stadium, but a new Monumental Stadium was constructed after he died at age 83 in 1996. The new stadium has a prominent statue of Fernández inside the front gate, and as a result, is also called the Lolo Fernández stadium.

Only two members of the 1936 Peru Olympic football team remain alive at this writing – goalkeeper Juan Valdivieso Padilla (b.06.05.10) and midfielder Carlos Tovar Venegas (b. 06.04.15). Both graciously consented to interviews at short notice in their homes.

Carlos Tovar was interviewed on 9 July 2004. Tovar played for Universitario alongside Lolo Fernández for a decade, then retired to Chancay, north of Lima. The Carlos Tovar football club still stands near his house. Tovar's gates are unmarked, but he lives in a small traditional house on about half an acre located directly on a cliff overlooking the Pacific Ocean. The view is spectacular, with a bird's eye view of the Castillo de Chancay (the Chancay castle) and the constantly maneuvering fishing boats. He was 89 years old, and bundled up with sweaters against the windy winter weather. Tovar had outlived his immediate family, surviving the deaths of his son, then his wife, and most recently his daughter, but he still has three grandsons from the marriage of his daughter and 1936 teammate Arturo Fernández' son. Tovar had lived the past decades with the caregiver family of Purificacion and Carlos Juarez.

Tovar was in a wheelchair, from which he rarely rises, his legs atrophied from arthritis. But he appeared well taken care of and quick of mind, and was more eager to discuss the topics of the day than football games of long ago. He appeared incredulous that modern players now demanded money before appearing in international games for their country, putting his fist to his chest, declaring, "We played from the heart, for pride, we would have died for our country." He brought out all his old photos from the 1930s and 1940s, but his long-term memory failed him, as he could not recall the details of Berlin from the many other games he had played in Europe. Tovar did, however, retrieve the medal awarded to the Peru football team after they arrived back in Lima. The inscription reads "*A los futbolistas peruanos campeones olympicos 1936*" ["To the Peruvian Football Players, 1936 Olympic Champions"]. Clearly, the team was viewed as champions in Peru despite the crude manner in which the Europeans had them eliminated [Figure 131].

Juan Valdivieso was interviewed on 15 January 2003 at his immaculate home in Lima. Valdivieso spent much of his life in football, coaching several teams, and eventually serving as the Peru national team coach in the 1950s. He also spent 30 years working for the municipality of Lima, much of it in sports development. Valdivieso is still revered as the greatest goalkeeper of his club Alianza Lima, and of the nation of Peru. On 15 February 2001, at the age of ninety, Valdivieso received an ovation in the Alejandro Villanueva Stadium (popularly known as "Matute") in Lima, having been invited as a special guest to the centenary celebration of his old club, Alianza Lima (see Chapter 12).

Although Valdivieso walked with a cane, his mind was sharp and he remained the perfect gentleman at ninety-two years of age. When asked about his recollections of the 1936 Olympics, he initially replied sadly, "I don't remember much, it was so long ago." But then he brightened and gave more than an hour of his recollections of his career. On the annulment of the Peru win over Austria, he said, "there was no way they would let a European team be beaten." This was Valdivieso's gentle way of saying that xenophobia buried his countrymen's dream and quest for Olympic gold and glory.

The interview revealed the 1936 Olympics was still painful for Valdivieso to recall, because once that kind of opportunity is stolen away, the chance has been lost forever. After all, *how many opportunities does one have to slay a dragon*? The dragon in this case was not only Austria and Italy, but also the festering fascist and racist ideals of the time. By Peru losing their chance to show their magic and power in the semi-finals and finals, the world lost the chance to see the ingenuity of human diversity triumph in sport's most popular game. The world would have to wait until well after the Second World War's destruction to witness that phenomenon, when Brazil conquered all in the 1958 World Cup in Sweden.

FIFA 1936 documents of the Peru-Austria match

In communications to the IOC in 2001, their representative acknowledged IOC's oversight responsibilities of all FIFA actions in the 1936 Olympics soccer tournament, but claimed no documentation of the Peru-Austria game in 1936 was available. Further inquiries to FIFA over the next year (2002-2003), including a hand-delivered request to FIFA headquarters in Zurich, brought some relevant documents – excepting the minutes of the FIFA committee meeting that determined that the Peru-Austria game should be replayed. FIFA provided no information as to the persons present at that meeting, nor the vote given for the replay. The author repeatedly requested but never received these critical documents.

FIFA-IOC Disgrace

There are many parts of the official FIFA story that make little sense. FIFA records document that earlier in the 1936 tournament, the Italian players were totally out of control in the Italy-USA game:

> In Italy's 1-0 victory over the United States, for instance, two American players were injured when the referee ordered Achille Piccini off the field. The player refused. Several *teammates surrounded the official and covered his mouth with their hands* Piccini, for some reason, remained in the game [italics author].[15]

This FIFA history report documents that the Italians were able to intimidate and actually attack the referee during the game, and yet suffer *no disciplinary consequences by FIFA or the IOC*. The proper response by FIFA would have been to dismiss the Italian team from the tournament for team intimidation and assaulting the referee. *Yet Peru was sanctioned for inconsequential actions that FIFA acknowledges that the Peru team did not execute and had no part of.*

In addition, FIFA's official explanation of annulling the Peru-Austria game is inaccurate:

> Peru rallied from a two-goal deficit in the final 15 minutes of normal time. During extra-time, Peruvian fans ran onto the field and attacked an Austrian player. *In the chaos*, Peru scored twice and won, 4-2. Or so the South Americans thought Austria protested and the International Olympic Committee ordered a replay without any spectators. Peru refused and their entire Olympic squad left in protest as did Colombia [italics author].[16]

This explanation makes no sense, as this official FIFA rendition contains several inaccuracies:

---

[15] FIFA soccer history: http://www.fifa.com/en/comp/olympicsmen/0,2482,114-OLY-1936,00.htmlwww.fifa.com.
[16] Ibid.

(1) FIFA lays the blame of rescheduling on the IOC, but this is impossible as FIFA was running the tournament, and documents reveal that it was a FIFA committee that ruled a replay.
(2) Scoring twice *in the chaos* is a ludicrous statement. FIFA makes it sound like a riot was going on the field during play favoring the Peruvians, when clearly it was Peru who was subjected to an "away" crowd. Peru scored fair and square on the same field as the Austrians.
(3) FIFA says the incident occurred in overtime, rather than regular time.
(4) The alleged incident was the action of spectators and not players, which FIFA claims were Peruvians without any proof (because there was none). In the Decision of FIFA's own Appeals Court from August 10, 1936 – signed by Jules Rimet himself – FIFA admits they did not know the identity of the spectators.[17]
(5) Colombia did not even bring a soccer squad for the competition, but temporarily resigned from FIFA. None of their Olympic squad left in protest, although they had offered to do so in solidarity with the Peruvians.

How was it possible that Italian players were not punished for personally attacking the referee themselves, yet Peru was punished to the point of annulling a fairly played victory for actions not even taken by their players? The only plausible explanation for the unjust and unsportsmanlike ruling was xenophobic and racist conduct by FIFA and the IOC against the Peruvians. The actions were likely influenced by fascist Nazi and Italian bias, and/or intimidation of those making the replay decision. The documents FIFA has provided offer no other credible explanation of the events.

The IFFHS is the only international soccer organization to condemn the 1936 Olympic soccer tournament, stating "after two victories, Peru's Olympic debut ended with a miscarriage of sports justice by part of the IOC and FIFA. The loser was definitely Olympic football."

Other sources have added to the confusion over the years, still attempting to insinuate that the Peru team was somehow responsible for the annulment. In a book about the Olympics, it was reported "Italy won the soccer after Peru had been disqualified for refusing to replay a match they had won against Austria *when it was discovered they had illegally used a substitute.*"[18] This explanation is also false as (1) neither IOC nor FIFA presented this argument as a reason for a replay, (2) a game with an ineligible player would result in an outright forfeit, and (3) soccer matches did not even allow substitutes until 1970.

FIFA is obviously ambivalent about their actions taken against Peru in the 1936 Olympics. On FIFA's website, Peru's record was placed at 2-0-0, with 11 goals scored and 5 conceded for the tournament. If the Peru-Austria result was ruled as illegitimate, why is Peru recorded as having won two games? And if they "won" the game against Austria, why play again? According to FIFA's bizarre ruling, the second game should be labeled cancelled, and the Peru record set back to 1-0. Also, Lolo Fernández does not figure into their published list of high scorers of the games, which includes all who had more than five goals. Fernández' first five goals against Finland would justify his place on the list. Contrast this treatment with the IFFHS's meticulous documentation, which credits both Peru games and lists Fernández with six goals, and Villanueva with four.

This event, occurring just prior to World War II, was one of the darkest hours of international football – one of profound dishonor to the game itself and of disgraceful racism to the Peruvian team (and by extension, all of South America and the non-Western world). Further Peruvian soccer success at the 1936 Games could have brought critical awareness to the German people; a decent sensibility the Nazis had so successfully stifled. A sensibility

---

[17] This FIFA letter in French states: "Que notamment il a été impossible d'empêcher des spectateurs d'entrer dans le terrain de jeu et que particulièrement l'un d'eux, après avoir pénétré sur le terrain a pu porter un coup à un joueur."
[18] Arnold, Peter. *Olympic Games.* 1983. Optimum Books, London.

embracing the notion that people halfway around the world can play a beautiful organized sport as well or better than they, and who are not automatically their enemy. This vital lesson of tolerance of others "who do not look like carbon copies of us" – could only have helped human history.

Postscript: Nazi Attempt to Control the IOC After 1936

Hitler was extremely pleased with the platform and propaganda boost that the 1936 Olympics had given the Third Reich. German filmmaker Leni Riefenstahl made her *art nouveau* film "Olympia" about the 1936 Olympics, which satisfied the propaganda requirements of the Nazis.

Hitler rapidly commissioned Albert Speer to design a stadium at Nuremberg, which was planned to have a *crowd capacity of 400,000 and would house the Olympics for all time*. The Nazis effectively planned on annexing the Olympics permanently to Germany, presumably by operating through their control of IOC members.

The 1940 Olympics had originally been awarded to Sapporo, in Japan, but was later changed to St. Moritz, in Switzerland. Japanese and Swiss withdrawals on the eve of World War II gave the Nazis a chance to commence with their dream of permanent Olympic host. In June 1939, the IOC awarded the 1940 Winter Olympics to Nazi Germany, to be held in Garmisch-Partenkirchen as they were four years before. The IOC voted unanimously to return the Olympics to Germany "in the interests of sport and the Olympic movement," and claimed to have made the decision "regardless of political considerations."

In November 1939, however, the Nazis withdrew from hosting the Games in order to concentrate on more urgent matters. It was two months after Germany had invaded Poland (on September 1, 1939), and initiated World War II.[19] As a result, the 1940 Games were never held.

---

[19] United States Holocaust Memorial Museum (www.ushmm.org/museum/exhibit/online/olympics/zcd073.htm) has a picture of the Olympic and Nazi flags flying together in a poster for the 1940 Nazi Germany Winter games that were never held.

Soccer Future

Chapter Fourteen

Soccer: The USA Way

'What matters is the skill level of the player, which doesn't come from organized soccer. It comes from a love affair with the ball and playing games with and against players of all ages.'

'The coach is really a substitute voice. We want the players to hear the silent voice, the game. The game is actually talking to you.'

Manny Schellscheidt[1]

USA soccer development has followed an uneven course. Although the USA was one of the earliest countries to receive soccer in the 1860s it was eminently peculiar in not adopting it as a dominant sport, in large part because the USA developed multiple competing indigenous sports that continue to dominate the professional sport landscape. Because the USA remains the largest world market that soccer has yet to conquer, it will likely play a significant role in the future of soccer.

Soccer's Early Travels from England to Boston and New Jersey

The USA was the first country outside of England to organize a soccer team, the Boston *Oneida Football Club* in 1862. The Oneida club was named after a Native American tribe that was part of the Six-Nation Iroquois Confederation,[2] and drew student members from upper-class secondary schools in Boston (primarily the Dixwell Latin School). A famous *Oneida* match took place on November 7, 1863 against students of the Boston Latin and Boston English schools, and the vulcanized rubber ball used in that game is still preserved at the Soccer National Hall of Fame in Oneonta, New York.[3] The *Oneida* club took on all challengers for four years, and *won every match by a shutout* on the fields of the Boston Common.

---

[1] Manny Schellscheidt led SC Elizabeth to US Open Cup wins in 1970 and 1972, and several professional soccer teams to titles in the NASL and ASL. He subsequently coached all levels in the USA, including youth, university, and professional, and the USA Olympic and national teams. He was granted the first ever "A" coaching license by the USSF, and is an esteemed member of the USA Soccer Hall of Fame.

[2] The Six-Nation Iroquois Confederation (the native name is "Haudenosaunee," meaning "People Building a Longhouse") was made up of the Cayuga, Mohawk, Oneida, Onondaga, Seneca, and Tuscarora indigenous American nations, and is one of the oldest continual participatory democracies in human history. The Confederation is also credited by some historians as influencing the structure of the nascent USA government.

[3] Charles Goodyear patented vulcanized rubber in 1836, and "footballs" (soccer balls) made of several rubber panels glued together first appeared in 1855. The first basketball game organized by basketball inventor Dr. James Naismith on December 21, 1891 was also played with a soccer ball of this type; the score of that first basketball game was a "soccer-like" 1-0.

Perhaps bored by their excellence, the *Oneidas* mysteriously disappeared from the horizon after only four years. The exact rules under which they competed are lost, and some have questioned whether it was real soccer (as supported by the 1863 London Rules) or a revised version of the 1848 Cambridge Rules that had merely separated the "dribbling game" from the "handling game." Indeed, the match the Oneidas played against Boston Latin and Boston English was a scant thirteen days after the Laws of Football were codified across the Atlantic Ocean in London on October 25, 1863, so it would have been impossible for the first Oneida games to have used those modified rules. But it is possible that the Oneidas received the London rules by 1864, and subsequently adopted the new rules for their games.

Seven surviving members of the team erected a monument on Boston Common in 1925 commemorating the existence of their historic club [Figure 14A]. The Oneida Football monument reads: "ON THIS FIELD THE ONEIDA FOOTBALL CLUB OF BOSTON THE FIRST ORGANIZED FOOTBALL CLUB IN THE UNITED STATES PLAYED AGAINST ALL COMERS FROM 1862 TO 1865. THE ONEIDA GOAL WAS NEVER CROSSED."[4]

By the 1870s soccer had infiltrated the northeastern universities, with the first university match played between New Jersey colleges Rutgers and Princeton on November 6, 1869 in New Brunswick, New Jersey. The game was played using the 1863 London Rules that are the foundation of modern soccer, although both teams employed 25 men (see Chapter 1 for further details).

In 1873, the Rutgers, Princeton, Columbia, and Yale universities formed the Intercollegiate Football Association in order to standardize university soccer rules, and by 1880, the USA universities had agreed on an eleven versus eleven-man soccer format.[5] Shortly thereafter, university soccer was nearly forgotten by the meteoric rise of the indigenous USA-football, and USA soccer was forced to hibernate in immigrant enclaves for much of the next century until the breakout of youth soccer in the 1960s.

Soccer Name Games in the USA

Soccer was generally labeled "football" in the USA until well after 1900. In the early 1900s, the USA had two competing soccer associations, the American Amateur Football Association (AAFA) and the American Football Association (AFA). However, as a condition for USA entrance into FIFA in 1913, FIFA insisted on enforcing the rule that each country has only one controlling Football Association. The AAFA then forced a merger with the AFA, changed its name to the United States Football Association (USFA), and was admitted to FIFA in 1914. "Soccer" terminology was finally introduced only in 1945, when the USFA became the United States Soccer Football Federation (USSFF). In 1974, the USSFF finally eliminated "football" and became the United States Soccer Federation (USSF).[6]

In contrast, some of the leagues in the USA used the "soccer" terminology by the early 20th century, including the professional *American Soccer League* from 1921-1933. However, the *German-American Soccer League* (GASL) only used their soccer name for four years (1923-1927), and then changed their official name to the *German American Football*

---

[4] Below the inscription on the monument front is printed "This monument is placed on the Boston Common November 1925 by the seven surviving members of the Team." The reverse of the monument documents the original "MEMBERS OF THE ONEIDA TEAM," which are listed top to bottom as: GERRIT SMITH MILLER Founder and Captain, EDWARD LINCOLN ARNOLD, ROBERT APTHORP BOIT, EDWARD BOWDITCH, WALTER DENISON BROOKS, GEORGE DAVIS, JOHN MALCOLM FORBES, JOHN POWER HALL, ROBERT MEANS LAWRENCE, JAMES D'WOLF LOVETT, FRANCIS GREENWOOD PEABODY, WINTHROP SALTONSTALL SCUDDER, ALANSON TUCKER, LOUIS THIES, ROBERT CLIFFORD WATSON, HUNTINGTON FROTHINGHAM WOLCOTT.

[5] Note the use of "football" in the early formation of USA soccer associations. The word "soccer" was not invented until around 1886, presumably by Oxford student Charles Wreford Brown – who later captained the English national team on two separate occasions.

[6] The USSF is also called US Soccer, with website at www.ussoccer.com.

Association (GAFA) for the next fifty years, until a further change to the *Cosmopolitan League* in 1977.

Modern professional soccer leagues in the USA such as the NASL (*North American Soccer League* operated from 1967-1984), and the MLS (*Major League Soccer* operating from 1996 to the present) have always used "soccer" in their titles.

Ethnic and Working Class Contributions to USA Soccer Development

Industries hiring large numbers of working-class immigrants in the late 1800s and early 1900s - especially in Missouri, Massachusetts and Pennsylvania - took a particular interest in promoting soccer and invested money in their factory teams. A read-through of the US Open champions (the USA championship that is incredibly the oldest continually operating soccer tournament in the world) from the first part of the 20th century reveals such industrial representatives as Bethlehem Steel, St. Louis Scullins Steel and St. Louis Central Breweries; the runner-up in 1928 and 1931 had the incredible moniker of the Chicago Bricklayers.

Clubs formed by one or more ethnic group also kept the soccer dream alive, often supplementing their fanaticism with soccer news and players from the "old country" (meaning practically anywhere in Europe or the Americas). The first of these "ethnic teams" to win the US Open Cup was New York Hakoah in 1929, a team made up of Jewish immigrants, many of who had played in Europe. They were followed by Philadelphia German-American in 1936, Brooklyn Hispano in 1943, Fall River Ponta Delgada (1947), New York German-Hungarian (1951), SC Eintracht (1955), Philadelphia Ukrainian Nationals (1960-61, 1963, 1966), New York Hungaria (1962), New York Ukrainians (1965), New York Greek-Americans (1967-69, 1974), SC Elizabeth (1970, 1972 – see Chapter 18), New York Hota Bavarians (1971), Los Angeles Maccabee (1973, 1975, 1977-78, 1981), New York Pancyprian Freedoms (1980, 1982-83), New York AO Krete (1984), San Francisco Greek-Americans (1985, 1994), Washington Club España (1987), Brooklyn Italians (1991), and San Francisco CD México (1993).

Even the modern NASL league had a team with a prominent ethnic emphasis – the Toronto Metro-Croatians – for which Eusébio (see Chapter 7) led to the NASL title in 1976. However, no USA professional soccer league enrolled a team that carried an ethnic reference after 1978.

USA Soccer from 1930-1990

The USA men's soccer team was initially very successful in international play, as they participated in three of the first four World Cups (1930 Uruguay, 1934 Italy and the 1950 Brazil World Cups). USA striker Bert Patenaude was the first player to score three goals (a "hat trick") in a World Cup game, as the USA advanced to the semi-finals in 1930.[7] Moreover, in 1934, eventual champions and host Italy narrowly beat the USA 1-0.

It is ironic that the only Olympic Games since 1900 that failed to host a soccer tournament was the 1932 Olympics held in Los Angeles. The reason for the 1932 omission was ostensibly a disagreement over the concept of amateur and professional soccer credentials. Although the USA has qualified for and competed in twelve of the twenty-three Olympic soccer tournaments held so far, it has never earned a soccer medal.[8] The best USA finish was fourth in 2000, but they did not qualify for the 2004 tournament.

---

[7] Patenaude was long denied this accomplishment, as his second goal was often ruled an own-goal or instead scored by USA captain Tom Florie. Guillermo Stábile of Argentina was previously credited with the first World Cup hat trick, scoring three goals two days later in the 1930 tournament. FIFA has finally acknowledged that Patenaude scored the first World Cup hat trick.

[8] Twenty-three of the twenty-five Olympic Games held from 1896-2004 hosted a soccer tournament (1900-1928, 1936-2004), with no Games in 1916 due to World War I, none in 1932 because of a amateur-professional definition conflict, and none in 1940 and 1944 due to World War II).

However, in 1950, the USA enjoyed the most unexpected result ever in the World Cup; beating heavily favored England 1-0 in Brazil.[9] The scorer of the goal was Joe Gaetjens, a Haitian who later returned to his native country and disappeared during the dictatorship of Papa Doc Duvalier (he is assumed to have been killed by Duvalier's personal terrorist squad, the Tonton Macoute).

Thereafter followed a forty-year hiatus in World Cup appearances from 1950-1990, in which the USA failed to qualify for nine consecutive World Cups. Those decades encompassed the expansion of the professional baseball, basketball, USA-football and ice hockey leagues, as the USA populace was seduced by the four native North American sports and neglected soccer. However, during those four decades a series of professional soccer leagues were formed, culminating in the ambitious NASL that existed for eighteen years (1967-1984, see Chapter 18).

USA Back in the World Cup After 40 Years
1990 Italy World Cup

On 19 November 1989, Paul Caliguiri scored a spectacular 30-yard goal in a 1-0 away win over Trinidad and Tobago, thereby enabling the USA to qualify for the 1990 World Cup Finals. Of note, the CONACAF group was not very competitive that year because powerhouse Mexico had already been suspended from the competition for using over-age players in a youth tournament.

However, the USA re-entry into World Cup soccer was ultimately bittersweet as the team lost all three games, scoring only two goals while allowing eight. The lone bright spot was holding host soccer power Italy to a 1-0 score, thanks to a well-organized defense.

Still, watching that USA-Italy game on USA television was excruciating for a genuine soccer fan. Television commercials frequently interrupted the broadcast making a travesty of soccer as a free-flowing sport; the Italian goal came during such one such interruption. The commentators made continual irrelevant references to other sports as play was continuing, as if those inane references would somehow enlighten viewers as to the intricacies of the soccer match. Soccer "analogies" were made to basketball ("floppy basketball socks"), USA-football (the "pressure of a field goal kick"), and baseball ("popped up behind second base"). Each time a player penetrated into the penalty area, the commentators speculated as to whether he would "pull-the-trigger" (to "shoot the ball") – a mindless gun-fighting reference. The level of "dumbed-down" analysis made a mockery of intelligent commentary, which experienced fans expected and new spectators required.

1994 USA World Cup

Watching the 1994 World Cup Finals hosted by the USA was an easier task, because during the English-language channel commercials there was the option of immediately switching to the Spanish-language Univision channel. The Univision broadcast was without commercial breaks and had sophisticated commentary by Andres Cantor (famous for his long *Goooool!* calls and book by the same name – see Chapter 17). In actual fact the best option was to watch the games exclusively on Univision, thereby escaping the tedious chatter and commercials on the other channel. The USA advanced to the second stage in the 1994 Cup only to gallantly succumb to eventual champion Brazil 1-0.

The 1994 World Cup was hailed to be an unqualified financial success, especially by people like World Cup Organizing Committee's Chairman and Chief Executive Officer Alan Rothenberg – who pocketed a cool $7 million after the event. Rothenberg had shrewdly declined a $350,000 per year salary for four years, and in opting for a bonus made a net increase of $5.6 million over the four years. Journalist Hank Hersh described Rothenberg's bonus as an "unconscionable" amount of personal renumeration for purporting to work in a

---

[9] This result was such a surprising upset that when the news was cabled to England, the press initially assumed that it was a typographical error and that England had really won 10-0.

voluntary capacity for a (supposedly) non-profit organization.[10] Rothenberg took the $7 million despite the fact that thousands of 1994 World Cup volunteers *were paid nothing*, and that that US Soccer could have sorely used that money for youth soccer development in urban areas.

1998 France World Cup

The USA men's national soccer team earned some good results between the 1994 and 1998 World Cups, particularly a 3-0 win over Argentina in the 1995 Copa America in Uruguay, and a 1-0 win over Brazil in the 1998 Gold Cup. But while the USA played up to their potential in the 1994 World Cup, the team imploded from the misguided machinations of coach Steve Sampson in the 1998 Cup. Shortly before the World Cup, Sampson dismissed captain John Harkes from the team for a minor infraction, thereby disrupting team morale. Additionally, the entire defense was overhauled at the last minute, as stalwart defenders Alexi Lalas and Jeff Agoos did not play at all, and Marcelo Balboa was allotted only eight minutes in the last game. Sampson's psychological and personnel changes were a complete failure, and embarrassed the country at a time that an improved performance was needed to impress the USA soccer audience.[11]

After the 1998 debacle the USSF procrastinated before hiring Bruce Arena, the obvious choice to replace Sampson. Arena had compiled an impressive record of five university championships at the University of Virginia, and had won the first two MLS championships with the D.C. United club in the new MLS league. Arena had worked successfully with many international players on the D.C. United MLS championship teams, most notably star Bolivian midfielder Marco Etcheverry. Arena's knowledge, flexibility, and leadership in guiding the USA to the World Cup quarterfinals in 2002 revealed his quality, and fortunately for the USA he was contracted to coach the national team through the 2006 World Cup.

2002 Japan – Korea Republic World Cup

The USA gave an excellent performance at the 2002 World Cup, exiting only after a close quarterfinal loss to eventual Finalist Germany [See Chapter 9 and Figure 14B].

2006 World Cup and Beyond

The USA has the potential to really shine in the 2006 and 2010 World Cups, when players such as Landon Donovan, DaMarcus Beasley, and Ed Johnson could be peaking at the same time. Donovan in particular has shown signs of being the USA's first world-class "number 10," a creative midfielder who can score.[12] All of these players would benefit from more international seasoning; by 2005 Beasley had played for PSV Eindhoven in the European Champions League semi-finals but Donovan had returned from Germany's Bayer Leverkusen to the MLS Los Angeles Galaxy. Donovan's creative playing style is likely more compatible with the Spanish First Division than the Bundesliga.

The USA has another potential star in Freddy Adu, who played in the 2005 U-20 World Cup just after turning 16 years old (he skipped over the 2005 U-17 World Cup hosted by Peru). Adu emigrated from Ghana at eight years old, and began to play professionally in the MLS at the astonishing age of 15. Adu will be just 17 years and one week old on June 9, 2006 when the 2006 World Cup begins, and if he plays he would be more than seven months younger than Pelé was when he took the Sweden 1958 World Cup by storm [see Chapter 10].

---

[10] Sugden, John and Tomlinson, Alan. *FIFA and the Contest for World Football: Who Rules the Peoples' Game?* Polity Press, Cambridge. 1998.
[11] An incisive parody of the self-inflicted 1998 USA World Cup failure is in the inaugural July 1998 issue of the online magazine ThreeSixOne at www.kenn.com/361/. Also, John Harkes' book, *John Harkes: Captain for Life and Other Temporary Assignments* (1999, Sleeping Bear Press, Michigan) is basic reading for anybody who wants to understand USA soccer in the 1990s.
[12] Midfielders Ricky Davis, Tab Ramos, and Claudio Reyna were all excellent number 10s, but Donovan has the potential to surpass their feats.

USA Men's Soccer Team Achievements

Despite the USA public's lack of knowledge of the national men's soccer team's performance, the team has had identifiable international success over recent years. The following list documents their increasing accomplishments, culminating in their fifth consecutive World Cup appearance in 2006.

Like many countries the USA has a history of narrowly losing to top team Brazil; a notable exception was their 1-0 win in the 1998 CONCACAF Gold Cup.

1930 FIFA World Cup semi-finalist; fourth place.
1950 Beat England 1-0 in the biggest World Cup upset ever.
1990 FIFA World Cup appearance, exited after the 1st Round.
1991 CONCACAF Gold Cup champions.
1992 US Cup champions.
1993 CONCACAF Gold Cup runners-up.
1994 FIFA World Cup appearance, exited after the 2nd round (lost to Brazil 1-0).
1995 Copa America semi-finalist, fourth place.
1996 CONCACAF Gold Cup; third place (lost to Brazil 1-0).
1998 CONCACAF Gold Cup runners-up (USA beat Brazil 1-0 in semi-final).
1998 FIFA World Cup, exited after the 1st round.
2000 US Cup champions.
2002 CONCACAF Gold Cup champions.
2002 FIFA World Cup, exited after the quarterfinals.
2003 CONCACAF Gold Cup; third place (lost to Brazil 2-1 in overtime in semi-final).
2005 CONCACAF Gold Cup champions.
2006 Fifth consecutive FIFA World Cup appearance – Ranked 4th in world (April 2006)

USA Men's Youth Teams: Biggest Success To Date

The Under-17 (U-17) Youth team has so far been the most successful USA men's national team. Similar to Brazil being the only country to participate in all seventeen Men's World Cups, *the USA is surprisingly the only country to have participated in all eleven U-17 Youth Cups*. Most recently the USA participated in the 2005 U-17 World Cup in Peru, where they topped their group but yielded to the Netherlands in the quarterfinals 0-2 [Figure 14C].

The USA took fourth place in the 1999 U-17 Cup, the USA's highest finish in any male World Soccer championship since 1930. Landon Donovan was voted the MVP of that tournament, an unprecedented honor for a USA soccer player.

The 2001 U-20 World Cup USA team featured striker-midfielders Landon Donovan, DaMarcus Beasley, and Bobby Convey, but they were not able to elevate the USA into the 3rd round. The 2005 USA U-20 World Cup team started with great promise as they finished top of their group, beating favorites Argentina and tying Germany. However, they exited in first elimination game, losing to Italy 1-3.

The Under-23 World Soccer Championships have been supplanted by the U-23 format at the Olympic games (the Olympics allow three over-age players on each team). Despite the Olympics' original amateur intent, virtually all players in modern Olympic soccer tournaments are already professionals. The USA's best Olympic and U-23 showing was in 2000, when they advanced to the semi-finals only to be beaten by eventual silver medalist Spain 3-1 (the USA finished in fourth place). The USA did not travel to the 2004 Olympics in Greece, as Mexico and Costa Rica qualified from the CONCACAF group.

Impediments to USA Soccer Development
Other Sport Competition and the Reluctant Development of USA Soccer

More children play soccer in the United States than any other sport except basketball. Although the sport battle appears to have been won with children, soccer needs to make further gains in the adolescent, adult, and professional spheres before soccer is taken seriously in the USA sports world.

The USA is the only country in the world with many competing indigenous professional sports. Basketball, baseball, and USA-football all have wealthy professional leagues that declare they have no serious competition worldwide, although there are many other quality national baseball and basketball leagues elsewhere. Since these sports were locally developed, the USA populace naturally wants to believe they must play them better than anybody else. USA Major League Baseball (MLB) calls their champions "World Champions," although potentially equivalent teams from Japan and Cuba are not invited to compete.[13] What better way to be a "world champion" if serious international competition is not confronted?

To combat that elitist attitude, sports globalization has finally arrived for the USA Big Four sports in the form of the immigrant athlete. Because athletes from all over Europe, Asia, Africa and the Americas now compete in the USA professional sports leagues, the days of knee-jerk USA sports nationalism may be waning.[14]

However, three of the Big Four USA sports have experienced the following significant negative events in 2005, and soccer may therefore have a chance to capitalize on the evolving sport preferences of the USA adolescent population.

- The 2005 steroid scandal of MLB threatens to destroy much of baseball's recent history, as the glamour players who established recent home run and other records are suspected of steroid and other medication abuse.
- The NBA basketball league experienced an increased on-court violence level in 2004-5 that alienated fans and media alike.
- The NHL hockey league cancelled their entire 2004-2005 season, and will likely take years before it regains lost ground after abandoning the season.

Concept of International Competition Outside of Olympic Games

Even in 21st century USA, it is a strange concept that a national soccer team routinely competes against other national teams, and that the professional MLS club teams play foreign club teams in tournaments like the CONCACAF Cup. This rarely happens within the other Big Four sports, which usually only compete domestically.

The Olympics are held every four years and host basketball, baseball, ice hockey and soccer tournaments – virtually the only time the first three sports face international play. So when a professional "Dream Team" of NBA basketball stars or MLB baseball stars fail to dispatch nations with less significant basketball or baseball traditions and resources, it is a profound shock to the USA public who wonders what happened to the "natural balance" of USA sport superiority.[15]

Where this attitude matters within the USA sports psyche is if the USA soccer team loses to some of the world's top soccer powers, some fans may withdraw their marginal

---

[13] Japanese teams beat MLB teams in preseason games, and Cuba won three of the past four Olympic baseball tournaments (1992, 1996, and 2004). The first true world baseball tournament, the World Baseball Classic, took place in the USA in March 2006, and the USA was eliminated before the semi-finals. Japan beat Cuba in the Final.
[14] The MLB has Caribbean, Central American, South American, and Asian players, the NBA has Africans, Europeans, and South Americans, the NHL has Europeans, and even the NFL has a few foreigners.
[15] The professional USA basketball team lost to Lithuania, Puerto Rico, and Argentina in the 2004 Olympics, and was lucky to finish in third place; and the all-professional USA baseball team lost the inaugural World Baseball Classic in 2006, *with the Japan-Cuba Final featuring only two professional players.*

support, as the team has not proven their worth of the "We're Number One" mantra that (mis)guides USA sport policy in general.

Lack of Professional Soccer Tradition

The most tradition-bound teams in all countries are the oldest teams. In the United States the oldest teams are the baseball teams, followed by USA-football, basketball, and ice hockey teams. A significant history problem for USA soccer is there is no continuous professional first division league tradition. Although professional outdoor soccer leagues have existed in the USA for more than eighty years, all have eventually gone out of existence (even the popular NASL 1967 – 1984).

Major League Soccer (MLS) is only ten years old (1996-2005) and the tradition is growing but is still weak. Some of the weakness can be explained by other sport competition, but MLS has made several blunders that will likely erode consumer confidence in the league.

(1) A major *faux pas* is playing the MLS season through a World Cup competition, such as the 1998 and 2002 World Cup tournaments, and *again scheduling games through the 2006 World Cup in Germany*. No serious soccer fan would be caught watching a MLS game during a World Cup tournament – the premier world sports event every four years.

To make matters worse, MLS players participating in the World Cup (mostly USA players) are conspicuously absent from their club during crucial league games. Still, there is no attractive option for MLS in World Cup years, as it is one of the few leagues in the world that runs a spring to autumn season.

(2) Another MLS gaffe was scheduling a league game the same day as a USA international match – no other world league would dare schedule games when an international match was due to be played by their host country. As a result of this scheduling conflict, on 22 April 1997 Alexi Lalas was forced to perform in two games; the USA–Mexico match and in a game for his New England Revolution club.

(3) New MLS names are not necessarily helping soccer traditions grow, with two examples standing out. The new MLS team in Salt Lake City was given the pre-name *ReAL Salt Lake*[16], which is seen as a silly imitation name (in this case of Spanish giant club *Real Madrid*) that will cause confusion. The "Real" in Real Madrid simply means that the team has been favored by the Spanish monarchy, but the Spanish word addition has no relevance in the USA. The new Houston team (actually the relocated *San Jose Earthquakes* franchise) was originally named *Houston 1836*, but this had to be rescinded because it offended the Mexican-American community – exactly the core audience the team wanted to attract![17]

(4) The New York/New Jersey MetroStars were sold to Austrian drink company Red Bull with the understanding that the team change name to the preposterous *New York Red Bulls*. This mirrored its earlier purchase of SV Austria Salzburg, which when changed to Red Bull Salzburg brought protests in Austria. Besides alienating many supporters that object to such in-your-face product branding of "their team," the new name ignores the state of New Jersey altogether – despite the team actually playing in that state. Naming a team after a product is a risky action, even in the overly-advertised world of 21st century USA.[18]

In 2005, the International Federation of Football History and Statistics (IFFHS) ranked the eighty best football leagues in the world, placing MLS at an incredible 64th, behind such

---

[16] This is not a typographical error. Real Salt Lake is really spelled ReAL in their insignia, ostensibly to ensure correct Spanish pronunciation of the ludicrous pre-name by non-Spanish speaking persons. There is also a ridiculous crown over the small "e."

[17] Houston was founded in 1836 after defeating the Mexicans. Actually, only DC United and FC Dallas have club names in the worldwide geographic tradition. The other ten teams in MLS are identified by their nicknames as much as their locations. If MLS cannot make team names correct the first time, how can they run a soccer league?

[18] Because of either high taurine, glucuronolactone, and/or caffeine ingredients, The Red Bull drink product is restricted in several European countries, required a warning label in Canada, and is not recommended for children and pregnant or lactating women. If restrictions of this type are introduced in the USA, the Red Bull soccer team venture could prove risky indeed.

soccer non-entities such as Qatar (57th), Albania (50th), and Azerbaijan (48th). Even though the USA has qualified for five successive World Cups, eleven of the leagues ranked above them were in countries that had never made one World Cup finals appearance. The MLS will have to convince some people that their league ranks much higher if it is to gain international credibility.[19]

Sub-Standard Soccer Stadiums

The lack of proper soccer stadiums has been a problem faced by many USA clubs. Most large professional stadiums in the USA were built for baseball or USA-football, and the MLS (like the NASL that preceded it) routinely plays matches on fields marked by USA-football or baseball lines.[20] That a professional soccer league cannot remove other sport lines in favor of soccer-only lines is a painful embarrassment for USA soccer, and makes for a pitiful sight on television.

The state of fields was a constant embarrassment even in the NASL era. For example, the New York Cosmos played in a USA-football stadium (NFL New York Giants Stadium) with an artificial turf pitch too narrow for first-class soccer. Additionally, the artificial turf slanted downward from the middle for drainage runoff, and the concrete under the turf made the ball take many high and unnatural bounces.

It was later determined that USA-football players sustained a higher rate of serious knee injuries while playing on artificial turf than on natural grass, and that information led to the banishment of artificial turf from nearly all USA-football stadiums. FIFA has embraced a new generation of artificial turf, but it remains to be proven whether it will be proven to be more "joint friendly" than previous generations of artificial turf.[21]

All-Star Games

All-Star games appear to be a USA contribution to world sport, as each of the USA Big Four sports hosts an all-star game (usually between the east and west divisions of their league). These matches are usually low-intensity affairs that give the best players of the league a chance to show off their skills.

In its heyday the NASL held successful All-Star Games, and the MLS has continued this USA sports custom. For example, the 2001 MLS All-Star game was a spectator-pleasing goal-fest ending tied at 6-6, with Landon Donovan getting four goals for the West side. However, there is debate on whether the MLS All-Star game helps to develop USA soccer at all.

As a rule, international soccer leagues do not host All-Star matches. However, there are two international soccer parallels to the All-Star games of the USA leagues.

(1) FIFA occasionally gathers a group of top players they designate a "FIFA XI" or "World Stars" for a special match against a top club or national team. Being invited to a FIFA match is a tremendous honor for each player, as he will be performing alongside and against top players that he may never encounter again.[22]

(2) A *testimonial match* is a game for a retiring player, whereby guest players are invited to perform against the team of the retiring player. The proceeds most often go to the retiring player and perhaps to charity (see Chapter 18). Pelé's testimonial game poetically matched

---

[19] IFFHS rankings can be examined at www.iffhs.de. With due respect to the IFFHS and their excellent website and publications, their national league rankings are as inconsistent as FIFA's country rankings.
[20] Even in the 2005-2006 season, MLS's most successful club DC United has been forced to share their home field with the new MLB team Washington Nationals. Fans watching from the stadium or on television are treated to a sorry sight of a soccer match played on a baseball field, with the baseball infield covered over by substitute turf.
[21] Up to date FIFA artificial turf recommendations are at: www.fifa.com/en/development/pitch/index.html, and preliminary results indicate that the new artificial turf is safer than the older models.
[22] A recent match was the "Football for Hope" match benefiting the FIFA/AFC Tsunami Solidarity Fund, which was played at the Barcelona Camp Nou Stadium on February 15, 2005.

his former team Santos against his then current team Cosmos, and he played one half of the game for each team.

USA University Underdevelopment of Soccer Players

Because of the lack of the quality and quantity of competition during the crucial phase of a young player's learning curve, university soccer has been accused of being a liability for the development of men's soccer in the USA. In other countries it is a rarity for soccer players to attend university, and if they do, they likely play for a professional team associated with the university (such as Hugo Sanchez did at Universidad Nacional Autónoma de México [UNAM] in Mexico). Adding in the factors of poor financing and amateur coaching in the university ranks, young players from the USA have always been at a distinct competitive disadvantage compared to their international peers. It is impossible to compete with young foreign players of university age who normally play in the junior or senior levels of a professional team, perform in 50 or more games per year, and train and learn with the best professional players and coaches.

Although USA university soccer quality has likely improved, the young university based player who wishes to become a professional is still at a disadvantage to a comparable foreign-based player. The Brigham Young University men's club soccer program tried a new angle in 2003; it now competes in the semi-professional United Soccer Leagues' Premier Soccer Development League rather than against fellow universities. This challenge to NCAA hegemony may become more frequent among universities that want to offer their students a more competitive soccer environment or to sidestep Title IX restrictions (which mandate that women be granted equal athletic opportunities).[23]

For the past thirty years, several successful university soccer teams have recruited foreign students to play soccer. The 1976 Division I NCAA (National Collegiate Athletic Association) Soccer Championship was held just as the professional NASL was becoming popular, and characterized the foreign student soccer athlete situation perfectly. That year the four semifinalists were Clemson University, Hartwick College, Indiana University, and the University of San Francisco (USF was defending its 1975 NCAA championship). The composition of the four teams that year highlighted the quality dilemma of either combing the USA for the best domestic student players, or to search the international market for foreign student players (foreign student players were invariably coached better as youths).

- Hartwick's Jim Lennox recruited nearby homegrown talent in the immigrant soccer hotbed of New Jersey. Reaching into Howell, Bloomfield, Paterson, Trenton, and Kearny, he extracted most of his national talent from this small state. Only five of the twenty-two man squad was international – three from England and one each from Canada and Columbia. Lennox's starting lineup usually consisted of three international students.
- Indiana's Jerry Yeagley had all USA players, most of which had developed in the soccer breeding grounds of Midwestern Chicago and St. Louis.
- USF's Steve Negoesco went semi-international, mixing fourteen Nigerian, Liberian, Norwegian, Guyanese, Salvadoran, and English players in with ten USA based players (nine from California). Negoesco's USF starting lineup usually had three USA players.

---

[23] Some universities ignore men's soccer or soccer completely while glorifying USA-football at any cost. For example, Tulane University in New Orleans sponsored only a women's soccer team but eliminated it after the 2005 hurricane Katrina flood – but allowed the far more costly USA-football men's team to continue. Still maintaining the money-losing USA-football team (about $14 million annually), the Tulane administration terminated 35% of their medical school faculty – thereby revealing their preference of a USA-football team over the continuity of health care of their fellow citizens.

- Clemson's I.M. Ibrahim went nearly all international, with twenty-one of his twenty-two players from Guyana, Nigeria, Ghana, Jamaica, or Lebanon. Clemson's starting lineup was all internationally based.

Thus forty of the ninety-two participating players (43%), and fully half of the starting players from the top four university teams in the nation were from overseas. These numbers illustrate perfectly the difficulty of cracking the starting lineup in a top USA university team for a native USA-based player in the mid-1970's, which more than anything, was due to a lack of proper coaching and playing opportunities at the youth level.

The two teams that maintained a USA-international student balance won the 1976 and 1977 NCAA soccer championships. USF won the 1976 championship (and also won in 1978 and 1980), while Hartwick won in 1977, beating USF in the final. Clemson won in 1984 and 1987, and Indiana won in 1982, 1983, 1988, 1998, 1999, 2003, and 2004.

Fortunately, the situation is not as extreme today. Home grown USA talent is present throughout top university teams, and has to a large degree supplanted the search for foreign talent to win championships. Still, there is always a venue for quality foreign nationals in the university game, such as Trinidad and Tobago's Brent Rahim and Liberia's Chris Gbandi, who both performed for the 2000 NCAA winning University of Connecticut team.

In summary, soccer globalization started in earnest in the USA university setting in the 1970s with the objective of increasing quality on the field. Over time, the improved domestic development of USA players has made this strategy less essential. Still, in the 1990s, creative midfielder Claudio Reyna decided to skip his final year of university eligibility to sign for Bayer Leverkusen, and the new tendency for top young players is to skip university completely. Many of the new USA soccer breed now join European clubs as teenagers in order to acclimate to the world of professional soccer. This is not necessarily an anti-intellectual or anti-university trend, as these young men confirm by their comportment that travel abroad and the "university of the street" more than compensates for classroom learning. Rather, they have determined that if they want to maximize their soccer potential, it will likely happen only on the more competitive fields of European club teams and international competitions. Both Landon Donovan at Bayer Leverkusen and Jovan Kirovski at Manchester United played on the development squads of those top teams, although their experiences were not entirely satisfying because they did not get first team experience. Their colleague John O'Brien persevered longer and eventually became a regular for Dutch powerhouse club Ajax, and DaMarcus Beasley is a regular at PSV Eindhoven.

The Media and USA Soccer

Although soccer is the second most popular participation sport for USA youth today, the mainstream USA media hardly ever presents significant soccer news. This includes the major newspapers (Washington Post, USA Today), and magazines (Sports Illustrated). Newspapers have special sections for professional, college, and even high school basketball, USA-football, and baseball, but one often has to mine through several USA newspapers just to find one story on soccer. The New York Times publishes a few soccer stories, but when the Times' website was redesigned in 2001, the soccer news link was temporarily eliminated until they received several complaints from readers.

General sport magazines in the USA are no better, as the media are more likely to satirize or exhibit outright hostility to soccer. For example, Sports Illustrated characterized soccer's nomination for the Nobel Peace Prize in 2001 as "This Week's Sign of the Apocalypse," and their preview analysis of the 2002 World Cup was so unsophisticated it was embarrassing. As a result, serious USA soccer fans must buy specialty magazines for coherent soccer information and analysis.

Despite the pathetic performance of USA newspapers and magazines, the television coverage has been even worse. While television coverage of the World Cup extravaganza is free in most countries, it is not in the USA. Only a handful of World Cup games have ever been shown on free English-language television in the USA, with most of those involving the USA team. As a result, only access to special cable packages (most likely with Spanish-language channels) or satellite television can satiate the USA soccer aficionado.

Even today, when soccer is played more often in the United States than nearly any other sport, with the development of the MLS professional soccer league, the appearance of the men's national team in five straight World Cups, and the women's national team winning two of the first four women's World Cups; there is a better chance of watching marginal "sports" such as bowling or billiards on the major television channels than a soccer match.

Why the USA media chooses to ignore the international phenomenon of soccer and its increasing popularity in the USA seems to be fourfold:

(1) <u>Limited soccer expertise in the press</u>. Very few writers are of age where they themselves played serious soccer (at least university level), and even less have any international experience with soccer. As a result, many published articles have glaring errors of fact and interpretation of the game.

(2) <u>Limited soccer interest in the press</u>. Culturally speaking, the press has a hard time presenting soccer on its own merits, and makes irrelevant comparisons between soccer and other sports. For example, the Central and South American contribution to USA soccer is rarely appreciated, resulting in the alienation of a large part of the USA soccer audience that truly understands the game.

(3) <u>Limited soccer monies</u>. Although soccer has a massive following in the USA, the press treats it as a small market sport with a small audience. This is partly because of a lack of money and marketing in USA soccer; if there is no "big money" the so-called independent press is not interested.

(4) <u>Lack of the big picture</u>. This could be restated as "lack of the global picture." The Big Four sports have an arrangement whereby a North American team will always be champion[24], although they sometimes erroneously refer to these champions as "World Champions." Soccer does not have the liberty of such a setup, as USA soccer has to compete on the international scene with major soccer powers. That "guaranteed success" the Big Four sports have locked in is lacking for the USA men's soccer team. The press wants to sell "success," even if it is artificially constructed and presented as a "world" triumph.

The USA national team was terribly manipulated before a television appearance in 2001. Because of a conflict with a USA-football game, the USA-Honduras World Cup qualifying match was played at the absurd hour of ten o'clock in the morning. The USSF had been given a choice to play the match at 10 am on Saturday, September 1, or 4 PM Sunday, September 2. A 4 PM start would have been a logical game time, but was forbidden on the Saturday because of the USA-football match. It was decided to play the game on Saturday morning because the USA was scheduled to play in Costa Rica the following Wednesday September 5th, and a Saturday game would give them more time to recuperate and travel. To add insult to injury, the match was held at JFK Stadium in Washington, D.C., making it nearly a home game for the Hondurans whose fans were more visible and vocal. The sport television ratings that influenced the timing and scheduling of the match likely had a direct effect on the USA men's national team performance, as the USA looked flat and lost 3-2 to Honduras, seriously endangering their 2002 World Cup qualification at the time.

The lack of soccer expertise and interest in the USA press feeds upon a vicious cycle that dates back to the NASL days; without decent press there will be limited television and sponsorship monies injected into the game. After all, sponsors are looking for good media

---

[24] The MLB (baseball), NBA (basketball), and NHL (ice hockey) all have a few teams in Canada, but the overwhelming majority of the teams are in the USA.

coverage, which brings more spectators, which brings more media coverage, etc. To be fair, much of the responsibility of soccer promotion in the USA lies with the USSF, but there has been little evidence of cooperation from the mainstream USA press. However, the USA youth population is increasingly interested in global soccer, and the first media outlets that capture the attention of this audience will find themselves rapidly expanding their demographic base.

Best USA Players in the Modern Era 1958-2006

Choosing the best USA players in the Modern Era (using the same criteria as Chapter 7, including must have played for the national team by 1994) is a difficult challenge. Most eligible candidates played an integral part in the ascendance of the USA squad in the 1990s, which finally elevated the USA as a world soccer power to be taken seriously. There are several candidates for best USA player, but one in particular stands out for his overall commitment, technique and improvisation.

Marcelo Balboa was a midfielder-defender with better than average speed and quickness, but with extraordinary anticipation and technique. He organized the USA defense for the better part of a decade (1988-2000), the team era most crucial to the USA development and eventual success. Balboa had the talent to play the midfield positions, and he played a total game, looking to score even when burdened with defensive duties. His thirteen goals for the USA national team is a great accomplishment for a defensive player.

Balboa created what was perhaps the most exciting move during the entire 1994 World Cup when he executed a perfect bicycle kick from the 18-yard line against Colombia; unfortunately the ball went centimeters wide of the left post (this play is memorialized in an exhibit in the US Soccer Hall of Fame in Oneonta, New York). Balboa was able to score on a similar bicycle kick during the 2000 MLS season, and the video replay was available from the MLS website (www.mls.com) and several other websites worldwide (such as www.futvol.com). Balboa always exhibited a tremendous desire for the game that few players realize, as his complete recovery to potential after a horrific knee injury demonstrated. Balboa was a player flexible and talented enough and could have performed well for any national team.

Four midfielders were standouts: Tab Ramos, sometimes described as the most technically gifted USA player; Ricky Davis, who anchored the USA team in the 1980s and was an exciting native player to watch alongside the foreign contingent on the New York Cosmos; Cobi Jones, the national team appearance leader with 164; and Claudio Reyna, captain of the successful USA team in 2002 World Cup. Also in the Top 10 USA players are striker Eric Wynalda, the all-time leading USA scorer with 34 goals; John Harkes, a defender-midfielder who achieved soccer success in England; defender Alexi Lalas, who was the first (and so far the only) USA player to perform in the Italian Serie A in the Modern Era (1958-2006)[25]; midfielder Ernie Stewart, who led the USA in World Cup qualifying goals; and defender-midfielder Paul Caliguiri, who scored the goal which brought the USA to the 1990 World Cup after an absence of forty years. In the second group of ten best USA players in the modern age would be defenders Jeff Agoos, Peter Vermes, Fernando Clavijo and Eddie Pope, midfielders Thomas Dooley, Roy Wegerle, and Hugo Perez, and strikers Brian McBride, Joe-Max Moore, and Bruce Murray.

The USA has had an abundance of excellent goalkeepers that could have started on almost any national team. Tony Meola kept goal in the 1990 and 1994 World Cups and was backup in the 2002 Cup. Meola also won the MLS MVP award in 2000 after a stellar campaign with champions Kansas City. Along with Tab Ramos and John Harkes, Meola

---

[25] Colin Jose has pointed out that two USA-born men, Alfonso Negro and Armando Frigo, played in Serie A before and during World War II. Negro even played for the Italian national team in the 1936 Olympics as an *oriundi* (foreign Italian), scoring one goal in his only appearance, the 2-1 semifinal win over Norway.

completes the remarkable trio of USA national players from the single town of Kearny, New Jersey. Brad Friedel has played for Liverpool and Blackburn in the English Premier League, Kasey Keller played in Europe for fifteen years in the Spanish, English and German top divisions, and Tim Howard began performing for Manchester United in 2003. All four have proven themselves to be world-class keepers.

Arnie Mausser was a formidable talent as USA national team goalkeeper in the 1970s and 1980s, and played professionally for numerous NASL teams. Another stellar goalkeeper was Shep Messing, who played on the 1977 NASL winning Cosmos team with Pelé and subsequently had a long career in indoor soccer. Messing also wrote (with David Hirshey) "*The Education of an American Soccer Player,*" a book that documented the difficulties USA players had in breaking into their own national league (the NASL) in the 1970s. During that era, Mausser kept Messing out of the national first team with his excellent goalkeeping form.

Why have USA goalkeepers shown world-class talent despite lack of early experience? An obvious reason could be because they were exposed to more ball-handling sports such as basketball, baseball, and USA-football at an early age, which was part of any typical USA soccer player's youth experience.

USA Soccer Future

Successes

Billions of people in the world necessarily monitor USA government policies because there are cultural, economic, and even military consequences.[26] But the world is also becoming more aware of USA soccer, which just twenty years ago was struggling to raise finances and boost organizational capacity. Since then, the USA women's national soccer team was ranked number one in the world for much of the past decade, and the men's national soccer team was ranked as high as number four in the world in 2006 (April 2006 ranking).

Failures

Despite those achievements, a relevant question is whether USA soccer has already reached its zenith and in danger of decline. After all, the professional women's soccer league (WUSA – Women's United Soccer Association) went out of business in 2003, and after ten years of existence the MLS is only ranked 64th in the world. The next Men's and Women's World Cup results will perhaps give an indication of which direction USA soccer is heading.

Media Knowledge

Despite occasional foolish media denials, much of the USA populace has the soccer passion.[27] What the USA needs now is an enlightened media to highlight the improved soccer quality and development beyond the previously demonstrated substantial grassroots involvement.

Soccer Culture

Individual development requires only heart – the desire to play and improve. But proper community soccer development requires a soccer culture, which is at present still evolving in the USA. A massive help was hosting the 1994 World Cup, which the USA was extremely fortunate to host – FIFA had never before allowed a country without a first division soccer league to host the ultimate soccer spectacle. Thousands of unpaid volunteers helped make the 1994 World Cup a success, although is was to be two more years before a professional men's league was jump-started (MLS).

USA soccer culture has benefited most from extensive international connections that exist for no other USA sport. Playing the beautiful game often necessitates traveling to other countries and exposing USA citizens to individuals from other cultures and belief systems. This international person-to-person interaction gives individuals special insight into the human condition that their homebound compatriots often lack.

Soccer Style

The USA soccer style is currently a mish-mash of *Latin technique* and *European power* styles. While past USA teams may have emphasized fitness over technique, the current national teams fortunately demonstrate as much technique as fitness. But the USA style still has more in common with rapid European team movement than the South American rhythm and possession style (which requires the highest level of soccer technique). Knowledgeable soccer critics such as Paul Gardner have frequently questioned the absence of many Latin players in the USA teams, pointing out that many have excellent technique and should be given a trial with the national squads.

---

[26] A short list in 2006 includes the bludgeoning myopia and corruption of the Bush administration and its subsequent effects on lives in the Middle East (superfluous Iraq war that has fueled extremism and killed thousands of innocent people), Africa (missing and slow delivery of promised aid for AIDS), and South America (runaway destruction of the world's remaining rainforests spearheaded by multinational corporations and unethical governmental policies).

[27] In 2005, one bow-tied conservative television interviewer emphatically called soccer "un-American" (meaning anathema to the USA), a nonsensical assertion when millions of USA children play soccer.

The MLS Experiment

The MLS was created in the image of USA professional sport and the "cult of the owner", –except that the owner IS the league. The league effectively owns clubs, controls salaries, and transfers players as they see fit. This "one-owner" model of the MLS has not been a major success on the world scale,[28] and will likely not be the most beneficial plan for the USA in the long run. Major problems include:

(1) Despite paying low salaries, the MLS has not made a profit in a decade of existence.
(2) According to the IFFHS, the MLS world league ranking in 2005 was a miserable 64th.
(3) The MLS Player's Association sued the league to try and break up its monopolistic structure. The lawsuit failed due to technicalities and the league still owns player's rights even after their contracts have expired (no true "free agency," which is counter to the Bosman agreement in place in Europe).
(4) The MLS's affluent investors are starting to remove their financial commitment.
(5) The fans are not substantially emotionally invested in the MLS club structure.

USA "Cult of the Owner"

Because the USA has such a strong grassroots soccer history, it would be a shame to continue the "cult of the owner" structure, whereupon teams are answerable to one controlling individual or institution. Otherwise, it is possible the MLS will follow the history of the privately-held NASL, which failed to survive in the 1980s despite the importation of many of the best players in the world.

USA Community Club Model

The USA soccer community should seek to embrace the "community club model" that has so far been the backbone of world professional soccer (see Chapter 5). The community club model would involve hundreds or thousands of community investors in each regional club with the board of directors accountable to them, the shareholders. This is the most promising paradigm that will create tangible links between community and club, and which would ensure sustainable and high-quality soccer in the USA.

---

[28] Except for the 1998 DC United and 2000 Los Angeles Galaxy championships in the CONCACAF Cup, the club championship for North and Central America.

Chapter Fifteen

The Penalty Paradox

"Thank God we were luckier during the penalty shoot-out."
Egypt coach *Hassan Shehata,* after Egypt won the 2006 African Nation's Cup on penalties against Ivory Coast.

The penalty kick is an integral part of the game during full and extra time, but when used to settle matches it has become an alien and regrettable element. That is the penalty paradox of soccer.

On February 8, 2002, the BBC website carried an African Nations Cup final headline that read: *Cameroon take African title over Senegal 3-2*.[1] But closer inspection of the story revealed that this was yet another Final decided by the pseudo-competition of the after-time penalty kicks. In actuality, the championship match had ended scoreless, but in an effort to make the result exciting news copy, the article title was presented as if the goals happened in full time.

And soccer fans can well imagine this possible future nightmare scenario:

> Dateline 2010:
> Team A won their first World Cup today with a negative scoreless display of soccer, but prevailing 5-4 in penalty kicks over Team B after full and extra-time. Unfortunately for the Team B, they had a goal annulled because of a wrong judgment by the linesman and referee.

Penalty Kicks Deciding Important Matches

Writing as a fan and a soccer player, penalty kicks are an abomination when used to decide important matches. Most fans derive little or no joy, and cannot tolerate many more matches decided by the penalty kick lottery. People would prefer endless sudden death, or a fair replay after tied matches.

Many fans do not consider the team that made one more penalty kick an authentic winner. By this standard, Brazil's 4th star on their canary yellow shirts representing the 1994 World Cup penalty win is forever tainted by an asterisk, by virtue of a scoreless tie and penalty kick competition in the Final.

Penalty kick shootouts take away the essence of the game, and when they are used to decide major competitions, after-time penalties remain a major embarrassment for the sport of soccer.

---

[1] The BBC ran a similar headline on February 10, 2006, *Egypt win Cup after penalty drama*; another drab Final decided by penalties.

The following is a partial list of major soccer cups decided by the penalty kick lottery:

(1) *FIFA World Cups* (National Team World Champion)
    1994 Men's World Cup - Brazil over Italy.
    1999 Women's World Cup - USA over China.

(2) *Copa Libertadores* (South American Club Champion)
    1999 Palmeiras over Deportivo Cali.
    2000 Boca Juniors over Palmeiras.
    2001 Boca Juniors over Cruz Azul.
    2002 Olimpia over São Caetano.
    2004 Once Caldas over Boca Juniors.

(3) *European Champions Cups* (European Club Champion)
    2001 Bayern Munich over Valencia.
    2003 AC Milan over Juventus.
    2005 Liverpool over AC Milan

(5) *Copa America* (South American National Team Champion)
    1995 Uruguay over Brazil
    2004 Brazil over Argentina.

(5) *European Championship* (European National Team Champion)
    1976 Czechoslovakia over West Germany.

(6) African Nations Cup (African National Team Champion)
    1992 Ivory Coast over Ghana
    2000 Cameroon over Nigeria
    2002 Cameroon over Senegal
    2006 Egypt over Ivory Coast

These penalty contests are detrimental to the game, an *anti-soccer* negating all that occurred over the previously contested 120 minutes on the field. How did international soccer ever get to this point?

First Penalty Kick Elimination

Penalty kicks were introduced in soccer in 1891 – for the express purpose of giving a player in the 18-yard box another opportunity to try for a goal after an attempt was denied by a major foul.

Penalty kick shootouts were first introduced in a major competition in the 1976 European Championship. Czechoslovakia had been leading West Germany 2-0 in the Final until the West Germans equalized in the final minute. There were no more goals in overtime, and the teams assumed there would be a replay. But the Finals committee had agreed to host the first penalty kick tiebreaker if necessary, which West Germany subsequently lost. The Germans lamented that loss, and have since been very successful at penalty kick shootouts.

The World Cup saw its first game decided by penalty kicks in 1982, and it was a doozy. The semi-final between France and West Germany decided who played Italy for the championship. West German winger Littbarski scored in the 17th minute, only to have Platini equalize from the penalty mark in the 26th minute. In the 62nd minute, West German keeper Schumacher committed a vicious attack against Patrick Battiston (see Chapter 6), which should have brought a mandatory red card and expulsion for Schumacher (he was not even assessed a yellow card). These events left the French team in a daze, not even knowing if their teammate would survive his horrific cranial injury.

In extra time, French defender Maurice Trésor scored on a beautiful volley, and then a driven shot from 18 yards by midfielder Alain Giresse, all in the first eight minutes. However, West Germany's less-than-fit captain Karl-Heinz Rummenigge came off the bench in the 96th minute to hustle in a goal in the 102nd minute, and Klaus Fischer equalized in the

108th minute, making the final score 3-3. Four goals in extra time! What soccer fan wouldn't pay money to see a replay of this game? Of course, FIFA should have thrown Schumacher out of the tournament after reviewing his attack on Battiston, as the referee missed the obvious ruling.

But there was no *Golden Goal* rule in 1982, whereby France would have won the game on Trésor's spectacular volley; and no replay was scheduled. The penalty kick competition that followed simply trivialized the great game just completed. In addition, Schumacher faced France's penalty kickers with Battiston's medical uncertainty weighing on their minds. Unjustly (because of Schumacher's participation), West Germany won the match on penalty kicks 5-4, and this travesty of soccer play continues today.

Flood of Penalty Kick Eliminations
World Cups

Penalty shoot-outs have played a vital part in recent World Cups, the most important soccer tournament in the world. After the *West Germany-France semi-final of 1982*, there was a deluge of penalty kick eliminations in subsequent World Cups:

- Two quarterfinal matches in 1986.
- One quarterfinal and *both semi-finals* in 1990.
- One quarterfinal and *the Final* in 1994.
- One quarterfinal and *one semi-final* in 1998.
- One quarterfinal in 2002.

It is an organizational shame that in order to determine which teams enter the Final, and even the result of the Final itself, have been decided by penalty kicks rather than wide-open football.

The 1994 World Cup Final ending was a major embarrassment for soccer. Both teams played in an overly defensive mode; Brazil was reluctant to play a wholeheartedly offensive game, even with Italy's Roberto Baggio and Franco Baresi hampered by injury. Brazil certainly remembered losing to Italy 2-3 in the 1982 World Cup, when they maintained an offensive posture after needing only a tie to advance (a rampant Paolo Rossi had a hat-trick for Italy in that game). Despite Brazil controlling the 1994 game, Italy still had a chance for goal with the ever-dangerous Baggio playing.

If the 1994 Final had continued indefinitely, the odds would have favored Brazil scoring first. As it was, Italy lost as the battle-scarred Baggio and Baresi missed their penalty kicks. Even though Brazil dominated the game and won their 4th World Cup, many people do not consider that they really "won" the World Cup (although I doubt many of them are Brazilians). The 1994 Final will always be a win with an asterisk, won on a static penalty contest.

How could this be? A World Cup won on penalties? Impossible. What if Italy had won the penalty contest and their 4th WC, especially after demonstrating less possession and offense? Would that have been fair? What a footballing nightmare.

Argentina and West Germany/Germany have the best records in World Cup penalty kick shootouts, winning all three they have participated. Italy has been the most unfortunate, as they have been forced to participate three times, and have lost three heart-breaking penalty kick elimination shootouts in a row (1990, 1994, and 1998), eliminating the *azzurri* from the World Cup each time.

A new chapter on World Cup penalty kicks was introduced in 2005, when *Australia became the first team to qualify for a World Cup on a penalty kick contest* (beating Uruguay).

European Champions League Competitions

The 2001 European Champions League Final between Bayern Munich and Valencia was a prime example of the penalty kick lottery debacle. Actually, the whole game was a penalty-festival fiasco, as Valencia received a penalty kick in the 3rd minute and Bayern in the 50th, both of which were phantom penalties. The Valencia kick resulted when a Bayern player fell down and could not get up as he was in the thick of the action. The second was when Bayern's Stefan Effenberg played the ball over Valencia's Jocelyn Angloma with no hope of recovering it in bounds. The creative midfielders took the kicks – Valencia's Gaizka Mendieta converted while Bayern's Mehmet Scholl missed. Then there was a *third* penalty kick, this one against Valencia again, occurring when German striker Carsten Jancker of Bayern *forcibly pushed Amedeo Carboni's arm into the ball* in the penalty area, which the referee from his angle could only view as intentional. That penalty should not have been a foul of any type against Carboni, as it was an unintentional handball. Effenberg scored that penalty for Bayern to tie.

At the end of regular time and the 30-minute overtime, the game was still 1-1. Statistically, Bayern dominated the game, but that does not and hopefully will never decide a soccer match. Bayern led in shots 19-9, corner kicks 10-3, and time of possession. By any of the wacky proposed statistical ideas as alternatives to penalty kicks (e.g., counting corner kicks, number of shots, or time of possession), Bayern would have won. Valencia had an equal chance in the penalty kick contest, but Bayern eventually won the penalty kicks.

The game was refereed by Dick Jol, a competent referee from the "international human rights city" of Den Haag, Holland, and site of the International Court of Justice. The problem was not Jol, but as outlined above, the insurmountable problems faced by all professional referees. One solitary referee does not have a chance of catching all important fouls or non-fouls appearing to be fouls.

The 2003 European Champions League Final matched AC Milan against fellow Serie A club Juventus. The year 2003 was a vindication for Italian soccer, because the Serie A had had only one total representative in the Champions League quarter-finals in the three previous (2000-2001-2002) editions, prompting suggestions of deteriorating quality of Italian football. This opinion was apparently premature, as Italian teams made up three of the four semi-final teams in 2003 (AC Milan, Inter Milan, and Juventus). But once it was reported that creative midfield stars Rivaldo (AC Milan) and Pavel Nedved (Juventus) would not play, it did not bode well for the quality of the Final. The 2003 Final was a boring 0-0 affair, which AC Milan won on penalties.

The 2005 European Champions League Final featured AC Milan again, this time against Liverpool in Istanbul. AC Milan led 3-0 after dominating the first half, but Liverpool made a tremendous effort to equalize 3-3 within 15 minutes after the half time break. The rest of regular time and extra time was end-to-end action, but no further scoring. A penalty kick contest followed this gripping match, which Liverpool won 3-2 to raise the trophy. For the third time in five years the penalty lottery trivialized European soccer's greatest occasion; this time after one of the best European Finals ever.

Copa Libertadores

The Copa Libertadores championship is the South American equivalent of the European Champions League. While the ECL Final is a one-game affair held in a neutral city, the CL is still a two-game home and away competition, leading one to believe there might be less of a chance of encountering a penalty kick shootout. However, this has not proven to be true.

The 2002 edition of the Copa Libertadores was determined by a penalty kick lottery-fest, which was eventually won by Paraguayan centenary team Olimpia (1902-2002) over Brazilian upstart Sao Caetano (a club founded as recently as 1989). Olimpia nudged into the Final, *after beating Brazilian powerhouse Gremio on penalty kicks in the semi-final.* Sao

Caetano reached the Final after defeating Peñarol (Uruguay) in the quarterfinals and Universidad Católica (Chile) in the round of 16, *both on penalty kick competitions.*

The first game of the 2002 Final was played in Estadio Defensores del Chaco in Asunción, Paraguay, and home team Olimpia disappointed their fans hoping to celebrate 100 years of club life with a victory, losing 1-0 to the tough Brazilians. The next game was held in Estadio Pacaembú in São Paulo, and Sao Caetano scored first through Aílton in the 31st minute. It looked grim for Olimpia at half time, being down 2-0 in total score, but somehow they were able to score twice in the second half through Córdoba and Báe. After Olimpia won the penalty kick contest 4-2, the centenarians had won their third South American championship, following their 1979 and 1990 wins.

Incredibly, this was *the fourth year in a row the Copa was decided by penalty kicks.* The other three years had Palmeiras (Brazil) over Deportivo Cali (Columbia) in 1999, Boca Juniors (Argentina) over Palmeiras in 2000, and Boca Juniors over Cruz Azul (Mexico) in 2001. Furthermore, the 2004 Copa Libertadores was also decided on penalties, as newcomer Once Caldas (Colombia) beat Boca Juniors. The Copa was also decided by penalties in 1994 (Vélez Sarsfield – Argentina over São Paulo – Brazil), and 1992 (São Paulo over Newell's Old Boys – Argentina).[2]

Boca Juniors has learned by experience that teams that live by the penalty can die by the penalty. Although Boca won the Copa Libertadores on penalties in 2000 and 2001, they lost the championship match to Once Caldas of Colombia in 2004 and the 2003 Recopa (played in 2004) to Cienciano of Peru, both on penalty contests. However, Boca won the Copa Sudamericana in 2005 on penalty kicks over Pumas UNAM of Mexico.

To have seven South American champions (Copa Libertadores) in the last thirteen years crowned by the crapshoot of the penalty kicks – is seven too many.

African Nations Cup

Fully half of the last eight African Nations Cups have ended in a penalty contest. The 1992 Final started off the trend when Ivory Coast beat Ghana 11-10 after 24 shots were taken. Ivory Coast had beaten Cameroon in the semifinal only after a penalty contest. Since both games ended 0-0, Ivory Coast won the semifinal and Final without scoring one goal.

After normal Finals in 1994, 1996, and 1998, the 2000, 2002, and 2006 versions also ended in penalty shootouts. Only the 2004 edition broke the penalty monotony as Tunisia beat Morocco 2-1.

International Club Cup championships

Boca Juniors won the 2003 Intercontinental Cup against AC Milan on a penalty competition after extra-time, after Milan had won the European Champion's league on penalties, while Porto (Portugal) won the 2004 Intercontinental Cup against Once Caldas (Colombia) on a penalty competition after extra-time, after Once Caldas had won the Copa Libertadores on penalties. Live by the penalty, die by the penalty.

The 2001 Intercontinental Club Cup in Tokyo was unique, as it was the *only ICC ever matching two penalty kick winner continental champions* - Boca Juniors (CL) and Bayern Munich (ECL). The Final nearly came down to penalties once again, but Bayern's Ghanaian central defender Samuel Kuffour fortunately scored in the second overtime period.[3]

The previous Intercontinental Cup won on penalty kicks was in 1995, when Ajax beat Gremio. Before that, Nacional beat PSV Eindhoven in 1988, and Juventus beat Argentinos Juniors in 1985 on penalty kick shootouts.

---

[2] For the 2005 Copa Libertadores competition, the away goals rule was introduced. Ironically, all of the Copa Libertadores championships from 1999-2004 that had been won by penalty kicks – excepting Boca Juniors in 2001 – would have been won by the opposite team if the away goals rule had been in effect.

[3] The deserving Kuffour did not win the 2001 African Player of the Year award, demonstrating the apparent difficulty for a defender to win highest individual honors.

FIFA Club World Championship

The *FIFA Club World Championship* has so far been held only twice, in 2000 and 2005. Four years elapsed between tournaments as FIFA sorted out its faltering finances and dubious marketing strategies.

The 2000 competition invited the 1998 Intercontinental Cup winners (Real Madrid), 1998 Copa Libertadores winners (Vasco da Gama – Brazil), 1999 UEFA Champions League winners (Manchester United - England), 1998 Asian Super Cup winners (Al Nassr – Saudi Arabia), 1999 Concacaf Champions Cup winners (Necaxa - Mexico), 1999 Oceania Champions' Cup winners (South Melbourne - Australia), 1999 Africa Champions' Cup winners (Raja Casablanca - Morocco), and 1998 Brazilian champions (Corinthians).

This was a competition too young for its time, as the Asian and Oceania teams were out of their depth. The format was poor (similar to the 1978 World Cup) with two groups of four teams each, and the top two teams going to the Final. In a shocker to English football, Manchester United elected not to contest the English FA Cup in order to concentrate on this new tournament, and finished an embarrassing 3rd in their group after Vasco da Gama and Necaxa. More and more, the potential of *Big Money* trod on tradition.

Corinthians advanced to the Final only by besting Real Madrid on goal difference (4-3) in the three games. Vasco da Gama won all three games against Manchester United, Necaxa, and South Melbourne, to advance and ensure the Final was an all-Brazil affair. The Final however, was a 0 – 0 bore, with Corinthians winning the title on the penalty kick lottery 4-3. Necaxa beat Real Madrid for third place; also on (surprise!) penalty kicks after a 1 – 1 tie.

The 2005 FIFA Club World Championship was a more classic competition with Sao Paulo beating Liverpool 1-0 in the Final, and none of the seven tournament matches was decided by penalty kicks.

December 12, 2004: Double Penalty Day Depression

On the same day that Porto won the 2004 Intercontinental Cup over Once Caldas on penalties, the African Champion's League was won by Nigerian club Enyimba over Etoile du Sahel of Tunisia, also on penalty kicks. These two major continental or intercontinental championships decided by the penalty kick lottery on the same day set a new low for the determination of soccer champions.

Enyimba also won their semi-final against Espérance of Tunisia on a penalty kick competition. Enyimba employed a novel strategy to win the penalty kick competition in both the semi-final and final matches, substituting their first team keeper (Nigerian national team keeper) Vincent Enyeama with penalty specialist Dele Aiyenugba. Interestingly, Enyeama was substituted in the Final after he had already scored a regular time penalty kick himself! And incredibly, reserve keeper Aiyenugba saved a kick in each competition to put Enyimba ahead! This is new (and dubious) ground that Enyimba has broken, deliberately substituting a talented goalkeeper in a major tournament for the express purpose of a specialist goalkeeper attempting to save penalty kicks in a penalty competition. One wonders if after Enyimba's success, more specialty goalkeepers will crop up in other competitions.

May 2005: Yet Another Double Penalty Depression

Within four days, two of the most prestigious European Finals ended in penalty kick contests. On 21 May 2005 the 124th English FA Cup (the oldest football Cup in the world) ended 0-0 after a scoreless battle between archrivals Arsenal and Manchester United. Arsenal took the trophy after penalties. Then on 25 May 2005 the European Champions League Final ended 3-3 between AC Milan and Liverpool, and Liverpool won on penalties. The irony is that both games were played at the highest level, yet the tremendous efforts of the players were effectively disregarded once the penalty lottery started.

Anti-Football: Penalty Kick Eliminations

The soul of the game is being ripped out by penalty lotteries. Fans are tired of watching marquee players like Roberto Baggio and Samuel Eto'o, after playing their hearts out for 120 minutes, sky their elimination penalty kicks over the bar.

The penalty kick pressure is all on the penalty taker; if the goalkeeper guesses wrong nobody can fault him. Because of this element of luck for the goalkeeper, the whole event is heavily weighted on chance. Sure, there is some skill involved, but luck is often the tiebreaker, and the whole event is therefore a gamble. Might as well flip a coin to see who wins the match.

There is a real danger that *penalty kicks deciding matches* will damage both facets of the game; the aesthetic/athletic art side and the business side. Teams that are being outplayed but still find themselves in a tie match after half-time, inevitably "play ugly" to arrive at the penalty kick tiebreaker. On the business side of the game, some people were making more cash than ever on football, but the golden times have dried up with the world recession and the overpayment of superstar salaries. Fewer fans have been willing to spend their hard-earned money to see games decided by penalty kicks.

The static penalty elimination is the epitome of Anti-Soccer. Simply put, *penalty kick eliminations are a severe design deficiency of the modern game,* and are not a sporting ending. Please, three decades, 30 years (1976-2006) of this foolishness is enough!

The End of the Exciting Golden Goal

The "*Golden Goal*", or "sudden death" winning goal in extra-time, was a good idea which was long overdue. With the Golden Goal rule in place, it would have been France rather than West Germany (as Marius Trésor had scored the first overtime goal) playing Italy in the 1982 World Cup Final, and Romania would have advanced to the 1994 World Cup semi-finals instead of Sweden (Florin Răducioiu put Romania ahead 2-1 in the 100th minute, but Kennet Andersson equalized in the 115th minute and Sweden won the subsequent penalty kick contest).

There were only a few important matches affected by the Golden Goal rule in the decade it existed (1994 to 2004). But what an exciting and fair way to end a match![4] The 1996 European Championship Final won by Germany over the Czech Republic (substitute Oliver Bierhoff scoring the equalizing goal in regular time, then the winning Golden Goal in overtime), the 1998 win by host France over Paraguay (defender Laurent Blanc scoring the Golden Goal past keeper José Luis Chilavert to finish the scoreless deadlock), the 2000 European Championships with France first beating Portugal in the semi-final (on a Zinedine Zidane penalty kick Golden Goal), then beating Italy in the Final (on a David Trézéguet Golden Goal), and the 2002 World Cup with Senegal beating Sweden (on Henri Camara's wonderful Golden Goal move), South Korea beating Italy (on Ahn Jung-Hwan's header Golden Goal), and Turkey beating Senegal (on a brilliant Golden Goal by İlhan Mansız). Every match had a thrilling finish, rather than a possibility for an after-extra-time penalty kick lottery.

The *Golden Goal* did not purge soccer of penalty eliminations; it just prevented them when one team scored in the overtime. But this positive change in the game was unfortunately abandoned by FIFA in early 2004, as it ruled that the full overtime period would be completed once again, even if a first "Golden Goal" was scored. However, returning to the old system will inevitably result in more penalty kick shootouts, as teams can recover and equalize the game again.

---

[4] After all, this is not "sudden death" as in USA-Football, where a coin-flip determines which team "goes on the offensive" first; a massive advantage in that sport. Soccer is so dynamic that no matter which team kicks off in overtime, both teams have an equal chance to score and win on the golden goal.

Indeed, in the Portugal-England quarterfinal of the 2004 European Championship, Portugal's Manuel Rui Costa scored in the 110th minute (which would have won the game as a Golden Goal a few months earlier), but England's Frank Lampard equalized in the 115th minute, thus ensuring another penalty kick contest (Portugal won 6-5 to advance to the semifinals). What would have been a clear victory for Portugal with a Golden Goal was placed into question as the penalty kick contest followed.

Below are some ideas on what should replace the nightmare penalty kick lottery contests at the end of tied tournament matches.

A. Solutions for Penalty Kick Eliminations
(1) Good Dynamic Ideas

A *game replay* is the optimal solution for fairness. In the past tied matches were replayed, and they were usually very well replayed. Game replays last occurred in major tournaments in Europe in the 1968 European Championship Final (Italy beat Yugoslavia 2-0 in the replay, after an initial 1-1- draw), and the 1974 European Cup Final (won by Bayern Munich 4-0 against Atlético Madrid on their second try as the first match was tied 1-1). Occasionally even the replay is tied, such as the scoreless 1979 Copa America Final replay between Paraguay and Chile. Paraguay was finally determined to win the tournament on a better three-game goal difference (for the home-and-away and replay series with Chile).

With a replay, team depth will help produce a fair final result. Unfortunately, a return to this best solution of replays in this age of instant television advertising is unlikely. Why would advertisers agree to a replay system if they have paid to sponsor a Final, but the Final is a draw? Well, *maybe because they would have another opportunity to advertise*?

Why not play *overtime for a golden goal without goalkeepers*? One or more of the defenders would then attempt to defend the goal closely, but the opposing team has a greater chance of getting a goal from a distance. Surely many spectacular goals will be scored, perhaps even from midfield. The weakest part of this solution is that it removes a key player from the field, and therefore is not standard football. Also, it will introduce another asterisk into the game (mark * for goals scored without goalkeeper), and as argued before, football is not a game of statistics, no matter how much some USA-based journalists and marketing types endeavor to present it as such.

Perhaps it is time to take a look at how the USA Big Four Sports end a tie game. Baseball, basketball, ice hockey, and USA-football all play *endless extra-time* to settle a match. This might be a solution for soccer, but one must bear in mind that soccer is the most physically demanding team sport, and the players are exhausted after 120 minutes of play (including full time and extra-time). Baseball is a slow and mostly static game, basketball action halts every minute or so, ice hockey has four groups of "lines" that freely enter the game multiple times, and USA-football has complete offensive and defensive squads and plenty of substitutes. Rarely in those games does even one player perform for the whole match, while that is the rule in soccer. In addition, those games allow higher scoring, so the match conclusion is guaranteed within a certain time frame. The only way that soccer could conceive of playing endless extra-time until a sudden-death goal occurs is by allowing extra substitutes after 120 minutes.

(2) Good Static Ideas

Instead of boring penalty kicks that are essentially a contest of luck, why not *allow free kicks anywhere along the 18 yard circle*? Soccer professionals should convert free kicks from this distance with only a goalkeeper to beat about 20% of the time. At this distance a goalkeeper cannot guess which way to move– if he even leans in the wrong direction he can be beat. He must simply wait for the kick to come and rely on his reflexes. It is the ultimate static challenge between defense (goalkeeper) and offense (free-kick taker). Therefore when a goal is scored there will be more of a feeling that a legitimate goal was scored, removing the negative psychology from the endgame wherein a player is a "goat" if he misses. Here a player is a hero when he scores.

To allow self-expression into the contest, players would be permitted to place the ball anywhere along the 18-yard circle. If the ball were placed at the intersection of the circle and the 18-yard line, the ball would be at 18 yards from the goal, but at an angle. If the ball were placed in the middle of the circle, it would be 22 yards away from the goal, but in the center. Some players would prefer an angled shot, while others would prefer a longer middle path.

Goalkeepers could move anywhere after the whistle is blown, but in this design there would be no incentive to move forward because of the greater distance (as the ball could float over their head).

Free kicks are more challenging than penalty kicks, and each team has several free kick specialists. But all eleven players (including goalkeepers) would kick before being allowed to attempt again.

It could be a "sudden death" contest – the first team that scores without the other team converting on their turn, wins.

(3) Bad Ideas

(1) *Coin toss or Drawn lots*: this utterly arbitrary option has been employed before. In the 1968 European Championship held in Italy, the home country won a *coin toss* after a tough 0-0 semi-final tie in Napoli with the Soviet Union. Italy went through to the Final, which they ultimately won in a replay against Yugoslavia in Rome.

In the 1975 Copa America competition, Peru went through to the Final, which they won in a replay against Colombia in Caracas, only after they *drew a lot* over Brazil, whom they had tied in a home and away series. In that unusual series, the home team lost each game, and although Peru had superior away goals, there was no away goal rule in that competition.

(2) *Counting infractions or possession*: there are some who advocate counting corner kicks or time of possession, and the team with the most should be declared the winner. These ludicrous ideas would lead to the "statistification" of the game (such as with the USA Big Four sports), and alter the aim of the sport, which is to score goals. Soccer is not a game of statistics, which is a key reason why it remains the beautiful game.

(3) *Shootouts:* In the event of a tie game, the defunct North American Soccer League used to have shootouts starting from the 35-yard line. The shootout was slightly more dynamic than penalties as the players were moving, and while slightly interesting to watch, they are now dismissed as silly. The shootout setup also involved the possibility of collisions and resultant injury to players, which should be minimized or eliminated after a full match.

Penalty Paradox Summary

Transforming the penalty pseudo-competition to decide a game winner will be a main challenge in the coming decade to those responsible for the Laws of Football. Although the after-time penalty competition rule has been in effect for only 30 years, the fans have already seen enough. Despite the game's inherent simplicity, the penalty paradox mocks soccer's essence by creating a superfluous and frivolous endgame. If soccer authorities cannot organize an effective, fair, and entertaining finish to the grand spectacle of a championship soccer match, the sport may well be headed for an international decline.

Chapter Sixteen

Soccer Future

Football is Sport and Sport is Peace. *FIFA[1]*

Soccer needs to free itself from the pharmacists and accountants. *Zdeněk Zeman[2]*

Soccer Change: Positive or Negative?

The future of soccer is uncertain, but not for want of speculation. Thousands of sportswriters and general reporters opine daily on the subject, and even scholarly reviews have appeared.[3] The only certainty is that soccer is dynamic and will change with time.

Rodney Marsh made a prescient statement in the early 1980's when he said, "in fifteen years the face of soccer will have changed completely."[4] Marsh suspected soccer would change, but few could have predicted a surplus of multi-millionaire players, ubiquitous advertising on uniforms and surrounding the pitch, and a faster, more violent, and often, a less creative game than 20 years ago.

Marsh's observation of soccer change will likely be repeated every 15 or 20 years. Indeed, Zeman has now identified two of the most pervasive negative modern changes; the search to make the game more physical through pharmaceutical means, and the increasing importance of money over the essence of soccer ("winning above all else"). But the most essential aspect of future soccer is that it must be positive; to create *positive play*, *positive sportsmanship*, and a *positive societal impression*.

Positive Play

The importance of *positive play* was noted by Rivaldo after the second Brazil-Turkey match up in the 2002 World Cup (which was a much less creative affair than the initial enthralling match), when he said, *"destroying the opponent is easy, but creating the game is difficult."* When the opposition is not just attacking the ball but also the opposing players with careless and violent tackling, the *creative forces of both teams are affected* and the game is most often a boring affair.

---

[1] From FIFA's *Fair Play* Code of Conduct for Football.
[2] *Zdeněk Zeman[2]* is a renowned Czech-Italian coach of many Serie A teams, and one of the strongest advocates for a fair football culture.
[3] A representative academic work is Garland, Dominic, and Rowe's edited volume: *The Future of Football: Challenges for the Twenty-First Century*.
[4] Rodney Marsh was a talented English player sometimes called the *"Clown Prince of Soccer,"* and *was* dubbed a *"Football Jester"* by anthropologist Desmond Morris. Pelé gave him his highest compliment of "plays like a Brazilian."

Soccer players are fitter than they were 20 years ago and now run 20% more in a game, and this increased movement means less space and time to manipulate the ball. But a higher fitness level without a high technique level also results in more violent off-the-ball contact, with tighter spaces and shorter times leading to more instances of "missing-the-ball" but "fouling the player" errors. Defensive players now commonly "play the man" (which is quite illegal) rather than "play the ball" (the actual point of the game).

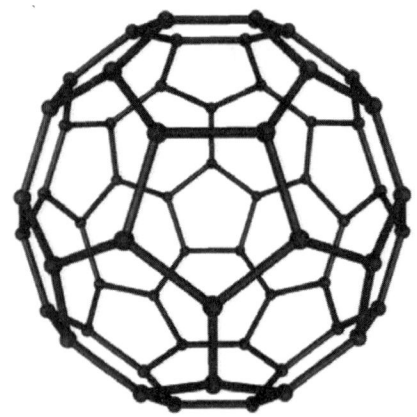

Will soccer continue to speed up – is it even possible for more speed? Twenty years hence, will players continue to be faster, further constricting space and time? Has soccer *already crossed the line in which athletics is more important than technique*? The brilliant BBC science fiction series *Red Dwarf* envisaged soccer three centuries from today, as lead character Lister idolized a player named Jim Bexley Speed who played 24th century "*Zero-G football.*"[5] This "evolved" soccer is presumably played in zero gravity using jetpacks on a three-dimensional cubic field in space. Perhaps a future "space soccer ball" will be made up of C_{60} *buckminsterfullerenes* – a form of pure carbon making up a polyhedron of 12 regular pentagons and 20 regular hexagons that form a perfect soccer ball model of 32 parts (model above).[6] If soccer continues to speed up, this scenario may not be far off.

Retired Brazil midfielder Sócrates proposed an elegant solution to restrain the seemingly inevitable trend of a more "physical" game of increased speeds, more collisions and violence, and less creativity. In Sócrates' view, modern soccer should be changed to a *nine versus nine* format rather than the current *eleven versus eleven* man game. The new configuration would presumably bring back the spaces of the game, thereby allowing more attractive creativity.[7]

Positive Sportsmanship

Good sportsmanship has unfortunately become less important in the modern hyper-competitive soccer world, where the line between marketing and sport has been increasingly obscured.

Under the new speed, stress, and high-money stakes of the modern game, even millionaire superstars lose their cool on the field and react violently in public temper tantrums against other players, the referee, or even the public. Examples of these phenomena are plentiful:

- Jose Luis Chilavert spat at Roberto Carlos near the end of his stellar career.
- Multiple Portuguese players manhandled the referee in the 2002 World Cup game against South Korea.
- Roy Keane admitted in his autobiography that he intentionally tried (and succeeded) to injure Manchester City player Alf Inge Haaland.
- Eric Cantona jumped into a grandstand and attacked a spectator with a karate kick.

---

[5] Red Dwarf website at: http://www.bbc.co.uk/comedy/reddwarf/.
[6] C_{60} is a third form of pure carbon discovered after graphite and diamonds. The C_{60} form is a type of *fullerene* – an allotrope of carbon in spherical, ellipsoid, or tubular form – also called a *buckminsterfullerene* (named after Buckminster Fuller, the architect who popularized the geodesic dome). Spherical fullerenes are also known as *buckyballs* – the C_{60} *buckminsterfullerene* is a truncated icosahedron buckyball. The C_{60} model is courtesy of Michael G. Ströck and Wikipedia.
[7] Socrates' plan is summarized in Alex Bellos' book, *Futebol: Soccer, The Brazilian Way*.

Three more examples from 2004 stand out:
- Francesco Totti spat at a Danish player in the European championship and was suspended three games. He also committed a horrific foul that could have ruined an opposition player's career.
- Marcelo Gallardo of River Plate head-butted a player, and then in the melee afterwards, gouged the face of Boca's goalkeeper Roberto Abbondanzieri, drawing blood. Gallardo was shown the red card and ejected from the match. Incredibly, both players are Argentine national players.
- Cuauhtémoc Blanco of Club América (Mexico) returned to the field after being ejected from the match to attack Sao Caetano (Brazil) players in the 2004 Copa Libertadores competition. For practically inciting a riot, he was suspended through the 2004 Copa America and banned from South American competition for one year.

All of the above actions are inexcusable, and these incidents by top players show that bad manners, poor sportsmanship, and violence are somehow acceptable – even for so-called superstar role models. Even if players are verbally abused, that is no excuse for violence interrupting the sanctity of the game. If taunts concern a player's national heritage or religion, then it is incumbent on the club teams, fan clubs, player associations, Football Associations, Football Confederations, FIFA and even the local legal system to protect players from these human-rights offenses.

It would also be prudent for players and even coaches to take a human diversity and tolerance course, in order to erase idiotic bigoted taunting. The full education of players and coaches will be a necessary first step to the elimination of racist taunting on the terraces.

Positive Societal Impression

Soccer has a long history of leaving a positive *societal impression* at the local level, but there is opportunity to do much more globally. Locally, soccer keeps children healthier and "off the streets," and they are less likely to become involved in drugs, gangs, and violence. Globally, soccer can and should combat the negative forces of xenophobia, gender inequality, and economic inequity more effectively, in order to contribute to basic human rights of societies.

Soccer cannot be neutral in these aspects, precisely as Michel Platini realized, that human rights cause is also soccer's cause. Platini said, "the future of soccer lies with the women," and his statement is really a revolution, for the development of women's soccer in different nations of the world will likely parallel women's improved economic, social, and political development [see Chapter 3 and Figure 4A].[8] To this end, World Soccer has more responsibilities to humanity than other sports, precisely because it is the most important global sport.

More women in soccer will hopefully humanize it more and allow soccer to fulfill its societal potential. Giulianotti and Williams recorded a women's soccer team opinion in 1993, when their shirts bore an illustration that from left to right depicted *a caveman, a USA-football player, a male soccer player, and a female soccer player*. Under the picture was the comment EVOLUTION. And why not? The women's game retains the beauty yet is so far without the violence and xenophobia of the men's game. It is evident the soccer men in

---

[8] Physical education is usually part of general education, and it is proven that the more education women obtain the healthier their societies become (better economies, better child health, etc). Soccer can fulfill an empowering role in women's education worldwide, thereby improving societies. Malcolm X predicted this in 1963, when he said "To educate the man is to educate an individual, to educate the woman is to educate and liberate a nation." In the West, the ascendance of women's soccer in the USA was started by the 1972 Title IX ruling prohibiting sex discrimination in education. Title IX subsequently elevated women's university sports opportunities and women's status as equals in society.

power have important things to learn from women in sports, politics, and society – including giving up some power so that women can realize their and humanity's potential.

FIFA is experimenting with new societal angles to promote soccer; for example, organizing a friendly match between the Brazilian and Haitian national teams in August 2004. The original purpose of the match was ostensibly to help curb violence and remove guns from the street in Haiti. However, the original plan of exchanging guns for tickets to the game had to be scrapped for practical reasons. The game also disturbed members of the Brazil national team, as the Brazilians from AC Milan were not allowed to participate, and captain Cafú (who desperately wanted to go to Haiti), was temporarily dropped from the national team. In addition, a golden chance was missed to enhance HIV education in Haiti – the country worst hit by the HIV epidemic in the Western hemisphere – although Ronaldo made an HIV awareness message in Haiti as he has done before in Brazil. If FIFA desires to organize well-meaning social-type games in the future, they must be better thought out and planned, or they will possibly create more animosity than goodwill. Brazil won 6-0 in a game closer than the score indicated, with three wonderful goals supplied by 2004 and 2005 *World Player of the Year* Ronaldinho.

Soccer Globalization

Soccer globalization[9] is now a reality, which carries both positive and negative connotations for the game.

The <u>positive</u> is that players from other countries are playing together on club teams, and even some national teams. This can only be good for international relations, as players become familiar with each other and realize that inherently people are not all that different. The mixture of playing styles potentially makes soccer art richer provided negative-thinking coaches do not inhibit player talents. When one watched the 2005-2006 teams of AC Milan, Arsenal, Barcelona, Lyon, Roma, and Villarreal, one witnessed both human diversity and football creativity at a high level.

The <u>negative</u> aspect of globalization is that the business/financial side of the game is attempting to dominate the aesthetic and tactical side – and often succeeding). Because of the enormous sums of money laid out for select players, teams consider adopting a *playing not to lose* style instead of engaging in the free-flow of attacking soccer they are capable of.

When confronted with a team that is technically superior, many teams will use *defensive shutdown and counterattack* tactics rather than play a creative technical game at the height of their abilities. Using this negative strategy, Liverpool was able to tie Barcelona 0-0 away, and continue to the UEFA Final in 2001. Ironically, Liverpool then won the UEFA Championship in a thrilling end-to-end 5-4 match against impressive Deportivo Alavés of Spain.

Still, defensive soccer tactics have made a comeback, as the game has concentrated on more man-to-man marking. Defensive players have become as fast as offensive players (which is good for the game) but there are more frequent and egregious fouls on the pitch (not good for the game). From a fan's viewpoint, these fouls destroy the creative flow and style of the football.

Firm defensive tactics were used to perfection by Otto Rehhagel's Greek team in the 2004 European Championship. Greece won their first European competition by scoring only seven goals in six games, an average of only 1.16 goals per game – the *lowest goal average to ever win a major soccer championship*. Not to begrudge Greece's accomplishment, but their best assets were fitness and defensive organization, with less of the creativity and offensive flair that fans expect to see from the "beautiful game."

---

[9] For the purposes of this book, "soccer globalization" refers to the more frequent involvement of "foreign" elements in international soccer, including more "foreign" players in national leagues, as well as increased foreign capital and control in clubs and even national teams (through foreign coaches and sponsors).

Soccer Rule Changes

Rule changes are inevitable in soccer, but as the sport design is already simple and beautiful, the Laws should be "tweaked to perfection," and amended rather than altered.

Substitutions were not permitted in soccer matches before the 1970 World Cup Finals,. If a player was injured, even if intentionally, he was forced to uselessly hobble about the field, or retire from the game altogether, leaving his team a man short.

Introducing substitutions may have seemed like a radical change in the game, but in reality was a natural extension of the rules allocating fit players to perform on the pitch. The substitution rule inevitably introduced new tactical changes; perhaps the earliest example was the 1970 Italian World Cup team that shared creative midfielder duties between Sandro Mazzola and Gianni Rivera. With the rule change, teams attempted to exploit their team depth, especially in a two game home-and-away series.

Below are some suggestions on soccer rule changes that may be forthcoming in the coming decades:

I. Game Architecture
Soccer Goes Metric

Most of the world uses the metric system, and the only strict remnants of inches, feet, and yards in soccer are in the original goalpost measurements of 24 feet long by 8 feet high, the 6 yard and 18 yard boxes and the 12 yard penalty kick spot.

Metric field dimensions are already specified by FIFA standards, but in the future the goal area and goal measurements may change slightly to make the game purely metric. The 6-yard box could be the 6-meter box, the penalty kick spot would be from 12 meters, and the 18-yard box would be the 18-meter area. However, this change would increase the respective distances by 11%, thereby seriously altering the field dimensions.

To make metric measurements more accurate to the current Old English style measurements (less than 0.3% difference), the new distances could be the 5.5-meter box, the 11-meter penalty kick spot, and the 16.5 meter box (the 5.5-11-16.5 setup preserving the 1-2-3 ratio); but this ratio is perhaps not so poetic as the original 6-12-18.

Goals could be slightly enlarged to 7.5 meters long by 2.5 meters high. This would keep the goal length: height ratio at 3:1, lengthening the current goal dimension by 7 inches and raising it by 2.4 inches, thereby increasing the distances by only 2.5%.

II. Soccer Art versus Brute Force

The escalation of more destructive physical strategies of soccer restricts the art and brutalizes the spirit of the sport, and teams that engage in these tactics are inevitably inferior in technique to their rivals. Two foul modes that seem to be continually executed in the game today are (1) pulling the shirt and (2) hands on the body - both infractions commonly occurring off-the-ball as well as on the ball. These foul types should be addressed for the good of the game, by amending existing rules and perhaps designing new equipment.

Shirt pulling rule and uniform flexibility

Shirt pulling has become an epidemic, ranging from ubiquitous shirt grabbing with the ball under contention, to Fernando Hierro's near disrobing of Niall Quinn in the 2002 World Cup (which backfired badly, earning Ireland a match-tying penalty kick).
Tighter shirts such as the figure-hugging Lycra suits (common for sprinters) would prevent most shirt pulling. The 2002 Italy shirts were very snug and hard to pull, and were one of the most stylish shirts of the competition. If one wanted to prevent pants-pulling as well, one could opt for a radical all-in-one figure-hugging uniform such as speed skaters use. Cameroon tried a unitard uniform at the 2004 African Cup, but the team was penalized for their usage, as FIFA did not approve of this design.

Hand checking rule

A soccer player should be able to freely move into space on the soccer field. Players *should not* be allowed to put their hands on another player, simply to impede his progress of moving into space that is not occupied. Players holding or grabbing, or otherwise impeding another player, should be cautioned (yellow card). This will especially give the forwards the needed freedom to get open, without being subjected to mugging tactics prevalent today. FIFA should consider this type of "hand-check" rule that has been a massive success in promoting free-play in the National Basketball Association in the USA (NBA rule B.1.d. – Fouls).

III. Control and Guidance of the Game

After a number of awful referee decisions that affected the outcomes of several first and second round games during the 2002 World Cup, FIFA President Sepp Blatter was quoted as saying, "A World Cup that receives the best players and teams in the world should be overseen by the best referees regardless of their nationality. From now on we will call in the best, full stop, even if they come from just a handful of countries."

Blatter unfortunately implied that certain countries could not provide top referees, while it is the *lack of referee training opportunities* inside their countries that result in inexperienced referees. An optimal solution would be to plan for a *professional and international referee cadre* that would be properly trained and experienced, and would be responsible for important matches and competitions. Otherwise, regular referees will probably not be able to keep up with the game speed of soccer's highest caliber competitions, and refereeing decisions will disappoint and outrage once again.

Finally, FIFA needs to keep their best referees in the game. After the 2005 Barcelona – Chelsea UEFA Champion's League match, Chelsea coach Jose Mourinho made some unfounded and harsh remarks towards Swedish referee Anders Frisk, who had done a good job. The subsequent email barrage from Chelsea fans and threats on his life were enough to make Frisk withdraw from the game permanently.

The UEFA brought charges against Chelsea and their staff, stating, "By further disseminating these wrong and unfounded statements, Chelsea FC allowed its technical staff to deliberately create a poisoned and negative ambience amongst the teams and to put pressure on the refereeing officials." UEFA identified exactly what was wrong with the statements coming from Chelsea, and is seemingly determined to derail this new negative trend before it can spread and damage soccer further. Still, even after being fined and suspended by UEFA, Mourinho failed to learn his lesson and later questioned the linesman after Chelsea was eliminated from the competition by Liverpool.

In the ultra-competitive modern soccer world, there has apparently developed a need for the reining in of provocative and false comments for the protection of soccer official's basic human rights; otherwise, soccer will be left without any of its best referees and linesmen.

IV. Trickery, Cheating, and Poor Refereeing

Despite ever-present video coverage, cheating in soccer is more prevalent than ever. Maradona's now-distant "Hand of God" hand-ball goal against England in the 1986 World Cup was scandalous and risky, as he could have gotten thrown out of the game for intentional handling of the ball. Maradona would never have then scored the "Goal of the Century" later in the game, nor would Argentina likely have played for the championship. Even a normally classy player such as Raúl Gonzales of Real Madrid beat Barcelona in 2001 with a "Hand of God" hand-ball goal.

The 2002 World Cup also featured some non-Fair Play action. During the first Turkey-Brazil match, although a foul against Luizão occurred outside the penalty area, Turkey was assessed a penalty kick, which Brazil's Rivaldo duly converted. A frustrated Hakan Unsal was then red-carded after he kicked the ball at Rivaldo's knees. Rivaldo faked the severity of the foul, and ultimately received a token fine of 11,250 Swiss francs by FIFA, which is not a credible deterrent to preventing future bad behavior. After the game, both Rivaldo and Luizão admitted faking the injury or foul. In Brazil, the advantage brought by faking is called "*malandragem*," and is unfortunately accepted in some countries as being a "smart play". The play-acting of "malandragem" does not bode well for soccer – what these players must realize is that the fans have much more appreciation for true skill than theatrical deception.

Are players so desperate to win that they have to cheat? Don't they realize that cameras are running and everybody can see the replays? Who is applauding the cheating? Not the vast majority of fans, who want to see good, clean, technical football. Where is the purity of the game, the Fair Play that FIFA promotes?

In short, ugly and cheating football is often winning out over aesthetically pleasing and honest football in the professional realm. So what to do?

A. Two Referees

It has unfortunately become routine in professional soccer that certain players will seek any advantage, including well-disguised illegal actions. The amount of punching, pulling, pinching, kicking, and illegal shirt-pulling in the modern game is distressing, and has everything to do with *playing the man rather than playing the ball.* Soccer occasionally evolves into a form of "Rollerball" even in the presence of competent referees, which is not an auspicious development for the future of the game.

One referee cannot be everywhere and see everything. Missed calls are increasingly deciding important games, and with tremendous monies and "honor" at stake, cheating players may be encouraged to continue.

How best to address this problem? Why not have two referees, or increase the power of the two assistant referees (the linesmen)? Regarding the latter proposal, however, it is probably impossible for the assistant referees to increase their duties due to the crucial importance of making the offside calls correctly.

Why might the lone referee need additional help? One needs only to compare the *referee to area to player* ratio to other professional sports to see the difficulty soccer referees have enforcing the rules of the beautiful game:

- Professional basketball has *two referees* to referee an area less than $1/10^{th}$ the size of a soccer field, with less than half the men (ten men on the court at one time).
- USA-football has a *crew of seven,* to police a field smaller than a soccer field with the same amount of players.
- Ice hockey has a *crew of three or four* (one or two referees and two linesman), to control an area ¼ the size of a soccer field with half the men (twelve men on the ice at one time).

Two referees for soccer matches are a possible, even an optimal solution. Following the lead of ice hockey and basketball, they would have equal powers. Although two referees have been tried out in a non-league format in England without apparent improvement over the single referee system, FIFA should not be so easily discouraged by an initial design failure.

B. Video-Assisted Refereeing (VAR)

Television and video allow the fans to immediately witness poor and often completely wrong refereeing decisions, which lead to unjust penalty kicks or offside rulings on justifiable goals. These decisions ruin the fan experience, as the game appears to be mocking its own Laws. There is no question that video refereeing, as performed by the NFL in USA-football, results in more correct calls, but is it right to do it? This question is even more important in soccer because it is a fluid game broken up only by offside and foul calls.

FIFA president Joseph Blatter initially stated that as long as he was in office, there would be no technological help for referees, rationalizing "If our game becomes scientific then we will take away its emotion and *no one would wonder* if someone was offside or onside, or whether a foul was inside the box or out (italics author)."

Blatter began to change his mind during the 2002 World Cup, as nobody is wondering now if Joaquin crossed the ball before it went over the line, resulting in Morrientes heading a Golden Goal that should have sent Spain on to play Germany in the semi-finals of the 2002 World Cup. It is on the video for all to see – the linesman made a 20 cm error that made all the difference in the match. The cruel irony is that the linesman was in perfect position to make the correct call. Even clearer was Vieri's onside status when he scored a goal against Croatia; he was ruled offside and his goal was annulled. A further example was Totti receiving a red card against South Korea for play-acting when a penalty should have been awarded to Italy, as Totti was fouled inside the 18-yard box.

These match circumstances illustrate perfectly why instant video replay will be necessary for World Cup Games and other important tournaments in the future. Spain had formerly underachieved in the World Cup, but in the 2002 Cup they had competed fairly in the host country, only for their historical misfortune to continue. As for history, the excellent but lucky South Korean team was the first Asian team to reach the semi-final level of the World Cup.

Critics have said that video-assisted refereeing will break up the flow of the game, but this is an unlikely outcome if VAR is properly organized and equipped. Frankly, *the chaos that occurs over gross refereeing errors takes up far more time than a quick video review and correction would.*

In 2003, FIFA began to advocate an electronic system consisting of a chip placed inside the ball to determine when it has completely crossed the goal line. Such a "smart ball" was successfully tested at the 2005 FIFA U-17 World Cup in Peru, but FIFA decided in December 2005 that the system was not yet ready for the 2006 Germany World Cup.

In January 2005, German firm Cairos Technologies proposed a 12-gram positional chip (called Smartball technology) to be inserted into game balls to ensure an accurate goal decision once the ball travels completely over the line. Their announcement came shortly after Tottenham Hotspur were denied victory against Manchester United on January 4, 2005 after an obvious 50-yard goal by Spurs player Pedro Mendes was not recognized by the three-man officiating team. Apparently the officiating trio were fooled by Manchester United's goalkeeper Roy Carroll throwing the ball back after it was *more than one meter over the goal line.* Some English bookmakers were so incensed by the officiating insult to soccer integrity that they paid out money to "winning" bettors – who had wagered that Mendes would score a goal.

The one point that Manchester United were erroneously awarded and the two points that Tottenham lost affected Tottenham's final standing in the Premiership. If the goal had stood and Tottenham won the match, they would have finished in eighth place ahead of Manchester City. As it was, Tottenham finished in ninth, tied on points with Manchester City but behind on goal difference. Both team finished just out of the European competitions and money.

After the match, a fan astutely pointed out that *"human error is part of the game, but blatant incompetence is not,"* a sentiment that this sorry episode exposed. Blatant officiating errors also raise the possibility of whether they are influenced by corruption (similar to events surrounding Germany's 2005 referee corruption crisis), which would not be a welcome investigation for any referee.

A similar ridiculous error occurred during a 1997 Bolton-Everton match, when Bolton had a clear goal ignored and the game ended 0-0. Not awarding the goal *cost Bolton their place in the Premiership*, as Bolton was relegated at the end of the 1997-1998 season on goal difference, despite being tied on points with – yes – Everton. True justice would have been Everton relegated three points behind Bolton.

In the Italian league game between Juventus and Chievo on 13 March 2005, the referees again failed to recognize a legitimate goal, in this case by Chievo's forward Sergio Pellissier. Shortly after half-time, Pellissier struck a tremendous shot that hit the Juventus upright, bounced into the goal, hit the upright again, and bounced out of the goal. Instant video replays from numerous camera angles proved the ball traveled well over the goal line. Juventus scored and won the game 1-0, taking three points instead of one. As league co-leaders Juventus and Milan stood even on points as well as goal difference after that match, the erroneous non-goal could have affected the Italian league championship. Luckily, Juventus eventually won the 2005 championship by a clear seven points. However, Chievo would have finished in 8th place instead of 14th place if Pellissier's goal had stood.

FIFA has still not reconciled the need for electronic assistance during the game, but gross and unavoidable refereeing errors suggest it is inevitable. In December 2005 FIFA announced that Smartball technology would not be used at the 2006 Germany World Cup, even after an apparently faultless debut at the 2005 U-17 World Cup in Peru. Perhaps FIFA is wisely taking its time to get the technology right.

The next necessary electronic referee aid (after the goal-line electronic measurement) would be an offside system similar to what is used on television replays, where a line is drawn and player positioning is clearly seen at the point of the pass release. The assistant referees would receive a signal when a true offside occurs, which could be via a handheld device or a light system along the sidelines. This electronic system could then free the assistant referees for the important duties of detecting infractions on their side of the field. A German company has already developed an electronic system that would help in correcting erroneous offside calls, but was not fully evaluated for the 2006 World Cup in Germany.

The 13 October 2004 World Cup qualifier between host Brazil and Colombia necessitated both a VAR and offside electronic system for the accurate resolution of the match. Colombia struck first with a legitimate goal that was wrongfully annulled (the ball had been played off a Brazil defender, and the goal scorer was not offside). Brazil's Adriano then struck a powerful shot off the underside of the bar, which crossed Colombia's goal line by at least 40 centimeters. The goal was annulled by the referee for *not* crossing the line, despite the video replay confirming a goal. A game that ended scoreless should have ended tied 1-1.

Entering into the video confirmation debate is the fact that *video is already playing a prominent part in the game, particularly in the disciplining of players*. For example, the English Football Association reviews game film before finalizing punishment concerning player incidents. Players can be adjudged as to the severity of infractions, and even be exonerated when previously thought guilty. After video review within 48 hours, an English referee may amend his decision for a yellow or red card, and even rescind his decision to send off the player. As a result of this retroactive "referee justice," the player would not serve a suspension (but of course he did miss the rest of the match by the referee's error). Listed here are some examples of video affecting disciplinary decisions in England:[10]

- In 2002 Birmingham's Aliou Cisse was sent off against Arsenal; after viewing the video evidence referee Riley decided that his decision was wrong and recommended no suspension for Cisse.
- In 2004, Chelsea's Didier Drogba and Portsmouth's Ricardo Fuller had their yellow cards for diving revoked by the match referees.
- In 2005, after reviewing the video evidence, Newcastle's Jermaine Jenas had his red card decision reversed by referee Bennett in his match report.

---

[10] FIFA does not yet condone video review for reviewing disciplinary actions, and is in disagreement with the English FA over rescinding yellow and red cards. The FIFA position is there must be no appeal for correction made on a disciplinary yellow or red card after a game, unless it is based on a case of mistaken identity.

- In 2006, Chelsea's Asier del Horno had his suspension reduced from three games to one game after a series of dangerous fouls on Barcelona starlet Lionel Messi. His red card was not revoked.

Referees should not perceive VAR as competition, but a tool to help them perform their jobs better, or even flawlessly. Technology that will improve decision-making on the field while not disrupting the flow of the match is well within grasp. The 21st century is the computer age, and if electronic assistance is not used in Mr. Blatter's tenure, it surely will be for the next FIFA President.[11]

V. Future Playing Surfaces

Although grass was not mentioned in either the original 1863 Laws of Soccer (they used the generic "ground"), or the modern FIFA Laws ("field of play" is used), the optimal surface for soccer has always been a perfect grass pitch. Soccer matches have always been subject to the whims of the environment, and keeping grass in good condition in a northern European stadium in the winter is expensive, as it demands considerable groundskeeper skill and equipment. It is also difficult to keep a field in good playing condition in other parts of the world due to drought or overly rainy weather conditions. Even when a grass field is in good condition, it is liable to be damaged due to overuse.

Even in this age of multimillionaire players, top division matches have taken place on substandard pitches. For example, in a 2003 match between Chelsea vs. Sunderland, the field was described as "playing on a sand pitch" (Chelsea won 4-1 on their substandard home field). A grievance was filed with the English FA to overturn the result, which was eventually denied. The Chelsea field surface was again in poor shape for their 2006 home European Champion's League match against Barcelona, but the visitors won 2-1 and therefore did not make a formal grievance. After the Barcelona loss Chelsea replaced their pitch with new grass, but they could only tie 1-1 in the return match at the impeccable pitch in the Camp Nou stadium in Barcelona (Barça advanced to the next round).

Hence the invention of artificial playing surfaces, designed to make field conditions predictable and less expensive to maintain. The original artificial turf in the 1970s had short blades of "grass" with resultant high bounces, as the concrete foundation underneath had insufficient padding. A few soccer teams in England and the North American Soccer League (NASL) used the first generation artificial turf as a cheaper and more convenient alternative to real grass. Professional soccer players universally detested the first generation turf, as it was much less forgiving than a grass surface.

However, modern technology has apparently made a better artificial turf, and FIFA has been sufficiently impressed that it is now keen to introduce the latest generation artificial turf to a worldwide setting, especially in locales that would have difficulty maintaining a traditional grass field. The latest plastic turf has longer blades and a rubber-sand foundation, which gives a truer ball bounce and has more "give" for the ankle and knee joints.

Because of the necessity to include the new generation artificial turf in soccer's rules, only as of July 1, 2004 were field materials included the Laws of Football (*Law 1 – The Field of Play*). The addition proclaimed, "If permitted under the applicable competition rules, matches may be played on a natural turf or artificial turf surface. In the case of artificial turf, the surface must meet the requisite quality standards (i.e. the FIFA Quality Concept for Artificial Turf or the International Artificial Turf Standard)."[12] The 2005 version was

---

[11] The main arguments against technology in soccer is that it is "un-natural" and that it will create a divide between the professional and amateur game. Both of these arguments are true, but if major (game-altering) errors are to be avoided in big competitions in the future basic technology must be used.
[12] 2004 FIFA Laws of Football; www.fifa.com/en/media/index/0,1369,74381,00.html?articleid=74381.

shortened further, "Matches may be played on natural or artificial surfaces, according to the rules of the competition."

The new generation artificial turf had already been used in the 2003 FIFA U-17 World Cup in Finland – even before it was included in the Laws of Football. Ten matches, including the Final, were played on the artificial turf, with more positive responses than negative. Adding to the positives was an apparent lack of serious injuries from the new pitch surface, which boded well for its acceptance elsewhere.

At the 2005 FIFA U-17 World Cup in Peru, new generation artificial fields were installed in all the participating stadiums, meaning that all thirty-two matches were played on artificial turf. The turf was so new that powdered rubber jumped from the field with nearly every strong kick. But the most surprising aspect of the tournament was that the Estadio Nacional (National Stadium) in Lima – historically the most important stadium in Peru – was outfitted with artificial turf. This change directly affects the Peruvian First Division soccer, as many of the league games are played at the stadium (including most of the "superclasicos" between top teams). Most of Peru's national team games have been played at the stadium, leaving the question open whether FIFA will sanction national team games on the artificial turf there, or whether Peru's future games will have to move to the privately owned Estadio Monumental in Ate in eastern Lima.

Not all are passionate about the new generation turf, especially in professional soccer. For example, successful ex-Celtic coach Martin O'Neill was vocal about his First Division team having to play on Dunfermline's artificial field at East End Park. Apparently, O'Neill has a permanent nostalgia for a good grass pitch – a sentiment surely shared by most professional coaches at this time.

The Non-Joy of Soccer: Violence and Xenophobia
A. Soccer Violence

"Hack-men" are players who harass "skill players" by illegally tackling in actions that are dangerous and may be meant to injure – in short, playing the man rather than the all. Hack-men were numerous in England and Argentina in the 1960s, and the hack credo unfortunately spread throughout Europe by the 1980s.

Some skill players in the 1970's, such as Rodney Marsh and Peter Osgood, tried to get their licks in with the hack men first, so as to discourage them. George Best simply tried to embarrass the hack-men, as he nutmegged and ran past them time after time.

Many players started using shin pads again in the 1980's, as hard play became the norm. Occasionally, a skill player would wear only one shin guard, to protect an injury inflicted by a hack-man. But without referee protection, even after the supposed banishment of the tackle from behind, skill players have had to adapt their game and their equipment.

FIFA mandated that shin pads be worn immediately before the 1990 World Cup in Italy. The exact reason why FIFA enjoined this rule is uncertain, but a lucid argument can be made that *its enactment has protected the hack-man as much or more than the skill players.* One argument for this rule was that the hack-men could ostensibly bring down the skill players with less damage. This is a poor rationale as a plastic shin pad does not in the least protect skill players from getting their ankles and knees ruined by hack men. Another argument was that shin pads were mandated because of the emergence of AIDS. This makes no medical sense, as leg injuries are rarely bloody and dangerous to other players. Facial injuries are the most common bloody accidents in soccer, and it would therefore be justifiable to focus attention on those injuries, regarding the infinitesimally small HIV and Hepatitis B risks in actual soccer play.[13]

---

[13] FIFA Circular No. 438 (July 6, 1990) states in general, "The referee should prevent a player who is bleeding profusely from taking further part in a match, until he has been adequately treated and the bleeding has stopped."

The only solution to the proliferation of hack-men is to enforce the rules and protect the skill players from the hacks. The 1990 World Cup was the first Cup to mandate the wearing of shin pads, and perhaps not accidentally, was the worst and most boring World Cup ever. There was little skill demonstrated, even from Maradona and the Argentina team that made the Final; in fact, Argentina was hacking pretty well themselves. Maradona had to wear not only shin pads but also bulky ankle guards to protect himself, thus losing his best touch on the ball. The next two World Cups in 1994 and 1998 brought the spectacle of *historically creative and goal-happy Brazil scoring zero goals in two consecutive World Cup Finals*, despite 240 minutes of regular and overtime play.

Brazil and the beautiful game returned to the World Cup Final again in 2002. But perhaps not coincidentally, many in the Brazil team were wearing tiny shin guards that would not inhibit their feel of the ball on their feet, but still placed them within the confines of the modern Laws of the Game.

B. Soccer Stadium Violence

Scotland's legendary player and coach Kenny Dalglish had the freak misfortune to witness three of soccer's worst crowd disasters: the 1971 Celtic – Rangers match in Glasgow that resulted in 66 deaths, the 1985 Liverpool – Juventus European Cup Final in Brussels that resulted in 39 deaths, and the 1989 Liverpool – Nottingham Forest FA Cup semi-final in Hillsborough that resulted in 95 deaths, the latter of which remains the worst sporting disaster in British history. Dalglish witnessed the first disaster as a spectator, the second as a player, and the third as Liverpool coach.

After Hillsborough, England finally got serious about stadium and fan safety, and demanded that their stadiums be of "all seat" design. The days of standing on the terraces were over, but the reward has been a lack of crowd disasters since.

Still, much of the world does not have all-seater stadiums, or worse, has poorly trained and/or motivated security personnel. Most of the modern stadium disasters (since 2000 there have been a few in African stadiums) still result from poorly trained staff, which are not trained to open gates in the event of over-crowding, and who inappropriately expose crowds to tear gas that results in stampeding and death.

FIFA still has a job to do with crowd control in much of the world, and should publish a handbook on which are the best stadium designs and crowd control methods.

The 2005 European Champions League brought the 20th anniversary and memory of the 1985 *Liverpool – Juventus* Final alive in the quarterfinals. In a measured statement, Dalglish appealed for peace and calm before the matches, as hooligans had instigated the 1985 Brussels disaster. The two games came off without serious problems, thereby best honoring those who died in the previous era of uncontrolled hooliganism and poor and ultimately inhumane crowd control. However, it was Milan's turn to become violent in the tournament, as the *AC Milan – Inter Milan* second leg quarterfinal had to be abandoned due to widespread flare and rocket throwing by Inter fans (Inter was losing 3-0 on aggregate). Something is very wrong when two teams from the same city – who even share the same San Siro stadium – cannot play a tournament game without senseless rioting.

C. Soccer Xenophobia

Xenophobia ("fear of the foreign," which encompasses ethnophobia and racism) has been a part of every modern culture to different degrees, but through the 20th century efforts of people like Mahatma Gandhi, Martin Luther King, Nelson Mandela, Malcolm X, Frantz Fanon, Rigoberta Menchú and many others, humanity has made great strides in attacking this nefarious stain on the species.

Xenophobia in soccer has not been limited to hooligans, but has also infected the ranks of the players, coaches, and administrators. Sometimes xenophobia is manifested in the most shocking places. For example, the city of Oxford, home of Oxford University, one of the world's most important academic institutions, is a place that should be free from xenophobia. However, it is also the home of Oxford United, who in 2001 suffered the shame of having their coach (ex-England player Mark Wright) fined and suspended for making a racist remark to a referee.

Spain has been an increasing focus of hooligan xenophobic behavior. The English team was subjected to shameful racist taunts when they visited Madrid to meet Spain for a friendly match in 2004. That game had been preceded by Spain coach Luis Aragones racially abusing star French striker Thierry Henry, a slur recorded for posterity by a Spanish television crew. Although the Spanish FA apologized for Aragones' remarks, Aragones did not and was fined a pitiful € 3,000 with no suspension. In 2006, Cameroon and Barcelona striker Samuel Eto'o tried to walk off the field after enduring racist taunts from Real Zaragoza's hooligans. His coach Frank Rijkaard, teammate Ronaldinho, and even opponent Ewerthon finally convinced the distraught player to continue, and he subsequently created Barça's second goal to seal a 2-0 victory. Eto'o had previously been abused at Real Zaragoza in 2005, the team drawing only a pitiful € 400 fine from the Spanish FA. The latest incident drew a € 9,000 fine – still woefully inadequate to affect hooligan behavior. The thoughtful Eto'o suggested that closing Zaragoza's La Romareda stadium for one year might be appropriate behavior-changing punishment, which would be a significant blow to Zaragoza's efforts to attract the 2014 Olympic games.

Aragones and others will continue to feel vindicated and remain at liberty to racially or ethnically slur players if the Spanish FA, UEFA, and FIFA do not take further action. All of the Anti-Racism efforts made by soccer fans worldwide will be in vain if this vile behavior is allowed to carry on unchecked.

In 2005, Lazio player Paolo Di Canio gave fascist salutes to crowds after matches. The player disingenuously claims he is a fascist and not a racist, ignoring the historical reality that racism has always been a prominent part of fascist ideology. It is obvious that this kind of gesture could easily lead to a riot, notwithstanding the gross indecency and outright aggression of this action against diverse people who suffered and died during World War II. The player was initially fined only 10,000 Euros, less than one week wages, and suspended only one game.[14] At Lazio (ex-dictator Mussolini's favorite team) games in 2005, their hooligan fans routinely wave Nazi flag and banners proclaiming "Rome is fascist," *despite these actions being against Italian law*. If the clubs and Italian justice refuse to enforce their own anti-xenophobia laws, then UEFA and FIFA must punish those clubs involved by banning them from European competitions.

Some public figures have stepped forward to join the anti-xenophobia effort that organized soccer seems incapable of addressing correctly. Juan Alberto Belloch, the mayor of Zaragoza, invited Eto'o as an official guest to showcase the city's multicultural aspects that contrast the horrendous treatment he has received at the soccer stadium. Walter Veltroni, the mayor of Rome, invited both Rome soccer teams (Roma and Lazio) to listen live to the stories of Jewish survivors of WWII. Many players were sensitive and appreciative of the opportunity to meet such historic figures, but Di Canio preferred to remain ignorant, saying, "I have my ideas."

---

[14] It does not help matters that two congressmen loyal to Italy's right-wing prime minister Silvio Berlusconi proposed to pay Di Canio's fine. Berlusconi also owns massive media companies and the AC Milan club, and appears to have lost his re-election bid in April 2006.

Soccer and Human Rights

Until FIFA develops a firm human rights policy for their sport and dispenses severe penalties for xenophobia, these behaviors will continue to do real harm to individuals and irreparably damage soccer's integrity. FIFA should take note that xenophobia has been clinically proven to negatively affect human health[15] – an additional reason beyond the ethical basis for abolishing such attacks at soccer matches. The xenophobic cancer is of existential importance to soccer's progressive investment on human diversity, and has the potential to override much of the immense virtue the game has delivered.[16]

Additionally, FIFA must enforce the United Nations Universal Declaration of Human Rights at all times. This apparently happened in 2004 when Israel was impeding the travel rights of Palestinian players. If Israel had not relented to FIFA pressure, they might have found themselves kicked out of the 2006 qualifying competition – which would have been extremely unpopular with the Israeli public. Still, if FIFA is to fully embrace human rights in its policies and actions, it must first acknowledge its own past transgressions (Chapter 13).[17]

Soccer in Life Perspective

Consider the differences between a poorly paid teacher, who has a direct effect on students' lives, and a professional soccer player, who is increasingly pampered, overpaid, and rapidly losing his roots to egoism and materialism. One educator described the dichotomy as such:

> "I have heard it said that there are two main differences between the high-priced athlete and a teacher. The first is that only a few athletes can compete at such a high skill level, whereas teachers are a dime a dozen. The second is that people won't pay to watch someone teach, whereas they fill stadiums to watch star athletes...
>
> My perspective is a little different. In one of those jobs you begin every new day with wild anticipation, wondering how you will react to what comes your way. Will you be up to the challenge? Will you make the play, or even better, get to the goal, or will you miss the ball? You are determined to do your best because you know how important you are to the team and what it means. Your life is focused and you can't think of any other place you'd rather be.
>
> The other job is just a bunch of men playing a game."[18]

The secret to a professional player's contentment is to stay true to oneself – stay close to your roots, remain humble, resist overt materialism, and support your community - be it local, national, or international - according to your abilities. That is how professional soccer can contribute far more to humanity than just the impressive aesthetic and athletic aspect of the beautiful game.

A wonderful example was made by retiring Sunderland and Ireland national team player Niall Quinn, who donated monies from his 2002 testimonial game (over $1.5 million), to charities in Ireland, England, and Calcutta. Quinn partially justified his decision as also being a gift to himself, explaining, "I have abused the privileged life I've had, and if this match is

---

[15] First noted by Dr. Frantz Fanon's studies in Algeria in the 1960s (documented in his book *The Wretched of the Earth*), and clinically proven in many studies since   Fanon died of lymphoma at the age of 36 in 1961 – the same age Bob Marley died in 1981.
[16] FIFA also needs to address gender inequality at FIFA sponsored events, such as the matches played in Iran that women are legally forbidden to attend.
[17] On 17 March 2006, FIFA rushed into effect an anti-racism punishment scheme of 3 points deduction for the first offense, 6 points for the second, and relegation for the third offense. Member associations must follow the guidelines or risk being suspended from FIFA for two years, which would also rule out that country's national team from competing. These guidelines are a start, but it remains to be seen whether they will be enforced or effective at curbing xenophobic behavior at select soccer games.
[18] Slightly altered from Jim Yerman's excellent book, *So You Want to be a Special Education Teacher?* 2001. Future Horizons, Inc. Arlington.

anything, it is me paying my debt. I am uncomfortable with the way football is going, has gone. If I hadn't become a professional footballer, if I'd stayed in Ireland and got a job, I think I would have been a far better person. I am convinced of that. That's the debt and it's something that crosses my mind every week."

Soccer Art Future

Art gave comfort to Early Man, allowing him some control over an environment in which he was in near constant danger. Today, Art provides consolation and meaning, counteracting the chaos of modern daily existence.

As Art is a universal possession of humanity, the Art of Soccer belongs to all. One need not venture far to appreciate this art – it is in the street just outside your door, or down the block at the neighborhood field. This "street" or "pickup" game model was the artisan and eventual artist model for Pelé, Cruyff, Maradona, Rivelino, and Beckenbauer. Even master soccer artist Rivelino's autobiography is titled *"Get out of the Street, Roberto!"* – a phrase he heard constantly from his mother in his childhood. But he has no regrets, saying, "The street formed me as a man and as a footballer." Rivelino and others believe that the cluttering up of Brazil's cities has led to a drop-off in street soccer, which means less talented young footballers in Brazil. If the progression from the street was good enough for the older stars, it should be good enough for the rest of us.

There are tens of thousands of high quality soccer artists that never make it to the professional world. *Ironically, it is on the non-professional playing fields around the world that aesthetic football is still predominant.* Often times, watching the apprentice hone his craft is as rewarding – if not more so – than watching the finished product that may be vastly overpaid and over-rated.

The soccer finished product has changed a lot in the last twenty years. Soccer is enduring a battle between the yin and the yang, the soft and the hard, the creative and the destructive. It is too early to predict which side will prevail, but it is not too early to predict that the popularity of football will decrease if the thug mentality of the hack-men wins out.

If professional soccer ceased to exist tomorrow, there would be just as many fans watching football, only it would be down the block at the local field instead of on television. Street and park soccer will hopefully always be the most accessible and ultimately important showcase of the talent and imagination that makes soccer the greatest team sport on earth.

Soccer, World Peace and the Human Future

Soccer is an important part of life, but its existence is not the salvation of humanity. Soccer is a tool, one that can be used to construct great works of art in the athletic realm – but it can also be much more.

Because of the privilege and burden of being the World Sport, soccer has an opportunity and obligation to be a major positive force for humankind. Some will say that this idea is untenable – that soccer is just a game. But South Africa ex-President and Nobel Peace Prize-winning Nelson Mandela's perceptive statement, *"We can reach far more people through sport than we can through political or educational programs. In that way, sport is more powerful than politics,"* cannot be ignored. Soccer is not just a game, and it remains soccer's responsibility to harness its aesthetic and harmonic power for the good of humanity.

The nomination of the Sport of Soccer for the 2001 Nobel Peace Prize by Swedish politician Lars Gustafsson was an inspired choice,[19] which however, was criticized for being premature.[20] For example, as long as Aragones' and Di Canio's action are barely punished, soccer has no chance at the award. But Gustafson's nomination remains much more worthy than previously awarded (Henry Kissinger – 1973) or nominated (George W. Bush – 2004) individuals, which had not only *not* fulfilled the Nobel Peace Prize requirements, but actively contradicted them.[21]

---

[19] Gustafsson's nomination letter on 18 January 2001 read: "Although modern sport has enhanced the understanding between people of different races and religions in different countries, it has never been awarded the Nobel Peace Prize. Therefore, to put notice on and encourage sports ability to create positive international contacts, a contribution to a more peaceful world, I hereby nominate football, the greatest sport of all, as a candidate for the Nobel Peace Prize for 2001. I propose that the recipient of the prize should be the *Federation Internationale de Football Association*, FIFA. Football seems to be a game that has attracted people for a very long time. In many different places, archaeologists believe themselves to have found evidence showing that we played a game similar to football 2 000 years ago. The modern form of football originated in Great Britain in mid-19th century and was elaborated in 1863 with permanent rules. Today it is clearly the most widespread game of all with an estimated 200 million active practisers (sic) and a global audience of billions. Taking part in the game of football, either as a player or as a spectator, is a way of expressing oneself in a universal language. With its common rules and principles of understanding, football creates a public meeting-place with no hindering boundaries. The game links people together from most nations of the world, from different continents and with varying history and culture. FIFA was established in 1904, gathering seven member countries, and was able to pass a milestone in 1930 when the organisation arranged the first World Championship in Montevideo, Uruguay. In 1998, FIFA counted 203 member countries. Given this, FIFA should not and cannot be seen as anything but a truly global organisation. Through the last nine decades, football has acted in a world suffering two world wars and innumerable conflicts between and within ethnical (sic) groups. But there are several notable accounts of positive border-transcending relations between peoples that were facilitated, or even made possible, through football. One example is when North and South Korea sent one common national team to the 1991 Junior World Championship in Portugal. Well ahead of political negotiations between the two countries. Another event of a similar kind was when Iran, Iraq, North- and South Korea met for talks regarding the arrangements for the Asian qualification-tournament to the 1994 World Championship. These meetings were held in a spirit of friendship and peace. Football has played and will continue to play an important role on the global arena, with reference to its ability to create understanding between different peoples. Because of its non-political purpose, football has proven to be very suitable for serving peace and understanding. Therefore it is time to notify, reward and encourage the game of football, its practicers (sic) and spectators, with a well-merited honour, The Nobel Peace Prize." Signed: Lars Gustafsson, Member of the Swedish Parliament, The Swedish Christian Democrats.

[20] The USA sports establishment was horrified, surely because none of the Big Four sports would ever be considered for the award. Not surprisingly, historically soccer-unfriendly magazine *Sports Illustrated* placed the story under their hyperbolic banner of "Signs of the Apocalypse."

[21] The Nobel Peace Prize committee requires that the recipient, according to Alfred Nobel's will, "*shall have done the most or the best work for fraternity between nations, or the abolition or reduction of standing armies, and for the holding and promotion of peace congresses.*" The Nobel Prize Committee needs to be more careful to whom it awards the Peace prize, such as the 1973 prize that was co-awarded to USA Secretary of State Henry Kissinger and Democratic Republic of Vietnam negotiator Le Duc Tho (Lê Đức Thọ) for signing the Vietnam Peace Agreement. However, Le Duc Tho declined to accept the award with Kissinger, as he viewed the prize as an inappropriate memorial of the end of an illegal war of Western hegemony perpetrated upon his people. Something is very wrong with the Peace Prize decision when one winner declines to accept.

Kissinger always tried his best to force his way to the side of kings, whether it was "King Tricky Dick" Nixon, soccer "King" Pelé, or old-blood monarchy figures. Kissinger was inexplicably named vice chairman of the 1994 World Cup USA organizing committee, although he should have been rebuffed on the basis of his obstruction of human rights of millions of Vietnamese and Cambodian civilians and even USA soldiers during the Vietnam War. For details on Kissinger's role in the history of the Vietnam War, see *Sideshow: Kissinger, Nixon, and the Destruction of Cambodia*, by William Shawcross (1979), and *The Trial of Henry Kissinger*, by Christopher Hutchins (2001). Also, on 23 March 2006 – just one day before the 30th anniversary of the Argentine coup that "ushered in the dictatorship that may have been the most murderous in modern South American history" (per Larry Rohter at the New York Times) – new documents obtained by the National Security Archive clearly show Kissinger encouraged the Argentine military junta even after being warned that repression in Argentina would be markedly increased – thereby setting an irrevocable course of USA support for the military dictatorship.

Bush initiated a military invasion of Iraq under false pretenses in 2003 – an action never sanctioned by the United Nations and opposed by most governments in the world (and even Pope John Paul II). UN Secretary General Kofi Annan and many other diplomatic and legal experts concluded that the invasion almost surely violated international law, and the war has since been challenged by millions of protestors around the globe.

It is certain that soccer means more to the world than any other single sport, and Gustafsson is on the right track to defining what soccer has meant to humanity and its sociopolitical framework. Whether that means that Soccer the Sport deserves the Peace prize is not yet obvious.

Soccer is both a mirror and metaphor of life, reflecting and illuminating a story of human joy and sometimes despair. As people celebrate the beautiful things in soccer – the soccer art and public service – there remain the unsightly aspects of hooliganism, xenophobia and violence. Soccer as the World Sport can do much more in terms of world public service, and definitely needs to control any violence derived from supposed passion for the sport.

Before FIFA would accept the prize for the Sport, they need to clean house for at least the next decade and prove to be corruption free. FIFA has squabbled with the European soccer federation UEFA and there has even been talk of UEFA succeeding from FIFA; this is unhealthy for the sport. There needs to be less ego and posturing and more progressive leadership from the FIFA administration. Although it is true that soccer promotes international fraternity, and soccer authorities have held some significant "peace" congresses (such as Anti-Racism conferences), it has not yet reduced any standing armies (although eliminating hooligan violence would be a first step).

Soccer in its organized form, which presumably would be FIFA accepting the prize, is not yet ready for a serious nomination. There is as of yet no human rights committee amongst the twenty-nine standing committees of FIFA, and such a committee will be a necessity for FIFA to seriously entertain winning the Peace Prize in the name of global soccer. Soccer can promote human rights like no other sport, and soccer's authorities must rise to the challenge.

The prime human health challenge for soccer is easily the HIV epidemic, as affected players have faced the ugly stigma of society and withered away without significant support. This needs to change immediately, with players becoming involved by the thousands in HIV prevention and support campaigns all over the globe. Soccer must take a leadership position against a disease that will soon have caused the demise of more humans than any other epidemic in history, *especially since the next World Cup is in 2010 in South Africa*, a country estimated to have more HIV-infected individuals than any other nation. In many ways, soccer is the ideal human creation to remove the savage stigma that has been placed on persons with HIV/AIDS by twisted traditions and bureaucracies – principally because modern societies revere these young people that play the beautiful game, and these youth are in prime position to save their own generation. A proper HIV/AIDS education and empowerment effort will take an unprecedented amount of time and planning from both soccer players and administrators before and during the 2010 World Cup.

Organized Football still needs more Fair Play in every aspect of the game – on and off the field – and needs to do far more good works in the international community. A rough first step for FIFA was promoting the Brazilian national team to travel to Haiti in August 2004, to try and rid the Haitian countryside of guns in exchange for tickets to the match. But because of social problems, it turned out to be largely just a football match, and did little to disarm the country. But however inauspicious the end result was, it signaled the much needed entry of *organized soccer* into the most important subject of the 21st century: human rights. A subsequent FIFA match for Tsunami relief played in Barcelona on February 15, 2005, was an appreciated event for a conscientious international sport ("Ronaldinho & Friends" beat "Andriy Shevchenko & Friends" 6-3). One year later, FIFA president Blatter stated that FIFA was not yet finished with the Tsunami Task Force – a welcome signal that FIFA is invested in the future of the region.

Soccer Essence – Human Essence

What soccer is more than anything is the Beautiful Game of the Global Village. And through this physical and intellectual beauty comes understanding – perhaps better than any other known to man.

Man communicates through Language, but there are hundreds of major languages in use. One must then use a translator, but what about untranslatable words and concepts? Music was said to be the universal language, but music is a cultural phenomenon not intuitively translatable to other cultures, and requires explanation as to the lyrics, music style, and interpretation. Even the lyrics of world musician Bob Marley require translation to be fully appreciated.[22]

Then there is soccer, the World's Game. If you take two people from around the globe and put them on a pitch, there is a good chance they will start communicating right away. Juggling and passing, they begin to understand each other through a physical language that is the door to all other forms of communication. That is the essential beauty of soccer, and the basis for its potential contribution to world peace.

---

[22] Football was also important to Marley's fellow musician and human rights activist John Lennon, as the cover of his album *Walls and Bridges* is a football game illustration he painted as a 12-year-old boy. Lennon was the author of *Imagine*, a song about the brotherhood of humanity, which was voted the number one all-time pop song in the 2005 Virgin Radio poll (www.virginradio.co.uk/music/top500/vote.html).

Chapter Seventeen

Soccer References and Resources

Ludere Causa Ludendi ["To play for the sake of playing"]   QPFC motto[1]

Arte Et Labor ["By Skill and Labor"]   Blackburn Rovers FC motto[2]

Soccer Books in English

There are thousands of soccer titles available in English; below are listed a selection of sixty of the most appealing in alphabetical order by author or editor. Most are recently published thoughtful and well-written works commenting on soccer's place in society and history as well as soccer's attributes as an athletic endeavor. A few older classic works are exceptional inclusions, as are four sports-oriented medical texts.

1. Allaway, Roger, Jose, Colin, Litterer, David. **The Encyclopedia of American Soccer History.** Scarecrow Press, Inc. 2001.
   Definitive book for history and statistics of the USA soccer experience, covering all aspects of USA soccer from the 1860's to 2000.

2. Armstrong, Gary, and Giulianotti, Richard, Eds. **Entering the Field: New Perspectives on World Football.** Berg, Oxford. 1997.
   A soccer sociology collection that includes essays on Brazilian, Italian, Argentine, Scottish, English, Palestinian, and African soccer. Explores topics such as, "Successes and Contradictions in 'Multiracial' Brazilian Football," and will reward the reader interested in investigative works about soccer and society.

3. Armstrong, Gary, and Giulianotti, Richard, Eds. **Football Cultures and Identities.** Macmillan Press, London. 1999.
   Excellent selections including "The Brazilian Style of Football and its Dilemmas," and "Everything in Moderation: The Swedish Model." For the reader who wants to understand why football is often not "just a game," but an integral part of the human cultural experience.

---

[1] "Ludere Causa Ludendi" is the Latin motto of Glasgow club Queen's Park Football Club (QPFC), which has been an amateur outfit since their inception in 1867 (www.queensparkfc.co.uk/home.htm). QPFC organized the first ever international match that occurred between Scotland and England on 30 November 1872, which ended in a 0-0 draw. All eleven of Scotland's players were QPFC players in that game.
[2] Blackburn FC is a founding member of the English Football League (1888) and the Premier League (1992).

4. Armstrong, Gary, and Giulianotti, Richard, Eds. **Fear and Loathing in World Football.** Berg, Oxford. 2001.

Another fascinating Armstrong and Giulianotti edited work exploring ethnic, class, and other societal contributions to the creation of soccer rivalries worldwide.

5. Back, Les, Crabbe, Tim, and Solomos, John. **Changing Face of Football: Racism, Multiculturalism and Identity in the English Game.** Berg Pub. Ltd. 2001.

A comprehensive investigation into racism and English football by three contributors of the anti-racism movement in Britain. Examines in detail the reaction of football culture to the integration of English society, the resulting increase in player diversity, and the public face of racism in football. Does anybody at the FA read these important books?

6. Bellos, Alex. **Futebol: Soccer, The Brazilian Way.** Bloomsbury, New York. 2002.

A fresh look at the all-consuming nature of *futebol* in Brazil. Bellos' research and interviews of both regular Brazilian citizens and soccer stars lead to surprising conclusions, some laugh-out-loud funny. The new definitive introduction to Brazilian soccer attitude in English, it also contains an invaluable listing of classic soccer works in Portuguese.

7. Bowler, Dave, and Bains, Jas. **Samba in the Smethwick End: Regis, Cunningham, Batson, and the Football Revolution.** Mainstream Publishing, Edinburgh. 2000.

A work documenting the rise and difficulties of "black" players in England in the 1970s and 1980s; specifically the trio of Laurie Cunningham, Cyrille Regis, and Brendon Batson at West Bromwich Albion. Public and institutional racism is thoroughly examined in this period in England. Whoever had the luck to see this trio perform will find an honorable account of their remarkable histories and skills. How a myopic and ineffective England team could have better used their talents!

8. Brooks, David. **The All-Time World Cup.** Parrs Wood Press. Manchester 2002.

One hundred and seventy-five page hallucination of what a World Cup would look like if all history's players were available. Games, goals, and events are invented out of thin air, all in good fun and mystery – *of what could have happened.*

9. Burns, Jimmy. **Hand of God: The Life of Diego Maradona, Soccer's Fallen Star.** Lyons Press, New York. 1996.

The *unofficial* autobiography of Diego Maradona, an exceptionally well-researched book written in an enjoyable prose. Examines all the personalities that influenced Maradona and his career, and in the process Burns necessarily introduces elements of exploitation, politics, and corruption in football. Young soccer players aspiring to be professionals should read this book to be aware of encounters and events to avoid – in order to reach their full soccer and personal potential.

10. Burns, Jimmy. **Barça: A People's Passion.** Bloomsbury, London. 1999.

A history of FC Barcelona, the historic soccer organization and the representative team of the Catalan region. Because Catalonia (Catalunya in Catalan) had their own language and culture officially repressed during the fascist Franco era, FC Barcelona has evolved from a simple football team into a symbol of self-identity and freedom. Written for the FC Barcelona's centenary year (1899-1999).

11. Butler, Richard. **Soccer and the Soul.** Queensgate, London. 1999.

Explores the existence and essence of British football featuring tons of great quotations from players and other individuals in football.

12. Caligiuri, Paul, and Herbst, Dan. **High-Performance Soccer.** Human Kinetics, Champaign. 1997.

A lucid analysis of the technical and mental aspects of soccer. Written by one of the USA's most important players ever, Caligiuri teaches techniques and tactics in an experienced and inspirational manner. Book should be read by young players intent on maximizing their potential and/or advancing beyond amateur soccer.

13. Cantor, André. **Goooal!** Simon & Schuster, New York. 1996.

A World Cup memorial written by the commentator famous for bringing the Goooal (Gooool in Spanish) celebration cry to the USA for the 1994 World Cup. Cantor reveals in this entertaining and informative work that he is a good journalist as well as an excellent play-by-play man. Each World Cup roundup is accompanied by a Cantor interview of one of the protagonists, including players who performed as far back as the 1930 World Cup!

14. Cashmore, Ellis. **Beckham.** Blackwell Publishers, Oxford. 2002.

An incisive work by a British Professor of Culture, Media, and Sport, which examines all three subjects with regards to worldwide soccer marketing and celebrity cults. Less an autobiography than an analysis of modern superficial celebrity status in an era when people are more famous for being famous than for tangible accomplishments.

15. Clifford, Simon. **Play the Brazilian Way.** Boxtree, London. 1999.

Enjoyable book written by a British football coach investigating what makes Brazilian soccer so fabulous. Introduces Brazilian *futebol de salão* (also called *futsal*) – which uses a heavier, smaller ball to encourage skill development – to the English-speaking world. The book also contains many excellent color photos demonstrating a variety of soccer techniques. Best book prose occurs when he attempts to describe some top players' favorite moves. Still, some moves are almost impossible to detail in words and would need a video series to do them justice.

16. Evans, Robert and Edward Bellion. **For the Good of the Game.** Youth Sports Publishing. 2001.

Comprehensive book written for amateur and professional referees. Examines all aspects of quality refereeing – including good positioning, foul calling, interactions with players, and psychology. Should be mandatory reading for all referees; players would also benefit from studying this book and realizing the tremendous challenges of the job.

17. FIFA. **FIFA Museum Collection.** Edition Q. Berlin. 1996.

Nearly 300-page quadruple language book of the history of soccer according to FIFA. An important historical work that is especially strong on historical items and old photos. A reference for the serious soccer history buff (See also below the 1904-2004 centenary FIFA book in Spanish).

18. Foer, Franklin. **How Soccer Explains the World: An Unlikely Theory of Globalization.** HarperCollins, New York. 2004.

Not necessarily a comprehensive theory of the effects of "globalization" on international soccer, this book weaves politics and sociology in coherent samplings of the new soccer order.

19. Freeman, Simon. **Own Goal! How Egotism and Greed are Destroying Football.** Orion. London. 2000.

Freeman's book chronicles the contemporary soccer slide into the massive wealth of the haves and have-not players and clubs, and the concessions required thereof. Well-written book in a penetrating style by a veteran British journalist.

20. Galeano, Eduardo. **Soccer in Sun and Shadow.** Verso, London. 1998.

A book of short stories – almost poems – about soccer experiences. Almost unique among soccer books, his short subjects are both magical and insightful. By a well-known Uruguayan writer, translated from the Spanish.

21. Gardner, Paul. **The Simplest Game.** 3rd edition. Macmillan, New York. 1996.

A wonderful look into the history and tournaments of soccer from the beginning to modern day soccer. Chapters on tactics and how soccer has changed are incisive. A British expatriate, Gardner is the most insightful soccer writer in the USA, and one of the best in the English language. Foreword by Pelé.

22. Gardner, Paul. **SoccerTalk: Life Under the Spell of the Round Ball.** Masters Press, USA. 1999.

A 30-year collection of magazine columns covering nearly every aspect of the game from the sterling soccer analyst. Foreword by USA national team coach Bruce Arena.

23. Garland, Jon, Dominic Malcolm and Michael Rowe, Eds. **The Future of Football: Challenges for the Twenty-First Century.** Frank Cass, London. 2000.

Presented as a football journal, it comprises fifteen articles addressing important subjects in the modern game, including community football, refereeing, and the effects of globalization, European law and racism on the game. An academic yet readable work.

24. Garland, Jon, & Rowe, Michael. **Racism and Anti-Racism in Football.** Palgrave, New York. 2001.

One of the best books on this subject, it addresses not only the history of racism and xenophobia but also the all-important strategies to identify and combat these human rights violations in soccer.

25. Giulianotti, Richard. **Football: A Sociology of the Game.** Polity Press, Cambridge, U.K. 1999.

A modern sociological study of soccer. Thoroughly referenced, it is written in a clear style for any reader. Recommended study for any player active in the professional soccer, in order to give them a more complete understanding of how the game affects the public, and how society affects them as players.

26. Giulianotti, Richard, and Williams, John, Eds. **Game Without Frontiers: Football, Identity, and Modernity.** Arena Ashgate Publishing, Aldershot. 1994.

Another excellent collection of football sociology studies from all over the world. The USA chapter is entitled "Stillborn in the USA?" and investigates (and forecasts) the fusion of soccer, commercialization, and materialism in the USA.

27. Glanville, Brian. **The Story of the World Cup.** Faber & Faber, London. 2001.

Story of all the World Cups from 1930 to the France triumph in 1998, written by prolific British author and soccer analyst Brian Glanville. The text has beautiful descriptions of field play, which is characteristic of Glanville's many soccer books.

28. Glanville, Brian. **A Book of Soccer.** Oxford University Press, New York. 1979.

A splendid effort by Glanville that captures the essence of soccer from the pre-Association days until the 1978 World Cup. Unparalleled for descriptions of soccer trends and events during the 20th century.

29. Goldblatt, David. **World Soccer Yearbook 2002-2003: The Complete Guide to the Game.** DK Publishing, New York. 2002.

This book is a cross between Jelinek & Tomeš' *Atlas* and Radnedge's *Encyclopedia*. Slightly less detailed than these definitive works, it provides a comprehensive overview of the modern game and contains excellent color photos.

30. Harris, Harry. **Pelé: His Life and Times.** Robson Books, London. 2000.

Modern-day biography of Pelé, which effectively follows up on Pelé's 1977 autobiography. Contains all appearances and goals in appendix form, and contains Pelé's comments on the modern game.

31. Hong, Fan. & Mangan JA, Eds. **Soccer, Women, Sexual Liberation: Kicking Off a New Era.** Frank Cass, London. 2004.

Excellent collection of articles on the development and struggle of women's soccer in societies. An international overview, with chapters not only on the USA and northern European countries but also on Korea, China, India, Brazil, and African soccer. Importantly points out that "South African society was not only segregated by race, but also by sex, in a system that exacerbated patriarchal "traditions" across different cultural groups." For example, football was forbidden for women as it was not deemed a "ladylike" sport. These are important points to recognize for combating the South African HIV epidemic.

32. Hornby, Nick. **Fever Pitch.** Riverhead Books, New York. 1992.

Apparent real-life story of a total football supporter: a lad is all consumed by his football team (in this case Arsenal), and obsessive condition persists into adulthood. An astute read into the neurotic world of an English football super-fanatic of the last 30 years. Sometimes pathetic, often hilarious. The book was made into a British movie in 1996, and later adapted to baseball(!) in the 2005 USA version.

33. Jelinek, Radovan, & Tomeš, Jiří. **The First World Atlas of Football.** Infokart. Prague. 2002.

The title says it all – the initial and therefore seminal atlas of international football. Filled with maps and crammed with football information ranging from top clubs and countries to tiny amateur outfits. The authors are cartographers, and as expected the maps are beautiful. Does your soccer-crazed boy or girl need to learn how to read maps? Get this book and they will teach themselves.

34. Jose, Colin. **NASL: A Complete Record of the North American Soccer League.** Breedon Books Sport. Derby. 1989.

Definitive book of the heavily foreign player North American Soccer League (NASL), beginning from its initiation in 1967 and ending in its demise in 1984. Contains all the stories and statistics of this epic league, which ultimately failed to fully incorporate soccer as a premier professional sport in the USA.

35. Kapuściński, Ryszard. **The Soccer War.** Vintage International, New York. 1992.

A Polish war reporter details his football observations within war zones. Kapuściński was at the Congo, Algeria, and Nigeria conflicts, and the Honduras-El Salvador soccer war, and presents the extreme but very real end of the spectrum of the inter-relations of football and society. Originally published in Polish (1978) as *Wojna Futbolowa*, and in Spanish as *La Guerra del Fútbol y Otros Reportajes*.

36. King, Colin. **Offside Racism: Playing the White Man.** Berg, Oxford, 2004.

An important and insightful look into the deeper pressures of racism in society and on the field. This book addresses some concerns not yet widely recognized and is thereby important.

37. Kuper, Simon. **Football Against the Enemy.** Orion, London. 1994.

The author has an eye for coincidence and controversy in football from his travels around the globe, and the essays of connected observations make an absorbing read. Kuper also edits the "Perfect Pitch" series of books that attempt to promote the "best new football writing."

38. Lanfranchi, Pierre. & Taylor, Matthew. **Moving With the Ball: The Migration of Professional Footballers.** Berg, Oxford. 2001.

The most complete and entertaining work concerning the early "globalization" of football labor and the migrations of footballers to new and promising shores.

39. Lyons, Andy, and Ticher, Mike, Eds. **Back Home: How the World Watched France 98.** WSC Books, London. 1998.

Twenty-five writers describe how the 1998 World Cup was observed in their native or adopted countries. A unique look at how the world's most popular game and most popular event is seen globally and in situations in which the fans have no chance to actually be present.

40. MacDonald, Tom. **The World Encyclopedia of Soccer: A Complete Guide to the Beautiful Game.** Anness Publishing, London. 2001.

A good overview of world soccer in 250 large format pages, many of which carry classic pictures of top players. Good history text and photos, including a picture of the England team giving the Nazi salute in Berlin in 1938 (before hammering the German team 6-3).

41. Markovits, Andrei S., and Hellerman, Steven L. **Offside: Soccer and American Exceptionalism.** Princeton University Press, Princeton. 2001.

This work examines how soccer was introduced into the USA in the 1860's yet did not achieve mainstream success – as opposed to the indigenous games of USA-football, baseball, and basketball. Examines USA sports sociology and postulates how soccer could achieve USA success in the era of globalization.

42. Morris, Desmond. **The Soccer Tribe.** Jonathan Cape, London. 1981.

Morris has written the most complete and entertaining anthropological work on soccer. The author – a noted popular anthropology writer (*The Naked Ape* and *Manwatching*) – wrote this book while a director of the British soccer club Oxford United. Besides the excellent writing, the book has copious high quality photographs. Indeed, one of the best-photographed soccer books ever published.

43. Murray, Bill. **The World's Game: A History of Soccer.** University of Illinois Press. 1998.

Written by a Scottish history professor living in Australia, this book explores the inter-relations between soccer, society, and historical events. Excellent piece of writing and research.

44. Pelé, with Robert Fish. **Pelé: My Life and the Beautiful Game.** Doubleday, New York. 1977.

The autobiography of soccer's greatest player, the book text finishing after his time with the New York Cosmos. The book is remarkable for revealing Pelé's emotions and experiences through his career, and his insights of Brazilian and international soccer in the 1950s-1970s.

45. Radnedge, Keir. **The Complete Encyclopedia of Soccer.** Carlton Books, London. 2000.

A standard for soccer information in the English language, it is well written and presented at 650 pages with numerous photographs. The British edition is of course, *The Complete Encyclopedia of Football.*

46. Reilly, Thomas & Williams, A. Mark, Eds. **Science and Soccer.** Routledge, London. 2003.

A good synopsis of the scientific aspects of soccer containing many excellent chapters on biomechanics and behavioral science topics, and an excellent short section on altitude training.

The authors acknowledge that soccer is an art: "That soccer itself is an art rather than a science is exemplified by the craft of great players like Zinedine Zidane or Brazil's Rivaldo, the erstwhile guile of Diego Maradona, the precision of David Beckham or the speed of Michael Owen. The game is aleatory and is partly determined by chance or strokes of individual genius. This uncertainty of outcome is part of its [universal] appeal." They then explain their book's purpose, "A scientific approach towards preparation for play can nevertheless enhance the enjoyment of both players and spectators. It can achieve this goal by enabling the team to play to its potential."

47. Rühn, Christov, Ed. **Le Foot: The Legends of French Football.** Abacus, London. 2000.

Edited by an expatriate Frenchman living in London, this book gives a good account of England's recent attraction to French footballers. Interesting chapters on both standard (France wins the 1998 World Cup) and offbeat (Fabien Barthez falls in love) topics. Best-known contributor is novelist Salman Rushdie.

48. Smith, Dave, Edwards, Pete, and Ward, Adam. **Step-By-Step Soccer Skills.** Hamlyn, London. 2000.

A very good introduction to soccer skills as practiced in modern Britain, presented in a large-format with lucid text and photos. Some football tricks included are associated more with Latin football than British, which must be an agreeable effect of football globalization.

49. Spurdens, David. **World Soccer Skills.** Hamlyn, London. 1984.

A top-notch skills manual for players who aspire to be quality footballers. Contains continental and radical moves, as well as some South American styles. Remains the most comprehensive individual skills book published in English. The book is only limited by the static medium of paper, which sub-optimally demonstrates dynamic actions.

50. Steen, Rob. **The Mavericks: English Football When Flair Wore Flares.** Mainstream Publishing, Edinburgh. 1994.

Details the story of seven English flair players – Stan Bowles, Tony Currie, Charlie George, Alan Hudson, Rodney Marsh, Peter Osgood, and Frank Worthington – who followed in the path of skill king George Best. Fascinating account of what English football could have been with the unleashing of their most creative players in the early 1970's. Boring English soccer and the absence of England in the 1974 and 1978 World Cups might have been averted had England gone the "skills" route rather than continue the outdated "work-rate" soccer model. Contains incisive interviews and enjoyable prose.

51. Sugden, John and Tomlinson, Alan. **FIFA and the Contest for World Football: Who Rules the Peoples' Game?** Polity Press, Cambridge. 1998.

A comprehensive investigation of FIFA's growth and shaping of world football. Details especially the reign of long-standing President João Havelange that ended in 1998.

52. Sugden, John, and Tomlinson, Alan. **Great Balls of Fire: How Big Money is Hijacking World Football.** Mainstream, London. 1999.

Excellent critique and documentation of the history of sponsors and their demands influencing/corrupting the world of football. Examines the evolution of the corporate control of football worldwide, including clubs and national teams.

53. Varley, Nick. **Parklife: A Search for the Heart of Football.** Penguin, London. 1999.

A journalist and fan's view of British football from the 1960s until 1998. *Parklife* covers many angles in its nine simply named chapters: Changes, Roots, One Spring Day, Winners, Losers, Bigots, Spectators, Players, and France. An honest and hopeful read of the modern British game.

54. Vasili, Phil. **Colouring Over the White Line: The History of Black Footballers in Britain.** Mainstream Publishing, Edinburgh. 2000.

A seminal work that documents from 1883 the involvement of "blacks" (in this book anybody not of pure European ethnicity) in British football. As the British empire collapsed in the 20th century Britain experienced explosive immigration, and the immigrant sons went on to excel in football despite ridiculous xenophobic barriers erected. An essential read for those who seek to understand the history of diversified societies and its contribution to football in nation-states. Author is active in the British FURD project (Football Unites, Racism Divides), and the foreword is by Trinidad and Tobago and 2006 World Cup goalkeeper Shaka Hislop.

55. Wagg, Stephen. **The Football World: A Contemporary Social History.** Harvester Press, Brighton. 1984.

An overview of soccer on the cusp of change, including "Soccer Slaves: Behind the Fight Against the Maximum Wage," and a prescient chapter on "Footballers in the Age of Publicity." Also has good insight on soccer and politics, including the import placed by pre-WWII fascist regimes.

56. Walvin, James. **Football and the Decline of Britain.** Macmillan, London. 1986.

Written by a prolific historian in direct response to the two British 1985 soccer disasters of Bradford and Brussels (the Heysel Stadium European Cup Final between Liverpool and Juventus). The book is divided into two parts; *People on the Inside* and *Outside Forces*, and contains excellent early chapters on *Racism and Fascism, The Distorting Mirror: The Media and the Game,* and *Politics and Sport.* More recently (2000), Walvin wrote "The People's Game," a revisit of soccer history.

57. Wesson, John. **The Science of Soccer.** Institute of Physics Publishing. Bristol. 2002.

Written by an English physics professor, this book contains all the physics formulas, diagrams, tables, and graphs that explain why a football bounces the way it does. Addressing shots off the crossbar, game theory, and statistics, this book is a must for every high school or "A" level Physics student who plays soccer.

58. Whittington, E. Michael. **The Sport of Life and Death: The MesoAmerican Ballgame.** Thames & Hudson. New York. 2001.

Unique book edited by a museum curator that documents the art-history exhibit of the same name. Documents the world's only creation story based around a ballgame (the *Popol Vuh*), and the oldest ballgame from 3,200 years ago in MesoAmerica. This new information would likely place the oldest origins of football in the New World rather than in the Old World (China) as previously assumed. Also, the MesoAmericans used bouncing rubber balls 2,700 years before the rest of the world caught on.

59. Widdows, Richard. **The Arco Book of Soccer Techniques and Tactics.** Arco Publishing, New York. 1983.

One of the best visual books of soccer, with hundreds of color photos of the best professionals and unambiguous illustrations by Paul Buckle. Has all the soccer basics information, plus flair extras such as the "nutmeg."

60. Yallop, David. **How They Stole the Game: The Book the FIFA President Tried to Ban.** Poetic Publishing, London. 1999.

Investigative journalist Yallop demonstrates that even if FIFA is officially apolitical, there is very little the FIFA administration did that was not driven by politics. The comeuppance of ex-FIFA President João Havelange, it is a fascinating read but would benefit from more complete documentation.

Soccer Books in Spanish

Below are a selection of eighteen of the author's favorite soccer books available in Spanish. Book authors and/or editors are from Argentina, England, France, Germany, Peru and Spain.

1. Alabarces, Pablo, Editor. **Futbologías: Fútbol, Identidad y Violencia en América Latina [Soccer Identity and Violence in Latin America]**. CLACSO, Buenos Aires. 2003.

    A compilation of fifteen articles in three parts that examine the sociology and economy of Latin American soccer. The cover contains an alarming photo of Atlético Madrid fans giving the fascist salute, an image illuminating one of soccer's major problems that the book endeavors to deconstruct. Also has interesting discussion of globalization and "gol-balization" in soccer.

2. Cappa, Ángel. **Y El Fútbol, Dónde Está? [And Where is Soccer?]**. PEISA, Lima. 2004.

    A book of soccer life observations by the well-traveled and successful Argentine coach. This is Cappa's polemic against both bad soccer and bad societal influences, which are seemingly more and more intertwined. He dedicates his book to his neighborhood and to the international fight against injustice.

3. Di Stéfano, Alfredo, with Enrique Ortego and Alfredo Relaño. **Gracias Vieja: Las Memorias del Mayor Mito del Fútbol [Thanks, Old Man: Memories of the Biggest Legend of Football]**. Aguilar, Buenos Aires. 2000.

    The autobiography of Alfredo Di Stéfano, published in the same year as his compatriot Maradona's autobiography. Performing for River Plate in Argentina and the renegade Millionarios in Columbia, and finally for the spectacular Real Madrid team that captured the first five European Cups – Di Stéfano had a successful career unlike any other.

4. Eisenberg, Christiane, Lanfranchi, Pierre, Mason, Tony, and Wahl, Alfred. **FIFA 1904-2004: Un Siglo de Fútbol [FIFA 1904-2004: A Century of Soccer]**. Pearson, Madrid. 2004.

    A concise history of soccer, naturally loaded with information of the history of FIFA. The best part of the book is the collection of historical photographs, prints and documents. The worst is the glorification of Henry Kissinger and Coca-Cola – the latter's propaganda merits nine free images in the last sixty pages of the book.

5. Federación Peruana de Fútbol. **Once Historias de Fútbol [Eleven Soccer Stories]**. FPF, Lima. 1997.

    A wonderful collection of soccer writings from eleven authors – including three Nobel prize winners. Albert Camus, Camilo José Cela, Gabriel García Márquez, and eight others narrate their football memories.

6. García Candau, Julián. **Épica y Lírica del Fútbol [Epics and Stories of Football]**. Alianza Editorial, Madrid. 1997.

    Twenty-eight chapters about different aspects of the game, with stories annotated by the most poignant soccer poems from Latin America. Four chapter title examples are: The Goal, Number 10, Football Makes Music, and Football and Religion.

7. García Candau, Julián. **Madrid - Barça: Historia de un Desamor [Madrid – Barça: Story of a Loathing]**. El País. Madrid. 1996.

    Book covers the history of the world's greatest derby between Barcelona and Real Madrid. Documents important historical details, including players forced into exile or jailed during the Spanish Civil War. Many excellent photos, including one of Alfredo Di Stéfano wearing the colors of Barcelona.

8. Maradona, Diego, with Daniel Arcucci & Ernesto Bialo. **Yo Soy el Diego de la Gente [I am Diego of the People]**. Planeta, Buenos Aries. 2000.

    The *official* autobiography of the Argentine supernova, who had as many serious problems (drug addiction, extra women, tax problems) as brilliant successes (World Cup winner, Serie A winner). More than an illumination of his career, it is a dubious celebration of his life and style since he avoids the most damaging events. Features frank opinions of persons and situations, and many pictures including a semi-nude. As usual, Maradona does not evade controversy – he sees himself as a simple worker providing entertainment for his people. An intriguing section is where he names his hundred favorite players (thirty-seven are Argentines), and Pelé is number one despite their public squabbling over the years. Maradona avoids the issue of who was better by stating his list is not a ranking. Advise as a companion read with Burn's book *Hand of God*, to find out what made Maradona tick.

Some sections are written in a street slang style that make a literal English translation challenging. Book was eventually published in England in 2004 as *El Diego: The Autobiography of the World's Greatest Footballer Diego Maradona*.

9. Marías, Javier. **Salvajes y Sentimentales: Letras de Fútbol [Savageness and Sentiments: Football Letters]**. Aguilar, Madrid. 2000.

A collection of short essays mostly recounting Real Madrid and Barcelona football stories, and enriched with notations from around the world.

10. Milliones, Luis, Aldo Panfichi & Victor Vich. **En el Corazón del Pueblo: Pasión y Gloria de Alianza Lima 1901-2001. [In the Heart of the People: Alianza Lima's Passion and Glory 1901-2001]**. FECP, Lima. 2002.

Written by three academics, it is the definitive history of Alianza Lima, the oldest and most storied club in Peru, the club of Alejandro Villanueva, Juan Valdivieso, Teófilo Cubillas, Hugo Sotil, Cesar Cueto and other soccer legends. Alianza won the Peruvian championship on its 100th anniversary in 2001.

11. Perryman, Mark. **La Filosofía del Fútbol: Patadas y Pensamiento. [Published in English as: Philosophy Football: Eleven Great Thinkers Play it Deep]**. Edhasa, Barcelona. 1999.

Perryman introduces his all-star cast of philosophers who dabbled in soccer or its tangents: Albert Camus in goal, Friedrich Nietzsche and Ludwig Wittgenstein in central defense, Simone de Beauvoir and Jean Baudrillard as attacking defenders, William Shakespeare and Sun Zi in central midfield, Oscar Wilde and Bob Marley as extreme creators, and Umberto Eco and Antonio Gramsci as center forwards. The book evolved into the internet website www.philosophyfootball.com, where one can find all sorts of "inspirational" soccer products.

12. Relaño, Alfredo. **Futbolcedario [Football Alfabet]**. Aguilar, Madrid. 1996.

Not a children's book, but an insightful look at the Spanish and international phrases of football arranged by letters of the alphabet. Accompanied by relevant photos.

13. Relaño, Alfredo. **Futbol: Contado con Sencillez [Soccer: Simply Told]**. MAEVA, Madrid. 2001.

Relaño's short interpretation of soccer history from English birth to the present. Particularly valuable for soccer insights concerning the Spanish and Second World Wars.

14. Sánchez León, Abelardo. **La Balada del Gol Perdido: Lima, la Seducción de la Nostalgia [The Ballad of the Lost Goal: Lima, the Seduction of Nostalgia]**. PEISA, Lima. 1998.

Book of essays on what football means to the Peruvian community, with many national and international references.

15. Sebreli, Juan José. **La Era del Fútbol [The Time of Football]**. Editorial Sudamericana. Buenos Aries. 1998.

Mixing in philosophy, sociology, and anthropology, Sebreli comments on the essentials of the football life in thirteen simply named chapters. Favorite chapters are Football and Money, Football and Magic, Football and Eros, Football and Violence, Football and Politics, and Football and Civilization. Also has a chapter on Maradona (The Maradona Myth), where he chronicles the defects of his life and the limitations of his game – concluding that Maradona was not the best ever soccer player.

16. Ternero, Freddy. **Si Se Puede! La Conquista de un Sueño.** [Yes You Can: The Conquest of a Dream].

The part autobiography/diary of coach Freddy Ternero, who led Peru team Cienciano to the 2003 Copa Sudamericana and Recopa titles (see Chapter 11). Ternero was subsequently made Peru's national team coach in 2005.

17. Thorndike, Guillermo. **El Reves de Morir. [The Reverse of Dying].** Mosca Azul, Lima. 1978.
   Highlights the history of the early Alianza Lima teams, the life of star player Alejandro Villanueva, and the Peruvian soccer team experience in the 1936 Berlin Olympic games. A soccer documentary work written in descriptive style.

18. Valdano, Jorge. **Los Cuadernos de Valdano. [Valdano's Notebook].** Aguilar, Buenos Aires. 1997.
   Breezy book of football observations and other distractions by the footballing compatriot of Maradona. Valdano – whose football nickname in Argentina was El Filósofo (The Philosopher) – went on to coach Real Madrid and later entered club management.

Medical Books

1. Harries, M, Williams C, Stanish WD, Micheli LJ, Eds. **Oxford Textbook of Sports Medicine.** 2nd edition. Oxford University Press. Oxford. 2000.
   A complete text on sports medicine and injuries, with a new edition expected shortly. The first chapter is the philosophical *Man as an Athlete*, and it also contains important chapters on nutrition, sports psychology, and the growing and aging athlete.

2. Hornbein, TF, and Schoene, RB, eds. **High Altitude: An Exploration of Human Adaptation.** Marcel Dekker, New York. 2001.
   A comprehensive work on altitude medicine written in an eminently readable style. For the medical professional and/or coach that needs to understand the possibilities and side effects of playing at altitude.

3. Sherry, Eugene, and Wilson, Stephen, eds. **Oxford Handbook of Sports Medicine.** Oxford University Press, Oxford. 1998.
   Nine hundred-page pocket summary of virtually any sports injury, as well as nutritional and preventive medicine information. Relevant reference for the interested player, coach, or medical provider.

4. West, JB. **High Life. A History of High Altitude Physiology and Medicine.** Oxford University Press, Oxford. 1998.
   Another comprehensive work on altitude medicine, with an unparalleled history of the subspecialty presented, including many rare photographs.

Soccer Books in German

One recent German book is notable for its idiosyncrasies and copious information (although much is glorious trivia). A breezy and humorous read for the German *fussball* fan.

1. Augustin, Eduard, von Keisenberg, Philipp, Zaschke, Christian. **Fussball Unser: Was Man Nicht Alles Wissen Muss [Our Football: Trivia].** Suddeutsche Zeitung Edition, Munich. 2005.
   This new entry presents itself as a football Bible (the title is a play on "Vater Unser" [Our Father]), complete with black leather binding, gilt-edged paper and a cloth bookmark. Dozens of idiosyncratic soccer lists and stories are its main attraction. A big hit in Germany, but will be difficult to translate to other languages because of it dominant focus on German soccer events.

World Soccer Magazines

A Bola. (Portugal).   www.abola.pt
A major football magazine from Portugal, with a nice website with minimal advertising.

Don Balón. (Spain)   www.donbalon.es
Barcelona-based magazine concentrating on Spanish football, but also publishes international football stories.

El Grafico. (Argentina).   www.elgrafico.com.ar
The major sport and football magazine for Argentina, which mostly covers their national scene.

FourFourTwo. (England)   www.fourfourtwo.premiumtv.co.uk
English magazine cheekily named for the 4-4-2 soccer formation. Tons of information about British football, with less on international topics. Generally well written, the *FourFourTwo* style is longer in-depth informative and entertaining articles, off-beat pieces, and interviews.

Fanatik. (Turkey)   www.fanatik.com.tr
The main sports (mainly football) magazine from Turkey.

France Football. (France)   www.francefootball.fr
One of two major French language football magazines.

Kicker. (Germany)   www.kicker.de
German-based football magazine concentrating on Bundesliga information, with some international stories.

La Gazzetta dello Sport. (Italy)   www.gazzetta.it
Covers all sport, but a large amount of football, especially Serie A and the *azzurri*.

O Jogo. (Portugal)   www.ojogo.pt
Portuguese sport magazine with great concentration on the Portuguese football scene. Competes with *A Bola*.

Onze Mondial. (France)   No website
One of two major French language football magazines, and names their European Footballer of the Year (Onze d'Or).

Placar. (Brazil)   www.placar.com.br
The major football magazine from Brazil, it is also responsible for handing out various *Placar* awards.

Soccer America. (USA)   www.socceramerica.com
Covers mostly the MLS (Major League Soccer) league, other domestic semi-pro leagues, university, amateur, and youth soccer in the USA.

Voetbal International. (Holland)   www.vi.nl
Dutch magazine covering club and national teams, as well as many overseas Dutch players. Up-to-date website accompanies the magazine.

When Saturday Comes. (England)   www.wsc.co.uk
Touted as the "half decent football magazine," it has intelligent commentary from a fan's perspective. Also has a welcome mischievous side, poking usually deserving fun at players, managers, and organizations alike.

World Soccer. (England)   www.worldsoccer.com

    The definitive soccer magazine in the English language (based in England but British soccer is not overemphasized). Has all international information, with an emphasis on the European soccer scene. Even the original 1960 *World Soccer* issue contained important international information. The writing style is concise pieces and interviews with little excess, and excellent commentary.

Internet Sites

    There are thousands of soccer/football websites on the Internet. Below are listed some important sites that will provide the soccer enthusiast with relevant information and links. Soccer websites are divided into two general categories:

(1) **Informational:** Many of these are official sites representing organizations, or sites set up by soccer enthusiasts. The general sites listed below are some of the best.

(2) **Entertainment and Marketing:** These soccer portal sites aim to entertain, with video, animations, games, and more to keep the enthusiast engaged. These sites invariably offer merchandise for sale.

Many sites integrate both categories. For example, many team sites have excellent information as well as entertainment, and have a shop attached.

I. General Informational Sites:

1. Rec. Sport. Soccer Statistics Foundation [RSSSF].   www.rsssf.com

    This is the best informational site, an awesome international soccer archive that is the most complete statistical soccer page existing. Has virtually any historical soccer information, not only results of games, but often has the actual lineups.

2. FIFA. Fédération Internationale de Football Association.   www.fifa.com

    Many useful areas on this site, including the Laws of the Game, regional and national football federation sites, and latest news from FIFA. The confederation sites have basic information on many country members of FIFA, as well as links to many club teams.

    The six Confederation websites are listed below:

    (1) **AFC. Asian Football Confederation.**   www.the-afc.com

    (2) **CAF. Confédération Africaine de Football.**   www.cafonline.com

    (3) **CONCACAF. Confederation of North, Central American & Caribbean Association Football.**   www.concacaf.com

[CONCACAF acronym is derived from **CO**nfederation of **N**orth, **C**entral **A**merican & **C**aribbean **A**ssociation **F**ootball].

    (4) **CONMEBOL. Confederación Sudamericana de Fútbol.**   www.conmebol.com

[CONMEBOL acronym is derived from **CON**federación suda**ME**ricana de Fút**BOL**].

    (5) **OFC. Oceania Football Confederation.**   www.oceaniafootball.com

    (6) **UEFA. Union of European Football Associations.**   www.uefa.com

3. National Soccer Hall of Fame. [USA]   www.soccerhall.org

    Superb site from the US Soccer Museum located in Oneonta, New York. Contains the complete US Soccer archives, US Open Cup results, and much more information of USA soccer history.

4. National Football Museum. [England]   www.nationalfootballmuseum.com

    Introductory website to the English football museum located in Preston North End's Deepdale stadium. As of printing time, still not much information on the website.

5. World Stadiums. www.worldstadiums.com
Basic information about many of the world's football stadiums.

6. Fussballdaten. www.fussballdaten.de
Comprehensive site in German that gives career data on most professional players.

6. World Cup sites.
  (1) www.worldcup-history.com
     Excellent unofficial site of World Cup statistics and information.
  (2) www.rsssf.com/tablesw/worldcup.html.
     From the main RSSSF site.
  (3) www.fifaworldcup.yahoo.com.
     Official FIFA site covers only the most recent World Cup action in depth.

7. Federation and National Team sites.

ARGENTINA [Asociación del Fútbol Argentino]. www.afa.org.ar

BRAZIL [Confederação Brasileira de Futebol]. www.cbfnews.com.br

ECUADOR [Federación Ecuatoriana de Fútbol]. www.equafutbol.org

ENGLAND [English Football Association]. www.thefa.com

HOLLAND [De Koninklijke Nederlandse Voetbalbond]. www.knvb.nl

ITALY [Federazione Italiana Giuoco Calcio]. www.figc.it

FRANCE [Fédération Française de Football]. www.fff.fr

GERMANY [Deutscher Fussball-Bund]. www.dfb.de

MEXICO [Federación Mexicana de Fútbol Asociación]. www.femexfut.org.mx

PARAGUAY [Asociación Paraguaya de Fútbol]. www.afp.org.py

PERU [La Federación Peruana de Fútbol]. www.fpf.com.pe

SPAIN [Real Federación Española de Fútbol]. www.rfef.es

SWEDEN [Svenska Fotbollförbundet]. www.svenskfotboll.se

SWITZERLAND [Schweizerischer Fussball-Verband]. www.football.ch

URUGUAY [Asociación Uruguaya de Fútbol]. www.auf.org.uy

USA [United States Soccer Federation]. www.us-soccer.com

Also informative is: www.sams-army.com, website of the "unofficial supporters club for the United States National Soccer Team."

The rest of the website addresses of the national football federations can be found by clicking on the confederation links at the FIFA site:
http://www.fifa.com/en/organisation/confederations/index.html.

II. Entertainment and Marketing

There are thousands of soccer portals and shopping sites existing, and the numbers are growing. Listed alphabetically below are five sites for a unique soccer experience.

1. Futbolmasters.   www.futbolmasters.com

Website setup by Top Modern Era players Teófilo Cubillas, Eusébio, Elias Figueroa, Kevin Keegan, Gerd Müller, and Roberto Rivelino, and now includes dozens of other players.

2. Futebol: The Brazilian Way of Life.   www.futebolthebrazilianwayoflife.com

Excellent website by author Alex Bellos, which covers many aspects of Brazilian *futebol*. Even has a musical section that plays important Brazilian music pieces of various styles that have football themes.

3. Johan Cruyff Academics International   www.cruyffacademics.org/eng/index.asp

Academic programs for empowering athletes and students, created by Johan Cruyff's academic team. Specializes in educational innovation and sports management.

4. PhilosophyFootball.com.   www.philosophyfootball.com

Soccer fan store features shirts with dozens of quotations by players such as Pelé, Johan Cruyff, and George Best, and personalities such as Che Guevara, Bob Marley, and Friedrich Nietzsche.

5. The Global Game.   www.theglobalgame.com

Very well informed international soccer site run by several editors, with back issues from 2003. Current incisive commentary featured on all soccer subjects.

Epilogue

Chapter Eighteen

Modern Soccer Odyssey

Love…Love…Love. *Pelé[1]*

It [fútbol] is not just a simple game. It is a weapon of the revolution. *Che Guevara[2]*

Every person who has played soccer seriously has a story about how, when and where they developed soccer skills, learned the nuances of the sport, and fell in love with the beautiful game. I must admit an initial reluctance to share my story because it might seem egotistic and/or irrelevant. After all, my official soccer "career" was only university and semi-professional soccer until I pursued a career in medicine and public health.

So this chapter was originally written only to commit to paper the soccer experiences in my life, never intending to publish. But at the conclusion of recording the soccer tokens of my memory, I realized this chapter both explores human diversity and illustrates the mystique of soccer in a life; two international themes that merit further investigation.

It is my sincere hope that including my experiences will allow the reader to flow back into time and reminisce of how and with whom they learned and enjoyed the game. This chapter also serves as a memoriam to those who helped me appreciate this most human sport. Real life names are mentioned not to embarrass anyone, but rather to remember the good times, and how much I enjoyed playing with them.

---

[1] These are Pelé's words to the crowd at his testimonial game in Giants Stadium in New Jersey (USA), which matched his first club Santos against his last club Cosmos.
[2] Ernesto "Che" Guevara was an Argentine doctor and Cuban revolutionary who helped oust Cuban dictator Fulgencio Batista in 1959. Guevara's quote epitomizes his love for the game, and the recognition that soccer is integral to South American identity. In his first book *Mi Primer Gran Viaje* (*My First Big Trip* - made into the movie *The Motorcycle Diaries* in 2004), he tells of going to a famous match in Bogotá between Millionarios of Colombia and Real Madrid of Spain – the best of South America soccer versus the best of Europe. This match would have been one of two games Real Madrid met Millionarios in 1952 (either July 6th or 9th), both of which the home side Millionarios won by 2-1 scores. After those matches, Real Madrid was intent on signing Millionarios' star player Alfredo Di Stéfano, which signaled the beginning of the best South American players migrating to Europe for club, and often new country, careers (Di Stéfano initially played for Argentina but later played for his adopted country of Spain). *The Motorcycle Diaries* shows Guevara playing soccer at the San Pablo leprosy colony in Peru (he excelled as a goalkeeper probably because of his chronic asthma condition).

Early Years

I was born in 1957 in New York City to my expectant parents and cheerful two-year-old sister. My father had immigrated to the United States from Bern, Switzerland seven years earlier, seeking an outlet for his artistic talent and bringing a European's appreciation of Jazz music. My mother was a native New Jerseyan, also a fine artist with an aptitude for mathematics.

The year 1957 must have been especially memorable for Dad because his hometown football team, the Young Boys, won the first of four consecutive Swiss championships. Young Boys' previous championship had been won in 1929, so the inhabitants of the Swiss capital city could at last celebrate after a lackluster three decades of local soccer. After consecutive championship number four (vier/quatre/quattro/quatter[3]) in 1960, YB (pronounced "E-Bay" in Switzerland) failed to win another championship until 1986, and even dropped out of the Swiss First Division in the 1990's, to be promoted back in 2001. Young Boys, along with Grasshoppers from Zurich, are the only two First Division Swiss teams to have English names, which honor the English contribution to the development of soccer in Switzerland.

My birth year was only seven years after the USA national team shocked the world by defeating England 1-0 in the 1950 World Cup Finals held in Brazil. This historic victory had gone largely unnoticed in the USA, as the soccer standard in America was still the semi-professional league ("semi-pro" players would be paid a stipend for weekend games after a full work-week at various jobs). It was in this relative USA soccer vacuum that I began to develop.

When I was a few months old, our pediatrician Dr. Heller recognized that I had a congenital condition called *talipes* (commonly called "clubfoot"). This meant that my right foot was growing in the wrong direction, and if uncorrected it would develop into a non-functioning limb and impede walking for life. Initially my clubfoot was put in a cast, and then my feet were placed in a dual foot brace to hold them together. Both feet had to be stabilized – the right to grow correctly, and the left to hold it in place [Figure 18A]. As a result I started walking later than usual, but luckily I had received the proper care to effect a cure of this uncommon congenital ailment.

During my work as a physician overseas, on occasion I encounter children and adults with common correctable congenital conditions – such as clubfoot or cleft lip – that never had a chance to be repaired. Even today, a child with an untreated clubfoot in parts of Africa, Asia, or the Americas is doomed to a life of crawling in the dust, or propelling themselves on a small cart or crutches. But for a small investment made in correcting their talipes earlier, they would have led a normal and fully productive life. These children never fail to illustrate how our birthplace determines our immediate condition, how we develop as individuals, and that one's fateful fortune requires sharing amongst those who have less.

Youth Soccer 1965 – 1970

By the time I was eight years old, we had moved to Tenafly, New Jersey, a suburb five miles outside New York City. Dr. Fernando Ottati, a Brazilian pharmacist, had started a youth soccer league with Armenian coach Jack Hajinlian. Mr. Hajinlian (as he was known to us) was all of five-foot four, but he was a giant to the children who were given the opportunity to learn soccer skills from him at that impressionable age. Jack (as I came to know him as an adult) was ever present on the fields encouraging all kids to participate. The

---

[3] Switzerland has four official languages: German, French, Italian, and Romansch, and a good percentage of the populace also speak English. However, most of the "German" speaking parts of Switzerland actually converse in Schwyzerdütsch, (literally "Swiss-German"), a series of unwritten dialects that are practically unintelligible to the average German speaker.

thing about Jack that impressed me most was that he always made an effort to know every child's name and treated everybody with respect, no matter how small.

Although my father's first sports love had been ice hockey, like all Swiss boys he had played *fussball* all through his school years. Therefore my father was immediately drafted into the league as my first coach.

Like many youth soccer leagues, much of the coaches' time was spent assuaging parents' anxieties about their children, and yelling to their players "Shoot the ball!" "Get back!" and especially "Don't bunch up!" There were no formally trained coaches and few teaching aids. It was in that league that I learned the basics – how to strike the ball with the instep, to dribble, pass, and shoot. We played an ancient 2-3-5 formation - outdated around 1950 - which allowed half the kids to be strikers. Some inexperienced coaches would try to keep their five forwards in a perfectly straight line! It was mostly good fun without any pressure or serious training; exactly what children need at that age.

I later learned advanced ball and body movements primarily by watching talented older players, and by practicing with my Dad (and my sister and Mom, too). By the time I entered high school, I was eager to learn everything about soccer.

Tenafly High School 1971-1974

The Tenafly youth soccer league started by Ottati and Hajinlian presumably gave an advantage to players when they reached high school. I was the center-midfielder on our freshman soccer team coached by mathematics teacher Bill Strohmeyer in 1971, and we had no serious competition as we won fourteen games without loss.

During the summer of 1972 I broke my big toe playing beach soccer and missed much of that season. During my recuperation, I discovered the German magazine *Kicker* in a foreign newspaper store in New York City. *Kicker* was the only contemporary soccer magazine available in any language that I could find. I could practice the German language by reading it, and in the process discovered the world of European football. I was especially fond of Bayern Munich, FC Köln, and the spectacular Dutch team Ajax Amsterdam. Thereafter, I would stencil the number 14 on my T-shirts (for Ajax and Holland's Johan Cruyff), as well as number 10 (for Pelé). Who didn't love Pelé and Brazil? In high school I wore number 5 (for Beckenbauer) at the midfield position.

The 1972-1974 seasons were very successful at Tenafly, which won the BCSL (Bergen County Scholastic League) league and established an enduring dominance amongst similarly sized Group 2 towns. Those 1972-1974 teams were led by forwards Rich and Billy Jaeger, Bill and Jeddy Duggan, Bruce Bokor and Bruce Ottati, were anchored by midfielders Mark McCracken, Mark Sherry, John Van Ost, and Felipe Salgado, and had the elastic Roger Roux in goal. I began to understand the rigors of competition by observing those skilled and dedicated players. Many of that team went on to soccer success at the university level, and Bruce Bokor even auditioned for the Chicago Sting in the professional North American Soccer League (NASL). Unfortunately, the NASL was almost exclusively signing foreign players and not seriously developing native USA talent (for complete details, see Colin Jose's book *NASL: A Complete Record of the North American Soccer League*).

In the summer of 1972 I attended a summer soccer camp at Ramapo College. There I met Kenny Kropkowski, a very smooth defensive player from the neighboring town of Dumont. Kenny had developed an ambidextrous ball-handling ability, and would boom goal kicks 60 yards with either foot. Although I was not a "one-footed" player, I wanted to kick with my left as well as my right. After a week of constant practice I could almost kick as well as Kenny, and subsequently was voted the most improved player of the camp. Becoming a true two-footed will give any player great confidence, and since that time, I strangely scored most goals with my left foot, as I developed a quick move from left to right that was hard to defend.

Finding soccer supplies was difficult in 1972, as the main sports stores had a poor selection of soccer boots. The only solution was to hop on the bus going over the George Washington Bridge from New Jersey to New York City, and take the AA subway down to the Museum of Natural History exit at 81st Street and 8th Avenue. From there I would walk across Manhattan, meandering through Central Park, and eventually arrive at the Soccer Sport Supply store at the junction of 90th Street and 1st Avenue. The store is still a specialty soccer shop run by the Doss family, and at that time they had a much wider display of soccer boots and equipment than all other sports stores combined.[4]

On one of our forays into New York, my friend Dave Shelton and I discovered a store in the Bensonhurst section of Brooklyn that had soccer boots manufactured in Italy. Although Dave was probably a genius, he was also a soccer fanatic and the goalkeeper for his Horace Mann High School team. Like Albert Camus and Che Guevara, Dave wasn't the best field player so he excelled at goalkeeper. We would often play pickup ball with Jason Forsythe near his house, discussing philosophy and politics in between shots. As we pummeled shots at him, Dave would throw his body around making saves when he could – we would often shoot two balls at once! Dave was a great sport and conversationalist who also had a great heart. After he scored a perfect 1600 on his SAT university entrance exam, Dave eschewed university and did human rights work organizing farm workers before entering Harvard University. I was studying in the Caribbean five years later when the news reached me that Dave had died. I had not been aware that he was recently suffering from manic-depressive illness, which at times made life unbearable for him.

I'll never forget Dave, he was a one-in-a million person, and not just for his intellect but especially his heart. Most of his life he was a rock-steady individual seeking the essence of humanity, but in one depressive moment he was lost. Even though he was not a top player, I think soccer had been a major stabilizing factor in his life. When he left high school he left much of the art and camaraderie of the game behind to pursue intellectual excellence and social change. I sadly sense it might have been different if we had stayed in contact more instead of wandering the globe in opposite directions. Dave died so young, but had given so much back for his time. He had shone like a diamond through the grey northeast sky.

Around that time I saw my first World Cup game ever, an eight millimeter film of the 1974 World Cup final between Germany and Holland. Incredibly, the world's biggest sporting event was not available on any USA television station. I thought it was because the USA had not qualified for the 1974 Cup, and therefore was no impetus to broadcast soccer. However, even in later years when the USA did qualify, there was still great reluctance by the television networks in the world's greatest power to broadcast the World Cup – probably they were afraid of the world's greatest sporting event with all those foreigners. The dearth of soccer television coverage on in the USA sometimes led to the defection of soccer players to other sports that were more "socially acceptable."

The 1974 season marked my last year playing soccer in high school. Coach Charles Billings was a former college soccer player, and had us playing a 3-3-4 system (four strikers). The senior leaders on the team were Victor Ottati and Ray and Gerry Roux as forwards, Jason Forsythe, Billy Blank, and me as midfielders and defenders, and Shelly Blumenthal in goal. The team suffered a major pre-season loss when top defender Greig Smith developed peritonitis and was out for the year.

---

[4] The Soccer Sport Supply store is a USA historic soccer landmark ("The Home of Soccer since 1933" at website www.homeofsoccer.com). Founded by German immigrant Max Doss in 1933, it became the East Coast's leading soccer shop. Max and his wife Dorothy were fixtures in the store, attending to each customer graciously. Soccer Sport Supply was also the first soccer venue to operate their own factory (on Prince Street in New York City), although they also imported quality soccer supplies from France and West Germany on which they placed their family name. The Doss gear were often less expensive than the "name brands," but just as good quality. The store is still operating at the same location and is managed by Max's son Herman and grandson Jeffrey.

The Roux brothers were 50% of the forward line – Ray a roving winger and Gerry the goal poacher. Victor – befitting his Brazilian ancestry – played the creative role of the withdrawn forward. Billy and I shared the center midfield position, as coach Billings had devised two tactical schemes. The offensive scheme was called "Point Blank," with Billy playing an attacking center-midfielder position, and the defensive scheme was called "Point Back," when I played a central defensive midfielder role. We saved Point Back for when the other team had a star goal-scorer. Billing's "Point Blank – Point Back" plan was intuitive because Billy was a better attacker while I was the better defender. Whoever was not in the center played the left or right midfield position; it didn't matter as we were all "two-footed" by then. Jason was the central defensive back, although with Greig recuperating he did not have the liberty to exercise his more natural *libero* position he modeled after his hero Franz (Beckenbauer).

The year started smoothly, winning our first games 5-0 and 4-0. We then played Dumont on their home field. During the game, our friend and nemesis Kenny Kropkowski boomed a free kick 22 yards from the left side of goal heading for the far post that Shelly had covered. A player in the defensive wall thrust up his foot a meter off the ground in a valiant effort to stop the shot, but instead succeeded in deflecting it into the near post corner. That was the game winner and the first Tenafly league loss for many years. We focused our newfound humility on the next opposing teams, defeating them by scores of 8-1, 10-0, 8-0, 7-0, and an incredible 15-0 in a freak October snowstorm (scoring 48 goals with only 1 against in the five games). The return Dumont game in Tenafly was my turn for revenge; Ray Roux alertly passed to me directly from a corner kick and I left-footed the ball from 18 yards into the left lower-hand corner for the game winner. Thanks a lot, Ray. As they say in New Orleans, "There's no gumbo without the roux."[5] Kenny and I had a good laugh over our dueling goals.

Some of our high school USA-football team classmates would razz us that they were tougher than we were (see analysis of this USA-football myth in Chapter 6). The last laugh was on them, as the USA-football team lost all their games. Our soccer team actually outscored the USA-football team 81 to 72 for the year, which is insanely difficult to accomplish when USA-football games typically have scores like 35-24, and each score counts for seven points.

We had lost Tenafly's undefeated league streak that had lasted for years, but still won the league with only one loss. By then many other towns had developed their own youth leagues and there was evolving parity. A good example was Dumont with quality players like Kropkowski and "Deke" DeMatteo. In the county tournament we lost to eventual winners Ridgewood, a larger Group 4 school with quality players like the Van Doren brothers, Craig and Dirk.

In the state tournament, we played Vailsburg, a team with a phenomenal striker named Vito. We played the "Point Back" formation, as I was to man-mark Vito. Early in the game I gave him a little too much room after he received the ball, and he turned quickly and blasted a shot from the 18-yard line into the top corner. Shelly had had no chance to save and we were down 1-0. I then had a revelation while walking back to the center spot; I would shadow Vito around the field and deny him the chance to even properly receive the ball. That way he couldn't turn on me if he didn't have the ball – or at least didn't have it exactly where he wanted it. The tide of the game started to turn as we scored the equalizer and the go-ahead goals. My defensive strategy worked, Vito never had another good chance for goal, and the result was a 5-1 win for us. After that big win we let down our guard and lost 2-1 to North Plainfield, finishing our season with 14 wins and 3 losses. Despite the 3 losses, the team scored 81 goals and allowed only 10 for the year.

---

[5] A *roux* in French or Louisiana Cajun cuisine is a vegetable base that adds sustenance and flavor to a dish; particularly the multi-ethnic influenced *gumbo* stew in New Orleans.

Watching my teammates play during that year was very satisfying - Ray slashing his way to 20 goals, Gerry bulling and finessing his way to 19, Victor in the middle finding the free man yet also getting his goals, Billy beating the opposition with his patented "stepover" move, Jason a streak in the back as he defended primarily with speed (teams were not used to that as the speedier players usually played offense), and Shelly making great saves and distributing flawlessly with his point-guard overhand motion. All the senior leaders made the league all-star team. Speedsters Bob Duzoglu and Mark Shirvan, Ottati protégé Dave Wexler, handyman Andy Weiss, and defensive stalwart Adam Kubler also performed very well for us.

There were many opposing players who also impressed me that year. The best were Zoran Ivanov from Cliffside Park, Craig Baumann and Carlos Sanchez from Saddle Brook, Gerry Roach from Englewood, Toussaint Potter and Craig DeJaeger from Teaneck, Jairo Sierra from Hackensack, and the aforementioned Ridgewood and Dumont players.

Tenafly High School has kept up the tradition and continued to field excellent teams over the years, winning their share of the honors. Tenafly won the state championship under Coach Billings in 1976, and former star striker and present soccer coach Billy Jaeger has sustained the academic and soccer excellence.

One ex-resident of Tenafly, Gregg Berhalter, represented the USA national team in the 2002 FIFA World Cup. Although Berhalter had lived in Tenafly, he attended the successful St. Benedict's Prep soccer program in Newark along with future USA national team captain Claudio Reyna. An outstanding defender, Berhalter later played with Crystal Palace in England and Cottbus Energie in Germany. Berhalter had a special moment in the quarterfinal game against Germany in the 2002 World Cup. He had ranged far forward and his close-in shot clearly beat keeper Oliver Kahn, but defender Torsten Frings blatantly blocked the ball on the goal line with his left arm. No penalty was called, and Germany won, 1-0 (see Chapter 9 for details).

Haledon Lyceum Amateur League Soccer 1975

After the high school season was over, I wanted to continue playing soccer. I was lucky to live in New Jersey, the adopted home of countless soccer-playing immigrants, and consequently one of the few states that had all-year soccer playing possibilities. The off-season amateur soccer teams were most often immigrant run "ethnic" teams.

Soon I was playing at a February game in Paterson, New Jersey for a team called *Olympic*. We had never practiced together before, and the only player I knew was Carlos Sanchez from Saddle Brook. It was zero degrees Centigrade on the field, and it ominously started snowing shortly after kickoff. Thankfully I had brought my gloves, but we were all wearing shorts of course. It was an average game notable for one event; during halftime the coach's assistant removed a tall pyramidal bottle of yellow liquid out of the trunk of his car. To us kids, the bottle appeared to be nearly as tall as his portly 5-foot frame, and he proceeded to pour a shot-glass for each of the players. He said, "drink this, it will warm you up," in an accent I had not fully identified. I was later to clarify it was a bottle of *Galliano*, an Italian liquor. None of us had reached drinking age or had imbibed anything remotely like Galliano before. It went down fiery and fruity, and we momentarily felt a bit warmer once we entered the snow-covered field for the second half, when Sanchez put away a chance for us to win 1-0.

The Galliano must have had a placebo effect, because alcohol dilates the peripheral blood vessels, thereby making the body feel colder. In cold weather alcohol actually increases the risk of hypothermia, while in hot weather alcohol will increase sweating and lead to dehydration. There was no common knowledge in 1975 about electrolyte drinks for replacement therapy; we kids were just hungry for more soccer. The medical lesson is that no matter the environmental conditions, one should never drink alcohol while participating in sports; especially such a demanding sport as soccer.

The following week Saddle Brook goalkeeper Craig Baumann called to invite Jason and I to join a new team with star North Jersey players. Although I was already playing with Olympic, the club did not look particularly organized, so Carlos and I agreed to check it out at the scheduled meeting. My new club was Haledon Lyceum, based in the hamlet of Haledon next to multi-cultural Paterson. At the meeting we were introduced to the coach, a jovial German named Fritz. Our teammates were our top opponents during the season, and others we knew only by name since they played in Passaic or Union County. Our strike team was impressive, as we had the three top scorers from the area; Tommy Hochkeppel from Fair Lawn, Jeff Karpovich from Ramsey, and Carlos Sanchez from Saddle Brook. We also had two outstanding strikers from Newark, Alberto and Steve Hammond. Alberto was also the backup keeper, specializing in flying across the goal and knocking out balls with his forearms. Jason and I were in the midfield, with Rodney Irrizarry from Fair Lawn and Kenny Kropkowski from Dumont in defense, and Craig in the goal. We received warm-up suits before we even played a game, making us feel very welcome at the club.

Playing with Haledon Lyceum in the spring would mean missing the baseball season. Since I was a co-captain of the baseball team, the baseball coach was not thrilled to hear of my new plan. But although I was the field captain as catcher, hitting the smaller baseball was always difficult because the vision in my left eye was poor, and I could never adjust to the small ball coming in fast with two eyes with different refractive capabilities. Soccer did not pose this problem, as the ball was so much larger and my eyes were able to track it well. Anyway, I enjoyed soccer much more than baseball, and had no regrets with my decision to retire. The baseball team did fine, so they never missed my presence.

Our Haledon Lyceum team won 18 games without a loss. The most memorable game was playing against the Paterson team with two great skill players, forward Viorel Oldja and midfielder Pedro Machado. They were an example of being so good that it was easier to watch them instead of guard them, even if we ended up winning 2-1. Unfortunately, our season then ended in the state competition held in the old Newark Ironbound stadium. Overall it was a fantastic experience playing with such high caliber players from the region. For the first time I was able to play soccer year-round, a necessary element for developing high quality players.

New York Cosmos, Pelé, and the NASL 1974-1984

The North American Soccer League (NASL) had started play in 1967, but was only becoming noticed in 1974 when the world's top player Pelé joined the New York Cosmos. Pelé had retired from his Santos club the year before, but received an opportunity to advance soccer in the United States when he signed with the Cosmos for 2.4 million dollars, a massive sum at the time. Developing professional soccer in the big market arena of New York City was very challenging, as the city already had eight professional teams (two USA-football teams, two baseball teams, two ice hockey teams, and two basketball teams).

My Dad arranged for the family to attend Pelé's first Cosmos appearance at the Randall's Island Stadium east of Manhattan. As we were advancing on the ticket booth, a woman came up to me and asked, "Do you want these four tickets [for free]?" So by that unusual circumstance we saw Pelé's first Cosmos appearance for free (maybe she thought the Cosmos played USA-football).

The game was not sold out, nor was the old rundown Stadium the proper venue for Pelé, the King of World Football. Pelé's technique was so far above the others that at times he seemed to be playing by himself. In short order, the Cosmos moved over to the 78,000-person capacity Meadowlands Giant Stadium in New Jersey, and hired some top-notch players to accompany Pelé.

The Cosmos brought in other top players, such as defenders Franz Beckenbauer (Germany), Carlos Alberto, Marinho (both Brazil) and Andranik Eskandarian (Iran);

midfielders Ramon Mifflin (Peru), Johan Neeskens (Holland) and Vladislav Bogicevic (Yugoslavia); and strikers Giorgio Chinaglia (Italy), Dennis Tueart and Steve Hunt (both England). Shep Messing, Ricky Davis, Jeff Durgan, and Werner Roth were the standouts from the USA on the Cosmos. When Pelé was on the field, he continually made everybody look, feel, and play better [Figure 18 B is of a ticket to his testimonial game].

A major embarrassment for the Cosmos was that their world-class team labored on an artificial turf pitch in a USA-football stadium, which was too narrow (60 yards wide) for proper first-class soccer (should be 75 yards wide). The artificial turf slanted downward from the middle for drainage runoff, and the concrete under the turf made the ball bounce much higher than a normal grass pitch. Still, Pelé's graceful play brought out the best in everybody, even on a substandard field.

It was doubly uncomfortable watching the Cosmos play on the first-generation artificial turf, because of fear of injury to Pelé or another player on the unforgiving plastic surface. Later it was proven that USA-football professionals sustained a higher rate of serious injuries playing on artificial turf compared with natural grass. That study led to the belated banishment of first generation artificial turf from nearly all USA-football stadiums. The obvious incentive for artificial turf was that it was cheaper for the owners to maintain, regardless of the athletes' necessities.

Soccer competition on artificial turf was an acknowledged aberration present in some USA stadiums, but the turf had also infiltrated the British professional scene. Six British football stadiums used first generation artificial turf during the 1970's and 1980's; the most prominent was the Queen's Park Rangers stadium in London.

There are no formal studies proving more soccer injuries on first-generation artificial turf than natural grass. But if USA-football players suffered more injuries on artificial turf, than almost certainly soccer players suffered as much, since they run a much longer distance during games. The subject of injuries on artificial turf has arisen once again, as there is a new generation of artificial turf now available, which FIFA is actively promoting for areas where it is difficult to maintain a grass pitch. This new artificial turf has longer blades of fake plastic grass, as well as a rubber and sand base that appears to make it more forgiving and similar to a natural grass surface.

The extraordinary Cosmos team had great skill and teamwork, but the crowds were impressive as well. The cosmopolitan city of New York was just a few miles away, so the Meadowlands stadium was often near full capacity, with several games attracting more than 70,000 fans. Immigrant ethnicities brought their soccer cultures to be represented at the Cosmos games. After all, the Germans had Franz and Hubert, the Italians had Giorgio, the English had Tueart and Hunt, the Brazilians Pelé, Carlos Alberto, and Marinho, the Peruvians had Ramon Mifflin, the Iranians had Eskandarian, the Paraguayans had Romerito and Roberto Cabañas, and the USA had Ricky Davis, Jeff Durgan, Werner Roth and Shep Messing.

The multi-ethnic crowds were not soccer fans in the often-overzealous style of their homelands. The Meadowlands was an all-seater stadium, and there was not a lot of raucous cheering or singing of songs. But the fans brought an electric and worldly atmosphere, with no risk of violence. Families could enjoy an exciting game together, something that remains unthinkable in many world stadiums because of macho hooligan soccer culture. The wildest the Cosmos crowd would get was when they performed "the wave," rising in sequential unity after a Cosmos goal.

After Pelé arrived, the NASL got busy obtaining the best talent in the world. Even if some stars were past their prime, it was still priceless to see these "flair" players perform in person. Others who graced the NASL clubs were: Johan Cruyff, Johan Neeskens, Rudi Krol, and Rob Rensenbrink (all Holland), George Best (Northern Ireland), Teófilo "Nene" Cubillas (Peru), Eusébio and António Simões (both Portugal), Bobby Moore, Geoff Hurst, Gordon

Banks, Rodney Marsh, Alan Ball and Trevor Francis (all England), Elias Figueroa (Chile), Kazimierz Deyna (Poland), and Gerd Müller (Germany). The best USA players not on the Cosmos were Dallas midfielder Tony Bellinger, and Tampa Bay goalkeeper Arnie Mausser.

The NASL was criticized for hiring international players past their best days, but to their credit the league also looked for young international talent. The following are some NASL players recruited while young and who made excellent first impressions before leaving the NASL:

(1) *Hugo Sánchez*, Mexico's best striker ever, played for the San Diego Sockers in 1979 and 1980, scoring 26 goals in 32 games. He later became a long-time player for Real Madrid, and was leading goal scorer (called the "Pichichi") in the Spanish First Division five times. Sánchez also performed in the 1978, 1982, and 1986 World Cups for Mexico. He came back to the USA and played briefly for the Dallas Burn in 1996, thus becoming one of only two players to have performed in both the NASL and MLS.

(2) *Peter Beardsley* was a winger who played with the Vancouver Whitecaps from 1981-83, then signed for Newcastle, and performed for England in the 1986 World Cup. He later played for Liverpool for years.

(3) *Mark Hateley* was another English striker who made the 1986 England World Cup team; he had played for the Detroit Express in 1980 when he was only nineteen.

(4) *Graeme Souness* was a midfielder who played with Montreal Olympique in 1972 when he was nineteen. He later played for Liverpool and the Scottish national teams (where he was captain), and also performed for Juventus.

(5) Midfielder *Julio César Romero* and striker *Roberto Cabañas* were two twenty-year-old Paraguayan players recruited by the New York Cosmos in 1980. Romero had 24 goals in 74 games for Cosmos, and was later named the 1985 South American Player of the year while playing for Brazil giant club team Fluminense. Both Cabañas and Romero played for Paraguay in the 1986 World Cup.

In addition, the Cosmos would occasionally invite an All-World team to play against them in New York. One of those teams had the left-footed Brazilian wizard Roberto Rivelino (Diego Maradona's idol), and he dazzled the crowd with his stellar "pull-back top-of-the-ball" technique. Iconoclastic Argentine keeper Hugo "El Loco" Gatti entertained the crowd with his dribbling forays out to midfield.

To their discredit, the NASL did not sufficiently cultivate young USA talent. Granted, the foreign players drew in the "ethnic" crowd base that still identified strongly with their ancestral nations. But most teams had only one or two USA citizens on the roster, and they often did not play for long stretches. As a result, USA soccer players started developing at an international level only when they went overseas in the late 1980s and early 1990s.

Rensselaer Polytechnic Institute 1975

After high school I attended university at Rensselaer Polytechnic Institute (RPI) in upstate New York. I knew nothing of the soccer team or players before I arrived. Soccer scholarships were nearly unheard of in the 1970's, but the Big Four USA sports of USA football, basketball, baseball, or ice hockey routinely provided full athletic scholarships. For example, RPI gave priority to ice hockey scholarships. This absence of soccer scholarships contributed to the underdevelopment of the university game in the USA for decades. Fortunately, I had received an academic scholarship so my situation was covered.

Still, RPI had some excellent soccer players, such as All-American goalkeeper Evans Nestorides from Greece, Nigel Peacock from England, and smooth ball handler Tony Phongsathorn from Thailand. Steve Proscino and Arnie Einhorn were the top American players, both with solid fundamentals who could break open a game. Steve taught me a valuable lesson in front of goal: control the ball and shoot as quickly as you possibly can before the defense and goalkeeper expects a shot. That way, if the shot is not optimal, there is still the element of surprise.

Coach Al Goodyear tried to mold a team of smart (and smart-alecky) guys into a smooth operation. The team did well in most of the games, including losing by only a 2-1 score against Hartwick College, the eventual 1976 Division 1 University Champions.

Hartwick College was one of the remarkable stories of USA soccer; a small college with no scholarships that always had great teams. Their teams were impressive because they had a quality coach, Jim Lennox, who respected his players and ensured that they received a quality education at Hartwick.

I started out the year on the junior team, and remember a tremendous shot my classmate Dominic Stroud took from fifty yards in one game - the ball smashed against the right post. Dom had been frustrated all game, but made a one-in-a-million shot where his dynamic momentum and foot placement just crushed the ball perfectly. Our junior goalkeeper was also quite a character – he had had both his kneecaps removed through injury and wore heavy wraps on his knees, but was still able to get around the goal well. Along with Dom, midfielder Jeffrey Wahl from Vermont was one of our best players.

Against Williams College in Massachusetts, I had a shock after being hacked in the right knee after having already distributed the ball. It was my first serious injury and it was very scary – I was out for the season. An orthopedic surgeon recommended operating to "take a look inside," but in 1975 there was no CT scanning or arthroscopic surgery, just the large vertical incision exploratory knee surgery that took many months or years to heal. Rehabilitation of serious knee injuries was really in its infancy, so I decided to wait. Although at first I couldn't walk without pain and was on crutches for 6 weeks, after four months I could run again.

After my knee felt better, I was itching to get some soccer action. At an indoor tournament at Keene State, one of our opponents was our nemesis Hartwick College again. The tournament was played on a basketball-type wood surface, and bouncing the ball off the walls was not allowed. The rules for this tournament were similar to Brazilian futsal (*futebol de salão*), which is designed for a high skill level. At that time Hartwick had Angrik Stepanow, Zeren Ombadykow, and Khyen Ivanchukov, three players of Mongolian heritage from Howell, New Jersey. They all had a wonderful touch on the ball and ran rings around us as they instinctively knew where their teammates would be; we lost 2-0.

The next indoor tournament was at the RPI indoor facility, which had a hard rubberized floor. I was full of energy when the coach sent me into the game. I had been practicing bicycle kicks with a Thai friend who was an amateur kick boxer, and when the opportunity presented itself, I put practice into play. The opposition defense cleared the ball poorly and the ball was coming over my head; I just levitated and smashed the ball over my head towards the goal 18 yards away. Landing on my back I rolled over just in time to see the ball smack off the crossbar, just missing a goal. Landing on the hard surface didn't hurt a bit, perhaps because of the adrenaline and because I landed correctly (the bicycle kick may look dangerous, but if executed correctly with commitment there is very little danger – see Chapter 2). After that game, my soccer confidence returned to my pre-injury status.

Tenafly Summer Soccer League 1976-1977

In between academic university years, the North Jersey summer soccer leagues provided a great opportunity to meet old acquaintances and to improve soccer skills. Over these summer sessions, former opponents from other towns learned from each other and became friends.

Jed Duggan set up the Tenafly Summer Soccer League (TSSL), with a seven versus seven league format. The idea of the TSSL league was to have fewer players on the field resulting in more time on the ball, thereby providing more opportunity to create openings and exhibit skills. This was a very successful idea; players were very happy with six field players per team on a 70-yard long field, with goalkeepers guarding smaller 16 foot long by 8-foot high goals. Jed ran the league the first year, and I ran the league the second and third years with Jason Forsythe. It was an open league, but we made a point of inviting the top players in the area to enroll.

The best players in the league were probably Mark Staropoli of Old Tappan and Paul Kitson from England. Mark had been an All-American in university and had a full range of skills; dribbling, creating, and shooting were his modes of dominating a game. Previously in the Englewood league I had seen him take a 50-yard laser shot that had beaten the goalkeeper. Mark later played for the GAFA (German-American Football Association) team Doxa in New York City, which had several Greek ex-national team players, and was drafted by both the professional ASL and NASL (Fort Lauderdale Strikers) soccer leagues.

Paul Kitson had played professionally for Watford in England before moving to the USA. Paul was very quick, had slick moves, and a fierce shot. Paul later played professionally for teams in the ASL, and the San Jose Earthquakes in the NASL. After those leagues died out, he played for years on the indoor circuit in the Major Indoor Soccer League (MISL). In 1985 he had 39 goals in 43 games for the Baltimore Blast, and he made the MISL All-Star team several times. Paul finished up his playing career with the Montreal Impact in the NPSL in 1998 at the age of 42, and is now a professional coach in the USA and Canada.

Other players from that league which impressed: Seth Roland was an attacking midfielder from Teaneck who went on to play for the USA Maccabi team in Israel four times, and to coach them twice again. Seth is currently the coach of the successful Fairleigh Dickenson University soccer team in New Jersey. The indomitable defender Albert Demateis and Mark's brother Frank were also great players to watch, as were Al Barrios and his talented Hackensack team.

The great success of the Tenafly Summer Soccer League was twofold: (1) having good players at a high skill level, and (2) the seven versus seven format that gave everybody at least 30 percent more time on the ball.

Elizabeth Sports Club 1976

After transferring to Rutgers University, I was forced to withdraw from competition for one year (called being "red shirted"), simply because I changed universities. This was an idiotic NCAA rule; how could I be recruited from a school that had no soccer scholarships to another, also without soccer scholarships? Sports scholarships at Rutgers, the State University of New Jersey, were again reserved for USA-football or basketball, despite New Jersey's critical historical importance in soccer's growth in the USA.

Rutgers was in a hotbed soccer state supplying top players to the whole country, but did not support soccer as should have been the State University's mandate. New Jersey was a soccer leader with the German-American Football Association (GAFA) and many pockets of immigrants who had always played serious soccer. New Jersey had top-level amateur and semi-pro clubs like the Kearny Scots, the Elizabeth S.C. "Germans," New Brunswick Hungarians, and Trenton Extension. New Brunswick later became home to a wave of Peruvian immigrants who supplied their own superb players.

As a result of being red-shirted, I would only be allowed to practice with the university team for my sophomore year. This was not satisfactory to me, and I soon found myself playing with the Elizabeth Sports Club, a semi-professional team that had a superb soccer pedigree. GAFA team Elizabeth S.C. was founded in 1924 and had twice won the US Open Challenge Cup (1970 & 1972), the official USA club championship.

Many of the first successful teams in the US Open competition were organized by industries that sponsored their immigrant workers' teams. These included Bethlehem Steel of Pennsylvania, and Scullin Steel and Central Breweries, both of Missouri. Teams in the ethnic semi-pro leagues, such as GAFA teams in the New Jersey-New York City area, subsequently became dominant in the US Open competition.[6]

Team names in these leagues represented which area they originally came from, which town they were currently living in, and/or their ethnic designation. Examples include the New York German-Hungarians, Eintracht FC, New York Hungarians, Greek-Americans, and the Brooklyn Italians (all from New York), the Ukrainian Nationals (Pennsylvania), Greek-Americans and Maccabi Los Angeles (California), and Elizabeth SC (New Jersey). All of the above-mentioned teams won the USA Open championship at least once. These ethnic semi-pro teams reigned supreme in the US Open until recently; the Brooklyn Italians last won in 1991, and the Greek-Americans from California won in 1994.

The USA did not have a full professional league until 1967 when the NASL was started. The NASL unwisely chose not to have their teams play in US Open competition, which would have bolstered both league and Open prestige. However, since the new USA professional soccer league Major league Soccer (MLS) started in 1996, MLS teams have entered the U.S. Open and won nine out of the past ten years – the exception being the Rochester Rhinos upset in 1999. Rochester winning the US Open was the equivalent of a third division team in England winning the FA Cup against a Premiership club (such as if Millwall beat Manchester United).

Elizabeth SC was informally known as the "Elizabeth Germans," as most of the club members and the former team members were of German ancestry. Manny Schellscheidt anchored the Elizabeth teams that won the U.S. Open in 1970 and 1972. Manny subsequently coached the USA Men's National and Olympic teams, coached championship teams in the ASL and NASL, and is still coaching at Seton Hall University in South Orange, New Jersey. Manny's contributions to USA soccer have already justified his induction at the USA Soccer Hall of Fame in Oneonta, New York.

The so-called ethnic teams eventually realized that talent from different areas was available, and started selecting players regardless of ancestry. For example, I was one of only three players from the 1976 Elizabeth team that could pass for German. One of the others was midfield general and captain Jürgen Armbrüster, who had a tremendous left foot, able to propel the ball like an arrow coming out of a crossbow (fittingly, Armbrüster means "crossbow maker" in German). We also had two members of the 1974 Haitian World Cup team playing for us, Herbert Austin and Fritz "Phito" Leandre. Herb was the best central defender I've ever played with, nearly impossible to pass, and a very nice guy who was never shy to demonstrate technique. Fritz was a striker known in Haiti for his incredible speed. I remember one match crossing the ball to him from the left touchline to the right side of the penalty box; Fritz ghosted in behind his defender and spectacularly volleyed the ball into the net. Fritz played on the biggest stage of all when he appeared in the 1974 World Cup Finals match against Argentina.[7]

Elizabeth SC was located right off Route 22 in New Jersey, about 20 miles west of New York City. There was a modest clubhouse and a lighted field called Farchers Grove. Like many fields in the GAFA, "Farchers" was no bargain, devoid of grass in many places, and well endowed with bumps, hollows, and stones. Other fields in the league were in similar shape or even worse, such as the notorious Metropolitan Oval in Queens that had a surplus of "moon holes," but not a blade of grass. It seemed that nobody interested in soccer could pay for good land or afford a groundskeeper. The poor state of grounds has been among the most

---

[6] The US Open Cup is the USA's equivalent to the F.A. Cup in England, and is the longest running continually-operating soccer Cup competition in the world, having started in 1914. The European Cup competitions were interrupted by two World Wars.

[7] Pictures of Fritz Leandre and Herbert Austin, as well as the history of Haitian soccer, can be found at Manno Sanon's website at: www.haitifoot.com.

disappointing attributes of USA soccer for decades. The Metropolitan Oval is still in use today, finally getting a makeover with new lights and a new generation artificial turf in 2001.

Having no car, I hitchhiked the 30 miles from my university to the Wednesday night practices and Sunday games. I averaged about three rides and 90 minutes to arrive at Farchers. Eventually I hooked up with another player to get rides up to Farchers.

At nineteen years old I was the youngest on the team. The mean age of the team was about twenty-five, and the others had already played in the league or in their home countries for years (we had players from El Salvador, Haiti, Mexico, Romania, Turkey, and the USA). I was placed in a wingback position as we already had enough skilled midfielders. Herby showed me how to play the outside back position, where my only definite responsibility was to not let the wing forward pass me. Other than that, I was free to overlap on offense when opportunities arose.

We were paid for the games, the amount depending on the end-result. It was a basic financial incentive for results; most for a win, less for a tie, and the least for a loss. The fees were above the NCAA rules, but I was blissfully ignorant of their rules that inhibited soccer development. Needless to say, the ex-World Cup players were paid the most.

My best performance was against Hotels Bermuda, the Bermuda champions in 1975 and 1979, which fielded some Bermuda national team players. Despite being a small state of 60,000 people, Bermuda had several players in professional leagues and was not a pushover for the USA national soccer team. To demonstrate, the USA lost to Bermuda in 1979 and 1991.

Hotels got into the game quickly, and after forty minutes they led 2-1. Just before halftime, Herby gave me a beautiful pass on an overlapping run up the left side that I blasted into the top left corner of the goal from 20 yards, tying the game. Fifteen minutes after halftime, Jürgen gave me a nearly identical ball – and from the same position I shot the ball low into the right hand corner to make it 3-2 to us. They were my only two shots of the game, both left-footed. I guess I was the star of that game, having scored the tying and winning goals from the a wingback position. We won 5-2, and after the game the bratwurst washed down with soda (or German beer) in the clubhouse tasted real good.

The GAFA changed its name to the Cosmopolitan Soccer League in 1977, and still exists in the New York City area (website at www.newyorksoccer.com). Unfortunately, Elizabeth SC is not active in the league in 2005.

Rutgers University 1977

As a university junior, I was finally able to play soccer for Rutgers University. The best player on the team was captain Ricky Young, a clone of national team attacking midfielder Ricky Davis. Unfortunately, Ricky suffered a horrific broken leg in the 108th anniversary game of the first soccer game ever in the USA (Rutgers versus Princeton in 1869 - see Chapter 1), and his leadership was sorely missed for the rest of the season.

The coach had his favorites from the year before, and new independent players like myself were not in favored player status. I started getting uncomfortable when several excellent players who tried out for the team were summarily released. The best-excluded players happened to be Gabe Kalu and Sree Raghavan, both brilliant foreign students.

Gabe, from Enugu, Nigeria, had excellent control of the ball and incredible shot technique. He had a cannon shot with either foot, and could also kick what is known as the "Zico shot," hitting the ball above the center causing the ball to knuckle and act unpredictably. Gabe was a constant threat to score from inside 30 yards, and also had exquisite dribbling skills. While Gabe had the best talent, he was actively harassed from joining the team. Like any good student-athlete, Gabe was concerned about his courses, and when he came late to a practice because of a chemistry laboratory, he was warned that to do so again would mean dismissal. This did not happen with the coach's core of favorite players. The only explicable reason why he was actively discouraged from continuing was the coach's xenophobic personality. Gabe was not the type to back down from adversity. After all, he had lived through the Biafra War, and Gabe subsequently went to medical school and became a physician.

Sree Raghavan was a wing-forward from Kuala Lumpur, Malaysia, who had played on youth teams for his country. Sree had devastating dribbling skills, and could take it all the way downfield and center beautifully or cut in to shoot. Sree later received a doctorate degree in the nutritional sciences. Another Nigerian ignored was John, a lightning-quick goalkeeper who was superior to the regular team keepers. John's specialty was catching the most difficult shots rather than punching them away.

While the best university teams in the country had coaches who were happy to incorporate their foreign students and accommodate their student-athlete status needs, the Rutgers coach and administration did not. Steve Negoesco at the University of San Francisco and Jim Lennox at Hartwick College were winning national championships using players from Europe, Africa, and Central and South America. These players not only elevated the USA players' abilities, but also improved cultural sensitivities. Rutgers actively discouraged foreigners from participating in the soccer program in those years, which damaged a program that had much more potential than it subsequently demonstrated.

The sports administration at Rutgers was not bothered by the situation. After the season, I led a group of players to an appointment with the athletic director. It was made clear during the meeting that Fred Gruninger had no concept of what New Jersey meant to soccer history in the USA, or the responsibility of Rutgers as the State University of New Jersey to promote this special soccer relationship. We found out that the entire budget for varsity soccer was under $10,000; no wonder we had old uniforms, no equipment, second-class fields, no overnight trips, and meals consisting of junk food. The RPI program (in a school $1/10^{th}$ the size of Rutgers) had been a much classier program.

Anyway, I try to forget about that year, as the "all-American" Rutgers soccer team did not play up to its potential. Teams rarely can play to their potential when there is rampant player favoritism, and emotions are mixed against the coach. Practices were depressing, and I often dreaded going to them. I would frequently see my friends Gabe and Sree who should have excelled on the team, and felt guilty.

I played sub-par most of the year. My best play was saved for the last practice of the year. Dave Grimaldi, a graduated captain and 1976 USA Olympic team player, was on the other team. That night it was my job to cover this brilliant player, which I attempted to like I blanketed Vito years before. Dave was a very creative player, and my only option was to try to prevent him from getting involved. On one play near the half-line he received a pass belt-high that he trapped just a little too far away. I flicked the ball away with my right foot, and then immediately volleyed the ball with my left as hard as I could, shooting for the goal 45 yards away. With that shot I let out all my frustration for that year. I had by chance hit the ball perfectly, and it took a knuckling action, making it hard for the goalkeeper to predict which side it was favoring. I felt little joy as it snuck into the left-hand top corner for a goal, just relief that the year was over.

The next year, my senior year, I avoided playing for the team as the situation had not changed; the same myopic coach and athletic director remained. I thought I would have a better time playing for Elizabeth SC again, or as it happened, for a team at Rutgers simply called the "International Team."

The Rutgers International Team 1978

I had a heavier academic load in my last university year that prevented me from traveling to Elizabeth. I looked around for another opportunity to play locally, perhaps with the Hungarians or with the newer New Brunswick immigrants, the Peruvians. One of my new roommates, Eric Bennett, informed me there was going to be a team based out of the *International Center*, the advisory office for foreign students at Rutgers.

The *International Team* was founded by Ravee Raghavan (Sree's older brother), who was the director of the International Center. Ravee was a skilled ballplayer, having played for top teams in Malaysia. He had heard complaints of discriminatory activities by the varsity coach, and wanted to set up an alternative playing structure for anybody who wanted to play.

The team was a small United Nations, as we had players from every part of the world. We had Keith Constantine and Tony from Trinidad, Eric Bennett and Teddy from Jamaica, Gabe Kalu, Rashid Ali and keeper John from Nigeria, François from Cameroon, Roberto from Mexico, Reza and Mohammed from Iran, Mohammed from Morocco, Mohammed from Gambia, Sree, Suresh, and Ravee from Malaysia, and Bruce Heckinger, Dan Yafet, Greg, and myself from the United States. We had so many Mohammeds that we had to identify them by their country. That was natural, as Mohammed is supposed to be the most common name in the world [Figure 18C].

At that time Bruce, Dan, Eric and I lived in a four-room second-floor apartment in New Brunswick, directly above a notorious greasy spoon called *Greasy Tony's*. "Greasy's," as it was locally known, proudly placed on its front window its culinary doctrine, "*No charge for extra grease.*" Clearly we were residing in a classy neighborhood. Greasy's specialty was the "Philly cheese steak," a dietary abomination comprised of unidentified compressed meat products and generic yellow cheese, which when thrown on the fryer would account for one's daily recommended caloric intake and an impending coronary attack.

Life above Greasy Tony's was rarely dull. Every three months the Greasy's crew would bomb out their cockroaches, and thousands of *cucarachas* fleeing the chemical attack would swarm upstairs into our apartment. We never had advance warning of extermination; why, that would have taken away the surprise! After Greasy's exterminated, there were so many roaches in our apartment they didn't even try to hide when the light was turned on. The next day we would retaliate by spraying the cockroaches in our apartment, whereupon nature's little wonders would then scamper back downstairs where they could entertain the clients of that estimable joint. We would then saunter downstairs, order a soda, and watch the roaches hop all over the seats in Greasy's.

Greasy's clientele included hustlers and bar hoppers of all types, and they stayed open until four in the morning. Their late hours benefited us, as their heat rose through the floor and kept us comfy until a big snowstorm arrived in March. An improbable punch line ends this story: traveling through Tempe, Arizona in 1994, I came across a *second* Greasy Tony's – Greasy's was a two-restaurant chain! Only in the USA could such a gastronomic aberration be cloned.

The International team had superior talent and playing ability to the varsity squad. We had a very powerful and creative strike force with the dominant Gabe as central striker, Teddy or Mohammed-Iran as withdrawn forward, and Reza and Sree patrolling the wings. Midfielders included Tony, Eric, Mohammed-Gambia, Bruce, Dan, and me. Keith Constantine was a formidable center back, extremely quick and almost impossible to beat, and helping him on defense was Mohammed-Morocco, Rashid Ali, Roberto, Roger, and/or Greg. In goal was the spectacular John or François. Ravee would coach the team and join in practices. We would play against any of the club teams in the area, and usually beat them in one of the city parks of New Brunswick or Piscataway.

Nearly all the players would later earn a graduate degree, so schoolwork came first. If somebody had a late class, they would come to practice or game late. Through his office Ravee tried to arrange a friendly game against the university team, but the varsity coach would not consent. Having known several of the players on our team, he knew it would cause more morale problems on the varsity team if they were badly beaten. However, we Internationals had great camaraderie all year, and it was an ideal team to complete my university career.

World Cup Argentina 1978

The 1978 World Cup was to take place in Argentina, but for those of us in the USA it might have well have been on Mars. The World's grandest sports extravaganza was again denied public access, as no games were televised. I saw an ad in the sports pages that the State Theater in Newark would show the Final live, which would feature host Argentina and Netherlands. Being an admirer of the "Total Football" of the Dutch, I was wearing an orange Netherlands shirt when I arrived, only to realize that I was the only "orange-man" in the theater. There were a lot of *albiceleste* (sky blue and white) shirts in the theater, as most of the fans were from Spanish-speaking countries and supporting Argentina. My orange look led to some good-natured ribbing.

My friends and I were disappointed that Johan Cruyff was not playing on the Dutch team that year. Nobody knew exactly why he was not playing, and in the absence of information the rumors on Cruyff ranged from (1) he was boycotting the Finals because of human rights abuses of the Argentine junta that should have changed the venue of the World Cup, (2) poor team security, (3) his wife forbid him to attend, (4) his ego had gotten too big for the team, and/or (5) he refused to dress for the Orange anymore as it supported the Dutch monarchy of the House of Orange instead of the Netherlands flag (which is red, white, and blue). Whatever his reasons, Holland still had Johan Neeskens, Rudi Krol, Johnny Rep, and Rob Rensenbrink, all of them playing in their second World Cup Final in yet another host country (Holland had lost to host West Germany 2-1 in 1974).

The lights went out, and the screen filled with an image of the Estadio Monumental pulsating in the Argentine colors of sky blue and white. A tiny section of the stadium confined the Dutch supporters defiantly displaying their *oranje* (see www.oranje.nl for fanatic Dutch supporter website). As the game began, the quality of play was very good as both teams were in an offensive mode. The 1978 Final was even more closely contested than the 1974 Final, because in the final minutes Rob Rensenbrink received a pass on the left side of the goal and beat keeper Ubaldo Fillol with his shot, but it agonizingly hit the left post.

If that shot had gone in and Holland had won the match, it is probable Argentina's history would have changed because Argentina was ruled by a military junta that was heavily invested in a World Cup triumph. There might have been major riots that could have accelerated the downfall of the Argentine generals, or conversely, may have led to a military crackdown and consolidation of power. As it was, Argentines would have to wait four more years until after the Falklands/Malvinas war debacle, when the military dictatorship was weak enough to be kicked out. (For a complete synopsis of soccer and politics in that sad era in Argentina, see Jimmy Burns's book, *Hand of God*.)

In any case, in the first overtime periods in World Cup history, Sampson-haired Mario Kempes scored his second goal and Daniel Bertoni added a third to make the final 3-1 in favor of Argentina. Holland again had a great team, but is very difficult to beat the host country, especially when the final takes place in a cauldron of host support. That Dutch team still rates as one of the 10 best national teams, even though they lost the two Finals.

Jamaica 1979

In the winter of 1979, Dan Yafet and I flew to Jamaica, where we met up with our roommate Eric Bennett. From Eric's base outside Spanish Town, we went to Kingston to see the prime Jamaican club rivalry of the time, Santos versus Boys Town. The Jamaican style of soccer play is very attractive to watch, akin to a mixture of Brazilian skill and English velocity. Santos had won the Jamaican championship from 1974-1977, and would win again in 1980. Boys Town was coming into their own, soon to win championships in 1984, 1986, and 1989. It was a very competitive and exciting game, with two young dreadlocked players showing remarkable creativity in going forward and scoring. Those two probably had the talent to play overseas, but at that time Jamaica had no conduit in which to send players for a professional soccer opportunity.

Soccer was beginning to heat up in Jamaica, partially fuelled by Bob Marley, the first and still greatest international reggae star. Marley was a soccer bum who could never pass up a ball game, whether a pickup game while on tour or an arranged game with his own team, the *House of Dread*. He packed his team with some quality players including his friend Alan "Skilly" Cole, the best Jamaican player of his time. Watching film of Marley "kick ball," the viewer can see he was a quality player who probably fancied himself a "number 10."

I witnessed firsthand the power of the Bob Marley and the Wailers message and music experience in a concert at the Apollo Theater in Harlem in 1979. I have noticed through my international travels and work that Marley's "message music" resounds in more places in the world than any other artist; more than Michael Jackson, Madonna, the Beatles, or any new pop creation. Next to dirt playing fields in the West Indies, Nigeria, or India - even in non-English-speaking countries like Indonesia, Japan, or Peru – after the local music you are more likely to find Marley's music being played and sold on the street, undoubtedly without copyright permission.

Eric had suspected that security in the stadium area would be deficient, and although there was no violence at the game, we left quickly before darkness arrived. This was the era of political election violence between the supporters of Michael Manley's PNP and Edward Seaga's JNP. Despite Marley attempting to form a peace pact between these two politicians at the "One Love Concert," more than 600 Jamaican lives were senselessly taken before the elections. Marley himself had just escaped an assassination attempt on his life at his home in Kingston, purportedly arranged by JLP supporters.

The next day, we awoke to the *Jamaica Gleaner* newspaper headline detailing the shooting deaths of three policemen at the National Stadium police station after the game the night before. That news demonstrated that political violence was increasing, even occurring around a soccer match. Still, plenty Jamaicans braved the bad political situation to come out and watch their native sons play the beautiful game.

Only two years later in 1981, Marley died aged thirty-six of metastatic malignant melanoma, an aggressive type of skin cancer. When statues are placed outside national stadiums, they are usually of politicians, generals, or athletes. But fittingly, a statue of native son Bob Marley – soccer fanatic and the world's most famous international music star – stands outside the National Stadium in Kingston, Jamaica [Figure 18D].

West Indies 1980-1983

After graduation from university I decided to become a physician, and applied to a variety of domestic as well as international medical schools because I was attracted by the idea of studying medicine outside my immediate world. For two reasons I settled on a British-American school in the West Indian country of Grenada. The first was that they had garnered a good academic reputation in a short time, using a combination of USA (scientific) and British (excellent clinical) style training. The second reason was that there was a social experiment going on in Grenada that was intriguing to witness firsthand; the New Jewel Party of charismatic populist Maurice Bishop had overthrown the preceding corrupt government and was promising a more equitable society.

The first semester I had to get acclimated and work hard to make sure I would get through my studies. There were a few soccer players in my class; Steve Wilson was the best and we became roommates. That semester we only had the opportunity to play at a local Sugar Mill field called "the pasture." It was just an ordinary cow pasture, which was occasionally used for local cricket and soccer games.

Grenada is a volcanic mountainous island country, and the "cow pasture" was by no means level, but had undulations like a mogul ski run. The main hazards were the ubiquitous "cow chips"; if the ball hit a fresh one it might stick there. Some of the better student soccer players were Walter Bokun, Jerald Thompson, Marshall Asonye, Larry Egbuchulan, Peter Musuka, and Emmanuel Yamusah. Our team included players from the USA, St. Vincent, Ghana, Nigeria, and Zimbabwe, as we ran with the locals of Sugar Mill in spirited games in the pasture.

Grenadians, like many West Indians, often have colorful nicknames that may escape memory as to exactly how they were conceived. These nicknames usually stay with them for life, through jobs, marriage, family, and even death. Even the Prime Minister is more likely to be called by his nickname than his real name. I once asked a player named Rabs, "Rabs, how did you get your name?" Answer: "Cyaan really tell, man, tink I had a rabbit when I was pickney, oui?" [Translation: "I don't really remember, but I think I had a rabbit when I was younger, you know?"]. Two very likable Grenadian players who were cousins had the rather incredible nicknames of Lousy and Shittee. I never bothered to ask them how they received their nicknames.

The next semester, Steve and I moved into Tanteen Terrace, located on the outskirts of the capital town of St. George's. From our porch we overlooked a school and its small field, which had been audaciously christened "Old Trafford" (the name of the Manchester United Stadium). Pickup games between Grenadian dockworkers and visiting Italian, Greek, or British ship workers would take place after their ships unloaded at the harbor. That was how Steve and I met members of the Carenage United Football Club (CUFC), who played in the First Division of the Grenada Football League (GFL). Local players Boyo, Blanca, BJ, Pie-yee, Ben, Ba-boy, and Grabowski would regularly turn out and usually beat the visiting seaman's team at Old Trafford. Occasionally, the larger Tanteen field across the street would be available for matches when not being used for cricket or school games.

Along with the two other capital teams, Queens Park Rangers and Honved, CUFC was one of the three top teams in Grenada. The team was named after the Carenage, the U-shaped harbor located in the center of St. George's. City rivals Honved had borrowed their name from the great Hungarian team, while QPR could have been named after the London team or the Grenada National Queen's Park stadium, the home venue for all these three capital teams. Queen's Park is an expansive field on the Caribbean Sea just to the north of St. George's, and soccer matches there were routinely broadcast on the government radio channel Radio Free Grenada (RFG).

CUFC was a workers team, in particular the dockworker's team. Their captain was *Boyo* Thomas, a former dockworker who had elevated himself into the Ministry of Tourism. Boyo had multiple nicknames, including the regal *Remo* and *King*, and the ironic *Caboose* – hardly anybody knew his real name was Augustine. His nicknames signified the natural leader status he had held since his youth days.

Boyo was also the Grenada national soccer team captain. Grenada had players with more skill on the ball, but there wasn't a better ball-winner or bolder field leader in the country. Boyo had the perfect soccer body - tree-trunk legs with a lean muscular chest - and he could run all day. He was a two-way force in midfield, running the ball down and tackling expertly and fairly [Figure 18E].

Boyo also had three brothers: winger Bobby (also known as *Grabowski* or *Dalglish*), creative midfielder *Blanca*, and "*Dopey*," a team supporter. Other players were *Booce*, an organizing and scoring midfielder who also led the Angel Harps steel-band orchestra, and *Pie-yee*, the goalkeeper and also a steel-pan master (Pie-yee may have gotten his nickname from the Spanish word *pie*, meaning foot). *Maitland*, otherwise known as "*Botswanna*," was the outside left winger, short and fast and a excellent swimmer – he had won the cross-Carenage harbor swim race against many taller swimmers. Young *Ben* was a center back with a cannon shot; despite his tender age he took accurate booming free kicks. *Preacher* was an outside back of cunning effectiveness. Preacher was not a religious man – his name simply reflected a penchant to opine. *Claudio* was a youngster who could play with the big boys. Carenage United's *piece de resistance* was perhaps national team center forward *BJ* (Barry James), a rapier thin center forward who had great dribbling and passing talents, and who had an incredible double-pullback move that I have never seen duplicated [Figure 18F & G].

Most of the players were still working on the docks. Once in a while one would get a job on a cruise ship and disappear for some months. Cruise jobs did not pay very well, so after a period of travel the player would come back home to perform with CUFC again.

I missed many Carenage practices because of my university courses and A-Level Biology teaching schedule. Still, Boyo would show up at our door at dawn, and kick me out of bed to "run up the Lane." "The Lane" was Lowthar's Lane, a torturous 800 foot vertical run straight up from the ocean to the Psychiatric Hospital.[8] I was 25 years old, Boyo in his late 20s, but by determination and stamina he could run up that hill faster than anybody on the team. Later, Boyo proudly built a house at the top of that hill for his family.

Carenage United was a very popular club and would get a good turnout for home games. We looked pretty smart in our all-red uniforms – shirt, pants, and socks. In my initial CUFC match, RFG radio commentator Ray Roberts creatively announced that I was a "new German player." As the only European-looking player in the league, I was a bit of a novelty.

It was even more dramatic when we played in "up country" towns like Gouyave, Grenville, or Victoria, because there were no stadiums, just a field beautifully set next to the ocean. Hundreds of supporters would gather around the field and follow the play. If the ball was on the other side of the field, the crowd would creep five yards onto the field. If play switched quickly, they would recede off the field like a slow-moving wave. Sometimes the spectators failed to make it off the field on time, and players then found themselves dribbling on the field, but also amongst the crowd desperately trying to move back.[9]

CUFC usually beat all the country teams, but we would look forward to playing Victoria, as they were the best team outside the capital. Victoria's team was known as "Hurricane," and they certainly looked the part. Hurricane players were all rock-solid fishermen, with massive thighs sculpted from dragging their nets in the surf every morning. Their technique was less sophisticated than the town teams, but they were the fittest team in the league and had tremendous heart.

Our game against Hurricane was memorable. When we arrived, there were so many people we had a hard time making it on to the field. When we reached the pitch, some spectators exclaimed, "*white man play football!*" as if they never had seen anybody European-looking play soccer before. Early in the match, I was anxious receiving a belt-high pass at the 18-yard line. Time slowed down as I looked to pass to BJ, but failing to locate him I tried a shot. The volley took off for the upper right hand corner, and following the trajectory I thought, "That was the best possible shot I could have made, a sure goal." But their athletic keeper jumped high and turned the ball onto the crossbar where it ricocheted back on the field, only to be cleared by the defense after a short scrum in the penalty box. As I received a pass near the sideline, a human wave fell back like dominoes to the touchline to allow play. I was exhausted after the game; we had our technique but it was their house and natural fitness. The game against Hurricane was like playing a school of flying fish; they were flapping about everywhere. The final score was 2-1 to them, but a thrilling game nonetheless.

Because Steve and I were associated with the Carenage team and lived in town, we became well known in St. George's. People knew who we were, but did not really know our

---

[8] The Psychiatric Hospital was later stupidly destroyed by USA artillery during the 1983 invasion of Grenada, resulting in heavy civilian patient casualties (callously called "collateral damage" in USA military doublespeak).
[9] The Nike company designed a television commercial on this theme that was broadcast in 2005, the premise being Brazilian star Ronaldinho dribbling on the field with a crowd immediately behind him. This advertisement was no doubt based in the spectator reality of such games as I participated in Grenada.

names. They knew we were Steve and Ritchie, but couldn't remember who was who. When we walked together it was not a problem, they would call out "Ritchie....Steve," and we would return the greeting with "Hail" or "Irie." But when we walked alone, we would get the same greeting of "Ritchie....Steve," or "Steve....Ritchie"; two names for the price of one! When I checked with Steve, he routinely received the same treatment from people. People were so friendly that they wanted to show they knew your name, but figured they better cover themselves with both names. It was amusing to get the same name treatment because we are fairly distinct individuals – Steve is shorter, more muscular, and has a darker complexion than me [Figure 18H].

Those were great times in Grenada; there is nothing better than playing soccer with good players on a field next to the Caribbean Sea. After the league season ended, we would play "court-ball" or "small-ball" on concrete courts in St. George's or Grand Anse. These were basketball or netball courts, in which small metal goals about 2 by 2 feet were placed at the ends. Play was with a plastic or rubber ball the size of a number 3 soccer ball, and it required great skill to maneuver it into the small goals. Court-ball was a smaller form of "futsal," expertly designed to improve ball-skills.

On 11 May 1981, we were playing court-ball in St. George's when we received word that reggae king Bob Marley had died. People were visibly stunned, as Marley was the best-known person to ever come out of the Caribbean, and was widely admired by young people worldwide for his brilliant "message music." After hearing the news with disbelief, everybody lost the desire to play. Somebody put on Marley's music on a loudspeaker next to the court, and right then - in the middle of the day - workers began to leave their jobs, some crying in the street. That day turned into a forced holiday; the death of a man who was a modern-day musical prophet, and a dedicated football player.

The time came to leave Grenada for a five-month stint in the neighboring country of St. Vincent. A geographically similar island country to Grenada, St. Vincent is mountainous in the middle with picturesque beaches on the shores. Being there on a short stay, it was impossible to play routinely with a team. The best I could find was regular pickup games in Calliaqua on yet another field directly on the turquoise Caribbean Sea. The locals had plenty of energy, and after the game we would refresh ourselves at the corner shop with *Giant* malt or "sea moss", a white concoction of seaweed and condensed milk, which reputedly "gave you the ability" (a natural Viagra). When in the capital of Kingstown I played a few times with the first division players. They were of good caliber, and St. Vincent still ranks at the top of the small island countries in the Caribbean.

I was to miss my Carenage colleagues tremendously in the future. The coming invasion of Grenada by USA military forces was just ten months away, and the Reagan administration was making disingenuous claims that Grenada's new airport was to be a Russian air base, and that they were building a submarine base at Calvigny Bay. To counter these fabrications, the British engineers working the construction projects held press conferences showing that the "missile silos" were in fact standard buried fuel tanks, and that it was impossible to put a submarine base in Calvigny Bay because it had an average depth of only 20 feet! But concrete facts had little effect on the USA government propaganda machine. The USA military would invade Grenada, and hundreds of people (mostly civilians) would needlessly lose their lives. The Caribbean Council of Churches had almost finished negotiating an agreement to end the political stalemate in Grenada, but Reagan steam-rolled the effort to have "his war." Even the parents of the medical school students – under whose pretense the USA was invading – begged Reagan NOT to invade as they deemed that was an action that would put the students in MORE danger.

After the invasion fiasco, Preacher was thrown in jail for 10 months for defending his country against the foreign invaders, and the invincible Boyo took ill with swollen lymph glands. Boyo had developed advanced Hodgkin's lymphoma, and despite urgent treatment administered by our colleague Yamusah, he succumbed at the tender age of thirty-four. Both Boyo and Bob went way too early.

Bern, Switzerland 1982-1983

During the summer of 1982 I went to discover my ancestral roots in the Swiss capital of Bern. The Altstadt (Old Town) of Bern was founded in the year 1191, and was constructed of ancient elegant stone buildings with archways to walk underneath. The ice-cold Aare River curls around the city, having protected it from invaders over the centuries.

My grandparents Alfred and Margrit lived in Bümpliz, a suburb of Bern, but since they lived an ocean away we were still relative strangers. While my grandmother could speak some English, my grandfather spoke the local dialect of *Schwyzerdütsch*.

Almost immediately I got a job in the Altstadt pouring wine and making sandwiches in the Rathaus (*Town Hall*) Restaurant. While working one afternoon (May 31st, 1982), there was an interesting scene in front of the restaurant after the Sion club beat Basel to win the Swiss Cup at the historic Wankdorf Stadium. Sion is in the French-speaking area of Switzerland, and their club has very active supporters. The Sion fans descended to the outdoor square of the restaurant encircling an ancient fountain, singing their team songs as they rang huge cowbells hanging around their necks – brrrrring, brrring, brrring – directly into the restaurant's clients faces. The alcohol was flowing as one of their drunken supporters relieved himself into the square's fountain. All in all, a classy Swiss football celebration.[10]

I left the Rathaus shortly thereafter, and started work at the Inselspital Kinderklinik, the University of Bern Children's Hospital. This was no ordinary hospital, but a research facility sixteen floors high, yet containing only about 80 inpatients. I worked in the kitchen and the operating rooms, and would occasionally get together to play soccer with my friend Stefan Hüggler, who was a master baker.

That 1982 summer was also memorable for the World Cup in Spain. I was in heaven, as I would come home after work and flip on the television to Swiss, Italian, German, or French television, and watch whatever game I wanted (over and over). The channels had coordinated their schedules so that on one channel you would see one game, and the other would have another game. Almost every night I would watch 1½ to 4 ½ hours of World Cup football. What a change from the dearth of World Cup coverage in the United States!

The final was between West Germany and Italy, and when Italy won, the Swiss joined the Italians in the streets of Bern to celebrate. Most Swiss fans I met favored the Latin flair over the Teutonic technician approach to soccer. Many also remembered the historic Swiss defeat of Germany in 1938 World Cup, knocking the Germans out of the competition on the eve of World War II. To put that game in perspective, by 1938 Switzerland's neighbor Austria had already been annexed by Germany, and the Swiss feared they were to be the next victim of Nazi hegemony.

For eight months in 1983 I went back to work in the Inselspital Kinderklinik. After a spell on the cleaning crew, I worked in the operating rooms. Although the hours were long, I looked to play soccer whenever possible. I found what appeared to be the only serious pickup game in all of Bern, on Wednesday afternoons with the university graduate students. Most of the players were foreigners - from Ghana, Egypt, Turkey, and Italy - all with good skills and an unselfish playing style as we played on a 7 versus 7 format. The students found a perfectly flat grass field adjacent to the university, which served well for a game that welcomed all comers.

In professional soccer in Bern, the Young Boys club still played their home games in historic Wankdorf Stadium, the same stadium where the "Battle of Bern" (between Brazil

---

[10] Sion has appeared in nine Swiss Cup finals since 1965 (1965, 1974, 1980, 1982, 1986, 1991, 1995, 1996, and 1997), and has a perfect record winning all nine; thereby giving their fans reason to celebrate in style.

and Hungary), and the World Cup Final (between Germany and Hungary) were staged in 1954. At the Wankdorf Stadium on August 5, 1983, I witnessed the Final of the inaugural Phillips Cup between top Swiss team Grasshoppers from Zurich and Atlético Mineiro from Brazil. The Swiss champion "Hoppers" had a very good team, with national team players striker Claudio Sulser, most ever capped midfielder Heinz Hermann, Andy Egli in defense, and keeper Roger Berbig. The Brazilian team had left midfielder-winger Eder, a special talent from the 1982 World Cup. Eder's specialties were dribbling and shooting from long range, and taking long free kicks. He had made some spectacular goals in the World Cup, and Eder did not disappoint that day in Bern.

Wankdorf stadium was not as big as most American stadiums, and I was able to get very close to the pitch at the center of the field. During the game, a foul was committed against the Brazilians on the left side of the field about 35 yards away from the Swiss goal. I was only 20 yards away and could see the action very clearly. Eder went up and delicately placed the ball on the grass and slowly backed away. He took his typical 10-yard run-up and blasted the ball with his left leg, launching it with tremendous power without spin. The knuckleball movement of the ball fooled Berbig as there was no spin to predict exactly where it was going; it initially looked like it would sail into the right side of the goal. By the time the bewildered Berbig knew where the ball was going, it was already there, safely nestled in the upper left hand corner of the net. He had no chance with Eder's magic act. Eder, watching the results of his technique, then capped his performance with his characteristic somersault and celebration. That shot was the greatest dead-ball goal from distance I ever saw live; and from one of the all-time masters.

Atlético Mineiro tied the Grasshoppers 2-2, but "won" the Final on penalty kicks 6-5. The lineup from that entertaining game:

Grasshoppers: Berbig, Wehrli, In-Albon (46' Schällibaum), Egli, Ladner, Koller, Ponte, Hermann, Jara, Marchand, Sulser.
Atlético Mineiro: Leite, Fred, Nelinho (62' Niranda), Heleno, Salvador, Marcelo (72' Ricardo Eugenio), Renato, Valenca, Formiga, Paulinho, Eder. Goals: Sulser 7', Nelinho 35', Eder 51', Hermann 69'.

London, England 1984

In 1984, I had clinical rotations scheduled in London hospitals. Based in Edmonton in northeast London, I was a jog from White Hart Lane, the Tottenham Hotspurs Football Club ground. Thus, by proximity I became a "Spurs" supporter.

Tottenham had an excellent team in the early 1960s, but experienced a success drought for the next decade. Tottenham then became the first English team to incorporate Argentine players, bringing in creative midfielder Osvaldo Ardiles and forward Ricky Villa after Argentina's World Cup victory in 1978. With their South American skills Tottenham returned to glory, as they won the FA Cup in 1981 and 1982 and the UEFA Cup in 1984.

The English welcome for the Argentines was interrupted by the foolish Malvinas/Falklands war, which was waged over the mostly sheep-populated islands in 1982. Ardiles had to leave Tottenham and London to play in France during the war, but he persevered and after the conflict ended and the generals were kicked out in Argentina, he again helped bring success to Tottenham.

Standing on the terraces at White Hart Lane was a novel and intimate experience for one used to all-seater stadiums in the USA. Spurs' stadium was smaller than USA stadiums, because the standing areas allowed more people per square meter. The crowds on the terraces could be captivating as they would rhythmically sway as they sang inspirational songs to their teams. Occasionally however, on those enchanted evenings at White Hart Lane, a fan drank too much beer, swayed, and ultimately vomited on his neighbors. Charming.

I attended as many Tottenham games as my schedule allowed, and enjoyed the skills of Spurs players such as Ardiles, Clive Allen, Steve Archibald, Alan Brazil, Garth Crooks, Steve Perryman, Glenn Hoddle, and Ray Clemence, as well as many others in the First Division (now called the Premier League).

Tottenham's most important match of the year is always against archrival Arsenal. Separated by just a few miles from the White Hart Lane train stop to the Arsenal underground subway line, Arsenal-Tottenham is still the principal rivalry or "derby" in London (although it is rivaled in Britain by the important Celtic-Rangers and Manchester United-Liverpool derbies). Arsenal also had a good team that year, with some classy players like Kenny Sansom, Charlie Nicholas, Viv Anderson, Paul Mariner, Tony Woodcock, and keeper Pat Jennings.

Emerging from the Arsenal underground, I encountered a sea of people controlled by mounted policemen. Upon eventual arrival at the ticket booth, I was asked if I was a Tottenham or Arsenal supporter. Trying to inject some humor into what I thought was a strange question, I replied, "I'm from the colonies, mate, just came to see the game." The ticket seller then informed me it was a serious matter to choose from which spectator area (Arsenal or Tottenham) I wanted to watch. Off I went into one Spurs section in the corner of the field.

The Arsenal supporters were separated from the Spurs fans by a metal hurricane fence. All was relatively peaceful until the game commenced, whereupon the Gunners' fanatics immediately tried to tear down the fence. The police frantically rushed over in an attempt to contain the mayhem. Then, like a military operation, the Gunner's fans opened a second engagement. Some Arsenal hooligans had already infiltrated the Tottenham section, and were stationed on the top of our terraces. These moronic yobbos would then run down the middle of the terrace with flying elbows, knocking down all they encountered; Tottenham supporters were laid out all over the terrace. But because the Arsenal fans were pretending to be Spurs fans until they went on their rampages, the police seemed powerless to prevent these crimes until they had already been committed.

Before the first half ended, there were two policemen on each step of the terrace, and each hooligan who was caught was led around the field to the cheers of the Arsenal supporters. All game long these idiots were being led around the field to the exit. Maybe that was their objective anyway, as they only could get close to their heroes by being arrested as the game was being played.

The police on the terraces appeared shocked and helpless, as there was little preventive action they could take until spectators were already damaged. As the English police were not armed, they had to perform effective riot control with only sticks and a badge. It was a truly frightening experience being immersed in the mob atmosphere and witnessing people being cowardly assaulted from behind by hooligans while simply watching a football match.

I began to wonder about the state of British football. The sad thing is, I don't remember the score of that game or even which team won. It was the beginning of the hooligan era on the continent.[11]

---

[11] For a good analysis of the hooligan period see Bill Buford's *Among the Thugs* (1990). Written by a USA expatriate literary expert, Buford studied the phenomenon up close (sometimes *too close* for comfort).

London Caribbean Team 1984

While I was in London, I played with a local team in Edmonton, just north of Tottenham. Once again I was playing on an "all-Caribbean" team, as the other players were transplants or offspring of West Indian immigrants. Most carried London accents and displayed more of the toughness characteristic of the English game rather than the crafty skills present in the West Indian game. I missed quite a few games due to night duty in the hospital, but we participated in two memorable competitions.

We entered a tournament contested at the Hackney Marshes in London, which has the largest collection of soccer fields in the world (about 120 football pitches placed in its confines). Over two thousand players can compete at one time at the Marshes, making it a fitting tribute to soccer in the land where the Laws of Football were codified. Upon arrival, we were told we had *three games* that afternoon, although the games had been shortened to 70 minutes each. By the end of the third match everybody was completely *knackered* (English term for "exhausted"). After all, this was English football and everybody was running full tilt. We won the first, tied the second, and were one goal down in the third game when, at 210 minutes played in the last minute of the last game, I was tripped up from behind and broke my wrist. What I learned from that experience is *that it is possible to overdose from playing soccer*. Still, a soccer overdose is probably better than other societal overdose alternatives.

I had a cast fitted from my colleagues in the North Middlesex Hospital, and started playing again a month later in an indoor tournament in South London. One of our opponents was a Watford FC squad. Pop star Elton John had bought controlling interest in the club, and helped Watford make a remarkable run from Division 4 to Division 1 in only five years (from 1978-1982). Watford's star of that era was John Barnes, one of England's first national team players with some African ancestry.[12] Our London Caribbean side tried our best, but we were outmatched and lost 2-0 to the Watford reserve side in an intense 20-minute game.

New York City 1985-1988

After medical school, I underwent further medical training in the Bronx area of New York City. My initial training was at St. Barnabas Hospital on 183rd Street and 3rd Avenue, which was home to several ethnic neighborhoods; Italian, West Indian, Central American, African, and Puerto Rican. As I was working about 110 hours per week in the hospital, there was little recreational time for soccer, but I soon found good pickup games twice a week at nearby Fordham University. I would show up at the field in terrible condition, as sleep was a rarity during the on-call nights every 2nd or 3rd night. But there were some very useful players at those games, and I was sometimes the only person without a foreign accent.

There were some players from the lower Italian leagues living in the Bronx section of Arthur Avenue, an Italian-American enclave in which Italian was spoken as freely as English. One Italian, Alfredo, was unbeatable on the dribble and could pass beautifully as well. Nearly all his goals were perfectly placed in the corners. It was easy to see how he played in Italy, but did he give up his professional career just to immigrate to the USA? It was 1985 and the NASL had just collapsed, and there was no full-field professional soccer existing in the USA.

Later in my training, as I started working "only" 80 hours a week at Lincoln Hospital located in the "Fort Apache" area of the South Bronx, I was able to play more soccer. On the northwest side of Manhattan, Fort Tryon Park was a wonderful field located right on the

---

[12] Barnes had made a slalom "Maradona-type" run for goal, when England beat Brazil 2-0 in a friendly shocker result in the Maracana in Rio de Janeiro in 1984. The astute Brazilian press nominated Barnes' skill goal as the best *Brazilian* goal of that year.

Hudson River, where ex-university players would gather on Sunday afternoons. Another promising pickup game was on the opposite end of Manhattan, at the east end of Houston Street next to the East River. A variety of Latins, Africans, and West Indians would play there on the weekends. Occasionally, I would go down to Brooklyn and play with Caribbean teams in Prospect Park.

And that is how it went for three long years, a time that passed almost in a sleepless blur. Instead of sharpening my game in my middle 20s, I was honing my work-numbed brain in a quest to become a quality doctor. Only a few players have been able to play top quality soccer and earn their medical degree at the same time, such as Socrates (pediatrics) and Hugo Sanchez (dentist). However, the long hours required for advanced medical training are dreadfully incompatible with serious soccer training, and must be postponed until the playing days are over.

Boston 1988-1990

In 1988 I went to Harvard University in Boston to do a course in public heath. While waiting for a separate license to practice medicine in Massachusetts, I would drive back to New York City every two weeks to work forty-eight hours straight (from 8 AM Saturday to 8 AM Monday morning) in the hospital. I would then drive like mad to try and make my 10:30 AM class in Boston. I never made that class; I usually pulled over by the side of the road to get some much needed sleep. As I was working all weekend, I couldn't play with my friends in New York, so I found some places to play in the Boston area.

Across from Harvard Medical School was a small gymnasium in Vanderbilt Hall, where students would play indoors twice weekly. It wasn't very fancy, only a way to keep in shape during the cold Boston winter. There I met a group of workers from the Dana-Farber Cancer Center who entered a team in an indoor league in Hingham, about 15 miles south of Boston. The field was about the size of a hockey rink with artificial turf laid down. We had no star players but went on to win the league anyway, mostly due to the overachieving nature of our cancer-fighters.

My second year in Boston I worked at Harvard University Health Services in Cambridge. One evening in the emergency room, I saw a young goalkeeper with a strange soccer injury. He had been hit with a fast-traveling ball right between the eyes, saving a goal in the process. But after the incident, whenever he pinched his nose and blew out air, his left eye moved! I asked him to show me, and he did, whereupon I exclaimed, "Don't do that again!" as his left eye performed a disconcerting dance. I suspected a blowout fracture of his left orbit, the delicate bone cavity holding his eye in place. I immediately packed him off to the "Mass Eye and Ear" (Massachusetts Eye and Ear Hospital in Boston) to get a CT scan and further management. The goalkeeper turned out to be the brother of an ex-New York Cosmos player.

During that year, I started looking for an opportunity to study infectious diseases in more depth, and the best opportunity turned out to be located way down south in New Orleans.

New Orleans 1990-1992

New Orleans is located in Louisiana, a territory formerly controlled by Spain and France. As a result, Louisiana has many Spanish and French named towns, and New Orleans has many buildings and streets of Spanish and French origin. The United States acquired greater Louisiana from Napoleon Bonaparte for 15 million dollars in 1803, in a country-building deal (or steal) called the Louisiana Purchase. Louisiana still maintains some French idiosyncrasies such as calling their counties "parishes," and unlike the other 49 states in the USA, Louisiana state law is still based on the Napoleonic code.

New Orleans was historically somewhat of an oasis in the Deep South, where people of African ancestry were freed long before the Civil War ended slavery. New Orleans is also known as the birthplace of Louis Armstrong and the indigenous music form called Jazz.

Besides the original French influence that led to Creole society in Louisiana, French immigrants from snowy Arcadia migrated 2000 miles south to the tropical swamps of Louisiana. These "Cajuns" continued with their culture, after being subjugated in Canada because of their Catholic religion. It is into this cultural gumbo that I have resided intermittently for the last sixteen years (1990-2006). The first two years were spent in specialized medical training at Tulane University Medical School, but my hours were not so rigorous as before (only 60 active hours a week).

In 1990, there were two main places to find a quality pickup soccer game in New Orleans. The first was Cabrini Park in the historic Vieux Carré, popularly known as the French Quarter. Located on a half-block of Barracks Street between the 1200 blocks of Dauphine and Burgundy Streets, Cabrini Park was the only place to play soccer in the downtown CBD (Central Business District) area. We would set up a small goal game on this good quality pitch, with up to seven on each side. Many players were foreigners in the culinary or hotel fields that are New Orleans specialties. Some became successful restaurateurs, such as Jacques who runs the *Degas* restaurant (named after the French painter Edgar Degas, who spent time in New Orleans) on Esplanade Avenue, Nanoo who runs the *La Crepe Nanoo* on Robert Street, and brew master Wolfgang who runs the *Crescent City Brewhouse* in the French Quarter. Also playing were French bakers, deliverymen from Belize and Senegal, Latin American hotel workers, and international students and faculty from the nearby Tulane School of Public Health and Tropical Medicine. Some players had very good skills, which were enhanced by the increased time on the ball from the small game format. Soccer games are no longer permitted in this quaint French Quarter Park, which has regrettably been turned into a dog park.

The second pickup game locale was in uptown New Orleans at the Riverfront Park in back of the Audubon Zoo (for some reason, this park is also called "The Fly"). The fields are located directly on the levee crest holding back the mighty Mississippi River, thereby providing a panoramic view of the tankers and riverboats negotiating the tricky currents of the USA's mightiest river. Pickup soccer games have been played in this area since the 1920's, originally between foreign ship crews at the Port of New Orleans. There still are pickup games during the week and on Saturday afternoons, but not between ship crews anymore. The players were a mix of Central and South Americans, Africans, Europeans, and USA players from various universities. Hondurans were well represented at that time, including Garifunas (people of mixed Arawak and African ancestry whose ancestors had been sent against their will from the island of St. Vincent to the isle of Roatan off the coast of Honduras). A few of the Hondurans had performed for their national team, and I recognized one of them from a summary videotape of the Spain 1982 World Cup.

On Sunday afternoons during the summers, Ben Franklin High School soccer team players would show up at "the Fly." I particularly enjoyed playing with them because they sought the creative seams of the game, with good technique and unselfish play as their rule.

There were several soccer leagues in the area, mostly located in Lafreniere Park in Metairie, ten miles west from downtown New Orleans. However, large games of 11 versus 11 players with few moments on the ball can be boring for busy adults seeking serious soccer recreation. Smaller games with more time on the ball are often more enjoyable.

New Orleans had a lower-level professional soccer team, called the Gamblers, who played at the Pan-American stadium in the 1990s. The Gamblers eventually went out of business, but New Orleans began to host another soccer team in 2003, called the Shellshockers, who played their home games on the latest generation of artificial turf at Tulane University.[13]

---

[13] After the collapse of several New Orleans levees from hurricane Katrina in August 2005, polluted waters flooded over 80% of the city, including the Pan-American Stadium and Tulane fields. Lafreniere Park was turned into a massive dumping ground, leaving only "The Fly" as a soccer ground in greater New Orleans.

Peru 1992–1998

I originally came to Peru in 1992 to investigate epidemic deaths in an isolated Amazonian tribe. My home base was the city of Iquitos, located directly on the Amazon River. Although Iquitos has 330,000 inhabitants, it is only accessible by river or by air because there are no roads to this jungle city. The Iquiteños' life by the largest river in the world is hot, humid, and full of the daily challenges of work, housing, and disease. In the last decade alone, the city has experienced severe epidemics of cholera, drug-resistant malaria, and dengue fever. Still, people have to recreate, and in 1992 Iquitos had their Colegio Nacional de Iquitos (CNI, pronounced *say-enna-ee*) football team in the first division of Peru (more on CNI and Amazon soccer in Chapter 12).

A favorite soccer locale of mine was at hospitals or medical schools in Peru, as nearly every hospital and medical school in Peru has their own field or *futbito* court. In Iquitos, matches would be played at the Amazonas Regional Hospital and Hospital Apoyo Iquitos, where after making their patient rounds on Saturdays, the doctors and health workers would play several matches. In Lima, I was able to play futbito with the faculty and medical students of Cayetano Heredia University Medical School, while in Cusco I played with the students at UNSAAC and the IPSS hospital. I was enthusiastically accepted into these games and made several good medical acquaintances when competing in these friendly matches.

Lima Teams

Soccer in the overflowing capital city of Lima is an ever-changing phenomenon. While many professional players developed their ball skills playing "street soccer," because of increased vehicular traffic it is now too unsafe to play in most streets. Many poor neighborhoods (which encompass most of the greater Lima area) have no parks or even playgrounds in which children can play soccer. Perhaps as a result of poor urban planning with little green space, Peru's stature in the global game has dropped.

Lima teams ruled the professional game until 1972, when decentralization opened the first division up to the rest of the country. Lima still has the three largest and most successful teams in the country: Alianza Lima (founded 1901), Universitario (founded 1924), and Sporting Cristal (founded 1955). They have dominated the national championships as well: Universitario winning 25, Alianza with 20, and Cristal with 14 championships. Smaller club Sport Boys (founded 1927) from Lima's port zone of Callao contributes 6 championships.

Sporting Cristal was the strongest Peruvian team in the mid 1990's, and went the farthest in the South American championship (Copa Libertadores). Their stars were Roberto "Chorri" Palacios, Jorge Soto, Flavio Maestri and Brazilian-born and Peruvian nationalized Juninho.

Sporting Cristal played a home and away match in 1996 against top club River Plate of Argentina. The first match was home for Cristal, which meant playing in front of more fans at Lima's Estadio Nacional (National Stadium) than their cozy San Martin de Porras home stadium. Cristal played flawless football against River Plate that night, and hardly made a wrong touch. Cristal won easily by 2-0, but it should have been 5-0, and they only needed to tie or lose by one goal in Argentina to go through to the next round. The away match at River Plate was a different story, however, as Cristal lost 5-2 with a young Hernan Crespo scoring on a spectacular bicycle kick from the 18-yard line. That finished the 1996 Copa for Cristal.

Cristal came back stronger in 1997, and made it all the way to the Copa Final, where they lost to Cruzeiro of Brazil 1-0 on aggregate. That was the best finish ever for a Peruvian team in the Copa Libertadores.

Estadio Nacional

Lima's Estadio Nacional (National Stadium) is the site of national team games, and many of the city's "classicos" (classic games between the Big Three – Alianza Lima, Sporting Cristal or Universitario). In 2004, the stadium hosted the first-round games, semi-finals and Final of the Copa America [Figure 18J and K]. The stadium also contains the offices of the Instituto Peruano de Deporte (IPD), which is responsible for all sport in Peru (IPD website at www.ipd.gob.pe).

Despite its seeming ordinariness, the Estadio Nacional is the site of one of the most horrific football disasters in history.[14] In 1963, when the Estadio Nacional was relatively new (inaugurated in October 1952), an Olympic qualifying match between Peru and Argentina was hosted, and the result would determine which country would qualify for the 1964 Olympics. Peru scored near the end of the game, but the referee disallowed the goal, and pandemonium ensued. The undermanned police used tear gas to try and control the crowd, but instead, instigated a stampede that left 314 people confirmed dead. The Peruvian President then placed the city under martial law for the following month. Somewhat surprisingly, there is no memorial to that horrific event at the stadium, nor on the IPD website description of the National Stadium. It is as it never happened, and the stadium went on to host the 2004 Copa America and 2005 U-17 World Cup.

Even today, the strategy of police tossing tear gas into crowds resulting in stampedes causes many of the mass injuries and deaths in soccer matches worldwide. More expert oversight of stadium police tactical crowd control is still necessary after so many instigated stampedes at emotional football matches.

Globalization Hyperbole – Claudia Schiffer and Lalo Maradona

There are few things that can cause a daily buzz for months in the Lima newspapers. National elections, border skirmishes with Ecuador, an embassy taken over by terrorists – these were the usual stories that were dragged out on the front pages in the late 1990s. Two other far less significant stories were reported in Lima in 1997-8 that nonetheless instigated newspaper hyperbole for far longer than warranted.

The first was that the German model Claudia Schiffer was hired to launch a new bank credit card in Peru. This story appeared months before she arrived, and her picture appeared on the front pages like the second coming of Mary Magdalene. Unfortunately, the undue attention fostered on a foreign model by multinational companies discounts the inherent beauty of Peruvian women. Finally Schiffer arrived, and her presence swamped the newsprint for the week she was in Peru. Thankfully the coverage decreased after she left, except for the omnipresent billboards of her image aiming to sell credit cards to Peruvians looking for their next meal.

The second story was that Deportivo Municipal (an out of favor club also known as "Muni") was searching for a player to elevate their club status to match their former halcyon days of the 1940s and 1950s. Muni eventually signed Lalo Maradona, the brother of Argentine superstar Diego Maradona. Lalo did not have a soccer pedigree anywhere close to his brother's, but to look at some of the newspaper articles you got the impression it was the second coming of Diego himself. The build-up occurred weeks before he arrived, and continued when he started playing for Municipal. Eventually Muni's directors realized that although a few more fans had temporarily been attracted to their games, Lalo's lack of "Diego-ness" was a liability to the team's play, and he was eventually released. Muni was subsequently relegated from the First Division, and has not been promoted since.

The Claudia and Lalo affairs won the Hyperbole Awards that year, for the most sensational stories embellished by Peru's newspapers.

What was not exaggerated was the performance of Brazilian Eduardo Esidio in the First Division from 1997 to 2001. The newspapers properly understated his HIV status, while appropriately covering his personal and team's success (league top scorer, World Silver Boot winner, and four consecutive Peruvian championships). Esidio's remarkable story is covered in detail in Chapter 6.

---

[14] The 1963 Peru-Argentina pre-Olympic qualifier is often labeled the most lethal soccer disaster ever. Some are convinced that a 1982 Russian soccer stampede in Lenin Stadium in Moscow claimed 340 lives, but not surprisingly, the USSR government never confirmed that estimated mortality figure.

Cusco Soccer

In Cusco in 1997, I would exercise a few times a week with my fiancée Massiel at the Inca Garcilaso de la Vega Stadium. The stadium was named after one of the greatest of Peruvians, who was the progeny of an Inca princess and a Spanish soldier. Garcilaso de la Vega developed into one of the 16th century's leading intellectuals, and his "Los Comentarios Reales de los Incas" (Lisbon, 1609) is unsurpassed in detailing the Spanish conquest and consequent deterioration of the Inca civilization. As Cusco was the urban nucleus of the ancient Inca Empire, the stadium appropriately carries de la Vega's name. It is incredibly refreshing to find a stadium named for a historic intellectual figure, but I would not hold my breath for corporate named stadiums in the USA and Europe to follow suit.

The Estadio Garcilaso stadium belongs to the public, as it is owned by the government Instituto Peruano de Deporte. Because it is a public stadium, the public has full use rights. This means that ordinary citizens may utilize the stadium, even when the professional soccer team Cienciano is practicing. The physical proximity to the team and players probably reinforces the strong feelings Cusqueños have for their home team.

Massiel and I would typically run and lift weights, and once a week I would play *futsal* on a inside grass court with some of the university students from the UNSAAC Cusco national university (Universidad Nacional de San Antonio Abad Cusco). One day, when Massiel and I wandered into the stadium to exercise, the professional Cienciano team was practicing on the field. Small groups of children were on the opposite side, and a few dozen people were running on the track. We sat in the stands watching the players loosen up and start to kick the ball.

Massiel informed me that the Cienciano coach was Argentine-born goalkeeper Ramón Quiroga, a nationalized Peruvian who represented Peru in the World Cups in Argentina (1978) and Spain (1982). He was known as "El Loco" (Crazy), as many flamboyant players – especially goalkeepers – in Latin football are called.

Quiroga performed well in the 1978 Cup until Peru had to play Argentina in Rosario, which also happened to be his hometown. Argentina was required to beat Peru by at least four goals to enter the Final, otherwise archrival Brazil would meet Holland in the Final (this ridiculous non-knockout format was fortunately abandoned in subsequent World Cups). After a good start, Peru had a bad day and was humbled 6-0. The Brazilians suspected that the Peruvians had been bribed, but a review of that game tape discounts this theory. First, in the beginning of the game Peru almost scored twice, hitting the post, and secondly, the goals that Quiroga allowed were really not his fault. After an initial scare, the *albiceleste* slowly gained confidence, their first goals came, and they finally turned in a stupendous performance in their home country to arrive in the Final. The Argentines were well motivated as hosts in their own country, but they also wanted to avenge the 1970 World Cup qualifier loss from which Peru eliminated Argentina and went to the Finals instead.

Quiroga was looking into the stands in our direction. He then walked over to the edge of the field and shouted "Rubio, no quiere jugar?" (Hey blondie, do you want to play?). As the only "blondie" around, I realized that he was talking to me. I shouted back, "Por supuesto, como no?" (Sure, why not?), and went under the stadium to enter on the field. I had not brought my soccer boots, but he quickly arranged for an old pair that was at least one size too big. So there I was, playing *futbol* with professionals at nearly 11,000 feet above sea level, with minimal altitude conditioning, at the age of thirty-nine.

The experience gave me an unparalleled chance to see how modern professionals trained and performed at altitude. The Cienciano players, including Uruguayan defender Mario Rebollo, goalkeeper Maurinho Mendoza, and young attacker Paul Cominges, had excellent skills. After an hour or so, we went to full field play. After 10 minutes, I felt my heart palpitating, but continued to play – I was having too much fun! One of my passes went short as my large left shoe went flying off – the small crowd got a kick out of that. Later Cominges went flying past me like a condor – he was a real speedster but his shot went over Mendoza (Cominges later scored two goals in the 1997 Copa America, then played in Greece and Venezuela). After the game, we took some direct kicks and I managed to put a couple past Mendoza. I later went back to practice with Cienciano, but my medical project schedule then took precedence

Quiroga took Cienciano as far as they could that year, finishing in fourth – an excellent effort for a team outside of Lima. He coached mostly by motivation, and he knew well the psychological state of his players and how to inspire them to fulfill their potential. While Quiroga moved on to coach for big Lima club Universitario in 2003, it was ironic that his previous "small" club Cienciano won the continental Copa Sudamericana championship against Argentine giant River Plate that year.

Atlanta 1998

I spent 1998-1999 in Atlanta at the Centers for Disease Control and Prevention. Modern Atlanta is best described as an unplanned "boomtown," with has few soccer fields that are not associated with a school or university. The best Atlanta soccer field was the billiard-table flat recreation fields of Emory University, and three times a week those fields would attract the best soccer talent. Eventually Emory officials became weary of chasing off non-student soccer players, and shut the games down completely.

The large Piedmont Park located in the center of Atlanta has two bumpy soccer fields, always drawing an international crowd of players. The park has been in relative disrepair for years, however, leaving no decent public soccer field available in all of Atlanta.

However, the suburban areas around Atlanta have become a hotbed of soccer action in the last decade. USA national team members Clint Mathis and Josh Wolff are quality soccer products from around the city of Atlanta.

Peshawar, Pakistan 1999

The World Health Organization sent me to the Afghanistan-Pakistan border to work on the Campaign for the Global Eradication of Polio in 1999. Pakistan is not a nation known for soccer, as its national sport is cricket, yet another game the British exported. Since the national cricket team has been successful cricket still has the momentum in Pakistan. But just across the border the situation is reversed; the national game in Afghanistan is definitely soccer.

The one place to find soccer was in Peshawar, the capital of the North West Frontier Province (NWFP) area of Pakistan. Peshawar lies at the doorstep of the Khyber Pass, which enters Afghanistan on the southern route of the famous Silk Road, only twenty miles away from the city. In 1999 Peshawar was a bustling city of over a million people, with an additional million Afghan refugees in camps surrounding the city. The NWFP contains 23 million people, a majority of them belonging to the Pathan ethnic group, a fiercely independent and well armed people. The town of Darra in the tribal areas specializes in making customized weapons, and one can routinely hear machine gun fire while passing through this town. There are seven distinct tribal areas in NWFP that are normally off limits to outsiders and even to Pakistani government activity (the government uses a *political agent* to interact with the Pathan populations). Having traveled inside six of these areas, I have found the tribal zones full of loyal and independent people, but the societal dynamics can be similar to the Wild West.

Sporting activities were permitted in NWFP in 1999, but were forbidden across the border in the Taliban controlled areas of Afghanistan. The best soccer fields in NWFP were at the University of Peshawar and the ornate Islamia College. The University of Peshawar hosted a variety of foreign students, mostly from Muslim nations. The best players were Palestinians, Kurds, Afghanis, and Kenyans, and they accepted me enthusiastically into their matches. Many of the students were of refugee status, and were not sure where they would go after they finished their studies. So soccer was a welcome respite from the worry of studies and life's uncertainties.

Some players belonged to more conservative Muslim sects, and would play soccer in their *shawar kameez,* or local dress composed of a long-sleeved shirt and long baggy pants. They were a sight, as cotton would go flying everywhere as they streaked down the field. Sometimes you would lose sight of the ball, as it got lost in their robes.

Even if Pakistanis do not play soccer very much, the country is very much involved in world soccer, as about 80% of the world's soccer balls are manufactured in Pakistan! Unfortunately, child labor frequently has been used in the Pakistani soccer ball industry, an egregious human-rights violation that the international FoulBall Campaign is attempting to address.[15] Pakistan is also known for expert counterfeiting skills (especially items like CDs and DVDs), and in a sporting goods store in Peshawar, I was able to buy a beautiful Adidas soccer ball for only eight USA dollars that declared itself *Made in France.*

Florida 2000-2001

As this book came to fruition, we found ourselves living in the coastal hamlet of Hobe Sound, 100 miles north of Miami. This area of Florida has some beautiful playing fields, with golf course caliber grass laid down on a topsoil and sand base. The result is very soft and smooth fields, almost the quality of top European fields.

Every Wednesday and Sunday night a wide assortment of players showed up for soccer at the Hobe Sound fields. The USA citizens were mostly young adults who enjoyed playing with and learning skills from the immigrants that settled in the surrounding area. The age range of players was from 13 to 61 years old, and the 61 year old could flat out play; one week he had a well-taken hat trick!

So thanks to Adrian, Santiago, Jesus, Beto, Rafael, Ossie, Luis, David, Cesar, Leno, Fernando, Carlos, Pėpe, Uziel, Jose, Josh, Shane, Max, Ozzie, Hank, Stan, David, and John who brought their soccer experience and talents to Hobe Sound from Mexico, El Salvador, Guatemala, Columbia, Peru, Paraguay, Argentina, Brazil, Honduras, Jamaica, England, Czech Republic, and Germany. Also thanks to USA players Al, Alex, Jerimiah, Dan, Daniel, Donovan, Hansen, Kevin, Kiwi, Shea, Taylor and Troy for being open-minded footballers.

New Orleans 2001-2006

I arrived in New Orleans once again in 2001, and try to fit in soccer at least twice a week. There are still games up on "The Fly" today, but most of the New Orleans soccer fields were inundated for weeks after the levees broke from the August 2005 Hurricane Katrina storm surge (The Fly remained dry and immediately playable – a sampling of the New Orleans devastation is pictured in Figures 18L & M). The New Orleans devastation has brought in thousands of new workers from Mexico and Brazil (among other countries), and when they have leisure time away from the heavy reconstruction effort, they of course exhibit their culture and play soccer at The Fly and elsewhere in the greater NOLA area.

A new indoor soccer arena was built with the latest generation artificial turf laid down on three differently sized fields, and several leagues going on at all hours of the day and night. Unlike artificial turf fields in New York, the New Orleans indoor site is more useful in the Louisiana summer than the New York snowy winters, as the heat and humidity of the New Orleans summer replicates the oppressive Amazon or Singapore conditions. I therefore remain able to participate in the beautiful game both indoors and in nature, and as a source of physical fitness as well as camaraderie in the New Orleans area.

---

[15] See: www.laborrights.org/projects/foulball/, & www.dol.gov/ilab/media/reports/iclp/sweat4/soccerft.htm.

Conclusion

Over the course of a forty-year "career" I have probably sustained the average number of injuries playing soccer: two broken toes playing barefoot soccer on the beach, a broken wrist, two facial lacerations, a thigh laceration, three severely sprained ankles, a couple of hip pointers, a few strained ribs, right and left knee contusions, and a partial knee ligament tear. A few splints, a few stitches, and one arthroscopy, and I feel lucky for surviving so much soccer with so few injuries. Counting the one severe knee injury, which resulted in the loss of a full year, a total of two years were involuntarily soccer free (only about 5% of soccer life lost to injury). Others have not been so fortunate.

This chapter is necessarily unfinished, as I hope to enjoy many more soccer adventures in the future. I expect soccer to continue "breaking the ice" in domestic and international situations, and to help unite people in many different circumstances.

In writing this book, I would ask the reader to appreciate the many varied international names of the individuals recorded within. These are authentic names, and reflect the very real and dynamic diversity of many areas of the USA and the world. Indeed, if the reader comes away with nothing else from this book than a better appreciation of human diversity from absorbing the rhythmic cadence of people's names, the author will be satisfied. This book ends with soccer photos from various venues showing children and adolescents playing the beautiful game – starting with the fantastic talent demonstrated at the 2005 FIFA U-17 World Championships in Peru [Figures 18N to Z].

The USA's soccer history reveals that it has long been a nation of diversity, despite domestic politicians' recent discovery of this fact. The state of New Jersey – where I was raised in a soccer friendly community – is adjacent to New York City, and these areas, which include Ellis Island, were the first landing points for countless immigrants from all continents of the world.[16] Most immigrants today, however, disembark at John F. Kennedy International Airport or Newark International Airport in New York City and New Jersey, respectively. Some arrive nearly empty-handed, but they retain their own soccer traditions that further contribute to the evolving understanding of world cultures in the USA.

---

[16] Ellis Island was the port of entry for nearly all immigrant ships to the east coast of the USA in the early part of the 20th century. See http://en.wikipedia.org/wiki/Ellis_island for further details and links.

Appendix I

British Football Association: 1863 Laws of Football

(1) The maximum length of the ground shall be 200 yards, the maximum breadth shall be 100 yards, the length and breadth shall be marked off with flags; and the goal shall be defined by two upright posts, eight yards apart, without any tape or bar across them.

(2) A toss for goals shall take place, and the game shall be commenced by a place kick from the centre of the ground by the side losing the toss for goals; the other side shall not approach within 10 yards of the ball until it is kicked off.

(3) After a goal is won, the losing side shall be entitled to kick off, and the two sides shall change goals after each goal is won.

(4) A goal shall be won when the ball passes between the goal-posts or over the space between the goal-posts (at whatever height), not being thrown, knocked on, or carried.

(5) When the ball is in touch, the first player who touches it shall throw it from the point on the boundary line where it left the ground in a direction at right angles with the boundary line, and the ball shall not be in play until it has touched the ground.

(6) When a player has kicked the ball, any one of the same side who is nearer to the opponent's goal line is out of play and may not touch the ball himself, nor in any way whatever prevent any other player from doing so, until he is in play; but no player is out of play when the ball is kicked off from behind the goal line.

(7) In case the ball goes behind the goal line, if a player on the side to whom the goal belongs first touches the ball, one of his side shall be entitled to a free kick from the goal line at the point opposite the place where the ball shall be touched. If a player of the opposite side first touches the ball, one of his side shall be entitled to a free kick at the goal only from a point 15 yards outside the goal line, opposite the place where the ball is touched, the opposing side standing within their goal line until he has had his kick.

(8) If a player makes a fair catch, he shall be entitled to a free kick, providing he claims it by making a mark with his heel at once; and in order to take such a kick he may go back as far as he pleases, and no player on the opposite side shall advance beyond his mark until he has kicked.

(9) No player shall run with the ball.

(10) Neither tripping nor hacking shall be allowed, and no player shall use his hands to hold or push his adversary.

(11) A player shall not be allowed to throw the ball or pass it to another with his hands.

(12) No player shall be allowed to take the ball from the ground with his hands under any pretext whatever while it is in play.

(13) No player shall be allowed to wear projecting nails, iron plates, or gutta percha* on the soles or heels of his boots.

*Gutta-percha was a hard natural latex made from the resin of the *Isonandra Gutta* tree.

Postscript

Some of my friends have asked me, "Why are you writing a soccer book? After all, you have been in medicine for twenty years." My answer is both simple and complex.

The simple part of the answer is *soccer is pure joy and beautiful art – the expression of the human spirit in athletic form.* Indeed, why else would anybody write a book about soccer, other than a love for the game?

The complex part of the answer stems from the fact that my regular day (and night) job in medicine can at times be quite depressing. One is obviously exposed to more human suffering in the front lines of medicine than working in other fields. But it is *not the human suffering in medicine that is depressing – that is to be expected and remedied.* After all, a doctor or nurse's job is to help a patient through his illness, to place the patient in a mental and physical framework in which they may become well. The conquest of suffering is the reward for both patient and doctor.

What is most depressing in medicine are the walls of greed and barriers to health that have been constructed by business and political forces. When one sees the results of these obstructions to human rights, it is devastating to humanity within and outside the USA. I confess to believing that all people in the world deserve adequate and equitable health care, a concept of a basic human right enshrined in the United Nations Universal Declaration of Human Rights (Article 25). However, in the eyes of the USA political and medical communities where the "business of medicine" takes precedence over comprehensive healing, this conviction designates myself an outsider.

It is disheartening to work in the wealthiest country in the world, and yet so many poor and lower middle-class families have inadequate and prohibitively expensive health care (the USA has more than 45 million uninsured people with uncertain medical care and at imminent threat of poverty from catastrophic illness). Doctors must daily defy the Hippocratic Oath, as health providers are obliged to prioritize financial status over standard-of-care medical practice and privacy issues.

In my field of infectious diseases and public health, there is always the optimistic possibility of cure or prevention of disease, but recent evolution in infectious diseases has brought new and terrible surprises. The most notorious is the AIDS epidemic, which has decimated large parts of the human population, and has so far elicited a woefully inadequate political and public health response at home and abroad. Looking backwards, just a few dozen forward-thinking politicians and public health officials could have averted so much disease and suffering over the past twenty-five years. Even now, when AIDS is soon to be the largest lethal epidemic humanity has ever experienced (after 40 million deaths are surpassed AIDS will have killed more humans that the bubonic plague), the control and treatment efforts have generally been unexceptional. I have addressed this major health and human rights issue as it relates to international soccer and the human potential (Chapter 6).

However, like professional medicine, professional soccer appears to be in an unhealthy state of flux. In many ways, the "Hippocratic Oath of Soccer" (First Do No Harm to the Essence of Soccer) is constantly being fractured, as the imperial business of winning and "success" has become paramount over the sublime essence of the game. The sport is distressed by negative defensive play, lack of inspired offensive play, episodes of horrific sportsmanship, and frivolous penalty contests determining major championships. Select players, administrators, coaches, and agents make buckets of money – often under dodgy ethical standards – while fans are subjected to ever-increasing mind-numbing advertisements for non-soccer related products. For all the increased money in the sport, the fans expect and deserve a quality and improved product, and that has not yet happened.

Of course there are exceptions. FC Barcelona still refuses to allow advertising to stain their jerseys, and also plays the most attractive soccer on the planet. If only more clubs would follow their community and aesthetic lead.

Still, soccer is unpredictable and fans often root for the underdog (the "little guy"), a known and admired paradoxical attraction of the human spirit. It brings happiness to see the underrated players outperform (to "play above their heads") the over-hyped "superstars" or "galacticos." Lower division teams routinely play against top division teams (especially in Cup competitions), and on any given day, the less favored can succeed against a team that – at least on paper – should beat them easily.

One needs only absorb these remarkable results to grasp the power of the underdog in soccer:

- USA beat England 1-0, in the World Cup's most remarkable upset ever in 1950.
- Queen's Park Rangers as a *Third Division team* beat First Division West Bromwich Albion 3-2 to win the 1967 English League Cup after being down 0-2. Another third division club, Swindon Town, duplicated the feat two years later as they beat Arsenal 3-1 in 1969.
- A team made up mostly of semi-professionals from Malmö, Sweden won their way to the European Cup Final in 1979, losing 0-1 to champions Nottingham Forrest.
- Tiny Bermuda (population 60,000) beat the USA (population 260,000,000) 1-0 in 1991. The USA's population was more than four thousand times larger than Bermuda's.
- Cienciano of Peru and Once Caldas of Colombia, then two minnows of South American soccer, beat Santos, River Plate, and Boca Juniors, among others, on their way to the 2003 Copa Sudamericana & 2003 Recopa, and 2004 Copa Libertadores championships, respectively.
- *Non-league* Exeter City tied most successful Premiership side ever Manchester United in a third-round FA Cup match at Manchester United's own home Old Trafford ground in January 2005. Manchester United tied another non-League team, Burton Albion, in another FA Cup match in January 2006.

In soccer, anything can and likely will happen. But most importantly, aficionados can always find some quality attractive football on the streets or in the lower divisions, where the dog-eat-dog world of win-or-die business football does not hold as toxic an embrace.

One firm lesson I have learned through my global soccer experiences is that *professionals do not retain and will never have a monopoly on the beautiful game.* Fans – many of whom are players themselves – love to see soccer excellence, but preferably in a wholesome form and in a community forum. Here's hoping that modern professional soccer finds the way back to its unadulterated roots, so everybody can just concentrate on the Art.

With this book I have temporarily turned my creative efforts from the labor of medicine, which I still love, to the athletic expression I love, soccer, or as it is more properly named all over the world – football. I have been a soccer participant in many parts of the world in roles as player, fan, coach, and referee. This is my first foray into soccer writing, and I can confirm that many of my soccer obsessions have been successfully exorcised by the therapeutic writing of this book. I sincerely hope readers will enjoy and learn something important about soccer and the world, as I have repeatedly experienced from researching and writing this book.

Index

AIDS/HIV, xii, 32, 110-118, 457
  Southern Africa, 114-115
Altitude soccer, 323-338
  Altitude sickness, 328
  Oxygen availability, 326
Amazon soccer, 340-346, 449
American Ball Games, 4-6
Ancestral Ball Games, 4-6
Anti-football, 29, 385
Artificial turf, 104-105, 398-399
Atlanta, 452
Aztec, see Tlachtli
Autism, xii
Beach soccer, 12-13
Beckham, David, 95-96
Berlin "Nazi" Olympics 1936, 347-359

Best Players, 131-193
  Goalkeepers
    Banks, Gordon, 135
    Chilavert, José Luis, 136-137
    Fillol, Ubaldo, 135
    Jennings, Pat, 137
    Maier, Sepp, 136
    N'kono, Thomas, 137-138
    Schmeichel, Peter, 136
    Yashin, Lev, 134
    Zenga, Walter, 137
    Zoff, Dino, 134-135
  Defenders
    Baresi, Franco, 140
    Beckenbauer, Franz, 139
    Bergomi, Giuseppe, 148
    Blanc, Laurent, 144
    Brehme, Andreas, 147-148
    Breitner, Paul, 143
    Cafú, 144
    Charles, John, 146
    Chumpitaz, Hector, 149
    Desailly, Marcel, 147
    Facchetti, Giacinto, 144
    Figueroa, Elías, 139-140
    Gamarra, Carlos, 148
    Hansen, Alan, 147
    Hierro, Fernando, 147
    Koeman, Ronald, 145
    Krol, Ruud, 142
    Maldini, Paolo, 141
    Matthäus, Lothar, 142
    Moore, Bobby, 140
    Passarella, Daniel, 143
    Rijkaard, Frank, 141-142
    Roberto Carlos, 148
    Ruggeri, Oscar, 146
    Sammer, Matthias, 145
    Santos, Nilton, 143
    Scirea, Gaetano, 146
    Torres, Carlos Alberto, 141
    Trésor, Marius, 145
    Vogts, Berti, 149
  Midfielders
    Ardiles, Osvaldo, 163
    Boniek, Zbigniew, 162
    Brady, Liam, 165
    Ceulemans, Jan, 166
    Charlton, Bobby, 155
    Cubillas, Teófilo, 156
    Dalglish, Kenny, 159
    Deyna, Kazimierz, 157
    Di Stéfano, Alfredo, 152
    Didí, 155
    Etcheverry, Marco, 166
    Falcão, 161
    Figo, Luis, 164
    Francescoli, Enzo, 158
    Gérson, 160
    Gullit, Ruud, 155-156
    Hagi, Gheorghe, 158
    Kopa, Raymond, 159
    Laudrup, Michael, 160
    Maradona, Diego, 153
    Masopust, Josef, 161
    Mazzola, Alessandro, 162
    Michel, 165-166
    Nedved, Pavel, 164
    Neeskens, Johan, 156-157
    Overath, Wolfgang, 162
    Platini, Michel, 153-154
    Platt, David, 167
    Raí, 163
    Redondo, Fernando, 165
    Rivaldo, 157-158
    Rivelino, Roberto, 159
    Rivera, Gianni, 160

Robson, Bryan, 164
Romero, Julio César, 165
Schuster, Bernd, 163
Sócrates, 161-162
Suárez, Luis, 157
Valderrama, Carlos, 166-167
Zidane, Zinedine, 154-155
Strikers
  Albert, Flórián, 184
  Altafini, José João, 180-181
  Baggio, Roberto, 176
  Batistuta, Gabriel, 179
  Bebeto, 185
  Bergkamp, Dennis, 186-187
  Best, George, 172
  Blokhin, Oleg, 184
  Cantona, Eric, 186
  Careca, 184
  Cruyff, Johan, 170-171
  Eusébio, 171
  Fontaine, Just, 177
  Garrincha, 172
  Greaves, Jimmy, 181
  Hurst, Geoff, 187
  Jairzinho, 177-178
  Keegan, Kevin, 181-182
  Kempes, Mario, 176
  Klinsmann, Jürgen, 182
  Lato, Grzegorz, 183
  Law, Denis, 177
  Lineker, Gary, 180
  Milla, Roger, 182-183
  Müller, Gerd, 174
  Papin, Jean-Pierre, 187
  Pelé, 170
  Puskas, Ferenc, 175-176
  Rensenbrink, Rob, 185
  Riva, Luigi, 185
  Romário, 175
  Ronaldo, 174
  Rossi, Paolo, 181
  Rummenigge, Karl-Heinz, 184-185
  Sánchez, Hugo, 179
  Schillaci, Salvatore, 187-188
  Seeler, Uwe, 180
  Stoichkov, Hristo, 182
  Šuker, Davor, 183
  Tostão, 178
  Van Basten, Marco, 173
  Vavá, 186
  Völler, Rudi, 187
  Weah, George, 178
  Zico, 173
Best Teams
  Club teams
    AC Milan 1989-90, 213
    AC Milan 1993-94, 216
    Ajax Amsterdam 1971-73, 212
    Ajax Amsterdam 1995-96, 216
    Barcelona 1992, 218
    Bayern Munich 1974-76, 214
    Benfica 1961-62, 215
    Boca Juniors 1977-78, 215
    Boca Juniors 2000-04, 218
    Borussia Dortmund 1997, 218
    Estudiantes de la Plata 1968-70, 219
    Feyenoord 1970, 219
    Flamengo 1981, 217
    Independiente 1964-65, 217
    Independiente 1972-75, 215
    Internazionale 1964-65, 216
    Juventus 1985, 219
    Liverpool FC 1977-78, 214
    Manchester United 1968/1999, 217
    Nottingham Forest 1979-80, 216
    Peñarol 1960-61, 217
    Real Madrid 1956-60, 213
    Real Madrid 1998/2000/2002, 214-215
    São Paulo 1992-93, 214
    Santos 1962-63, 213
  National teams
    Argentina 1978, 204
    Argentina 1986, 201-202
    Brazil 1958-1962, 202-203
    Brazil 1970, 197-198
    Brazil 1982, 206-207
    Brazil 1994, 206
    Brazil 2002, 199-200
    England 1966, 205-206
    France 1984, 205
    France 1998, 200-201
    Italy 1970, 209-210
    Italy 1982, 203-204
    Italy 1990, 208
    Italy 1994, 208-209
    Netherlands 1974, 199
    Netherlands 1978, 207-208
    Netherlands 1988, 205
    Poland 1974, 210

West Germany 1974, 198
West Germany 1990, 210-211
Bhutan, 295
Blackburn FC motto, 407
Body types and sizes, 25-26
Bosman decision, 86-87
Boston, 447
British influence, 32-35
Buckminsterfullerene C_{60}, 390
Buddha, 347
Busby, Matt, 59
Cambridge rules, 6
Camus, Albert, 3-4
Calcio, 6
Carenage United Football Club, 440-442
Centenary, 32
Charleroi case, 69-70
Chelsea, 84
   Oil money, 84
Cienciano, 323-38, 451-452
Club identity, 35-36, 69-70, 82-84
   Branding 83-84
   Charleroi case, 69-70
   Wealthiest, 82
Clubfoot, see talipes
Colegio Nacional de Iquitos (CNI), 340-342
Communities, 78-81
Copa Sudamericana 2003, 333-335
Cubillas, Teófilo "Nene," 28, 156, 327, 349
Cruyff, Johan, 15, 20-21, 170-171
Di Stéfano, Alfredo, 15
Derby matches, 47-50
Diversity, human, ix, 39-43, 60-66, 454
Doping, 126-127
Episkyros, 4
Elizabeth Sports Club, 433-435
Estadio Inca Garcilaso de la Vega – Cusco, 330-334, 451
Estadio Nacional – Lima, 449-450
Esidio, Eduardo, 112-113
Fantasy footballers, 193
Fascism, 347-359
   Franco, 347-349
   Mussolini, 347-349
   Hitler, 347-359
Fernández, Teodoro "Lolo", 349-358,
FIFA, ix, 6, 8, 11-13, 389
   Olympics 1936, 347-359
   Politics, 67-75
   World Cups, 37-38, 71, 221-320, 438

Fish, Mark, 32
Florida, Hobe Sound, 453
Football Associations, 67-69
Franchise model, 79-80
Futsal, 11-12
Games
   Hungary – England 1953, 33-34
   Rutgers – Princeton 1869, 7
   USA – England 1950, 33
Globalization, 31, 81
Golden goal, 385-386
Grenada, 439-442
Guevara, Che, 63, 423
Hagi, Gheorge, 31
Hairstyles, 55-56
Haledon Lyceum, 429-430
Harpastum, 4
HIV/AIDS, xii, 32, 110-118, 457
Human diversity, ix, 39-43, 60-66, 454
Iquitos, 340-343
   FIFA 2005 U-17 Fair Play award, 343
Intolerance, 43-46, 60-63, 65
Individual player identity, 37-38
Infant mortality, 32
International Olympic Committee (IOC), 347-359
Jamaica, 438-439
Kemari, 5
KesselsKramer, 295
Labor rights and salaries, 86-88
   Bosman decision, 86-87
Land mine injuries, 121
Laws of Football, 6, 455
LineCrushBall, see USA-football
London, 444-446
London rules, 6
Major League Soccer (MLS), 370-378
Malaria, xii, 32
Maná, 339
Mandela, Nelson, 32
Marley, Bob, 3, 406, 439, 442-443
Mental development, 128
Miller, Charles, 8
Montserrat, 295
National Football Museum (England), 8
"Nazi" Olympics Berlin 1936, 347-359
New Orleans, 447-448, 453
New York, 446-447
New York Cosmos, 429-431
Nobel Peace Prize, 403-405

461

North American Soccer League (NASL), 370-378, 429-431
Nutritional Supplements, 127
Olympic games
   Berlin "Nazi" Olympics 1936, 347-359
Oneida Football Club, 8, 363-364
Pakistan, 452-453
Pelé, 170, 423, 429-431
Penalty kicks, 379-387
Peruvian soccer, 323-359, 449-452
Platini, Michel, 31, 153-154
Plautus, 347
Polio, 120-121
Popol Vuh, 3,
Queen's Park Football Club, 407
Quiché Maya, see Popol Vuh
Quiroga, Ramón, 451-452
Recopa (South American) 2003, 335-337
Red Dwarf soccer, 390
Rensselaer Polytechnic Institute (RPI), 431-432
Rickets, 120
Rijkaard, Frank, 141-142, 339
Rivalries, 50
   Argentina—Brazil, 50
   England—Argentina, 50
   Germany—Netherlands, 50
Ronaldinho, 3, 132, 314
Rutgers International team, 436-437
Rutgers soccer, 7, 435-437
Sanon, Emmanuel "Manno," vii, 104, 188
Schellscheidt, Manny, 363
Shakespeare, William, 5-6
Shehata, Hassan, 379
Shrovetide football, 5
Soccer
   Age and play, 3, 11
   Altitude, 323-338
   Art, 15-29, 403
   Business, 77-97
      Financial difficulties, 89
      USA business interests, 85
   Culture, 31-57
   Differences v. other sports, 8-11, 16
   Dishonor, 347-359
   End of the world, 339-346
   Future, 389-406
   Globalization, 392
   Human rights, x, 76, 402-406
   Injury/Illness prevention, 127
   Injuries, 99-109
   Illnesses, 110-120
   Indoor soccer USA style, 12
   Marketing, 90-97
   Names, i, ix, 7-8, 364-365
   Oneida Football Club Boston, 8
   References and Resources, 407-420
      Books, English, 407-413
      Book, German, 416
      Books, Medical, 416
      Books, Spanish, 414-416
      Internet sites, 418-420
      Magazines, 417-418
   Religion, 57
   Rule changes, 393-399
   Skills, 16-25
   Soccer – rugby distinction, 7
   Top of the world, 323-338
   Toxicities, 122-126
   Violence, 45, 399-400
   Xenophobia, 400-401
Sócrates, 161-162, 390
Soule, 5
Sportsmanship, 13, 96-97
Stein, Jock, 77
Switzerland, 424, 443-444
Talipes, 120, 424
Tenafly, 424-428, 432-433
Ternero, Freddy, 330-338, 415
The Other Final, 295
Tlachtli, 5
Tsu-Chu, 4
Tuberculosis, xii
Türkyilmaz, Kubilay, 45
Uniforms, 51-55, 66, 90-91
   Advertisements, 55, 90-91
   Advert-Shirt Tottenham, 77-78
   Monarchy influences, 66
Universal appeal, 13
Urarina, 344-346
USA-football, 7
   First games played, 8
USA National Soccer Hall of Fame, 8
USA soccer, 363-378
   Best USA players 1958-2006, 375-376
   Ethnic and working class contributions, 365
   Men's soccer team achievements, 365-368
   Soccer future, 377-378
Valdivieso, Juan, 52, 349-357

Villanueva, Alejandro, 349-356
Wars and Conflicts, 71-76
West Indies, 439-442
Wimbledon FC, 80-81
Women's soccer, 64-66, 391
World Cup, FIFA, 37-38
  Appearances by country, 320
  Argentina 1978, 438
  Germany 2006
    Assigned groups/strength, 302
    FIFA confederations & teams 300-301
    Group A: Germany, Costa Rica, Poland, Ecuador, 304-305
    Group B: England, Paraguay, Trinidad & Tobago, Sweden, 306-307
    Group C: Argentina, Ivory Coast, Serbia & Montenegro, Netherlands, 308-309
    Group D: Mexico, Iran, Angola, Portugal, 310-311
    Group E: Italy, Ghana, USA, Czech Republic, 312-313
    Group F: Brazil, Croatia, Australia, Japan, 314-315
    Group G: France, Switzerland, Korea republic, Togo, 316-317
    Group H: Spain, Ukraine, Tunisia, Saudi Arabia, 318-319
    Odds, 303
    Official Emblem, 13
    Schedule, 310-319
    Special historical significance, 299
  Japan—Korea 2002, 221-295
    All-star teams, 284
    Assigned groups/strength, 225
    Best sixteen young players, 285
    FIFA confederations & teams 222-223
    Final Brazil – Germany, 279-281
    Final summary, 282
    First round summary, 263
    Group A: France, Senegal, Uruguay, Denmark, 227-230
    Group B: Spain, Slovenia, Paraguay, South Africa, 231-235
    Group C: Brazil, Turkey, China PR, Costa Rica, 235-239
    Group D: Korea, Poland, USA, Portugal, 240-244
    Group E: Germany, Saudi Arabia, Ireland, Cameroon, 245-249
    Group F: Argentina, Nigeria, England, Sweden, 250-254
    Group G: Italy, Ecuador, Croatia, Mexico, 255-259
    Group H: Japan, Belgium, Russia, Tunisia, 259-262
    Magic moments, 286-288
    MVP Golden Ball, 283
    Not so magic moments, 289
    Odds, 224
    Preparations, 221-22
    Quarterfinals, 270-274
    Scheduling inequities, 226
    Second round, 264-270
    Semifinals, 275-276
    Sex, 224
    Third place match, 277
    World Cup summary, 290-294
  Most important global sports event, 297
World Football Dream Teams, 192
Young Boys, 424
Zeman, Zdeněk, 389

About the Author

Richard Witzig grew up in the soccer hotbed of the New York-New Jersey area of the USA, and graduated from both Rutgers and Harvard universities – the sites of the first soccer and USA-football games in the USA, respectively. He played with amateur, university, and semi-professional teams until entering medical school. At various times in his life, he has lived in Switzerland, England, Peru, and the West Indies, in addition to multiple areas in the USA. Since becoming a physician, he has practiced medicine and public health in South America and Asia, in addition to the USA. He has worked at Harvard, Johns Hopkins, and Tulane universities, at the USA Centers for Disease Control, and as a consultant to the World Health Organization.

Dr. Witzig's medical specialties are medicine, infectious diseases, tropical medicine, public health, and health and human rights, and he has published on malaria, tuberculosis, and AIDS in the scientific press. He currently maintains international medical projects, and has discovered that playing soccer within a community allows him to quickly socialize and form professional and friendly relationships when working with people on complex health problems worldwide.

Figure 1. 1974 Haiti World Cup team in practice, prior to traveling to Munich.
Standing: Henri Francillion, Mario Leandre, Claude Désir, Serge Ducoste, Arsene Auguste, Claude Legros (coach). Kneeling: Claude Barthélemy, Phillipe Vorbe, Manno Sanon, Guy St. Vil, Guy François.

This team of mostly semi-professionals met up with powerhouses Italy, Argentina, and Poland in 1974 World Cup's "Group of Death" (with eight Best Players Kempes, Lato, Deyna, Zoff, Facchetti, Mazzola, Rivera, Riva – Chapter 7), and won over the West German crowds with their infectious enthusiasm for the game. Haiti managed two goals by Manno Sanon – his dribbling goal around Dino Zoff broke the Italian's record 12-international game unscored-upon streak. Photo: Manno Sanon.

Figure 1A. One of two stone hoops at the ball court at Uxmal, Yucatan, Mexico.
Each hoop protrudes from the center of one of the court's walls.
The object of the ball game was to manipulate a rubber ball through the hoop
goal without the use of the hands. Photo: Edgar Martín del Campo.

Figure 1B.

Figure 4A.

Page 470, Figure 1B. The birth of the cradle-rocking celebration in 1994, as Bebeto was joined by Brazil teammates Mazinho (left) and Romário (right). Photo: Getty Images.

Page 471, Figure 4A. A Bangladeshi women's team celebrates its victory in the first ever female soccer tournament in Dhaka, Bangladesh; 4 October 2004.
Photo: Farjana K. Godhuly / AFP / Getty Images.

The People's Game

Figure 1C. Street Futsal from above – Iquitos, Peru, 1999.

 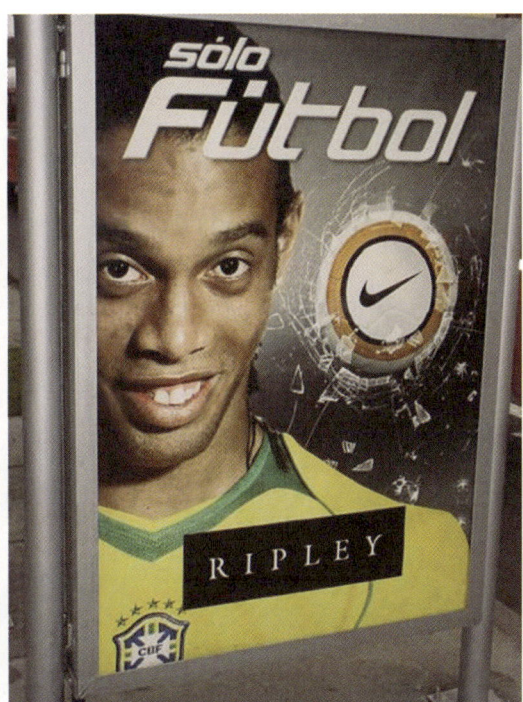

Figure 5A. Some differences between the Beckham and Ronaldinho images.

Big money paid for David Beckham's image to crash the 2004 Copa America in Peru, as the CCCI billboard advert in Lima during the tournament shows. CCCI heavily promoted Beckham's image even though the England team was not even eligible for the competition, and there were far more Beckham posters on Lima's streets than any other footballer – including all South American stars.

Although 2002 Brazil World Cup winner and 2004 & 2005 World Player of the Year Ronaldinho (Lima poster at right) was rested for the competition, his country won the 2004 Copa tournament.

Beckham (Vive el Futbol - "Live Football") promotes the upscale *Saga Falabella* chain store with a vacuous look in a Real Madrid shirt, while Ronaldinho (Sólo Fútbol – "Only Football") promotes the less luxurious *Ripley* chain with real expression in a Brazil jersey (pages 96-97).

CCCI emblem under Beckham street billboard in Lima, Peru.

Figure 6A. Peru school campaign to include special and handicapped children.
"Put yourself in my shoes" [Ponte en mis zapatos], and
"I can play with crutches" [Yo sé jugar con muletas].

Figure 6B. Eduardo Esidio (number 11 in stripes) leading the Alianza Lima attack against Cienciano in February 2001, at the Estadio Inca Garcilaso de la Vega in Cusco at 3360 meters above sea level. Cienciano goalkeeper Maurinho Mendoza clears the ball.

Figure 6C. Eduardo Esidio (third from left) also played defense against Cienciano, in an end-to-end performance at 11,024 feet above sea level.

Figure 6D. A photo from the Johan Cruyff anti-tobacco video (details page 123), with Cruyff kicking away the cigarette pack after juggling it sixteen times.

The Cruyff video was sponsored by the Generalitat de Catalunya (GENCAT) Departament de Salut (Catalan Department of Health), and is still viewable on the GENCAT website at: www.gencat.net/salut/depsan/units/sanitat/html/ca/tabac/doc6816.html.

Figure 11A. Peruvian *Club Cienciano* training at 3555 meters above sea level, at the Sacsayhuamán Inca archeological site above Cusco in 2001. The largest stone at the site is at left sitting atop two smaller stones.

Figure 11B. *Cienciano* coach Freddy Ternero (left) and trainer Luis Cuba oversee the training at Sacsayhuamán. The stones are at least 100 meters distant.

Figure 11C. The 2001 *Cienciano* Centenary shirt; "Cc" *Club Cienciano* crest is at upper right. Shirt made by local Cusco company ARIES, and sponsored by Peruvian beer Cusqueña.

11D & E. Two shirts made in Peru for the 2003 Recopa (actually played in 2004). At left is a half-Peru and half-*Cienciano* shirt with message "Cienciano es el Peru" ["Cienciano is Peru"] – the number 10 is suitably designed of Inca stonework. At right is a half-Boca and half-*Cienciano* jersey with message "*Rumbo a Los Angeles*" ["Meeting in Los Angeles"] – denoting the original venue of the match. Both quality jerseys were made by local Cusco shirt maker ARIES.

Figure 11F & G. Action sequences from the 2003 Recopa in Fort Lauderdale (Chapter 11). Left, in an attempt to score, *Boca Juniors'* striker Martín Palermo jumps high over *Cienciano's* Santiago Acasiete, but goalkeeper Oscar Ibáñez recovers the ball (right).

Figure H. *Cienciano* defender Manuel Arboleda attempts to keep *Boca Juniors'* 2003-2005 South American Player of the Year Carlos Tévez under tight control in the 2003 Recopa.

Figure 11I. Euphoric *Cienciano* team carries off the gold 2003 *Recopa* championship Trophy, displaying the Peruvian flag after beating *Boca Juniors*. Note the MACA advertisement on the right front of the shorts.

Figure 11J. Lockhart Stadium security personnel in Fort Lauderdale forcibly interrupting the *Cienciano* celebratory "Olympic lap" after their Recopa triumph. Captain Oscar Ibáñez (wearing gray shirt at center) and seven other *Cienciano* players attempt to reason (without success) with the nine USA security personnel pictured.

Figure 12A. CNI team at their sandy practice field in Iquitos in 2001.

Figure 12B. CNI [*Colegio Nacional Iquitos*] versus *Universitario* in Lima, 1984.
Standing: Roy Ramirez, Roberto Areducea, Pedro Belver, Rino Giordino (Argentina), Cesar Adriazola, Ramón Quiroga (Argentina – in gray and black shirt). Kneeling: Ernesto Guillen, William Huapaya, Jorge Lovera, Jose Carranza, Jacinto Diaz. Masajista Willy Hurtado standing left, and utilero Pastor Shapiama kneeling right. Peruvian soda manufacturer Inca Kola was the sponsor.

Figure 12C. Both feet and soccer balls were obscured in the Urarina's first soccer games in 1992. Tabuina attempts to round Ufquasiri's defensive stance (ball is nearly hidden between players).

Figure 12E (left). Seven *minga* participants hewing a jungle clearing by machete prior to a Urarina soccer game. Note the constructed goalposts in the background, and the "wall of green" that makes up the Amazonian rainforest in all three pictures.

Figure 12D. (right). Urarina prodigy Kookuri demonstrating his volleying skills near the touchline (delineated by the log behind him). Note the grass height, which reaches his knees.

Figure 13A. The 1933 "Equipo Pacifico" team meets a German team in the snow in Munich, one of 33 matches played in less than two months in Europe.
Pictured from left: Lolo Fernández (first from left), Juan Valdivieso (third in dark sweater), Carlos Tovar (fourth), Alejandro Villanueva (fifth), Arturo Fernández (seventh).
Provided from the collection of Juan Valdivieso.

Figure 13B. 1936 Peru Olympic soccer team.
Standing: Juan Valdivieso at extreme left, Alejandro Villanueva second from right.
Carlos Tovar and Lolo Fernández are kneeling, fourth and fifth from the left.
Provided from the collection of Juan Valdivieso.

Figure 13C. Members of the 1936 Peru Olympic Team with Jesse Owens in Berlin.
Standing from left: Portal (basketball), Carlos Tovar (football), Anderson (track & field),
Ruiz (basketball), Jesse Owens, Paredes & Zacarías Flores (boxing).
Kneeling: Juan Valdivieso and Raul Chappel (football).
Provided from the collection of Juan Valdivieso.

Figure 13I. Carlos Tovar still has his medal that reads "*A los futbolistas peruanos campeones olympicos 1936*" ["To the Peruvian Football Players, 1936 Olympic Champions"].

Figure 13D. Peru soccer legend Alejandro Villanueva (wearing Alianza Lima uniform). Early photo circa 1927, when he led Peru in their first-ever international game. Provided from the collection of Juan Valdivieso.

Figure 13E. Juan Valdivieso at full stretch making a courageous save in the 1930s. Provided from the collection of Juan Valdivieso.

Figure 13F. "El Mago" Juan Valdivieso was a beloved figure in Peru, and is still rated Peru's best goalkeeper ever. Early 1930s; provided from the collection of Juan Valdivieso.

Figure 13G. Juan Valdivieso striking a pose before a game in the 1930's, wearing a heavy sweater in the Lima winter, and as was the custom at the time, a hat of some type (here a wool beret, in 13E a cap – Lolo Fernández sometimes wore a hairnet).
Provided from the collection of Juan Valdivieso.

Figure 13H. Lolo Fernandez' statue in front of the new Estadio Monumental in Lima.

Figure 14A. Oneida Football Club monument still located on the Boston Common.

Figure 14B. USA national team at practice in 2001 for the 2002 World Cup.
Left to right: Chris Armas, Tim Howard, Coach Bruce Arena, Tony Sanneh.

Figure 14C. Jeremy Hall (white shirt, center) scores for the USA U-17 team against Ivory Coast in the 2005 U-17 World Championships in Peru. The team had earlier beaten Italy 3-1 and North Korea 3-2, but lost to third-place Netherlands 2-0 in the next round.

Figure 18A. Author (left) as infant wearing low-technology foot-brace cure for talipes deformity. Note the right leg forcibly turned inward.

Figure 18C. 1978 Rutgers University International Team
Standing: Danny Mitchell, Mohammed-Morocco, Sree Raghavan, author, Bruce Heckinger, Mohammed-Iran, Roberto, Reza, Greg, Eric Bennett, Ravee Raghavan. Kneeling: Rashid Ali, Roger, Teddy, Francois, Gabe Kalu, Keith Constantine, Dan Yafet.

Figure 18B. Ticket to Pelè's last game, a testimonial between the New York Cosmos and Brazil team Santos in New Jersey in 1977.

Figure 18I. Ticket to Diego Maradona's last Argentina international game – a 1994 World Cup match against Nigeria in Boston.

Figure 18D. A young fan by the Bob Marley statue outside the National Stadium in Kingston, Jamaica.

Figure 18E. Grenada national team captain Boyo Thomas, with son David in the Caribbean Sea, 1982.

Figure 18F & G. Grenada national team striker Barry James (# 9) showing off his quick turning technique (left), and "rocking" three defenders in "small-ball" (small goal is the white square to the right of the post).

Figure 18H. Author, Emmanuel Yamusah, and Steve Wilson in Grenada (1982).

Figure 18J. Estadio Nacional (National Stadium) in Lima, Peru has been through the most extreme events in soccer history. In 1963, 314 people died after a stampede after an Olympic qualifying match between Peru and Argentina. The stadium later successfully hosted the 2004 Copa America and the 2005 U-17 FIFA World Championship (below).

Figure 18K. Near capacity crowd at the Estadio Nacional in Lima for the 2005 U-17 World Championships, continuing the successful rehabilitation of a traumatized stadium.

Widespread Devastation in New Orleans 2005-2006 – After Hurricane Katrina Provoked a Levee Failure and Caused 80% of City to Flood

Figure 18L. A roof appears all alone without a house post-hurricane and flood. In the left background lie other flattened houses.
Photo courtesy of David Maxwell.

Figure 18M. A truck is flipped upside down and then pinned down by an unmoored house – in the flooded 9th Ward of New Orleans.
Photo courtesy of David Maxwell.

Figures 18N & O. At left, Brazil's Anderson takes on the Mexican defense in the 2005 U-17 World Championship Final, just before succumbing to injury. At right, talented Gambian forward Momodou Ceesay alarms the Netherlands defense.

Figure 18P. Mexico's U-17 team wins the 2005 World Championship (held aloft at center). Carlos Vela (at right in white shirt) holds his Golden Boot top goal scorer award, while Giovani Dos Santos (third from right) holds his Silver Ball award.

Figure 18Q & R. After the Final, Brazil's Anderson (left on crutches) and Mexico's Giovani Dos Santos display their Gold and Silver Ball awards as the top two players of the 2005 U-17 World Championship, while the official llama mascot appears to signal his approval.

Figure 18S. Children in the "Floating City" of Belen, Iquitos play water soccer.

Figure 18T. Football as celebration. El Coco, Costa Rica, 1992.

Figure 18U. A young Albert Camus (Chapter 1) learns about life between two garbage bags for goal posts. The youngest and smallest children are often relegated to goalkeeping duties, but this talented boy performed fearlessly against his bigger opponents. (Costa Rica 1992).

Figure 18V. The ball can comfort in many ways. Child near San Pablo in the Peruvian Amazon.

Figure 18W. A toddler can always depend on his ball for stimulation.

Figure 18X. Facing a large longhouse, an Urarina community field awaits the local talent.

Figure 18Y. A small secluded field in the Andes mountains awaits the local talent.
Photo courtesy of Anand Roy.

Figure 18Z. *Punch* "poster-type" magazine cover from 9 November 1960. Mr. Punch grabs the sun instead of punching away the ball entering the net, perhaps signifying the pre-eminence of the natural world over man-made pursuits (the reader can fill in his or her punch line here).
Fred Witzig is the poster artist.